Joseph Ramée

Joseph Ramée

International Architect of the Revolutionary Era

Paul V. Turner
Stanford University

This book originated with the Architectural History Foundation. It was also made possible in part through subventions from the National Endowment for the Humanities, the Graham Foundation for Advanced Studies in the Fine Arts, and the School of Humanities and Sciences of Stanford University.

Published by the Press Syndicate of the University of Cambridge
The Pitt Building, Trumpington Street, Cambridge CB2 1RP
40 West 20th Street, New York, NY 10011-4211, USA
10 Stamford Road, Oakleigh, Melbourne 3166, Australia

First published 1996

Printed in the United States of America

Library of Congress Cataloging-in-Publication Data

Turner, Paul Venable.
Joseph Ramée : international architect of the revolutionary era / Paul Venable Turner
p. cm.
Includes bibliographical references and index.
ISBN 0-521-49552-0 (hc)
1. Ramée, Joseph Jacques, 1764–1842. 2. Architects—France—Biography. 3. Landscape architects—France—Biography. I. Title.
NA1053.R35T87 1995
720'.92—dc20
[B] 95-18456
CIP

A catalog record for this book is available from the British Library

ISBN 0-521-49552-0 Hardback

for Michael E. Moors

Contents

List of Illustrations

COLOR PLATES

Acknowledgments

During my decade-long reconstruction of Ramée's life and work, through archival and on-site research in several countries, I have been assisted by hundreds of people. Three of them deserve special mention for the unusually generous and repeated help they provided me: Didier Coupaye, of Paris; Hakon Lund, of the Art Academy in Copenhagen; and Hermann Hipp, of the University of Hamburg.

Most of the people who assisted my research on specific parts of Ramée's career are acknowledged in the appropriate sections of the notes to this monograph. Others, whose help was of a more general nature, include: Lorenz Eitner, Michel Gallet, Philippe Grunchec, Estelle Halévi, Lisbet Jørgensen, Roger G. Kennedy, Robin Middleton, Michelle Morran, Monique Mosser, Jean-Marie Pérouse de Montclos, Adolf K. Placzek, Daniel Robbins, Pierre Rosenberg, Damie Stillman, Frederic Stout, Werner Szambien, Robert Tricoire, Anthony Vidler, Dora Wiebenson, and Henri Zerner.

I am grateful to the following organizations that provided financial support for parts of my research or for the preparation and production of the book: the National Endowment for the Humanities, the Graham Foundation for Advanced Studies in the Fine Arts, the Architectural History Foundation, and the School of Humanities and Sciences of Stanford University.

Acknowledgment is also due to the late Harold A. Larrabee, of Union College in Schenectady, New York. Following the discovery in 1932 of many of Ramée's drawings for the college's buildings and grounds, Larrabee conducted the first research into the architect's forgotten career. The records of these efforts, preserved in the Union College archives, provided the initial basis for my own research.

It seems appropriate here to note the genesis of my interest in Ramée, and the personal significance of his work for me. I was born and raised in Schenectady, near the Union College campus. As a child, I often walked or bicycled through the campus and wondered about the old buildings facing each other, mirrorlike, across the broad field with the massive domed structure at its center. This place, so clearly the work of a creative mind, was one of the things that aroused my early interest in architecture and history. Later, as an undergraduate student at Union, I learned of Ramée and his 1813 design of the college. But so little was known about the rest of the architect's career that it seemed of minor interest to me as an object of investigation.

Graduate study in architecture and art history followed, then work on various subjects in French and American architecture during my early years of teaching at Stanford University. Only as I was writing *Campus*, my book on American college planning, did I begin to realize the importance of Ramée's

Union College design. It was then that I conceived the idea of reconstructing the architect's entire career. Conducting preliminary research at the Archives Nationales and elsewhere in Paris in 1983, I had the good luck to make some significant discoveries early on. Thus encouraged, I arranged for further research in France, Belgium, Denmark, Germany, and the United States; the rich potential of the subject soon became apparent. I would have been fortunate to pursue it even if I had no personal connection with Ramée's work. But given this lifelong connection, the enterprise has taken on special meaning and pleasure for me. As another acknowledgment, therefore, I recognize the power of architecture itself, to inspire us and to shape our lives.

PAUL VENABLE TURNER
Stanford, California
October, 1993

Introduction: The Architect Without a Country

The Blérancourt Museum, near Noyon in northern France, has a portrait of the architect Joseph Ramée, part of a small collection of Ramée family documents that were given to the museum in 1937 (Fig. 1).[1] The only known representation of Ramée, it was painted in 1832 when the architect was sixty-eight years old and shows him looking healthy and confident. If the image is faithful in this regard, Ramée must have had great fortitude, for his life was filled with difficulties that forced him to lead an almost nomadic existence.

Ramée's career coincided with the turbulent period in Europe inaugurated by the French Revolution. Repeatedly, after he had started an architectural practice somewhere, war, economic collapse, or some other disaster forced him to move on and reestablish his career elsewhere. Practicing a profession that normally requires stable residence in one location (to acquire a reputation, understand local building practices, and cultivate relationships with clients), Ramée was an anomaly: an architect on the move.

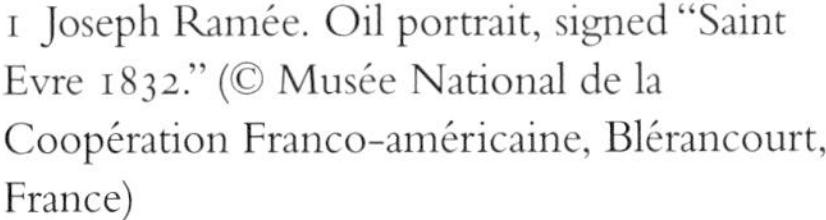

1 Joseph Ramée. Oil portrait, signed "Saint Evre 1832." (© Musée National de la Coopération Franco-américaine, Blérancourt, France)

Born in 1764 at Charlemont, near the border of France and Belgium, Ramée was trained by the architect François Joseph Belanger and began his career in Paris in the final years of the *ancien régime*. In 1793 he fled the Reign of Terror of the French Revolution and practiced architecture briefly in Louvain in Belgium. He then went to Germany, where he worked in several cities and principalities, most successfully in Hamburg and its environs. By 1800 he also was receiving important commissions in Denmark. Napoleon's imperial wars and other events soon made work in these places impossible for Ramée. He returned to France around 1810 and tried to start his career anew, but he was lured to America by one of his clients who promised that great opportunities awaited him there.

Ramée arrived in the United States just as the War of 1812 broke out, undermining his client's plans for land development in northern New York. Although Ramée was the most experienced European architect in America in this period and did important work (especially the design of Union College, the most ambitious American collegiate plan up to that time), he did not get enough commissions to satisfy him. In 1816 he returned to Europe, where he again practiced successively in Belgium, France, and Germany. As late as 1839, three years before his death at the age of seventy-eight, Ramée was still pursuing his career. A letter he wrote in that year, in a shaky hand, reveals that he was traveling through northern France to supervise the execution of landscape designs (see Fig. 299).[2]

Ramée's nomadism was certainly harmful to his career and reputation. With the possible exception of Hamburg, he stayed nowhere long enough to establish a really solid practice, and not enough of his work survives in any one country for him to be remembered as a major national architect. Indeed, he is virtually unknown today in many of the places where he practiced, including his native France, and some of his works have been misattributed to other architects.

But Ramée's internationalism is also the main reason for his significance. He transmitted many of the latest concepts of architecture and landscape design from one country to another, and he adopted regional forms encountered in his travels, producing at times a unique synthesis of esthetic traditions and innovations. Ramée himself was proud of the international character of his work. In publications of his designs toward the end of his life, he noted that he had worked "in different parts of Europe and North America" and that his designs were suitable to "diverse localities."[3] Ramée's multinational experience is reflected also in the work of his son, Daniel, who as a child accompanied him on his travels. Daniel Ramée learned the profession of architecture from his father, and went on to have an important career as an architectural restorer and historian with an unusually international perspective. Daniel's story is summarized in the epilogue of this book.

Another reason that Joseph Ramée is largely unknown today, besides his nomadic life, is a scarcity of documentation. Except for his surviving buildings and the designs he published in the 1820s and 1830s, few records of Ramée's career are known and almost nothing has been published about his life or work as a whole. The architect's personal papers evidently were dispersed in the late nineteenth century, after the death of his son. To reconstruct Ramée's life and career, I have had to accumulate fragmentary bits of information from widespread sources, producing a mosaic that still has missing pieces.

But if Ramée himself remains somewhat shadowy, many of his clients were famous and their lives are well documented. Ramée's clientele was remarkably varied. It included members of the French aristocracy, officials of the Revolutionary government of France, English writer William Beckford, several German dukes, the great author Goethe, prominent merchants and bankers in Hamburg and Copenhagen, Danish poet Frederikke Brun, international financier David Parish, American college president Eliphalet Nott, and other notable figures. These clients, with strong personalities and opinions, often played forceful roles in the architectural process and influenced the nature of Ramée's designs. The architect–client relationship is therefore of special interest in the case of Ramée, and the stories of his clients are an important component in reconstructing his work.

Just as Ramée's clientele was diverse, so was the scope of his work. Not only an architect of buildings, he was a landscape designer, an interior decorator, a furniture and wallpaper designer, a military engineer, and an urban planner. Although such diversity can be found in other architects of the period, in Ramée's case it was intensified by the unusual circumstances of his life: just as his nomadism required him to move from one kind of clientele to another, so did he have to be ready for any type of work. Ramée was somewhat like a chameleon, able to adapt quickly to different environments and to assume many roles or identities. His work thus does not have the continuity it might otherwise have had, but it reflects well the multifarious age in which the architect lived.

During Ramée's lifetime, European architecture underwent radical changes, which have shaped developments in design up to the present time. Trained in Paris, where the architectural ferment was most intense, Ramée absorbed many of the innovative concepts, as well as certain contradictions and ambiguities that accompanied them.

Neoclassicism was the main context in which Ramée worked. Seemingly devoted to the revival of the art of ancient Greece and Rome, neoclassicism was in fact a complex phenomenon, containing seeds of its own destruction. An increasingly important aspect of the neoclassical ideal in the eighteenth century was the search for fundamental principles of architecture. This search gradually led beyond antiquity itself, as seen in Marc Antoine Laugier's *Essai sur l'architecture* (1753), which attempts to identify the most primitive and therefore the purest elements of architecture. Another component of the search for first principles was the attraction to pure geometry, epitomized by the radically cubic and spherical forms of Claude Nicolas Ledoux and Étienne Louis Boullée toward the end of the century.

Rameé embraced these ideas while still a student. His teacher, Belanger, remarked that Ramée respected the pure architecture of antiquity but "has proposed purifying it even further."[4] Much of Ramée's architecture reveals this tendency in its emphasis on simple geometry and its unconventional use (or outright avoidance) of standard classical elements such as columns and porticos, relying instead on plain walls, arched openings, and other rudimentary elements of construction. In these ways, Ramée's work is similar to that of Ledoux and Boullée, but in contrast to the solid and massive forms of these two architects, Ramée's surfaces and details often produce an impression of lightness and insubstantial volume – like bubbles about to burst – almost prefiguring the forms of International-Style modernism of the 1920s and 1930s.

Another more insidious idea in the eighteenth century was esthetic relativism. The view that traditional architectural canons were the result of arbitrary human invention had been suggested in the late seventeenth century by the scholar-architect Claude Perrault; although too threatening to classicism to find much acceptance at that time, the notion persisted in various guises through the eighteenth century. This view encouraged the study of architectural history and contributed to the interest in nonclassical styles – the Gothic, for example, and even non-Western modes such as the Chinese. These styles appeared first in the harmless form of garden pavilions and other "follies," but by the late eighteenth century they were beginning to be seen as valid alternatives to classicism.

In this new eclectic climate, the architect had a wide range of styles at his disposal. Although most of Ramée's work was in the neoclassical mode, he showed his interest in eclecticism in the buildings he produced that incorporated Gothic, Egyptian, and other kinds of nonclassical forms. Toward the end of his life, he even published a collection of cottage designs presenting a broad repertoire of exotic styles (see Figs. 280–98).[5] It is perhaps significant that despite his extensive travels, Ramée apparently never went to Italy, the traditional pilgrimage goal of architects seeking their classical roots. His orientation was rather toward northern Europe. At first, this was probably just because the events in his life took him to Belgium, Germany, and Denmark. But he soon became enamored of nonclassical, northern modes of architecture, such as vernacular timber structures and even log-cabin construction. This architectural equivalent of certain literary trends of the period, which celebrated Germanic and Celtic legends over the classical epics, is one of the ways in which Ramée's work reflects the romantic spirit that was spreading through European culture at this time.

In Ramée's lifetime there were important innovations in architectural theory. Among the new ideas were some that concerned the expressive and symbolic potential of architecture, viewing it as a kind of language.[6] In the writings of A. C. Quatremère de Quincy, for example, architecture was seen as expressing the distinctive character of the people who built it, the culture they represented, and the climatic and other geographic conditions of their homeland. We do not know if Ramée was interested in these theoretical currents. But his career itself exemplified an increasing internationalization of the arts, which both reflected and stimulated the theoretical attention to architectural diversity. Ramée was not the only international architect of the period; there were many others who worked in more than one country.[7] But the extent of

Ramée's itinerant practice was extraordinary and epitomizes this characteristic of the age.

A subtle innovation of late eighteenth-century architecture was a new manner of composition. First described in detail by the historian Emil Kaufmann, this new esthetic replaced the unified and hierarchic patterns of Baroque design with forms that were independent of one another and created strong contrasts of size, shape, or texture.[8] Among the architects who pioneered in this approach were Ramée's teacher, Belanger, and others who influenced the young architect in the 1780s. Kaufmann, in fact, cited one of Ramée's works, the altar of the *Fête de la Fédération* of 1790, as a prime example of the new esthetic (see Fig. 33). It remained a trait of Ramée's work throughout his career, apparent in the cubic composition of his country houses in Denmark, or the isolated chapel at the center of his design for Union College in New York State (see Fig. 187).

Ramée was also involved in the eighteenth-century transformation of landscape design, in which the geometric Baroque park gave way to the irregular or picturesque garden. Not just one style of landscape, this type of design went through many phases of development, was interpreted differently in different places and was still evolving when Ramée began to devote much of his architectural practice to park and garden design. In France, Ramée had been trained in the complex "*anglo-chinois*" manner of landscape design popular there before the Revolution, but when he settled in Germany he was exposed to the more "natural" landscape patterns favored in England at the time. Ramée combined various elements of these picturesque garden modes, creating his own landscape style, which he employed in the region around Hamburg, in Denmark, and in the United States.

Moreover, Ramée developed a special attitude toward the relationship between architecture and landscape. Because of the difficulties of practicing architecture in foreign countries, he was forced at times to work mainly as a garden designer; devoting more attention to landscape than other architects of the period, Ramée came to think of architecture in a very broad sense – as encompassing, ideally, the entire environment of a building. This attitude can be found in other artists of the period, but it was particularly marked in Ramée and was perhaps his most important contribution in some of the places where he worked.[9] In the United States, especially, Ramée's designs were remarkable for their creation of totally integrated environments of man-made and natural components.

The term "universal" might be applied in certain ways to Ramée's work: in its neoclassical ideal of geometric purity, its fascination with all historical periods and geographical areas, and its integration of architecture and nature in total or environmental design. The circumstances of Ramée's life encouraged his universalist mentality. As an architect without a country, who was forced repeatedly to adapt to new conditions and types of clientele, Ramée had to seek common denominators that could make sense of the diverse components of his career.

Documents, Missing and Known

Most of what is known of Ramée's life comes from scattered surviving documents: his baptismal and death certificates; a petition he wrote in 1800, asking to have his name removed from the official list of French émigrés; an article on him in a biographical dictionary of 1830; about twenty letters written by Ramée himself; and various references to him in other people's correspondence and miscellaneous documents. In addition are Ramée's surviving drawings and three collections of engravings and lithographs of his work that he published in the 1820s and 1830s. But only about sixty drawings by Ramée are known to exist, and his published designs represent only a portion of his work.

One of the mysteries about Ramée is what happened to his personal papers. Despite his wanderings, he surely preserved many of his architectural drawings; at the very least, he must have saved the plans he eventually published toward the end of his life. After Ramée's death in 1842, his drawings probably were kept by his son, Daniel, who was close to his father and had collaborated in some of his later work. Daniel died childless in 1887. Daniel's widow died eight years later, leaving her estate to a young woman unrelated to the Ramées.[10] It was this woman, Edmée La Chesnais, who gave to the Blérancourt Museum the Ramée material now preserved there, which includes Ramée family portraits and documents, as well as personal papers of Daniel – but almost nothing from Ramée *père*. A clue to the fate of the elder Ramée's papers is the fact that a plan by him of Union College (a plan that is clearly the source of one of the lithographs he published at the end of his life) was discovered in 1890 in a print shop in Paris (Fig. 2, and see Fig. 197).[11] It seems, therefore, that soon after Daniel Ramée's death his father's drawings were sold or otherwise disposed of. Whether any of them still survive, apart from the drawing found in 1890 (now safe in the Union College archives), is not known.

The most important source of information on Ramée is an article published in 1830 (when the architect was sixty-six years old and living again in France) in a book entitled *Biographie ardennaise,* a collection of biographies of notable natives of the Ardennes region of northern France, compiled by a certain Abbot Boulliot.[12] A list of subscribers to the publication includes Ramée's name, and the article on him contains details of his personal and professional life that could only have been provided by Ramée himself. One suspects that the architect (or perhaps his son) actually wrote the piece for Boulliot. Despite its promotional tone, the article proves to be essentially accurate: nearly all its statements that can be verified independently turn out to be correct. The article is reproduced here as an appendix and its information will be examined as Ramée's life unfolds in this study.

Boulliot's article provides valuable clues to Ramée's life and work, but it omits much. Its account of Ramée's youthful career in Paris, for instance, stresses his work for the Comte d'Artois, brother of Louis XVI, and makes no mention of the design of the revolutionary *Fête de la Fédération* in 1790. The reason for this becomes clear when we realize that in the late 1820s (when

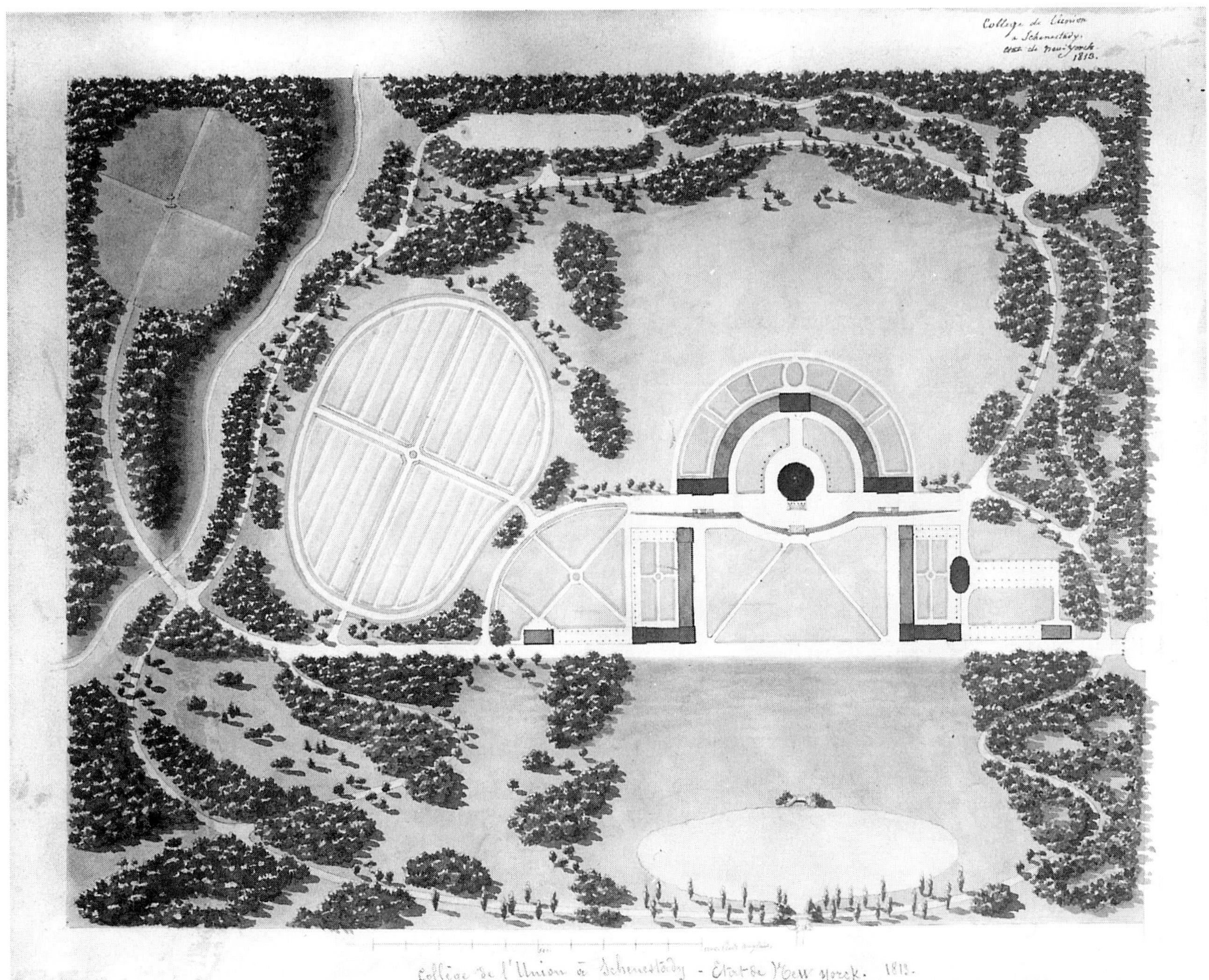

2 Plan of Union College, Schenectady, New York. Ink and wash drawing, c. 26 × 36 cm. Inscribed "Collège de l'Union à Schenectady, Etat de Neu-Yorck, 1813." (Schaffer Library, Union College)

Ramée provided the information for Boulliot's article), he no doubt hoped to obtain work from the restored Bourbon monarchy, headed by Charles X – none other than the former Comte d'Artois, bitterest enemy of the French Revolution. Any publicity about Ramée's involvement in the *Fête de la Fédération* could have been detrimental to his hopes.

This was not the only time that Ramée had to suppress part of his career. A petition he presented to the French government in 1800, describing his work up to that time, did exactly the opposite of the article in Boulliot: it emphasized his work for the Revolution and was completely silent about his services to the then-exiled Comte d'Artois.[13]

Ramée's selective career-descriptions suggest the political pitfalls and uncertainties with which he continually had to contend as he moved from one type of clientele to another, often making his previous connections useless or even dangerous. This also illustrates the problems facing the Ramée historian, dealing with documents that may be incomplete or distorted for unexpected reasons.

More frustrating than the distortion of documents has been their scarcity. In some cases, only one document or a passing reference to Ramée is all I found as evidence for an entire phase of his career or aspect of his life. His work in Thuringia and that in Mecklenburg-Schwerin, for example, were completely unknown, except for brief mention in Boulliot's article, until my research in these two parts of Germany. A reference in the 1800 petition was the only clue I had in searching for Ramée's early buildings in Paris. And a letter written by an acquaintance of the architect in America, in 1812, provides almost the only description of Ramée's personal character. Writing to his fiancée and having no reason to flatter Ramée, the man said: "You will also see Monsieur Ramée. I very much regret your not being conversant with the French [language]. He is so good hearted a gentleman, to whom I am so much indebted for salutary advice and friendly admonitions when I stood in need of both. . . . I am much attached to M. Ramée."[14]

Even Ramée's name is a matter of some mystery. His baptismal certificate gives his father's family name as "Poisramé" and a later document indicates that the architect was known by both surnames in his home town, but the reason for this discrepancy is not known. As for Ramée's Christian names, they are given variously as Jean-Jacques (one copy of his baptismal record), Joseph Guillaume (his petition of 1800), Jean (a military document of about 1810), Jean-Jacques Joseph (his death certificate), and Joseph Jacques (a second copy of his baptismal record and the biographical article of 1830). This last version became standard in references to Ramée in the late nineteenth century, and twentieth-century historians have continued to use it. But for the last thirty years of his life, the architect himself and his family considered his name to be simply Joseph Ramée. This is how he was known while in America; how he identified himself on the title pages of all three of his publications; how he is named by his son and brother-in-law in documents toward the end of his life; and how his name appeared on his tombstone. This, therefore, is the way he should be known – Joseph Ramée – the name he himself used in his later life.[15]

Origins in the Ardennes

Chapter 1

In the forested Ardennes region of northern France, the small city of Givet lies on both shores of the Meuse, only a few kilometers before the broad river crosses the frontier into Belgium. The twisting border here gives France a dagger-shaped intrusion into Belgium; the area has belonged to many governments over the centuries and has often been the route of invading armies. The older part of the city, called Givet-Saint Hilaire, lies on the left bank of the Meuse and is dominated by an extraordinary topographic feature: a massive rocky promontory, part of a high bluff that follows the river north, ending in steep cliffs that throw their shadow over the southern edge of the town (Fig. 3).

In the sixteenth century, Charles V, Hapsburg emperor and king of Spain, extended his Netherlandish possessions to include this region along the Meuse and created a fortified town on the great rock above Givet, giving it the name Charlemont. In 1678 Louis XIV acquired the place for France and had his military engineer, Sebastien Vauban, rebuild and expand the fortifications of Charlemont, which still largely survive. It was here in the lofty fortress village of Charlemont that Joseph Ramée was born on 26 April 1764.[1]

Little is known about Ramée's family. Boulliot's article on the architect does not even mention his parents, though it does refer to an uncle who was a priest in Louvain, Belgium. The devastation of northern France in the First and Second World Wars destroyed many archival records in the Ardennes region and only fragmentary evidence of Ramée's parentage can be found in documents there and elsewhere. These include surviving copies of Ramée's baptismal certificate; some records concerning his mother's side of the family; a statement that Ramée was related to the architect François Joseph Belanger, his teacher in Paris; and other miscellaneous bits of information.[2]

Ramée's baptismal certificate is known from two copies – one in Latin, the other French – preserved in the Ramée papers at the Blérancourt Museum.[3] The copies were made at the town hall of Givet in 1817, shortly after Ramée returned from America and perhaps needed proof of his birthplace in order to resettle in France. The information in the Latin and French versions of the certificate is identical, except for Ramée's first names. The text reads in part: "Born on the 26th of April, 1764, and baptized the following day. . . , Josephus Jacobus [Jean Jacques, in the French version], legitimate son of Jacques Poisramé and Anne Dieudonnée Lambert, his father and mother in legitimate marriage. . . ."[4]

Most puzzling here is the father's surname, given in the text as "Poisramé." Meaning roughly "staked peas," it is a peculiar name, of which I have found no other example. At first I thought that "Pois" was an error in the copy of the baptismal certificate; then a reference to the architect was discovered in a nineteenth-century publication about Givet, stating that Ramée "is also

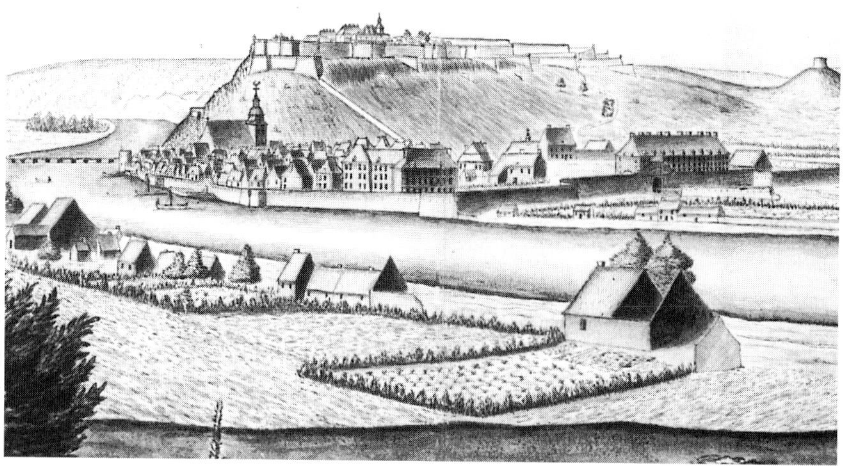

3 Drawing of Givet and Charlemont, from right bank of Meuse River, c. late eighteenth century, detail. (© cliché Bibliothèque Nationale, Paris)

called Poix-Ramée."[5] So it seems that Ramée's family was known locally by both names. But it is unclear whether Poix (or Pois) was part of the original family name or was adopted by the father; nor is it known when the name was shortened, or why. As for the surname Ramée, it is rare but is found especially in northern France and southern Belgium, where there are a couple of villages called La Ramée ("the arbor"). The history of the region records several notable individuals and families named de la Ramée.[6] But the origins of the architect's father remain mysterious, as does his occupation and nearly everything else about him.

More is known of Ramée's mother. The information in Boulliot's article that Ramée had an uncle who was a priest in Louvain (a maternal uncle, it turns out) has led to the identification of the mother's home town: the village of Aubrives, just south of Givet. The parish records of Aubrives reveal that Anne Dieudonnée Lambert was born in 1720 (and therefore was forty-four years old when Joseph was born); her family was long established in the region and had ties with local seignorial families.[7] Especially relevant is the fact that her godfather was from Charlemont, of a family that produced directors of fortification construction – the field in which Ramée was first to be trained.[8] Another recently discovered document reveals that Ramée's mother was a widow when she died, about 1802, and that she bequeathed a house in Givet to a daughter and to Joseph (who returned at that time from Hamburg to sell his share of the property to his sister).[9]

In the mid-eighteenth century, Givet was enjoying a peaceful period and the fortress of Charlemont had a small population – sometimes fewer than a hundred civilians, although the army barracks could accommodate over 2,000 soldiers.[10] In 1764, the year of Ramée's birth, a geographical dictionary of France said of the place:

> The city of Charlemont occupies a small area and has a very irregular form. One enters it through two gates, one of which gives on the mountain, the other toward Givet. There is quite a handsome town square, streets laid out neatly, and pretty houses. There is but one church and one storehouse. As for other buildings, only the Governor's house is worthy of mention.[11]

Since Ramée's father's occupation is unknown, it is impossible to say whether the architect was born in Charlemont because his parents lived there or because of his mother's family connections with the place. Ramée's father may have been a military man, temporarily posted at Charlemont, but he was more likely part of the local population, like his wife.

The livelihood of this population depended largely on service to the military. Givet's most famous native, the composer Étienne Nicolas Méhul, born just one year before Ramée, was the son of a wine merchant and restaurateur, both common professions in the town.[12] Méhul and Ramée probably knew each other from attendance at Givet's only school, the École des Récollets; when they both later went to Paris to pursue their precocious careers (Méhul at the age of fifteen, Ramée at sixteen), they may well have remained in contact – two children of obscure families from a provincial town, each to become a significant figure in his artistic field.

The accomplishments of the young Méhul and Ramée are all the more remarkable as Givet was hardly a center of the arts. Its character as a military town was suggested by the Abbé d'Expilly in 1792, in his chatty *Voyage dans les départements français*:

> This city has almost no commerce. . . . There are no industries here, where there are many men but they have little to spend, where the sword rules, and where men are prisoners from dusk to dawn. . . . The only thing that strikes one in Givet is the beauty of the people: it is as rare to meet an ugly woman here as it is often difficult to find a pretty one elsewhere. The only monuments worth seeing are the barracks. They are superb.[13]

The barracks were everywhere in Givet and Charlemont. One of them, the Caserne Rougé (destroyed by the Germans in 1914), extended along the Meuse for 500 meters and was famous as the longest barrack structure in France (Fig. 4). In their simplicity, regularity, and heavy stone construction, the barracks typified the character of nearly all the architecture of Givet and Charlemont. Even the main church, St. Hilaire, had been rebuilt by Vauban in 1682 as a massive structure (whose bold rhythm of arched windows is its main adornment), meant to serve as a last refuge for the city's defenders in time of war.

But the greatest architectural work was the citadel of Charlemont itself (Fig. 5). As originally planned under Charles V in 1555, it was one of the earliest fortresses to use fully the new type of military architecture invented in

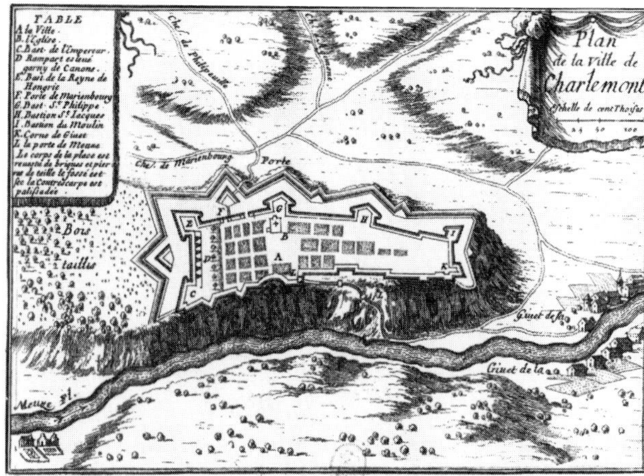

4 Caserne Rougé, Givet, seen from the Meuse with Charlemont in the background. Constructed c. 1700, destroyed 1914. (Postcard, c. 1900, courtesy of Pierre Hubert)

5 Plan of Charlemont, c. 1680. (© cliché Bibliothèque Nationale, Paris)

response to advances in fire power. Instead of the high walls and round towers of medieval castles, now vulnerable to cannon fire, the new manner of fortification employed series of low and massive bastions, extending outward from the fortress at angles calculated for the optimal positioning of cannon and for the defense of the flanks of the citadel. The engineer Vauban was the most briliant practitioner of this system of design, refining it in response to individual topographic and military conditions. Starting in 1680, he expanded the fortifications of Charlemont, constructing multiple levels of sharp-angled bastions around the summit of the rock.

To the child Ramée, this fortress must have made a deep impression – especially its great walls and bastions, fanning out in zig-zag patterns down the cliffs. Here architecture assumed the power and scale of nature itself. A mountain had been reshaped by man and turned into a habitable structure; the irregular form of the natural landscape had been given precise angles, edges, and surfaces. It is not surprising that Ramée later recalled (as stated in Boulliot's article) that as a child he had "spent his time drawing shapes, seeking to copy them regularly and correctly, before he even knew their names or was aware that there was a science concerned with them."[14]

As an architect, Ramée was to be an ardent proponent of pure geometric neoclassicism, often using cubic forms stripped of nearly all details and ornament, to a degree remarkable even for his period. One suspects that the powerful geometric nature of the place where he was born contributed something to this predilection. The buildings at Givet and Charlemont also had great simplicity and structural clarity. Designed to withstand military assault, their paramount traits were solid workmanship and strength; they therefore embodied clearly the fundamental parts of architectural structure: walls, spanning beams, arches. The great portals leading into the city and the fortress were massive barrel-vaulted structures that demonstrated with striking clarity the principles of stone arch construction. The façade of the cistern at Charlemont, built in 1725, is an elegant work, relying on a simple repetition of arched openings, with the pattern of masonry courses and the voussoirs of each arch neatly emphasized (Fig. 6). The clear expression of basic structural

6 Cistern, Charlemont, constructed c. 1725. (Author)

forms, especially arches and plain walls, was to be a major interest of Ramée's throughout his career and would distinguish many of his designs.

According to Boulliot, Ramée "at the age of twelve was employed by the military corps of engineers [*le génie militaire*] to draw fortification plans." One wonders if Ramée's father was connected with this engineering corps, perhaps as a local contractor involved in the maintenance of the fortifications, as members of Ramée's mother's family had been. But even without a family connection, the employment of a twelve-year-old boy in this activity is not as unlikely as it might sound. The Génie Militaire was still in a formative stage in the mid-eighteenth century: Vauban had attempted to create a permanent and professional organization of military engineers, but only gradually was the groundwork laid for this profession whose importance to modern warfare was first recognized fully by Napoleon. In the 1770s, the engineers had just been separated from the artillery and were in the process of organizing themselves.[15] In peacetime, officers of the Génie Militaire were dispatched to local garrisons to undertake the repair or expansion of fortifications, but they did not normally have large or well-trained staffs. Especially in an isolated place such as Charlemont, an engineer might gladly have taken on a local boy who showed talent for drafting as an apprentice.

Such an apprenticeship was an excellent introduction to the profession of architecture. Military engineering in the eighteenth century still played an important role in architecture, as it had for Renaissance architects. Military engineers in fact performed many of the functions of today's civil engineers, designing not only defensive fortifications but roads, canals, bridges, public squares, and other large-scale works. In eighteenth-century France, members of the Génie Militaire were often involved in the design and execution of royal palaces and parks (including those at Versailles), because of the structural and logistical problems these enterprises entailed.

As an apprentice or assistant to a military engineer at Charlemont, the boy Ramée would have learned the rudiments of practical architecture: the use of drafting tools, the standard types of architectural drawings, the principal structural systems, something of the strength of materials, and the art of constructing walls and arches of stone. Perhaps also included was instruction in the classical orders, for even fortification architecture sometimes employed them, particularly the robust Doric. At Charlemont, the orders are found especially on the entry gates, but in a rudimentary, almost cubist form, without capitals or other niceties.

In 1840, two years before Ramée's death, his son Daniel published a small treatise on architectural drawing, *Théorie du dessin linéaire*.[16] It consists mainly of engraved plates, presenting visually the fundamentals of architecture for beginners. Daniel had been trained as an architect by his father (having followed him, as a boy, to all the places where he worked) and this architectural primer probably reflects Daniel's own introduction to the art at his father's drafting board. It is similar to traditional architectural treatises, but with a special emphasis on practical matters (devoting as much attention to construction techniques as to the classical orders) and stressing geometry as the basis of the art of architecture. This approach may have been influenced by J. L. Durand's *Précis des leçons d'architecture* of 1802, but it also probably reflected Joseph Ramée's own introduction to architecture, as an apprentice to the Génie Militaire in the angular rock-fortress of Charlemont.

Louvain

After stating that the twelve-year-old Ramée was employed by the Génie Militaire, Boulliot's article provides the only other information about the youth before he went to Paris in 1780: "One of his uncles, a canon of the church of St. Pierre in Louvain, having brought [Ramée] to that city, quickly recognized his talent; he provided him with a Vignola and compasses, and at the age of fifteen his nephew was giving architectural lessons."[17]

In my reconstruction of Ramée's life, identifying the architect's unnamed uncle became one of my peripheral fascinations. A search of ecclesiastical records in Louvain produced only one suitable canon of St. Pierre in the mid-eighteenth century: Charles Joseph Lambrechts (Lambrechts being the Flemish form of Lambert, Ramée's mother's name). Lambrechts, it turned out, was an important historical figure, who renounced the church and eventually became a high official in the French government; his career and connections seemed to explain some of the mysterious episodes in Ramée's life. But in a demonstration of the risks of speculative scholarship, I then discovered that Ramée's uncle was not Lambrechts at all, but a certain Jean-Louis Lambert, a *chaplain* of St. Pierre (a considerably lesser post than that of canon).[18]

Little is known about Lambert. He attended the University of Louvain as a scholarship student. Later, as chaplain of St. Pierre, he lived in one of the old houses that were built right against the back of the church, and records reveal that one or more of his relatives lived there with him.[19]

Although we cannot say what influence Lambert had on the young Ramée, we can be sure that the city of Louvain itself was important in his education. In contrast to the provincial military town where Ramée was born, Louvain was cosmopolitan and architecturally diverse. Capital of the duchy of Brabant before the rise of Brussels, Louvain in the fifteenth century had become the seat of one of the major universities in Europe. Many of the fine buildings that still distinguish the city are colleges or other university structures, most dating from the sixteenth to the eighteenth century. Louvain, in fact, has excellent examples of nearly every northern European architectural period and style and must have served as a splendid living history of architecture to the young Ramée.

Among the medieval structures of Louvain is the church of Saint Pierre (behind which Ramée probably lived with his uncle), a fine example of the Brabant High Gothic, in which large windows, a dominating verticality, and the suppression of unnecessary details produce one of the clearest expressions of the Gothic system found anywhere (Fig. 7). Directly across from Saint Pierre in the center of Louvain, the fifteenth-century Town Hall represents the opposite tendency of the Gothic, with its multiple layers of decorative sculpture, niches, balustrades, towers, finials, and other ornament. Renaissance

7 View of Louvain with Town Hall at left and church of St. Pierre at right (showing houses behind church, where Ramée's uncle lived). Lithograph of 1828 by Gustav Kraus, after painting by Domenico Quaglio. (Katholieke Universiteit, Central Library, Print Collection, Leuven)

architecture in Louvain is represented at several of the colleges and there is a wide range of Baroque styles, from the full-blown Roman Baroque of the Jesuit church of Saint Michael to various types of northern Baroque buildings constructed of brick with stone trim. Neoclassicism is also well represented, by collegiate structures that had just been completed or were still under construction when Ramée was there in the 1770s, such as the quadrangle of the College of the Pope, with its elegant and simple arcaded portico (Fig. 8).

8 Courtyard of College of the Pope, Louvain, designed by Louis Montoyer, constructed 1776. (Author)

Besides such high-style architecture, the young Ramée saw a wide range of vernacular building in Louvain (much of which survives today, especially in the "Grand Béguinage" enclave), including traditional half-timbered structures and distinctively Flemish brick houses with steep gables (Fig. 9). Such Netherlandish house types may have helped cultivate the interest in vernacular architecture that Ramée was later to reveal in his own work.

When Ramée's uncle perceived the boy's talents, he gave him "a Vignola and compasses [*un vignole et des compas*]," according to Boulliot. In this context, the term "compasses" probably refers not only to the instruments that draw circles, but to drafting implements in general. Similarly, "Vignola" may mean any architectural treatise or handbook. Giacomo Barozzi da Vignola's book, *Regola delli cinque ordini d'architettura,* originally published in 1562, became so popular in the following centuries, in innumerable revised and translated editions, that the author's name was sometimes used generically.[20] But the book Ramée's uncle gave him in the 1770s probably *was* an edition of Vignola's work, for this was the standard introductory treatise on architecture. There were more than a dozen French versions of Vignola in the eighteenth century, ranging from small volumes that merely reproduced Vignola's plates and his brief preface, to heavily annotated editions and works that used Vignola as a point of departure for lengthy original texts.

It was probably one of the smaller and cheaper editions of Vignola that the young Ramée received from his uncle. Vignola's preface, included in nearly all editions, explains the purpose of the treatise and also suggests the reason for its great popularity. In contrast to most Renaissance architectural theorists, who painstakingly compared and analyzed the subtle differences in form and proportion of ancient Roman buildings in an attempt to discover the true standards of architectural beauty, Vignola took a simpler approach. Using classical prototypes as a basis, but not adhering to them slavishly or worrying about their discrepancies, Vignola devised a simplified canon of proportions for each architectural order, in which the larger dimensions (column height and diameter, distance between columns, etc.) were made standard multiples of a unit measurement or "module," allowing the easy translation of these proportions into forms of any size, using any national unit of measure (Fig. 10).

If followed precisely, Vignola's system tended perhaps to discourage subtlety of design, but it was relatively easy to learn and therefore was particularly suitable for students of architecture. Moreover, it would have had special appeal to someone like Ramée, who was to seek simplification and purification of architectural form. Used as an introduction to the theory of architecture, Vignola's treatise probably encouraged the development in Ramée of that trait that Belanger, his teacher in Paris, would later describe as a desire to "purify even further" the forms of classicism.[21]

9 Houses in the Grand Béguinage, Louvain. (Author)

Ramée's progress in his studies was remarkable, if we are to believe Boulliot's statement that at the age of fifteen he was giving lessons in architecture. These were perhaps lessons in drawing, offered to university acquaintances of Ramée's uncle or to interested students and townspeople. This early activity confirms that the boy had received good training in draftsmanship as an apprentice to the Génie Militaire in Charlemont, and that the drawing skill evident in Ramée's later sketches and watercolor renderings was already apparent.

One can also speculate on the types of training the young Ramée did *not* receive. There is no evidence that he received an education in classical languages or other academic studies. If he had, Boulliot probably would have mentioned it in his laudatory article on the architect. And Ramée's surviving letters are written in simple conversational French, rather than the formal language typical of much educated correspondence of the period.[22] Everything suggests that the adolescent Ramée, encouraged by his uncle in Louvain, directed his energies wholly to a practical career in architecture.

10 Plate from 1760 French edition of Vignola's treatise, showing modular proportions of the orders. (*Nouveau livre des cinq ordres d'architecture*, Paris, 1760, p. 8)

After Ramée moved to Paris in 1780, there is little evidence of further contact with his family. Following the architect's marriage in Hamburg in 1805, there are many indications of his close ties to his wife's relatives, but almost none to his own family. At least twice, however, the architect returned to live in the places where he had spent his childhood. After fleeing France in 1793, he practiced architecture for a while in Louvain, and in 1816, on returning to Europe from America, he settled in Dinant, just north of Givet. In the second instance, especially, it seems likely that some family tie or business connection drew him back to his native region. Like so much in Ramée's life, the picture of his family is shadowy and leaves parts of his career obscure.

Training in Paris

Chapter 2

At the age of sixteen, Ramée arrived in Paris and soon was working for François Joseph Belanger, architect to the Comte d'Artois, brother of Louis XVI. According to Boulliot's article on Ramée: "Having gone to Paris in 1780, his attention was directed immediately to the immortal masterpieces that decorate this capital. At the end of nine months he entered the offices of building works of the Comte d'Artois. . . ." [1]

Paris at this time was the Mecca for aspiring young architects. The French capital had its share of fine medieval, Renaissance, and Baroque buildings, but what really distinguished it was its modern architecture. Throughout the eighteenth century, Paris led the way for European architecture – in important construction, concentration of talent, stylistic innovation, and theory.

Besides the attraction of Paris itself, the young Ramée had a personal reason to move there: he was, it appears, related to Belanger, the man who became his teacher. This relationship, which has never been mentioned in the literature on Ramée, is revealed in a letter written in 1805 by Belanger's son Alexandre.[2] Listing his father's professional achievements, Alexandre Belanger noted the success of his many students; among these, he named three of his father's "relatives," including Ramée. It is clear that he meant this literally, for the other two students he named were definitely related to Belanger: Louis Belanger (his brother) and Jean Démosthène Dugourc (his brother-in-law). Even if Ramée was only a distant relative of Belanger, this fact helps explain how a teen-age lad was accepted into the office of one of the foremost architects in France, shortly after arriving in Paris from the provinces.

Two documents provide nearly all the known clues for reconstructing Ramée's training and early career in Paris, before he fled France in 1793: the account by Boulliot (whose information, we recall, must have been provided by the architect himself) and a petition that Ramée submitted to the French authorities in 1800. As noted in the Introduction, these two documents present conflicting views of Ramée's years in Paris, one suggesting that he opposed the Revolution, the other that he supported it. Boulliot's account, published in 1830 when Ramée was probably seeking work from the restored Bourbon monarchy in France, tactfully emphasizes the architect's aristocratic connections, especially his early work for the Comte d'Artois. Boulliot states:

> At the end of nine months [Ramée] entered the offices of building works [*bureaux des bâtimens*] of the Comte d'Artois, as Inspecteur, and contributed to the fitting-up of the pavilion and park of Bagatelle, as well as that of Saint-James in Neuilly.
>
> At the age of twenty-two, he constructed a house in Paris that used the first roof structure of circular form. In 1790, he was

> charged by Mr. Beckford to have a magnificent tent executed in the oriental style. Erected at the *Menus-Plaisirs du Roi,* the tent was transported from there to the shores of Lake Geneva, where the artist from Givet went to direct the *fêtes* that the wealthy Englishman presented there, which are still remembered.
>
> Having pronounced himself against the events of 20 June 1792, when he was Captain of the Grenadiers in his neighborhood, he was marked out as a suspect. [These "events" were the invasion of the Tuileries Palace by a mob and their confrontation of the King, the most radical action against the monarchy up to that point.] Threatened with prison, he escaped the assassins' daggers on September 2–3 [the night of revolutionary massacre in Paris] only by taking refuge in the Army of Belgium, commanded by Dumouriez, who employed him as a staff officer. But the defection of this general on 4 April 1793 led Ramée to Louvain, where he took up his first profession again.[3]

In contrast to this account, Ramée's petition of 1800, written when the architect was in exile from France, completely suppresses his aristocratic ties, emphasizing instead his supposed Revolutionary sympathies and his work for nonaristocratic clients. Preserved in the Archives Nationales in Paris, this document is a "*pétition de radiation,*" an application to have one's name "erased" from the lists of proscribed émigrés (see Fig. 38).[4] The petition includes Ramée's own statement (which he signed "Joseph Guillaume Ramée," the name he used at that period of his life) and supporting statements from four other people: his former teacher Belanger, the architect Jacques Cellerier, a client named Perregaux, and a French consul general in Hamburg (where Ramée was living in 1800), who vouched for his patriotism. The information on Ramée's early years in Paris is found mainly in the statements of Belanger and Cellerier. Belanger certified:

> That Joseph Guillaume Ramé [sic], architect, was my student during several years, that he distinguished himself in the study of that art, in which he made rapid progress up to the time when he was worthy of employing his talents for his own personal advantage. That he left my studio in 1790, having been named by Citizen Cellerier *Premier Inspecteur du Décor* of the *Fête de la Première Fédération,* in Paris. That he constructed in Paris a small *salle de spectacle;* the *corps-de-logis,* on the street, of the Perregaux house, in the Chaussée d'Antin; the house of Citizen Berthault on the rue du Mail; as well as gardens at Chantilly, etc., etc., etc. That the works of this artist have always shown a talent distinguished as much by its natural genius as by its taste for the Antique, which he has proposed to purify even further; by examination of the works of the Greeks and Romans, our veritable masters in this art. . . .[5]

Cellerier's supporting statement confirmed that he had named Ramée "inspector general" for the *Fête de la Fédération* of 1790, adding that previously he had employed him "in my works for more than two years." Cellerier also testified to Ramée's great talent, intelligence, and enthusiasm for his art, as well as his dedication to "the principles of the Revolution."[6]

Besides the statements of Belanger and Cellerier, several other artists added their signatures to Ramée's petition.[7] Most of these supporters, including the painter Jean-Jacques Lagrenée and the sculptor Louis Simon Boizot, had professional connections with Belanger. Especially intriguing is the signature of Charles Percier, who in 1800 had just begun the work for Napoleon and Josephine Bonaparte that was to make him the foremost architect of the Empire period. (The relationship between Percier and Ramée will be examined later.)

These two documents – Boulliot's biographical article and the petition of 1800 – provide our major clues for the reconstruction of Ramée's training and early career.

Belanger and the Comte d'Artois

François Joseph Belanger (Fig. 11) was one of the most innovative and prolific architects in France when Ramée entered his office.[8] Trained at the Académie Royale d'Architecture, Belanger had been a student of Contant d'Ivry and the pioneering classicist David Leroy (author of one of the earliest publications on ancient Greek architecture). Belanger had spent some time in the 1770s in England, where he was one of the first French designers to study picturesque landscape design. His subsequent work in France embodied many progressive trends in architecture, garden planning, and interior decor – anticipating, for example, the Directoire and Empire styles of design.

11 François Joseph Belanger. Medallion portrait by H. Roguier, on Belanger's tomb in Père Lachaise Cemetery, Paris.

Belanger also had useful aristocratic connections, largely through the help of the opera singer and courtesan Sophie Arnould, who had a special affection for Belanger (her *bel ange,* as she called him in her letters). Probably no other architect's office in the 1780s provided such an excellent opportunity for a wide-ranging and progressive education in the profession. There was only one disadvantage to training with Belanger: his lack of membership in the Royal Academy of Architecture.

By the late eighteenth century, architectural education in France had evolved to a complex state that made advancement difficult for students without the right connections.[9] The Académie Royale d'Architecture functioned on two levels: that of its public lectures and that of the *concours* or competitions, culminating in the coveted *Prix de Rome.* To enter the *concours,* a student had to be sponsored by a member of the Academy, and the number of possible entrants each year was limited (to about forty, in the 1780s). Since the Academy members tended to sponsor their own students or others having special connections with themselves, and since sponsored students often entered the competitions year after year, an outsider might effectively be locked out of the system. This was one of the reasons given for the suppression of the Academy in 1793 and its reorganization when it later emerged as the architectural department of the École des Beaux-Arts. Belanger, although professionally successful, was apparently not a member of the Academy; nor was Jacques Cellerier, the other architect under whom Ramée apprenticed in Paris.[10] Ramée therefore could not be sponsored for competitions by his teachers, and his position in their offices may actually have made it harder for him to find other sponsors, owing to professional rivalry.

The advantage of participation in the Academy and its competitions is difficult to assess, especially as complete records of the institution do not survive. Success in the *concours* certainly bestowed prestige and launched many important careers. Yet some of the major Parisian architects of the period had never taken an Academy prize, including Claude Nicolas Ledoux (creator of the royal tollhouses that ringed the city), Jacques Denis Antoine (architect of the Hôtel des Monnaies, the royal mint), and Jacques Germain Soufflot (designer of the church of Sainte Geneviève, now the Panthéon). Most of the best-known architects had participated in the Academy, even if they had not won prizes; but a few, such as Ledoux and Antoine, seem to have had nothing to do with the Academy as students.[11]

Since a full list of *concours* entrants does not exist, it is possible that Ramée did, in fact, enter Academy competitions during the 1780s. In any case he might have done so later if the Revolution had not intervened. In the late eighteenth century, the average age at which architectural students participated in the Academy's competitions was about twenty-five, and entrants in their thirties were not rare.[12] Ramée was twenty-five when the Revolution broke out in 1789. As so often in his life, events and timing conspired to disrupt his career.

Belanger's main post was *Premier Architecte* to the Comte d'Artois. Bourliot's statement that Ramée entered the office of Artois's building works, nine months after arriving in Paris in 1780, means therefore that Belanger took on the young man as an apprentice or employee within this part of his practice.

12 The Comte d'Artois, later Charles X of France. Print after portrait attributed to Elisabeth Vigée-Lebrun.

The Comte d'Artois (Fig. 12), one of the younger brothers of Louis XVI, was popularly seen as epitomizing the worst traits of the French nobility: wastefulness, arrogance, and general uselessness. Artois received large government stipends (over two million livres a year by 1789) besides the revenues from his properties, and he made no secret of his view that the state existed principally to provide the royal family with whatever it wished. In 1787, when royal ministers proposed economies to relieve the government's increasingly grave financial problems, Artois answered disdainfully that "the expenses of the King [and his family] cannot be regulated by his receipts; his income must be regulated by his expenses." The French controller-general during this period, Loménie de Brienne, wrote in his memoirs that Artois "regarded the public treasury as an inexhaustible source of plunder."[13] The favorite amusements of the royal brother were lavish parties, gambling, the company of prostitutes, hunting, and architecture. Belanger was well qualified to satisfy Artois's wishes in the last area, being adept in the latest fashions in design, not only French but English (Artois had Anglophile tendencies), and having a natural disposition to design in a light and elegant style.

13 Bagatelle, in the Bois de Boulogne, Paris, designed by Belanger, c. 1777. Engraving by Née, after L. Bellanger, showing the entry façade.

Belanger's work for Artois included remodeling his numerous townhouses and *châteaux,* erecting new ones, and laying out extensive gardens in the irregular "English" style, which Belanger helped introduce to France. His most spectacular achievement for Artois was the design and execution of the pleasure house Bagatelle in the Bois de Boulogne, west of Paris (Fig. 13) – a task accomplished in only sixty-four days in 1777 in order to win a 100,000-franc bet that Artois had waged with his sister-in-law Marie Antoinette.[14] Belanger also was involved in land-development schemes for Artois, such as a projected new neighborhood in Paris, to be called La Nouvelle Amérique (with a Place Franklin as its focal point), conceived in the first flush of French enthusiasm for the American War of Independence.

Throughout the 1780s, Belanger also retained his post as architect in the office where he had begun his official career in 1767, the *Menus-Plaisirs du Roi.* This bureau was charged with all manner of ephemeral and decorative designs for the French court, such as theatrical presentations, *fêtes,* and the furnishing of royal residences. Besides his official positions, Belanger was busy with outside commissions, designing private houses and gardens. He also was involved in engineering projects: he experimented with innovative structural designs (including one of the first uses of iron trusses, about 1785) and worked on an hydraulic pump system for the Paris water supply.[15]

Ramée, when he later moved from country to country in search of work, found it advantageous to be able to present himself as either a designer of buildings, a landscape gardener, an interior decorator and furniture designer, a city planner, or an engineer. Belanger's office in the 1780s provided the perfect training for this multiplicity of architectural roles.

Ramée's official position in Belanger's office was a member of the Comte d'Artois's staff, although he also worked on some of Belanger's non-Artois projects and even assumed jobs outside Belanger's office.[16] The Comte d'Artois's diverse building activities required a large staff and an organization similar to that of the building works of the king himself. In charge of the whole enterprise was a *Surintendant des Bâtiments,* under whom an *Intendant, Premier Architecte, Contrôleur, Premier Commis,* and *Secrétaire* each had his area of responsibility.[17] Belanger, as *Premier Architecte,* was empowered to hire assistants as needed: the two main types of employee were *Dessinateur,* or draftsman, and *Inspecteur,* whose tasks included supervising the execution of a design. (A document that survives from 1777 names two *Inspecteurs* and a *Sous-Inspecteur* working under Belanger, each of whom received one-fifth of Belanger's salary; it does not name the *Dessinateurs* employed at that time.)[18]

When the sixteen- or seventeen-year-old Ramée entered Belanger's office, it surely was not as an *Inspecteur,* as Boulliot later stated, although Ramée did assume this position at some point during his roughly ten-year employment with Belanger. Belanger himself referred to Ramée simply as his "*élève,*" in his statement supporting the 1800 petition and in a later document.[19] One gets the impression that in Belanger's office there was no clear distinction between being a student and a paid employee – even an employee with the title *Inspecteur.* Education and employment merged into one another, as was typical of the traditional apprentice system, and therefore it is impossible to say exactly when Ramée's "training" ended and his "career" began.

According to Boulliot, Ramée's work in Belanger's office included "contributing to the fitting-up [*l'arrangement*] of the pavilion and park of Bagatelle, as well as that of Saint-James" (an estate near Bagatelle). These two commissions occupied much of Belanger's attention during the early part of Ramée's tenure in his office. Even though Bagatelle was largely completed in sixty-four days in 1777, work on it continued for a number of years, especially on its gardens and interior furnishings.[20] Typical of Belanger's work, the plan of the house included a variety of geometric shapes, with circular, square, elliptical, and octagonal rooms, as would later be found in some of Ramée's own designs.

In Belanger's houses of the 1780s, he experimented with forms of ornament that later typified the so-called Directoire style. Belanger was, in fact, the principal creator of this style, which Ramée was to introduce into Germany and Denmark.[21] As a stylistic term, "Directoire" designates the art of a period much longer than the four years of the Directorate government in France (1795–9). The style appeared first in the reign of Louis XVI, developed in the 1790s and merged into the Empire Style after 1800. Some historians view the Directoire as the early phase of the Empire style; others feel it should be called simply neoclassicism.[22] Whatever one calls it, the style has certain distinctive characteristics, such as simple geometric forms, especially circles – circular bas-reliefs being common in the designs of Belanger and Ramée (Fig. 14). Another trait, which links the Directoire to the Adam style in England, is the faithful use of motifs from classical antiquity, including the light and airy "arabesque" decorations that had earlier been unearthed at Pompeii and other Roman sites. The sculptor Nicolas François Lhuillier, Belanger's frequent collaborator, had studied this "Pompeiian" style in Italy and helped popularize it in France.

14 Salon in Belanger House, Rue des Capucines, Paris, designed by Belanger, c. 1785. (J. C. Krafft and N. Ransonnette, *Plans, coupes, élévations des plus belles maisons*, Paris, 1801–3, pl. 93)

Gardens

Ramée, who was to devote much of his career to landscape architecture, had an excellent teacher in this subject, for Belanger was the foremost designer of gardens in France in the 1780s. His prominence was due in part to his wealthy, garden-loving clientele, but also to the fact that he was one of the few French architects who knew English gardens from personal experience, as he had visited Britain at least once in the 1770s. One of Belanger's sketchbooks contains drawings of several of the important picturesque parks in England, including those at Stowe, Stourhead, and The Leasowes.[23]

In the 1770s and 1780s, Belanger received many commissions to lay out gardens in the manner that the French called "*anglais*" or "*anglais-chinois*." This style was based partly on English prototypes and fanciful notions of Chinese landscape design, but also on French landscape painting, written criticism of the formal French garden, and romantic literary themes of the period, such as those found in the writings of Jean-Jacques Rousseau. The "*jardin anglo-chinois*" tended to include as many twisting paths, exotic pavilions, and peculiar topographic features (artificial hills, grottos, odd-shaped lakes) as could fit in a given area. Among Belanger's gardens in this style – besides those at Bagatelle and Saint-James – were ones executed, starting in the 1770s, for the Prince de Ligne at Beloeil in Belgium, Monsieur de Laborde at Méréville, and the author Beaumarchais in Paris.[24]

For Belanger, gardens ideally were "picturesque" in the literal sense of creating images as in a painting. Writing to one of his clients, a certain Madame Joly, Belanger defended with the following remarks his inclusion of a bridge in her garden, even though there was no water under it (which she evidently thought odd):

> As a garden is the full-scale model of a landscape painting, it should not be deprived of the objects that can embellish the pic-

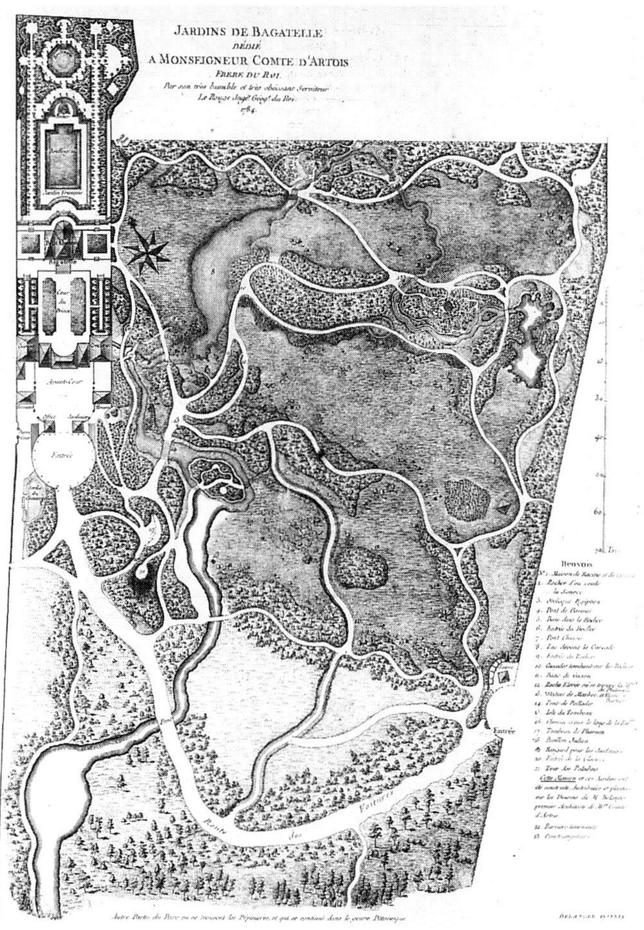

15 Bagatelle, plan of the gardens. (G. Le Rouge, *Jardins anglo-chinois*, vol. 12, Paris, 1784, pl. 2)

> torial perspective. . . . Therefore, Madame, charged with creating a garden for a lady of taste, I did not believe it sufficient to lay out sinuous paths at random, but had to offer [more] for her eyes. . . . You must rise above the criticism of those who think that a bridge should always have a river or stream flowing under it.[25]

The gardens at Bagatelle probably introduced Ramée to irregular landscape design. The story of their design is complex, extending over several years and involving at least three people: Belanger; Georges Louis Le Rouge (the *Ingénieur Royal,* whose extensive publication on *anglo-chinois* gardens is a major document of the art); and the Scottish gardener Thomas Blaikie, whom the Comte d'Artois hired in 1778 as his "*jardinier anglais.*"[26] Blaikie's diary reveals that he disapproved of many aspects of the French *anglo-chinois* gardens, with their complexity and exoticism.[27] Blaikie represented the more naturalistic style in England of Capability Brown, which emphasized larger and simpler effects, with broad expanses of lawn and masses of trees creating tranquil vistas.

The Bagatelle gardens evolved as a compromise between these two concepts of the irregular or English garden, although the more complex *chinois* esthetic predominated (Fig. 15). All the standard types of exotic features were

16 Bagatelle, views of the "Chinese" bridge and one of the lakes in the garden. (J. C. Krafft, *Recueil d'architecture civile*, Paris, 1812, pl. 119)

represented, with circuitous paths and waterways, pavilions of various sorts, an obelisk, a "Chinese" bridge, a "Pharaoh's Tomb," a "Philosopher's Monument," a "Paladins' Tower," and several "*rochers*" or artificial rock formations (Fig. 16).[28] But Blaikie gradually put his own stamp on the grounds as well, by "opening up Lawns" and creating "perspectives," as he noted in his diary.[29]

Ramée, executing Belanger's plans and probably working closely with Blaikie in the field as an *Inspecteur,* thus became familiar with the current debates about irregular landscape design. His own later garden plans – in Germany, Denmark, and America – are much less *chinois* than those of Belanger and are more in the spirit of Capability Brown's naturalism. Yet Ramée's own landscape style was to combine elements from the many traditions to which he was exposed in his nomadic career. And he was to retain an awareness – typically French – that garden design is fundamentally artificial, no matter how "natural" one attempts to make it. When Ramée published his *Jardins irréguliers* in 1823, he included on the title page a quotation from Jean-Jacques Rousseau's essay on nature in his novel *La Nouvelle Héloïse,* an essay that had done much to popularize romantic garden design in France:

> Nature flees frequented places; it displays its most touching charms on mountain tops, in the depths of forests, and on desert isles. Those who love nature but cannot travel that far to find it are reduced to do some violence to it, to force it somehow to come live with them; and this can be done only with some illusion.[30]

Near Bagatelle was the even more extensive estate known as the Folie Saint-James, where, according to Boulliot, Ramée also worked. The wealthy and eccentric government official Claude Baudard, Baron de Saint-James, hired Belanger in the late 1770s to create for him a house and gardens that would surpass those of his neighbor Artois. Baudard's instruction to Belanger reportedly was, "Faites ce que vous voudrez, pourvu que ce soit cher (Do whatever you wish, provided it's expensive)."[31] Belanger took Baudard at his word especially in the gardens, where he created extravagant examples of the Anglo-Chinese fashion. Most remarkable is a construction called the "Grand

Rocher," an artificial hill with a massive arch made of rough boulders, sheltering a Doric temple portico out of which issued a "spring" that fed a small lake, and with passageways leading into underground chambers accommodating a bath, a gallery, and other amusements (Fig. 17). Predictably, Blaikie considered it "ridiculous" and "the greatest pitch of extravagance."[32] But this folly strikingly combined two of the aesthetic trends of the period: the attraction to "sublime" Nature and the passion for the pure forms of antiquity. Although created for aristocratic amusement, this juxtaposition of natural and classical forms was soon to be appropriated for use in Revolutionary pageants as an expression of republican ideals.[33]

17 The Grand Rocher at the Folie Saint-James, Paris. (Author)

If Ramée in the 1780s also worked on gardens at Chantilly – as Belanger later stated in Ramée's petition – he was further exposed to contemporary developments in French landscape planning. The vast estate of the Prince de Condé at Chantilly, north of Paris, had one of the most elaborate naturalistic gardens of the period, containing romantic pavilions of numerous types and even a rustic "*Hameau*" similar to that of Marie Antoinette at Versailles, with half-timbered cottages of a sort that Ramée was later to erect on estates in Germany and Denmark.[34]

The Circular "Comble"

Boulliot's article on Ramée includes this intriguing remark: "At the age of twenty-four [i.e., in 1786], he constructed a house in Paris that used the first roof structure of circular form [*le premier comble de forme circulaire*]." The French word *comble*, in this context, refers to the timber framework that forms the roof structure of a building.[35] Belanger's experiments in building technology help clarify the nature of this "*comble de forme circulaire*."

The late eighteenth century was a time of important innovations in construction technology, and Belanger was a leader in the field. He was one of the first in France to experiment with iron trusses, which he used in a group of houses built about 1785.[36] A couple of years earlier, in collaboration with an iron-fabricator, Belanger had proposed a revolutionary iron dome to cover the central space of the Halle au Blé (grain market) in Paris. Belanger's proposal was not accepted at that time, but the executed design, by the architects Jacques Molinos and Jacques Legrand, was equally innovative: the complex and heavy trusswork of traditional timber dome construction was replaced by long, simple arches made up of short pieces of wood bolted or strapped together, a kind of forerunner of the modern laminated wood arch.[37] This concept had been proposed originally in the sixteenth century by the architect Philibert De L'Orme, but was seldom used until the experiments of Molinos and Legrand and others in the 1780s.

This "De L'Orme system," as it is sometimes called, attracted widespread interest. Thomas Jefferson and Benjamin Franklin, in Paris in the 1780s, were fascinated by its use in the Halle au Blé, and Jefferson later had the architect Benjamin Latrobe use the system to cover the Chamber of Representatives in the United States Capitol. In 1797, the German architect David Gilly published a book advocating the use of these "*Bohlen-Dächer*," as the roofs were called in German.[38] Belanger himself used this system, or something similar to it, in rebuilding the Château de Buzancy about 1784.[39]

This structural system is no doubt what Boulliot's article on Ramée means by "*comble de forme circulaire*." In fact, Ramée is known to have used the system later, in his design for a warehouse in Louvain in 1793 (see Fig. 41). And a slightly modified version of the system can be seen in Ramée's section drawing of the house he built in 1789 on the Rue du Mail in Paris, forming the circular roof (see Fig. 24). If Ramée constructed a house with a similar roof three years earlier (perhaps while acting as *Inspecteur* for Belanger), it could well have been the first use of the system in a domestic design, as stated in Boulliot's article.

Circular roofs, whether using the De L'Orme system or not, became increasingly common in Paris in the following years, as seen in the buildings that line the Rue de Rivoli, designed by Percier and Fontaine about 1805.[40] Their popularity may have been caused partly by interest in the new structural technology, but more likely by the appeal of the shape itself, circles being so essential in the neoclassical esthetic of this period.

Ramée and Cellerier

In his statement supporting Ramée's petition of 1800, the architect Jacques Cellerier wrote that he had employed him "for more than two years" and that Ramée's talent led him to entrust the young architect with the "*inspection générale*" of the *Fête de la Fédération* in 1790. Ramée himself stated that he had been a "student" of Cellerier, by which he probably meant the same kind of apprenticelike employment he had with Belanger.[41] Aside from the *Fête de la Fédération* itself (to be examined later), the identity of Ramée's work for Cellerier is not known for certain, but we can speculate about it.

Cellerier and Belanger were close friends, having been fellow students of Leroy.[42] And they developed similar architectural styles. They both were attracted to decorative motifs from Antiquity (Cellerier had spent a year in Rome as a *Prix de Rome* winner and thus had direct knowledge of newly-discovered ancient decoration). They also both favored circular forms, in their ground plans as well as in decoration. Cellerier's Hôtel Laval-Montmorency in Paris, of 1774, with a semicircular series of stables at the end of a courtyard, foreshadowed designs by Belanger as well as Ramée's Union College in America, with its ranges of buildings linked by a semicircular arcade.[43]

Cellerier was not as prolific as Belanger, nor is his work as well documented. But among the buildings attributed to Cellerier are an unusually large number of theatres, both public and private, which constituted his main specialty.[44] (The diminutive Théâtre des Variétés, built by Cellerier in 1807, still graces the Boulevard Montmartre in Paris and serves its original function.) Belanger designed a couple of theatres in the 1780s, but they were not executed.[45] Therefore, when Belanger stated in 1800 that Ramée had "constructed in Paris a small theatre [*une petite salle de spectacle*]," he probably was referring to one of Cellerier's works. One possibility is the *salle de concert* that Cellerier added to the Hôtel Laval-Montmorency in 1786 (Fig. 18): a small concert hall similar in certain ways to an auditorium-chapel that Ramée later designed for Union College (see Fig. 190).[46] And the interior ornament of the Laval-

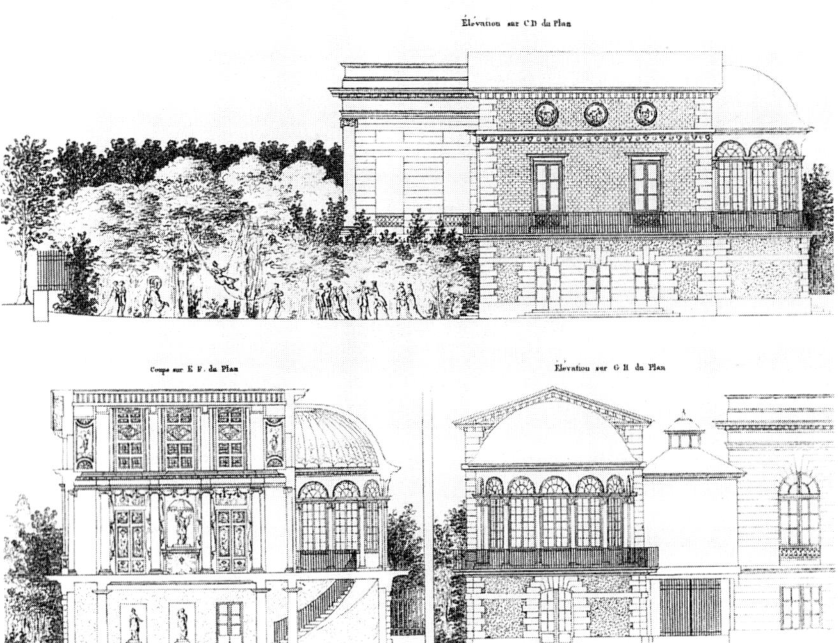

18 Salle de Concert of the Hôtel Laval-Montmorency, Paris, designed by Jacques Cellerier, 1786. (Krafft and Ransonnette, *Plans*, pl. 42)

Montmorency theatre is similar to Ramée's ornament in his buildings in Germany and Denmark.[47] If Ramée did "construct" this *salle de concert* for Cellerier, he probably was serving Cellerier as an *Inspecteur,* the position he held in Belanger's office for the Comte d'Artois.

Also in 1786, Ramée may have assisted Cellerier in the construction of one of his most remarkable buildings, a large stable for the Duc de l'Infantado, which stood on the Rue Saint-Florentin near the present Place de la Concorde.[48] The circular interior courtyard of this building was covered by a conical timber roof, over sixty feet in diameter and surmounted by a large lantern.[49] Cellerier would have had good reason to borrow one of Belanger's assistants to help in the erection of this structure, since Belanger was a leading innovator in roof systems. Ramée's construction of buildings using a pioneering circular roof suggests that he was a principal assistant to Belanger in this area.

The young Ramée, studying and working under Belanger and Cellerier in the 1780s, was thus involved in the latest developments in architecture, interior design, landscape planning, and construction technology. He probably came to know many of the other avant-garde French architects of the period, such as Alexandre Théodore Brongniart (designer of the Paris Bourse and a close friend of Belanger), Claude Nicolas Ledoux (friend of both Belanger and Cellerier), and the visionary Étienne Louis Boullée (who worked for the Comte d'Artois on occasion).[50] Ledoux in particular seems to have influenced Ramée, in ways that will be examined later.

Ramée's training may have lacked the prestige of participation in the Academy. But in all other respects, his education and practical experience prepared him well for what could have been a successful career in France if the Revolution had not intervened. This potential is indicated also by the first works Ramée produced independently, which form the subject of the next chapter.

First Works in France

Chapter 3

Ramée, forgotten in many of the places where he worked, has been neglected even in his native country. He is rarely mentioned in histories of French architecture, and then only as someone who practiced in foreign lands; no acknowledgment is made of buildings by Ramée in France. There is evidence, however, that Ramée established an independent and promising architectural practice before he fled France in 1793.

Belanger, in his statement supporting Ramée's petition of 1800, certified that his student left his office in 1790 and constructed in Paris a small theatre and houses for men named Perregaux and Berthault.[1] When Belanger wrote that Ramée "constructed" these works ("*il a construit. . .*"), it is hard to know if he meant that Ramée actually designed them or only supervised their execution for another architect. The phrase is as ambiguous in French as in English. In the case of the small theatre (*petite salle de spectacle*), we have seen that Ramée may have overseen its construction for Cellerier. The same may be true of the house with a circular roof structure, which Boulliot's biographical article states, equally ambiguously, that Ramee "constructed" in Paris. But in the cases of the houses for Perregaux and Berthault, there is evidence that Ramée acted fully as their architect. Moreover, Boulliot says that Ramée was hired directly by William Beckford to produce festive constructions in 1790. There is also a tradition that Ramée created the design for the central altar of the *Fête de la Fédération* of 1790, the first great public ceremony of the French Revolution.

Considering that much of this work occurred as the Revolution had just begun, with architectural activity in sharp decline, it is remarkable that the young Ramée found as much work as he did. Writing about architecture in Paris during the Revolution, Louis Hautecoeur has noted, "A few houses were completed in 1790 and 1791, but by the spring of 1792 inactivity in construction was almost total."[2] If Ramée had begun his career at almost any other time, his first works probably would have signaled the start of a successful professional practice in France.

The Perregaux House

Belanger's statement in Ramée's petition of 1800 mentions that Ramée constructed "the detached building, on the street, of the Perregaux house in the Chaussée d'Antin [*le corps de logis, sur la rue, de la maison Peregaux Chaussée d'Antin*]."[3] This was the property of Jean Frédéric Perregaux, the successful banker who played a prominent role in the Revolution, was named by Napoleon a senator in 1799, and was one of the founders (and first president) of the Banque de France.[4] Perregaux himself wrote a statement in support of Ramée's petition, in which he certified that "Citizen Ramée, in his capacity as

Maison de Melle Guimard située à la chaussée d'Antin.

19 Pavillon Guimard, Paris, designed by Claude Nicolas Ledoux, c. 1770. (Daniel Ramée, ed., *Architecture de C. N. Ledoux*, Paris, 1847, pl. 176, courtesy of Princeton Architectural Press)

architect, conducted the works of the building that I occupy on the Rue du Montblanc."[5] (This was the name of the Rue de la Chaussée d'Antin during this period, when it was one of the most fashionable streets in Paris.)

The structure referred to by Belanger and Perregaux was in front of the famous house that the architect Claude Nicolas Ledoux had built, starting in 1770, for the dancer and courtesan Marie Madeleine Guimard (Fig. 19). Ledoux's elegant Pavillon Guimard, with its unusual niche screened by Ionic columns (surmounted by a sculptural representation of the crowning of Terpsichore, muse of dance) was one of the most admired buildings in Paris during this period and came to be called "*le Temple de Terpsichore*."[6] Its admirers included Thomas Jefferson, who lived in Paris from 1784 to 1789 as ambassador to France and later used the house as a model for one of the buildings at the University of Virginia.[7] Ramée himself was later to use the "Guimard motif" – a niche screened by columns – in several of his designs.

On the street, in front of the Pavillon Guimard and serving as an entry to it, Ledoux had built a structure with a theatre on its upper floor, in which Mademoiselle Guimard presented performances for her friends.[8] In 1786, an impoverished Guimard had to dispose of her luxurious house and shortly thereafter the property was bought by the banker Perregaux, who moved his family into the main pavilion and rebuilt the structure on the street for use as his banking house.[9] This building on the street is the "*corps-de-logis*" erected by Ramée. In the 1790s, Perregaux's establishment was a center of financial and social activity in Paris, even providing the setting for romantic stories and novels.[10] In the mid-nineteenth century, both Ledoux's pavilion and Ramée's banking house were demolished to make way for the commercial structures that came to dominate this street, just a block east of the Paris Opera.

20 Rue de la Chaussée d'Antin, Paris, with Perregaux House at right. Anonymous watercolor drawing, probably 1790s. (courtesy of Mr. and Mrs. Theodore Kiendl, Jr.)

Little documentation of Ramée's building for Perregaux survives. A ground plan of the property, in a Paris block map of about 1820, shows that the structure covered roughly the same area as Guimard's previous theatre on the site, but had a different interior arrangement, with a large stairway leading to the banking hall on the upper floor.[11] The only known representation of the façade of the house is a watercolor drawing of the Rue de la Chaussée d'Antin, probably of the 1790s (Fig. 20).[12] The building on the right in this drawing has previously been identified as Mademoiselle Guimard's theatre structure, but it must be Ramée's new *corps-de-logis* for Perregaux: for one thing, it has four floors, whereas the Guimard building had only two.[13] Moreover, the unusual design of the façade points to a student of Belanger as its architect.

21 House on the Rue Pigalle, Paris, designed by Belanger, 1788. (Krafft and Ransonnette, *Plans*, pl. 63)

This façade has an unorthodox combination of architectural elements and surface treatments. On the rusticated lower floor is an arched doorway with a pediment over it; the upper part of the façade is smooth but framed by rough quoins; the main windows are topped by unusual semicircular panels, above which are square windows and a frieze of paterae, or round disks, under the cornice. All of these elements are found in the work of Belanger, especially during the years 1787 and 1788, when Belanger was experimenting with an almost Mannerist combination of unconventional forms and textures. Examples in Paris are his house on the Rue Neuve-des-Capucins of 1787, his three contiguous houses on the Rue Saint-Georges of 1788, and his house of the same year on the Rue Pigalle (Fig. 21).[14]

Most distinctive is the semicircular over-window that Belanger used at this time, formed by a broad projecting band supported on voluted female heads and containing either a fan-light or relief sculpture – the same element found on the façade of Perregaux's house. Ramée clearly was under the spell of his teacher when he produced this design, using the motifs that fascinated Belanger during this brief period (although not quite as boldly as Belanger himself would have used them). For this reason, it seems likely that Ramée designed the Perregaux House in 1787 or 1788, especially when one considers that by 1789 he had come under the influence of Claude Nicolas Ledoux and produced a house in a very different style.

Perregaux's statement that Ramée constructed his house "in his capacity as architect [*en sa qualité d'architecte*]" indicates that Ramée was its architect in the full sense of the word, not just a construction supervisor. If the house was designed in 1787 or 1788, when Ramée was about twenty-four years old, it may well have been his first independent commission. As might be expected, it shows the fledgling architect relying on the example of his master.

The Berthault-Récamier House

Belanger's statement in the petition of 1800 notes also "the house of Citizen Berthauld [sic], on the Rue du Mail," as one of the buildings Ramée constructed. Recently discovered in the Archives Nationales are documents pertaining to this building, dated 1789, as well as the architect's drawings of it – which make it possible to identify the house itself, still standing on the Rue du Mail, near the Place des Victoires in Paris (Fig. 22). It is one of the few works by Ramée that survive in France. The house is also of interest for its connection with the famous beauty Madame Récamier, who lived there for several years in the 1790s (before she moved, by an odd coincidence, into the building next to Perregaux's house on the Rue de la Chaussée d'Antin).

The documents in the Archives Nationales consist of an application by the property owner, Jacques Antoine Berthault, for permission to demolish an existing house on the Rue du Mail in order to erect a new one, and an eight-page report by a building inspector, on the existing structure and the proposed plans.[15] The drawings are attached to these documents. Official signatures and notations at the end of the report indicate that approval for construction of the building was given on 20 June 1789, less than a month before the storming of the Bastille.

Neither the written documents nor the plans identify the architect of this house. But the handwriting on the plans is in Ramée's distinctive script.[16] Previously, the identity of the architect of this building was the subject of speculation. Jacques Hillairet's monumental *Dictionnaire historique des rues de Paris* attributed it to the architect Louis Martin Berthault, a nephew of the man who built it; but Berthault was only eighteen or nineteen years old in 1789 and the attribution is unconvincing.[17] It is possible, of course, that Ramée collaborated with Belanger or someone else on this design. But the drawings in Ramée's hand, as well as Belanger's statement that the house was one of Ramée's works, indicate strongly that the design was his. The owner of the property, Jacques Antoine Berthault, was a successful master-mason and building contractor who had previously done construction work for Belanger.[18] Perhaps he asked Belanger to design his new house, but Belanger

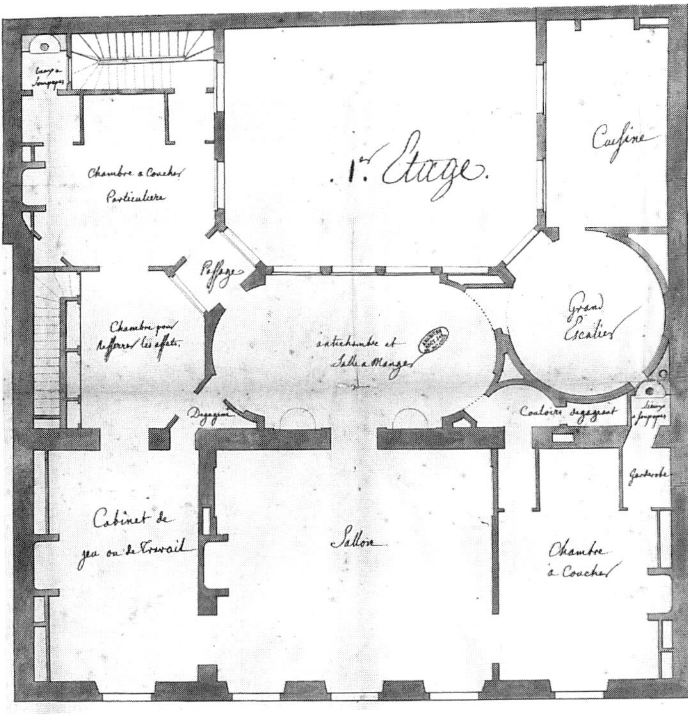

22 Berthault-Récamier House, Paris, façade on the Rue du Mail. (Author)

23 Berthault-Récamier House, plan of main floor. Ink and watercolor on paper, 49 × 52 cm. (Archives Nationales, Paris)

was too busy (this was the most active period of his career) and recommended his assistant Ramée.[19]

Ramée's drawings for the house consist of three floor plans, a section drawing, and an elevation of the street façade, all executed in ink and watercolor wash (Figs. 23–5 and color plate 1).[20] Except for some details, the house was constructed as shown in the drawings.[21] It has a U-shaped plan, enclosing a small interior courtyard. The ground floor contained shops on the street and stables behind, above which were three floors of living space, plus an attic. The plan of the main living floor reflects the architectural taste of the period, especially that of Belanger, in its variety of room shapes: rectangular, circular, elliptical, and semioctagonal.

The façade of the house, however, reveals the influence of another contemporary architect: Claude Nicolas Ledoux. Especially telling is the lower part of the façade. With its pattern of large arched openings (between which are smaller doors and windows), its prominently banded rustication, and its arches of alternately large and small voussoirs (in Ramée's drawing), it is

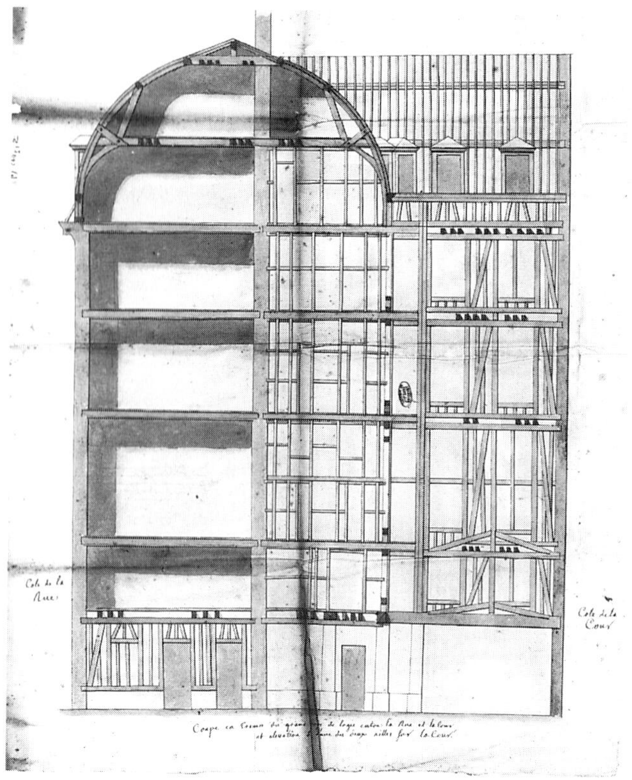

24 Berthault-Récamier House, section drawing. Ink and watercolor on paper, 52 × 68 cm. (Archives Nationales, Paris)

25 Berthault-Récamier House, elevation drawing of street façade. Ink and watercolor on paper, 36 × 45 cm. (Archives Nationales, Paris)

remarkably similar to several buildings by Ledoux, especially one of his structures at the royal salt-works of Arc et Senans, constructed in the late 1770s (Fig. 26).[22] Also consistent with Ledoux's work is the flat surface of the upper façade, with plain windows cut neatly into it – except for the windows of the principal floor, which have delicate classical frames, and pediments in the case of the three central windows.

This design established certain traits of Ramée's subsequent work, such as smooth wall surfaces, simple neoclassical details, and geometric clarity.[23] The influence of Belanger, too, is seen in Ramée's mature work, especially in his interior designs; but Ledoux seems to have played a major role in the development of Ramée's architecture. Even the most radically stripped-down of Ledoux's designs, such as his visionary plans for the Utopian city of Chaux, are echoed occasionally in Ramée's work, as in several of the house designs he published toward the end of his life (see Figs. 294–5).

It is worth recalling Belanger's remark that Ramée's talent was "distinguished as much by its natural genius as by its taste for the antique, which he has proposed to purify even further [*distingué tant par son génie naturel que par son goût pour l'antique, qu'il s'étoit proposé d'aller encore épurer*]." The revolutionary idea that ancient architecture might actually be improved by a process of purification or simplification was embodied most strikingly in the work of Ledoux. Belanger too took liberties with classical precedent, but not as radically as did Ledoux, and not generally through simplification. Thus, reading between the lines of Belanger's statement, we may detect a subtle criticism of

26 Ledoux, design for salt manufactory, Arc et Senans. (Daniel Ramée, ed., *Architecture de C. N. Ledoux*, pl. 132, courtesy of Princeton Architectural Press)

Ramée for his audacity in proposing to "purify" classicism, especially as Belanger followed this remark with a reference to "the Greeks and Romans, our veritable masters." One wonders if Belanger resented Ramée's falling under the influence of the more radical Ledoux.

There is no proof that Ledoux and Ramée knew each other personally, but they probably did. Ledoux and Belanger were friends and their professional paths often crossed, as when Belanger designed a house for Sophie Arnould, to be built next to Ledoux's Pavillon Guimard. Cellerier was an even closer friend of Ledoux and published a eulogy of him at his death in 1806.[24] So Ramée had the opportunity to meet Ledoux through either of his two mentors.

27 Berthault-Récamier House, bas-relief in salon. (Author)

28 Berthault-Récamier House, bas-relief in salon. (Author)

Moreover, Ramée's son Daniel, who became a prominent architectural writer and historian in the mid-nineteenth century, apparently acquired the engraved plates of Ledoux's designs, which he published in 1847.[25] Cellerier had been one of three people chosen by Ledoux, shortly before his death, to oversee the publication of this work. Especially as the elder Ramée had worked for Cellerier, one suspects that Daniel Ramée published Ledoux's plates because of some connection his father had with Ledoux, a question that is explored in the Epilogue of this book. These facts, as well as the nature of Ramée's work itself, suggest that he knew Ledoux personally and was strongly influenced by him in the late 1780s.

The interior of the Berthault House has been partly transformed, having been used for various purposes over the years. But some details remain of its original decoration, especially in the salon on the main floor (the room with the three pedimented windows on the street façade).[26] For the most part, this decoration is in the refined, neoclassical style that Belanger, Cellerier, and others had created in the preceding years. Around the ceiling of the salon is a cornice of projecting volute-brackets, alternating with rosettes. On the upper walls are bas-relief panels with classical motifs typical of the interior decor of Belanger and his associates.[27] On the side walls are reliefs of seated female figures shown in profile, one feeding an eagle, the other a goat (Fig. 27). On another wall is a relief showing flute- and pipe-playing youths flanking a Greek vase (Fig. 28) – virtually the same as a relief in the Hôtel Gouthière in Paris, constructed somewhat earlier by Pierre Gouthière, a master sculptor who worked with Belanger in the *Menus-Plaisirs du Roi*.[28] The same type of neoclassical bas-relief decoration was to be used by Ramée in his houses in Germany and Denmark.

29 Madame Récamier. Portrait of 1800 by Jacques Louis David, as etched by Jules David. (Jules David, *Le Peintre Louis David*, vol. 2, Paris, 1882)

It is not known if Berthault built the house on the Rue du Mail to live in himself, or to lease or sell. By the mid-1790s, however, it was inhabited by the businessman Jacques Rose Récamier and his beautiful wife, Jeanne. Only fifteen years old at the time of her marriage in 1793, Madame Récamier became the most fashionable ornament of Paris society by the end of the decade, when Jacques Louis David painted his famous portrait of her, reclining on her neoclassical couch (Fig. 29). She and her husband lived in the Rue du Mail house from soon after their marriage until late 1798, when they purchased the house of Jacques Necker (former finance minister of Louis XVI and father of Madame de Staël), on the Rue de la Chaussée d'Antin next to Perregaux's house.[29] It was the Chaussée d'Antin house that Madame Récamier made famous with her Directoire-style renovations. But her previous residence on the Rue du Mail was also appropriate to the artistic ideals she espoused, in its chaste simplicity and delicate neoclassical details.

Beckford's Oriental Tent

Boulliot's 1830 article on Ramée makes an intriguing statement: "In 1790, he was charged by Mr. Beckfort [sic] to execute a magnificent tent in the oriental style. Erected at the *Menus-Plaisirs du Roi,* this tent was transported from there to the shores of Lake Geneva, where the artist from Givet went to direct the *fêtes* that this wealthy Englishman presented there, which are still remembered."[30] Although no visual record of this work has been found, its story sheds additional light on Ramée's activities at this time.

30 William Beckford. Engraved portrait, after painting by P. J. Sauvage, c. 1792.

The eccentric William Beckford (Fig. 30) – best known for his romantic oriental novel *Vathek* and his neo-Gothic creation, Fonthill Abbey – spent much of his time in the 1780s and 1790s traveling about Europe, indulging his extravagant taste in art and luxury.[31] He was in Paris in 1789, then visited England but returned to the French capital in October 1790, despite the increasingly unsettled state of affairs there. In fact, Beckford took advantage of the disorder in France by purchasing art and fine furniture at bargain prices and engaging the services of the unemployed musicians, artists, and other retainers of the fleeing aristocrats. In February of 1792 Beckford wrote from Paris to his friend Sir William Hamilton in Naples, asking him to find an Italian palace he could rent for the following winter and noting, "I must have terraces & gardens, with views of the sea, & capabilities of placing pavilions, tents, & awnings in an Oriental fantastic style."[32]

This must be what Beckford had hired Ramée to create for him. Boulliot's remark that the "magnificent tent in the oriental style" was "erected at the *Menus-Plaisirs du Roi*" reveals that Beckford employed the royal workshops to manufacture his festive decorations. These workshops naturally were less and less active during this period; they were, in fact, shut down in 1792.[33] Beckford's tents and other paraphernalia would have been fabricated at the Hôtel des Menus-Plaisirs on the Rue du Faubourg-Poissonnière in Paris (the street, incidentally, that Ramée gave as his Paris address in his petition of 1800). As noted earlier, one of Belanger's posts was *Architecte des Menus-Plaisirs.* Ramée may well have assisted him in this position, thereby acquiring the expertise that led Beckford to hire him to design festive decorations. Ledoux, a friend of Beckford, may have introduced him to the young architect.

In July of 1792, Beckford traveled to Lake Geneva with a large entourage of servants, including an entire orchestra of former royal musicians.[34] At the end of the month, he wrote from Évian to Hamilton:

> I left Paris just in time to avoid a scene of the most frightful confusion, & am quietly established in one of the wildest forests of Savoy, on the borders of the lake. My pavilions are in a style you would like, and Lady Hamilton be in raptures with. They have been planned, executed, & adorned by the first artists of Paris, who are all here in my suite. . . .[35]

An English traveler who was entertained by Beckford at this time described the festivities, which Ramée (according to Boulliot) had gone to Lake Geneva to organize:

> The dinner was sumptuous. . . . During the repast we were entertained with a concert, performed by a select band of twenty-four musicians, which [Beckford] keeps constantly in his pay. . . . Afterwards the carriages were announced: the whole company were conveyed. . . to a most delightful wood, in the midst of which was a garden laid out in the English taste, adorned with statues. . . . Here, while we sauntered, our ears were often unexpectedly struck with the softest music, the performers of which were to us invisible, and the sounds were reverberated, with ravishing melody, by the echoing mountains which surrounded us, so that the whole appeared the effect of enchantment.[36]

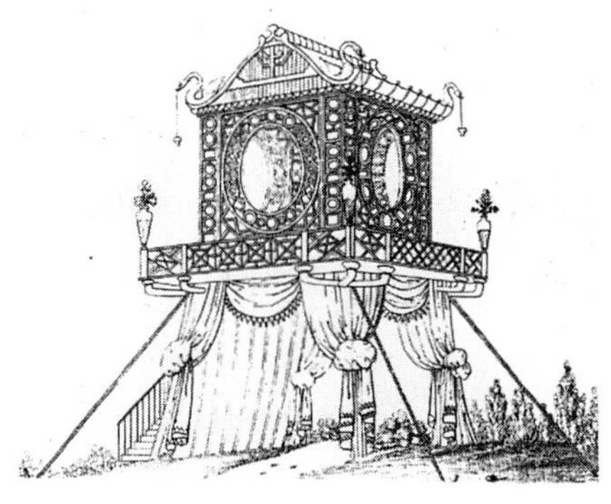

31 The "Chinese Tent" at Bagatelle. (J. C. Krafft, *Recueil d'architecture civile*, Paris, 1812, pl. 119)

32 "Turkish Tent" at Monceau Garden, Paris. Detail of engraving from Carmontelle, *Jardin de Monceau*, Paris, 1779.

Beckford was living like a king. These were the kinds of entertainment the staff of the French monarch's *Menus-Plaisirs* were trained to produce. Ramée no doubt worked at the site for some time before Beckford arrived at Lake Geneva, setting up the pavilions and readying other accommodations, as well as creating the "garden laid out in the English taste," if it did not already exist. (Landscape designers of the period were adept at producing gardens quickly; Ramée had the example of the first garden at Bagatelle, which Belanger had created in sixty-four days.) After making the preparations, Ramée must have left Évian before Beckford actually arrived, if Boulliot's statement is correct that Ramée was in Paris on 20 June 1792 when a mob invaded the royal family's apartments and he spoke out against the direction the Revolution was taking.

As for Ramée's "oriental tent" for Beckford, no representation or description of it is known.[37] But there are records of other exotic pavilions of the period, which were popular for *anglo-chinois* gardens. Belanger had erected a "*tente chinoise*" at Bagatelle (a latticework structure on stilts, draped with curtains) and a "*pavillon chinois*" at the Folie Saint-James; there also was a "*kiosk chinois*" at Chantilly and a "*tente turque*" in the garden of Monceau in Paris (Figs. 31, 32).[38] Something about tents appealed to the romantic temperament of the period. Even rooms in houses were made to look like them, such as Belanger's bedroom for the Comte d'Artois at Bagatelle, and, later, Percier and Fontaine's bedroom for Josephine Bonaparte at Malmaison.[39] Ramée too was to create tentlike rooms, in Germany and Denmark (see Figs. 66, 91, 92). Beckford's tent may have been "Arabian" in character, in keeping with the atmosphere of his novel *Vathek, conte arabe,* which he had published shortly before he hired Ramée.[40]

Even without more details, the story of Ramée's work for Beckford shows that the young architect was capable of performing the functions of a staff member of the king's *Menus-Plaisirs,* thereby suggesting that he had served as an assistant to Belanger in this activity. It is further evidence of the

33 *Fête de la Fédération* on the Champ-de-Mars, Paris, 14 July 1790. Engraving by I. S. Helman, after C. Monnet. (Stanford University Museum of Art)

breadth of Ramée's training, although in this case it was a type of training Ramée did not find many opportunities to draw upon in his later career. Few clients were like the king of France or William Beckford.

The Fête de la Fédération

Ramée evidently supported the Revolution in its early days, as did both of his mentors. (Cellerier, in fact, was appointed by the first revolutionary mayor of Paris, Jean Bailly, as deputy for public works, to supervise such projects as the demolition of the Bastille; both he and Belanger later managed to survive the Reign of Terror, despite their previous ties to the aristocracy and royal family.)[41] In his petition of 1800, Ramée stated that he had "served from the first days of the Revolution, with all the devotion of a true patriot, in the battalion of the Faubourg Montmartre."[42] Even Boulliot's article, which otherwise suppressed Ramée's ties with the Revolution, noted that in 1792 he was a "*capitaine des grenadiers*" in his neighborhood in Paris.

On 14 July 1790, exactly a year after the storming of the Bastille, the first great ceremony of the French Revolution took place, the *Fête de la Fédération* (Fig. 33). Organized by the National Assembly and held on the Champ-de-Mars in Paris (where the Eiffel Tower now stands), the event was intended to promote national unity and order by demonstrating mass support for revolutionary principles within the context of a constitutional monarchy – an ideal that still seemed possible at this stage of the Revolution. National Guard units

34 The Marquis de Lafayette at the *Autel de la Patrie, Fête de la Fédération.* Engraving by Moret, after Scheffer.

from all parts of France converged on Paris and assembled with the local populace in a vast elliptical circus formed by earthen embankments on the Champ-de-Mars. At one end of the space was a temporary triumphal arch, at the other a loggia accommodating the National Assembly and Louis XVI himself, who had reluctantly agreed to participate in the event with his family. The physical plan of this setting, using ancient Roman forms to express Enlightenment ideals, has been called the most innovative architectural creation of the French Revolution.[43]

In the center of the circus, raised on a platform, was the *Autel de la Patrie* (Altar of the Fatherland), the focal point of the ceremony. After a mass was performed, the Marquis de Lafayette, commander of the National Guard and popular hero of this phase of the Revolution, ascended to the altar and swore an oath of fidelity to "the nation, the law, and the king," with pledges to support public order (Fig. 34). The oath was repeated, in varying forms, by the guard units, the general populace, and the king himself. Contemporary accounts agreed that the hundreds of thousands of participants in the ceremony experienced a euphoria of goodwill and optimism about the future of the Revolution.[44] Madame de Staël reported the high point of the event: "Monsieur de Lafayette approached the altar to swear faithfulness to the nation, law and king; both the oath and the man who spoke it gave rise to a great feeling of confidence. The spectators were intoxicated; the king and liberty now seemed to them completely reunited."[45]

As National Guard commander, Lafayette had played the major role, along with the mayor of Paris, in planning this event and the logistics of handling the multitude of troops that came to Paris to participate. The job of making the physical plans for the ceremony had been given to Jacques Cellerier, probably because of his position as the mayor's deputy for public works.[46] Cellerier's assistant in the project was Ramée. In their supporting statements for Ramée's petition of 1800, both Belanger and Cellerier emphasized his role in the *Fête de la Fédération*. Cellerier stated that Ramée had been entrusted with "*l'inspection générale des travaux* [the construction supervision]"; Belanger said that Cellerier had named Ramée "*premier Inspecteur du Décor*" of the event; and in the margin of Ramée's own statement in the petition, Belanger added a note that "it was Ramée who executed the plans of Cellerier on the field of the Federation."[47]

Moreover, Ramée has been credited (at least since the mid-nineteenth century) with the actual design of the *Autel de la Patrie*.[48] No proof of this attribution has been found. But the form of the *Autel* is so distinctive that it is important in Ramée's career regardless of whether he designed it or merely executed it for Cellerier.[49]

The altar itself was a cylinder, raised on a series of circular tiers or steps (Figs. 35, 36). These tiers were in the center of a square platform, with additional steps on all four sides, the corners of which were filled by cubes with inscriptions and allegorical reliefs on their faces and incense-burning tripods on top. These elements stood in the center of a large circular platform, surrounded by additional steps which raised the central altar to a height of nearly

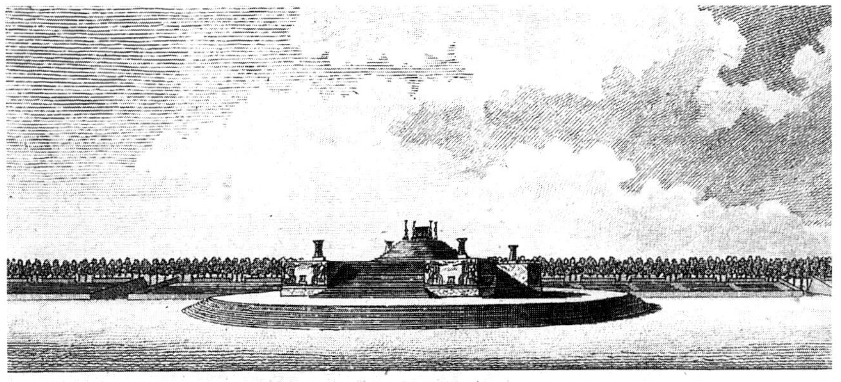

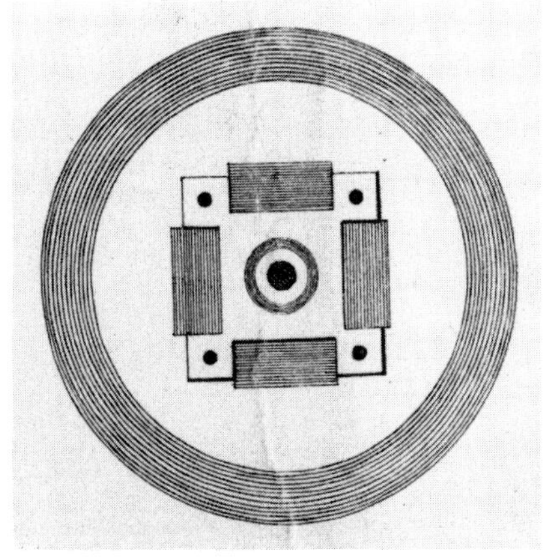

35 The *Autel de la Patrie*. Engraving by Meusnier and Gauché. (© cliché Bibliothèque Nationale)

36 Plan of the Autel de la Patrie. (J. N. L. Durand, *Recueil et parallèle des édifices de tout genre*, Paris, 1801, detail of pl. 42)

37 Funeral ceremony on the Champ-de-Mars, 20 September 1790, for soldiers killed in Nancy. Engraving by Berthaut after Prieur.

thirty feet above the ground.[50] The design was a superb solution for the functions required, allowing broad ranks of guard units to ascend from all sides for the oath-taking ceremonies, and making the rites at the elevated altar visible to the vast throngs in all directions.

The design was also a brilliant expression of the esthetic spirit of the time, with its reliance on the purest geometric forms – circles, cylinders, squares, cubes – each of which kept its formal integrity while being part of a unified whole. The design was considered a great success at the time. It was reused for other revolutionary rites, including a memorial ceremony in 1792, in honor of soldiers killed in Nancy in 1790, for which the cylindrical altar was replaced by a sarcophagus (Fig. 37).[51] In its abstraction and clarity, the design had a universal quality that allowed it to be used for various purposes and to become a symbol of the abstract ideals of the Revolution.

Ramée himself was later to employ the plan of a circular volume in a large open space in his design for Union College in America, with its cylindrical chapel in the center of a broad rectangular terrace (see Fig. 187).[52] Like the Berthault-Récamier House of the previous year, the *Autel de la Patrie* of 1790 was a pivotal design for Ramée, establishing patterns that would appear in his later work.

Between the time of the *Fête de la Fédération* and Ramée's flight from France in 1793, we know of no professional activity by him (aside from his work for Beckford). It is possible that none occurred because of the increasingly chaotic political and economic circumstances in France. When a mob invaded the king's apartments in the Tuileries Palace on 20 June 1792, Ramée spoke out in protest, according to Boulliot, making him suspect and endangering his life on the night of 2 September, when a massacre of over a thousand people suspected of disloyalty took place in Paris. Ramée joined the army of General Dumouriez and then fled France in April of 1793, for reasons that will be seen in the next chapter.

Although still in his twenties when he left his native country, Ramée had accomplished much. His training under the versatile Belanger had prepared him to work as an architect, engineer, interior decorator, city planner, or landscape designer. His jobs as *Inspecteur* for Belanger and Cellerier had given him practical experience in construction. He already had obtained commissions on his own, notably his houses for Perregaux and Berthault. And his personal contact with some of the most advanced designers working in France – Ledoux, Blaikie, and Lhuillier, besides Belanger and Cellerier – prepared him to represent the latest French styles while he was abroad. But Ramée surely did not anticipate the adventures and difficulties that awaited him in exile.

Emigration to Belgium

Chapter 4

Ramée's flight from France in 1793 began three decades of wandering and working abroad – the greater part of the architect's career. Like so much in his life, the causes and circumstances of Ramée's emigration have been shrouded in mystery. It has generally been assumed that he left Revolutionary France because of his association with the Comte d'Artois: the historian Louis Réau, for example, writing about French émigré artists, spoke of Ramée as one of those who were "compromised by their attachment with the royal family or reduced to misery by the absence of commissions."[1] But Belanger, who was much more closely associated with the Comte d'Artois than was Ramée, stayed in Paris throughout the Revolution, as did other artists who had worked for the aristocrats. Nor was Ramée's emigration due to economic hardship. It had a more sinister cause.

In his 1800 petition to have his name removed from the French government's list of émigrés (Fig. 38), Ramée gave a misleading account of his departure from France. (One gets the impression, from the brevity of Ramée's statement in this petition and the ink-splattered carelessness of his handwriting, that he wrote it disdainfully and did not take the care even to make his

38 Ramée's personal statement in his petition to have his name removed from the list of French émigrés, 1800. (Archives Nationales, Paris)

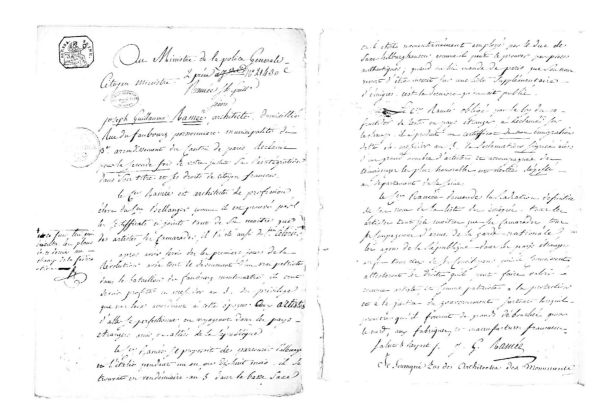

story very convincing.) Writing of himself in the third person and giving dates according to the Revolutionary Calendar, Ramée stated:

> After having served from the first days of the Revolution with all the devotion of a true patriot, in the battalion of the Faubourg Montmartre, he felt the need to take advantage, in Messidor of Year 3 [June–July 1795], of the privilege accorded to artists by our laws of that time, to perfect themselves by traveling in foreign countries that were friendly or allied with the Republic.
>
> Citizen Ramée intended to travel through Germany and Italy for a year or eighteen months. He found himself in Lower Saxony in Vendémiaire of Year 3 [September-October 1794], . . .[2]

Even disregarding the fact that the second date is illogically earlier than the first, this account does not make sense, as Ramée had been out of France for some time before either of the dates mentioned. Perhaps Ramée made a slip of the pen in writing them or was confused by the Revolutionary Calendar, whose use was required in official French documents. In any case, the statement suppresses Ramée's activities after he left Paris in 1792, probably because he knew that the true facts would jeopardize the success of his petition. The account in Boulliot's 1830 article (after the danger had passed) gives somewhat more accurate details:

> Having pronounced himself against the events of 20 June 1792 [the invasion of the Tuileries Palace by a mob], when he was Captain of the Grenadiers in his neighborhood, Ramée was marked out as a suspect. Threatened with prison, he escaped the assassins' daggers on September 2–3 [the night of massacre] only by taking refuge in the Army of Belgium, commanded by Dumouriez, who employed him as a staff officer. But the defection of this general on 4 April 1793 led Mr. Ramée to Louvain, where he took up his first profession again.[3]

39 Charles François Dumouriez. Nineteenth-century engraved portrait.

The cause of Ramée's emigration was his involvement with General Dumouriez and his treason against the French government. Charles François Dumouriez (Fig. 39), a successful commander under Louis XVI, supported the Revolution in its early days and urged the declaration of war against Austria. (Goaded by the émigré aristocrats already based in Germany, Austria was threatening an invasion of France.) When the Marquis de Lafayette turned against the increasingly radical revolution and was relieved of his command in August 1792, Dumouriez was named his successor and took charge of the Army of the North, to defend the border and invade the Austrian Netherlands. One wonders if Ramée's position as aide to Dumouriez may have been a continuation of a similar post under Lafayette, for whom Ramée had worked on the planning of the *Fête de la Fédération*.

Among Dumouriez's first military actions were engagements with the

Austrian and Prussian forces along the frontier in the Ardennes region, where the strategically located Givet and its fortress, Charlemont, were major military objectives.[4] Ramée may therefore have helped to defend his home town. In any case, he joined Dumouriez's staff before 11 October 1792, when the name "Ramé" appears on a list of the general's officers as one of six "*adjoints*" or aides.[5] (One of the other aides was named Torréry, perhaps the man of that name who later became the architect's brother-in-law.)[6] Whether or not Ramée owed his staff position to connections with Lafayette, his qualifications for it no doubt included his knowledge of engineering, from his work with Belanger, and of military fortification, from his youthful training in the Génie Militaire at Charlemont.

If Ramée was on Dumouriez's staff by 20 September, he was probably involved in the crucial Battle of Valmy, in which the French forces halted the Prussian advance to Paris and gave the Revolution its first military victory, turning the tide that most observers had thought would sweep the disciplined Austro-Prussian armies to a swift conquest of the inexperienced revolutionaries. (The author Goethe, present at the Battle of Valmy as a staff member of one of the German armies, proclaimed, "Here and now a new epoch in world history has begun."[7] Ramée was later to work for Goethe in Weimar.) After reinforcing his French troops and regrouping along the border, Dumouriez invaded Flanders in November, issuing declarations calling on the Belgian people to help expell the Austrians.

Following Dumouriez's victory at Jemappes on 6 November, Brussels fell to the French on 14 November, Liége two weeks later, and by the beginning of December Dumouriez was master of virtually all present-day Belgium. Now his problems were with Paris more than with foreign forces. The French government of the Convention distrusted Dumouriez's intentions (there was talk that he wanted to make Belgium his own personal kingdom) and it ordered him to invade Germany. In reply, he accused the Convention of providing his army with insufficient resources and supplies, resulting in dreadful conditions for the troops. In his memoirs, Dumouriez recalled the winter of 1792–3:

> The army consisted of forty-eight battalions, with 14,000 to 15,000 infantry soldiers. The cavalry totaled about 3,200 men. The soldiers were without shoes; most of them, camped in the mud, had their feet wrapped in hay. The rest of the clothing was in nearly the same condition. . . . This army had stopped at the banks of the Meuse [near Liége] because of the lack of provisions, and if General Clairfayt [the Austrian commander] had known of its distress, he could easily have attacked it, for the artillery equipment was nearly destroyed and 6,000 horses had died in December alone, for lack of fodder. There were less than 10,000 fire-arms in working order. The cavalry was without boots, saddles, coats, rifles, pistols, or sabers. Money was absolutely lacking and often the staff officers [*l'état-major,* which included Ramée] assessed themselves to furnish a day's pay.[8]

Louis XVI was now on trial in Paris. Dumouriez, distressed by the radical turn of events, which were nearly as dangerous for him as for the royal family, went to Paris to try to outmaneuver his enemies in the government and to save the monarch's life. But on 21 January 1793, the king was taken to the guillotine and the course of the Reign of Terror was set. Having returned to his army in Belgium, Dumouriez now laid plans to overthrow the Paris government and, as he later recalled, "save the unfortunate queen and her son, reestablish a constitutional monarchy and wipe out the hideous anarchy that was heaping opprobrium and misfortune on France."[9]

With reinforced troops, Dumouriez began an invasion of Holland, but the campaign went badly. He retreated and regrouped his army near Louvain; morale and discipline were low and there were many desertions. On 18 March 1793, Dumouriez's Army of Belgium met the Austrian forces of the Prince of Saxe-Coburg at Neerwinden and was defeated. Dumouriez decided on a desperate course of action: to collaborate with the enemy and to persuade the French army to march on Paris and overturn the government there. By the beginning of April, Dumouriez had drawn a number of his staff officers into his plot (including the young Duc de Chartres, later to be King Louis Philippe) and arrested some who opposed it.[10] On 2 April, when the French Minister of War and four members of the governing Convention arrived at Dumouriez's camp at St. Amand on the French border to take Dumouriez to Paris, the general was forced to action.

Dumouriez's account of this episode (written in the third person) emphasizes the role played by his still-loyal staff, of which Ramée was a member: "All the officers of the general staff filled the room [where the delegation from Paris confronted Dumouriez]. Sharing their general's views, . . . his fate became theirs." When the delegation asked Dumouriez to go into a private room with them, "the staff officers did not allow the door to be shut." The conference lasted two hours, with the delegates insisting that Dumouriez return to Paris; Dumouriez attacked the present government, "dominated by the monster Marat," and said that if he went to Paris he would simply be "giving his head to the tigers." The delegates then conferred among themselves, and their leader, Camus, announced to Dumouriez that he was relieved of his command and must obey. "A murmur of indignation arose. 'Give me the names of these men,' Camus cried, indicating the officers who surrounded him. . . . The general saw that the anger of his officers was at a pitch and about to explode."[11]

Dumouriez had the government officials seized and delivered them to the Austrians to hold as hostages (Fig. 40), thus sealing his fate in French history as a traitor. He still entertained hopes of rousing his remaining troops to join him in rebellion; but instead most of them turned on him, and on 4 April Dumouriez escaped, with his closest staff officers, into Austrian-held territory.[12]

Ramée must have been one of the officers who supported Dumouriez in these actions. Otherwise he would not have fled France at this time. Only the knowledge that he could be identified as one of Dumouriez's coconspirators would lead him to this desperate flight, which was to prevent his returning

40 Dumouriez's arrest of the Convention delegates. Engraving of 1790s.

home for many years. Even Napoleon, who was generally favorable to the return of the émigrés to France, remained adamant in regard to Dumouriez. In his petition of 1800, Ramée therefore had to suppress any mention of this period of his life. Only with the restoration of the Bourbon monarchy in France, many years later, was it possible for Ramée to acknowledge his association with Dumouriez.

Louvain

According to Boulliot's article on Ramée, Dumouriez's defection "led Ramée to Louvain, where he took up his first profession." Ramée, we recall, had spent part of his youth in Louvain with his uncle, a chaplain at the cathedral of St. Pierre. This uncle, Jean Louis Lambert, had died in 1789, but Ramée perhaps returned to Louvain because of other acquaintances or contacts in the city. Ramée stayed in Louvain only about a year and the sole evidence of his architectural work there is a design recently discovered in the Archives Nationales in Paris (Fig. 41 and color plates 2–4).[13] The finely executed drawings for this unbuilt project are on a large sheet of paper, labeled "General plan, section and elevation of a projected warehouse [*Entrepôt*] for the city of Louvain," and signed "Ramée, architect in Louvain."

The civic *Entrepôt* in Louvain was used for the storage of commodities for the city's merchants, especially its famed brewers. In 1787, Emperor Joseph II granted Louvain tax duties to pay for a new *Entrepôt* to replace the cramped existing facility on the Dyle River in the northern part of the city.[14] Plans were drawn up by an engineer named De Brou and construction began; but work on the building stopped during the short-lived Belgian revolution of 1789–90. Even before this interruption, the merchants of Louvain had complained that De Brou's plan was unsatisfactory, as it did not provide enough space either for storage or for the circulation of wagons and carts in the courtyard of the warehouse, and that it was not sufficiently enclosed to be secure from theft.[15]

Ramée's proposed new *Entrepôt,* which he designed sometime between April and June of 1793, would have satisfied these requirements.[16] Located partly on the site of the old facility, Ramée's building was to be a large structure with a central court and only one entrance. Ramée also designed a new street plan around the *Entrepôt,* to facilitate access from the nearby canal and provide an appropriate setting for the monumental building.

Around all four sides of Ramée's proposed *Entrepôt* is a continuous space for storage, on two levels, opening into the central courtyard through arched openings (color plate 3). A horizontal band on the wall between these openings is nearly the only decoration inside the building. The roof was to have a curving profile and be supported by a system of wooden arches – probably the same kind of "*comble de forme circulaire*" that Ramée claimed he had introduced to Paris domestic architecture in the 1780s.

Ramée's elevation and section drawings of the *Entrepôt,* at the top of the sheet of drawings, are rendered in ink and watercolor and presented in a *trompe l'oeil* manner, as if on a separate piece of paper, slit to reveal the ground plan beneath – a device found especially in engineers' drawings of the period.[17] The elevation drawing of the façade reveals some of the latest architectural tendencies of the period (color plate 2). The façade is almost brutal in its simplicity, appropriate to the commercial function of the building and reflecting the fashion for architectural primitivism of the time. Ramée created a kind of tension, however, between this brutalism and certain elements of refinement. The two long, unbroken wings of the façade are absolutely plain, in contrast to the three projecting pavilions at the center and ends of the building. These pavilions combine flat upper walls and heavily banded rustication below, but decorative details are placed on these surfaces in unconventional ways: within panels set in the banded rustication (on the end pavilions), and as separate decorative motifs on the plain wall of the central pavilion. This central pavilion, with its three arched openings and banded rustication, is similar to the Ledoux-inspired ground floor of Ramée's Berthault-Récamier House in Paris. Most unusual is the placement of the relief sculpture on this wall, especially the figures fitted tightly under the eaves of the roof.

In its combination of plain surfaces and idiosyncratic ornament, Ramée's *Entrepôt* façade is similar to certain competition designs of the Academy of about the same time, such as a Grand Prix design for a civic market by Charles Normand, of 1792.[18] Ramée's design for the Louvain warehouse exemplified the latest trends in French architecture; it also contains motifs that were to become staples in the architect's later work, such as the pattern of arched windows on the upper part of the central pavilion, linked by a horizontal band running across the façade.

In the lower right-hand corner of the sheet bearing Ramée's *Entrepôt* plan is a drawing of a triumphal arch, rich in sculptural decoration (color plate 4). This elegant design is puzzling. No such arch appears in the plan for the *Entrepôt* itself. Did Ramée invent the monument simply as an elaborate ornament for the title of the sheet, which is inscribed on the base under the arch? Or was it intended as an actual structure? It is one of Ramée's most fascinating designs, both for its architectural form and for the commemorative meaning revealed in its ornament and inscriptions.

Triumphal arches, invented by the ancient Romans, were used in the Renaissance and Baroque periods mainly as temporary structures celebrating royal events; occasionally they also were adapted for new uses, such as city gates and entries to great houses.[19] But it was the French Revolution that gave the

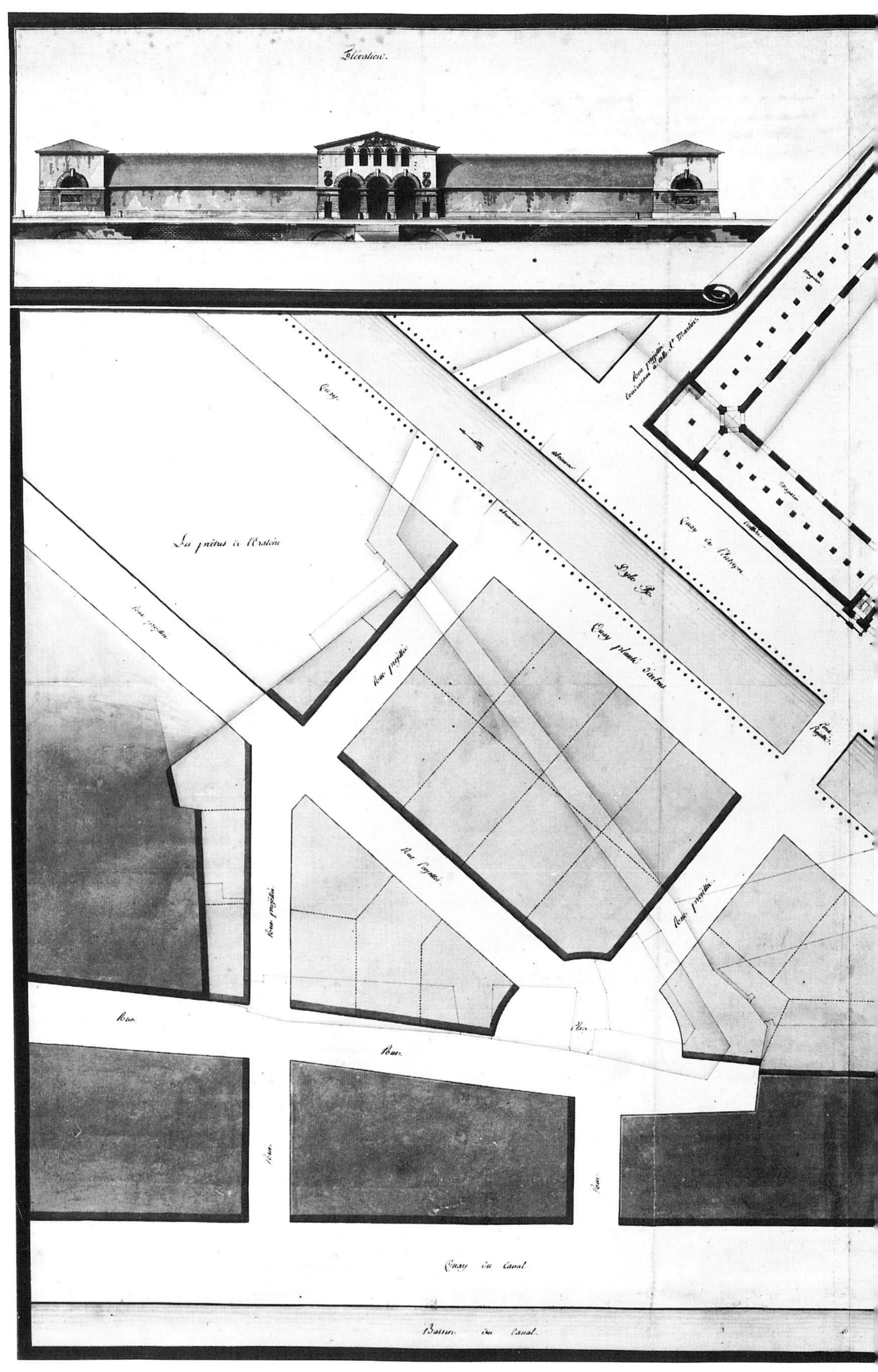

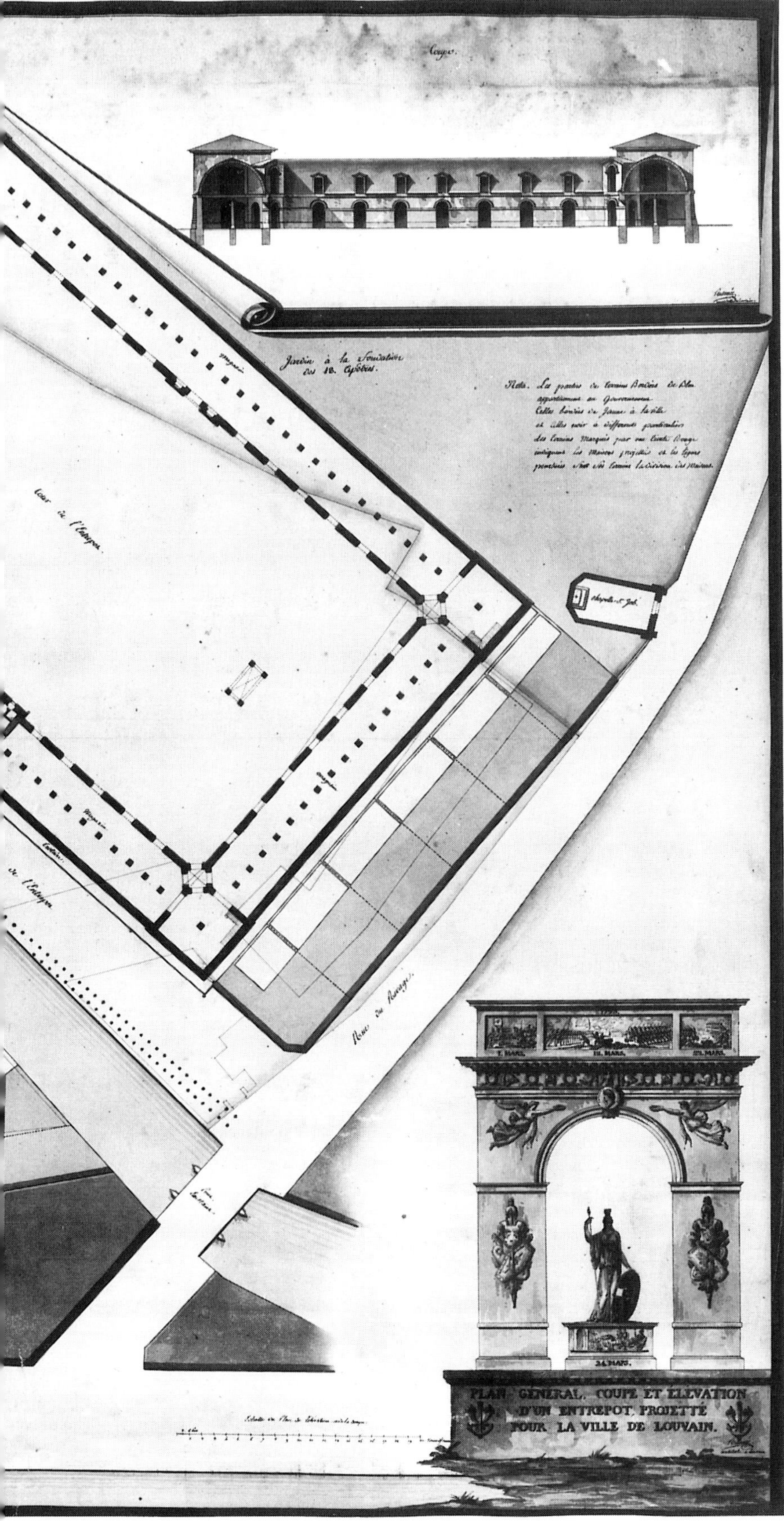

41 Plan of *Entrepôt* (civic warehouse) for the city of Louvain. Ink and watercolor drawing on paper, 98 × 120 cm, signed "Ramée, architecte à Louvain." (Archives Nationales, Paris)

triumphal arch its greatest popularity, imbuing it with new patriotic symbolism. It was used widely for revolutionary festivals, beginning with the three-arched structure that served as entry to the *Fête de la Fédération* of 1790, erected by Ramée's mentor Jacques Cellerier. Napoleon was to turn the form to his own propagandistic purposes, erecting numerous temporary arches in France and the conquered territories, as well as several great permanent arches, such as the Arc de Triomphe de l'Étoile in Paris.[20] The Revolutionary and Napoleonic obsession with the triumphal arch was the basis for its worldwide popularity in the nineteenth century; Ramée himself was to contribute to this trend, in 1813, with his design for an arch memorializing George Washington, in Baltimore.

Ramée's Louvain arch reveals a familiarity with earlier triumphal arches, but it is also innovative. Its overall shape, with a single opening and prominent attic, recalls the Roman Arch of Titus. The absence of columns and pilasters, however, is typical of late eighteenth-century designs, as is the way the principal sculptural decoration – the "trophies" on the legs of the arch and the winged "victories" above – float on perfectly flat surfaces. Ramée's arch is especially similar to one that figured in J. B. Le Febvre's design for a medical school, which took first prize in the *Grand Prix* competition of the Academy in 1789.[21] But if Ramée modeled his arch on Le Febvre's design, he also modified it, for example by adding an attic to accommodate the three bas-relief panels depicting battle scenes.

The most remarkable thing about Ramée's arch, however, is the presence of a statue under it. Traditionally, the passageways of triumphal arches were open, to allow unimpeded procession through them. Statuary was sometimes set atop them; but Ramée's placement of a statue within the arch was most unusual, with hardly any precedents.[22] In the case of this unbuilt Louvain design, we might suppose that the statue was merely a fanciful addition, which Ramée would not have proposed for a real or permanent arch. But in fact the architect was to repeat the innovation in his design for the Washington Monument in Baltimore (see color plate 18).

As for the intended purpose of Ramée's Louvain arch, its sculptural details reveal that it had a very specific – and unexpected – commemorative function. Inscribed at the top of the structure is the date 1793, below which are three bas-relief panels with battle scenes, dated 1 March, 18 March, and 22 March. The statue standing under the arch is an allegorical female figure, holding a shield bearing one of the heraldic devices of the Austrian Netherlands. On the pedestal beneath the statue is another bas-relief, representing figures in front of a city gate, dated 24 March. On the keystone of the arch is a medallion with a laurel-crowned head and inscribed "Carolus Ludovicus."

March 18, 1793, was the date of the Battle of Neerwinden, in which the Austrian forces of the Prince of Saxe-Coburg defeated the French army of General Dumouriez. The principal commander of the German forces in this battle was the twenty-two-year-old Austrian archduke Carl Ludwig – Carolus Ludovicus – who later had an heroic military career opposing Napoleon. On 1 March, Carl Ludwig had commanded his troops in the Battle of Aldenhoven (a prelude to Neerwinden); on 22 March he engaged in actions near Louvain, which drove the French from that city; on 24 March he entered Louvain, as the newly-appointed Governor General of the Austrian Netherlands.[23] Ramée's triumphal arch is therefore a memorial to Carl Ludwig's defeat of the French, which saved the Netherlands for Austria (briefly, at least). More specically, it is a monument to the Austrian general's "liberation" of Louvain.

The Austrian authorities in Louvain perhaps had proposed, or were considering, the erection of such a memorial to Carl Ludwig. Several temporary triumphal arches were, in fact, erected when the Austrian emperor entered Louvain in April of 1794.[24] But why did Ramée include this design on the sheet illustrating his *Entrepôt* project? Merely to advertise his talents to the authorities? One would think that Ramée must have found it painful to design a memorial to the man who had defeated his commander, Dumouriez, thereby forcing the two of them into exile from their country. Did Ramée simply decide that he would not let national or personal feelings stand in the way of his professional career? As an exile from his homeland, in an age of instability and change, Ramée was to be confronted with many such situations during his career, requiring quick shifts of loyalty or identity. To keep his self-respect, he perhaps began to consider himself simply an architect and a citizen of the world, not a Frenchman or a member of a particular political group.

The role of uncommitted wanderer may actually have appealed to Ramée. At several points in his life, he kept on the move even when it seems he could have remained settled if he had wished. An example is his decision to go to America in 1812: the architectural profession was not thriving in Paris (where Ramée was living at that time), but things were not so bad as to require him to go halfway around the world. It is also remarkable how easily Ramée moved from one social milieu or type of clientele to another – from Bourbons to merchants to frontiersmen. In an age of revolution, Ramée represents one kind of response to the problems of the period: an adoption of anonymity or universalism.

Ramée's architecture itself might be seen as mirroring this attitude. In its geometric clarity it is cool, abstract, even impersonal. Ramée sometimes added ornament or eclectic details to his forms (classical, Gothic, or other, depending on the circumstances), but these additions tended to remain superficial, in the literal sense of being applied to the surface, and in their interchangeability. Ramée's obsession with pure geometry was typical of the neoclassicism of his period, but his treatment of it was special. In contrast to the massive and powerful forms of Ledoux, for instance, Ramée's architecture became increasingly crisp, light, and almost insubstantial.

After hardly a year in Louvain, Ramée was forced to move again when the French staged a new campaign in Belgium and finally ejected the Austrians from the country. Boulliot tells us that "during the second conquest of the Netherlands by the French, after the Battle of Fleurus, 26 June 1794, Ramée left for Erfurt," in Saxony. During the next decade and a half, he was to live in Germany, practicing architecture and landscape design in several cities and principalities, and also in Denmark. Ramée's professional success during this period (when his career was not disrupted by political turmoil) was due in large measure to his facility with the latest styles in French design, which he helped introduce into the places where he worked. In some of these places, such as Denmark, Ramée was the only French architect active at that time. Everywhere he worked, he was seen as representing the most up-to-date Paris fashion.

How did Ramée stay abreast of French design during these years abroad? He apparently subscribed to Parisian architectural journals (issues of the *Journal des bâtimens* are mentioned in his correspondence in 1806), and he perhaps had access to more substantial publications, such as Percier and Fontaine's *Recueil de décorations intérieures* or J. N. L. Durand's *Précis des leçons d'architecture,* as well as collections of engraved plans of contemporary French designs, such as those published by J. C. Krafft.[25] But there is evidence that Ramée actually returned to Paris several times while living in Germany. Surprisingly, some of his visits took place even before he was granted amnesty by the French government in 1803. It is possible that he had to make these trips secretly, or at least in such a way as not to draw attention to himself while in France and still on the official list of émigrés.

One of these visits to Paris took place in early 1801, as revealed in a letter that the Marquis de Lafayette wrote to Ramée's business partner in Hamburg (quoted in Chapter 7). Ramée also may have been in Paris the previous year, to gather the letters of support for his amnesty petition, in which he actually identified himself as having a Paris address ("Joseph Guillaume Ramée, architecte, domicillié Rue du Faubourg-Poissonière," the street on which his teacher Belanger lived).[26] In February 1803, after the death of his mother, Ramée returned to his home town of Givet, as revealed by a legal document recording his sale of inherited property.[27] And in a letter of 1805, Ramée's partner, André Masson, referred to "our firm in Paris," implying that they had a branch office there or were associated with a Paris business.[28]

The most intriguing document in this regard is a French police report of September 1796, recording the death in Paris of one "Joseph Jacques Ramée . . . without known heirs."[29] The address of this person is given as the Rue Poissonière (the continuation of the street Ramée was to name in his petition of 1800). This, as well as the rarity of the surname Ramée and the fact that the architect himself sometimes used the names Joseph Jacques, makes it hardly likely that these two men were unrelated. Was the dead man the architect's father, who perhaps had come to Paris to live with his son before the Revolution? Or was it possibly the architect himself? If Ramée made a trip from Germany to Paris in 1796, he probably had to do so surreptitiously, since, at this early date, his émigré status and association with Dumouriez still would have put him in considerable danger. If his presence in Paris was discovered, Ramée perhaps fled and his friends somehow faked his death in order to aid his escape.

Ramée's petition of 1800 contains one more clue to his continued contacts with Paris. The petition bears the signatures of several French artists, the most significant of whom is Charles Percier.[30] In 1800, Percier and his partner,

Pierre Fontaine, had just begun their work for Napoleon which would make them the foremost architects and decorators of the period and the main creators of the Empire Style.[31] Percier must have known Ramée personally; otherwise, he surely would not have taken the risk, at this crucial point in his career, of supporting an émigré with a compromising past.

Ramée and Percier were the same age (both born in 1764) and they may have met first when they were students in Paris in the 1780s – Ramée in Belanger's office, Percier at the atelier of David Leroy, Belanger's own former teacher. Percier's signature on Ramée's petition suggests that they kept in contact following Ramée's departure from France and that they saw each other when Ramée returned periodically to Paris. If so, Ramée had the opportunity to play an unusual role during his years in Germany. Practicing architecture in Hamburg and elsewhere, but maintaining contact with artists in Paris, including the preeminent tastemaker Percier, Ramée was in a unique position to represent and disseminate French ideas abroad.

Thuringia and the Saxon Principalities

Chapter 5

Boulliot's article of 1830 provides nearly the only clues for reconstructing Ramée's work in central Germany after he left Belgium, a part of his career that has been virtually unknown until now. The article states: "During the second conquest of the Netherlands by the French, after the Battle of Fleurus, 26 June 1794, Ramée left for Erfurt, where the Prince Primate, Monsieur Dalberg, charged him with diverse constructions. This procured for our artist the putting in order of the parks of Saxe-Meiningen, Gotha, and Weimar."[1]

Ramée's petition of 1800 adds the information that "he found himself in Lower Saxony in Vendémiaire of Year 3 [late 1794], where he was briefly employed by the duke of Saxe-Hildburghausen."[2]

The cities of Erfurt, Meiningen, Gotha, Weimar, and Hildburghausen are close to one another in the region of Saxony called Thuringia. In the late eighteenth century, all of them except Erfurt were independent duchies, ruled by members of the Saxon royal family. Erfurt was subject to the archbishop-elector of Mainz, who was represented in Erfurt by a governor. If Ramée produced work in all these places in Thuringia, he therefore was working for at least five different clients.

Little evidence can be found of the specific projects ascribed to Ramée in Boulliot's article. But research in Thuringian archives has uncovered other work by the architect, including some remarkable drawings. Moreover, a survey of the places where Ramée worked, and of his clients, reveals the cultural environment and new ideas to which he was exposed, which helped shape his later work.

Erfurt, in the mid-1790s, was the destination of many French and Netherlandish émigrés, including the archbishop of Liége.[3] Ramée perhaps accompanied other refugees from Belgium to Erfurt, or he may have had an introduction to the governor of the city, who (according to Boulliot) then hired him. This man was Karl Theodor von Dalberg, a statesman and ecclesiastic with wide-ranging interests in the arts and sciences (Fig. 42).[4] After his university studies Dalberg had joined the staff of the archbishop-elector of Mainz; in 1772 he was appointed Staathalter (governor) of Erfurt, a post he held until he became elector of Mainz, in 1802, and arch-chancellor of the Holy Roman Empire. But Dalberg is known mainly for his later role in European history, after 1803, when he supported Napoleon's restructuring of Germany and was named by the Emperor "prince primate" of the newly-created Confederation of the Rhine, a political entity that collapsed when Napoleon fell from power.

42 Karl Theodor von Dalberg. Silhouette portrait.

In the 1790s, when he engaged Ramée, Dalberg had assumed ecclesiastical posts in several cities besides Erfurt, but he continued to reside mainly there, where he had instituted progressive policies in social welfare and education. Dalberg was a member of the Illuminati, an elite international fraternity

43 View of Domplatz (Cathedral Square) in Erfurt. Ink and watercolor drawing on paper, 44 × 65 cm., signed "Ramée, architecte, 1795." (Angermuseum, Erfurt)

of Enlightenment figures founded in 1776, and he befriended the writers Wieland, Goethe, Schiller, and others. His own writings, on theology, government, criminology, esthetics, mathematics, and music, reveal the philosophy that has been called enlightened despotism, a belief in Enlightenment rationalism but also in the need for a strong paternalistic state, to oversee the welfare of the people and to guide the arts and sciences.[5]

No evidence can be found of the "diverse constructions" that Ramée reportedly executed for Dalberg in Erfurt. But one document of the architect's stay in Erfurt survives: a remarkable watercolor drawing, preserved in the city's Angermuseum (Fig. 43 and color plate 5).[6] Signed by Ramée and dated 1795, it portrays the center of the city, dominated by the Domhügel or Cathedral Hill, with its two towering medieval churches, the Gothic cathedral of St. Mary and the older church of St. Severus. In the foreground is the square now called the Domplatz, with groups of citizens and marching troops. Surrounding the square are houses of traditional half-timbered construction. In the center foreground is the Minervabrunnen, a fountain that had been erected in 1784. To the right is an obelisk that had been put up in 1777 to honor the archbishop of Mainz, Dalberg's superior.[7]

This view of Erfurt is different from all of Ramée's other known drawings, which represent his own architectural and landscape designs. But it was surely not his first such drawing, for its skillfulness shows that the architect had experience with this kind of topographical rendering. It was perhaps commissioned by Dalberg or some other resident of Erfurt, to provide an accurate record of the city center. In fact, the most striking thing about the drawing is its detailed accuracy. Comparison with other visual records and with the structures that still exist on the site (the two churches, several of the houses, the obelisk, and the fountain) reveals that Ramée's drawing was based on precise and detailed observation.

The accurate portrayal of medieval buildings and cities was a relatively new phenomenon in the late eighteenth century. More common were impressionistic, romanticized, or idealized views of such scenes. Ramée's drawing reflects a more objective interest in medieval architecture, which was to develop in the nineteenth century and be embodied in France in the *Commission des Monuments Historiques*. It is interesting that one of the early employees of this government commission, in the 1830s, was Ramée's son, Daniel – who was born in Hamburg in 1806 and trained in architecture with his father. Daniel's drawings of medieval buildings and cities, many of which were published in the mid-nineteenth century, are similar in certain respects to his father's drawing of Erfurt.

In its lovingly rendered details, this drawing seems to reveal a genuine interest in medieval architecture on the part of Ramée *père*. Had the architect acquired this interest before he came to Germany? Or was it inspired in him by someone in Erfurt? There is no evidence that Dalberg had an interest in medieval architecture; his writings, in fact, reveal a general contempt for the Middle Ages and its arts (in 1802 he wrote of medieval man as "buried in the shadows of stupidity and barbarism" and stated that "the fine arts were forgotten" then).[8] This was the conventional view of the Middle Ages at the time. But at the end of the eighteenth century new attitudes were emerging. Goethe had contributed to this shift in 1772, with his essay on the cathedral of Strasbourg, in which he praised Gothic architecture – "German architecture," as he called it – for qualities of harmony and organic integrity, which Goethe was perhaps the first author to articulate clearly.[9] By the 1790s, when Ramée was in Erfurt, Goethe himself had largely transferred his enthusiasm from the Gothic style to the classical architecture he had seen in Italy in the previous decade; but he had sown the seeds of a new appreciation of medieval building. Ramée may well have encountered someone in Erfurt who represented the new attitude and who inspired him, or commissioned him, to make an accurate drawing of the city's ancient churches and houses.

Boulliot tells us that Ramée's work for Dalberg in Erfurt procured for him "the putting in order [*l'arrangement*] of the parks of Saxe-Meiningen, Gotha, and Weimar." All three of these parks existed before the architect arrived and they exemplified some of the most advanced landscape design in Germany. But Ramée evidently produced plans for parts of these gardens, and his study of them added to his knowledge of international trends in landscape planning.

Dalberg probably introduced Ramée to the dukes of Meiningen, Gotha, Weimar, and Hildburghausen. Although these rulers were Protestant and Dalberg was Catholic, they were all friends and had many common interests. The dukes of Gotha and Weimar were members of the Illuminati, like Dalberg, and all five rulers shared the friendship of Goethe and other intellectuals who frequented their courts.[10]

These dukes were all cousins, members of the Ernestine branch of the Saxon royal family.[11] Their duchies were small and relatively insignificant; unlike Dalberg, who had considerable political power, each of these dukes was simply one of the legion of rulers who held patches of land in the crazy quilt of eighteenth-century Central Europe. They were much more likely to make a cultural than a political mark in the world, a fact that these Thuringian dukes appreciated fully. Most notable in this regard was Karl August of Saxe-Weimar, who at the beginning of his reign in 1775 brought Goethe to his court (where the poet remained for the rest of his life), creating there one of the period's great centers of culture.

Karl August's ducal cousins were also important patrons of the arts, especially of the theatre. Ernst II of Gotha presented the dramas of Goethe and Schiller in the theatre in his palace, as did Georg I of Meiningen; even tiny Hildburghausen had its court theatre, presided over by its duke, Friedrich.[12] In Weimar, Goethe himself was director of Karl August's court theatre. Ramée, with experience in theatre design in Paris, may have been engaged to draw stage sets or plans for new theatres at these Saxon courts, as he was later to do in Hamburg and Copenhagen. In the mid-1790s, the theatre at Weimar was in need of rebuilding; the job was eventually done in 1798 by the architect Nicolaus Friedrich Thouret, but it is possible that Ramée was involved in the design three years earlier.[13] No records of this work are known. There is evidence, however, of other types of design by Ramée in Weimar: for parts of the ducal park and for interior design in the "Roman House" in the park. It appears that while Ramée was, strictly speaking, working for the duke, his more immediate client was Goethe (Fig. 44).

44 Johann Wolfgang von Goethe. Engraved portrait by J. H. Lips, 1791.

Interested in nearly every human activity, Johann Wolfgang von Goethe had a special interest in architecture and landscape design. One of his principal responsibilities in Weimar, in his job as a minister to Karl August, was overseeing the physical layout of the ducal properties.[14] For several decades, starting in the late 1770s, Goethe directed the rebuilding of parts of the ducal palace that had burned, the laying out of an extensive park, and the erection of various structures in this park.

The Weimar park, along the banks of the meandering River Ilm to the south of the ducal palace, was perhaps the most up-to-date landscape garden in Germany when Ramée worked there (Fig. 45).[15] Karl August and Goethe had initially been inspired by a visit in 1778 to the duke of Anhalt-Dessau's park at Wörlitz – the first great "English" garden in Germany – and also by C. C. L. Hirschfeld's treatise on landscape planning.[16] The park at Weimar, as it evolved mainly in the 1780s, typified the romantic garden, with a variety of wooded and open areas and picturesque structures. But Goethe imbued the park with a special character, reflecting his own wide-ranging interests.[17] It served as a laboratory for his scientific study of plants; it inspired many of his

45 Part of the Weimar Park, on the River Ilm, with Goethe's *Gartenhaus* to the left. Engraving by Jacob Roux, before 1809.

46 Goethe's "Gutes Glück" monument in the Weimar Park. (Author)

poems about nature; and it became the site of monuments expressing his esthetic ideas, such as the "Gutes Glück" sculpture he erected in his own part of the park (Fig. 46). This monument is a perfectly plain sphere poised on a cube, set amid foliage, epitomizing the neoclassical fascination with the contrast between the regularity of abstract thought and the irregularity of nature.

Another aspect of Goethe's landscape philosophy is suggested by remarks he made in 1778 in a letter to a friend: "My valley is getting more and more beautiful. . . as I am engaged in [improving] the neglected spots, . . . handing over the objects of art to dear obliging nature to attach and cover them."[18] Mainly due to Goethe's role in creating it, as an expression of his diverse views on art and life, the Weimar park quickly became one of the best-known naturalistic landscapes in Europe.

When Ramée arrived in Weimar, the major work in progress in the park was the Römisches Haus (Roman House), begun in 1791, which reflected Goethe's heightened interest in classical architecture following his sojourn in Italy in the 1780s (Fig. 47).[19] This building, perched above the river valley and shaped like an ancient temple (one of the first such neoclassical structures in Europe), contained several small rooms for the use of Karl August, for whom the building became a favorite retreat in his later years. Goethe had engaged the architect Johann August Arens to plan the structure, but the poet himself probably conceived the essential form, including the unusual basement entrance (at the lower end, facing the valley) with squat Doric columns reflecting the primitive associations of Greek architecture current at that time.

47 Römisches Haus (Roman House), Weimar. (Author)

A Weimar court account book for 1795–6 notes the following payment to Ramée (made probably in late 1795, judging from its position in the accounts): "26 Reichsthalers, to the French architect J. Ramée for various sketches and drawings for the Römisches Haus."[20] No further evidence of these drawings by Ramée can be found, but they probably had to do with the building's interior, which was being planned and executed at this time. The Dresden architect C. F. Schuricht had already been hired to design the interior of the Römisches Haus, and his drawings for the two main rooms survive.[21]

Perhaps Ramée's drawings were for another room in the building, the Yellow Room (Fig. 48), whose decorative details are similar to those of rooms Ramée later created in Hamburg and Copenhagen. Or Ramée may have contributed in some way to the execution of the rooms planned by Schuricht, which resemble the Directoire-style interior designs of Belanger in Paris. Whatever his role in the design of the Römisches Haus, Ramée here was exposed, perhaps for the first time, to the new interest in buildings shaped like classical temples (an interest stronger in Germany than in France), which the architect was later to display in his mausoleum at Ludwigslust (see Fig. 145). Another element was thus added to Ramée's experience of diverse artistic trends.

48 Römisches Haus, the Yellow Room. (Nationale Forschungs- und Gedenkstätten in Weimar)

Ramée also drew landscape plans in Weimar. The court accounts contain the following item (written probably in early 1796): "130 Reichsthalers, to the French architect Jos. Ramée for making a plan of the Rothäuser Berg and Fischhalter Platz, as well as several drawings which he made at the command of His Serene Highness, concerning the park."[22]

These drawings no longer survive, nor is it known to what extent they were implemented.[23] But this is the earliest documented case of Ramée's activity as a landscape designer (aside from his work as an apprentice to Belanger). Park design was to become a major part of Ramée's architectural practice in northern Germany, Denmark, the United States, and finally in France, where toward the end of his life Ramée was to publish many of his landscape plans. The fact that in 1795 the duke of Weimar – or Goethe – hired Ramée to make plans for parts of the ducal park shows that he was already able to present himself convincingly as an expert in landscape design.

The Rothäuser Berg was an area to the east of the ducal palace, to which Karl August had turned his attention in the late 1780s, in order to extend his parklands. (The Fischhalter Platz was an adjacent area, around a group of fish ponds.) After a farm called the Rotes Haus burned in 1785, the duke purchased the property, which became the Rothäuser Garten. There he erected in 1788 a group of three columns, evoking a ruined temple (Fig. 49). The duke gradually acquired additional lands to the east. This was hilly terrain, in contrast to the more level ground on which the earlier parts of the ducal park had been laid out along the banks of the Ilm. An interest in rugged, hilly land was a new trend in romantic park planning at this time, a departure from the previous preference for tamer, gently rolling terrain. Whatever was the nature of Ramée's lost plans for this part of the Weimar park, it is interesting that after the architect proceeded to Hamburg, he executed several plans for parks along the steep and rugged banks of the River Elbe, in which he took full advantage of the picturesque possibilities of this newly appreciated type of topography.

As for the other Saxon principalities in which Ramée is said to have worked, his activity in Hildburghausen remains a mystery. But Meiningen and Gotha provide some clues to his work there – and, in the case of Gotha, a wonderful discovery.

The duke of Saxe-Meiningen, Georg I, was a supporter of progressive social ideas and a patron of the arts. Best known for his court theatre and his

49 The Rothäuser Garten, Weimar. Drawing by G. M. Kraus, c. 1800. (Kunstsammlungen zu Weimar)

50 Gothic-ruin entry to the English Garden, Meiningen. Engraving by Wilhelm Thierry, 1794. (© cliché Bibliothèque Nationale, Paris)

friendships with Goethe, Schiller, and other writers, the duke also promoted the latest notions in garden design. Beginning in 1782 when he became duke, Georg gradually laid out an "*Englischer Garten*" which was somewhat different from that in Weimar.[24] Georg's special interest was the architectural constructions and "follies" that one could erect in such parks, and over the years he created a remarkable group of them: pavilions, bridges, grottos, a Gothic hermitage, a "fisherman's cottage" built of logs, and several artificial ruins. The most striking of these structures served as the entry to the park, simulating the ruin of a Gothic church (Fig. 50). It apparently was executed in 1793 by a builder named J. A. Schaubach, but like everything in the Meiningen garden, it was probably conceived by the duke himself. From 1794 to 1797, Georg had an architect named Wilhelm Thierry produce engraved views of his English garden, each view portraying one of its architectural structures.[25]

Ramée therefore worked in Meiningen during the period when Georg was largely completing his garden and recording it in engravings. We can only speculate on what Ramée's contributions may have been. Most interesting in this regard is the pavilion called the *Tempel der Harmonie*, a circular structure whose exterior had a purposely primitive appearance (with natural tree-trunks serving as columns) but whose interior was in a contrasting, classical style, with Corinthian columns, a finely decorated dome, and wall panels painted with rather Directoire-style "Pompeiian" motifs (Figs. 51, 52).[26] The date of construction of this Temple of Harmony is not known, but Thierry engraved it in 1797, which suggests that it had been completed shortly before then. Ramée may have had a hand in the design of this structure, especially of its interior, as he had done in the Römisches Haus at Weimar.

In the late 1790s, the duke of Saxe-Meiningen also laid out gardens at other properties he owned, so Ramée may have contributed to their design as well. The park at Altenstein, north of Meiningen, was especially important (Fig. 53). Situated in hilly country, it had a wilder, more irregular character

51 Temple of Harmony in the English Garden, Meiningen. Drawing by G. Lilie, c. 1900. (P. Lehfeldt and G. Voss, *Bau- und Kunst-Denkmäler Thüringens*, vol. 34, Jena, 1909, p. 240)

52 Interior of the Temple of Harmony. (P. Lehfeldt and G. Voss, *Bau- und Kunst-Denkmäler Thüringens*, vol. 34, p. 241)

53 View of Altenstein Park, with "Alpine Chalet" in background. Engraving by W. Thierry. (Staatliche Museum, Meiningen)

than the Meiningen Park, with precipitous rock formations and waterfalls (reminiscent of the artificial "rochers" created by Ramée's teacher Belanger at Bagatelle and the Folie Saint-James in Paris) and picturesque structures such as an "Alpine Chalet," Gothic "Knight's Chapel," and "Chinese Rotunda." The Altenstein park was executed starting in 1798, reportedly following the ideas of Georg himself, so it is possible that Ramée contributed in some way to the duke's plans.[27]

The duke of Saxe-Gotha, Ernst II, also had an English garden, to the south of his palace at Gotha. It was, in fact, one of the earliest such parks in Germany, having been laid out starting in 1769. Simpler than the gardens at Weimar and Meiningen, it consisted mainly of an hourglass-shaped lake with an island in it, surrounded by open and wooded areas; it had few architectural constructions, notably a small Doric temple, built about 1780.[28]

Ramée's garden plans for the duke of Saxe-Gotha, however, were probably in a different area. Starting about 1790, the fortification walls around the palace and the adjacent city were gradually torn down and replaced by boulevards and public gardens.[29] In the mid-1790s, when Ramée was in Gotha, the walls to the east and south of the palace had been removed, and it is in this area that Ramée likely produced plans for new gardens.[30]

No evidence of Ramée's garden plans can be found in the Gotha state archive or the former ducal library. But the library, still housed in the palace, possesses a group of splendid drawings by Ramée for a country house (Figs. 54–9 and color plates 6–8).[31] Drawn in ink and watercolor, they are on five sheets of paper, bound together as a volume that has been in the Gotha library since at least the early nineteenth century. Each sheet is signed and dated "Ramée, 1796." Each bears two drawings: at the bottom, a plan (a site plan and four floor plans); at the top, perspective, elevation, and section drawings of the house. The first sheet, with the perspective view and site plan of the house, is labeled with the only identification of the design: "Vue perspective et plan général d'une maison de campagne."

This country house is shown, in the site plan, at the end of a tree-lined avenue. A forecourt is bounded at the sides by two buildings serving as stables

54 Perspective view and site plan of country house. Ink and watercolor drawing on paper, 26 × 41 cm, signed "Ramée, 1796." (Forschungs- und Landesbibliothek, Gotha)

and servants' quarters, buildings whose walls have a continuous series of shallow arched recesses – a motif found especially in the work of Claude Nicolas Ledoux, and which Ramée was later to use as the unifying feature of his design for Union College in the United States.[32] The house itself, set in an irregular garden, is based more on the designs of Ramée's teacher Belanger than on those of Ledoux. On the front of the house (Fig. 55), above the portico, is an unusual pedimented projection with an arched opening in it, a feature found in the house Belanger built in 1787 on the Rue des Capucines in Paris (Fig. 56). On the garden façade (Fig. 57), the decorative arches over the central door and windows are similar to the overwindows Belanger used in two other Paris houses in the late 1780s (and which Ramée had included on the façade of his Perregaux House), although Ramée now placed the sculpted female heads within the arches, rather than under their ends.[33]

Inside the house, the rooms have a variety of shapes – rectangular, oval, polygonal – as in Ramée's earlier Berthault-Récamier House and in many of Belanger's houses. But especially reminiscent of Belanger is the decoration of these rooms, as revealed in the section drawing made by Ramée: an exquisite drawing showing in full color the minutest details of the wall surfaces, fabrics, and furniture in these rooms (Fig. 58 and color plate 8). The decoration is in the most elaborate version of Belanger's Directoire style of interior design, similar to his interiors in Bagatelle, the Hôtel Dervieux, and the Rue des Capucines house in Paris.[34] Distinctive details include the trompe-l'oeil fan decoration in the bed chamber, the striped fabric in the sofa and bed alcoves, the circular wall reliefs with cameo-like scenes from Antiquity, and the octagonal and lozenge-shaped patterns on the doors and wall panels. Later, in Hamburg and in Denmark, Ramée was to execute much interior decoration but it was to be simpler, employing mainly cast-plaster wall reliefs; only in the palatial Erichsen Mansion in Copenhagen (and probably in the now-destroyed Hamburg Börsenhalle) would Ramée create rooms comparable in their rich detail and color to those shown in the Gotha drawings. This interior design reveals that the house, despite its relatively modest size, was meant for a client with considerable financial resources.

For whom was this country house intended? Normally, drawings for such a design would indicate the name of the person who commissioned it. The fact that this design is identified only as a "*maison de campagne*" suggests that it may have been an imaginary project drawn by Ramée to show to prospective clients. Yet the architect must have presented or sold the design to a specific person; the drawings are too fine for Ramée simply to have discarded. And they were evidently intended for a German client, as indicated by the scale given in "*pieds de France*" (a specification that would have been unnecessary in France itself) and the fact that the basement plan includes a "*cave à bierre*" larger than the adjacent "*cave à vin*" (no French house would have had a beer cellar larger than its wine cellar).

The presence of these drawings in the duke of Saxe-Gotha's library certainly suggests that he or a member of his family commissioned them, or at least purchased them from Ramée. An intriguing possibility has been suggested

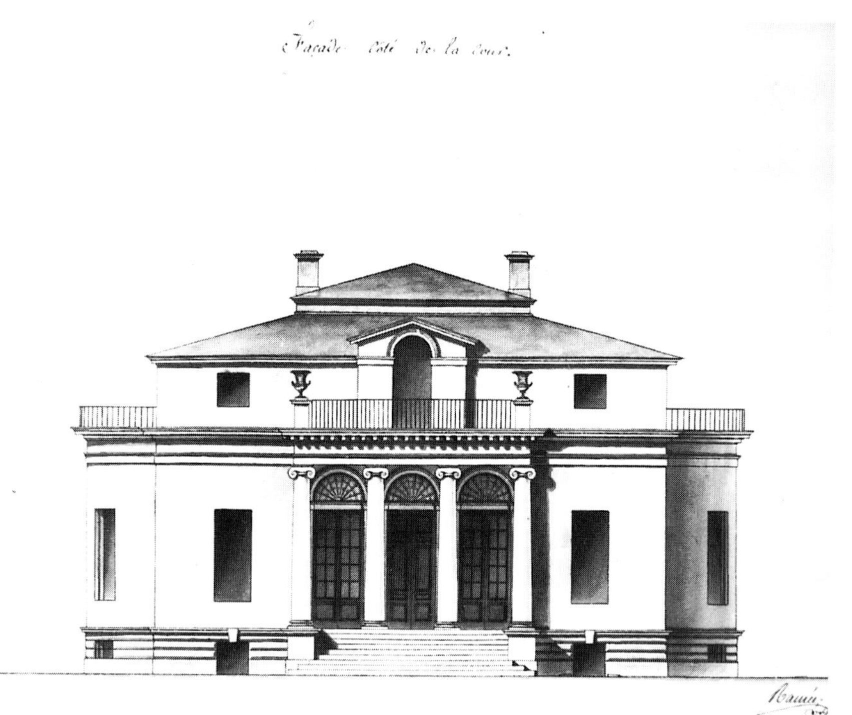

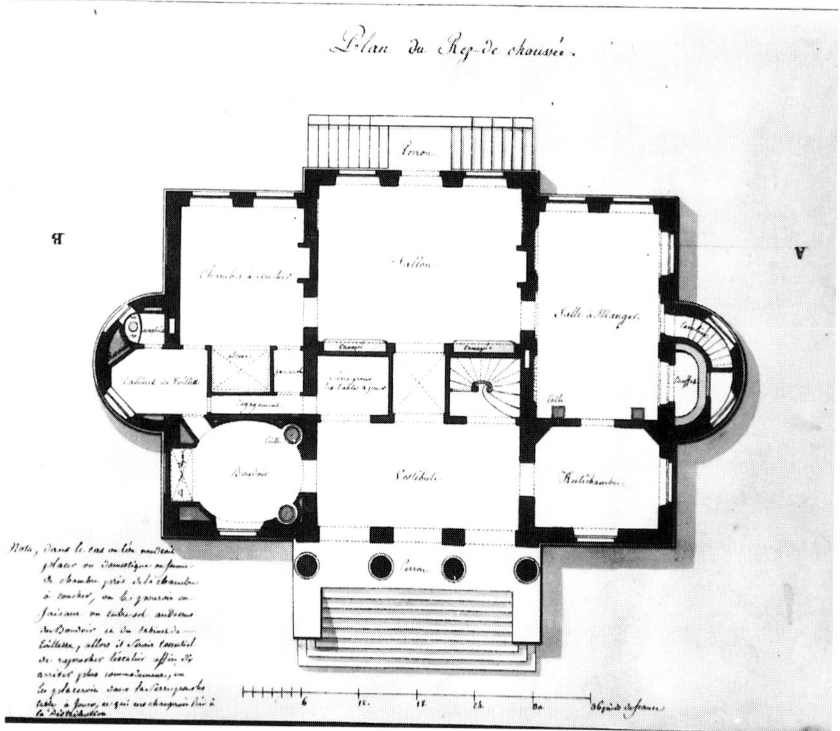

55 Entry façade and main floor plan of country house. Ink and watercolor drawing on paper, 26 × 41 cm, signed "Ramée, 1796." (Forschungs- und Landesbibliothek, Gotha)

56 Belanger House, Rue des Capucins (Rue Joubert), Paris, constructed c. 1787. (Krafft and Ransonnette, *Plans*, pl. 4, detail)

57 Garden façade and basement floor plan of country house. Ink and watercolor drawing on paper, 26 × 41 cm, signed "Ramée, 1796." (Forschungs- und Landesbibliothek, Gotha)

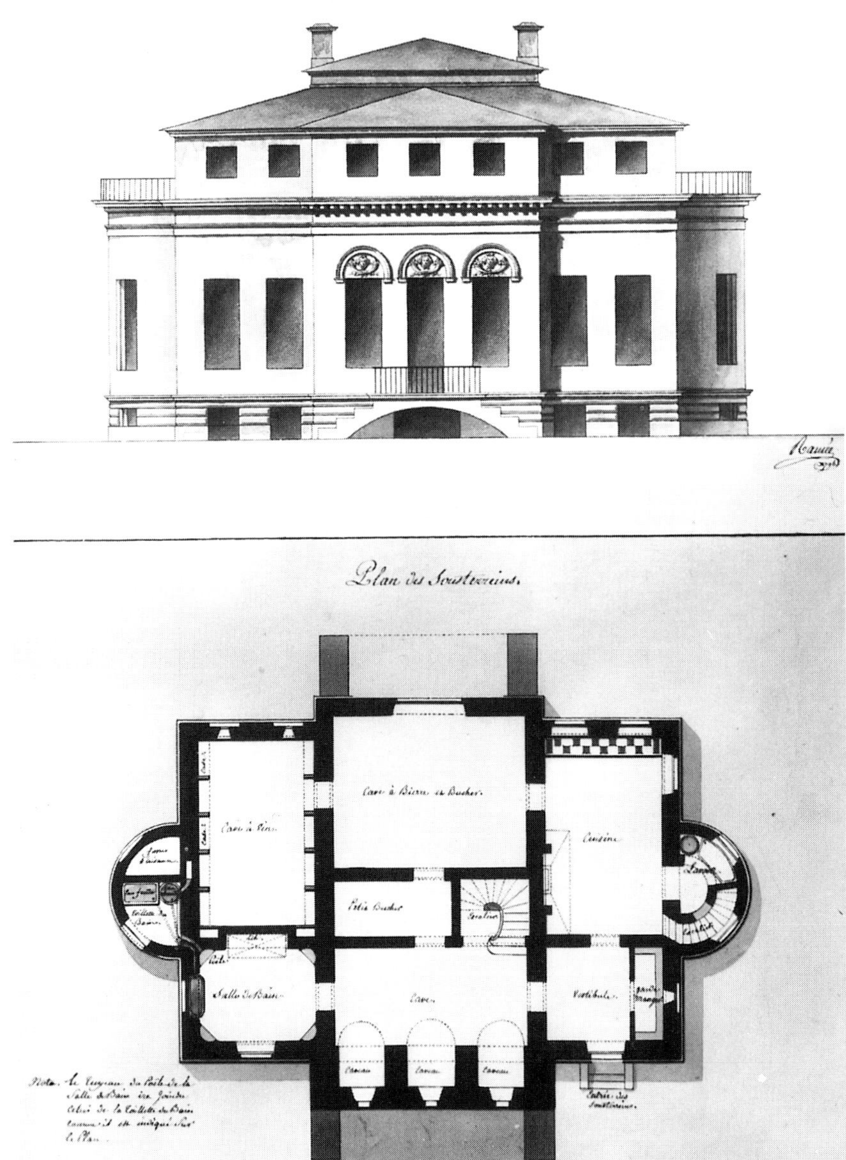

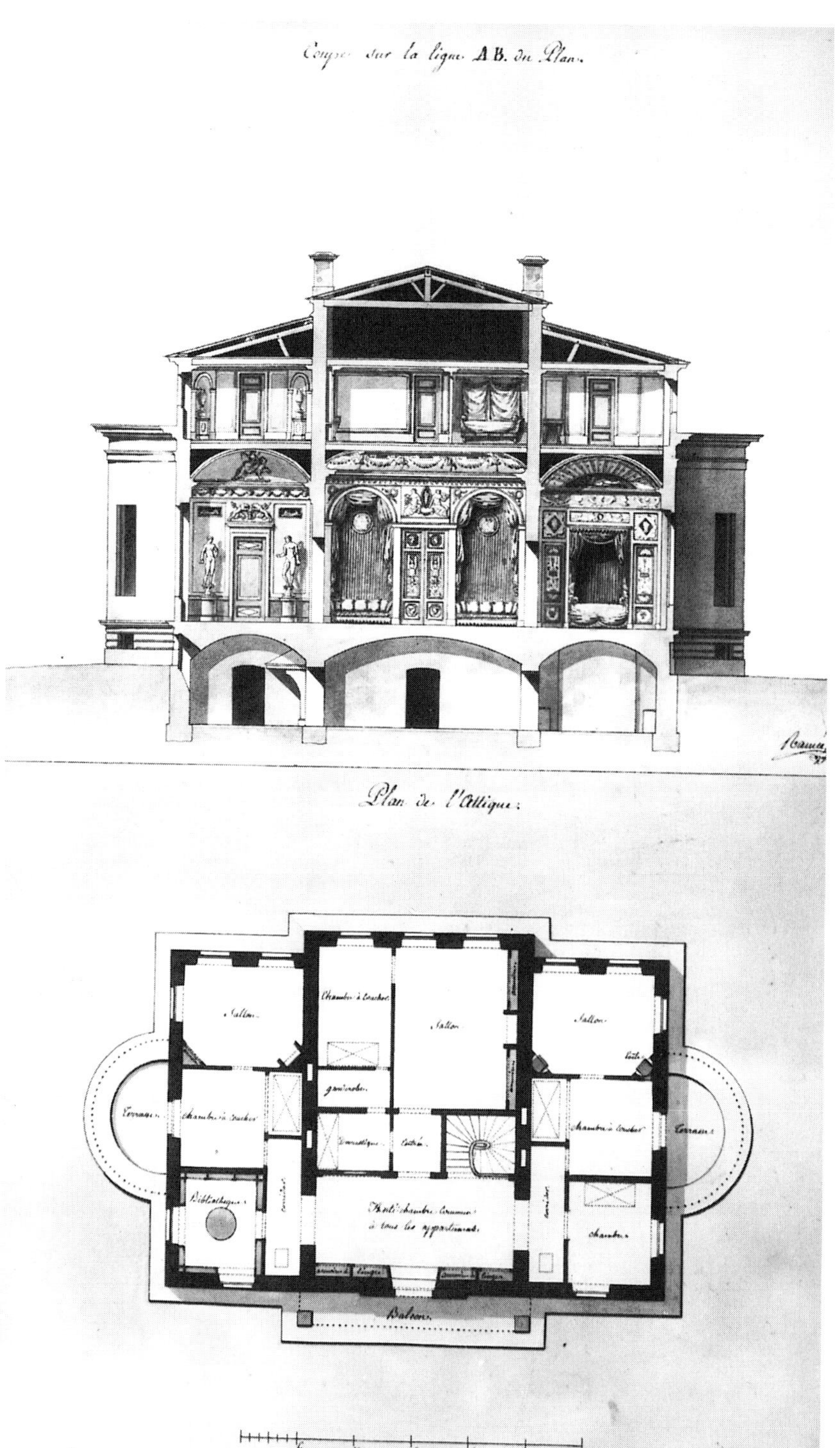

58 Section drawing and attic floor plan of country house. Ink and watercolor drawing on paper, 26 × 41 cm, signed "Ramée, 1796." (Forschungs- und Landesbibliothek, Gotha)

59 Side façade and roof plan of country house. Ink and watercolor drawing, 26 × 41 cm, signed "Ramée, 1796." (Forschungs- und Landesbibliothek, Gotha)

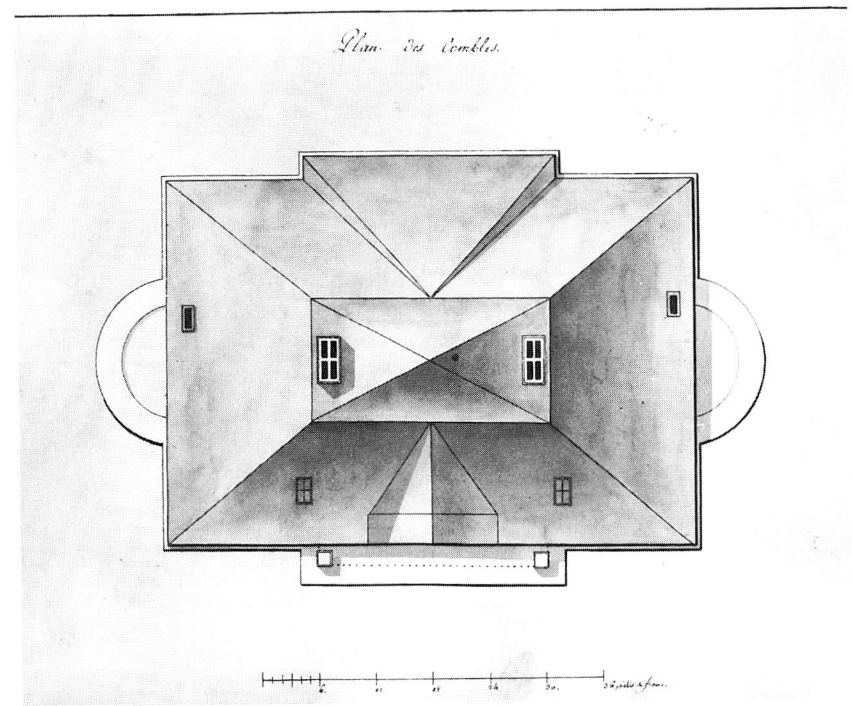

to me by Dr. Helga Raschke, a Gotha historian with whom I spoke after finding the drawings in the ducal library. Duke Ernst II was a devoted student of natural science, whose interests in nature and travel actually induced him, in the 1790s, to consider renouncing his throne and moving to America.[35] He went so far as to purchase land in Montgomery County, Ohio, and to assemble an "American library" of books to take to his new home. Nothing came of these plans. But did the duke ask Ramée to design an elegant house for the wilds of Ohio? If so, the anonymous identification of the design as simply a *maison de campagne* might be explained by the fact that Ernst II was keeping his emigration plans secret from his subjects.

Whoever was Ramée's client for this country house, the fine drawings for it show that already by 1796 Ramée was producing work in all the principal fields that would dominate his career in succeeding years: country-house architecture, interior decoration, and landscape design. The drawings also reveal that Ramée introduced into the Saxon principalities a synthesis of several of the latest styles of design from Paris. And they suggest the quality and richness of the work that Ramée reportedly executed for Dalberg in Erfurt and for his other Thuringian clients during the architect's brief period in this part of Germany.

Chapter 6

Hamburg and the Elbchaussee

Ramée settled in Hamburg about 1796 and stayed there for nearly fifteen years.[1] This period, when the architect was in his thirties and early forties, was the most stable and productive part of his career. During this time, Ramée was active not only in Hamburg and its environs – especially the region of the Elbchaussee along the River Elbe (Danish territory, at that time) – but elsewhere in northern Germany and also in Denmark proper. He worked in these places as a landscape designer as well as an architect, and he created an interior decorating and furniture business with another Frenchman, André Masson. Ramée's rapid success in Hamburg is indicated by the fact that as early as 1801 a local publication, *Skizzen zu einem Gemälde von Hamburg* (Sketches for a Picture of Hamburg), extolled him as one of the city's leading architects, landscapists, and decorators.[2]

Ramée also acquired a family in Hamburg. In 1805 he married the daughter of a local merchant; their son Daniel was born the following year, and several of Ramée's in-laws gave him architectural commissions and retained close ties with him for the rest of his life. In fact, Ramée later returned to Hamburg and worked there for a while in the 1830s. It seems likely that he would have stayed permanently in Hamburg from the start, if he had not been forced to leave in 1810, because of political events and the bankruptcy of his business with Masson – a disaster that was to plague him for years. (This business and its failure will be examined in Chapter 7.)

Ramée's petition to the French government in 1800, asking to have his name removed from the list of émigrés, implies that he wished to return to his native country. But when amnesty was in fact granted to him, in 1803, he did not leave Germany.[3] Did Ramée apply for amnesty simply as a kind of insurance, knowing well, by then, how suddenly his life could be unsettled by unforeseen events? Or did he need amnesty largely for business reasons? The firm of Masson et Ramée specialized in the importation of furniture and other goods from Paris; Ramée perhaps wanted a clean record with the French authorities in order to facilitate this business and his visits to Paris in connection with it. As noted earlier, Ramée made trips from Germany to Paris even before receiving amnesty.

Ramée's period in Hamburg was thus one of intense professional activity, in several fields of design and involving travel to France, Denmark, and other parts of Germany. Ramée in Hamburg also worked with a different kind of clientele from that which he had previously known. In France and the Saxon principalities, architects served mainly the aristocracy and the institutions allied to it. Hamburg, however, was a city-state without a ruling aristocracy, run principally by merchants, bankers, and other leaders of the bourgeoisie. Although these people often shared the esthetic predilections of the nobility, their lives and interests were different from those of aristocrats in certain ways that affected their patronage of architecture and the arts.

As a member of the Hanseatic League of free cities, Hamburg – on the Elbe River, with Holstein to the north and Hanover to the south – had long enjoyed a position of independence and prosperity. In the late eighteenth century it was the foremost commercial center of Germany. It prospered especially after the American Revolution, when Hamburg became the chief port of entry for United States trade, and after the French occupation of the Netherlands, which shifted business from Antwerp to Hamburg. Unfettered by autocracy, the city was diverse and innovative. Among its population, which by 1800 exceeded 100,000, there were many foreigners and citizens of foreign origin – especially British, French, Dutch, and Portuguese and Spanish Jews – some of whom were among the wealthiest citizens of Hamburg. John Parish, for example, whose son David was to take Ramée to America in 1812, was a native of Scotland who had settled in Hamburg in the 1750s and created there one of Europe's major banking houses.

Having intercourse with the rest of Europe and beyond, the leaders of this port city tended to be open to new ideas – artistic, intellectual, and social. Epitomizing this type was Caspar Voght, one of Ramée's first clients in Hamburg, who was a successful merchant but devoted much of his attention to the implementation of progressive ideas in the fields of art and public welfare.

Hamburg after 1790 also became a center for French émigrés, who flocked there and created their own community and institutions. Among these exiles were the future king Louis Philippe, who had served with Ramée under General Dumouriez in Belgium; the ever-resourceful statesman Talleyrand, who held posts in royal, revolutionary, and Napoleonic governments; and Dumouriez himself, who published his memoirs in Hamburg in 1794. These celebrities were naturally accompanied in exile by retinues of servants, ex-royalist officials, and miscellaneous others, including the former theatre company of the French court, which opened a French theatre in Hamburg in 1795. Many of the émigrés returned to France as soon as it was safe to do so, but others established themselves permanently in the Hamburg area; one of these was César Rainville, another former aide of Dumouriez, who acquired property along the Elbe and created a fashionable restaurant and inn there.[4]

Ramée perhaps went to Hamburg to join this community and seek architectural commissions from the French émigrés or through the influence of Dumouriez. But of all the work that Ramée executed in Hamburg and its environs, only one job is known to have been for French clients: the interior decoration of the playhouse of the French theatre company mentioned above. More likely, Ramée settled in Hamburg because it was a prosperous city whose citizens wanted the latest fashions in buildings and gardens. The evidence shows that he quickly made himself known to the Hamburgers and that his work appealed greatly to them.

Ramée was no doubt helped by the extensive social contacts between the French émigrés and the wealthy merchants and bankers of Hamburg. The memoirs of Vincent Nolte, member of a Hamburg commercial family, include a recollection of this social atmosphere, as well as a reference to Ramée:

> Madame de Genlis [author and educator], generals Dumouriez and Valence, the Duc de Penthièvre [later King Louis-Philippe], Prince Talleyrand, and other notables. . . could be seen in the various social circles. . . . The theatre continued to be my favorite activity. I was not content until I had infected my friend, Peter Godeffroy, Jr., with my mania; through him, his father [a Hamburg merchant] and then the whole family caught it; so that finally the French architect Ramée, the same one who had built our first Börsenhalle, received the commission to erect a theatre in Godeffroy's splendid premises, and there, in the course of the winter [probably 1804], we all made our debut. Our company consisted of thirteen persons, including four ladies from the first families of Hamburg.[5]

This passion for the theatre in Hamburg was due largely to the aristocratic French exiles and the actors, writers, and musicians who had followed them to Germany.[6] It is not surprising that Ramée – who had worked with the foremost theatrical architect in Paris, Jacques Cellerier, and had experience in the office of the king's *Menus Plaisirs* – received several commissions in Hamburg to design theatres and their interiors. Besides his construction of the private theatre for Godeffroy mentioned above (probably in Godeffroy's country house west of Hamburg), Ramée is said to have decorated the playhouse of the French company and to have proposed a theatre for the old cathedral square of Hamburg.[7] Unfortunately, no descriptions or views of these designs are known.

Although it was easier for a foreign architect to work in cosmopolitan Hamburg than in many other places, Ramée faced difficulties. Unlike painters and other artists who can often practice their skills abroad as easily as at home, architects are likely to encounter problems in a foreign place. Their profession requires precise communication with many people, knowledge of local building practices, and numerous social and business contacts. Language, for one thing, was probably an immediate obstacle for Ramée in Germany. Although most of his clients, being of the educated upper class, could no doubt speak with him in French, he must have had to learn German quickly in order to converse with construction foremen and others he had to deal with on a day-to-day basis.

In Hamburg itself, the design of buildings around 1800 was monopolized by local architects such as Johann August Arens. Outside the city, in Altona and along the fashionable Elbchaussee, the Danish architect Christian Frederik Hansen had an almost complete monopoly on work. This is probably the main reason that Ramée designed only a few buildings in the Hamburg area, and only one of major significance: the Börsenhalle (see Chapter 7). He had to supplement his infrequent architectural commissions with jobs in related fields, such as landscape design and interior decoration. Given these obstacles, it is remarkable that Ramée made an important impact on the arts in Hamburg during his decade there.

In Boulliot's 1830 article on Ramée, the account of his Hamburg period is oddly condensed; in fact, it is somewhat misleading:

> Having moved from Weimar to Hamburg, Ramée stayed there until 1802 and built the Börsenhalle, a place where the merchants assembled before going to the stock exchange. In Hamburg he also decorated the French theatre and put in order all the vast parks and gardens that neighbor this flourishing city. In 1802 he was called to Schwerin. . . . At the same time he made frequent trips to Copenhagen.[8]

It appears that Ramée, who must have provided this information to Boulliot, altered the facts a bit. Rather than leaving Hamburg in 1802, as suggested here, he remained active in the city for the rest of the decade. This is proved by the many designs Ramée executed in the Hamburg area after 1802, by documents such as his marriage certificate of 1805, and by his regular appearance in the *Hamburgisches Adress-Buch* until 1810.[9] Perhaps Ramée wanted to suppress the later part of his career in Hamburg in order to minimize his role in the disastrous business venture with Masson, by implying that he was no longer in the city when the firm failed and incurred its debts.

The Elbchaussee

The city of Hamburg was nearly surrounded by the duchy of Holstein, which in the late eighteenth century was subject to the king of Denmark. Therefore, as Hamburg grew and its prosperous citizens increasingly desired country estates, they had to create them mainly in Danish territory. The most popular location for these estates was the Elbchaussee (Elbe Road), a highway that follows the north bank of the River Elbe west of Hamburg, starting at the town of Altona and passing through Ottensen, Neumühlen, Klein Flottbek, Nienstedten, Dockenhuden, and Blankenese (Fig. 60).

The hilly topography of this area provided spectacular views of the river and surrounding countryside, which satisfied the new romantic attraction to rugged, natural scenery and was well suited to the laying out of irregular parks. The Hamburg bourgeoisie was very attached to its landscaped gardens. The young David Parish, having gone to America in 1805, urged his parents to join him there to escape the turmoil of Europe, but he admitted that the thought of abandoning their home was like "pulling up by the roots every tree and bush in the garden of Nienstedten"[10] By the end of the eighteenth century, the Elbchaussee was lined, mile after mile, by wealthy Hamburgers' landscaped estates, many of which still stand today.[11]

Most of the important houses constructed on the Elbchaussee in the 1790s were the work of the innovative architect Christian Frederik Hansen.[12] Eight years older than Ramée, Hansen had trained in his native Copenhagen, studied ancient and Renaissance architecture in Italy in the early 1780s, then

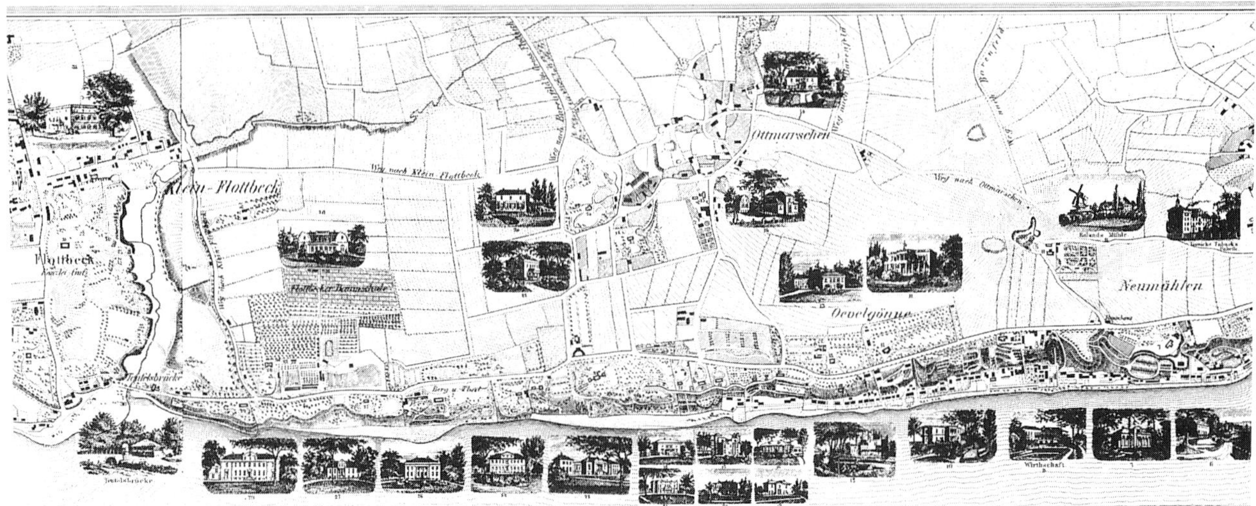

60 Part of the Elbchaussee on the Elbe River, from Neumühlen (at the right) to Flottbek (at the left). Portion of Fuchs's engraved map, c. 1850.

settled in Altona and produced many private houses in Danish Holstein over a fifteen-year period starting in 1789. After his return to Copenhagen in 1804, Hansen designed the great public buildings for which he is best known, such as the cathedral and city hall–law court complex, among the most powerful examples of neoclassical architecture in Europe.

When Ramée came to Hamburg in the mid-1790s, he must have recognized Hansen as the most significant architect working in the region, and as his principal rival. Hansen probably was interested in Ramée, too, not so much as a rival (since a foreigner had little access to major architectural commissions) but as a source of information on contemporary developments in France. Hansen's early work, such as his two houses on the Elbchaussee for Peter and J. C. Godeffroy, of about 1790, are rather conventional in their classical style (Fig. 61); but during the following decade, Hansen's work reveals the influence of the radical architecture of Ledoux and others in France.[13] Since Hansen apparently did not go to France himself, he must have learned of French developments through publications or other architects.

61 Peter Godeffroy House, Dockenhuden, designed by C. F. Hansen, c. 1790. Engraving by G. Lehmann, 1807. (Staatliche Landesbildstelle, Hamburg)

But despite the growing similarity between Hansen's and Ramée's works, differences remained. Hansen normally used the classical orders, with columns, pilasters, and other traditional elements such as rusticated masonry, which Ramée increasingly rejected. And Hansen generally followed the Renaissance and Baroque principles of composition, with the parts of a building bound together in a unified whole, whereas the parts of Ramée's compositions tended to be separate and isolated. In these respects, Ramée's work was perhaps more avant-garde than Hansen's, although Hansen was more innovative in other ways, as in his genius for inventing new combinations of forms in each design. More on the relationship of Hansen and Ramée will be said in the next chapter, in connection with Ramée's Börsenhalle in Hamburg.

Voght's Ornamented Farm

Ramee's first documented work in the Hamburg area was for the merchant Caspar Voght (Fig. 62), who epitomized the progressive Hamburg upper class.

Voght combined the practicality of the business world with the idealism of the Enlightenment and he was intensely interested in new ideas about society and the arts.[14] He counted among his personal friends the authors Lessing, Klopstock, and Goethe, and he was greatly interested in intellectual developments in England, which he visited several times. Representing a new type of client for Ramée, Voght's ideas on landscaping and architecture are of particular interest.

62 Caspar von Voght. Lithographic portrait by C. F. Gröger.

Beginning at an early age, Voght concerned himself with the welfare of the poor and was active in German and English movements for the reform of hospitals, prisons, and poorhouses. While traveling in Britain in 1794, Voght also became fascinated by English concepts of landscape planning, especially during a visit to The Leasowes, the estate of the poet and garden designer William Shenstone. Most appealing to Voght was the notion of the "ornamented farm," which he interpreted as combining the practicality of a working farm, the esthetic pleasure of picturesque landscape, and the morality of providing good housing and working conditions for employees.[15] Voght's idea of the ornamented farm (which he referred to in English, in his writings) was therefore different from the "*ferme ornée*" popular in late eighteenth-century France – usually a rustic imitation of a farm built to create a theatrical setting for aristocratic amusement.[16]

On his return from England, Voght began creating his own ornamented farm on land he had acquired in the 1780s at Klein Flottbek, above the Elbchaussee west of Hamburg. The architect Johann August Arens drew the plans for the house and park, but Voght provided precise instructions about what he wanted and called in specialists, such as the Scottish gardener James Booth.[17] Toward the end of his life, Voght wrote a description of his estate, in which he summarized his philosophy of landscaping:

> The art of garden design chiefly requires forming a series of landscapes, whose lighting is calculated for certain times of the day or the year, not only to provide enjoyment of nature and art . . . but to serve a higher purpose, with each of these landscapes having a special character . . . which by their total impression may calm or magically stir the spirit – in the new strength of awakening spring to excite joyful hopes in a beating heart, or in the soft impressions of autumn to rouse the echo of dear memories.[18]

Voght also had ideas about architecture, which led him to plan his house at Klein Flottbek in an unusual way (Fig. 63). Although it had to be large and elegant enough to accommodate the entertaining for which Voght was famous, he wanted it to be modest in appearance, at least from the outside. Reflecting new moral and esthetic sensibilities, Voght rejected the traditional assumption that a building ought to impress people. In 1794, he wrote from London to his architect Arens, stating his views about what he called "*meine Hütte*" ("my cottage"):

63 Voght House, Klein Flottbek. Drawing by J. Gensler, showing Voght and his secretary in foreground. (Staatliche Landesbildstelle Hamburg)

> I have kept hoping I would see something [in England] that could fix a certain type [of house] for me, but I find nothing – the rich are too rich, the poor too poor, and no one has any taste for good middle-class architecture or a sense of proportion. I am sending you Soane's Sketches [a book of house designs by the architect John Soane]; you will see how it is. I have seen countless interesting cottages, but they were too small and fussy to live in; I have seen very proper houses, but they were too beautiful, too big, too costly. I have seen Gothic dwellings, and would just as soon spend my days reading old fables as live in them. The only conclusion I have drawn is this resolution: to build a small, rustic, dry, warm, and comfortable house.[19]

In another letter, Voght added, "My house must fit in with the other buildings on the farm and not look foreign . . . not presenting to the eye a bulk meant to impress by its size, but rather many small parts, with pleasing relationships between them."[20]

These ideas reflected notions of the "picturesque" that were developing in England at this time, but Voght gave them his own individual character – sensible, homey, and informed by moral considerations. Ramée was already familiar with picturesque landscape design, but this was a different expression of the esthetic from what he had known in France. Toward the end of his career, Ramée was to publish a book of cottage designs; their character, and that of other works by Ramée, reflect some of the qualities of Voght's ideal house, especially in their unusual combination of rusticity and elegance.

Voght also gave careful attention to the design of the workers' housing on his estate, producing picturesque but solidly constructed structures, some of which still stand. Half-timbered and steep-roofed, these buildings too may have contributed to Ramée's evolving notion of cottage architecture.

The main block of Voght's house has a columned porch at one end, presenting a strangely asymmetrical face to the road. The addition of wings (which Voght realized, during construction, were needed for extra space) gave the house an even more irregular and informal shape. Voght later wrote: "To conceal its size, the house is partly hidden in shrubbery and intentionally made irregular, to avoid all architectural pretention and produce a dwelling that fits with the farm buildings. The inside had to perform more than the outside promised."[21]

Only the exterior of the house had to look modest. Inside, Voght had no reluctance about creating elegant rooms in the latest French taste. It was to design these rooms that he hired Ramée, probably in 1796.[22] Three rooms known to be the work of Ramée survive intact: on the ground floor, the *Festsaal* or main hall; adjacent to it, a small room for more intimate entertaining (which Voght called his "*Freundschaftstempel*" or Friendship Temple); and on the upper floor an octagonal boudoir or "*Kabinett*." These rooms were inaugurated with a ball in September of 1798. One of Voght's guests, Hermann Reimarus, wrote at that time:

> It is not easy to imagine how splendid is the salon [*Saal*], and how elegant and comfortable the whole house. Upstairs . . . is a boudoir that exudes pure softness; mirrors all the way to the floor, a sofa in a niche under a baldachin, lovely bookcases round about, and above them very beautiful oval paintings, ordered direct from Paris. . . . This Kabinett truly does great honor to Ramé [sic].[23]

Each of Ramée's three rooms has an individual character and style of decoration. The small *Kabinett* on the upper floor, described above, is ornamented with a series of paintings in panels: rectangular on the main walls, oval on the corner walls above the niches (Fig. 64).[24] The paintings, of high quality, represent scenes from Antiquity and possibly are the work of Pierre Étienne Le Sueur, the artist who soon was to work for Ramée's decorating firm, Masson et Ramée.[25] If these paintings were ordered from Paris, as Reimarus stated, it is possible that Ramée did not get exactly what he wanted, for the oval shape was somewhat out of style by this time. Circles were more typical of the Directoire style of the 1790s, and in this regard Ramée's other two rooms in Voght's house were more up-to-date.

The *Festsaal* is a long salon on the west side of the house, whose decoration recalls the work of Ramée's teachers Belanger and Cellerier (Fig. 65). At the juncture of the walls and the ceiling is a finely detailed classical cornice with doubled consoles or brackets. Just below, on the upper part of the walls, are separate pieces of relief sculpture drawn from classical prototypes: rectangular panels with female figures over the doors at the two ends of the room;

64 *Kabinett* on upper floor of Voght House. (Staatliche Landesbildstelle, Hamburg)

65 Salon, Voght House. North end of room. (Altonaer Museum, Hamburg)

circular bas-reliefs to the sides of these panels; urns and other classical motifs on the long wall opposite the windows.

These reliefs, cast in plaster, were no doubt ordered from Paris by Ramée. The circular reliefs, in particular, were popularized by Belanger, who used similar ones at Bagatelle and in his subsequent work. Identical examples of some of the Voght House reliefs, in fact, can be found in houses in Paris of the same period.[26] For example, the circular bas-relief of a satyr kissing a reclining maenad (whose source was a Pompeiian wall painting known from late eighteenth-century engravings) is found in the Hôtel Gouthière in Paris, the residence of an associate of Belanger, in which there are other sculptural reliefs also used by Ramée.[27] The designs of the two rectangular panels over the doors in Voght's salon, drawn from Roman bas-reliefs of dancing female

66 Small room (*Freundschaftstempel*) next to salon, Voght House. (Staatliche Landesbildstelle, Hamburg)

figures, were especially popular in Directoire (and then Empire) decoration. The originals, which were in the Villa Borghese in Rome in the eighteenth century, were taken to the Louvre by Napoleon in 1808.[28]

The doors at one end of the *Festsaal* lead into Voght's *Freundschaftstempel,* into which only his closest friends were admitted (Fig. 66).[29] The most striking feature here is the vaulted ceiling, stuccoed to create the illusion of stretched fabric. This is one of the most distinctive motifs of the Directoire style, one that had been developed by Ramée's closest associates in Paris: Belanger, Cellerier, and the decorator Dugourc.[30] The palmette frieze in this room is another motif used by Belanger which then became popular in the Directoire and Empire styles.

In these rooms for Caspar Voght, Ramée was thus using decorative motifs that had been developed largely by Belanger in the 1780s and which now represented the height of neoclassical Parisian fashion. In Hamburg, the novelty of this decoration must have drawn attention to Ramée and prompted him to establish a separate business for the production of interior decoration (to be examined in the next chapter).

Gardens

The statement in Boulliot's article that Ramée "put in order [*arrangea*] all the immense parks and gardens that neighbor this flourishing city" is perhaps an exaggeration (depending partly on what the French verb *arranger* means in this instance). But Ramée was, it seems, the most important landscape designer in the Hamburg area by the time he left the city in about 1810. More than anyone else, he popularized the picturesque garden in the region, and his landscape work there was remembered long after he left Germany. One late nineteenth-century Hamburg publication spoke of Ramée's "many garden designs [*Gartenanlagen*]" and another stated that he was "one of the best landscape architects of all time."[31]

The garden plans that Ramée published at the end of his life include eight in the greater Hamburg area, and there is evidence for two more. Of these gardens, five were on the Elbchaussee (gardens for Georg Sieveking, G. F. Baur, J. H. Baur, Richard Parish, and Salomon Heine), two were in suburbs north and east of Hamburg (the Hosstrup garden in Eppendorf and the Lengercke garden in Wandsbek), and three were farther afield in Holstein (at Perdöl, Hamfelde, and Plageberg).[32] The gardens for Parish, Heine, and Lengercke are identified by Ramée as dating from his second residence in Hamburg, in the 1830s. All the others probably date from his first period there.

When Ramée came to Germany in the mid-1790s, irregular or "English" gardens were confined largely to the noble estates of the German principalities; they were not yet well known in bourgeois Hamburg. Probably the first important irregular garden in the Hamburg region was Caspar Voght's "ornamented farm" at Klein Flottbek. As late as 1802, when F. J. L. Meyer devoted a section of his *Sketches for a Picture of Hamburg* to landscape design, he spoke of the English garden as "new" to Hamburg and admitted that he found it "a jumble of chaotic plantings [*einen Wirrwarr regelloser Pflanzungen*]."[33] Meyer spoke of the architect J. A. Arens as the principal garden designer of Hamburg in 1802, saying that Arens' first important landscape work was at Flottbek – that is, Voght's estate.[34] Although Ramée had not yet executed most of his gardens at Hamburg, Meyer mentioned him as one of the two other leading landscape artists at that time.[35]

Voght's landscaping at Flottbek reflected the style of park design Voght had seen in England, especially the modest, rural landscape of The Leasowes. There, William Shenstone had laid out a circuit path that took the visitor around the farmlike fields and past the vista points and simple monuments. The effect was midway between the complexity of William Kent's early-eighteenth-century gardens and the "naturalness" of those of Capability Brown, but with a sequence of wooded and open spaces intended to evoke poetic feelings in the viewer.[36] Working for Voght just after arriving in Hamburg, Ramée was thus exposed to another aspect of picturesque garden design.

Ramée also probably knew Christian Hirschfeld's *Theorie der Gartenkunst* (Theory of the Art of Gardening), whose five volumes were published, starting in 1779, in French as well as German.[37] Hirschfeld's work was based largely on English models and ideas (although Hirschfeld had not actually been to England) and presented the most complete case for the naturalistic English garden. Voght may, in fact, have been inspired by this publication to visit the landscaped estates of England such as The Leasowes.[38]

Ramée therefore had an unusually diverse training in picturesque garden design: first from Belanger, LeRouge, and Blaikie in Paris; from his knowledge of other French gardens such as those at Chantilly; from his experience of the gardens in the Saxon principalities; probably from the publications of Hirschfeld and other theorists; and from Voght's personal interpretation of recent developments in England.

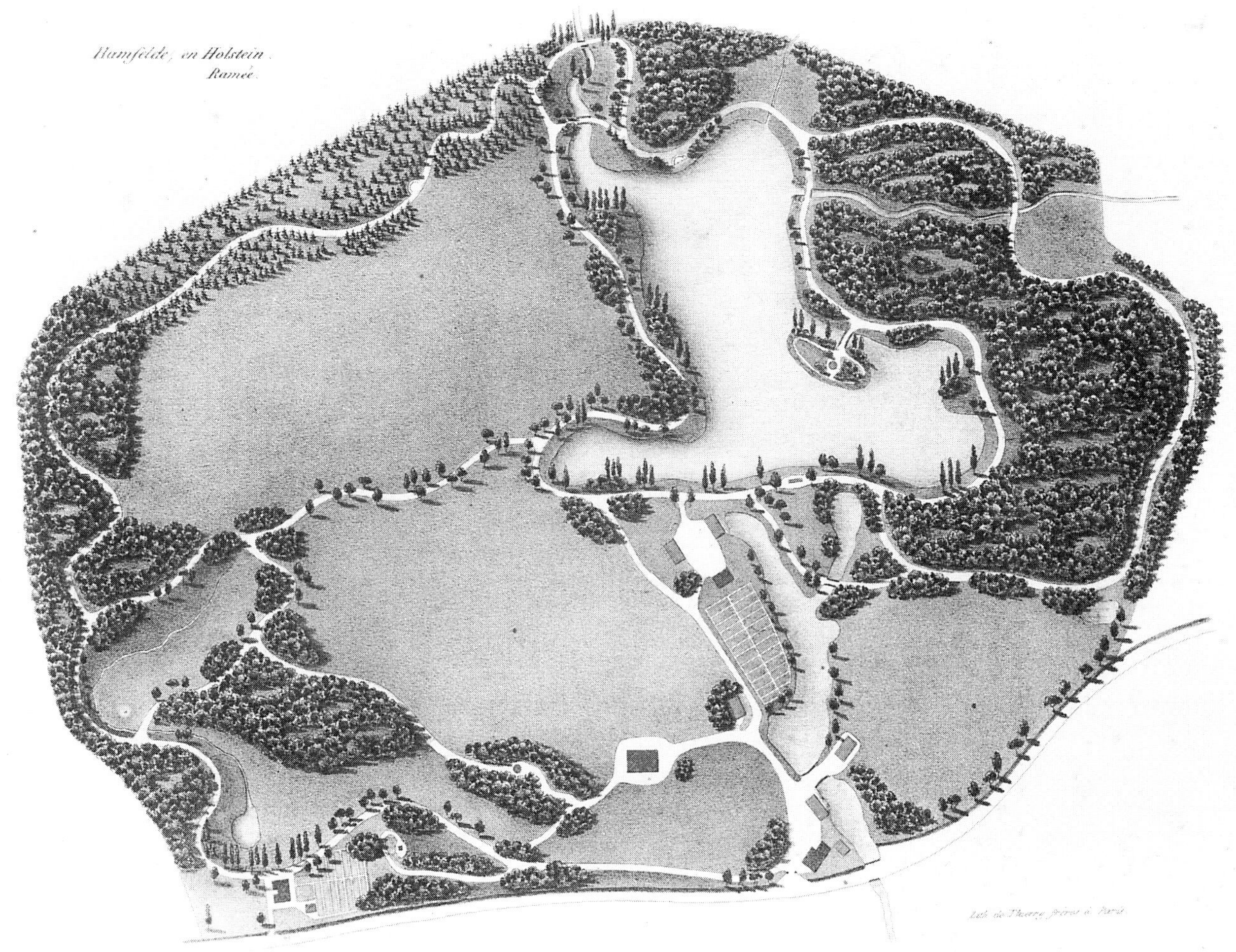

67 Hamfelde. Plan in Ramée's *Parcs et jardins*, pl. 17. (Schaffer Library, Union College)

This varied background is evident in the landscape designs that Ramée began creating in Hamburg in the 1790s. Although elements of Belanger's garden style can be seen, Ramée's designs are free of the crowded *chinois* intricacy that typified French gardens. Ramée's plans are closer in spirit to those of Capability Brown in England (whom Ramée perhaps first knew about from the Scotsman Blaikie), in their large expanses of lawn or meadow, their paths that make bold and sweeping curves rather than convoluted twists, and their irregularly shaped lakes, often created by the damming of a stream.[39]

Typical of Ramée's landscape style is his design for an estate at Hamfelde, in Holstein about thirty kilometers east of Hamburg (Fig. 67). The plan that Ramée later published in *Parcs et jardins* specifies neither the date of the design nor the client's name. But it was no doubt commissioned by Daniel Poppe, a relative of Ramée's wife who owned this property at Hamfelde until 1821.[40] Ramée laid out the grounds so that from the main house one would see nearly the entire estate, across the broad expanses of meadowland to the artificially created lake, screened only partially by small groups of trees. Today, the lake still has roughly the same shape as in Ramée's plan, with its small island on which Ramée sited a romantic temple. In the spirit of Voght's orna-

68 Stable at Hamfelde. (Author)

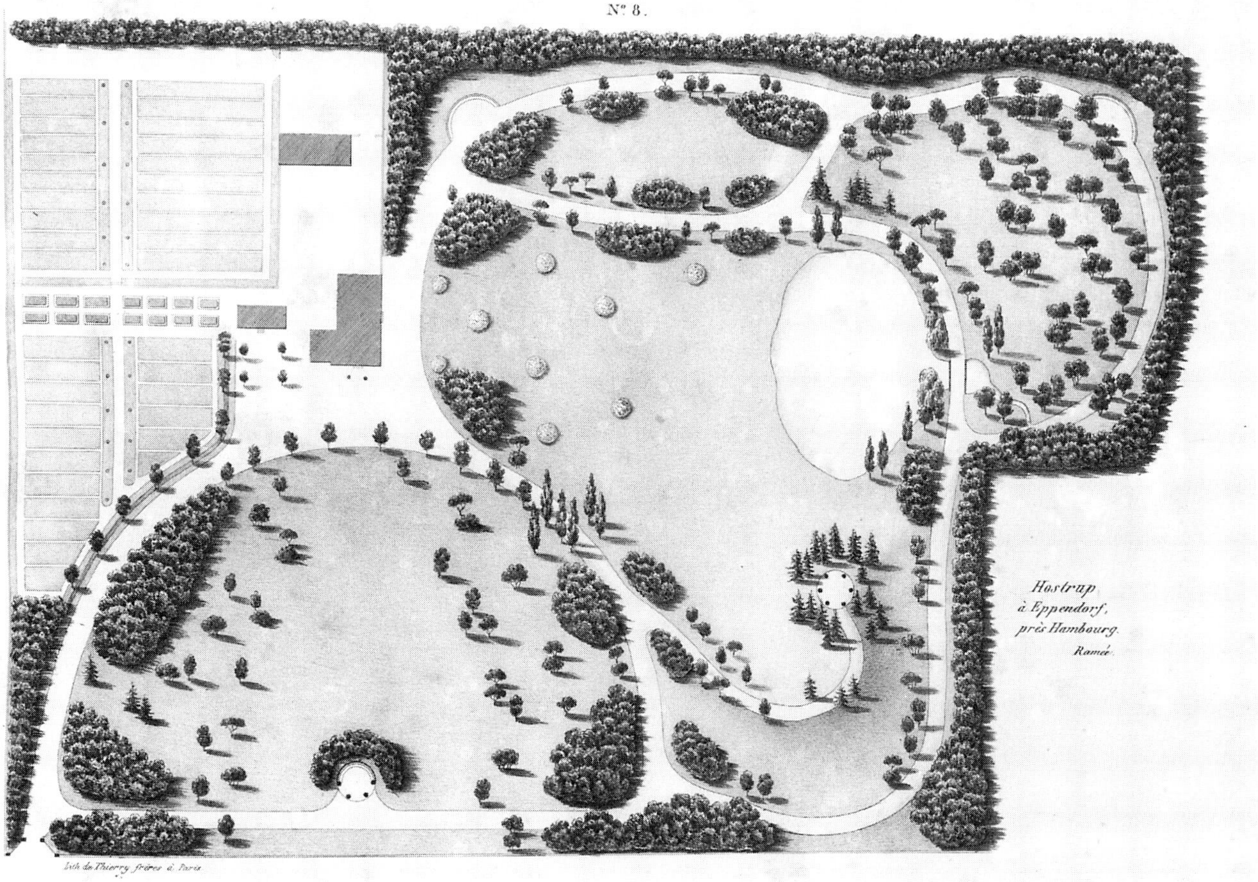

69 Hosstrup estate, Eppendorf. Plan in Ramée's *Parcs et jardins*, pl. 8. (Schaffer Library, Union College)

mented farm, Ramée even located some of the farm buildings at the shore of the lake, in view of the house. One of these structures, a stable, still exists as designed by Ramée, constructed in the half-timbered *Fachwerk* manner of medieval vernacular architecture of the region, but with the classicizing addition of half-round windows (Fig. 68).

Ramée's garden plan for the merchant Gerhard von Hosstrup, at Eppendorf just north of Hamburg (Fig. 69), also probably dates from this period around 1800, for Hosstrup commissioned Ramée at this time to design the Börsenhalle in Hamburg.[41] But the landscape plan at Eppendorf is different from that at Hamfelde. In particular, the trees are set out in smaller clumps, resulting in a less sharp distinction between open space and wooded area. This difference may have been due to the client's wishes or to Ramée's views about the types of landscape appropriate to different sites and circumstances. Ramée's plans reveal, for instance, that he made a distinction between "jardins" and "parcs": gardens were more domestically-scaled grounds for a house in an urban or suburban setting, whereas parks were larger and more heavily wooded grounds for a rural establishment. Moreover, each of Ramée's park and garden plans has special characteristics that distinguish it from the others. Ramée implied this himself, in remarks he later included on the title page of his publication *Parcs et jardins:* "The author hopes to be useful to garden lovers by offering them a series of the most varied designs, which are applicable to all sites . . . and which the different localities suggested to the author."[42]

Ramée's two most important landscapes in the Hamburg area illustrate how he responded to unusual site conditions. These are the parks he designed

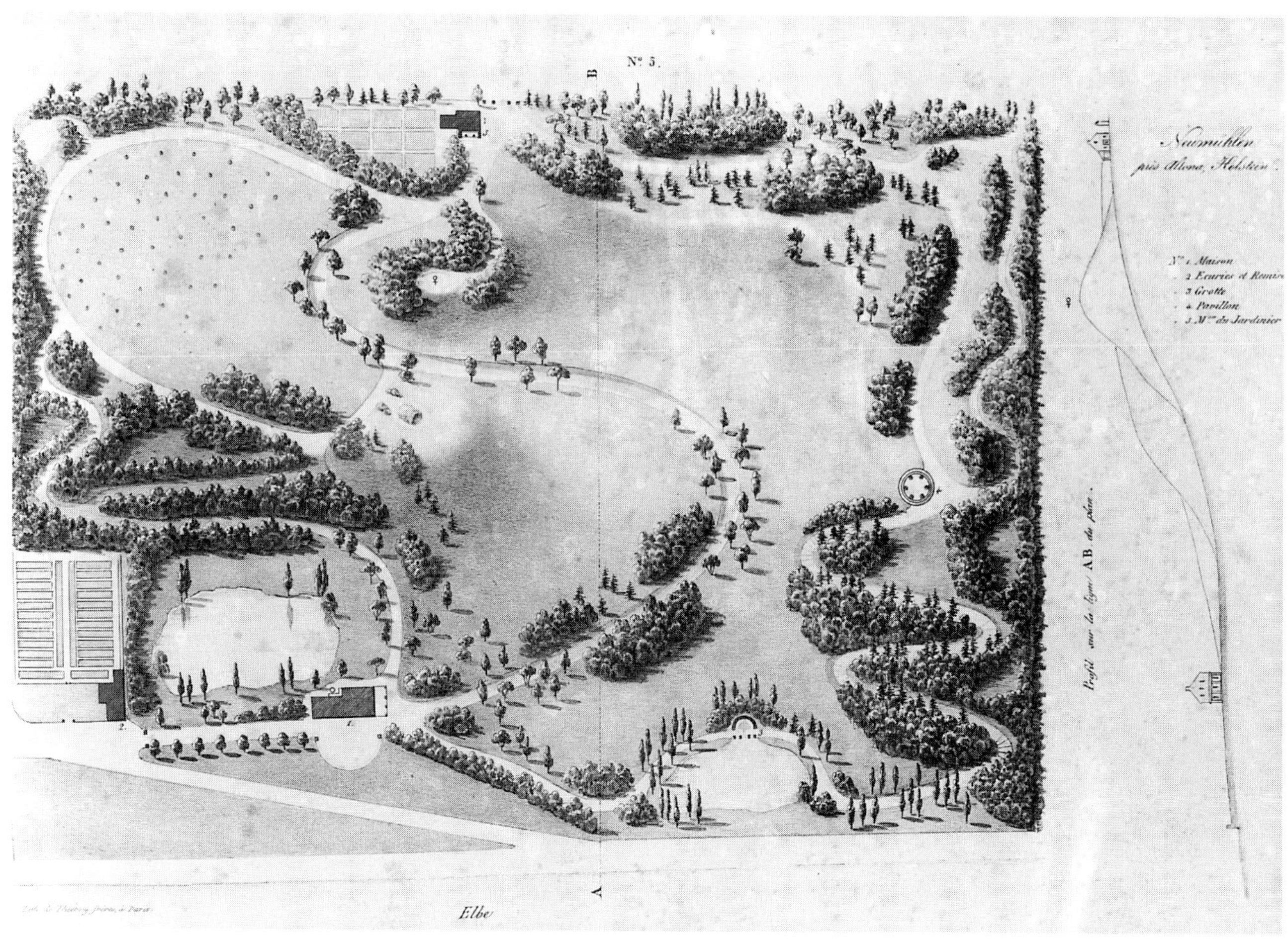

70 Sieveking estate, Neumühlen. Plan in Ramée's *Parcs et jardins*, pl. 5. (Schaffer Library, Union College)

for Georg Sieveking (Caspar Voght's business partner) at Neumühlen, and for G. F. Baur at Blankenese. Both of these sites are between the Elbchaussee and the river; each is steep and hilly, creating unusual topographical conditions.

Sieveking's park dates from 1797 or earlier and perhaps was Ramée's first landscape commission in the Hamburg area (Fig. 70).[43] In 1793 Sieveking purchased the Neumühlen property in collaboration with two of his close friends, merchant Conrad Matthiessen and publisher Pieter Poel, as a country estate for the three of them and their families to use jointly (they each had a city house in Hamburg or in nearby Altona). Ramée was hired to make gardens on the land that rose steeply from the river, where the large existing house stood, up to the Elbchaussee to the north. The land, which today is preserved as a public pleasure ground called Donners Park, does not rise uniformly; there are peaks and valleys in it. This topography led Ramée to create a more complex plan than usual, with several open spaces and serpentine paths ascending to the heights, where he placed pavilions and vista points.

The park was intended not only to provide picturesque views from the house, but to serve for recreational activity. The three families who shared the property entertained on a grand scale, their guests including many of the distinguished figures of the day (the poet Klopstock celebrated his birthday there every year), and the midday meal on Sunday was often attended by as many as eighty people.[44] The character of Ramée's park at Neumühlen is suggested in remarks made by a young woman who visited there in 1798:

> At this time I inspected the garden with Poel, especially the hilltop grove [*Bergboskett*] toward the Elbe. From a thatched cottage, to which the guests had found their way without prior arrangement, there is a splendid view of the Elbe and its islands. Another hill, which fell steeply down to the Elbe, has been leveled. Above, there has been a planting of fir trees, from which one has a view of the Elbe that is unique of its kind.[45]

Ramée's grandest landscape creation in the Hamburg area – and the best documented – is Baurs Park, on the Elbe at Blankenese, about twenty kilometers west of Hamburg. In 1802 the merchant and senator Georg Friedrich Baur began acquiring separate pieces of property at Blankenese and making them into a landscaped estate. The process extended over many years. The last piece of land was purchased by Baur in 1817; in 1829 he demolished the existing house to erect a new one, and the planning of the gardens was still continuing in the 1830s.[46] Although early maps, views, and other documents of the park exist, some aspects of its planning remain unclear, as the process was complex and involved several designers.

The lithographed plan of Baurs Park that Ramée published at the end of his life is labeled "Blank[enese] près Hambourg, Ramée 1805 & 1833." (Fig. 71)[47] That Ramée worked on the park during both of his periods in Hamburg, three decades apart, is confirmed by surviving records of fees and expenses that Baur paid to him in 1809, 1812, and 1833, totaling 14,026 Marks

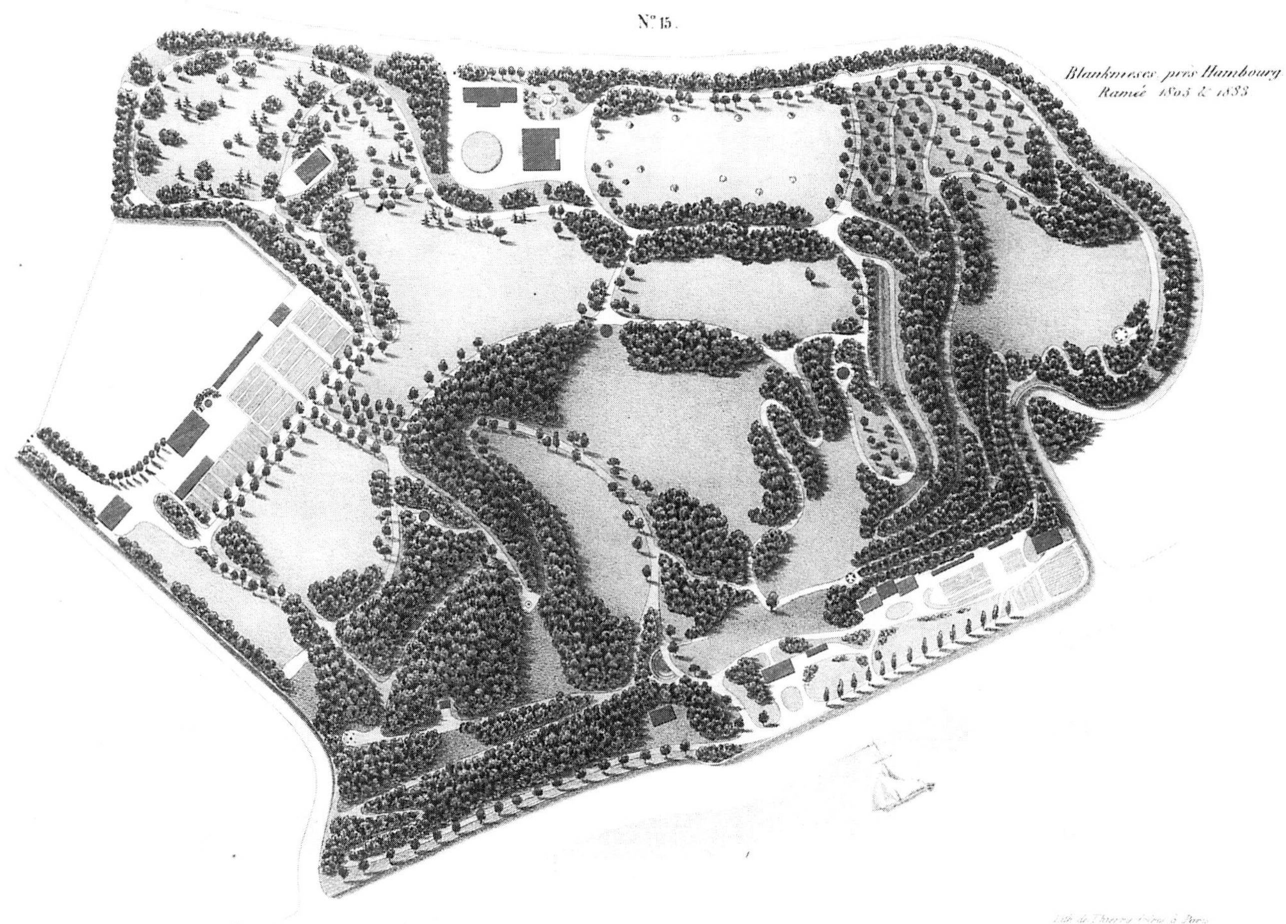

71 Baurs Park, Blankenese. Plan in Ramée's *Parcs et jardins*, pl. 15. (Schaffer Library, Union College)

Courant.[48] Other records reveal that Ramée and Caspar Voght's Scottish gardener James Booth imported unusual trees and other plants for Baurs Park, some from as far away as Holland and northern Italy.[49]

A remarkable drawing of Baurs Park, signed by Ramée and dated 1810, is preserved at the Blérancourt Museum, in its collection of Ramée family documents (Fig. 72 and color plate 13).[50] As 1810 is the year Ramée left Hamburg, he probably made this drawing in order to keep a visual record of the park and his plans for it. With the Elbe River and its ships in the foreground (including a three-masted ship flying the American flag), the drawing shows Baur's property in simplified form – the land flattened out to reveal the entire property – and shows several buildings that were not actually constructed, such as Ramée's proposed design for a new main house at the top of the hill (Fig. 73). But enough of the topography and architecture is accurate to confirm that this drawing does represent Baurs Park, as Ramée idealized it in 1810.

The most unusual thing about the land Baur assembled, and the most challenging for a landscape designer, was its wildly irregular topography, with precipitous hills rising from the narrow strip of flat land at the river, and deep

72 Baurs Park, seen from the Elbe. Watercolor drawing on paper, 36 × 50 cm, signed "Ramée, 1810." (© Musée National de la Coopération Franco-américaine, Blérancourt, France)

73 Detail of Ramée's Baurs Park drawing, showing main house.

ravines that cut through the property in various directions. When one visits the grounds today (they are maintained as a public park, largely as Baur left them), one is struck by this irregularity, which makes it impossible to walk straight across the property: in most places, one must follow serpentine paths cut into the hillsides, leading from one peak to the next.

This rugged topography explains the nature of Ramée's design for the park, which in its complexity of circuitous paths and irregular wooded areas looks more like the French *chinois* gardens than Ramée's other park plans. But while the labyrinthine paths of a *jardin anglo-chinois* were largely arbitrary, here they were necessary to get up and down the hillsides.

Ramée's drawing of 1810 may give the impression that he would have preferred Baurs Park to have a more normal topography. But in fact, he took advantage of the unusual site to create a new kind of landscape, wilder and more savage in feeling than the earlier gardens he had known. The actual character of Ramée's park is best suggested by a series of paintings that the artist Ludwig Philipp Strack executed for Baur in 1811, which show well the heavily wooded ravines and slopes as seen from the hilltop vista points created by Ramée (Fig. 74).[51] The spirit of the place is somewhat like that which was

74 View of Baurs Park, looking east from vista point, with Elbe at right. Painting by L. P. Strack, 1811. (Altonaer Museum)

being espoused at the time in England by Richard Payne Knight and Uvedale Price, who criticized Capability Brown's gentle parks and advocated wilder, more awe-inspiring picturesque environments.[52] A similar spirit of sublime landscape is found in the writings of Frederikke Brun, Ramée's main client in Denmark at this time, whose relationship with the architect will be explored in a later chapter.

Strack's paintings of Baurs Park also reveal new attitudes about the use and enjoyment of landscape. The people in the paintings are shown in casual dress – the women in simple, flowing, Empire-style garments – and they are devoid of pretention or formality. In one of the views, a group of women and children – members of the Baur family or their guests – are shown lounging on the grass and playing as a gardener pushes a wheelbarrow along a path near them. The scenes have a homey quality, different from the stately manner in which the European nobility traditionally had themselves portrayed in their gardens. Despite Baur's wealth and his extensive estate, he evidently led a relatively informal life there, just as Caspar Voght avoided unnecessary ostentation at his "ornamented farm."

75 Detail of Ramée's Baurs Park drawing, showing round temple over grotto.

Baur did, however, have a weakness for exotic garden pavilions and "follies," which he erected in a profusion more typical of the pre-Revolutionary gardens of France. Ramée's drawing of 1810 shows at least three such structures: a circular temple atop a subterranean grotto on one hillside; a multiturreted medieval tower on another; and a rustic wooden temple on one of the lower slopes (Figs. 75–7). The only one of these structures known to have been executed as designed by Ramée is the round temple over the grotto, which is recorded as having been constructed in 1809 and appears in Strack's paintings.[53] By the 1820s, when engravings and other views of the park were made, the medieval tower (later called the *Turmruine* or tower ruin) had been erected, but not quite following Ramée's design, and other structures included a "Chinese pagoda," "Japanese umbrella," "Egyptian temple," gazebos, and other amusements in miscellaneous styles. Some of these may have been built according to designs supplied by Ramée before he left Hamburg in 1810, but only the round temple and grotto can be ascribed to him with certainty.

A reference to this grotto-temple is found in the memoirs of one of Baur's granddaughters (who knew the estate starting in the 1840s), an account that also describes the park as a whole:

> The most magnificent terrain had been used [to create the park]. The upper part of the garden lay between three and four hundred feet above the lower part, which was directly on the Elbe. Seven different paths led from above to the river below, going through woods and valleys and by the most beautiful outlook points.
>
> A multitude of costly structures were erected in the garden . . . a large Chinese tower made of wood, with many roofs [etc.] Then there was a marvelous and beautiful grotto, which one could not see from outside. Through a small, dark passage, one came into a round room, all covered with moss, with a mirror on the ceiling and three large vantage points [*Aussichtspunkten*]. . . . Above this grotto was a Greek temple in the purest style, a circle of columns supporting a dome. This was a very beautiful work, full of charm and elegance, all of granite. . . .
>
> Let me not forget the Rose-Arbor, a pleasure pavilion completely overgrown with roses; the Vine-Arbor, a nicely situated pavilion made of wood-bark, completely covered with wild grapes. . . . Many paths and sections of the garden had also been laid out by French garden designers and were given their names. One path, for instance, is still called Ramée Way [*Ramée-Weg*].[54]

76 Detail of Ramée's Baurs Park drawing, showing medieval tower.

77 Detail of Ramée's Baurs Park drawing, showing rustic temple.

Buildings Possibly by Ramée

In Hamburg Ramée was known mainly as a landscape architect and interior designer. Aside from the Börsenhalle (examined in the next chapter), Ramée's only known buildings in the region are the structures in the gardens he laid out, such as the pavilions at Baurs Park and the half-timbered farm buildings at Hamfelde. But Ramée must have built other, more substantial structures, whose authorship is now forgotten. The chronicler of Hamburg's social and cultural life of the period, F. J. L. Meyer, noted in 1801 that the city's prosperity had attracted a number of architects from abroad, and he specified: "Among these, Ramé [sic], a Parisian, and Bunsen, a Dane, are the most important and have found much work. The first of these has erected several country houses, in the excessively light and airy French taste."[55]

Meyer's criticism of Ramée's architectural style indicates that he had, indeed, seen buildings designed by the architect. "Light and airy" is precisely the way Ramée's work must have appeared to people used to the more traditional forms of classicism.

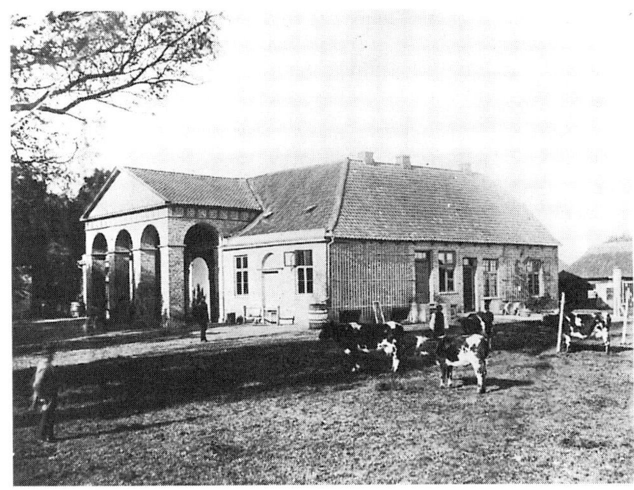

78 Klünder House, Blankenese. (Staatliche Landesbildstelle Hamburg)

79 Parish stable, Nienstedten. Photograph showing building before remodeling. (Staatsarchiv Hamburg)

What were the country houses to which Meyer referred? Perhaps one was the Klünder house in Blankenese, built about 1799, whose architect is unknown (Fig. 78).[56] A stark cube, whose only ornament is a prominent cornice, a balustrade (now removed), and a thin pediment over the large central door on the ground floor, this house has the skinlike flatness of surface (with windows sliced in as with a razor) that typifies much of Ramée's work.

One can attribute to Ramée more positively another building on the Elbchaussee, although it is not a country house: the stable at the Parish estate at Nienstedten (Fig. 79). This structure is now radically altered, but its original form is known from an old photograph. Parish family documents and insurance records indicate that it was constructed either in 1796 or 1806.[57] Ramée was in Hamburg at both these times, and the form of the building is fully typical of his work. The arcaded portico, projecting far from the rest of the structure (giving each of the two parts a kind of independence); the thin mouldings and other attenuated decorative details, emphasizing the geometric clarity of the forms; the use of square piers rather than columns – all these traits bespeak Ramée's special brand of neoclassicism, in contrast, for example, to that of C. F. Hansen.[58] It is known that Ramée was a close acquaintance of the Parish family, one member of which was to take the architect to America in 1812. The stable at Nienstedten is probably one of Ramée's designs for the family.

Despite these attributions, Ramée's "several country houses" mentioned by Meyer, in 1801, remain among the missing parts of the architect's work.

Just as this book is going to press, however, a nineteenth-century photograph has come to light, showing another, extraordinary house which was likely designed by Ramée shortly after Meyer referred to his work (Fig. 79A). Ramée's publication *Parcs et jardins* contains a plan for Plageberg (later renamed Charlottenberg), an estate near Itzehoe, in Holstein, about fifty kilometers northwest of Hamburg (see Fig. 279). The house on this property has been altered, but the newly discovered photograph shows its original form, and recent research by Ingrid A. Schubert has uncovered the probable facts of its

79A Plageberg (now Charlottenberg), near Itzehoe, Holstein. Photograph of the house, c. 1880s. (courtesy of Holger Vanselow)

construction.[59] The estate was purchased in 1804 by a merchant named Benjamin Jarvis, whose main residence was in Altona, on the Elbchaussee. Jarvis constructed his country house at Plageberg, overlooking the River Stör, probably about 1805. Square in plan, with a semielliptical ballroom on the upper floor, this house was built into a hillside, so that "from the upper floor one can walk into the garden," as a nineteenth-century description stated.[60] The photograph, taken probably in the 1880s, shows the house from the other, lower side, with its basement entrance through three arched openings, and a recessed loggia above, onto which the ballroom opened. Most remarkable is the contrast between the neoclassical, arcaded lower storey and the rustic upper parts of the house: the loglike columns of the loggia, the steep, thatched roof and the half-timbered, semicircular wall that projects from it (but contains a classical, Palladian window). All these elements can be found, individually, in Ramée's other designs of this period – the classical forms mostly in his country houses and more monumental buildings; the rustic elements in garden structures and outbuildings, such as those seen in the architect's drawing of Baurs Park, or those at Sophienholm in Denmark (see Figs. 72, 119–26). But combining the two modes so boldly in one design was most unusual and is not found in Ramée's other known works until later in his career, for instance in some of the designs in his 1830s publication *Recueil de cottages* (see Figs. 289, 293). The country house at Plageberg reveals an imaginative, even whimsical side of Ramée's artistic character. It also exemplifies his penchant for joining things in unconventional ways, whether styles from different periods, forms from different regions, or monumental and vernacular building traditions.

The Northern Attraction

In his petition of 1800, Ramée stated that when he first went to Germany, he intended to travel also to Italy.[61] This is Ramée's only known reference to the traditional goal of European architectural pilgrimages, the center of the study of classicism. As far as we know, Ramée never got to Italy, nor, in fact, anywhere in southern Europe. The fact that he worked exclusively in northern regions, both in Europe and America, was probably due mainly to the opportunities that presented themselves to Ramée during his career. But it also seems that he developed a special attraction to northern lands and their architecture. In the course of Ramée's career, typically northern architectural forms, such as steep roofs and Gothic arches, became increasingly important in his work. Many of the house designs that Ramée included in his publication *Recueil de cottages* have these characteristics, such as the designs showing board-and-batten walls or log-cabin construction, a Scandinavian type of building (see Figs. 297, 298). Even in Ramée's ostensibly classical designs, prominent roofs or vertical proportions often give the works a northern character, creating an idiosyncratic fusion of classical and nonclassical traits.

In late eighteenth-century France, Gothic and other nonclassical forms were normally used by architects only in garden pavilions and in other frivolous contexts. It was probably in Germany that Ramée acquired a more substantial interest in northern architectural traditions. Caspar Voght's concern for farm-workers' cottages and other vernacular building types of northern Germany no doubt contributed to Ramée's interest in this subject.

The tide of romanticism at this time was swelled by an enthusiasm for northern-European alternatives to Mediterranean classicism. In literature this is seen in the passion for the Gaelic Ossian epics and other real or fabricated relics of the ancient North. The Ossianic stories elicited particular excitement in Germany, largely through the writings of Gottlieb Friedrich Klopstock, close friend of Ramée's client Caspar Voght.[62] In France, Ossianic themes provided the subject of an opera by the composer Étienne Nicolas Méhul (Ramée's fellow native from Givet), and Madame de Staël's essay "De la littérature du Nord" enthroned Ossian and Homer as the contrasting paradigms of Nordic and Mediterranean temperaments. Madame de Staël was a close friend of Ramée's main client in Denmark, the poet Frederikke Brun, who also was attracted to northern themes.

80 Caroline Ramée at the age of forty-eight. Oil portrait, signed "Saint Evre 1835." (© Musée National de la Coopèration Franco-américaine, Blérancourt, France)

Thus in Germany Ramée was introduced to the new passion for northern European traditions and artistic expressions. This probably contributed to his willingness to forego the traditional architect's pilgrimage to Italy and to accommodate his principles to the northern regions through which he was to travel for the rest of his career.

Ramee's Marriage and Personal Life in Hamburg

In 1805, Ramée strengthened his commitment to Hamburg by marrying into a local family. For the rest of his life, in fact, Ramée retained closer ties with his wife's relations than with his own blood relatives – ties that influenced his professional activities and movements. A month before the wedding, Ramée revealed his happiness in a business letter to one of his clients, the Court Marshall of Mecklenburg. Declining an invitation to visit this man, Ramée wrote, "I am getting married soon and my young fiancée does not permit my absences to be any longer than necessary." He added that after the wedding it might be possible "to present Madame la Baumeister to you."[63]

Ramée's *Heiratsprotokoll* (a form of marriage license) is preserved in the Hamburg Staatsarchiv.[64] Dated 23 July 1805, it states that the civic marriage ceremony (*die Trauung*) was to take place on Saturday, 10 August, with the religious ceremony (*die Copulation*) to be performed at St. Catherine's church in Hamburg, a Lutheran church known for its affluent merchant congregation. The groom is identified as "Joseph Wilhelm Ramée, Bürger [citizen]." Ramée, who during this period used Guillaume or Wilhelm as a middle name, acquired Hamburg citizenship (*Bürgerrecht*) at about the same time as his marriage.[65] His profession, according to the marriage document, was *Kaufmann* (merchant), his residence was on the Fuhlentwiete (the street where the Hamburg offices of Masson et Ramée were located), and he is said to have resided in Hamburg for nine years. Ramée's bride was Caroline Dreyer, a native of Hamburg, daughter of Christian and Friederica Dreyer (Fig. 80).[66]

Caroline was born on 19 August 1787 and therefore was only seventeen when she married the forty-one-year-old Ramée in 1805. She was an orphan, her mother having died in 1797 and her father the following year, but she had seven brothers and sisters and many other close relatives in the Hamburg area. Caroline's paternal grandfather had established a tea and coffee business in Hamburg in the mid-eighteenth century; his seven children were successful in business and civic affairs and they married well. A genealogy of the Dreyer family, preserved in the Hamburg Staatsarchiv, observes that "this family is noteworthy especially because three of its members married into the important factory-owning family of von Lengercke."[67] The Lengerckes' cotton factory was at Wandsbek, northeast of Hamburg; its founder had married one of Caroline Dreyer's aunts, and two of Caroline's siblings also married Lengerckes. Other notable Hamburg clans into which Caroline's brothers and sisters married were the Poppe and Hey families. Joseph and Caroline Ramée retained contact with many of these relations for the rest of their lives, and Joseph produced architectural designs for several of them – including the country estate for Daniel Poppe at Hamfelde described above and a park for the Lengerckes at Wandsbek.[68]

A son, Daniel, was born to Joseph and Caroline on 16 May 1806 and was baptized in the great Baroque Lutheran church of St. Michael in Hamburg.[69] Daniel, who was to be trained in architecture by his father and have an important career as an author and a restorer of medieval churches, was apparently the only child that Joseph and Caroline Ramée had in their long marriage. Both wife and son were to accompany Ramée on his travels to America and elsewhere and to share in his tempestuous life until the end. But the family stayed in close contact with its Hamburg relatives: the Ramées returned and lived there for a while in the 1830s, and in Joseph's final days they shared a house with one of Caroline's sisters and her husband.

Almost nothing is known about Ramée's religious affiliations or beliefs. Although he was baptized a Catholic, the fact that his marriage and his son's baptism were Lutheran (following the religion of his wife's family) suggests perhaps that Ramée was not a practicing Catholic as an adult. Yet he evidently was a devout Christian. In 1843, the year after Joseph Ramée's death, Daniel published a history of architecture, dedicated to his father; at one point in the text, Daniel criticized the preference some people had for Greek culture over Christianity and recalled "the memories and affections of our youth, the moving instruction in Christian morality given us by a beloved father."[70]

Several additional details of Ramée's personal life during the Hamburg years are found in miscellaneous documents. A French police report on "Emigrés in Hamburg," compiled between 1796 and 1805, lists "Ramée, Jean [sic]" and states that he is "an architect in Hamburg, is practicing his profession with distinction, is living peacefully and removed from all sorts of intrigue."[71] On the death of his mother, probably in 1802, Ramée inherited property in his native city, Givet; a legal document, referring to him as "an architect and merchant," reveals that he returned to Givet and in February 1803 sold various interests to his sister and brother-in-law, for a total of 3,000 Francs.[72]

Ramée apparently took on an architectural student while in Hamburg: a young man named Pierre Philippon (or Phélippon), who had been born in Paris in 1784 and whose family were perhaps émigrés in Germany like Ramée himself. Later references to Philippon state that he studied under Ramée from 1800 to 1810 and assisted him with his work in Hamburg and Copenhagen.[73] Philippon then returned to Paris, entered the École des Beaux-Arts, and ultimately had a successful career as an architect in France.

Ramée's 1800 petition to the French authorities includes a supporting statement by a French consul general in Hamburg. This man, named Lagan, certified:

> It is well known, particularly to me, that citizen Joseph Guillaume Ramé [sic], architect, has resided [in Hamburg] and traveled within my jurisdiction [Lower Saxony] for about three years; that he has enjoyed the general esteem there; and that he has worn the national cockade since the moment when instructions were given that French citizens should wear this badge in foreign countries.[74]

The national cockade (*la cocarde nationale*), an ornament made of red, white, and blue ribbons, was the emblem of French revolutionary patriotism. If Ramée did indeed wear this tricolor badge while living in Hamburg, it is hard to believe that he did so out of true revolutionary fervor, given the trouble that the French Revolution had already caused him. The French consul in Hamburg may well have been a personal friend of Ramée, or may have been persuaded by Ramée's influential clients in Hamburg to support his petition and exaggerate his French patriotism.

The Firm of Masson et Ramée in Hamburg and Copenhagen

Chapter 7

While living in Hamburg but maintaining ties with Paris, Ramée was one of the first practitioners of the Directoire and Empire styles of interior design in Germany and Denmark.[1] Much of his work in this field was produced through the firm of Masson et Ramée, which he established about 1800 with a fellow Frenchman, André Masson.

Even before founding this firm, Ramée had become known for his interior designs. The rooms he created for Caspar Voght at Klein Flottbek around 1796 have been described. About the same time, he also installed a room for a certain "Madame Sillem," a job about which little is known except that it cost 15,000 Marks, a considerable sum.[2] The lavishing of great expense on interior decoration was, in fact, so pronounced in Hamburg during this period that visitors to the city frequently commented on it.[3] The opportunity this trend provided designers, for large fees, was no doubt a motive in Ramée's decision to enter this field, which was considered somewhat less elevated than architecture per se.

Masson et Ramée, although chiefly an interior-design firm, was also used by Ramée as the agency for executing some of his architectural commissions. The Börsenhalle, Ramée's only known building in Hamburg itself, was a commission executed by Masson et Ramée; so was the architect's principal work in Mecklenburg-Schwerin, the mausoleum of Helena Paulowna at Ludwigslust. Both were buildings with lavish interior decoration, which may explain why Ramée produced them through his business with Masson. But Ramée perhaps had additional reasons for this combining of architectural and interior-design business: it may have made bookkeeping more efficient or allowed cash advances to the architect from the company's assets.

When the firm of Masson et Ramée eventually failed, however, this intertwining of business activities had a disastrous effect on Ramée's entire professional practice. His relationship with Masson is therefore a crucial part of the story of Ramée's fortunes and misfortunes. Also of interest is the firm's connection with the Marquis de Lafayette, hero of the American Revolution and of the early days of the French Revolution.

Ramée and Masson were in partnership by 1800. Starting that year, their firm was listed in the Hamburg directory, first as a "wall-covering and furniture factory," then as a "furniture, wall-coverings, and French porcelain store."[4] But the business was more than this suggests. It was an all-purpose design firm, with a staff of painters and other artisans who executed various kinds of interior decoration. Masson was evidently in charge of the financial side of the firm, Ramée of the artistic.

Masson et Ramée quickly became known as the foremost source in Hamburg of fashionable furnishings and design, especially those in the French taste. (In his petition to the French government of 1800, Ramée claimed that he was serving his country by "creating large markets for French factories and manufacturers.")[5] In 1801, Meyer's *Sketches for a Picture of Hamburg,* surveying the current artistic climate of the city, described Masson and Ramée's company. Comparing it to a more established firm of similar type, that of Victor Petre, Meyer implied that the distinctive quality of the goods handled by Masson et Ramée was their neoclassical simplicity:

> A similar business, established recently by the Frenchmen Masson and Ramée, although not so large [as that of Petre], will soon take its place. It offers goods of all sorts, which are manufactured by a small French colony of workers not far from Hamburg, based on first-rate French and English models; moreover, [they have] wallpapers, marble and bronzed works, porcelain, and the like, from German and especially Parisian factories. Fine taste and a good selection of patterns distinguish this warehouse from several German and English establishments here, and particularly from a store of goods from factories in Berlin, where a superfluity of strange, multicolored decorations and curlicues is a prevailing and taste-corrupting fashion.[6]

Ramée's partner, André Masson, is a mysterious figure, whose career was linked with that of the Marquis de Lafayette. His full family name was apparently Masson de Neuville; he was called that in documents from his early years and again, in 1825, in a series of letters from the Swedish-Norwegian consulate in Paris to the French police, inquiring about his and Ramée's whereabouts.[7] Records in Hamburg give Masson's first name either as Andreas or Andrew; it is not known why he used the English form of this name. Nor is it known if he was the same person as a certain "colonel André Pierre Masson" who wrote a politically provocative work entitled "Les Sarrasins en France," the publication of which was forbidden under Napoleon.[8]

In the early days of the French Revolution in Paris, Masson de Neuville was an aide of the Marquis de Lafayette, at that time the commander of the National Guard. (We recall that Lafayette played a prominent role in the *Fête de la Fédération,* designed partly by Ramée, a fact which suggests that Masson and Ramée may have known each other already in Paris.) Masson was instrumental in uncovering the royalist plot of the Marquis de Favras in 1789, and he gave testimony at the sensational trial that followed.[9] After Lafayette fled France in 1792 and fell into the hands of the Austrians, Masson de Neuville helped coordinate the international efforts to secure the release of Lafayette and his family from prison. These efforts required Masson to shuttle between Paris, London, and Hamburg, where he conferred especially with the United States consul in Hamburg, John Parish (father of the man who later induced Ramée to move to America).[10]

In the mid-1790s, Masson, now minus the "de Neuville," settled in Hamburg. In April of 1796 he signed a "Fremdenkontract" with the city, which allowed him to carry on trade and to purchase property although he was not a Hamburg citizen. In 1797 he first appeared in the Hamburg directory, as "Andrew Masson & Comp. Kaufleute [merchants]."[11] This is the firm that Ramée joined as a partner, two or three years later.

Lafayette and his family were finally released by the Austrians in September of 1797. Their first days of liberty were spent in Hamburg, where Lafayette was greeted by supporters who had worked for his release, especially Gouverneur Morris, the American statesman; Johann Wilhelm von Archenholtz, editor of the journal *Minerva;* John Parish; and Masson.[12] Lafayette did not stay long in Hamburg, but he remained in contact with his friends there. Letters that Lafayette wrote to Archenholtz and Masson, now preserved at the Massachusetts Historical Society, reveal that Lafayette persuaded Archenholtz to invest in Masson's business, a recommendation that later caused Lafayette much grief when the firm went bankrupt and Archenholtz lost his investment.[13] Lafayette's letters also reveal that he knew Ramée, who visited him on occasion in Paris, where Ramée probably went to buy merchandise for the Hamburg business. In February of 1801, for instance, Lafayette wrote the following to Masson from his home outside Paris:

> My regards to your partner. I am much pleased with the success of your business and am sensitive to the feelings he has for me, as I have for him. You announced him for the month of January, but he has not yet come; perhaps I shall find him in Paris. . . . I shall be very glad to receive your friend Barbazan and I hope M. Ramée will bring him to see me.[14]

There is also evidence that Masson and Ramée's firm had a branch office in Paris or was associated with another firm there. In one of Masson's letters to a client in Mecklenburg-Schwerin in 1805, he made a reference to "our Paris firm [*notre maison de Paris*]."[15] And it seems that while in Hamburg Ramée established a wallpaper factory in the Belgian town of Dinant, at that time part of Napoleonic France.[16] Although little is known about these enterprises in Paris and Dinant, they confirm the wide-ranging scope of Ramée's business activities during this period.

In the Hamburg area, Masson and Ramée acquired two pieces of property for their business. One was in Dockenhuden, on the Elbchaussee several miles west of Hamburg. Called "Die Bost," it was bought by the two partners in 1800; a contract, dated May 20 of that year, records that the sale price was 30,100 Marks, half of which Masson and Ramée paid at that time.[17] The buildings there had previously been used for a starch factory and brickworks; Ramée and Masson turned them into carpentry shops, which produced the "goods of all sorts" mentioned in Meyer's publication on Hamburg of 1801, "manufactured by a small French colony of workers."

In 1804, Masson purchased additional property in Hamburg itself, at 15 Neustadter Fuhlentwiete, consisting of two adjacent lots and a garden. Several years later, this land was described as having two large houses on it, as well as a smaller dwelling, a shop on the street, stables, a pavilion in the garden, and a workshop.[18] Starting in 1804, the Hamburg directory listed this address on Fuhlentwiete both for Ramée himself and for the firm of Masson et Ramée. The business evidently operated from the shop on the street, while Ramée occupied one of the dwellings. (He previously had had another address in Hamburg, at 168 Herrengraben.)[19] When Ramée married in 1805, the marriage register also gave Fuhlentwiete as his address; he and his family probably lived there until 1810, when the property (and also the Dockenhuden property) were sold as part of the bankruptcy proceedings of Masson and Ramée's firm.[20]

The principal artist employed by Masson et Ramée was the painter Pierre Étienne Le Sueur. A native of Nîmes in southern France, Le Sueur had studied in Paris around 1780 and exhibited at the salons there in the 1790s, with paintings of subjects drawn from antiquity, and landscapes that one critic said were reminiscent of the works of Claude Lorrain.[21] By 1800, Le Sueur was in Hamburg working for Masson et Ramée. During the following two years, he is known to have contributed to at least four of the firm's works of interior decoration: those of the French theatre and the Börsenhalle in Hamburg, and the Erichsen Mansion and the Royal Theatre in Copenhagen.[22]

Of this work, only the decoration in the Erichsen Mansion survives, although H. H. Madsen, who has studied Le Sueur's career, believes he may also have created the oval paintings that are in the octagonal room Ramée executed in Voght's house on the Elbchaussee, about 1796 (described in Chapter 6).[23] In December of 1802, Le Sueur's career was tragically cut short when he and his wife died in a fire at their home in Hamburg. Masson and Ramée evidently were unable to find anyone to replace Le Sueur, for the firm's work after 1802 did not include the kind of fine painting he had done.

Interior Design in Denmark

Beginning about 1800, Ramée received commissions in Copenhagen and its environs for country houses, gardens, and interior decoration – mostly for the wealthy merchants who were profiting from Denmark's economic fortunes of the period. Ramée's architecture and landscape design in Denmark will be seen in the following chapter; his interior decoration, executed mostly by Masson et Ramée, is examined here.

A primary source of information on Ramée's Danish works is a gossipy diary written in 1802 by August Hennings, a German-Danish author who held bureaucratic posts in the Danish government. During a visit to Copenhagen in 1802, Hennings wrote a lively and opinionated account of the social scene in the Danish capital, which includes some revealing remarks about Ramée's work.[24] As he made the rounds of the prominent families, Hennings noted buildings, gardens, and interior decor newly created by the French architect. The unfamiliar nature of this work is suggested by Hennings's sometimes disapproving remarks. He also was surprised by how much people were willing to pay for Ramée's work; this extravagance disturbed Hennings's rather puritanical sense of economy and moderation. On 14 July 1802, he recorded his visit to Erich Erichsen's new mansion in Copenhagen, for which Masson et Ramée had provided the lavish decoration:

> The walls and ceilings of six rooms are painted most handsomely by Le Sueur, and a dining room is ornamented with Parisian stucco-work. One would think that such beautifully decorated rooms must accommodate London feasts of several hundred people. In fact, there is room for only about thirty. For this small number, the sumptuousness seems to me much too great. Ramé [sic] received 3,200 Rigsdalers for the decoration. There are some strange things here. In one room, the paintings over the doors show two bulls butting one another and a horse subduing a panther. On the walls are storm, sunrise, and moonlight scenes, and a figure combatting the storm. . . . In other rooms are mythological images; the arabesques and paintings are gently restrained, not gaudy, even when they are brightly colored. Ramé has also decorated state-councilor Brun's mansion, but Brun is unhappy about what he had to pay for it.[25]

The concluding reference is to the Copenhagen house of Constantin Brun (like Erichsen, one of the wealthiest Danish merchants at this time), whose wife, the poet Frederikke Brun, was Ramée's main supporter in Denmark. On 18 July, Hennings recorded a visit to the Bruns' house, noting especially a lavish bathroom that was being installed for Frederikke. Four days later, Hennings reported dining at the country house of C. G. Bernstorff (Danish minister of foreign affairs); the salon there, he said, "was decorated by Ramé, it seems," although this was perhaps incorrect.[26] Hennings reported also on Ramée's country houses and gardens outside Copenhagen, including the Bruns' estate, Sophienholm, which Hennings described as "the work of Ramée as artist and Brun as money-dispenser."[27] Hennings's cynicism about fashion and luxury was summarized in a final reference to Ramée in his diary in October 1802:

> Ramée is here now [in Copenhagen] and furnishes various houses, including those of Schimmelmann [government minister Ernst Schimmelmann] and Erichsen. He is unbelievably expensive, and therefore highly sought after. Surely it is great folly to pay 25 Rigsdalers for an armchair that is perfectly plain, as that is the current mode. Such value is quickly lost.[28]

These remarks suggest that Hennings's perplexity and disapproval of Ramée's work were due to the fact that this work was both luxurious and simple – seemingly contradictory qualities. Remarks by other people of the period, such as Frederikke Brun, indicate that Hennings was not the only one to be impressed, favorably or unfavorably, by the strange conjunction of elegance and plainness in Ramée's designs.

81 Erich Erichsen. Miniature portrait by J. B. Isabey, c. 1810. (H. H. Madsen, *Interiørdekorationer i Erichsens Palae*, Copenhagen, 1968, p. 7, courtesy of Den Danske Bank)

82 Erichsen Mansion, Copenhagen, designed by C. F. Harsdorff, constructed 1798–1801. Now the Danske Bank. (Author)

The decoration of the Erichsen Palae (Erichsen Mansion) in Copenhagen was probably the first large commission of Masson et Ramée. The interiors that the firm executed there, from about 1800 to 1802, are also its best preserved work and show the wide range of its decorative styles and techniques.

Erich Erichsen (Fig. 81) headed one of the largest shipping firms in Denmark, whose commodities included spices and fabrics from the East Indies and grain from the Baltic region, shipped to England and elsewhere.[29] From 1798 to 1801, Erichsen constructed his palatial mansion, with a portico of Ionic columns facing Kongens Nytorv (King's New Square) in Copenhagen, probably the most imposing private residence in the city (Fig. 82). The architect of the house, C. F. Harsdorff, died in 1799. Shortly after that, Ramée's firm was hired to decorate the principal rooms of the mansion, which were completed by the summer of 1802 when August Hennings described them in his diary. In the late nineteenth century, the building was acquired by a banking firm, the Kjøbenhavns Handelsbank (now the Danske Bank), which today still uses the structure as its headquarters. In the 1960s, the bank undertook a careful restoration of the rooms decorated by Masson et Ramée, a restoration that partly involved recreating lost work (where walls had been removed, for instance) but for the most part consisted of conserving the original decoration. This project was accompanied by thorough research and photographic documentation, which were published in a book on the subject.[30]

The rooms decorated by Masson et Ramée and now restored are the six principal rooms on the main floor of the mansion: a salon at the center of the main façade, a dining room, two more salons, and two smaller rooms, called the Alcove Room and Toilet Room (*Alkovevaerelse* and *Toilettevaerelse*). Each of these rooms has a somewhat different decorative character, but all of them are more highly ornamented than Ramée's other surviving interiors. (Only the Hamburg Börsenhalle had comparably lavish interior decor, judging from descriptions of the building before its destruction by fire in the mid-nineteenth century.)

The dining room of the Erichsen Mansion (Fig. 83) has no painted decoration (as the other rooms have), only plaster bas-relief ornament: what Hennings called "*Pariser Stukkatur*" (Parisian stucco-work). The walls of the room, which is semicircular at one end, are divided into sections by broad, flat pilasters that support a delicate frieze at the top of the wall, with the soffit of a Doric cornice decorating the edge of the ceiling. Between the pilasters, on the upper part of the walls, are bas-relief panels, mostly rectangular or circular, representing figures from classical mythology, in some cases drawn from contemporary engravings of Pompeiian wall paintings (Figs. 84, 85).[31] These reliefs are of the same type that Ramée had used in the salon of Baron Voght's house on the Elbchaussee; several of them, in fact, are exactly the same in design. Some of the reliefs can also be matched with ones used in Parisian houses of the period or somewhat earlier. One of the circular reliefs, for example, is the same as one found in the Hôtel Gouthière in Paris, of the 1780s.[32] These plaster reliefs were probably manufactured in Paris (perhaps by Belanger's brother-

83 Erichsen Mansion, dining room. (Madsen, p. 76, courtesy of Den Danske Bank)

in-law, J. D. Dugourc, who had a decorating firm) and ordered from there by Masson et Ramée.

More specifically Directoire in style is the relief ornament on the wall pilasters in this dining room: delicate arabesques in which stylized floral patterns merge into winged female figures and other motifs that are balanced atop one another (Fig. 86). Ultimately derived from ancient Roman wall decorations, these patterns are treated here in the crisp, dry manner typical of the Directoire style of the 1790s.[33] Also typical of this style, and of the emerging Empire style, is the palmette and garland frieze at the top of the wall in this room, which is similar to friezes in the work of Percier and Fontaine of the same time (Fig. 87).[34]

The other five rooms executed by Masson et Ramée in the Erichsen Mansion are different in character: their decoration is primarily painted (Figs. 88–90). These are the rooms that Hennings described in his diary as the work of the painter Le Sueur; it appears, though, that more than one artist was employed in their execution, since several different hands were identified during the recent restoration of these rooms.[35]

One might assume that the painted decoration in these rooms was conceived by Le Sueur or some other artist working for Masson et Ramée, rather than by Ramée himself. But much of the decoration is so similar to that of Belanger and the other artists (such as Dugourc and Cellerier) with whom Ramée was intimately associated in Paris, that one suspects that Ramée planned it, at least to the extent of determining the overall outlines and style. In the salon called the Corner Room (*Hjørnevaerelse*), for example, the walls are divided into panels whose decoration is very similar to the interior designs

84 Erichsen Mansion, two of the reliefs in the dining room. (Madsen, p. 37, courtesy of Den Danske Bank)

85 Erichsen Mansion, one of the round reliefs in the dining room. (Madsen, p. 36, courtesy of Den Danske Bank)

86 (left) Erichsen Mansion, relief ornament on one of the pilasters in the dining room. (Madsen, p. 77, courtesy of Den Danske Bank)

87 (above) Erichsen Mansion, frieze at top of wall in the dining room. (Madsen, p. 77, courtesy of Den Danske Bank)

88 Erichsen Mansion, Corner Room. (Madsen, p. 68, courtesy of Den Danske Bank)

89 Erichsen Mansion, room overlooking Holmens Kanal. (Madsen, p. 64, courtesy of Dan Danske Bank)

90 Erichsen Mansion, Alcove Room. (Madsen, p. 62, courtesy of Den Danske Bank)

91 Erichsen Mansion, ceiling of room overlooking Holmens Kanal. (Madsen, p. 66, courtesy of Den Danske Bank)

by Belanger for the Hôtel Dervieux in Paris, of about 1788, a seminal creation of the Directoire style.[36] In both cases, there are borders containing neoclassical ornament in simple geometric shapes (particularly an elongated octagon, an unusual form that was characteristic of Belanger); the centers of the panels are devoted to standing female figures, above smaller painted panels, which in the Erichsen Mansion are finely executed landscape scenes, no doubt from the hand of Le Sueur.[37] Above the doors in this room are the paintings of "two bulls butting one another" and "a horse subduing a panther" that Hennings found particularly noteworthy.

In the adjacent room (Fig. 89), which overlooks Holmens Kanal, the walls are subdivided by tall panels that contain the distinctively Directoire "arabesque" or "Pompeiian" type of ornament. Delicately drawn urns, garlands, wreaths, cameos, and other classical motifs are balanced atop one another in a decorative style that Robert Adam used in England starting in the 1770s and which Belanger and Dugourc introduced into France.[38] Between these arabesque panels are painted representations of bas-relief panels, with groups of neoclassical figures similar to those of the stucco panels that Ramée used in several of his interior designs.[39]

The painted ceilings in the Erichsen Mansion are the best preserved parts of Masson et Ramée's decorative work there (Figs. 91, 92). Each of the five ceiling designs is different in pattern, color scheme, and subject matter. But all of them recall the types of decoration Ramée knew from Paris. Circular panels are prominent, as in the decorative work of Belanger and Cellerier, and three of the ceilings are conceived as trompe-l'oeil representations of fabric canopies, stretched taut across the ceiling. This device, pioneered in Paris by Dugourc, Belanger, and Cellerier, and used already by Ramée in Caspar Voght's house on the Elbchaussee, was one of the most distinctive characteristics of the Directoire and then of the Empire styles.

The decoration of the Erichsen Mansion by Masson et Ramée thus

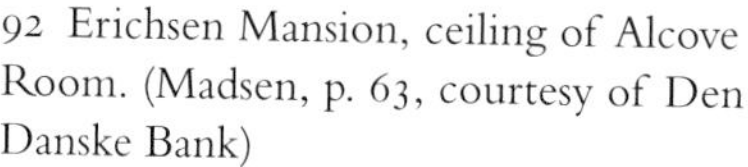
92 Erichsen Mansion, ceiling of Alcove Room. (Madsen, p. 63, courtesy of Den Danske Bank)

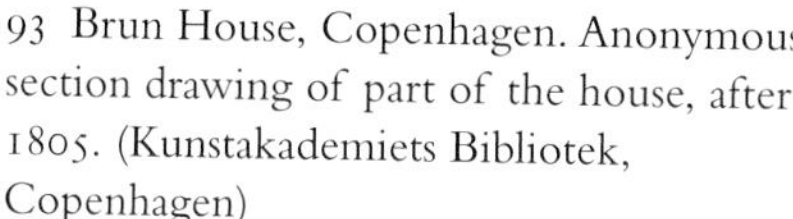
93 Brun House, Copenhagen. Anonymous section drawing of part of the house, after 1805. (Kunstakademiets Bibliotek, Copenhagen)

introduced to Denmark the latest French fashions in interior design. The prominence of this work, in the grandest private house in Copenhagen, brought Ramée and his firm strikingly to the attention of everyone in the Danish capital interested in the arts. August Hennings's fascination and puzzlement over Ramée's work were no doubt typical of the reactions of visitors to Erichsen's house. It was this commission, more than any other, that must have publicized Ramée's talents to Copenhagen society, resulting in the commissions for country houses that will be examined in the following chapter.

Aside from Erichsen, Ramée's principal clients in Denmark were Constantin Brun and his wife, the poet Frederikke Brun. The architect designed the Bruns' country estate, Sophienholm, and decorated their house in Copenhagen. This city mansion, situated on the corner of Bredgade and Dronningens Tvaergade, near the Amalienborg Palace, had been purchased by Brun in 1796 from the Queen Dowager of Denmark. Ramée remodeled its interior sometime before the summer of 1802, when August Hennings mentioned it in his diary (Fig. 93).[40] The rooms decorated by Ramée no longer survive, but one of them – an unusual bathroom – is documented in drawings by Ramée that survive in the collection of the Danish Art Academy.[41]

Frederikke Brun suffered from a skin disease, perhaps psoriasis, for which she took frequent baths.[42] Hennings, on his visit to the house in 1802, reported that Constantin Brun "lamented the illness and suffering of his wife, who presently is planning to travel to Italy to take the waters, and he showed me a bathroom that he is having built for her near her bedroom, for her use upon her return."[43] This bath was on the ground floor of the house, with a stair

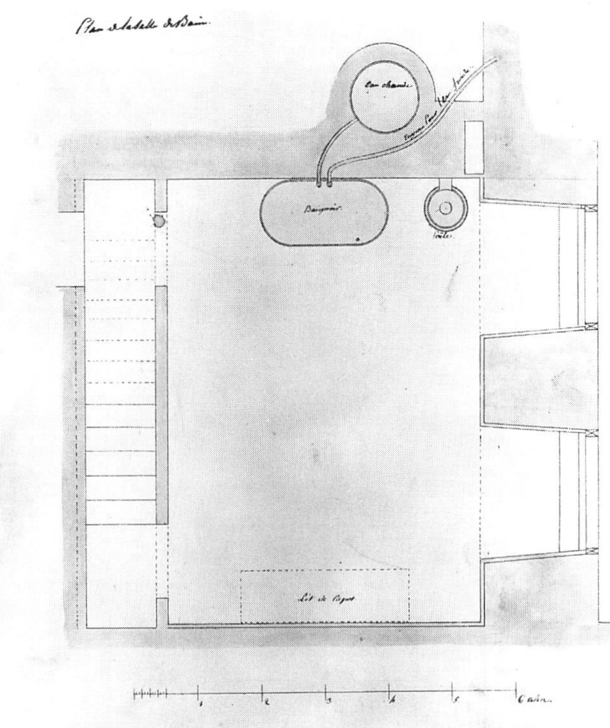

94 Plan of bathroom in Brun House. Ink and watercolor drawing on paper, 19 × 24 cm. (Kunstakademiets Bibliotek, Copenhagen)

leading up to Frederikke's bedroom. Ramée's drawings for the room, which are not signed but have notes in the architect's distinctive handwriting, consist of a floor plan and elevation drawings of all four walls, drawn in ink and watercolor (Figs. 94–6 and color plates 9, 10). Although small, the drawings are handsomely executed, with subtle washes indicating multicolored marbleized wall surfaces and circular wall reliefs with neoclassical bathing scenes. Also shown are the copper bathtub itself (connected by pipes to a hot-water tank and cold-water source in an adjacent room), a freestanding stove to heat the room, and a "*lit de repos,*" or couch, on the wall opposite the bathtub.

The design of this room replaces traditional classical elements (columns, pilasters, cornices, etc.) with a simple type of decoration: flat planes of different colors and surface patterns, on which circular reliefs float like bubbles. The inspiration for this style of interior decoration was perhaps the bathroom of the Hôtel Dervieux in Paris, designed by Belanger about 1790.[44] But Ramée's design departs even more from traditional classicism and reminds us of Belanger's remark that Ramée had "proposed purifying" the architecture of antiquity.[45]

In its radical simplicity, this design is part of the neoclassical movement of the period. But in contrast to the brutally plain work of architects such as Ledoux and Boullée, Ramée's design has a delicacy, a refinement of detail, even a kind of femininity: qualities appropriate to this design for Frederikke Brun, of course, but present to some extent in all of Ramée's work. The resulting ambiguity is one of the distinctive traits of Ramée's architecture. Is it simple or complex? Classical or anticlassical? Chaste or luxurious? It does not

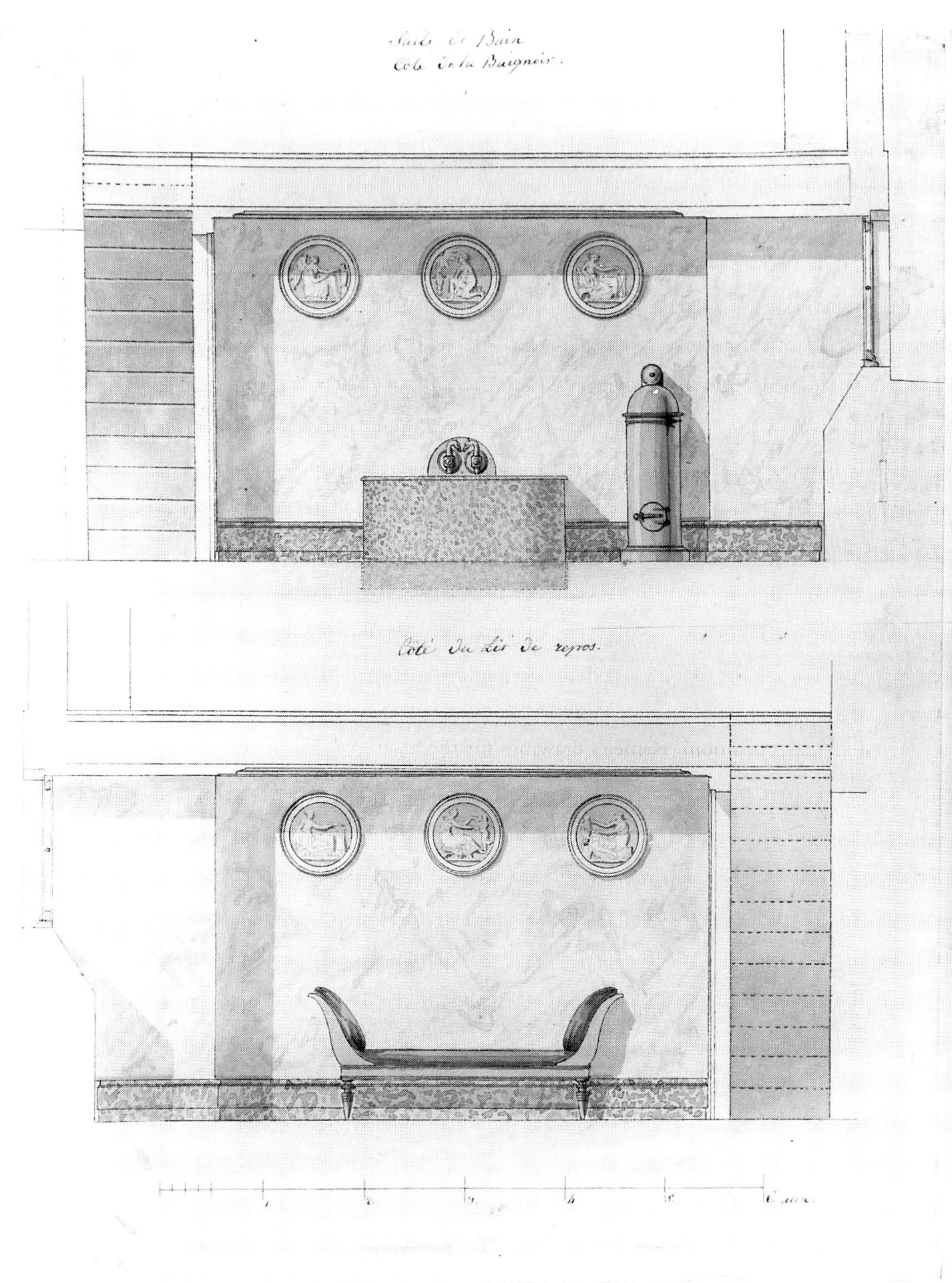

95 Sheet with two elevation drawings of bathroom in Brun House. Ink and watercolor on paper, 19 × 24 cm. (Kunstakademiets Bibliotek, Copenhagen)

96 Sheet with two elevation drawings of bathroom in Brun House. Ink and watercolor on paper, 19 × 24 cm. (Kunstakademiets Bibliotek, Copenhagen)

97 Frederikslund, dining room. (Kunstakademiets Bibliotek, Copenhagen)

fit easily into categories. People at the time apparently sensed this ambiguity and found it either appealingly original or (as did August Hennings) disconcerting.

Three country houses designed by Ramée survive in Denmark: the Bruns' Sophienholm, Frederic de Coninck's Frederikslund, and Johannes Søbøtker's Øregaard – all three built in the first decade of the nineteenth century and located just north of Copenhagen. The buildings themselves will be examined in the next chapter, but some observations on their interior decoration can be made here. In contrast to the houses in Copenhagen, the country houses contain no painted decoration, which suggests that the artisans of Masson et Ramée were not employed directly on these jobs; at the most, some of the plasterwork or carved woodwork may have been produced in the workshops at Dockenhuden.

The most highly decorated of the interiors is the dining room of Frederikslund (Fig. 97), whose walls are treated with Directoire-style plaster ornament: bands of acanthus and arabesquelike relief, ribbon-tied wreaths above the doors, and the circular bas-reliefs that Ramée had used in the Voght House on the Elbchaussee and the dining room of Erichsen's mansion. Here at Frederikslund, in fact, there are more of these circular reliefs than in the other houses: eight of them, each representing a different classical subject drawn from the art of antiquity. They were evidently mass-produced reliefs, for several of them are the same as those found in Ramée's other houses. Four are duplicates of reliefs in Voght's salon, and two of these four are found also in Erichsen's dining room. Some of the reliefs are also the same as, or similar to, relief sculpture found in Directoire-style houses of the period in France.[46]

Except for this dining room in Frederikslund, the interiors of Ramée's Danish country houses employ only simple architectural ornament: paneled

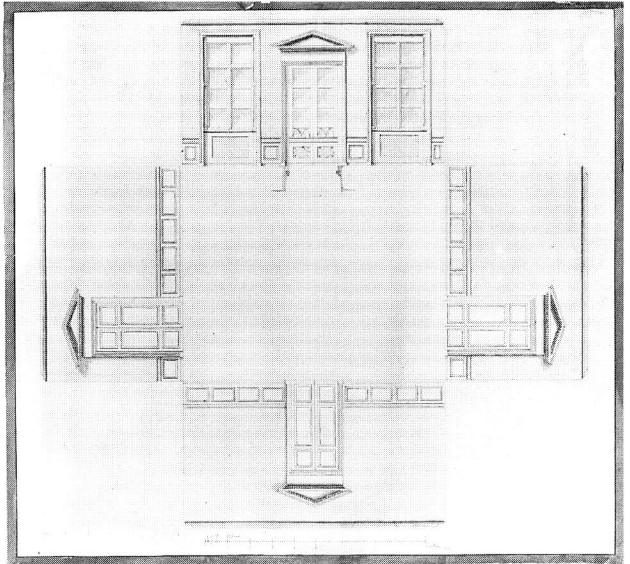

98 Sophienholm, elevation drawings of the four walls of the central salon. Ink on paper, 36 × 32 cm. (Kunstakademiets Bibliotek, Copenhagen)

99 Øregaard, central salon. (Øregaard Museum)

wainscotting, classical door- and window-frames and ceiling moldings. In the central hall or salon of both Sophienholm and Øregaard, attention is focused on the doors, which are provided with finely detailed pediments and have the attenuated proportions characteristic of the Directoire style.[47] A drawing possibly by Ramée, preserved at the Art Academy in Copenhagen, shows the four walls of the salon at Sophienholm, with its doors, windows, and wainscotting carefully delineated (Fig. 98).[48] At Øregaard, there are arched niches in the two interior corners of the salon (Fig. 99), which originally held room-heating stoves (later replaced by fireplaces).[49] A similar niche is found in the dining room of Frederikslund.

As noted earlier, Hennings stated that Ramée's work in Copenhagen included interior decoration for "Schimmelmann." This was Count Ernst Schimmelmann, finance minister to the King; but nothing is known of this job.[50] One Danish historian has suggested, moreover, that some of the French-style decoration in Valdemar's Castle, on the island of Taasinge, may have been the work of Ramée.[51] Even without such uncertain attributions, it is clear that Ramée was the foremost representative in Denmark of French interior design around 1800, and that his services were sought by some of the most prominent figures in the country.

Furniture

Although Masson et Ramée advertised itself chiefly as a producer of furniture, there are no known examples of the items it manufactured or sold. The firm had catalogues of its merchandise (in a letter of 1806 to one of his German clients, Ramée mentioned "a sale of luxury objects from our store" and said, "I shall [send] you some catalogues"), but none of them is known to survive.[52] We can only speculate on the nature of the furnishings produced by the firm.

Modeled largely on the latest Parisian designs, Ramée's products must have been in the neoclassical manner of the Directoire and Empire styles. Much of the furniture in these styles tended toward simplification. Ramée's designs probably showed this tendency to an extreme degree, both because of his innate preference for plainness and because simple models would be easier to manufacture in his firm's small factory outside Hamburg, without access to the specialized artisans of Paris. It is not surprising that observers of Ramée's furnishings mentioned especially their simplicity. As noted already, August Hennings wrote in 1802 that Ramée was in Copenhagen "furnish[ing] various houses," and he expressed amazement that people would pay so much for "an armchair that is perfectly *plain*."[53] (The German word used by Hennings is "*blos*," literally "naked.")

The only known furniture designs by Ramée are those shown in his drawings of rooms: the bed and sofas seen in his section drawing of a *maison de campagne* of 1796, and the *lit de repos* that appears in one of the drawings of the bathroom of the Brun House in Copenhagen (see color plates 8, 9). Based on ancient Greek or Roman furniture, this couch represents one extreme of neoclassical purity in French design of the period. It is remarkably similar, in fact, to the couch on which Madame Récamier is shown reclining, in David's portrait of her of 1800 (see Fig. 29).[54]

Madame Récamier, whose first house (on the Rue du Mail in Paris) had been built by Ramée, was a paragon of Parisian fashion around 1800. Ramée probably kept informed of the taste-setting interiors of her subsequent Chaussée d'Antin house, decorated by Louis Martin Berthault, and these designs no doubt contributed to Ramée's style of decoration in Germany and Denmark. Another source may have been the furniture of Percier and Fontaine, who around 1800 were creating the Empire style in their elegant work for Napoleon and Josephine Bonaparte. Ramée's connection with Charles Percier has been noted.

As for Masson et Ramée's major job of interior decoration in Copenhagen, the Erichsen Mansion, there are two pieces of furniture – an armchair and a large wardrobe – that are documented from Erichsen family records as being original to the house (Fig. 100). The Danish historian H. H. Madsen has suggested that these pieces were purchased in England by Erich Erichsen, during a buying trip he is known to have made to London in 1801.[55] If this is true, it seems likely that Erichsen was guided in his selection of furniture by the recommendations of Ramée, for these pieces represent exactly the taste for simplicity that we would expect of the architect. This is especially true in the case of the armchair: it is neoclassical in its overall shape, but so sleek and stripped of ornament that it could almost be of the twentieth century. It reminds us of Hennings's comment about Ramée's "naked" chairs.

100 Armchair from the Erichsen Mansion. (Madsen, p. 11, courtesy of Den Danske Bank)

One wonders, in fact, if these items of furniture may have been manufactured by Masson et Ramée, although possibly based on English models (as Meyer said that some of the firm's furniture was). It is interesting that another wardrobe, very similar in style to Erichsen's, is built into one of the rooms of the Voght House at Klein Flottbek on the Elbchaussee, which Ramée decorated in 1796, even before his association with Masson.[56] In any case, the wardrobe and armchair from the Erichsen House give us a notion of the kind of furniture designed by Ramée and produced by the workshops at Dockenhuden.

Suggestions of the variety of decorating services provided by Masson et Ramée are found in Ramee's extensive correspondence about his work for the Prince of Mecklenburg-Schwerin, from 1804 to 1808 (examined in Chapter 9). Ramée spoke of carpets for the mausoleum at Ludwigslust and for the prince's dining room at Schwerin; he referred to sample patterns and available stocks, revealing that the carpets came from the warehouse of Masson et Ramée.[57] Ramée also submitted bills for furniture supplied to the prince's apartments, including "thirty mahogany armchairs" and "twelve footstools," and he noted in one letter that he was enclosing a "prospectus" describing a new piece of furniture, for which he was soliciting "subscriptions."[58] He also sent the prince descriptions of a telescope that could be ordered from Paris. As noted earlier, Ramée's partner referred to "our Paris firm" in one of his letters, suggesting that Masson et Ramée had a branch office there, or were associated with another business enterprise.[59]

Wallpaper was another product sold by Masson et Ramée, as indicated by the firm's listing in the Hamburg *Adress-Buch*. Records of about 1805 show that the firm provided wallpaper for the newly erected house of J. H. Baur (brother of the man for whom Ramée laid out Baur's Park), at Nienstedten on the Elbchaussee.[60] Much of this product was no doubt supplied by Ramée's wallpaper factory in Dinant, although it is not known exactly when the architect established this enterprise.

Ramée also had close connections with the wallpaper trade in Paris. His teacher Belanger had designed wallpaper, and Belanger's brother-in-law, J. D. Dugourc, had a wallpaper business in Paris in the 1790s.[61] Dugourc also was involved in the manufacture of crystal and porcelain and was one of the foremost designers and producers of decorative objects in Paris in the 1790s, so it is likely that he was the source of some of Ramée's imports from France (at least until 1800, when Dugourc went to Madrid to be architect to the king of Spain). These were the imports that Ramée spoke of, in his petition of 1800, when he said that he was providing "large markets, in the North, for French factories and manufactures."[62]

Theatre Design

Several designs for theatres and theatrical decoration were executed by Ramée and his firm during his period in Hamburg. Ramée was well qualified for this kind of work, because of his apprenticeship with Jacques Cellerier, the foremost theatre architect in Paris, and because of his experience in the office of the *Menus Plaisirs du Roi,* in which stage scenery and related types of decor were produced for the French court. As suggested earlier, Ramée's expertise in this field may have been one of the reasons he first came to Hamburg, where there was a community of theatre-loving French émigrés. Unfortunately, none of Ramée's theatre designs are known to survive; all we have are tantalizing allusions to them.

Vincent Nolte's memoirs of his youth in Hamburg, quoted earlier, note that Ramée was hired about 1802 to erect a theatre on the property of Peter Godeffroy at Blankenese on the Elbchaussee, to satisfy the theatrical mania of Godeffroy's social set at that time.[63] And there is a reference in a biography of the statesman Karl Sieveking (a supporter of theatre in Hamburg in the early nineteenth century) to an 1806 proposal by Ramée to build a theatre on the Old Cathedral Square in Hamburg.[64]

Boulliot, in his 1830 article on Ramée, stated that the architect "decorated the French theatre in Hamburg." The theatre company of the French court, which had fled France during the Revolution and established itself at Brussels, was driven from there, too, when the French took Belgium; it went to Hamburg about 1795 and built a small theatre on land donated by Prince Potocky on the Drehbahn, in the northern part of the city.[65] The building itself, of light wood construction, was said to be the work of a French architect; one German writer in the late nineteenth century suggested that this might have been Ramée.[66] If so, it was the architect's first job in Hamburg and perhaps the reason he went to that city. But it is possible that Ramée's work was for a later remodeling of the theatre. In 1802, the theatre reopened with a newly decorated interior, executed by Masson et Ramée's painter Le Sueur.[67]

In Copenhagen, where Ramée received numerous architectural commissions starting about 1800, designs for two theatres are mentioned in Boulliot's article on Ramée: "The king [of Denmark] charged him with the decoration of the former royal theatre of that city and had him draw up projects for a new theatre [*salle de spectacle*] in Rosenborg Park."[68]

Research in Denmark has produced no trace of Ramée's designs for a theatre in Rosenborg Park. But there is some record of the decoration of the Royal Theatre in Copenhagen. In the archives of the theatre is a bill for services and a receipt signed by Le Sueur, acknowledging payment for work in the theatre. The document specifies "painting of two complete sets [*décorations*] and other separate parts made for different plays . . . by E. Le Sueur, painter, on the account of MM. Masson et Ramé [sic] of Hamburg, from 6 November 1800 to 27 February 1801."[69] The "two complete sets" are described as representing a "*Place Publique*" and a "*Palais Gothique*."[70] It seems likely that Ramée made preliminary designs for these stage sets, of an architectural nature, which Le Sueur then elaborated and executed.

Another work by Ramée that could be called theatrical was the design of a festival hall (*salle de fête*) for an official celebration of Napoleon's birthday in 1808, commissioned by the French governor of Hamburg, Jean Baptiste Bernadotte (later to be the king of Sweden), during the period of Napoleonic occupation of northern Germany.[71] But little is known of this work.

Despite the paucity of information about these many commissions, it is clear that theatrical designs constituted an important part of Ramée's work during the time he lived in Hamburg.

The Hamburg Börsenhalle

The building that brought Ramée the greatest fame in Germany was the Börsenhalle (Stock Exchange Hall), erected on Bohnenstrasse in Hamburg in 1803 and destroyed in the great fire that consumed much of the city in 1842 (Figs. 101, 102).[72] Not really a stock exchange, it was a kind of businessmen's club at which the city's merchants and bankers could meet to socialize or con-

101 Börsenhalle, Hamburg, engraved view before about 1825. (Staatsarchiv Hamburg)

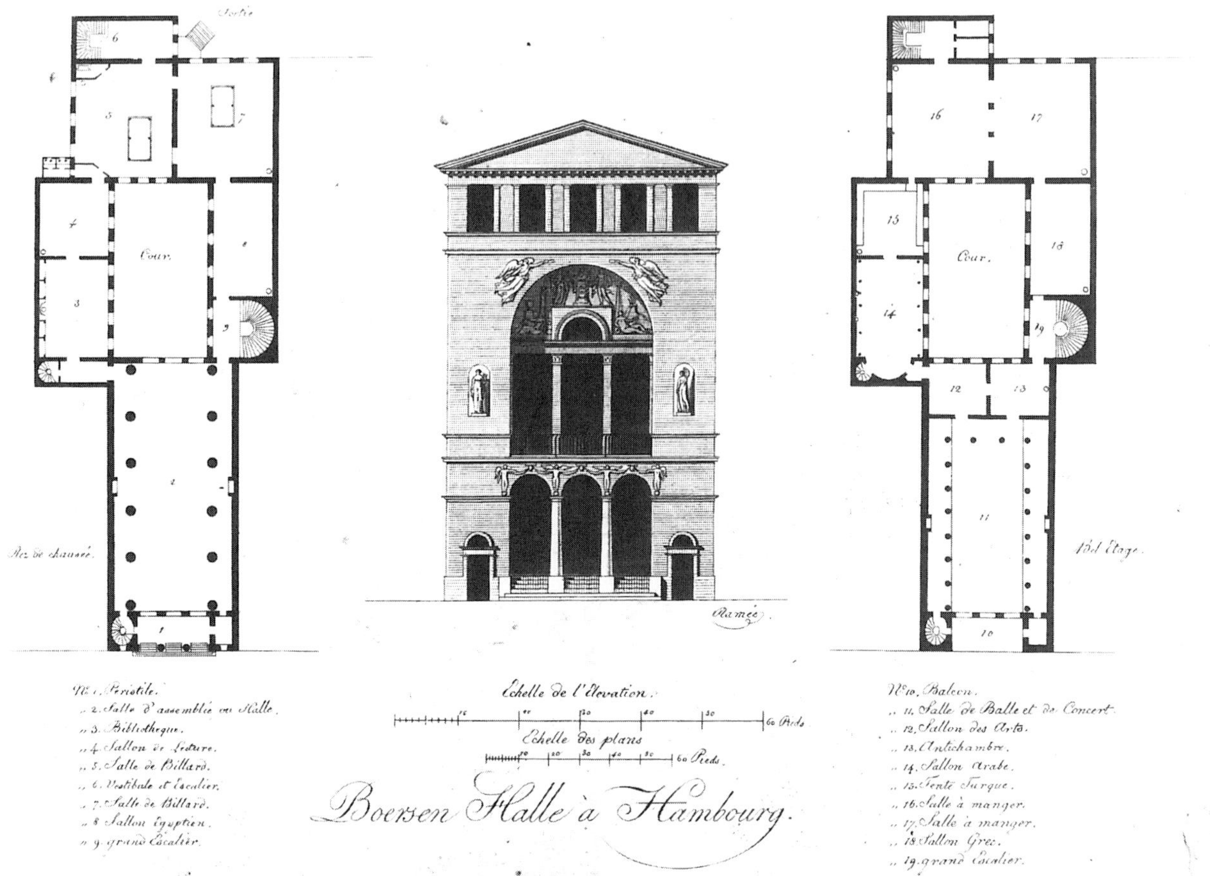

102 Börsenhalle, engraved plans and façade elevation, inscribed "Ramée." Published in *Zeitung für die elegante Welt*, 1804. (Staatsarchiv Hamburg)

duct business in a congenial atmosphere; the stock exchange itself (on the same street in Hamburg) was in an old and crowded structure.

The owner of the Börsenhalle was a merchant named Gerhard von Hosstrup, who also had Ramée design a garden for his estate outside Hamburg.[73] For the opening of the Börsenhalle in January of 1804, Hosstrup published a booklet about it, describing its business and social functions and stating that it was inspired by Lloyd's Coffee House in London.[74] But Hosstrup wanted to create something completely new. He suggested that he chose Ramée as architect of the Börsenhalle because Ramée was an innovator and could give the Börsenhalle a distinctive and avant-garde form:

> My wish was to erect something unique, which would borrow nothing from other places but would become a prototype itself. . . . A French architect, established in Hamburg, proved most useful to me in this regard, and fixed my resolution to spare no expense. This was Herr Ramée, partner in the firm of Masson & Ramée, known for its excellent furniture factory and its extensive trade in luxury goods; an artist celebrated for his remarkable taste, as well as the extent and novelty of his ideas, who had already made a

> name for himself in Paris before the Revolution. He undertook this enterprise with passion and, assisted by his similarly talented friend Masson, involved all the artists and workers of his firm in this job.[75]

103 Designs by C. F. Hansen for the Jacobsen House and the architect's own house, both in Altona, 1802 and 1803–4. (Kunstakademiets Bibliotek, Copenhagen)

The building Ramée designed for Hosstrup had a narrow frontage on the street, but widened toward the back, with rooms arranged around a courtyard; the latter appears, in an engraved view of the interior, to be covered by a glass roof (see Fig. 104).[76] The structure was four storeys high, three of them devoted to the Börsenhalle itself, the top floor serving as Hosstrup's residence and as the offices of a commercial newspaper he established in 1805.[77] The building's façade consisted of three parts. At the ground level was a three-arched entry way. Above this, the main portion of the façade had a large arched opening or niche, suggesting the form of a triumphal arch (complete with the bas-relief winged figures that traditionally decorated triumphal arches), as well as recalling Ledoux's Guimard House in Paris. At the top of the façade was an attic storey with five simple windows, surmounted by a pediment.[78]

Although Hosstrup stated that he had wanted his Börsenhalle to "borrow nothing," Ramée's design in fact represented some of the latest architectural trends in France. But they were largely new to Germany. Some of the distinctive traits of the design can be seen by comparing it with contemporary works of C. F. Hansen (Ramée's main rival in Hamburg), such as Hansen's own house and his Jacobsen House, whose façades were of the same size and overall proportions as that of the Börsenhalle (Fig. 103).[79] Hansen's buildings, despite their inventiveness, retained the standard elements of classicism, such as columns and pilasters, and adhered largely to traditional systems of proportion and design.

Ramée's Borsenhalle reveals a transformation that had begun in Paris about the time of the Revolution, especially in the unbuilt designs of the visionary Étienne Louis Boullée and in Academy students' projects. Columns and other classical elements tended to be isolated or play minor roles; they no longer controlled and organized a façade. As in the Börsenhalle, the façade was frequently a plain surface devoid of the major vertical elements that traditionally defined a classical façade. Sculpture and other decoration were not contained neatly within defined areas, but floated on the field of the façade plane. The underlying logic of classicism, in which the orders control and structure a design, was replaced here by a new esthetic of unbounded planes (or planes bounded only by horizontal divisions), on which ornament could be applied almost anywhere.

The freedom inherent in this system can be seen in the series of bas-relief figures extending across the center of Ramée's façade, just above the ground-floor arcade. This motif, which Hosstrup described (in his pamphlet on the Börsenhalle) as "genies carrying garlands of flowers and fruits," with "Mercury heads" over the centers of the arches, is similar to decoration on a theatre in Paris built by a student of Ledoux in the 1790s.[80] The simplicity and planarity of Ramée's design were evidently striking to people at the time. Hosstrup himself stated that the façade of the Börsenhalle was "in an elegant style" and made a point of noting that it was perfectly "flat [*glatt*]."[81]

The use of the triumphal-arch motif in the design of a façade is anoth-

104 Börsenhalle, engraved view of Assembly Hall on the ground floor. (Staatsarchiv Hamburg)

er reflection of contemporary French architecture. In the Börsenhalle, the arched opening created a large niche that served as a balcony for the principal room on the second floor, a ballroom or concert hall. On the back wall of this niche, life-sized bas-relief figures above the doors represented Minerva and Mercury honoring Abundance, flanked by allegorical representations of the River Elbe and of Science and Commerce – appropriate to the building's function and to Hamburg's mercantile prosperity.[82]

The interior of the Börsenhalle is known from Hosstrup's description in his pamphlet on the building, from floor plans shown in an engraving made by Ramée, and from an engraved view of the main space on the ground floor (Figs. 102, 104).[83] Numerous rooms were provided, on three floors, in which the club members could assemble for business or relaxation. Aside from the main hall on the ground floor, there was a library, a newspaper reading room, billiard rooms, dining rooms, the ballroom-concert hall on the second floor, and about eight additional rooms for general use, each with a special decorative theme.

Most interesting is the eclectic nature of these theme rooms. Besides a Salon of the Muses, a Salon of the Arts, and a Greek Salon decorated with caryatids and a panoramic mural of the ruins of Athens, there were rooms reflecting the new romantic interest in exotic architecture: an Arabian Salon furnished with "divans" and mahogany columns with golden capitals; a Turkish Tent with continuous "ottomans" around its periphery; and an Egyptian Salon

105 Friedrich Weinbrenner, design for Music Room of Karlsruhe Museum. Detail of plate 37 of Weinbrenner's *Architektonisches Lehrbuch*, 1810.

featuring granite columns with bronze capitals and murals showing the Pyramids and the Nile at flood time.[84]

This Egyptian Salon was the only one of these rooms to lie on the ground floor of the Börsenhalle. Significantly, the main space on the ground floor, the Assembly Hall, was also Egyptian in style. An engraving shows this long hall, with plain masonry walls and a dozen columns that had Egyptian palm capitals (Fig. 104). Ramée thus conceived the ground floor of the Börsenhalle as being in the "Egyptian" mode; it is one of the earliest examples of this style.

Napoleon's Egyptian campaign of 1798–9 stimulated great interest in the land of the Nile. It was the main force behind the Egyptian Revival style in Europe, especially after the publication of the multivolume official French report, the *Description de l'Egypte,* beginning in 1809.[85] But Ramée's Börsenhalle predates this true Egyptian Revival, which was based on accurate archaeological documentation; his design belongs to an earlier phase of interest in things Egyptian, the manifestations of which are rarer and in some respects more interesting.[86]

The occasional Egyptian motifs seen in European design in the eighteenth century were part of the eclectic repertoire of exotic styles, such as Gothick and Chinois, used in interior décor, garden follies, and the like. In Ramée's Börsenhalle, this tradition is suggested by the presence of "Arabic"

106 Börsenhalle, lithograph by J. Scheidel, c. 1840, showing additions made to the building between 1826 and 1836. (Staatsarchiv Hamburg)

and "Turkish" rooms along with the Egyptian ones. But at the end of the eighteenth century in France, the Egyptian mode assumed another significance. Some of the radical neoclassicists were attracted to Egyptian architectural forms because of their stark simplicity and geometric purity; Boullée, in particular, was inspired by the sublime scale of Egyptian monuments, their geometry and flat surfaces. It also is possible that Boullée's innovative treatment of ornament – floating on the surface of a façade, rather than neatly confined as in classical architecture – was inspired by the mural nature of ornament in Egyptian architecture, in which an entire wall, or any part of it, could receive decoration.

Ramée's Egyptian-columned room in the Börsenhalle, while not as stark as Boullée might have designed it, reflects this association of Egyptian architecture with geometric simplicity. In fact, it is one of the few executed examples of this phenomenon, as most of the "Egyptian" designs of this period remained unbuilt. Significantly, Hosstrup described this assembly hall as being "in the simple style [*im simplen Stil*]," a designation that Ramée himself may have employed to justify the unusual character of this room and its Egyptian columns.[87]

Seen in this light, Ramée's Egyptian hall is not so inconsistent with the façade of the Börsenhalle as it first appears. In both cases, the traditional classical principles of design are replaced by a new esthetic, in which plain surfaces reign and to which isolated bits of ornament are admitted: ornament that may be exotic in source, such as the Egyptian palm capitals, or placed in an unclassical manner, such as the relief sculpture on the façade.

Except for the Assembly Hall on the ground floor, the rooms in the Börsenhalle are known only from Hosstrup's descriptions of them. Their execution "involved all the artists and workers" of the firm of Masson et Ramée, who must have included painters, sculptors, stuccoists, woodcarvers, and metalworkers, judging from the nature of the rooms. The only artist specifically named by Hosstrup was Pierre Étienne Le Sueur, the painter who had collaborated with Ramée in Denmark; Hosstrup refers to a painting by Le Sueur in the vaulted ballroom of the Börsenhalle, representing Apollo in his chariot with a lyre and wreath.[88] Hosstrup also described the decoration in the adjacent Salon of the Arts (*Kunst-Saal*), which contained allegorical paintings of Poetry, Music, Sculpture, Painting and Architecture.[89]

Ramée took great pride in his design of the Hamburg Börsenhalle. A quarter-century after its erection, a footnote in Boulliot's article on Ramée (based, we recall, on information provided by the architect himself) made special reference to the critical reception of the Börsenhalle: "Mr. Weinbrenner, the celebrated German architect, said in one of his works that [the Börsenhalle] was the most beautiful and skillful [building] in Europe."[90] These remarks have not yet been found in the writings of Weinbrenner, but it is likely that Ramée's building did appeal to him. Friedrich Weinbrenner studied architecture in the 1790s in Vienna and Rome, and in the early years of the nineteenth century he became one of the major neoclassicists in Germany, especially with the buildings he erected in his native Karlsruhe. The Hamburg Börsenhalle may have been the first structure Weinbrenner saw that represented French architectural innovations around 1800, which were to help shape his own architectural style.

The influence of Ramée may be detected in works by Weinbrenner such as the Music Room of his Karlsruhe Museum (Fig. 105).[91] This room ends in a large niche framed by a wall conceived as a triumphal arch, like the façade of Ramée's Börsenhalle; it is similar even in the winged figures above the arch, delineated in the light, attentuated manner typical of Ramée and the Directoire style. Moreover, the upper part of the niche is treated as a canopied fabric, a motif typical of Ramée and his associates in Paris, and later of the Empire designs of Percier and Fontaine.

Hosstrup's Börsenhalle and the newspaper he published there prospered, and between 1826 and 1836 he enlarged the structure, replacing the two old adjacent houses with new buildings (Fig. 106).[92] These symmetrical additions to the Börsenhalle were reportedly designed by two Hamburg architects named Ludolf and Châteauneuf, the latter of whom was a student of Weinbrenner.[93] They followed Ramée's design of the Börsenhalle so closely in these additions (in the general proportions and even the lining-up of horizontal string-courses) that their admiration for Ramée's design is evident. One suspects that it was Weinbrenner's respect for this building that guaranteed the sympathetic treatment of its enlargement, by one of his students, more than twenty years after its construction.

The Failure of Masson et Ramée

No major commissions of Masson et Ramée are known after approximately 1805, and the firm evidently failed about 1808, for starting that year it no longer appeared in the Hamburg *Adress-Buch*. Two years later, bankruptcy proceedings were carried out against it, resulting in the sale of its properties in Hamburg and Dockenhuden.[94] It is possible that incompetence (or worse) on the part of Masson, the firm's business manager, caused the failure. But a more likely cause was the economic misfortune of Hamburg at the time.

Following Napoleon's defeat of the Austrian army at the Battle of Jena in October of 1806, the French occupied Hamburg and proceeded to divert its resources by tribute exaction and other means. The French blockade of trade with England further contributed to the decline of the city's prosperity. (For many Hamburgers, the results were devastating. John Parish and his family, for example, left Hamburg for good and he made this entry in a diary for 19 November 1806: "The fatal black Wednesday!, when the French occupied Hamburg.")[95] The kinds of luxurious products and services sold by Masson et Ramée were surely among the first economic casualties, especially since the firm's association with things French could only have hurt it in the eyes of the Hamburgers during this period of Napoleonic occupation.

Even before the French occupied Hamburg, blockades of the Elbe had damaged the city's economy and the work of Ramée's firm had suffered. In a letter of June 1806, Ramée lamented to the Court Marshall of Mecklenburg, "Times continue to be very bad for the city of Hamburg and particularly for us, who are doing almost no more work."[96]

Masson left Hamburg sometime between May 1808, when he paid a business tax, and June 1809, when the tax register notes that he had departed from the city.[97] According to the Hamburg directory, Ramée stayed in the city until 1810, so he was the one who had to deal with the problems of the firm's bankruptcy. In February 1811, the Marquis de Lafayette reported to his friend Johann von Archenholtz, who had invested in the business:

> I have no reply from Masson, no hope from his father-in-law or from his wife, and nothing satisfactory from my applications to his relatives. I have seen M. Ramée and I am well satisfied with the attitude he has shown to me; I am trying to be useful to him, but I have small means of doing so. He is skillfully working to bring himself before the public. . . . I expect nothing from Masson.[98]

Five years later, when Ramée was in America, Lafayette was still trying to get money from him for the family of Archenholtz (Johann von Archenholtz had died by this time). A letter survives, written to Lafayette from David Parish, Ramée's patron in America, in which Parish reports: "I have communicated to Mr. Ramée what you say respecting the Archenholdt [sic] family, & he has in consequence paid me $200 [for you] . . . Mr. Ramée is making a decent living . . . , but has not yet the means to liquidate the debts of his former establishment at Hamburg."[99]

So the shadow of his firm's failure followed Ramée even to the New World, and he continued there to try to fulfill his responsibilities in regard to it.

Country Houses in Denmark

Chapter 8

In 1807, the loss of its naval fleet ended one of Denmark's great eras of prosperity: "*den glimrende handelsperiode,*" the splendid age of trade. In the last several years of this period, Ramée worked as an architect, landscape designer, and decorator in Copenhagen and its environs.[1] As so often in his career, Ramée had the misfortune to establish his practice in a place just as decline or disaster was about to occur. But he nevertheless produced remarkable work in Denmark – which, moreover, has survived more completely than his work anywhere else.[2]

In the late eighteenth century, Denmark's leaders managed to stay neutral in the power struggle between France and Britain, thereby keeping the country's lucrative trade flowing. In 1801, Britain's anger over Danish commerce with France resulted in a naval battle in Copenhagen harbor, and Denmark was forced to withdraw from the League of Armed Neutrality it had formed with Russia, Prussia, and Sweden. France and Britain allowed Denmark to continue trading for several years, but, following Napoleon's military conquests of 1806 and Britain's imposition of naval blockades, Denmark's profitable neutrality was finally ended. In August of 1807, British forces bombarded Copenhagen and seized the entire Danish fleet; Denmark then allied itself with France and became entangled in the debilitating affairs of Europe.

The period leading up to these events in Denmark was also one of disruption in architecture and the other arts. French artists working in Denmark were preeminent throughout much of the eighteenth century, as in many other countries, but starting about 1770 there was a reaction against foreign influence in Denmark, which forced the departure of the major French artists there. In architecture, the main casualty was Nicolas Henri Jardin, who had taught at the Danish Academy of Fine Arts and trained a generation of Danish architects.[3] In succeeding decades, a spirit of artistic nationalism flourished in Denmark, bearing its greatest fruit in the works of the architect Christian Frederik Hansen and the sculptor Bertel Thorvaldsen.

During the years around 1800, however, there was a kind of vacuum in Danish architecture, at least in the capital. C. F. Harsdorff, who had dominated architecture in Copenhagen for many years (and was the architect of the Erichsen Mansion, whose interiors Ramée had decorated), died in 1799. Hansen was still working in Danish Holstein; not until 1804 did he return to Copenhagen permanently, to supervise the erection of his great public buildings there, such as the cathedral and the city hall and law-court complex.[4] The need for architects was especially great, as fire had destroyed a large section of Copenhagen in 1795 and extensive rebuilding was required in the following years.

Ramée seized these opportunities, about 1800, by presenting himself in the Danish capital as the only representative of current French design and naturalistic garden planning. The spirit of Danish nationalism prevented Ramée from receiving commissions for public or royal buildings, so he could not compete with Hansen in that area. (An exception is Ramée's design for a theatre in Rosenborg Park, if Boulliot's article is correct on this point.) But his services were eagerly sought by members of the wealthy merchant class and also by some government ministers. From about 1800 to 1806, Ramée introduced to Denmark the latest French styles of interior decoration (as seen in Chapter 7) and his own distinctive styles of architecture and landscape design. In the latter area, Ramée was one of the first professional landscape planners in Denmark to advocate the irregular garden (another was the royal gardner Johan Ludvig Mansa), and his country houses were perhaps the first in Denmark to be placed in irregular, naturalistic settings.[5]

There is no evidence that Ramée ever actually settled in Copenhagen. Living in Hamburg, he probably traveled to the Danish capital for brief periods of work. In May of 1805, for instance, Ramée's partner Masson mentioned in a letter that Ramée was in Denmark and would return to Hamburg in a week.[6] The trip took only about a day: by land from Hamburg to Kiel, then by boat to Copenhagen.[7] The commuting nature of Ramée's activity in Denmark is indicated by the remarks on this phase of his career in Boulliot's article on the architect:

> During the same period [circa 1802–7] Ramée made frequent trips to Copenhagen and the interior of Denmark, to carry out the planning of various country houses and parks. The king charged him also with the decoration of the former royal theatre in Copenhagen and had him draw up projects for a new theatre in Rosenborg Park.[8]

It is typical of Boulliot's article (written when Ramée was back in Bourbon-restored France) that work for royalty is emphasized. In fact, this was a minor part of Ramée's Danish activity. The designs for a theatre in the park of Rosenborg Castle were not executed, and the decoration of the royal theatre in Copenhagen consisted mainly of stage sets painted by Masson et Ramée's artist, Le Sueur, as described already. Most of Ramée's work in Denmark consisted of domestic houses, their interior decoration, and their surrounding gardens. Since Boulliot did not identify any of these projects by name, and Ramée included only one of them (Sophienholm) in his published designs, local records are the only sources of information about these works. In fact, almost the only indications of the names of Ramée's clients are found in the 1802 diary of August Hennings, as described in the preceeding chapter. We therefore probably know only a portion of Ramée's work in Denmark. (Some additional designs possibly by the architect have been suggested by Danish historians.)[9] But even the known work is fairly extensive: four important country houses, about six parks or gardens, and interior decoration in three or four mansions in Copenhagen.

Ramée's clients in Denmark exemplified the upper classes there.[10] Three of them – Frederic de Coninck, Erich Erichsen, and Johannes Søbøtker – were in the shipping business which was so profitable during this period. Erichsen's firm flourished through the trade of commodities that included spices and fabrics from the East Indies and grain from the Baltic region shipped mainly to England. Søbøtker came from a planter's family in the Danish West Indies. And de Coninck's shipping firm was involved in the infamous "triangular" trade on which the West Indian economy depended (slaves from Africa to the West Indies, plantation products from there to Europe, European goods to Africa).

Another of Ramée's clients was the Danish foreign minister and reformer Ernst Schimmelmann, who ended the slave trade with the Danish colonies in 1804. Ramée also reportedly worked for C. G. Bernstorff, the minister of foreign affairs who presided over Denmark's difficult international balancing act at this time. But the architect's most fruitful client-relationship in Denmark was with the Bruns: Constantin Brun, a merchant and a government official, and his wife Frederikke, an author of some importance and a friend of Goethe, Madame de Staël, and other literary greats of the period.

Ramée's introduction to his Danish clients probably came through connections in the Hamburg area. Since Altona and the Elbchaussee were in Danish territory, many of the merchants and bankers who lived there were acquainted with their counterparts in Copenhagen. The Hamburg banker John Parish, whose son was to take Ramée to America in 1812, was acquainted with several of the architect's Danish patrons.[11] And Frederikke Brun frequently visited Hamburg and Altona and knew there the poet Klopstock, the publisher Pieter Poel, and other associates of Ramée's clients Voght and Sieveking.[12]

August Hennings's opinionated remarks about Ramée's interior decoration in Copenhagen have already been quoted. Hennings's diary also contains references to Ramée's architecture and landscape design. On 15 July 1802, Hennings visited the country estate of Peter Erichsen (brother of the man whose house in Copenhagen was decorated by Masson et Ramée), at Ordrup outside the capital. He reported that the woodland there "has been laid out by Ramé in promenades."[13] Two days later, Hennings noted a visit to Constantin Brun's house in Copenhagen and said that "on Wednesday I shall visit Brun's country house [Sophienholm], Ramé's drawings for which Brun showed me. Ramé has also designed a temple for him, which like one at Erichsen's place at Ordrup is simply a plaything [*eine Spielerei*]. Playing, however, is the chief thing for most men."[14]

The next day, Hennings recorded a visit to Erich Erichsen's country estate at Hellerup, "where Erichsen is having Ramé erect a house, which does not please me. Surrounding it is a masonry-lined moat, with bridges, which will fill up with snow in the winter and be perilous for children, or for anyone at night. The garden is small and the promenades insignificant. The greenhouse is the main thing, and very well maintained."[15] The following month, Hennings gave a detailed description of Constantin Brun's country estate, Sophienholm ("the work of Ramée as artist and Brun as money-dispenser"), noting especially his walks through the landscape, which he called "Ramée's nature-painting [*Ramées Naturmalerei*]."[16]

The chronology of Ramée's Danish works is not clear, but it appears that most of his interior designs were executed first, from about 1800 to 1802. The Bruns' Sophienholm, begun about 1801, was probably the earliest of the country houses, with Hellerupgaard the following year and Frederikslund and Øregaard several years later. It seems that Ramée first became known in Denmark through the work of his decorating firm, Masson et Ramée, and the commissions for houses followed.

An exception would be the house built in Copenhagen by Frederic de Coninck in 1797, if its attribution to Ramée is correct (Fig. 107).[17] But there is little to support this attribution, which arose mainly because Ramée was known to have designed a country house for de Coninck. It is true that the undecorated wall surfaces and recessed planes of the façade of de Coninck's house are suggestive of Ramée. But the low proportions of the building and its asymmetry are not typical of the architect; nor is the use of exposed brick, as Ramée normally covered such walls with stucco. This, apparently, is a rare case of a building incorrectly attributed to Ramée. Only in Denmark (and possibly in New York State), where he is relatively well known, would this be likely to happen; elsewhere, works by the generally forgotten Ramée have been incorrectly ascribed to other architects, but not the opposite.

107 Frederic de Coninck House, Copenhagen, built 1797. (Author)

Ramée's four known country houses in Denmark are Sophienholm, Hellerupgaard, Frederikslund, and Øregaard, all constructed in the area just north of Copenhagen and all still standing except for Hellerupgaard. They constitute the largest group of country houses known to be by Ramée. Each of them has individual traits, yet they share qualities that make them a collective statement of Ramée's architectural principles.

The masonry structure of all four houses is covered with a coating of roughcast or stucco, which heightens the purity of their cubic volumes. In each case, these volumes consist of a large central block flanked by smaller masses. This design follows the Renaissance tradition of tripartite composition, but the way Ramée treated these forms is distinctive and reflects architectural currents of the period. Each of the volumes has an individual identity. There are, to be sure, unifying elements in the designs, such as continuous horizontal bands that hold together the parts; but there is a tension between the unifying forces and the forces of separation. A kind of unstable balance is established between submission to order and the liberated individuality of each member.

Ramée's Danish houses share, moreover, a remarkable starkness, with flat, plain walls and a minimum of ornamental trim. Although Ramée had always favored architectural simplicity, it is taken to a greater extreme here than in his earlier work. In contrast, for example, to the architect's country-house design for the Duke of Saxe-Gotha of 1796, the Danish houses suppress traditional cornices and wall mouldings, replacing them with flat strips or eliminating them altogether. Ramée in Denmark may simply have exerted more fully his natural inclinations. But it is also possible that he was influenced by certain traditions in Danish architecture itself, where one can find unusually plain and smooth surfaces, both in vernacular buildings such as farm structures and in some architect-designed buildings.[18] The possibility of Ramée's attraction to vernacular Danish architecture is especially likely, in view of the many other known cases of his interest in stables, cottages, and such structures.

Frederikke Brun and Sophienholm

Ramée's most remarkable client in Denmark was the poet Frederikke Brun (Fig. 108). She and her husband Constantin engaged the architect to redesign the interiors of their house in Copenhagen, as seen in the preceeding chapter. Ramée then refashioned their country estate, Sophienholm, whose main house, outbuildings, and gardens remain today in a fine state of preservation. It is likely that Frederikke Brun was, in fact, Ramée's first strong supporter in Denmark and introduced him to his later clients there. Luckily, a good deal is known about the Bruns, especially Frederikke, whose progressive artistic interests and international outlook probably attracted her to Ramée. In turn, the architect was apparently stimulated by her ideas and those of her friends, making her one of the clients (along with Perregaux in Paris, Voght in Hamburg, and David Parish in America) with whom Ramée had particularly fruitful relationships.

Friederike Brun – Frederikke in Danish – was born in 1765, the daughter of a German Lutheran minister who took a church post in Copenhagen.[19] In her youth, Frederikke's talents were nurtured by a circle of writers dominated by the romantic poet Gottfried Friedrich Klopstock, who had lived in Copenhagen in the 1750s and 1760s; later, Frederikke came to know Klopstock personally and visited him in Altona on the Elbchaussee. The ancient Gaelic epics of Ossian, which in Frederikke's youth had just been "discovered" (fabricated, actually, by James Macpherson) also inspired the teen-age girl, contributing to the fascination with natural scenery and northern-European subject matter that characterized many of her later writings. Written mostly in German, her works consist of prose descriptions of her travels and poetry that deals with nature and domesticity. Beginning in the 1790s, Frederikke's published writings attracted much attention and even Goethe admired her work.

108 Frederikke Brun, portrait of 1818, painted by Aldenrath. (L. Bobé, *Frederikke Brun og hendes kreds hjemme og ude*, Copenhagen, 1910, frontispiece)

In 1783, the eighteen-year-old Frederikke had married Constantin Brun, successful merchant and director of the Danish West Indies Company. His wealth allowed Frederikke to indulge her passion for travel and to cultivate friendships with the great literary figures of the age. (Besides Klopstock and Goethe, she developed a particularly close friendship with Madame de Staël, visiting her in Switzerland and becoming her "*précieuse amie,*" according to one of Staël's biographers.)[20] The Bruns had four children and Frederikke wrote tender poems about her husband and family, but the marriage was hardly conventional. In Geneva in the early 1790s, Frederikke fell in love with the Swiss writer Karl Viktor von Bonstetten; their relationship continued for many years, during which they often traveled together in France, Switzerland, and Italy. (In Rome in 1795–6, Frederikke was part of the artistic circle that included the Danish expatriate sculptor Thorvaldsen, whose work she was one of the first to appreciate and support.)[21] In 1798, Bonstetten returned with Frederikke to Denmark and actually lived for three years in the Brun household. One Danish historian has noted that the affair was "an open secret" in Copenhagen.[22]

During these years, Bonstetten became interested in the climatic differences between northern and southern Europe and their effects on the cultures of the regions. Years later, he summarized his views on this subject in a popular book entitled *L'Homme du midi et l'homme du nord* (1824), but in 1800 he wrote a more specialized essay on the effects of northern climate on garden design, which will be examined below with respect to Ramée's plans for Sophienholm.

Frederikke Brun's passionate poetry expresses many of the artistic trends of the period, such as the romanticism of wild nature and the creation of a new, northern subject matter, but also the desire to reconcile these ideas with the classical and Judeo-Christian traditions. Representative of Frederikke's work is the poem "*Chamouny beym Sonnenaufgange*" ("Chamounix at Sunrise"), included in several editions of her writings starting in the 1790s. Following are three typical stanzas and an English translation that was published in 1843.[23]

Aus tiefem Schatten des schweigenden Tannenhains
Erblick'ich bebend dich, Scheitel der Ewigkeit,
Blendender Gipfel, von dessen Höhe
Ahndend mein Geist ins Unendliche schwebet! . . .

Wer goss Euch hoch aus des ewigen Winters Reich,
O Zackenströme, mit Donnergetös' herab?
Und wer gebietet laut mit der Allmacht Stimme:
"Hier sollen ruhen die starrenden Wogen"! . . .

Jehovah! Jehovah! kracht's im berstenden Eis
Lavinendonner rollen's die Kluft hinab:
Jehovah! rauscht's in den hellen Wipfeln,
Flüstert's an rieselnden Silberbächen.

(From the still shadows of the tannen grove
Trembling I mark thee, as I gaze above,
Eternal Mountain, dazzling Summit, whence
My vaguely wandering sense
Departs upon its world-o'erpassing flight
Soaring aloft, away, into the Infinite. . . .

Who poured ye out, ye jagged streams that roar
In your descending course, from the abode
Of Winter, all unchangeable and hoar?
Who hath pronounced abroad
The voice of the Omnipotent behest:
Here let these surgy shapes for ever rest! . . .

Jehovah! yes, Jehovah sounds aloud
Where the tall Iceberg's massy form is rent,

And where the toppling Avalanche is bowed
Sheer o'er the thundering mountain's steep descent.
Jehovah rustles in the bright green trees,
And murmurs in the brooks, and in the breeze.)

Certain parallels might be drawn between Frederikke Brun's writings and Ramée's architecture, especially in the ways they combine contrasting principles. Frederikke's poetry expresses both a preoccupation with primeval nature and a desire for classical order and civilized society. Somewhat similarly, Ramée's designs combine elemental simplicity and elegant refinement. Frederikke was evidently attracted to this union of the radical and the refined in Ramée's work. She reportedly described the architect as "a new French landscapist and building revolutionary, who makes everything elegant regardless of climate or locality."[24]

It apparently was Frederikke Brun, rather than her husband, who was especially interested in Ramée's work and first decided to have him renovate their Cophenhagen house and then to transform their country estate, Sophienholm. Sophienholm deserves special attention, as one of Ramée's most distinctive and best-preserved creations.

In 1790 Constantin Brun bought this summer estate, on Bagsvaerd Lake about twelve kilometers north of Copenhagen (Fig. 109).[25] The property consisted of partially forested land, sloping down to the lake; a modest house that

109 Aerial view of Sophienholm on Bagsvaerd Lake. (Royal Library, Copenhagen)

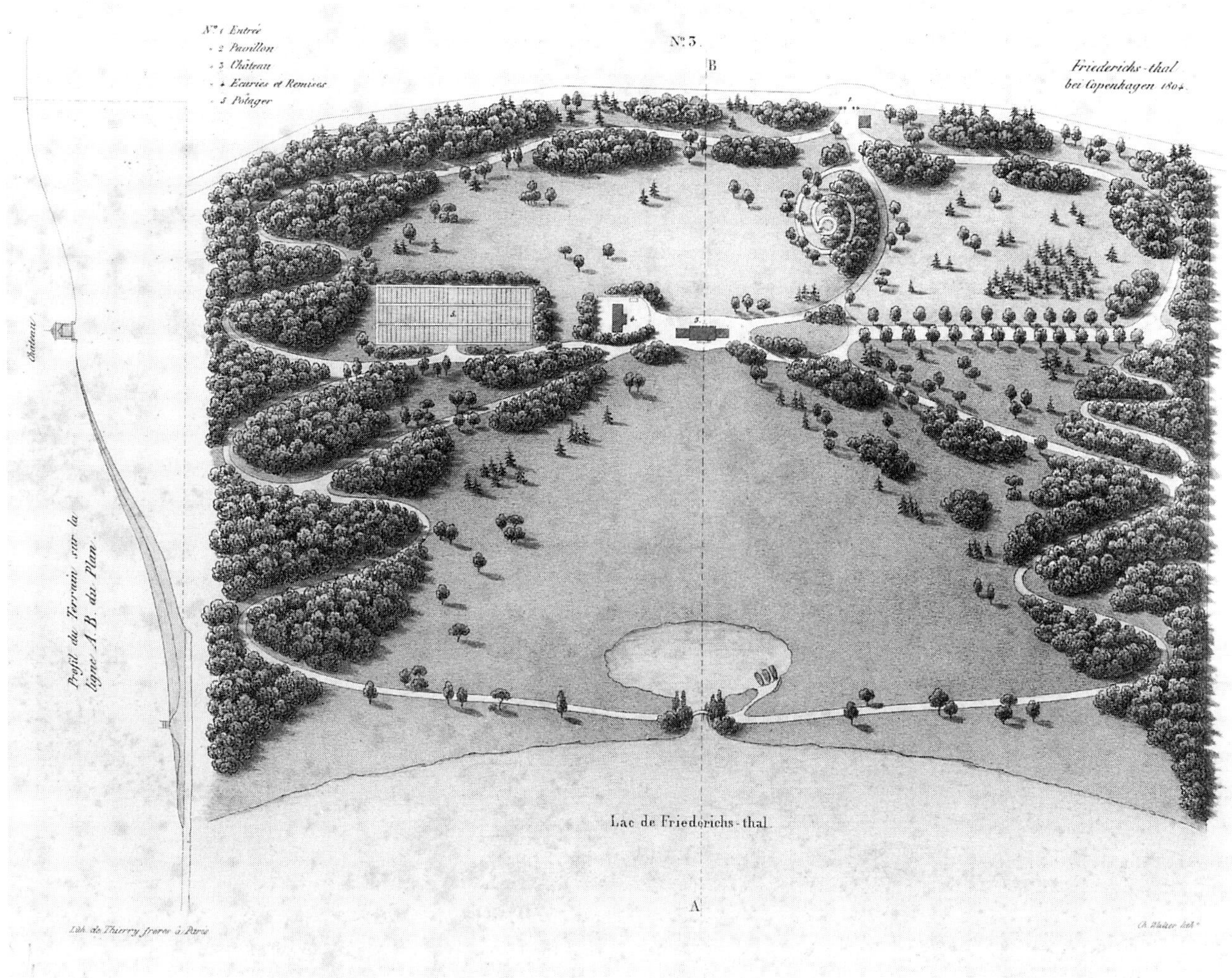

110 Sophienholm. Plan in Ramée's *Parcs et jardins*, pl. 3. (Schaffer Library, Union College)

had been constructed in 1767; and "wretched" stables, as Brun noted in a later description of the estate.[26] Sometime about 1800, Ramée was engaged to make improvements to the property. In the next couple of years he rebuilt the existing house, laid out a park on the surrounding grounds, and erected stables and other structures in Gothic, half-timbered, and other styles. A plan of the estate that Ramée later included in his publication *Parcs et jardins* shows the property largely as it was executed, except for the omission of some outbuildings and some differences in the pattern of plantings (Fig. 110).[27] Remarkably, nearly all the buildings and grounds at Sophienholm have been preserved as when the Bruns lived there. In 1963 the estate was acquired by the local municipality, the buildings were carefully restored, and the property is now open to the public.

Besides Ramée's published plan of Sophienholm, some of his original drawings for it are preserved at the Art Academy in Copenhagen: an elevation drawing and floor plans of the house (but missing the main floor plan), as well as drawings of some of the outbuildings.[28] There are also written descriptions of Sophienholm by Constantin Brun (in which he named Ramée as architect

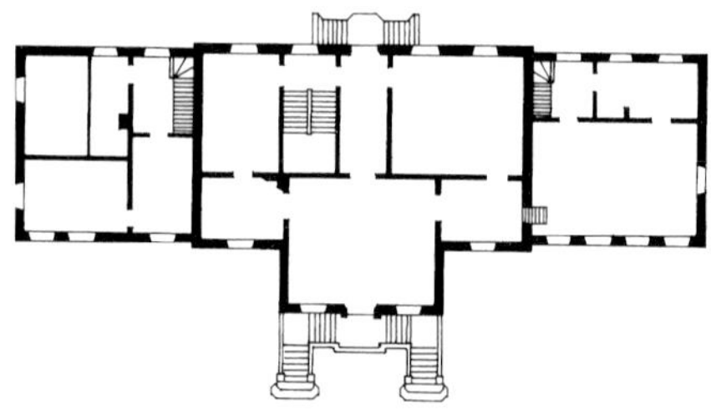

111 Sophienholm, plan of main floor. (Author)

of the main house and stables) and by August Hennings, when construction was still in progress in 1802.[29] References to Sophienholm appear in the writings of Frederikke and her friends, one of whom reported to the poet August Wilhelm Schlegel, in 1805, that she had visited "the spirited Brun at her charming Villa Sophienholm."[30] Later, Frederikke wrote to her fellow poet Friedrich von Matthisson, "You know well my Sophienholm and its mile-wide romantic surroundings. Come, come here! – with the swallows or later with the nightingales."[31]

The house itself at Sophienholm is one of Ramée's most distinctive buildings (Figs. 111–16). It forms a lengthy composition of cubes, with perfectly flat, plastered surfaces and almost no ornament (only a frame around the central door of the garden façade and simple pilasters at the attic storey), creating an impression so stark and volumetric that at first glance the building might be mistaken for an International Style work of the 1920s or 1930s. Equally remarkable is the degree to which the cubic parts of the house, especially the two-storey pavilions at the ends, have an independent character. This trait is found elsewhere in Ramée's work, and in that of other revolutionary architects of the period, but it is seen here in a particularly pronounced way.

One naturally wonders if this effect resulted from the fact that this was a remodeling of an existing building. A drawing of the original Sophienholm,

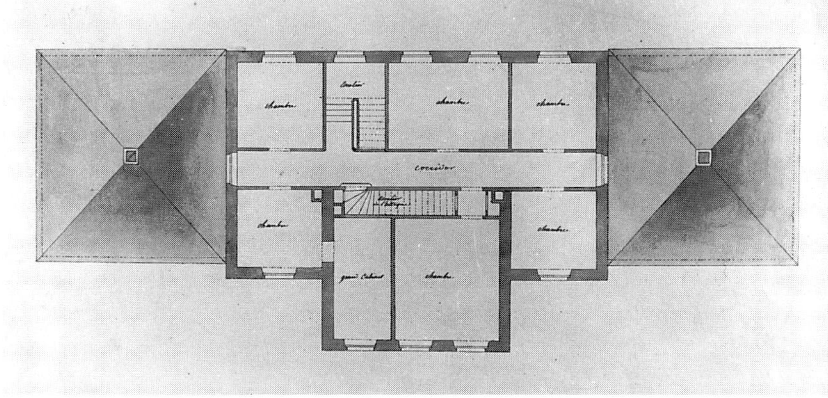

112 Sophienholm, plan of upper floor, inscribed in Ramée's hand, "Maison de M. Brun à Sophienholm / Plan du 2me Etage." Ink drawing, 44 × 27 cm. (Kunstakademiets Bibliotek, Copenhagen)

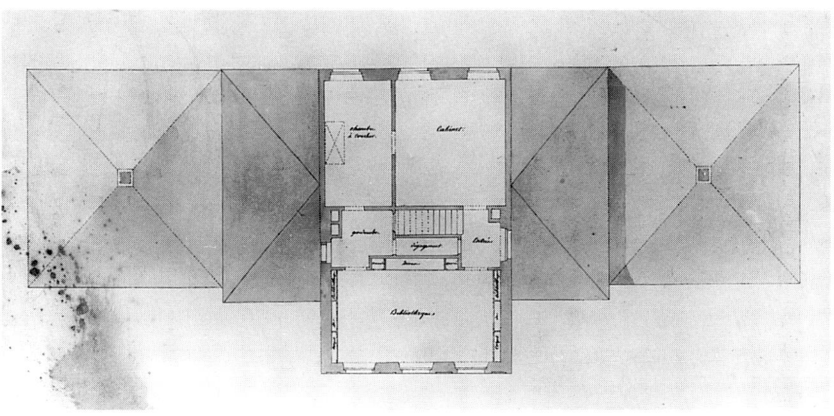

113 Sophienholm, plan of attic storey, inscribed in Ramée's hand, "Maison de Mr Brun à Sophienholm / Plan de l'attique." Ink drawing, 44 × 27 cm. (Kunstakademiets Bibliotek, Copenhagen)

114 Sophienholm, elevation drawing of south façade. Ink and wash drawing, 52 × 35 cm. (Kunstakademiets Bibliotek, Copenhagen)

as well as Constantin Brun's description of the property, reveal that the old house was small and had only one full storey, above which was a steep roof containing upper floors; the remodeling of this structure produced the central block of the present house, to which the side wings were added.[32] This process might have contributed to the independent appearance of the wings. But Ramée could have unified all the parts of the building if he had wanted to do so, by various means such as continuous cornices and rooflines. He chose to emphasize the cubic individuality of the parts, for example by giving the side wings pyramidal roofs, rather than roofs extending out from the central block. Ramée perhaps used the remodeling process as an excuse for the unusual effect he wished to achieve, but this effect was not dictated by the remodeling. Ramée probably recognized Frederikke Brun as someone sympathetic to his radical architectural ideas and saw an opportunity to execute a design that conventional clients would have found unacceptable, in its stark and seemingly disjointed form.

Especially unusual is the appearance of the attic storey of the central block of the house, the only part provided even with vestiges of the classical orders (the small pilasters framing the windows on the garden side) and separated from the lower storeys by a conspicuous cornice. To the extent that these devices make the attic seem separate from the lower floors, they are part of the esthetic of isolated volumes, suggesting visually that the attic is an independent object set on the block below. But there was also probably some symbolism involved here, a desire to set the attic apart in order to emphasize its special function, for this was Frederikke's personal domain: it contained her own "*bibliothèque,*" "*cabinet,*" and small "*chambre à coucher,*" as seen in Ramée's floor plan (Fig. 113). Tradition has it that when Frederikke visited Geneva in 1802 (during the construction of Sophienholm) and met Madame de Staël at

115 Sophienholm, seen from the south. (Author)

116 Sophienholm, seen from the north. (Author)

Coppet, she was inspired by Staël's top-storey library; upon her return to Denmark she had Ramée add such an attic to her own house.[33]

When August Hennings visited Sophienholm in August 1802, he noted in his diary that Constantin Brun was transforming the original, small house into an "Italian villa."[34] What made the house look Italian to Hennings (and to later Danish writers who have described it the same way)? It may have been partly the three-part composition, with wings flanking the central block, reminiscent of the Palladian tradition. But mostly, no doubt, it was the roofs, which are lower than traditional Danish roofs and have no gables.[35] As a result, the roofs of Sophienholm are minimally apparent to the viewer, especially from the lower vantage point of the garden side of the house – an unusual effect for a house in northern Europe.

Frederikke, who had lived in Rome in the mid-1790s, may have requested this "Italian" look for Sophienholm. It is unlikely that Ramée himself was very interested in emulating Italian villas, as his concept of classicism was highly abstract and universal. For him, the client's request for an "Italian" house would simply have provided another excuse to emphasize the geometric purity of the building, by eliminating as much as possible the roofs over its cubic parts. One of the surviving elevation drawings of Sophienholm shows the roofs of the central block drawn at a couple of different angles, as if Ramée was experimenting to see how low he could make them and still satisfy the functions of a northern roof (Fig. 114).[36]

Thus, in several ways – cubic purity, rejection of ornament, independence of the parts, and minimally apparent roofs – Ramée used Sophienholm as an experiment in pushing his architectural principles to the limit. Frederikke Brun was no doubt one of the few people who had the sympathy, resources, and adventurousness to support him in this effort.

Ramée's design for the rest of the estate at Sophienholm – its grounds and subsidiary buildings – is remarkable too. But it is less clear who collaborated most with Ramée on these parts: Frederikke, her husband, or her lover

Bonstetten. Most intriguing is the possible role of Bonstetten in the design. The Swiss author was living in the Brun household and spending summers at Sophienholm during the period leading up to and including Ramée's design of the country estate.[37] At the same time, Bonstetten was writing an essay entitled "On the art of landscape, especially in regard to northern countries [*Über die Gartenkunst, besonders in Rücksicht auf nördliche Länder*]."[38]

Published in 1800, Bonstetten's essay treats landscape design from the layman's point of view, revealing little interest in the stylistic fine points or controversies in garden planning of the period. One of Bonstetten's arguments is that visual appearance is given too much attention in most garden design. According to him, garden design should involve all the senses and deal mainly with practical matters, as well as "the moral purpose" of the art, which Bonstetten states is "to beautify our inner nature and country life."[39] The practical aspects of landscape design, according to Bonstetten, are especially important in northern countries, where the cold, wind, and dampness make life miserable during much of the year and are worsened by poor planning of buildings and grounds. Bonstetten apparently had been unprepared for the Danish climate when he went there in 1798 to live with the Bruns; he spent much of his time in Denmark suffering from the cold.[40] Regarding country estates, Bonstetten lambastes "our northern gardens, with their sun-destroying shadows," and complains that "we have ruins and hermitages, but we are usually freezing."[41] He recommends that everything be done to minimize wind and maximize sun, for example by leaving southern exposures free of trees, and he cites the Bruns' Sophienholm as a model in this regard: "At Sophienholm, a steep lawn faces south . . . [it] forms a circle and concentrates the rays of the sun. On the twentieth of November, 1799, I heard crickets or locusts chirping on this lawn, in warm sunshine, as if it were a summer day."[42]

117 Sophienholm, oval-shaped inlet from the lake, with bridge. (Author)

Bonstetten repeated this praise later in his essay, adding that flowers still bloomed at Sophienholm in late November and that "the frequent fog from the lake never rises up to the house, which is protected from the wind by the hilltop and the beech grove.[43]

Bonstetten here was describing Sophienholm before Ramée rebuilt the house and redesigned the grounds. But it is likely that Bonstetten's views, shared by Frederikke Brun, influenced Ramée's landscape plan (Fig. 110). In this plan, the south-facing lawn between the house and the lake was kept open and given a sweeping fan-shape, creating an axis around which the paths circulate; protective groves are formed around it to the north, east, and west, and in which Ramée's artificial inlet from the lake serves as a focal point (Fig. 117). Even the rebuilt house, whose wings produce an unusually long and narrow plan, may have been given its shape to present the maximum surface to the south and the sun.

Bonstetten disapproved of splendid, princely gardens, which he considered impractical and unnecessary.[44] His ideal was the modest estate, whose grounds and facilities have a natural relationship to the life of its owners. As a model, Bonstetten mentioned Wolmar's garden in Jean-Jacques Rousseau's essay on gardens in *La Nouvelle Héloïse* (from which Ramée was later to draw a passage for the title page of his *Jardins irréguliers*). Bonstetten quotes Rousseau's remark that "everywhere the useful has been substituted for the pleasing, and yet the pleasing has nearly always gained."[45]

Bonstetten spoke of the uplifting effects of a family's experience of simple agricultural activities – "the flower garden, the beehive, the fruit orchard" – and the educational benefits of garden work for upper-class children.[46] He described approvingly the estate of Marienburg on the Danish island of Moen, in which the dwelling house was immediately adjacent to the agricultural buildings, and he concluded his essay with the lofty dictum that "the true art of landscape must beautify every scene of human life. . . and attract Man to his true vocation, to industry and active life, and to lasting happiness."[47]

This moral aspect of Bonstetten's views may remind us of Caspar Voght's humane principles of the "ornamented farm." But in contrast to Voght's genuine involvement in rural reform, one senses a certain superficiality in Bonstetten's ideas about the ennobling effects of agriculture on the upper classes – a bit like Marie Antoinette's play-acting at her Versailles hamlet. Moreover, the replanned Sophienholm did not quite match Bonstetten's stated ideal. When the ever-practical August Hennings visited the estate in 1802, he was, in fact, struck most by its visual beauty and its divorce from real agricultural activity:

118 Sophienholm, *allée* of trees leading from the west to the front of the house. (Author)

> Lake, islands, woods, inlets, sinuous curves on all sides. . . create a composition that affords a new picture every hundred steps. . . . Everything is for pleasure, nothing for use or business. . . . Brun has only divans, paintings, mirrors, horse stables, a Swiss house [i.e., a peasant hut], gardener's house, Nordic house as a hermitage, Gothic gatehouse, Chinese pavilion, and not a cow to give him fresh milk or a field to provide him grain for bread.[48]

Despite the absence of a working farm at Sophienholm, Bonstetten's ideal of integrated rural life does seem to have influenced the replanning of the grounds, especially in the prominence given to the stables and other outbuildings, and their proximity to the main house. In particular, the stables and the large gardener's house are close to the main house and in full view from it.

Most of the outbuildings at Sophienholm still stand: the stable; the gardener's house and small greenhouses near it; the porter's lodge at the entrance to the estate; the original brick privy between the main house and the stable; and the rustic summer pavilion called the Norse House (now reconstructed). Even the landscape features created by Ramée survive well: the areas of wooded land and open space; the oval inlet at the shore of the lake, spanned by a rustic bridge; and the *allée* of linden trees to the west of the house (Fig. 118).

It is known that Ramée designed most of the outbuildings at Sophienholm. His drawings of the gardener's house, greenhouses, and privy survive. Constantin Brun stated that Ramée designed the stable.[49] Hennings said that he designed the "temple," which no longer survives.[50] And the style of the

119 Sophienholm, east side of the stable. (Author)

120 Sophienholm, interior of the stable. (Author)

121 Sophienholm, gate lodge. (Author)

Gothic gate lodge clearly points to Ramée. The diversity of these designs (not to mention the Norse House and "Swiss" and "Chinese" pavilions mentioned by Hennings, which Ramée may have designed) suggests that he purposely gave these structures an eclectic range of forms to contrast with the cool purity of the main house.

The stable has exposed half-timbered construction, but also half-round windows and a curved roofline over the entry, creating that combination of rusticity and elegance typical of Ramée (Fig. 119). The big surprise is inside the stable: the central corridor through the building is divided into a series of "Gothic" bays, with pointed wooden arches spanning the hallway and along the walls – a kind of abstracted version of medieval vaulting (Fig. 120). The

122 Pump house at the Folie Saint-James, Paris. (Krafft, *Recueil*, pl. 114)

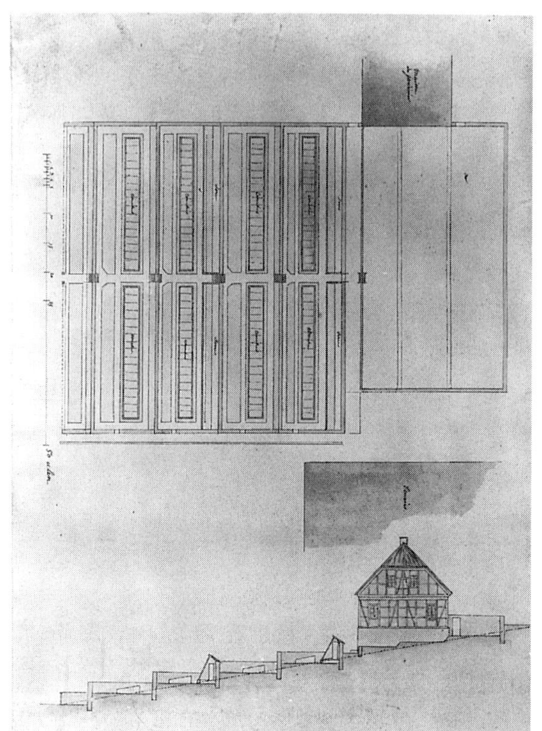

123 Sophienholm, plan and elevation drawing of gardener's house and planting beds, with notes in Ramée's hand. Ink and watercolor drawing, 24 × 37 cm. (Kunstakademiets Bibliotek, Copenhagen)

124 Sophienholm, gardener's house. (Author)

engaged columns, on which the pointed arches rest, are simplified Tuscan in order – the same kind of columns Ramée was to use, again in combination with Gothic arches, in a church in New York State. That Ramée would combine so many seemingly incompatible styles in one structure (Gothic, Tuscan, half-timbered vernacular, geometric neoclassical) reveals both an unabashed eclecticism and a touch of whimsy.

The same qualities are found in the gate lodge at Sophienholm (Fig. 121). Erected by 1802 (Hennings mentioned it in his diary of that year, as the "*gothisches Pförtnerhaus*"), the building is square in plan, has a hipped roof topped by a square chimney, a large Gothic-arched vault over the entry (with a circular window over the door), and a frieze of little pointed arches that runs

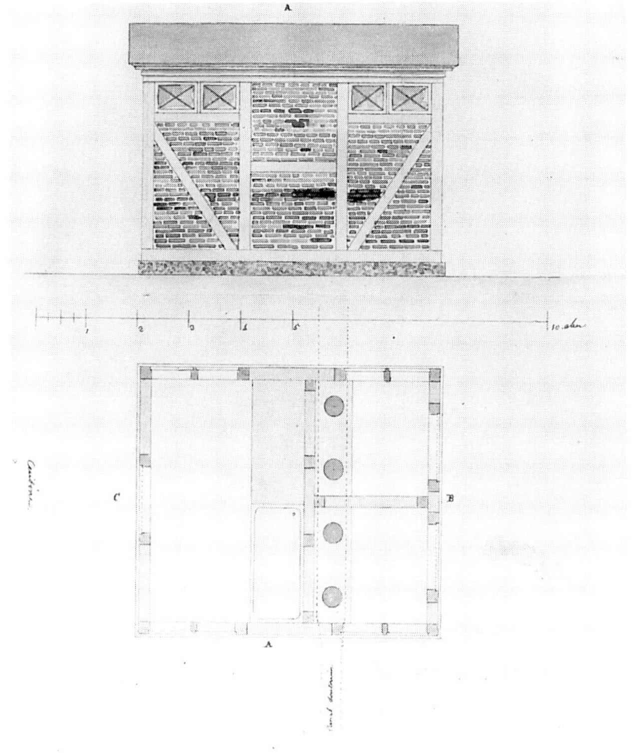

125 Sophienholm, plan and elevation drawing of privy, with notes in Ramée's hand. Ink and watercolor drawing, 19 × 24 cm. (Kunstakademiets Bibliotek, Copenhagen)

126 Sophienholm, privy, to the west of the main house. (Author)

continuously around the building at the top of the wall. Ramée may have had a specific building in mind when he created this gate lodge: the pump house at the Folie Saint-James in Paris, where Ramée had worked as François Joseph Belanger's apprentice (Fig. 122).[51] Ramée simplified Belanger's design, stripping it of most ornament, except for the pointed-arch frieze; he substituted a chimney for the pump-house's tower and expanded the Gothic doorway of Belanger's structure into the major feature of the design. The result is a building even more playful than Belanger's in its unconventional scale (the oversized entrance gives it a kind of dollhouse quality) and in the contrast between its stark, cubic forms and its fanciful Gothic frieze.

Ramée's design for the gardener's house and privy at Sophienholm can be seen on three sheets of drawings presently in the Art Academy in Copen-

127 Sophienholm, Norske Hus. (Kunstakademiets Bibliotek, Copenhagen)

hagen; they are unsigned but bear notes in French in Ramée's hand.[52] The large gardener's house is shown on a sheet devoted to the layout of planting beds and greenhouses, but one part of the sheet shows the east end of the gardener's house, with half-timbered walls and a thatched roof (Fig. 123 and color plate 12). The building now has a coating of stucco that covers the timber structure (Fig. 124). Constantin Brun's description of Sophienholm noted that this building contained, besides the gardener's quarters, a room for keeping plants in the winter, an area for furniture repair, and an ice cellar for food storage.

The privy, situated between the house and stables, is shown in meticulous detail on two sheets of drawings by Ramée, with a floor plan and three elevations (Fig. 125 and color plate 11). The plan shows two privy cubicles on one side of the structure and a washroom on the other. The elevation drawings, rendered in watercolor, show the half-timbered structure and brick infill, with small windows under the eaves. Surprisingly, as this kind of building is normally impermanent, the privy survives in perfect condition, exactly as shown in Ramée's drawing; the only change is that the infill between the half-timbering is now stucco rather than exposed brick (Fig. 126).[53]

As for the *Norske Hus* (Norse House), Ramée evidently did not design it, but he probably supported its inclusion at Sophienholm. Located on the hill at the end of the *allée* of linden trees, this garden pavilion was described by Constantin Brun as a "house brought by sea from Norway, built entirely of Norwegian beams."[54] Although now rebuilt, the original structure is known from photographs. These photos show that its exterior surface was made of vertical boards, overlaid in a board-and-batten manner (Fig. 127).[55] It was probably this construction method, unusual in Denmark, that made the building "Norwegian" in style. It is not surprising that Bonstetten and Frederikke Brun, with their literary interest in northern European traditions, and Ramée with his emerging interest in architectural forms of the north, sought out such a building type to include at Sophienholm.

The *Norske Hus* became one of Frederikke's favorite places at Sophienholm. A description of it, in a letter she wrote to her friend Friedrich von Matthisson, suggests the importance she attached to living close to nature – a concern that must have influenced Ramée's replanning of the whole estate:

> I wish you were here with me in the Norse House, actually made of fir beams and sailed here from Norway, complete to the roof. It stands on a steep terrace at the lake and is surrounded by such a dense and dusky circle of silver firs, Weymouth pines, and balsam birches, that kites and screech owls nest here. From below wafts the fragrance of blooming acacia, whose similarity to the scent of oranges transports me instantly from the North to Hesperia. The lake glistens below, bordered by beech-wooded shores that meander in and out alluringly. The contours of these gently rising banks are sketched lightly by the breeze and shaded in by the mirror of the water. Here, in my beloved solitude, I am working now on a revision of the third volume of my poems.[56]

References to Sophienholm occur also in Frederikke's poetry. The following romantic lines were published in 1801, just as Ramée was replanning the estate:

> Freystatt heiterer Ruh' und stiller Freuden der Seele,
> Lächelndes Sophienholm! sey mir voll Liebe gegrüsst!
> Leicht erduldet hier Psyche des Daseyns fesselnde Schranken,
> Und in den Becher voll Schmerz träufelt die Zähre des Danks.[57]

> (Refuge of serene rest and calm peace of the soul,
> Smiling Sophienholm, I greet thee with love.
> Here Psyche bears lightly the fetters of life,
> And sheds tears of thanks in the sorrowful cup.)

Ramée's transformation of Sophienholm could be seen as an architectural equivalent of Frederikke Brun's romanticism in literature. In both, nature is worshipped and an ideal nature is created by the artist. In both cases, this nature has an untamed character (the alpine glaciers of Frederikke's poetry, the irregularity of Ramée's landscape designs). But this wildness is tempered by elements of classicism (the allusions to antiquity in Frederikke's poetry, the cubic forms of Ramée's house at Sophienholm). The result, with both artists, is a peculiar tension between classicism and romanticism, restraint and passion. The architectural contrast at Sophienholm between the main house and the other structures (Gothic, half-timbered, Norse), which at first may appear

128 Conradshøj, plan of the estate, 1809. (Kunstakademiets Bibliotek, Copenhagen)

capricious, was no doubt a conscious expression of this esthetic of contrast and ambiguity.

Perhaps only artists intimately familiar with both the classical and the northern-European traditions could be so interested in combining them in this way. Frederikke Brun, the Dane who had spent long periods in Italy, and Ramée, trained in French classicism but now living in the north, both fashioned their art as a dialogue between conflicting traditions and principles. They no doubt recognized each other as kindred spirits in this regard, and both saw Sophienholm as a perfect opportunity to explore the new esthetic.

Conradshøj, Hellerupgaard, Frederikslund, and Øregaard

Besides Sophienholm, four estates just north of Copenhagen can be ascribed, in varying degrees, to Ramée. Of these, only Øregaard approaches Sophienholm in the present state of preservation of its house and grounds. At Frederikslund, the house remains in relatively good condition. Nothing survives of the other two estates, Conradshøj and Hellerupgaard. Yet each of these properties is of interest in one respect or another.

Conradshøj (also called Ordrupshøj), in Ordrup just north of Copenhagen, was the country estate of Peter Erichsen, brother and business partner of the man who hired Ramée's firm to decorate the rooms of his mansion in Copenhagen. Peter Erichsen had acquired the land in 1798 and two years later named it for his newborn son Conrad.[58] When August Hennings visited Ordrup in July of 1802, he noted that "Erichsen has the wooded land, which has been laid out by Ramé in promenades," adding that there was a "temple" in the garden.[59] Nothing of the estate remains today, as it was long ago subdivided and made part of the northern suburbs of Copenhagen; but a map of 1809 shows the layout of the grounds (Fig. 128).[60]

A puzzling thing about this plan of Conradshøj is its difference from Ramée's other garden designs. Here we see more-or-less uniform coverage of the terrain with twisting paths and undifferentiated wooded areas – almost *anglo-chinois* in character – in contrast to the simpler, more clearly defined type of landscape that Ramée had developed by this time. The contrast between

129 Conradshøj, view of the house. Detail of painting by N. G. Rademacher, c. 1880. (Øregaard Museum)

130 Conradshøj, farm building on lower part of the estate, now demolished. (L. Gotfredsen, *Gentofte fra Tuborg til Bellevue*, vol. 2, Hellerup, 1952, p. 167)

the plan of Conradshøj and that of Sophienholm is striking in this regard. Assuming that the 1809 map of Conradshøj is accurate, one wonders if Ramée worked under some constraints here, perhaps in collaboration with another designer, or with conditions imposed by the owner. It is interesting that the Conradshøj plan is similar to garden designs published in 1798 by Johan Ludvig Mansa, the other important creator of irregular landscaping in Denmark at this time.[61]

Erichsen erected two groups of buildings at Conradshøj: the residence on the hill and farm structures on the lower land.[62] The residence consisted of two structures, facing each other across a courtyard. A later nineteenth-century painting of the estate shows a building that may be one of these: an elegant pavilion with large, arched windows and a hipped roof (Fig. 129).[63] It is tempting to think that Ramée may have designed this country house, but the details in the painting are not clear enough to make a judgment. One of the farm buildings, however, is known from photographs, taken before its demolition in 1908 (Fig. 130).[64] Apparently the caretaker's house and the administrative center for the farm, this building is not typical of such structures in Denmark around 1800. Most unusual is the material used for the walls: vertical wooden boards (as in the "Norse" house at Sophienholm), instead of the traditional Danish half-timbered or masonry construction. Also distinctive are the large windows and the prominent central block that projected from the roof and had a small, circular window in its gable – features typical of much of Ramée's work.

Unlike many architects, who avoided the design of agricultural and other common types of buildings, Ramée was always willing to plan such structures and was genuinely interested in the forms they could take, as his drawings and later publications show. It seems likely that the farm structure at Conradshøj is one of Ramée's experiments of this sort, inspired perhaps by the unusual *Norske Hus* that had just been assembled at Sophienholm.

The three country houses of Hellerupgaard, Frederikslund and Øregaard can be considered as a group, as they are variations on a theme (Fig. 131). The first two are attributed to Ramée in documents of the period (Hennings's diary in the case of Hellerupgaard, the correspondence of Countess Sophie Reventlow in that of Frederikslund); and Øregaard has traditionally been ascribed to Ramée because of its similarity to his other works.[65] Hellerupgaard, erected in 1802 by Erich Erichsen (whose mansion in Copenhagen had just been decorated by Masson et Ramée), is known only from photographs and drawings, as it was demolished in 1954 to make way for a school in the borough of Hellerup (Figs. 132, 133).[66] Frederikslund, constructed about 1804 by the trader Frederic de Coninck for his son, was later enlarged by additions, but has now been returned largely to its original form; it is used as a training center for teachers in the borough of Holte (Figs. 134–39).[67] Øregaard, built about 1806–8 by another merchant shipper, Johannes Søbøtker, is superbly preserved and restored, serving now as the municipal museum of the borough of Gentofte, with its grounds a public park (Figs. 140–44).[68]

These three buildings are different from earlier Danish country houses in several ways. One is their roof design. Whereas the traditional Danish house had a high roof, often dominating its appearance, the roofs of these houses – as at Sophienholm – are so low that they are perceptually almost insignificant.[69] As a result, the cubic quality of the houses is intensified.

The plans of these three houses are also unusual. Traditional Danish country houses had relatively long plans, creating two broad façades (normally the entrance and garden façades) and two narrow ends. In contrast, the plans of Ramée's Danish houses, except for Sophienholm, are nearly square. The roughly cubic mass that results is composed, typically, of a central block oriented along the axis of entry (making the principal axis of Ramée's houses ninety degrees off that of traditional Danish country houses), with subsidiary blocks to the sides.

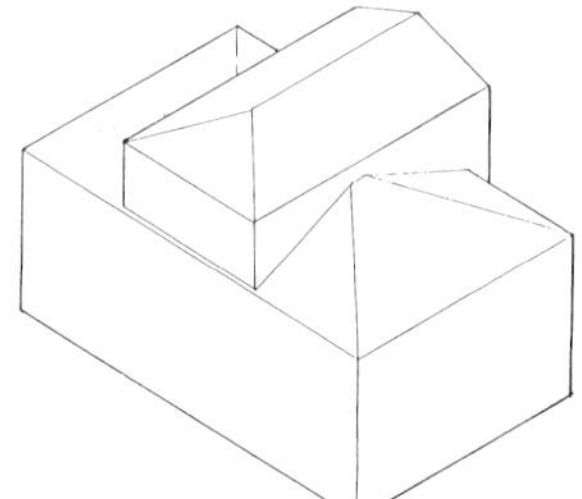

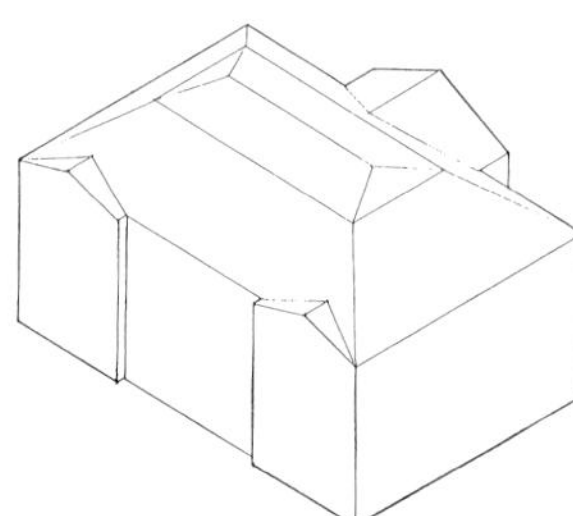

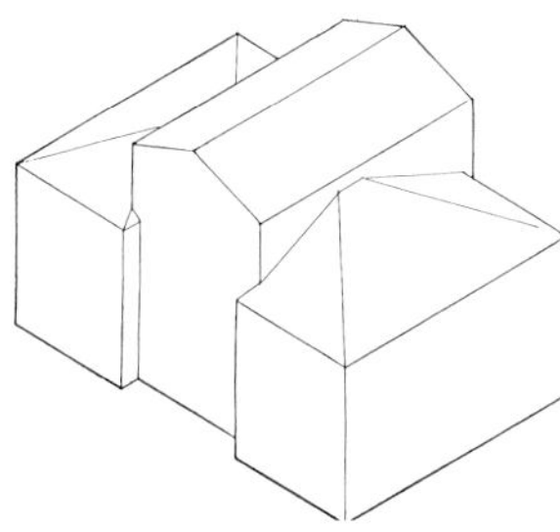

131 Schematic drawings of Hellerupgaard (top), Frederikslund (middle) and Øregaard (bottom). (Author)

132 Hellerupgaard, entrance façade of the house, now demolished. (Kunstakademiets Bibliotek, Copenhagen)

133 Hellerupgaard, garden side of the house. Drawing by I. F. Bredel, 1820s. Note: The proportions of the house in this view are vertically exaggerated. (Øregaard Museum)

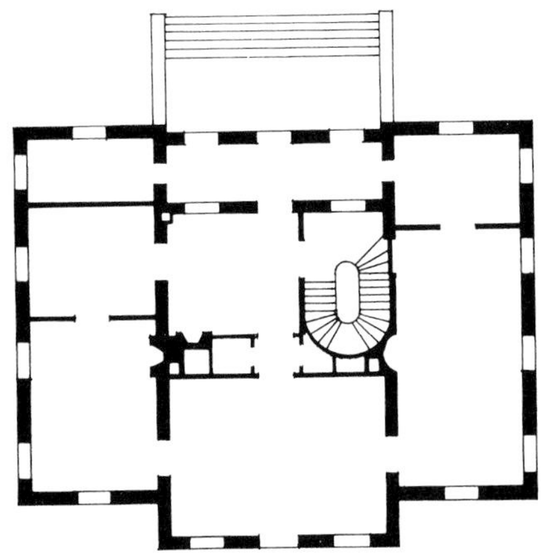

134 Frederikslund, plan of the main floor, as remodeled in the twentieth century. (Author)

135 Frederikslund, garden side of the house. (Author)

136 Frederikslund, entry side of the house. (Author)

137 Frederikslund, view of corner of the house, showing sunken area around base of the building and frieze of paterae under the roof cornice. (Author)

138 Frederikslund, detail of a drawing of the estate by Søren Lange, 1820. (Byhistorisk Arkiv for Søllerød Kommune)

139 Frederikslund, stable, now demolished. Photograph c. 1920. (Kunstakademiets Bibliotek, Copenhagen)

This basic pattern, however, is treated differently in each of the houses, and in each case is treated differently on the entry and garden sides of the house. The result is a kind of exercise of possible permutations (Fig. 131). At Hellerupgaard, the central block was pulled forward on the garden side and given a gable or pediment, while on the entry side the central block appeared only as a third-storey volume, above the main roof line and without a gable. (The semicircular garden room seen in photographs of Hellerupgaard was a later addition.)[70] At Frederikslund, the projecting central block on the garden façade is only two storeys high (rather than extending above the side wings as at Hellerupgaard), and on the garden façade the wings are given gables and made more prominent than the slightly-recessed central block. Finally, at Øregaard, Ramée made the central block dominant and gabled on both façades, but he recessed it on the entry façade while projecting it on the garden façade, thereby giving the building the form of three rectangular blocks of equal length, the central one shifted just slightly out of line from the other two.

This manipulation of elemental masses is somewhat like that found in the visionary designs of Ledoux (published in 1804, just as Ramée was building these Danish houses), or in the didactic exercises of J. N. L. Durand (whose *Précis des leçons d'architecture* appeared at the same time). But Ramée's experiments were conducted in executed buildings, not as theoretical operations.

Ramée also gave these country houses a new type of surface and ornament. Comparable buildings of the period in Denmark (including C. F. Hansen's houses in Danish Holstein) nearly always had at least some vestiges of the classical elements, such as pilasters, columned porticos, classical window frames and the like. But at Hellerupgaard, Frederikslund and Øregaard, all such elements are avoided, even more ruthlessly than at Sophienholm, where pilasters were admitted in the attic storey and around the main door. In the later three houses, only the most fundamental elements survive from the classical vocabulary, such as cornices and string courses that define certain areas of the walls.

In the few instances where Ramée introduced ornament that appears to be classical, he handled it in unconventional ways that actually underscore his iconoclasm. An example is the unusual frieze of circular "paterae" beneath the roof cornice at Frederikslund (Fig. 137).[71] Also, at Øregaard, the two ground-floor windows of the side blocks, on the entry and garden façades, are topped by decorative elements that bear some resemblance to classical window-pediments, but in fact are pure inventions. On the entry façade (Fig. 143), these "pediments" are so flat that their slope is hardly perceptible, as if Ramée was taking his low, un-Danish roofs and gables to a ridiculous extreme, to emphasize their foreignness. Moreover, these "pediments" are raised so high above the windows (to which they are connected only by a slight recess in the wall surface) that it is ambiguous whether they really are

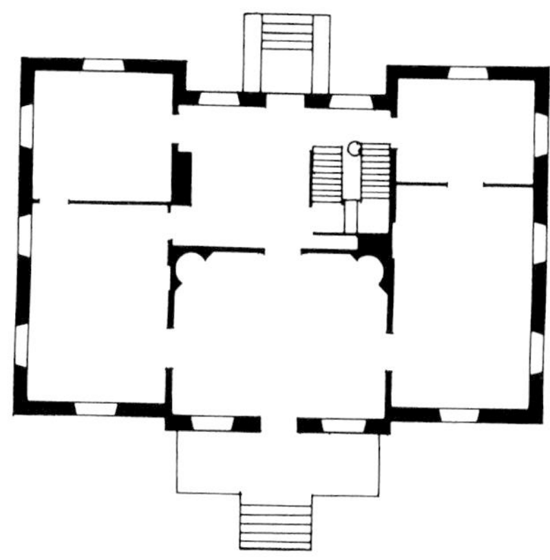

140 Øregaard, plan of the main floor. (Author)

141 Øregaard, lithographic view of the house and garden, c. 1850, from drawing by F. Richardt. (Øregaard Museum)

142 Øregaard, entry side of the house. (Author)

143 Øregaard, window on entry façade of the house. (Author)

144 Øregaard, window on garden façade of the house. (Author)

part of the windows or are simply free-floating elements on the walls. On the garden façade of the house (Fig. 144), only the upper edges of the "pediment" remain; the recessed plane between it and the window holds bas-relief sculpture within a lunette, creating a kind of exploded version of a classical pediment containing sculpture.

Another common feature of these three houses is the sunken area around them, almost a kind of moat, created in order to allow large windows for their lower or basement level (what Ramée called "*les souterrains*" on his floor plans). This feature was so unusual in Denmark that Hennings made a special point of criticizing it as a hazard to people who might fall into it, when he mentioned a visit to Hellerupgaard in his diary.[72] Besides providing illumination for the basement rooms, this device may have appealed to Ramée as a way to keep the houses lower than they would otherwise have been, as well as separating them from their immediate surroundings and heightening their geometric purity.

Geometry is also emphasized by the material used for the surfaces of these houses: roughcast or stucco, applied to the masonry walls. Especially when painted a light color (it is now grey at Frederikslund, nearly white at Øregaard and Sophienholm), this smooth, uniform surface increases the sense of volumetric geometry – in contrast to mass or weight – just as the International Style architects of the 1920s were to do using similiar surfaces.[73]

Little documentation survives about Ramée's plans for the grounds around these three houses.[74] But in the case of Øregaard, the surrounding park, as it appears in a lithograph of about 1850 and as it still exists today, is so close in spirit to Ramée's other landscape plans that it must represent his intentions (Fig. 141). In particular, the long, meandering, man-made lake (with its own island), which dominates the park at Øregaard, was one of Ramée's favorite garden features and is found in many of his plans (for example, that of Hamfelde, probably laid out about the same time).

An 1820 drawing of Frederikslund shows the house sitting in a wooded park and flanked by two identical outbuildings (Fig. 138).[75] These outbuildings do not survive, but one of them, a stable, is documented by photographs and measured drawings (Fig. 139).[76] The form of this stable, especially its curved roof, point to Ramée as its architect. The drawings show that the roof was made of curving beams, apparently the "*Bohlendächer*" or "De l'Orme" system of roof structure that Ramée had used in Paris and Belgium. Like the stable and other outbuildings at Sophienholm, it exemplifies Ramée's uncommon interest in common architecture.

Ramée's overall effect on Danish design is difficult to assess, especially as only some of his works there are known and documented. Although the architect spent only brief periods in Denmark, over less than a decade, he executed important work that introduced to the country new types of architecture, interior decoration, and landscape design. Some Danish writers have even suggested that Ramée influenced C. F. Hansen, the country's greatest architect of the period – for instance, in his setting of starkly cubic houses in irregular gardens.[77] More generally, it is likely that Ramée helped acquaint Hansen and other Danish artists with the latest French ideas in design.[78]

Because Ramée appeared in Denmark during a period of increasing nationalism, which tended to reject foreign cultural influences, his work did not have the effect that it might have had at some other time. It was mainly the sophisticated and individualistic clients such as Erich Erichsen and Frederikke Brun, with an international outlook and taste for the avant-garde, who were attracted to the work of the French "building revolutionary."

Mecklenburg-Schwerin and Napoleonic Paris

Chapter 9

Boulliot's article on Ramée states that in 1802 the architect "was called to Schwerin by the hereditary prince of Mecklenburg, to fit up [*arranger*] his palace," and that "five years later, he constructed the tomb of this prince's wife, sister of the emperor Nicholas."[1]

The duchy of Mecklenburg-Schwerin lay to the east of Hamburg and Holstein, on the shores of the Baltic Sea. Ramée's clients there were the duke, Friedrich Franz I, and his son, Prince Friedrich Ludwig. A letter preserved in Schwerin reveals that the duke first requested the architect's services in 1801.[2] The nature of these first services is unclear and little evidence is known of Ramée's work on the ducal palace mentioned by Boulliot; but the tomb of the princess still exists, and the story of its creation can be reconstructed in remarkable detail.

The young prince's wife, Helena Paulowna, was a daughter of Czar Paul I of Russia. She died in 1803 when she was only nineteen years old. Her grieving husband erected a splendid mausoleum in the park of the ducal palace at Ludwigslust, south of Schwerin – a mausoleum so grand that it ultimately came to serve as the tomb for much of the Mecklenburg dynasty (Figs. 145–8).[3] This structure has generally been attributed to the Danish architect Christian Joseph Lillie, who worked in Lübeck and elsewhere in northern Germany around 1800.[4] But extensive correspondence, preserved in the Mecklenburg National Archive, reveals that although Lillie drew preliminary plans for the mausoleum, it was Ramée who produced the final design and oversaw its execution. The correspondence is significant also in providing the most complete documentation, for any of Ramée's buildings, of the day-to-day problems of design and construction and of the architect–client relationship.

In March of 1806, the *Zeitung für die elegante Welt,* an illustrated journal published in Leipzig, printed a brief article on the mausoleum at Ludwigslust, accompanied by an engraved perspective view of the building (inscribed with Ramée's name) and floor plans (Fig. 145).[5] After singing the praises of the lamented Helena Paulowna, the anonymous author of the article described the tomb and its setting in the park of Ludwigslust and included an advertisement for its architect:

> The construction [of the mausoleum] was entrusted to the renowned Hamburg architect Ramée, whose excellent talents in architecture and landscape design have, unfortunately, not been sufficiently used in these times that are unfavorable to those arts. He is the architect of the splendid and tasteful Börsenhalle in Hamburg, which would certainly have remained unbuilt without this artist. The mausoleum was executed according to his drawings

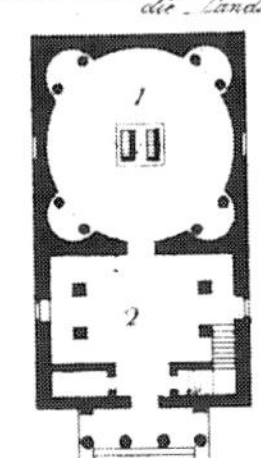

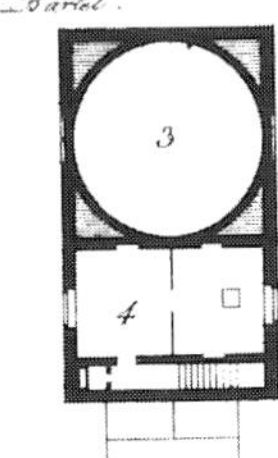

145 Mausoleum of Helena Paulowna, at Ludwigslust. Engraved view and plans, inscribed "Ramée inv.," published in *Zeitung für die elegante Welt*, 1806. The numbers on the floor plans refer to: (1) domed vault with sarcophagi. (2) entry hall. (3) upper part of vault. (4) chapel.

and under his direction. The site of the monument, chosen by the Prince at Ludwigslust, is thoroughly fitting: spacious, secluded, and removed from all noise, with beautiful oaks and beeches, as well as newly planted evergreens, willows, poplars, and flowering plants. . . . The mausoleum is of stone, seventy-four feet long and forty-four feet wide. A broad stairway of nine steps leads to the entrance, within a peristyle with four Doric columns, supporting a pediment that bears the inscription "Helenen Paulownen." The door is made of mahogany, with bronze fittings. From the peristyle, one enters the vestibule, from which a stairway leads up to the Orthodox Greek chapel, which is above the vestibule. The vestibule leads also to the vault itself, in the middle of which stand

146 Mausoleum of Helena Paulowna. (Author)

147 Mausoleum of Helena Paulowna, entry hall. At left, memorial to Helena Paulowna, P. Rouw, sculptor. (Landesamt für Denkmalpflege Mecklenburg-Vorpommern)

148 Mausoleum of Helena Paulowna, interior, drawing by R. Suhrlandt, 1842. (Staatliches Museum Schwerin, Kupferstichkabinett)

two sarcophagi. . . . Four bronze candelabra stand on the corners of the platform that supports the sarcophagi. A costly carpet of crimson velvet, embroidered with gold, covers everything. This burial vault is thirty-eight feet in diameter and its height is also thirty eight feet. It is lighted from above. The interior of the vault is covered with stucco work and is blue, with gilded bronze stars. . . . His Majesty the Czar of Russia has already given orders to the Russian mission in Berlin that two Orthodox priests visit Ludwigslust twice each year, to conduct religious ceremonies in commemoration of the dead.[6]

This article is accurate except for a couple of details. The mausoleum was not quite complete in 1806, as the article suggests, and it was not made entirely of stone; only the portico, pediments, cornices, and other trim were stone, the walls being brick covered with stucco or roughcast. In the late nineteenth century the main interior space of the mausoleum was transformed, but otherwise the building survives today as originally executed.[7]

Documents in the Mecklenburg National Archive reveal that in early 1804 the architect Lillie produced five separate designs for a burial monument at Ludwigslust.[8] But then Prince Friedrich Ludwig apparently replaced Lillie with Ramée. In May of 1804 Lillie wrote to the prince, submitting a bill for his plans and stating that he understood that "this commission is to be given to another architect."[9] For the next four years, extensive records document Ramée's design and execution of the mausoleum. The final design of the structure was clearly Ramée's. But it appears that his planning began as a modification of one of Lillie's projects, so the work might be considered a kind of collaboration between the two architects. This is also suggested by the actual form of the mausoleum.

The building has roughly the shape of a classical temple. This feature, as well as the presence of some elements that are Greek rather than Roman (such as the baseless Doric columns of the portico), associate this mausoleum with the new interest in Greek architecture that was captivating many architects of the period. But Ramée was not among them: seldom are Greek elements, or even porticos, found in his work. The attraction of the classical temple was particularly strong at this time among German architects, such as the Prussian Friedrich Gilly, who before his death in 1800 produced numerous designs for temple-shaped buildings, including mausolea.[10]

149 Ledoux, design for house, Rue Neuve de Berry, Paris, c. 1780s. (Daniel Ramée, ed., *Architecture de C. N. Ledoux*, Paris, 1847, pl. 213. Courtesy of Princeton Architectural Press)

The Ludwigslust mausoleum is unusual, however, in the reduced scale of its columned portico, creating a doubled image, or echo, of the pedimented façade. Gilly had a penchant for cubic buildings with relatively small porticos, but these buildings did not normally have gabled roofs.[11] Closer in shape to the Ludwigslust building is a design by Claude Nicolas Ledoux, of the 1780s, for a house in Paris that was never built but is seen in one of the plates of Ledoux's work that Ramée's son Daniel was to publish in 1847 (Fig. 149).[12]

Thus, although the mausoleum is not typical of Ramée's work and was probably based on one of Lillie's projects, it is a type of design with which Ramée was familiar. His correspondence about the building, as we shall see, reveals that his final design was a simplification of an earlier one that had multiple porticos. For Ramée, the building would have been of interest not because it was "Greek" or temple-shaped, but because it allowed the inventive manipulation of simple geometric forms: a cubic mass, triangular pediments, cylindrical columns, half-round windows. This geometry is seen also in Ramée's floor plan of the mausoleum, with the rectangular entrance hall leading into the domed vault: a circle inscribed in a square, with semicircular niches in the corners (see fig. 145). This is a type of plan found in the work of Ledoux, J. N. Durand, and other French architects of the period; it is also reminiscent of the plan of Ramée's altar at the *Fête de la Fédération* of 1793 (see Fig. 36).[13]

The only known representation of the original interior of the mausoleum is a drawing made in the 1840s (Fig. 148).[14] It shows the domed space with niches and other elements corresponding to Ramée's engraved plan and to the descriptions in his letters and in the 1806 article on the building. But this drawing also contains some details not known from other sources. Most interesting are the columns with Egyptian palm capitals, exactly like those Ramée had used in the Börsenhalle in Hamburg.

Another aspect of the mausoleum typical of Ramée is the naturalistic landscape that surrounds it, as seen in the engraved view of the building. There is no proof that Ramée designed this landscape, but it is likely that he did given the numerous references to landscaping in the remarkable correspondence about the mausoleum, preserved in the Mecklenburg National Archive.[15]

This correspondence includes nineteen letters written by Ramée to Ludwig Hermann von Mecklenburg, *Hofmarschall* (Court Marshall) of the prince who commissioned the mausoleum (Fig. 150).[16] The *Hofmarschall* was the prince's treasurer and manager, who served as an intermediary between the prince and the architect. There are also letters to the *Hofmarschall* from Ramée's partner, André Masson, dealing mainly with financial matters, and bills submitted by the firm of Masson et Ramée (Fig. 151). These communications reveal that Ramée's work on the mausoleum was conducted through the agency of his partnership with Masson. Also included are drafts of letters from the *Hofmarschall* to Ramée, as well as miscellaneous memoranda and notes. Typical of the linguistic dominance of French during this period, all the correspondence is in this language, except for some internal Mecklenburg court memos in German.

The correspondence contains references to designs by Ramée for a "*nouveau château*" for the prince, and for the remodeling and decoration of other ducal residences.[17] But most of the letters concern Ramée's work on the mausoleum at Ludwigslust. They reveal that Ramée made numerous trips from Hamburg to Mecklenburg-Schwerin to supervise construction of the tomb, and that even while in Hamburg he supervised operations closely through correspondence.

The earliest letter regarding the mausoleum was written by Ramée (from Ludwigslust) to the *Hofmarschall* (at the court in Schwerin) in September of 1804. It reveals that Ramée had already done some work on the mausoleum design, in an attempt – familiar to all architects – to reduce the estimated cost of an earlier plan and yet retain the grandeur desired by the client. Ramée wrote:

> The second plan for the monument, which I presented to the Prince, was rejected, and it is true that it would have been too modest [*mesquin*] for the beautiful location projected for it. I have been occupied with finding ways to diminish the cost of the first

Hambourg le 26 Juin 1805.

Monsieur le maréchal,

Nous avons reçu la lettre que vous nous avez fait l'honneur de nous écrire le 23. du c. Je compte partir pour Ludwigslust vendredi 25. Je suis très étonné des prétentions de Mr Calame, s'il n'est que sculpteur nous n'avons pas besoin de lui, car il n'y a pas un pouce de sculpture dans aucune des parties du Tombeau. J'espère donc le remettre à la raison, autrement j'enverrai [illegible] à Lubeck à la recherche d'autre tailleur de Pierres, mais on m'a assuré qu'il en existait peu dans cette ville.

agréez Monsieur le maréchal l'assurance de mon entier dévouement.

Ramée.

150 Letter from Ramée to Ludwig Hermann von Mecklenburg, *Hofmarschall* of the Prince of Mecklenburg-Schwerin, 26 June 1805. (Mecklenburgisches Landeshauptarchiv Schwerin)

> plan. There now will be only one portico, on the entry side. The chapel [on the upper floor of the mausoleum] will have a completely different form, but will still have its own entry, although without a projecting peristyle. All the columns of the interior and the vault are removed. I hope that by these revisions, which will change nothing of the grand conception of the first project, the cost will not exceed 20,000 Ecus. The difference of six or seven thousand Ecus between the first and second project should not be an obstacle to the execution of the first one.[18]

We can speculate on the early stages of the design that Ramée refers to here. The first plan for the mausoleum, probably one of Lillie's projects, was somewhat similar to the building as finally executed, but more lavishly ornamented, having two porticos, and columns on the interior. This scheme was considered too expensive. Ramée, having replaced Lillie, first produced a design that was very simple – probably with no porticos or columns at all – the result, perhaps, not only of the need for economy but of Ramée's own preference for radically simplified classicism. The prince and his advisers found this design excessively plain, so Ramée produced a kind of compromise, with a portico but otherwise as simple as possible.

In the same letter, Ramée went on to mention that "the master builder who will supervise the work has returned to Hamburg and will come back next Sunday" (revealing that Ramée brought some of his own assistants from Hamburg for the job); that he hoped to "complete the foundations this year if possible"; that the prince had spoken to him of a limestone deposit that might provide the material for the building; and that he was sending the *Hofmarschall* a plan of the foundations. Ramée added that he was leaving Ludwigslust that day for Wettin (a town near Leipzig) but would return in a couple of weeks, and that a "celebrated painter" he had recommended to the prince would be arriving soon from Hamburg. Ramée emphasized the need to economize if the building was to adhere to the stipulated budget, and he stated that he hoped "to show that one can do great things with little money." This budgetary concern was to dominate the entire project.

Over the next several months, Ramée's letters from Hamburg to the *Hofmarschall* reported on his inspection trips to Ludwigslust, on the slow progress of construction, problems with some of the workmen (Ramée dismissed a stonecarver and sent for others from Lübeck), and further revisions he was making in the design. Some of the architect's letters noted that he was enclosing drawings ("plans, sections, and elevations") and in April of 1805 he shipped a "model of the monument."[19] Several of Ramée's remarks suggest that the prince or his *Hofmarschall* wanted the monument to be more highly decorated than the architect was making it (despite their desire to keep the cost down), which led Ramée to defend architectural simplicity. At one point he described the pediment of the structure as being in "a pure style," and in July of 1805 he wrote:

> As for the rear wall of the monument, any decoration at all would be injurious to the general effect. Moreover, this wall will not be so simple, since it will be crowned with a very beautiful cornice with modillions and surmounted by a pediment. [Any additional features] would be superfluous and would take away that beautiful simplicity [*ôterait cette belle simplicité*] that ought to characterize such a monument.[20]

Ramée was no doubt concerned about the additional cost of more ornament. But one senses also a genuinely esthetic issue here, with Ramée promoting his stripped-down brand of neoclassicism to clients for whom it must have appeared almost shockingly plain. Just as Ramée had defended his Börsenhalle design in Hamburg by saying it was "in the simple style," he was making a similar connection between beauty and simplicity for his Mecklenburg client.

Ramée's letter of July 1805 also touches on more personal matters and reveals that a kind of social relationship had developed between the architect and the *Hofmarschall*. It is here that Ramée mentions his impending marriage:

> I would have been greatly pleased to accept your invitation to visit you at Plüschow, but I was too busy to go there. You should know, *Monsieur le Maréchal,* that I am marrying soon, and the young

> fiancée does not permit my necessary absences to be too long. The marriage will take place early next month, and about the fifteenth I plan to make a trip to Ludwigslust. As you should be spending part of the summer at Plüschow, let me propose visiting you there. It is even possible that I can present *Madame la Baumeister* to you there.[21]

Also in this letter, Ramée said he hoped to get the mausoleum roofed that year and to start the interior work that winter. In January of 1806, he reported the exterior nearly complete; by the springtime he was concerning himself with interior construction. A letter Ramée wrote to the *Hofmarschall* in June is worth quoting in full, as it touches on diverse aspects of the architect–client relationship, and also because it precipitated a crisis in this relationship:

> *Monsieur le Maréchal,*
>
> I have not had news from you in a long time, since you were on a trip the last time I was at Ludwigslust. I am writing in the hope that you are there now. I have to communicate to you some ideas about what remains to be done on the tomb. His Serene Highness the Prince has desired greatly that everything be finished by the end of summer, but the stucco work [*Stuck*] is what's holding us up. I had proposed that the vault be simply coated [*enduite*] and painted a clear sky-blue color, but His Highness let me know that he preferred to wait and have it stuccoed. I think I ought to make a further attempt in this regard, however, because stuccoing the vault will take a long time and cost us a lot. Moreover, sky blue on a well-made coating will have a better effect than stucco, in my opinion. We would have only the bottom part from the floor to the cornice to do, and the Italians could easily finish that in the course of the summer.
>
> I sent the carpet samples that the prince requested for the chapel, but he did not find any to his liking. There is one, however, that I feel would suit the purpose perfectly, a strong and inexpensive carpet, which would make a fine effect in the chapel. It is a gray jasper, with a flowered border. There is another that also could be suitable, one which imitates tiger-skin perfectly, but this would have to be ordered since we do not have any at the moment, and it will take three months to receive it. [This shows that materials were being supplied by Ramée's own firm.]
>
> Having found no great difference between the prices of the bronze factory and those of Paris, I ordered the stars in Ludwigslust, and also sent them the full-scale design for the inscription to go above the door inside. The candelabra that will be at the angles of the platform and support the two sarcophagi are in process and will be finished, I hope, at the end of this month. On these candelabra will be double air-current lamps, which will light the vault perfectly when necessary. During my last trip, I deter-

mined a way to have them made of bronzed wood rather than solid bronze, for as they must be large they would have been extremely expensive. The mascarons [grotesque masks] are being produced for the cornice and probably will be finished by the end of next week.

The son of my relative who regularly sends me good Champagne wine, of which I believe you have received some bottles, has been here for several days. He is going to Petersburg with a good quantity of this wine, which is presently at Lübeck. He wants to part with some of it, in order to cover some of his considerable expenses, and I am taking the liberty of sending you two sample bottles, a rosé and a white, both sparkling of course. You would oblige me greatly if you could bring them to the attention of the Duke and anyone else who might be interested, as it is really a very favorable opportunity, the wine being of the first quality, as you will see in tasting it. The price is three Marks and four Schillings of our money, at Lübeck, or three Marks and six if delivered to Ludwigslust, Schwerin, or Doberan. It is sold by fifty-bottle case.

I have another request to make of you, *Monsieur le Maréchal.* Times continue to be very bad for the city of Hamburg, and especially for us, who are doing practically nothing more. I believe this is a period when your coffers are being replenished, and if you could aid us in some way, you would be rendering us a great service. Our advance expenses are now about 2,000 Ecus, and half of this sum would be a great help for us on the fifteenth of this month.

During our absence, *Monsieur le Maréchal,* I have kept in correspondence with the gardener Schmidt, through whom the prince has transmitted his orders. This gardener has planted the area next to the tomb like a veritable cabbage planter, without reason or taste. I propose to rectify everything next autumn, with your help, *Monsieur le Maréchal,* but if it is not too much trouble, you could oblige me greatly by communicating your ideas and the prince's orders to me yourself, as in the past, because Schmidt is often unintelligible. I am certain that we could have saved 200 Ecus on the trees that were used in this planting, many of which are now dead.

Please accept, *Monsieur le Maréchal,* the assurance of my complete devotion.

Ramée.[22]

Poor Ramée surely had no inkling of the reaction this letter would provoke. The *Hofmarschall*'s resentments about unexpected costs in constructing the mausoleum were evidently triggered by Ramée's request for payment and were poured out in his next letter to the architect. The polite sarcasm of the *Hof-*

marschall's language (in contrast to Ramée's simpler writing style) only underscored his anger:

> Monsieur,
>
> The letter of June 6, which you did me the honor of writing me, arrived the day before yesterday in Schwerin, where I had the opportunity to speak with His Serene Highness the Hereditary Prince, regarding the stucco for the vault, which he consents to have simply coated and painted blue. I pray you to give at once the necessary orders and instructions.
>
> The choice of a carpet for the chapel has not yet been made. The samples are at Ludwigslust; I have not seen them, but shall write to you as soon as the Hereditary Prince has come to a resolution of this matter.
>
> I am sorry that I cannot be useful to your friend. The two samples of Champagne wine, which I had several people taste, did not find approbation.
>
> It is also with great regret that I find myself unable to send you the thousand Ecus that you ask of me. I assure you that I did not expect this request, and still less that your advances would have amounted again to 2,000 Ecus. How is that possible?
>
> I wish I had never got entangled in the construction of this sepulcral chapel, which is costing an enormous amount of money, despite your positive assurances.
>
> You forget completely your first estimate, which amounted to only 13,000 Thalers, including a considerable sum for unexpected expenses. It was on the basis of this calculation that we began the building. We certainly have economized as much as possible at Ludwigslust, and yet the money already spent surpasses the estimate so considerably, that already we approach its double. If it were only a matter of an excess of one or two thousand Ecus, I would not be surprised or alarmed, but this is much too much, and we are still not seeing the end of it.
>
> I hope, Sir, that you will be able to give me a justifying memorandum, explaining the reasons for such an astonishing difference between the estimate and the actual cost. No accident has taken place, no change has been made in the plans of the building or in the price of materials or labor. We must protect ourselves from reproaches. How do you think the Emperor Napoleon would greet bills that amounted to double what the architect had first asked of him?
>
> We shall not let everything get out of control, and I beseech you not to think that the required sum makes no difference to us.
>
> Surely you will not claim that making an accurate estimate is an impossible problem in architecture. I cannot conceive how an estimate made by you with care could depart so far from the actual

cost. On the other hand, you surely did not purposely make an inaccurate calculation in order to involve us in a considerable expense despite ourselves. Your manner of thinking, as well as the sentiments you have constantly expressed to me, attest that you would not have wanted to compromise me.

You will recall that last autumn, in December 1805, you made a new calculation of the things you still had to furnish us from Hamburg. Your account came to the sum of 2,000 Thalers, which according to you could only be exceeded by a small amount. These 2,000 Thalers were furnished to you in January, and you must agree that I am right to be somewhat surprised by the considerable advances you are requesting again. If you treat us to many more of these surprises, you will ruin us, and we shall be obliged to abandon the edifice, even if it is nearly completed.

Accept, Sir, the assurance of my civilities.

M. [Mecklenburg][23]

Six weeks later, not yet having received the requested "justifying memorandum," the *Hofmarschall* wrote again to Ramée, repeating his concerns and stating that his master was not to be taken advantage of, although he added graciously, "It is true that the Prince is very happy with the building."[24] He also returned several issues of the *Journal des bâtimens* that Ramée had lent him.

In early September 1806, Ramée finally answered the *Hofmarschall,* noting that "an absence of several weeks" had prevented his responding earlier. Perhaps as a result of the typical architect's experience with clients and cost overruns, Ramée remained unperturbed as he enumerated (not very convincingly) some reasons for the increased costs: revisions in the design, the need for more copper roofing than originally thought, the architect's inspection trips. And he suggested that he had actually saved the prince a good deal of money by various economies he had made.[25]

A detailed account sheet accompanied Ramée's letter (Fig. 151), listing all the materials supplied by the architect and his firm since November of 1804; his trips to Ludwigslust; and 1,000 Rixthalers for "architect's fees following the convention," for a total of 8,644 Rixthalers. Of this total apparently only 2,000 had already been paid to Masson et Ramée. Undaunted by the *Hofmarschall*'s cold shoulder to his earlier business propositions, Ramée even mentioned an upcoming "sale of luxury objects from our store" and added hopefully, "I shall take the liberty of sending you some catalogues and ask you to distribute them to your friends and acquaintances."

By this time, however, Germany was being transformed by the Napoleonic juggernaut. In July 1806, Karl Theodor von Dalberg, archbishop-elector of Mainz (and Ramée's former client from Erfurt), had led a large contingent of German kingdoms and principalities, including Mecklenburg-Schwerin, in withdrawal from the Holy Roman Empire and submission to Napoleon as the Confederation of the Rhine. The political and economic turmoil that accompanied this development affected the completion of the mausoleum at Lud-

151 First page of statement of expenses submitted by *Masson et Ramée* to the Prince of Mecklenburg-Schwerin, 5 September 1806. (Mecklenburgisches Landeshauptarchiv Schwerin)

wigslust. By May 1807, the previously condescending *Hofmarschall* was writing to Ramée and Masson with unaccustomed humility about his prince's difficulties in paying them:

> The state in which the Hereditary Prince's affairs naturally find themselves, due to the misfortunes that his country has suffered, and after all the Mecklenburg revenues have been taken from him, must excuse – for people as just and fair as you – the delays in His Serene Highness's payments.[26]

Work nevertheless proceeded, payments were periodically made, and by December of 1807 Ramée was concerning himself with the final interior details of the mausoleum and the landscaping around it. The last letters from Ramée, written in 1808, reveal that the building was completed and all that remained were minor matters such as replacing glass broken during the installation of the windows.

As always, money was a bone of contention. Ramée's requests for payment for his work on a "new palace" provide some details about this otherwise unknown part of his activity in Mecklenburg-Schwerin:[27]

> I mention again my request regarding the work done on the new

palace. I made four trips exclusively for this purpose, two of them with my young man. [This was perhaps Pierre Philippon, Ramée's student at this time.] I never have put anything on the bill except my actual expenses. There was also the general plan of the palace, a view of the garden façades, five drawings for the decoration of the *Grande Salle,* the family dining room, and the oval boudoir. Also a projected theatre, which was to be executed in the *Grande Salle,* all the cornice details for each room, the sculpture that was to decorate these cornices,. . . You will oblige me greatly, *Monsieur le Maréchal,* if you have the kindness to bring this to the attention of the Prince and to send me the moderate sum I am claiming for this work. I am planning within three weeks to leave Hamburg for several months, and I will tell you frankly that I have counted on this little payment to facilitate the trip. And if you could add to it the amount owed to the firm, or a part of it, you will render me a very great service, *Monsieur le Maréchal.* And if you could give me 100 marks for the glass to replace that which was broken, I would be very pleased.[28]

Ramée's difficulties – the lack of work in Hamburg, the impending bankruptcy of his business with Masson, the financial embarrassment of clients such as Mecklenburg who owed him money – were forcing him to consider leaving Hamburg for good. The architect's letters to Mecklenburg in 1808 imply that he wanted to reestablish himself in Paris but that something was preventing him from doing so. In March he mentioned that "the unencouraging letters I have received from Paris, as well as a few small jobs that have come my way, have made me put off my plans for another time."[29] In November he reported that "I will not think of returning to Paris soon."[30] About two years later, Ramée was finally to make the move, bringing to a close his fruitful but frustrating years of architectural practice in Germany.

Ramée's last letter to the *Hofmarschall,* dated 6 November 1808, mentions the only commission he is known to have received in Hamburg during this period:

I was [recently] very busy with the festival hall [*salle de fête*] that the Prince de Ponte Corvo built on the occasion of the Emperor's birthday.[31]

The Prince de Ponte Corvo was Jean Baptiste Bernadotte, the brilliant French soldier and statesman who later became king of Sweden. Napoleon had given him the Ponte Corvo title in 1806, in gratitude for his services at the Battle of Austerlitz; the following year, Bernadotte assumed the post of Imperial Governor of the Hanseatic cities, in Hamburg. It was in this capacity that he evidently hired Ramée to create a festive setting for the celebration of Napoleon's birthday (August 15) in 1808. The only known description of the event is found in a Hamburg newspaper account that appeared two days later:

> Four to five hundred invited guests came to the Prince's ball, at the residence of His Highness [i.e., Bernadotte]. . . . A hall, constructed in several weeks, decorated most splendidly and resembling a beautiful temple of Antiquity, provoked great admiration. The bust of His Majesty the Emperor Napoleon, situated in the sanctuary, was the first object that struck one's eyes, dazzled by the light of more than five hundred candles.[32]

One may imagine that Ramée was sensitive to the irony of participating in the adulation of the ruler whose conquests were destroying his architectural career. But the architect's feelings about Napoleon must have been ambivalent, for his next move was made in the hope of profiting from the prosperity of Napoleonic Paris.

Napoleonic Paris

Little is known about the approximately two-year period Ramée spent in Paris after leaving Hamburg and before setting sail for America. Two or three references to the architect and one drawing by him are all we have. Yet even this meagre evidence, when seen against the background of events in France at the time, suggests something about Ramée's activities in Paris and the reasons he went there and then departed.

Boulliot dispenses quickly with this episode in the architect's life: "Ramée returned to Paris in 1810, with the intention of settling there. But as the political horizon threatened new catastrophes, he went on to the United States of America."[33]

As noted already, Ramée's correspondence to the *Hofmarschall* of Mecklenburg in 1808 reveals that the architect had been planning to return to France, but postponed the move because of some work he obtained in Hamburg and also because of "unencouraging letters" he had received from Paris. The failure of the firm of Masson et Ramée and its resulting debts no doubt contributed to the architect's desire to leave Germany, but he did not try to escape the firm's creditors, as did Masson. The Marquis de Lafayette emphasized this in a letter of February 1811 to his old friend Archenholtz, who had invested in Masson and Ramée's business. After complaining of Masson's uncooperativeness, Lafayette told Archenholtz, "I have seen M. Ramée and I am well satisfied with the attitude he has shown to me." Lafayette then noted that Ramée was trying to reestablish his career in Paris: "I am attempting to be useful to him, but have small means of doing so. He is skillfully working to bring himself before the public."[35]

But Ramée probably returned to Paris mainly because that was where the professional opportunities looked best. He had stayed in Germany even after receiving amnesty from the French government in 1803, because he still was finding work in Hamburg, Mecklenburg-Schwerin, and Denmark. Following the Napoleonic occupation of northern Germany in 1806, economic conditions there deteriorated; then the British naval defeat of Denmark in 1807 crippled that country's commerce. France, however, was enjoying the victor's prosperity at this time, owing partly to tribute that Napoleon exacted from his conquered lands and to his policies calculated to stimulate the domestic economy and ensure full employment.[36] Architecture was naturally a beneficiary of these policies, especially in Paris, which Napoleon wanted to refashion as a expression of his glory.

Long before he became emperor, Napoleon is said to have boasted, "If I were master of France, I would want to make Paris not only the most beautiful city that ever existed but the most beautiful city that could exist."[37] When he assumed imperial power in 1804, Napoleon set about realizing this vision for his capital, with new public buildings, palaces, and parks; engineering works such as bridges, canals, fountains, and market halls; the demolition of old neighborhoods to create open spaces and new streets; and monuments to himself such as triumphal arches. A newspaper in 1804 reported that "it is unbelievable how many public works are underway in Paris at this moment." Each succeeding year brought new imperial plans: in 1808, for instance, an observer wrote that "the Emperor, after having visited the different quarters in Paris in which monuments are rising, returned to his palace with his imagination filled with new projects for the embellishment of the city."[38]

152 Halle au Blé, Paris. Dome executed by Belanger after 1808. (A. Pugin and C. Heath, *Paris and its Environs*, vol. 2, London, 1833, opp. p. 157)

This activity was of course a boon to architects and builders, many of whom had languished during the revolutionary years of the 1790s. Among these were Ramée's former mentors, François Joseph Belanger and Jacques Cellerier. Belanger had been arrested during the Reign of Terror in 1794 and was saved from the guillotine only by the overthrow of Robespierre; he found little work during the following decade and even in the first years of Napoleon's reign.[39] But in 1808 Belanger finally received important commissions: one for a central slaughterhouse in Paris, the Abattoir de Rochechouart; another for the rebuilding of the vast dome of the Halle au Blé (wheat market), which had burned six years earlier. Belanger's plans for the abattoir were never executed, but he did supervise construction of the Halle au Blé dome (completely in iron, as he had originally proposed in the 1780s), thus achieving one of the major engineering feats of the period (Fig. 152).[40] Napoleon took a personal interest in the progress of this work and inspected it several times during its construction.[41]

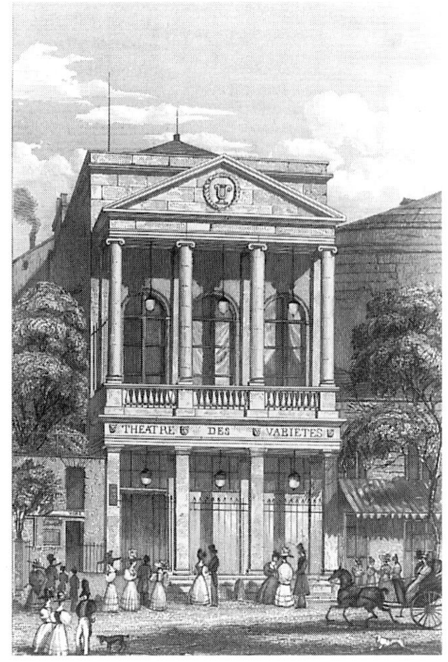

153 Théatre des Variétés, Paris, designed by Cellerier, 1807. (Pugin and Heath, *Paris*, vol. 2, opp. p. 109)

The career of Cellerier also revived during the Empire. Returning to his specialty of theatre design, he built in 1807 the Théâtre des Variétés, which still stands on the Boulevard Montmartre in Paris (Fig. 153). Cellerier also was entrusted with the rebuilding of the abbey church of St. Denis, devastated during the Revolution, which Napoleon wanted to restore as the burial place of French monarchs.[42] But Cellerier's most remarkable commission came in 1808, when he was chosen to design the "Elephant of the Bastille," a strange project conceived personally by the Emperor. It was to be an immense fountain on the Place de la Bastille, in the form of an elephant carrying a tower on its back (Fig. 154). The design went through various stages and was finally erected, after Cellerier's death in 1814, only as a mock-up in wood and plaster.[43] (It was this structure, in dilapidated condition, that was immortalized by Victor Hugo as the rat-infested home of the street urchin Gavroche in *Les Misérables*.)

154 Model of "Elephant of the Bastille," Paris. (Pugin and Heath, *Paris*, vol. 2, opp. p. 147)

Ramée, in dire straits in Hamburg, was no doubt in communication with Belanger, Cellerier, and other friends in Paris about the architectural possibilities there. His references in 1808 to letters from France, and his plans to return there, suggest that he was trying to arrange collaborations with other architects or commissions on his own in Paris. Jean Frédéric Perregaux, the powerful banker who had sponsored Ramée's petition in 1800, could surely have helped the architect reestablish his career in Paris; but Perregaux died in February of 1808. (Perregaux's death was perhaps the discouraging news Ramée alluded to in his letter to the *Hofmarschall* of Mecklenburg the following month.) Ramée may also have hoped for some kind of assistance from Charles Percier, who had signed his petition and was now one of Napoleon's chief architects.

In 1810, when Ramée finally returned to Paris, the building activity there was still intense. An observer that year wrote: "Seeing the upheaval everywhere [and] so many works begun at the same time, one would think that one hundred years will not be enough time to complete them."[44]

But the building boom was about to end. As so often in Ramée's life, his timing was unfortunate. In 1811 there was a severe depression in France, with bank failures, industrial bankruptcy, and large-scale unemployment, leading to riots and other disruptions. The domestic situation improved somewhat in 1812, but Napoleon's ill-fated invasion of Russia that summer began the process that would shortly destroy him and his empire. The resulting economic and political turmoil were probably the "catastrophes" that Boulliot later said Ramée had escaped when he left France in 1812. Three years later, a similar picture was painted by David Parish, the man who invited Ramée to America, when he referred to "my friend Mr. Ramée, . . . who at my suggestion left Europe when the reign of disorder prevailed."[45]

Only one record of Ramée's architectural work in Paris during this period is known: a small ink and watercolor drawing of the façade of a building inscribed "Loterie Impériale de France" (Fig. 155 and color plate 14).[46] Preserved at the Musée Carnavalet in Paris, the drawing is signed "Ramée, 1811."

The national French lottery had existed since the seventeenth century and Napoleon found it a lucrative tradition. Reorganized by one of his generals, the Loterie Impériale produced increasingly large profits for the government, over twenty-four million francs in 1810 alone.[47] The extension of the lottery into Napoleon's conquered territories, especially in Italy and Germany, further increased its revenues. The enterprise had a large administration with central headquarters in Paris, about ten regional offices, and hundreds of local bureaus that collected the moneys and disbursed the prizes. The small building designed by Ramée was probably meant to be one of the regional or local offices – perhaps a prototype design that could be executed in many places. Whether Ramée was commissioned to design it, or submitted it on his own or as part of a competition, is not known. In 1811 the lottery was being extended into new localities, such as Hamburg, so the administration was no doubt interested in architectural designs for new offices.[48]

Ramée's lottery design may appear at first rather ordinary or nondescript. But in fact it typifies some distinctive traits of the architect's work. There is

155 Design for "Loterie Impériale de France," inscribed "Ramée, 1811." Ink and watercolor drawing, 33 × 48 cm. (Musée Carnavalet, Paris)

an ambiguity about whether the focus is on the center of the building, with its arched windows and decorative features, or on the ends of the building, which project slightly from the façade (as in the residence buildings at Union College, which Ramée was to design two years later). There is also a tension between the full arches at the center and the low segmental arches over the doors at the ends, as if the architect were combining two different styles in one building. Segmental arches, and the very low-pitched pediments directly above the arches here, are features seen often in Ramée's work: in his Danish country houses, for instance, and later in his published designs for cottages.[49]

Another Raméean element in the lottery design is the little roof structure at the center of the building, framed by pilasters. It is the only use of the classical orders in the design and is thus similar to the attic storeys of Sophienholm in Denmark and the Börsenhalle in Hamburg. This roof pavilion serves a specific function in the lottery building: it contains a mechanism by which the winning numbers are displayed after each lottery drawing. So, following the principle of "*architecture parlante,*" the building itself is a statement of its function and an advertisement for it.

Despite the economic depression of 1811, Ramée surely found some work and produced additional designs (besides the lottery building) during his roughly two years in Paris. Whether the work was done independently or in collaboration with Belanger or other architects, and whether any of it was executed, is unknown. This period, just before Ramée escaped the "catastrophes" on the horizon by going to the New World, remains one of the mysterious chapters of his life.

The American North Country

Chapter 10

At the age of forty-eight, in 1812, Ramée made the boldest move of his nomadic life and came to the United States, bringing his wife and young son with him. He came at the behest of an acquaintance from Hamburg, David Parish, who had just made a fortune in America and wanted the architect to direct building projects he was planning near the Canadian border in New York State. Unfortunately, the War of 1812 and other events undermined Parish's plans. As Ramée was unable to get enough work from other sources to make a good living, he returned to Europe in 1816. But in this brief period the architect produced important work – in architecture, the decorative arts, landscape planning, and urbanism – which contributed to the development of American design.

Ramée is known in America for one great work: the buildings and grounds of Union College in Schenectady, New York, which constitute the most ambitious layout for an American college campus up to that time. But the architect also produced country houses, industrial and agricultural buildings, at least one church, and a project for a city square and monument. Ramée laid out parks and gardens, as he had done in Europe; he designed wallpaper and entered a business partnership for its manufacture in Philadelphia; and he produced other types of design when called upon to do so, such as military fortifications during the War of 1812. Ramée was well known in America during his stay and exhibited his designs publicly. Letters written by Benjamin Henry Latrobe, the foremost American architect of the period, reveal that he considered Ramée to be one of his principal rivals.

Ramée was, in fact, the most experienced European architect working in the United States in the 1810s. This in itself should have made him an eminent figure, for American architecture in the years following the Revolution was dominated by Europeans. Latrobe and several others were of British origin, but most of the important immigrant architects were French: Pierre Charles L'Enfant, who laid out the city of Washington; Stephen Hallet, who contributed to the design of the national Capitol; Joseph Mangin, designer of the New York City Hall; and Maximilien Godefroy, who erected buildings in Baltimore. Nearly all of these architects, however, had immigrated as young men and had established their careers in America.[1] Only Ramée had a background of lengthy and prominent professional practice in Europe.

Why, then, did Ramée not achieve more success in America? Perhaps the very fact that he immigrated at a relatively advanced age made it difficult for him to adjust to business in a strange environment. Language, for example, was no doubt a problem. A letter written by an acquaintance of Ramée soon after his arrival in America reveals that the architect did not speak English.[2] Although he surely acquired some facility in the language during his four years in the country, Ramée evidently preferred to communicate in his native language. All the known surviving letters to or from Ramée in America are in French, despite the fact that the correspondent in each case was an English speaker.[3]

Another problem was that Ramée came to America at an unfortunate time, just as the War of 1812 began. Besides the resulting economic disruption, there was a burgeoning spirit of nationalism, which tended to reject foreign architects in favor of the young American professionals who were beginning to appear on the scene. It is known that Ramée narrowly missed receiving at least one important commission – the Washington Monument in Baltimore – mainly because the competition jury wanted to choose an American architect.

Relatively speaking, however, Ramée did not fare badly in America. Architecture was still a young and risky business in the New World, where the professional architect as known in Europe had not yet fully emerged from the colonial traditions of craftsmen-builders and amateur "gentlemen-architects." Even the best-known architects in America had trouble making a decent living; many of them had long fallow periods between their few important commissions. Latrobe, for example, was plagued by bad luck at just the time that Ramée was in the country.[4] The difference, in Ramée's case, is that he had higher expectations. He had known success in Europe and had been enticed to America by the optimistic plans of David Parish. In 1814 and 1815, when Ramée had little work in the United States, political events in Europe – especially the fall of Napoleon and the restoration of the Bourbon monarchy – suddenly improved his prospects there. Not surprisingly, he returned home.

As in other countries, the brevity of Ramée's stay in America resulted in his being largely forgotten after he left. The extent of his work is not fully known. There is no contemporary account of his career in America and the remarks about it in Boulliot's 1830 biography of the architect are brief and incomplete. It seems that the architect (who must have supplied Boulliot with the information) mentioned only those aspects of his American stay that he thought would interest European readers:

> Mr. Ramée [after his brief period in Paris] traveled to the United States of America. From Philadelphia, he ventured to Ogdensburg, traversing primitive forests over a distance of 300 miles, relying only on a compass. England at that time was at war with its former colony. On the invitation of the American general Brocon [misprint for Brown], our man from the Ardennes fortified the small city of Ogdensburg, protecting it, in only a few days, from surprise attack. He also laid out several towns in New York State and constructed diverse establishments there. In the same state he was called to Schenectady, near Albany, where he built Union College, remarkable for its immense size and magnificent situation. Having returned to Philadelphia in 1812, he embellished that city and its

environs with several large and beautiful dwellings, and similarly in Baltimore, New York, and their surrounding areas.[5]

The statement that Ramée laid out towns in New York State is perhaps a reference to Parish's settlements, such as Parishville and Rossie, for which the architect designed the major buildings. Most intriguing is the remark that Ramée built houses in and around Philadelphia, Baltimore, and New York. Only one of these is known: Calverton, near Baltimore. It is unlikely that the statement is a fabrication, for Boulliot's article is generally accurate in its listing of Ramée's works. This, it seems, is a major part of the architect's American career about which we know almost nothing.

156 David Parish, engraved portrait, after a painting of c. 1810.

Missing from Boulliot's article is any mention of the man who brought Ramée to America, the international financier and adventurer David Parish (Fig. 156). An account of the architect's years in the United States must begin with the story of this most extraordinary of his clients.

David Parish

David Parish's father, John Parish, was from Scotland but had settled in Hamburg in the late eighteenth century and created there a great commercial and banking house.[6] The Parish family estate was at Nienstedten on the Elbchaussee, close to the country houses of Ramée's clients Voght, Baur, and others, and also near the furniture factory of Masson et Ramée at Dockenhuden. Ramée probably designed the Parishes' elegant stable at Nienstedten, as noted in Chapter 6. The architect's business partner, André Masson, also had connections with John Parish, for they both were instrumental in the liberation of the Marquis de Lafayette from Austrian captivity and his reception in Hamburg in 1797. Among the elder Parish's worldwide acquaintances were prominent Americans such as the statesman Gouverneur Morris, and Parish even served as the first United States consul in Hamburg.

All five of John Parish's sons followed him into commerce and finance, but David did so in the boldest ways. In 1803, at the age of twenty-five, David set up a business in Antwerp. He quickly made a small fortune through commodities speculation by taking advantage of the unsettled political conditions of the period, as well as tips provided by Napoleon's foreign minister Talleyrand, an old family friend. An unusual opportunity arose when the young Parish was chosen by an international syndicate of financiers to play a key role in a highly risky operation: a scheme to allow Napoleon to collect a large debt that Spain owed France, in spite of the British naval blockade that kept Spain's silver assets in Mexico from crossing the Atlantic. The plan involved a complex transfer of Mexican bullion into commodities in United States ports and from there to Europe on neutral ships. Parish was put in charge of the entire American part of the business, for a commission of one-fourth the syndicate's profits. In 1805 he went to New York and then established himself in Philadelphia. There he coordinated the operation through assistants who were dispatched to New Orleans, Vera Cruz in Mexico, and other cities. (One of these men, Vincent Nolte, later published an account of the affair, with many details about Parish's activities and personality – an account that inspired Hervey Allen's popular novel *Anthony Adverse* in the 1930s.)

Parish managed the enterprise skillfully and at its conclusion, about 1808, the profits were larger than anyone had expected; his share of the earnings made him suddenly one of the richest men in America.[7] In 1813 Parish joined John Jacob Astor and Stephen Girard in negotiating a sixteen-million-dollar loan to the United States government, saving the country from insolvency during the War of 1812.[8]

Parish had originally planned to return to Europe with his earnings when the Mexican bullion scheme was concluded. But after coming to America, he began to think about staying and investing his profits there; soon he decided that his investment would be in land, and by 1808 he was purchasing large wilderness tracts in northern New York State. One of Parish's motives was a desire to escape the political turbulence of Europe. Napoleon's occupation of Hamburg in 1806 had forced Parish's parents to flee Germany (they went first to Denmark, then England), and David's letters to them from America spoke of the United States as the only country offering "tranquility and security" in a troubled world.[9]

Parish also became convinced (wrongly, it turned out) that American land was an excellent investment. It seems that Parish was persuaded of this notion by Gouverneur Morris, the wealthy New Yorker who had known the elder Parish in Hamburg and who himself had large land holdings in northern New York. While in Europe in the 1780s and 1790s, Morris had encouraged acquaintances there to buy American property. One of these, Madame de Staël, acquired land in St. Lawrence County, New York, and for a while planned to move there; she never did so, but many of her compatriots did, making this "North Country" region of New York State a center of French *émigrés* (there was even a legend that Louis XVI's son, the "lost dauphin," escaped from France during the Revolution, came to America and became a missionary to the Indians in the North Country).[10] Morris took advantage of Europeans' romantic attraction to the American wilderness. Writing from France to an American friend in 1790, he noted that "Purchasers here are for the most part ignorant of geography. So, far from thinking the forests a disadvantage, they are captivated with the idea of having their *châteaux* surrounded by magnificent trees. They naturally expect superb highways over the pathless desert."[11]

When David Parish arrived in America, he was entertained by Morris and treated to his land-sales pitch. Morris's arguments can be found in a booklet he published at that time, in the form of a letter to an unnamed European acquaintance (possibly Parish himself).[12] Morris extolled the virtues of land in America, singling out for special praise the St. Lawrence River region of New York State, which he described as having tremendous agricultural potential and a mild climate – a blatant misrepresentation, as anyone who had spent a winter in upstate New York would have known.

In 1808, Parish bought extensive tracts of New York land from Morris, as well as from New York judge David B. Ogden and Jacques LeRay de Chaumont, one of the Frenchmen who had bought American land on Morris's advice and moved there. These lands were in Jefferson and St. Lawrence counties, on the southern shore of the St. Lawrence River. They were mostly forest lands (the present townships of Parishville, Antwerp, Rossie, and Hopkinton) but also included parts of the village of Ogdensburg, the main settlement and river port of the region. As soon as Parish's work for the Mexican-bullion syndicate was completed, he began making grandiose plans for his new domain. In contrast to men like Morris, who were interested in land mainly for financial speculation, Parish wanted to oversee the agricultural and commercial development of his property. With idealistic fervor, he envisioned the speedy creation of cities, complete with industries and cultural institutions. It was to make the physical plans for this dream that Parish brought Ramée to America.

Only certain parts of Parish's vision materialized and he returned to Europe after a few years. But in 1812, when he brought Ramée to America, Parish was at the height of his success and full of enthusiasm for his plans. Luckily, many records of his activities during this period survive, including extensive correspondence between Parish and his associates that contains information about Ramée.[13] The first references to the architect are in an exchange of letters between David and his brother Richard, in June 1812, revealing that Ramée sailed to America from Hamburg. (He perhaps returned there to wrap up business matters, or to join Caroline who may have gone there to bid her family farewell.) Richard Parish wrote from Hamburg that "Ramé [sic] is on the point of starting and I hope he and his party will join you in safety. You will find her [presumably Caroline] an amiable woman who improves on acquaintance – she is become quite a favorite with us." On 21 June, David responded from Philadelphia that "we are in daily expectation of the *Fair Trader* and the *Ariel* and from what you say about Ramée I presume he and his family are on board of the former vessel."[14]

During the four years that Ramée was in America, additional references in Parish's correspondence show that the architect's family remained with him the entire time.[15] This family included Ramée's young wife, their son Daniel, who was six years old when they arrived in the United States, and probably a female relative of Joseph or Caroline, as a couple of letters refer to Ramée and "his amiable ladies."[16] Later biographical articles on Daniel Ramée mentioned this American period as one of the significant events of his life. His first lessons from his father in architecture probably took place then, and his acquisition of English as a child gave him one of the linguistic skills that later distinguished his career as a scholar and author. As for Caroline, the only information about her in America is in a letter from Parish to an acquaintance in France, in which he wrote, "This lady is looking forward to receiving. . . the *Journal de Modes* that you have promised her."[17]

In September or October of 1812, after a brief time in Philadelphia, Ramée set out for the North Country, where Parish awaited him. This is the voyage that the architect later recalled proudly (to Boulliot): "He ventured to Ogdensburg, traversing primitive forests over a distance of 300 miles, relying only on a compass." In reality, Ramée did not make the trip in heroic solitude, as implied here, for it is

157 David Parish's house, Ogdensburg, New York. Photograph c. 1900. (Frederic Remington Art Museum, Ogdensburg, NY)

known that he was accompanied by at least one other person: Joseph Rosseel, a young Belgian immigrant to America who was Parish's principal North Country agent.[18] Even with guides and companions, however, the voyage was difficult and took the traveler progressively through the sublime American landscape that Europeans of a romantic temperament found so thrilling. The normal route was from Philadelphia to New York City by stage coach, up the magnificent Hudson River Valley to Albany, then following the Mohawk River west to Utica, and north through the forests to the St. Lawrence River.[19]

In mid-October, Ramée joined Parish at Ogdensburg, where the latter had already constructed a substantial brick house (now the Remington Art Museum) and a large stone warehouse on the river (now a United States customhouse) (Figs. 157, 158). The brick house is so similar, in its overall shape, to earlier buildings by Ramée – especially Hellerupgaard in Denmark – that one suspects it was based on drawings the architect had sent to Parish from Europe.[20] Once he arrived in Ogdensburg, Ramée supervised the interior decoration of the house and the laying out of its gardens.[21] In the dining room he constructed a "Russian stove" – made of brick and probably modeled on a type of room-heating stove Ramée knew from northern Germany – which proved so effective that copies of it became "all the rage" in Ogdensburg that winter, as one local resident reported in a letter.[22] Ramée involved himself in all sorts of architectural and horticultural matters, and after he returned to Philadelphia, Parish's manager in Ogdensburg complained that "the *Baumeister* promised me whole volumes of instructions" that had not yet arrived.[23]

158 David Parish's warehouse, Ogdensburg. (Author)

Despite the remoteness of Ogdensburg, Parish was determined to lead his accustomed civilized life while there. Besides his numerous agents and employees (including "an excellent French cook," as Nolte tells us in his memoirs) there were various guests, such as French miniature-painter Charles Hénard, whom Parish had brought to America mainly because he was a witty and entertaining companion.[24]

Joseph Rosseel, the young Belgian who was Parish's chief land agent, became a close friend of Ramée's. A letter that Rosseel wrote to his fiancée in November 1812 contains the most personal remarks we have about the architect:

> You will also see Monsieur Ramée. I very much regret your not being conversant with the French. . . . He is so goodhearted a gentleman to whom I am so much indebted for salutary advice and friendly admonitions when I stood in need of both, that I am ardently desirous you would make an attempt [to learn French]. . . so that when Monsieur Ramée returns next summer you may learn from him the particulars of the journey we made together. . . . Indeed, he has taken as much care of me, as if I had been his brother. I am much attached to M. Ramée whom I particularly recommend to your friendship.[25]

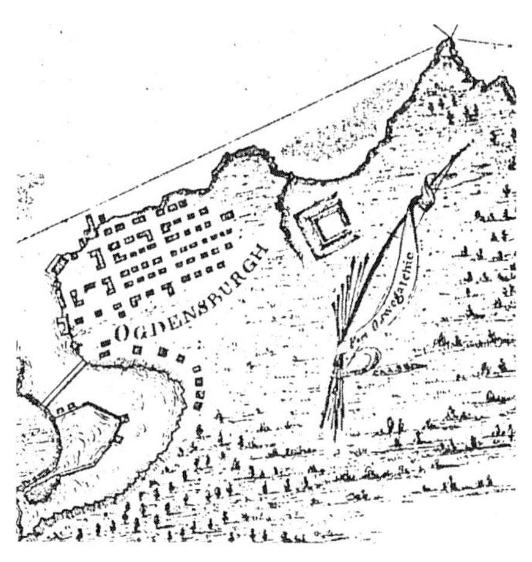

159 Fort Oswegatchie, Ogdensburg, as shown on map of 1818. (National Archives, Washington)

Ironically, Parish and Ramée, who had come to America partly to escape political turmoil, found themselves suddenly in the midst of war. In one of the first engagements of the War of 1812, the British invaded American settlements from the Canadian side of the St. Lawrence River. Ogdensburg was attacked just about the time Ramée arrived there; one of the first things he did was to lend his military-engineering skills to the American commander of the region, General Jacob Brown. In early November, the local Ogdensburg newpaper reported that a fort was under construction, planned by "Mr. Ramée, a French gentleman who resides in this village."[26] Fort Oswegatchie, as it was called, was not a permanent structure and no traces or records of it remain, except for schematic representations on maps of the period (Fig. 159). But Ramée thought the episode of enough interest to mention it to his biographer Boulliot.

Hostilities continued. In late November the British fired on Ogdensburg and it was reported that "Mr. Parish very narrowly missed being hit."[27] But the intrepid Parish was not to be deterred from plans to develop his lands and create new settlements. He turned his attention first to a tract east of Ogdensburg, a township previously called Cookham, which he renamed Parishville with the idea of making it the nucleus of his North Country empire.

Parishville

Parish situated his capital on the West Branch of the St. Regis River, a tributary of the St. Lawrence. He cut roads through the forest, leading to the new settlement, and laid out a grid of streets: possibly one of the town plans attributed to Ramée in Boulliot's article.[28] Parish envisioned the town as a model community, complete with housing for his agents, a large tavern or inn for visitors, an "academy," and unusual amenities such as a deer park. Parish's own country house was to be a couple of miles north of the town, at a waterfall in the river. In November 1812, he took Ramée to inspect the site. Parish's description of this visit (in a letter to his father) reveals his strong attraction to the natural beauty of the place, which must have been one of his motives for establishing his headquarters there:

> I have some of the most romantic situations [in Parishville] you can possibly imagine and Ramée, who made an excursion with me the other day to view them, declares he never saw anything as fine; the situation I have chosen is on the St. Regis River, the whole of which falls down 80 feet perpendicular and forms a most beautiful cascade, which will be close to and in full view of my house. . . . Ramée has been with me here for the last six weeks very busy making plans of the different buildings I intend erecting at Rossie, Parishville, etc.[29]

160 Allens Falls on the West Branch of the St. Regis River, near Parishville, New York. (Author)

Today, this waterfall is much reduced in volume, because of a diversion of the river upstream, but one is still struck by the scenery that so impressed Parish and Ramée (Fig. 160). In its wildness, grand scale, and contrasting features (jagged rocks, splashing water, angular fir trees), it exemplifies the late-eighteenth-century ideals of the picturesque and the sublime in landscape. Romanticized images of similar scenes abound in European art of the period – as seen, for example, in Alpine views that Frederikke Brun, Ramée's Danish client, used to illustrate her published writings (Fig. 161). Parish and Ramée thus sought out American landscape that fit their preconceptions of picturesque beauty. America simply provided it in greater abundance and primeval purity than Europe.

Ramée's plans for the buildings at Parishville were executed by Daniel Whipple Church, Parish's chief superintendent of North Country construction, and by Daniel Hoard, his land agent in the town. Surviving correspondence reveals that these down-to-earth Americans did not always think well of the strange and grandiose plans of Parish and his French architect, and that Parish often had to admonish them for deviations from Ramée's drawings. The most substantial buildings constructed in the town were the Tavern and the Academy. The Tavern, which burned in 1875 but is recorded in one photograph, was a large three-storey building with a hip roof and a porch with shallow arches similar to those of other buildings by Ramée (Fig. 162). Letters of 1813 reveal that the architect's plans for the Tavern had to be modified somewhat because of the restricted site on the bank of the river.[30] Ramée probably intended the central part of the building to be flanked symmetrically by side-wings, only one of which was constructed as planned. But even as executed, the overall proportions of the building, its roof, and its porch are reminiscent of other works of the architect, such as his country houses in Denmark.

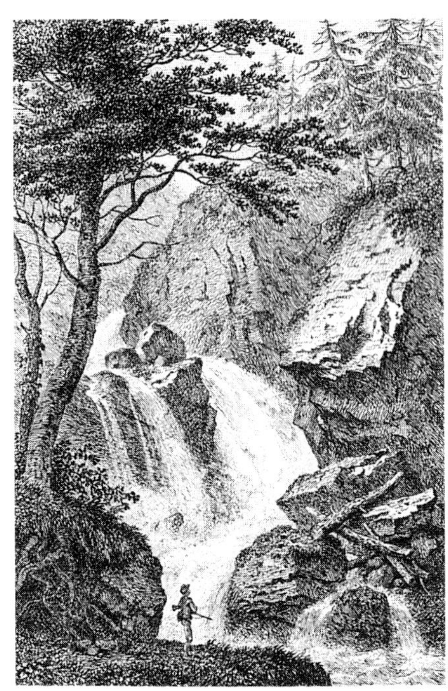

161 Engraved view of the river Arve, near Geneva. Frontispiece of Friederike Brun, *Prosäische Schriften*, Zurich, 1799.

The Academy in Parishville burned in 1854 and is known only from brief descriptions. David's brother George, visiting the North Country in 1816, called it "classically correct, surmounted by a Cupola and intended for a Public School."[31] Later references to it reveal that it contained one large room and was used as a town hall and a church as well as a school.[32]

The story of Parish's country house, north of Parishville, is complex but includes interesting details about the execution of Ramée's plans.[33] In the spring of 1813 construction began for a barn and a house about a quarter of a mile east of the river and the waterfall. Parish at first called this the "farm

162 Parish Tavern, Parishville. Photograph before 1875, when the building burned. (Parishville Historical Association)

house" and still planned to erect a building at the river, which he called his "Mansion House." In a letter to Daniel Church from Philadelphia, Parish approved certain alterations Church had proposed in the plans of the farm house, but cautioned him to execute them "in such a manner as to deviate as little as possible from Mr. Ramée's excellent disposition of these buildings."[34] Progress on construction was slowed by the disruptive effects of the war, but Daniel Hoard was able to report by the end of 1813 that the carpentry work on the house and barn was largely complete.

By the following spring, however, Parish had revised his plans, deciding not to build at the waterfall, at least for the present, and to expand the farm house to make it suitable for his own use. In March of 1814, he wrote to Hoard:

> I have determined on an addition [to the farm house] with which it will become a sufficiently large and convenient house for me and some friends. Enclosed you will find Mr. Ramée's plan of this addition, the execution of which I wish may be immediately undertaken – you will of course communicate it to Mr. Church and desire him not to deviate from this plan, which is I think perfect in all its parts. This addition is to be in the rear of the house and the entry into the covered passage from the back door. I have got the passage made 24 feet long, considering that a proper distance from the main building. Let particular attention be paid to the construction of the chimneys, on the plan formerly indicated by Mr. Ramée.[35]

Many letters about progress on the house survive, written between Parish, Hoard, Church, and Gilbert Smissaert, who was in charge of furnishing and staffing the house. Parish urged Church and Hoard to speed up work on the building, as he hoped to entertain guests there in the summer, including Ramée and his family.[36] But progress was slow, probably not only because of the war but because of the inherent problems of building uncommon architecture in the wilderness. In October 1814, Smissaert, who was occupying

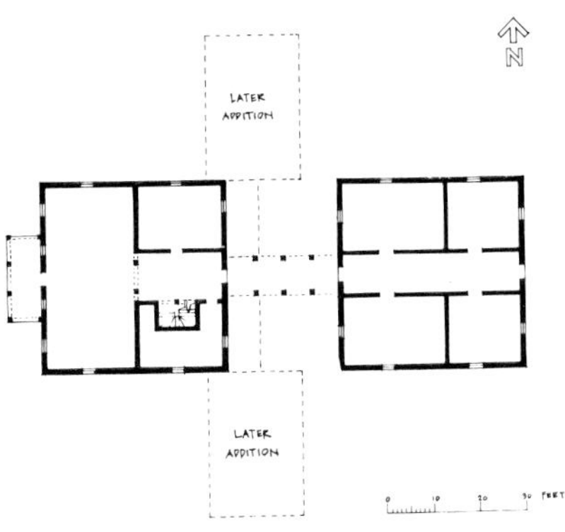

163 Parish House, Parishville, west front. Nineteenth-century photograph. (St. Lawrence County Historical Association)

164 Reconstructed plan of Parish House. The exterior form and dimensions of the west building (left) are more certain; the east building and the interior plans are more hypothetical. (Author)

the house with a couple of servants, vented his frustrations about its inadequacies, and gave Parish some advice about further construction:

> You cannot occupy the farm house without immediately discovering several insurmountable objections. I would therefore already make some preparation for building in brick. If I did consult Ramée, it would be merely for the outside dimensions. I do not wish to depreciate his *town*-talents, but his *country*-judgment I would not take as my guide. . . . Not a single door or window at the farm will open or shut. I well remember that this was the state they were in when more than a year ago I visited the house for the first time. Church says they ought not to be touched and will come right again, but when, God knows. Who would believe that to build a house here of good materials, will require four years?[37]

Throughout 1814 and 1815, Hoard continued to send Parish reports on the work at the farm: chimneys rebuilt, more land cleared, crops planted, sheep raised, and a bridge across the river constructed. It is not known whether Parish himself visited the farm during this period, which he spent mainly in Philadelphia, with few trips to the North Country. The mercurial adventurer was in fact growing tired of his life in America; he soon decided to return to Europe and let his younger brother George manage his properties. George was summoned from Europe in late 1815 and went north that winter to see the Parish lands. A journal kept by George during this trip provides a description of the Parishville farm:

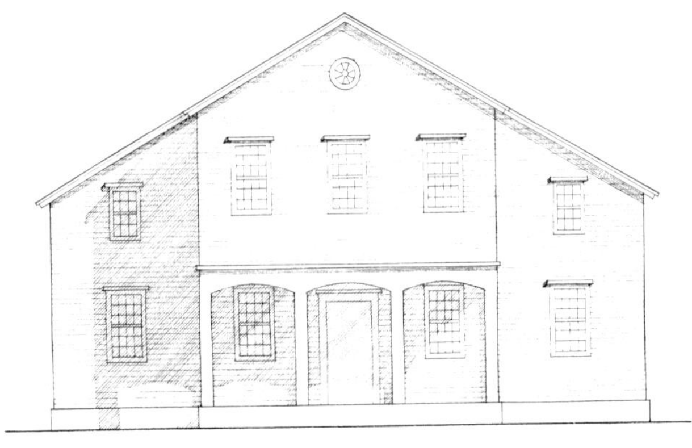

165 Reconstructed elevation drawing of the west façade of Parish House. (Author)

166 Design no. 17 of Ramée's *Recueil de cottages*, 1837. (Private collection)

> David has a comfortable house for his own residence, and a large barn built in strict imitation of a *Holstein Scheune* [a barn of the Holstein region of Germany]. The dwelling house is constructed in the cottage stile, the rooms not large, but comfortable. It is in charge of a German who married in America. Their duty besides is to superintend a Merino breed of sheep which David has introduced and already amount to seven hundred. [George continued with a passionate description of the "romantic" and "picturesque" waterfall near the farm.][38]

After David Parish's return to Europe, his North Country properties were managed first by George, then by one of their nephews. At Parishville, the barn survived until 1959 but the house burned in 1916 and is known only from descriptions and several old photographs (Fig. 163).[39] A plan of the unusual double house, its parts connected by a covered passageway, can be reconstructed, as can the west façade, which faced the river (Figs. 164, 165). The projecting central portion of this façade, the shallow arches of the porch, the simple classical details, and the round windows in the gables, all are typical of Ramée's earlier buildings, especially his country houses in Denmark. None of these elements was new to American architecture of the period, but the way Ramée combined them produced an innovative design. In particular, the expansive gabled roof, unifying the entire house under its bold sweep, was an unprecedented feature, giving the building a rustic, almost barnlike profile. It is very interesting that George Parish, in his journal, described the house as representing "the cottage stile," for this term suggests well the civilized rusticity that Ramée evidently had in mind in designing the building. Indeed, Ramée's later publication of cottage designs, *Recueil de cottages et maisons de campagne,* contains designs that are similar in character to the Parishville house (Fig. 166).

The barn, too, was remarkable (Fig. 167). Nearly one hundred feet long, it was by far the largest barn in the region, and its shape was unusual. Its roof

167 Parish Barn, Parishville. Nineteenth-century photograph. (St. Lawrence County Historical Association)

168 Detail of Ramée's drawing of Baurs Park, near Hamburg, 1810. (© Musée National de la Coopération Franco-américaine, Blérancourt, France)

came nearly to the ground, and it had half-timbered construction, with bricks filling the heavy timber framework of the walls. The building was, in fact, modeled on a traditional northern-German barn type, as George Parish recognized when he called it a "*Holstein Scheune*." It was surely designed by Ramée. Unlike most architects of the period, Ramée was genuinely interested in agricultural and farm structures, as we know from his careful design of stables and other outbuildings at Sophienholm and elsewhere in Denmark and Germany. In fact, the Parishville barn is very similar, in its overall shape and its pattern of half-timbering, to a barn that Ramée had included in his drawing of Baurs Park, on the Elbchaussee near Hamburg (Fig. 168). Ramée's interest in this kind of regional, vernacular building is characteristic of his work. For him, an architectural design ideally involved the entire environment; in the case of a country estate, he felt compelled to design not only the house but the grounds around it and even the farm structures. In America, especially, the idea may have seemed unusual to many people. But David Parish clearly was sympathetic to the notion and encouraged Ramée to use his North Country properties as models of environmental design.

Ramée's work for Parish also reveals a determination that northern-European forms of architecture were especially suitable to a region such as New York State. At a time when nearly all architects in America were enthralled by the classicism of Greece and Rome, this interest in creating appropriately northern models of architecture was remarkable. In this regard, it is significant that Ramée was also to design one of the first Gothic-Revival buildings in America.

Rossie

Another of Parish's tracts of land, along the Indian River south of Ogdensburg, was found to be rich in iron ore. At a waterfall in the river, Parish established a village that he named Rossie (after his sister's home in Scotland). There he erected mills and the first iron works in northern New York, with blast fur-

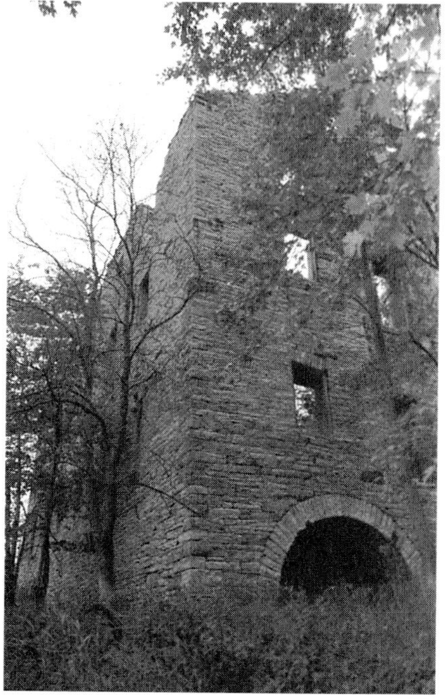

169 Ruins of Grist Mill, Rossie, New York. (Author)

naces and foundries.[40] Parish invested a lot of money in this enterprise, both in construction and in the importation of skilled personnel; despite technical problems, it soon became one of the important industries of the North Country. President James Monroe inspected it in 1817 and it was a source of iron and lead production during much of the nineteenth century. Its operations were eventually abandoned; Rossie is now nearly a ghost town, but the ruins of its massive stone structures on the rocky banks of the Indian River form a picturesque vestige of early American industry.

170 Iron Furnace, Rossie. Photograph c. 1895. (St. Lawrence County Historical Association)

In December 1812, Parish wrote (in the letter to his father quoted above) that Ramée was "busy making plans" for the buildings at Rossie. Unfortunately, there are no records showing what structures at Rossie were designed by the architect. Moreover, the construction dates of many of the Rossie buildings are not known precisely, so it is unclear which were erected while Ramée was in America. Despite these problems, the structures at Rossie are so remarkable that they merit consideration as possible works of Ramée. One suspects, for example, that the architect designed the Grist Mill, with its massive stone walls (still largely intact) and its great barrel-vaulted tunnel, running the length of the building at ground level — beautifully constructed and seemingly larger than required for its function as exit channel for the water passing through the mill (Fig. 169). But various dates after Ramée left America, from about 1820 to the 1840s, have been given for the erection of this mill.[41] It is possible, of course, that the building was based on an earlier design by Ramée, but in the absence of documentation only conjecture is possible.

171 "Rossie Furnace," detail of lithograph by Salathiel Ellis, 1838. (Collection of The New-York Historical Society)

172 Ledoux, design for iron forge at Chaux. (Daniel Ramée, ed., *Architecture de C. N. Ledoux*, Paris, 1847, pl. 150. Courtesy of Princeton Architectural Press)

Especially noteworthy is the great iron furnace at Rossie, no longer in existence but known from old photographs, which show it in ruin and without its chimney stack (Fig. 170).[42] One of the largest such structures in America in the early nineteenth century, it too suggests Ramée's hand in certain respects, such as the continuous horizontal band that marked the line where the angle of the sloping wall changed – the only decoration of this magnificently austere structure. A mid-nineteenth-century account of the iron industry at Rossie states that furnaces were built by David Parish in 1813 and were rebuilt in the 1830s and 1840s, but the description of them in this account does not match very well the structure seen in the photographs.[43] Complicating things further is a lithographic image of the "Rossie Furnace" of about 1838, one of a series of commissioned views of the Parish properties by the artist Salathiel Ellis (Fig. 171). This view shows a completely different type of structure: octagonal in plan, with a cone-shaped stack, and in a landscape different from the steep site of the furnace shown in the photographs.[44] Ellis's Parish views are inconsistent in their accuracy: some are faithful representations, while others take liberties with reality that suggest that the artist did not actually visit the sites.

The "furnace" in this view by Ellis lacks certain requirements of an iron furnace (such as the "charging bridge," from which ore was dropped into the stack), and its shape is completely unlike that of American iron furnaces, which were virtually always rectangular in plan.[45] Where did Ellis get this image of an octagonal structure with a conical stack? It seems unlikely that he simply invented it, as he was supposed to be portraying Parish's properties. One wonders if Ellis based his view on a drawing for a furnace by Ramée, unaware that it was a plan that had never been executed. One can easily imagine Ramée producing an unusual design like this, with its combination of primary geometric forms and its exaggerated portrayal of smoke pouring from the stack; it is similar in spirit to the iron furnaces designed by Claude Nicolas Ledoux for his utopian city of Chaux, the plans for which Ramée's son Daniel was later to publish (Fig. 172).[46] After designing it, Ramée may have learned that it was not practical and produced a more conventional design; but Ellis perhaps found the architect's original drawing in Parish's

173 Parish Barn, Rossie. Photograph before demolition of structure. (Elwood M. Simons)

papers and assumed that it represented the furnace as it had been constructed.

Aside from the mills and furnaces, there are several ordinary structures at Rossie that are said to have been erected by David Parish at the time Ramée was in America. Two of these are small but substantial brick buildings, reportedly erected between 1812 and 1815: the Land Office; and the David Parish House. The latter, built between 1812 and 1815, was a kind of double house with two front doors, which is said to have served as Parish's residence when he visited Rossie and also as the house of one of his agents.[47]

A more remarkable structure, which no longer exists but is known from an old photograph, is a large barn that Parish, an avid horseman, built in 1815 for stabling the race horses he kept at Rossie (Fig. 173).[48] This structure was unusual for an American barn, with its open arcade or passageway at ground level. But arcades of various forms are so typical of Ramée's work that it seems likely the architect designed the building, though its plans probably were modified in execution. Ramée no doubt intended the openings to have round-headed arches, as in the Parishville country house or the Parish stable at Nienstedten; the carpenters who erected the Rossie barn probably found it too difficult to fashion round arches and substituted the somewhat awkward angular openings. Such departures from Ramée's plans were common with the

174 St. Michael's Church, Antwerp, New York. (St. Michael's Church, Antwerp)

North Country builders, judging from Parish's repeated instructions not to "deviate" from his architect's designs.

Antwerp

About fifteen miles south of Rossie, in Jefferson County, was another of Parish's tracts of land. He acquired it in 1808 and named it Antwerp after the city where he had his European business office.[49] A settlement already existed there, and little is known about the physical improvements Parish made to the village, with one important exception. In 1816 Parish erected a church for the town, reportedly at a cost of about $10,000. In 1849 it became the Catholic church of St. Michael, and it still stands today, one of the oldest church buildings in northern New York (Figs. 174–7).

It is not known why Parish built churches in some of his towns and not in others. He evidently did not build one at Rossie, and at Parishville the Academy doubled as a meeting place for various religious denominations. But he erected a church in Antwerp (and possibly one in Ogdensburg), which he endowed for use by the Episcopal denomination but which could be used by other sects too. In early 1816, Parish's brother George wrote in a letter to their father: "Whilst on the subject of church establishments, I must notice that David is about building one at Ogdensburg, and another at Antwerp, and that he has made arangements with Bishop Hobart of New York for endowing them with regular church benefices."[50]

The fate of the Ogdensburg church is not known. But records show that the one at Antwerp was built in 1816 and that it is the same as the present St. Michael's Catholic Church.[51] Surviving copies of letters from Parish to his agent in Antwerp, Silvius Hoard, reveal that the construction of the building proceeded quickly. In April of 1816, Parish wrote to Hoard, "I have seen Mr. Thorp [probably a building contractor] in New York and advanced him $500 toward building a church. He says he wants no other plan than the one left

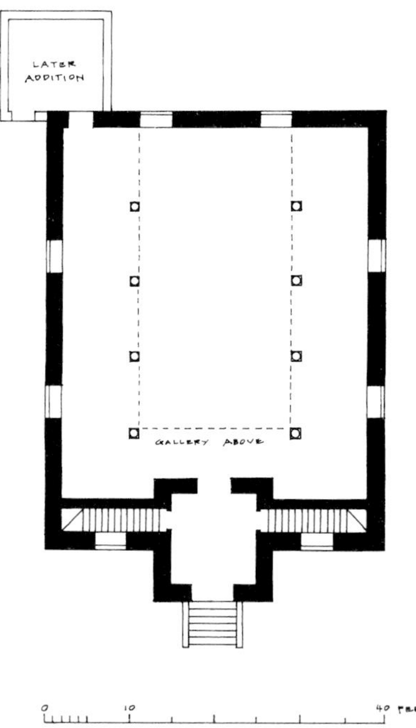

175 St. Michael's Church, floor plan. (Author)

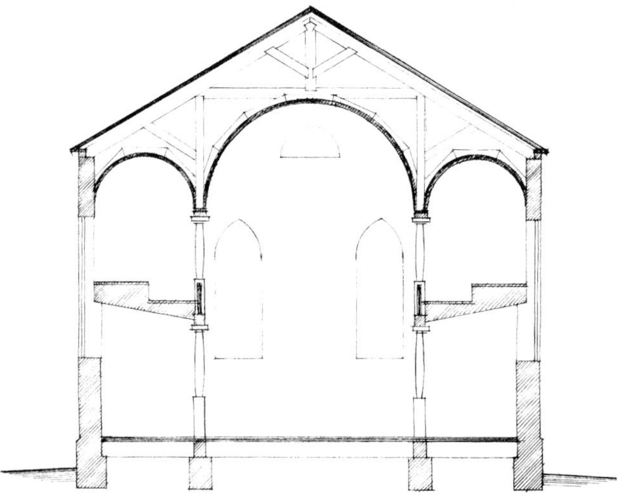

176 St. Michael's Church, section drawing. (Author)

177 St. Michael's Church, interior, from aisle beneath balcony. (Author)

with you, to which I wish you to be particular in making him adhere, except as relates to the dimensions." In April and May there are references to the bricks to be used for the church and additional funding of the job. And in mid-June Parish reported, "I am glad to find that the work connected with the church is coming on so well and that the ceremony of laying the cornerstone was attended to with decency and decorum."[52]

Nowhere is Ramée's name connected with this building. But it is highly unlikely that Parish procured plans for it from any other architect. Parish had brought Ramée to America with the promise of much work; his correspondence reveals that he felt a strong sense of responsibility toward his architect, and that when his own building plans diminished he took great pains to find other commissions for Ramée. This was especially true in 1815 and 1816, when the architect had little work and Parish attempted, unsuccessfully, to obtain public commissions for him in Baltimore and Washington. Parish surely relied on Ramée for the design of any building he erected that required an architect.

Moreover, the remarkable design of the Antwerp church points clearly to Ramée as its designer. The building has been beautifully preserved, both inside and out, with apparently no significant changes except the addition of a belfry atop the brick tower and a small vestry room at the rear of the church. Most unusual are the windows, with pointed arches, which make St. Michael's one of the earliest Gothic Revival buildings in America. Histories of the Gothic Revival identify only about a half-dozen American churches in the style before 1816 (St. Michael's, not mentioned in any of these studies, was apparently unknown to their authors).[53] Like most of the early examples of the style, St. Michael's is "Gothic" in only a superficial way: pointed windows are set in a building otherwise classical. On the main façade, the combination of round, half-round, and pointed windows creates a striking counterpoint of geometric shapes, neatly cut into the perfectly flat brick walls. Inside, a similar play of geometry results from the contrast between the pointed windows and the perfectly half-circular barrel vaults of the ceilings, the central vault having exactly twice the diameter of the vaults over the side balconies. It is all an exercise in geometry, in which the pointed arches introduce a variation on the circle.

This is the same type of "Gothic" found elsewhere in Ramée's work. In the gate lodge and stable at Sophienholm in Denmark, for example, pointed arches and circular windows are combined in a similar way to those at Antwerp (see Figs. 119–21). The pointed arches in the Sophienholm stable are supported on Tuscan columns that are almost exactly the same as those that hold up the balcony and the ceiling in St. Michael's (Fig. 177). This eccentric combination of the Tuscan order and pointed arches seems to be a distinctive feature of Ramée's personal brand of the "Gothic."

Parish's remark to Hoard, that he should be "particular in making [the builder] adhere [to the plan of the church], except as relates to the dimensions" is ambiguous. It could mean that the dimensions given on the architect's plan might be modified as long as the proportions of the building were kept the same; or that the proportions might be altered by the addition or subtraction of structural bays, or the alteration of vertical dimensions, or some such change. But Parish's admonition to "adhere" to the plan in all other respects reminds us of his earlier directive to his employees at Parishville, "not to deviate from [Ramée's] plan" for his farm house. Several aspects of St. Michael's church suggest that Ramée's plans were, in fact, followed carefully. Although the parts of the church are all relatively simple, there are subtle details. The wooden columns inside the building, for example, are distinguished by a graceful entasis, or bulge, which is difficult to execute and which a builder – especially one working in the wilderness – would not undertake unless it were specified by the architect. Everything suggests that St. Michael's church was executed in accordance with the plans of Ramée. It is one of his most distinctive and best preserved works.

Other Work in New York State

Shortly after Ramée arrived in America, Parish must have realized that he did not have enough construction work to keep his architect busy, for he soon tried to find other clients for him. During the four years he was in the country, Ramée produced work for a number of people, and in most cases there is evidence that Parish was instrumental in obtaining the jobs for him, by introducing him to prospective clients or simply by advertising his talents. In 1813, for instance, Parish wrote to Paul Hochstrasser, a business associate in Albany, telling him that Ramée would be visiting his city, and adding, "if . . . you can forward his professional views, you will oblige me and render service to your friends who may be disposed to build."[54]

Parish, in fact, often acted as a kind of agent for Ramée, transmitting messages between architect and client, especially regarding financial matters. Typical is a series of letters between Parish and Stephen Van Rensselaer of Albany. In June of 1813, Van Rensselaer reported to Parish that he had just seen "Mr. Rammé [sic]" and that the architect would visit him again shortly; in November, Van Rensselaer wrote that "the French gentleman who made a plan of a house etc. has not forwarded me his demand"; and in December, Parish responded with a reference to Ramée's bill for "200 dollars. . . for the plans he furnished you with last summer."[55] In this case, there is unfortunately no evidence of Ramée's plans or whether they were executed.

Parish's first successful promotion of Ramée was probably to the Ogden family, who owned large tracts of land in northern New York. David B. Ogden, a New York judge who had sold Parish some of his North Country property, decided about 1811 to make his home on a large island he owned in the St. Lawrence River (the Isle au Rapide Plat, later called Ogden Island), a few miles downstream from Ogdensburg. At approximately the same time, Gouverneur Ogden, David's brother, settled in the village of Hamilton (now Waddington) on the American side of the river, facing Ogden Island.[56] In November and December of 1812, the two brothers and their wives visited Ogdensburg and were entertained by Parish and other local notables. Parish no doubt introduced them to Ramée, who was being treated as a celebrity in Ogdensburg and whose "Russian stoves" were the talk of the town.[57] The details of Ramée's relationship with the Ogdens are not clear, but sometime in

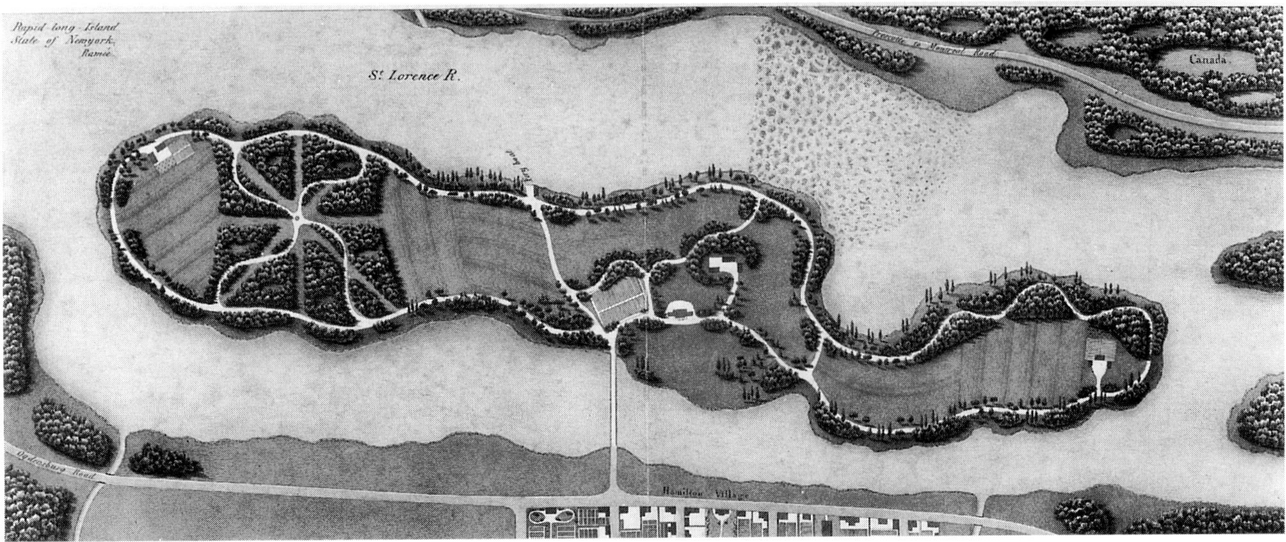

178 Ogden Island, St. Lawrence River. Plan in Ramée's *Parcs et jardins*, pl. 19–20. (Schaffer Library, Union College)

the following year he was hired by David Ogden to make designs for his island. A letter from Parish to the architect of March 1814 reveals that Ogden paid Ramée fifty dollars, perhaps only one of several payments for services rendered.[58]

Ramée later included his plan for Ogden Island in his publication *Parcs et jardins* (Fig. 178).[59] The plan shows the roughly three-mile-long island, connected by a causeway to the American shore and the village of Hamilton. Ramée's design transformed the island into a park, somewhat similar to those he had laid out in Germany and Denmark, with roads following wooded areas that define large open spaces, interspersed with groups of buildings. One difference from the earlier designs is that many of the open spaces seem to be intended as agricultural or grazing areas. An unexpected feature of the plan is the large wooded area near the western end of the island, with a geometric pattern of radiating and spiraling paths – more typical of earlier landscape traditions, which Ramée had largely rejected. Perhaps Ogden requested this feature, or perhaps Ramée introduced it as a contrast to the overwhelmingly rustic and irregular landscape of the island and its surroundings.

179 Ogden House on Ogden Island. Drawing, c. 1900. (William Ogden Wheeler, *The Ogden Family*, Philadelphia, 1907, p. 187)

The extent to which Ramée's plan for Ogden Island was executed is hard to determine. Later owners of the island used it mainly for agricultural purposes and may have altered the original landscaping; in the 1950s, the island was acquired by New York State as part of the St. Lawrence Seaway project, which raised the level of the river and greatly decreased the size of the island.[60] It is also unclear what buildings may have resulted from Ramée's design. The main house (shown on Ramée's plan just to the east of the point where the causeway joins the island) is documented in photographs and drawings made before it was demolished in the 1950s (Fig. 179). Its construction is said to have been started in 1811 but not completed until 1816; the cupola and side wings may have been later additions.[61] Nothing about the house specifically links it to Ramée. But his plan of the island shows the house with wings, giving it the shape of Sophien-

180 Coach House, Ogden Island. Photograph before demoliton of building. The dormers were not original. (Library of Congress, Prints and Photographs Division)

holm in Denmark. Even if the house was begun before Ramée's arrival, he may have suggested changes that were made during construction.

Another building on Ogden Island, however, can be ascribed to Ramée with some certainty: the coach house, which burned in 1926 but is known from photographs and descriptions by people who knew it (Fig. 180).[62] Most unusual in this structure were the arched, recessed panels, flanking the larger arched doorway and continuing along the sides of the building, to enliven the otherwise plain walls. This motif is very similar to the arched and recessed panels of Ramée's buildings at Union College in Schenectady, also of 1813. Other distinctive features, in both designs, are the horizontal bands running across the recesses, and the color contrast between the panels and the rest of the wall (in the coach house, the panels were stuccoed while the rest of the wall was exposed stone).[63]

181 St. Paul's Church, Waddington, New York. (Author)

The sophisticated design of this coach house contrasts sharply with the plainness of the façades of the main house on the island. One wonders if Ramée may have proposed the same arcaded treatment for the house, but that it was never carried out. The coach house may provide an intimation of grander designs that Ramée presented for the architecture of Ogden Island.

The bottom edge of Ramée's plan for Ogden Island shows part of "Hamilton Village" – now Waddington – its main road lined with buildings of various forms. None of these can be correlated with actual structures in the town, and Ramée may simply have drawn a generic village. But it is also possible that David Ogden, who owned much of this land, asked the architect to make designs for the town or its principal buildings.[64] Architecturally most significant of the early buildings of Waddington is St. Paul's Episcopal Church, a

182 Ellerslie (Gouverneur Ogden House), Waddington. Drawing by Gouverneur Ogden, early nineteenth century. The proportions of the house shown here are vertically exaggerated. (Professor Henry V. S. Ogden)

handsome stone structure which was built about 1816, under Ogden's supervision and with funds provided by his family and Trinity Church of New York City (Fig. 181).[65] A number of local historians have suggested that Ramée was the architect of this church.[66] It apparently was constructed by Daniel Whipple Church, the man who built many of Ramée's designs for Parish, but there is no documentary evidence of Ramée's authorship of St. Paul's and the form of the building itself is ambiguous in this regard.[67] The starkly cubic masses of the church and its large arched windows and doors are certainly compatible with the architect's work. But details such as the broken pediment above the main entrance and the flattened arch framing the chancel inside represent Baroque traditions not typical of Ramée. If he did draw plans for St. Paul's, they must have been modified during construction.

Another building in Waddington possibly by Ramée was Ellerslie, the house of David Ogden's brother, Gouverneur Ogden. Located on the river opposite Ogden Island, Ellerslie burned in 1843 and nothing remains of it today. It is known only from a couple of drawings and old photographs of its ruins (Fig. 182).[68] Consisting of a large central block flanked by low wings ending in pedimented pavilions, the building was remarkable in several respects for an American house of this period. The very large windows of the main block were unusual, as was the U-shape of this block, recessed in the center on the main façade – a form reminiscent of Ramée's country houses in Denmark, especially Frederikslund and Øregaard.

Also interesting is the exterior surface of Ellerslie: rough-cast or stucco (over brick and stone masonry) – again, not typically American, but Ramée's favorite wall surface. Only a few details were not typical of Ramée, such as the oval windows in the pediments, which Ramée would normally have made circular. The main difficulty in attributing Ellerslie to Ramée is that Gouverneur Ogden did not purchase the site and begin construction until a year after the architect returned to Europe. However, since Ogden must have known Ramée (both through his brother and through David Parish in Ogdensburg), it is possible that Ramée made plans for a house for him, which only later were used for the construction of Ellerslie.[69]

In January of 1813, Parish and Ramée left Ogdensburg to return to

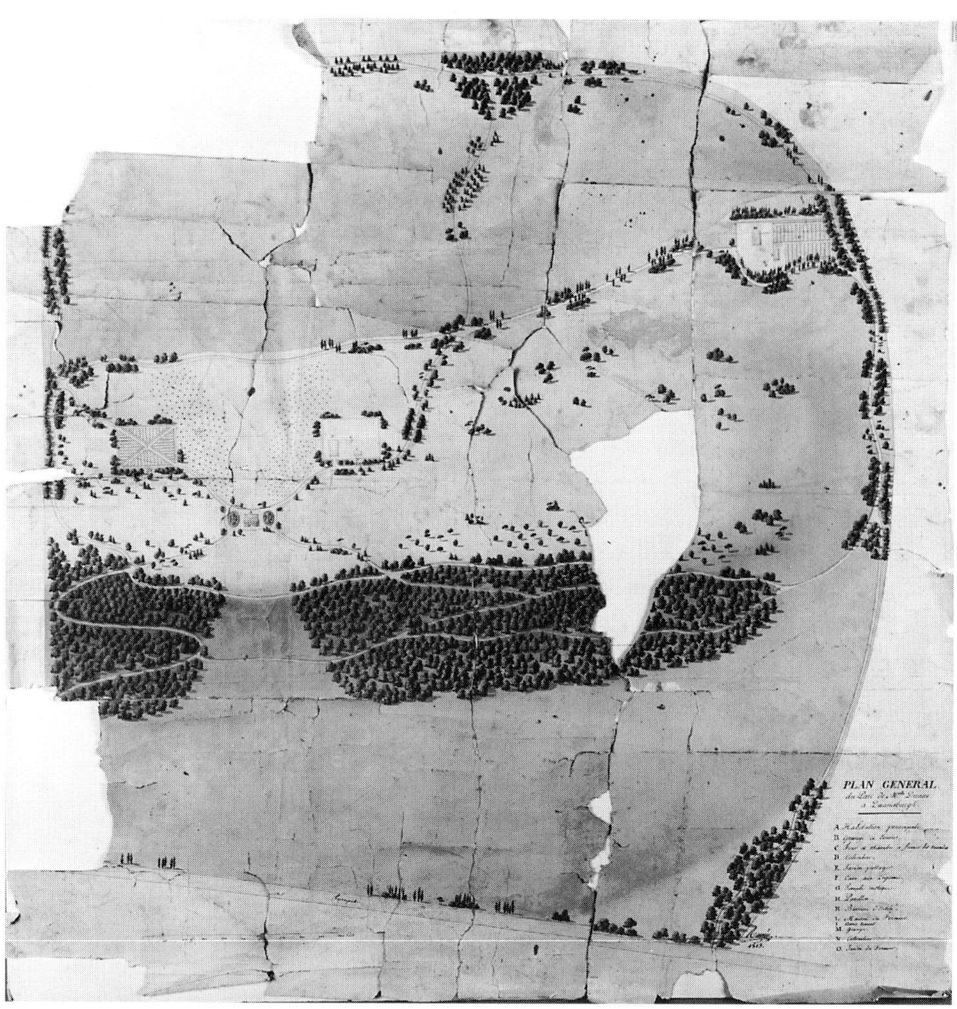

183 Duane estate, Duanesburg, New York. Ink and watercolor drawing, 81 × 81 cm, inscribed "Plan Général du Parc de M'elle Duane à Duanesburgh, Ramée 1813." (Mr. and Mrs. James Duane Featherstonhaugh)

Philadelphia. En route, the architect met the president of Union College in Schenectady and was hired to lay out a new campus for the institution (see Chapter 11). Ramée stayed in Schenectady only briefly at that time, but he returned several months later and it was probably then that he met another of his American clients: Catherine Livingston Duane. Miss Duane was the daughter of James Duane, who had been mayor of New York City in the 1780s; she was building a house for herself and her elderly mother on the family's land at Duanesburg, just a few miles west of Schenectady, and she engaged Ramée to draw plans for the estate.

Still in existence, though only fragmentary, is the architect's original plan for the property, drawn in ink and watercolor, inscribed "Plan Général du Parc de M'elle Duane à Duanesburgh" and signed "Ramée 1813" (Fig. 183).[70] It is similar to the lithographed plans of the estate that the architect later included in his publications *Jardins irréguliers* and *Parcs et jardins* (Fig. 184), except that the scale of the property was reduced in the published versions and a lake was added.[71] Ramée's design recalls his earlier plans for gardens in Germany and Denmark: it shows a circuit road around the periphery of the property, a variety of wooded and open areas, and an integration into the pleasure grounds of

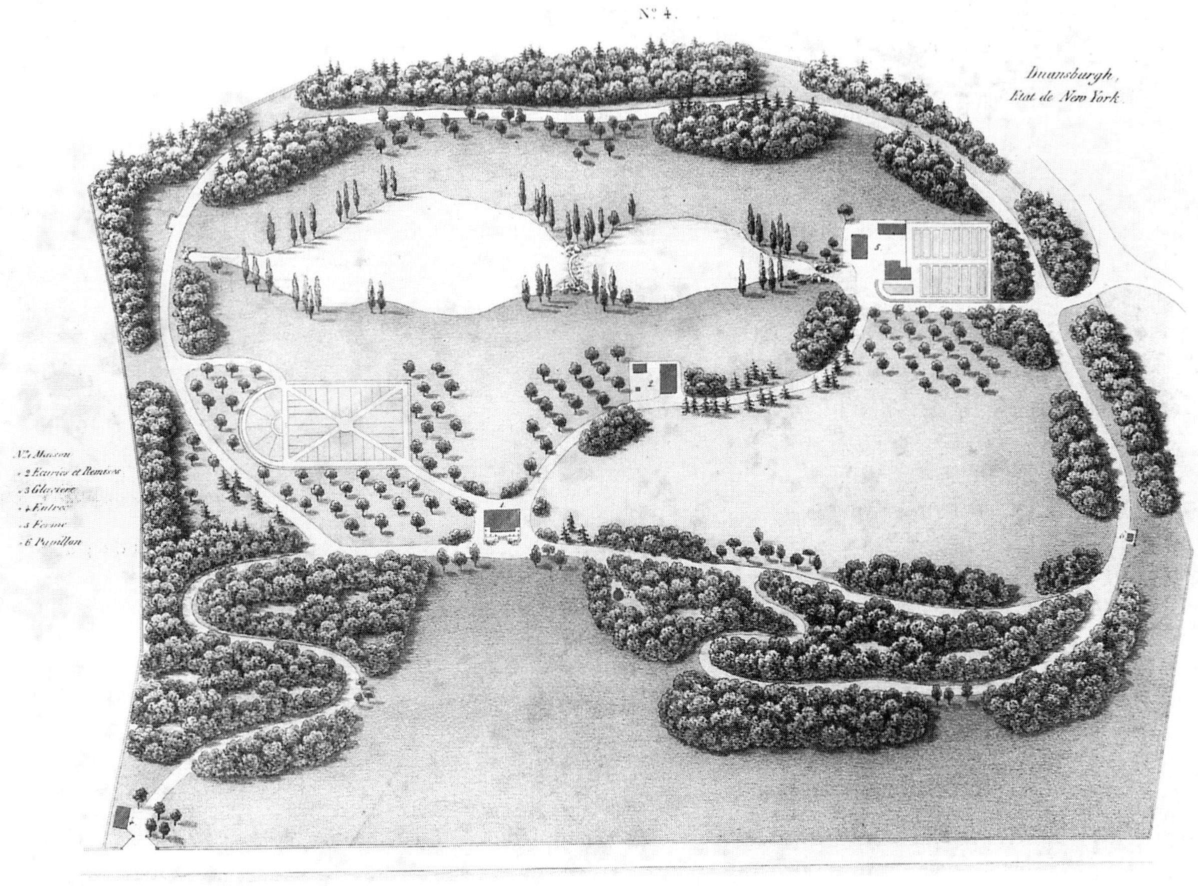

184 Duane estate, Duanesburg. Plan in Ramée's *Parcs et jardins*, pl. 17. (Schaffer Library, Union College)

farm buildings and small agricultural plots. As at Sophienholm, the Duane House was to be framed by wooded areas, defining a roughly triangular lawn or field, to afford a sweeping view from the hilltop site of the house. But it is unclear how much of the plan was executed — either its landscape features or the various pavilions and other structures shown on the drawn and lithographed plans.[72]

Most pertinent is the question of whether Ramée may have contributed to the design of the Duane House itself (Fig. 185). Its construction reportedly began in 1812 (too early for Ramée to have been the architect) but soon was halted due to the War of 1812; the structure was not completed until 1816.[73] Ramée, therefore, could possibly have revised a design originally prepared by someone else. The form of the house is unusual in certain respects, especially the porch on the north side, formed by a U-shaped cutting-away of the mass of the house under the roof, with two-storey-high columns (originally with Ionic capitals). Also distinctive is the low pitch of the roof, which emphasizes the overall cubic shape of the design, and the large round-headed windows along the porch, which suggest a French influence.[74] No house quite like this is found elsewhere in Ramée's work, and some of its details are not in his style (especially the small porches on the east, west, and south sides of the house, with their broken pediments).[75] But the building is so distinctive that one is tempted to suggest some contribution by Ramée. It is even more likely that Ramée designed the stable on the Duane property, which has a remarkable form for such a structure (Fig. 186). It has a tall, gabled section in the center, flanked by lower wings with arched doorways, resembling Ramée's Danish country houses in its overall shape.[76]

185 Duane House, seen from the garden side. (Author)

In recent years, a number of buildings in New York State have been attributed to Ramée, either because of some connection between their builders and David Parish, or because of their similarity to the work of Ramée.[77] In most of these cases, the evidence is not strong enough to make a clear determination. Two buildings in the town of Canandaigua, in western New York, are noteworthy as examples of these attributions. The Gideon Granger House, built about 1815, has been compared to Ramée's Øregaard and Sophienholm in Denmark; in fact, it is even more similar to Hellerupgaard, in the proportions of its façade and attic storey.[78] Roger G. Kennedy has also attributed to Ramée the First Congregational Church of Canandaigua, erected about 1816–18; its façade is dominated by a large arched opening, somewhat reminiscent of Ramée's Börsenhalle in Hamburg.[79] Kennedy notes that Gideon Granger, who was the United States Postmaster General under presidents Jefferson and Madison (and was on the building committee of the Congregational church), probably knew Ramée's Baltimore client Dennis Smith. If Ramée did provide plans to Granger for his house and the church, these plans must not have been followed closely in execution, for certain details of the two buildings are not fully compatible with the architect's work. But a cavalier interpretation of Ramée's designs on the part of builders in Upstate New York is thoroughly plausible. It is just what David Parish had continually to warn against in instructions to his building foremen.

186 Duane estate, stable. (Author)

It is interesting, moreover, that Ramée is sufficiently known in New York State that people would attribute buildings to him. The only other place where this is true is Denmark. Although Ramée spent only brief periods of time in New York, his work there was significant and made an impact on the architecture of the region. He seems to have affected local architects, such as Philip Hooker of Albany, whose works of the mid-1810s and later suggest Ramée's influence.[80] He also evidently had an effect on vernacular building in the region, judging from the unusual prevalence around Schenectady of nineteenth-century farm buildings with arcade-patterned walls (like the Union College buildings or the Duane stable) and around Parishville the prevalence of houses with circular gable windows (as in Parish's house). Ramée's more general impact on American architecture and landscape design will be examined in the next two chapters.

If David Parish's grandiose plans for the development of his North Country empire had materialized, Ramée would have had a much greater impact on New York architecture. Even in relative failure, Parish and his architect helped shape the physical environment of the region.

Union College

Chapter 11

In January of 1813, after three months in the North Country, Ramée set out to return to Philadelphia with David Parish. The journey across northern New York State – from Ogdensburg south through the forests to Utica, then following the Mohawk River east to Albany – was difficult at any time of year, but in midwinter it was an ordeal. Travelers had to pass through some of the coldest and snowiest country in the United States, largely by sleigh.[1]

A principal stop for travelers along the Mohawk was the old Dutch town of Schenectady, the site of Union College, one of the few institutions of higher education in America at that time. Parish, who always sought out the most distinguished citizens of the places he visited, was no doubt already acquainted with Eliphalet Nott, the energetic young president of Union College, and he probably knew that Nott was planning a physical expansion of the college. Looking for extra work for Ramée, Parish introduced the architect to the college president. In the middle of January, Parish noted in a letter he wrote from nearby Albany, "I have left Mr. Ramée at Schenectady where he will be charged with the building of a new college and laying out seventy acres of land in pleasure grounds."[2]

That January Ramée spent only a few days in Schenectady, before proceeding to Philadelphia.[3] He returned to Union College a few months later, and possibly again in 1814, but he did most of the designing of the college in Philadelphia.[4] Parish kept in contact with President Nott and transmitted messages from the architect; in one letter to Nott he wrote, "It gives me much pleasure to hear that the acquaintance you made with my friend Mr. Ramée has fully justified the opinion I . . . entertain of his taste and talents."[5]

Construction of two of the college buildings proceeded quickly and they were ready for occupancy in 1814. But it seems that Ramée continued to draw plans for the school, and he was paid his commission fee of $1,500 in three installments: in June 1813, March 1814, and March 1815.[6] Only a part of Ramée's sweeping plan for Union College was executed, but the entire design was well publicized in America. An engraving of it was made, drawings were exhibited in Philadelphia in 1814, and by the following year Parish could boast that the plan was "considered to be unrivalled in the United States."[7]

The essential elements of Ramée's plan for the college can be seen in the engraving made soon after the architect finished the design (Fig. 187).[8] On a large terrace made by leveling part of a hill outside Schenectady, buildings are arranged to form an immense courtyard, six hundred feet in width and open toward the west, overlooking the Mohawk Valley. Linking the buildings are arcades, one of which forms a semicircle at the back of the court. In the center of the space is a domed rotunda, intended as the college chapel. Surrounding the buildings are extensive landscaped grounds, in various kinds of garden and park design.

187 Union College, Schenectady. Engraving of Ramée's design, produced by J. Klein, W. Phelps, and V. Balch, c. 1818. (Schaffer Library, Union College)

The Union College design is Ramée's largest and most complex work. It is also the work best documented by drawings. In 1932, a long-forgotten portfolio of the architect's plans was discovered in an attic at the college.[9] Now preserved in the school's archives, these drawings, on thirty-four sheets of paper, range from thumbnail sketches to site plans and detailed working drawings of individual buildings. Although comprising only some of the drawings that Ramée must have presented to President Nott, this collection gives us a unique view of Ramée's working process and allows us to reconstruct the evolution of the design.

In American architecture, Ramée's Union College plan is important for introducing a new type of planning, involving many buildings related in complex ways to each other and to the surrounding landscape. It is also a milestone in the history of the American college campus. The most ambitious and comprehensive plan for a campus up to that time, the Union design became a model for collegiate planning.

This design reflects not only Ramée's architectural principles but President Nott's ideal vision for his school. Union College was founded in 1795 and embodied the liberal ideals of American education following the Revolution.[10] It was nonsectarian; it made efforts to modernize the restrictive classical curriculum, for example by offering French as an elective alternative to Greek; and it considered itself more democratic than its rival Columbia College in New York City. In 1804, after three short-term presidents had come and gone, the college hired Eliphalet Nott, an eloquent young preacher who was to remain as president for sixty-two years, the longest tenure in American college history (Fig. 188). Nott brought to the job great optimism, energy, and a combination of religious fervor and patriotism that led him to believe that America was to be the "new Zion."[11]

Nott continued Union College's policy of curricular innovation and liberalized the rules governing student behavior. But he also strengthened the school's collegiate character by instituting a plan to create a familylike community – a kind of Utopian microcosm of Nott's ideal society. Announced by the president when he took office, this plan specified that students were to be "separated from the great world," that each class was to constitute "the family of the officer who instructs them," that the students and the president, faculty, and their families were to "lodge in college and board in commons," and that emphasis would be on "the decorum, ceremony, and politeness of refined domestic life."[12] Over the years, Nott became famous for putting this familial policy into practice himself, acting as a friendly father figure to his students, in contrast to the traditional, stern college authority.

When Nott assumed the presidency in 1804, Union College had just erected a large new building in the town of Schenectady. But Nott's popularity soon swelled the student ranks (enrollments were surpassed only by those of Harvard and Yale) and additional quarters were needed. Nott decided that the college should have a new, spacious location outside town, appropriate to his vision of an ideal institution separated from the everyday world. In 1806, he began acquiring a large tract of land on a hill overlooking the Mohawk Valley. The site was described by an early graduate of the college:

188 Eliphalet Nott, engraving by Asher B. Durand, after portrait by Ezra Ames, 1820. (Schaffer Library, Union College)

> On the eastern border of the city the fields rise by a gentle slope to a plain of moderate elevation and of easy access. Near the upper edge of this slope the construction of a terrace a few feet high would afford a level campus of ample space, and a site for buildings that would overlook the valley, the river, and the neighboring city, while northward glimpses of mountains blue from distance, and southwestward ranges of hills dividing the waters of the Mohawk and Susquehanna Rivers, would present a panorama of peculiar loveliness. A gently murmuring brook issuing from dense woodlands flowed across the grounds just north of the proposed site, and in the rear alternating fields and groves extended several miles eastward to the Hudson.[13]

In 1812, foundations were laid for buildings on this site.[14] But the intended structures were not completed; at this point Ramée entered the picture, was hired by President Nott, and produced new plans for the school.

Why did Nott choose the French architect to plan his college? It was not a very practical choice in some respects. The architect's lack of English surely impeded communication about the project; and, living in Philadelphia, Ramée could only occasionally visit the college during the design process and for supervision during construction. Although talented architects were rare in America, Nott could have found some closer to home – notably Philip Hooker of Albany, who probably had designed the previous Union College building.[15] Perhaps Nott was persuaded by Parish that Ramée was simply the best architect available in America. Perhaps he felt that only a European artist could create a plan grand enough to be worthy of his own lofty vision of his college.

It is also possible that Nott saw qualities in Ramée's previous work (of which the architect probably showed him drawings) that he found appropriate to his educational ideals. Certain French Enlightenment ideals had influenced Union College in its early years, as reflected in the French motto on the college seal, proclaiming universal brotherhood through wisdom ("*Sous les lois de Minerve nous devenons tous frères*").[16] Although hardly an Enlightenment radical, Nott had some liberal ideas. He was a devoted enthusiast of science, which he introduced into the college curriculum to an unprecedented degree, and he was fascinated with technology. (He later became a successful inventor of cast-iron stoves, perhaps inspired by Ramée's brick "Russian" stoves which had aroused so much enthusiasm in Ogdensburg.)[17] Typical of his age, Nott saw astronomy and other sciences as explorations into aspects of divine creation. Nott's ideas about architecture are not recorded, but it is likely that he was attracted to simple geometric forms, and thus to Ramée's work, as another reflection of his ideal of a perfectly ordered cosmos.

The most popular plan for American campuses at this time was the Yale model: a straight row of buildings, in which dormitories alternated with a chapel and classroom structures, the row often facing a village green or set on the crest of a hill.[18] There is evidence that when Eliphalet Nott began planning his new college on the hill outside Schenectady, this was the pattern he intended to create: an alignment of buildings, looking west over the town and the Mohawk Valley. The college treasurer's records reveal that in 1812 foundations were built for "new college edifices" on the hill, and that one of these buildings was already called South College.[19] (At this time, American schools often used the word "college" to designate an individual building, especially a dormitory.)

After Ramée produced the new college plan, the first two buildings to be constructed were, in fact, South College and North College: two residence halls, at opposite ends of the line that a row of buildings would have followed. It seems, therefore, that the site of these two buildings was fixed when Ramée appeared on the scene. Since their foundations were already laid, Nott probably told the architect that they had to be incorporated into the new plan, for the sake of economy. This conclusion is supported by the fact that in all of

Ramée's drawings for the college, in which he explores different arrangements of the many proposed buildings, the positions of North and South Colleges are the only ones that remain fixed (see Fig. 196). Further evidence is found in a reminiscence made by Nott in his old age. In 1861, the college treasurer noted in his diary:

> [Nott recalled] the building of the college in 1812 – said they commenced building upon a horrible plan made by some one, David Burt perhaps [a local builder], and had progressed some ways when Remay [sic] was called to make the present plan, which cost 1500 Dollars, very dear at that. The foundations and walls already built had to be adapted to the new plan.[20]

In his design, Ramée therefore had to incorporate existing foundations that determined the location of two buildings. He also had to satisfy Nott's strong ideas about what the college should be. Ramée's surviving drawings reveal that the design process was complex and included at least one radical change in the basic concept of the plan. Reconstructing Ramée's design for Union College involves a variety of evidence: his surviving drawings, other representations of the design, written documents, and the buildings that were actually executed.

Most important is the portfolio of drawings found at the college in 1932. When discovered, they were accompanied by a list written in 1856 by Jonathan Pearson, a professor and the college treasurer at that time; it is inscribed "List of Plans drawn by Mr. Remay [sic] for Union College Buildings and Grounds."[21] Forty-three drawings are numbered and described on the list, but several of them (mostly drawings of the central rotunda) were missing from the portfolio when it was found. The surviving drawings are on thirty-four sheets of paper, seven of which have drawings on their backs as well. The sheets range in size from nine by eleven inches to twenty-three by thirty-four inches, and there is a great range of types of drawings on them – from small freehand sketches in pencil (mostly on the backs of sheets or in the margins around the principal drawings), to drafted plans, elevations, and section drawings in ink and watercolor.

The drawings include site plans, showing all the buildings; landscape designs; working drawings of individual buildings, showing their structural details (such as the wood framing of roofs); profiles of mouldings and column capitals, designs for doors, and even full-scale drawings of odd-shaped bricks that were to be manufactured specially. These drawings constitute a remarkable record for an American architectural design of this period. Nevertheless, they represent only a small portion of the drawings that Ramée must have produced during the year or more that he worked on the Union College design, and they are frustrating in their incompleteness. Many buildings are not represented at all, except in the site plans, and it is not clear how some of them relate to the overall scheme.

Most of the sheets have identifying legends or other kinds of writing on them. Except for a few notations that probably were added by the college treasurer in the 1850s, the writing is clearly original to the drawings. At least two styles of handwriting can be distinguished. One is recognizably the hand of Ramée which we know from his surviving correspondence and other documents: a cursive, informal hand with distinctive forms of certain capital letters. In the Union drawings, this hand is seen in several marginal notations in pencil, mostly written in French, and in isolated identifying words, some in English, some in a hybrid French-English ("Chapell," "Galery"). In contrast, the main inscriptions, centered on the sheets and identifying the drawings ("Second Story of the President's House," and so forth), are in more formal script. This second script might suggest that Ramée was aided by someone in producing these drawings, but it is more likely that the architect used different styles of handwriting, the more formal for the principal inscriptions.[22]

Ramée probably executed most of these drawings in Philadelphia and sent them to President Nott, receiving instructions from Nott and his subordinates at the college. In March of 1813, David Parish wrote to Nott that Ramée "is now occupied making plans for the Central Building, as also a sketch of his whole plan including the disposition of all the buildings, and of the grounds." Six months later, Parish reported to Nott that "Mr. Ramée has promised his attention to Professor McAuley's letter – the plans required of him will be forwarded shortly."[23] But some of the surviving drawings are too sketchy or exploratory to have been submitted by the architect to his client, so they probably were executed during Ramée's working visit to Schenectady in the summer of 1813, or on a later visit.[24]

Thirteen of Ramée's drawings form a puzzling group (Figs. 189–91).[25] Inscribed simply "Union College," they are floor plans, elevations, and section drawings of a large building that does not appear on any of Ramée's site plans of the entire campus. In fact, the building is incompatible with these plans; its symmetrical and imposing form shows that it was meant to be at the center of the campus, but there is no place for such a structure in the site plans. Moreover, the building was to contain practically all the collegiate functions except the dormitories (which were always intended for North and South colleges). In the central part of the building, there is a library on the ground floor and a large chapel above; in one of the side wings are several classrooms, extra library space, and a "Society Room"; in the other wing is a private residence that was probably to be the president's house.

These facts suggest that this large building was part of a plan for the campus that was very different from, and predated, the final design – a plan with only one main, central building and the dormitories. That it was earlier than the other plans is confirmed by the fact that two of the floor plans of the building are found, in fragmentary form, on the backs of two sheets of drawings; Ramée thus recycled these plans by cutting them to form sheets of different shapes, for making new drawings.[26] This large structure is probably the building Parish referred to in his letter of March 1813, when he reported to Nott that Ramée was "making plans for the Central Building."

It appears, therefore, that Ramée's first plan for Union College consisted

189 Central Building for Union College, front elevation. Ink and wash drawing, 56 × 85 cm. Sheet no. 6. (Schaffer Library, Union College)

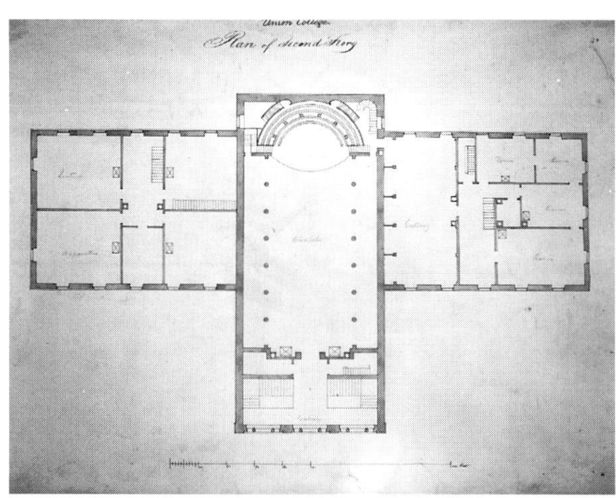

190 Central Building, plan of second floor, with chapel at center. Ink and watercolor drawing, 44 × 59 cm. Sheet no. 34. (Schaffer Library, Union College)

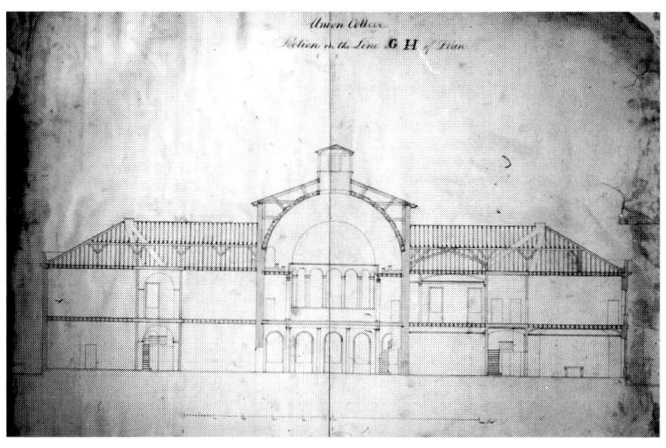

191 Central Building, longitudinal section, with chapel at center. Ink and watercolor drawing, 59 × 85 cm. Sheet no. 3. (Schaffer Library, Union College)

of this "Central Building" and two or more dormitories to the sides. Ramée planned to connect these structures by arcaded passageways, for the ends of two arcades can be seen at the edges of the elevation drawing of the Central Building (Fig. 189). Was this building to be lined up with the dormitories, or set back? Positioned in a straight line, the structures would have followed the tradition of the Yale Row, which was probably the kind of plan Nott originally conceived. But Ramée no doubt would have preferred a more dynamic arrangement, perhaps with the Central Building set behind the line of dormitories and the connecting arcades forming quarter-circles (Fig. 192) – a pattern similar to the rear portion of the final design for the college.

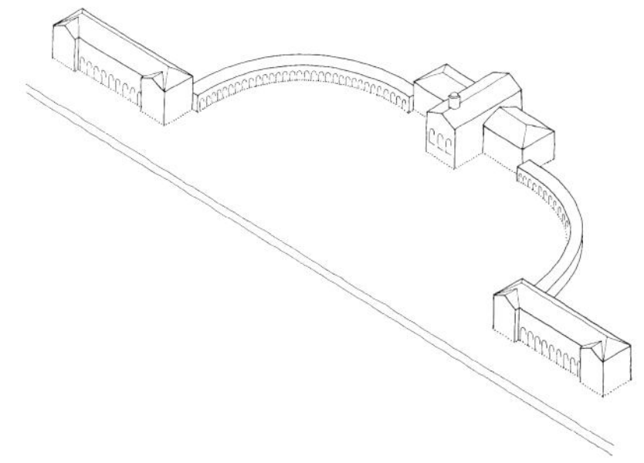

192 Hypothetical reconstruction of Ramée's first plan for Union College, with Central Building connected by arcades to North and South Colleges. (Author)

The design of the Central Building itself is puzzling, in that some of its features are not very typical of Ramée's work, while others definitely are. The main façade of the building is rather conservative in style, with a rusticated lower storey and Ionic pilasters on the projecting central section, framing "Palladian" windows; it is more in the manner of eighteenth-century English architecture than Ramée's radical neoclassicism.[27] One might suspect that this design was the work of another architect, except that Ramée's distinctive handwriting appears on the plans, and some parts of the design are fully typical of him. For example, the main interior space, the chapel, is dominated by simple circular forms: a barrel-vaulted ceiling and a half-domed niche behind the altar, supported on a series of arches. The design is reminiscent of ones Ramée knew from his period in Paris, such as Jacques Cellerier's concert hall at the Hôtel Laval-Montmorency, of 1786 (see Fig. 18). Echoing this geometry, the main wall of the rear of the building has a pattern of large recessed arches, the same motif that was to dominate Ramée's final design for the Union College buildings. One can only speculate on the cause of this building's stylistic discrepancies. Perhaps Ramée was constrained by certain requirements made by President Nott, for example that the main façade of the building adhere in style to an earlier design made by someone else.

In any case, when Ramée returned to Schenectady in May 1813 he no doubt presented his plans for the Central Building to Nott. Something, at this point, led to a rethinking of the entire design and a decision to make a more ambitious plan, unprecedented in American architecture. Perhaps Nott realized that one central building could not contain all the functions he envisioned for the college. This was the period of Nott's greatest optimism about the future of his institution. He was successfully lobbying the New York State Legislature for authority to raise large sums of money through public lotteries; he was planning additional purchases of land in order to enlarge the college site; and he thought he could plan on a grand scale, which later was to prove unrealistic.[28]

Ramée no doubt encouraged Nott's optimism. All architects naturally have a personal interest in talking their clients into more grandiose plans, which will keep them working longer and produce a larger commission fee. But in this case, Ramée had an esthetic motive as well. Increasing the number of buildings in the campus plan would allow him greater potential for the creation of architectural and spatial effects. It presented, in fact, an opportunity

193 Site plan for Union College. Pencil and watercolor drawing, 46 × 56 cm. Sheet no. 25 verso. (Schaffer Library, Union College)

that Ramée had never before had, to explore arrangements of many buildings and spaces – the types of compositions favored by French architects of the period.

In his new plan for the college, Ramée in effect disassembled the previous Central Building, turning its component parts into separate buildings. The chapel became a rotunda and remained at the center of the campus. The classrooms, president's residence, and other functions became separate structures. And additional dormitory or classroom space was provided in the arcaded links between the buildings.

Four of the sheets of drawings found in 1932 show Ramée's exploration of various ways these new buildings could be related to one another. In all, there are at least eight site-plan variations shown on these sheets (Figs. 193–6).[29] In addition is the lithographic plan of the college that Ramée later published in *Parcs et jardins* (Fig. 197), as well as the virtually identical ink-drawn plan that was discovered by a Union College alumnus in a Paris print

194 Site plan for Union College. Ink and watercolor drawing, 46 × 28 cm. Sheet no. 27. (Schaffer Library, Union College)

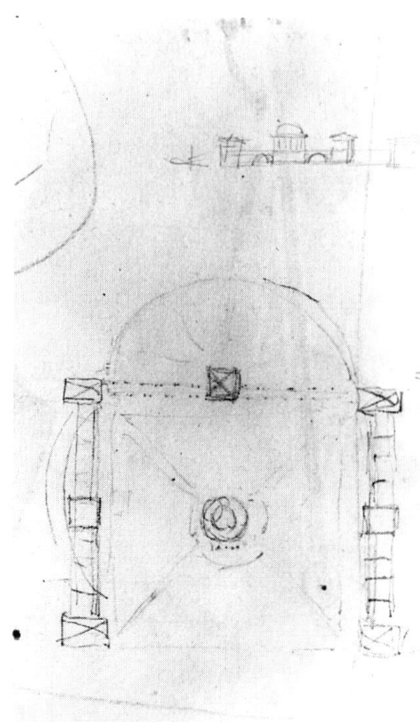

195 Thumbnail site plan, drawn in the margin of one of Ramée's sheets. Detail of sheet no. 22 verso. (Schaffer Library, Union College)

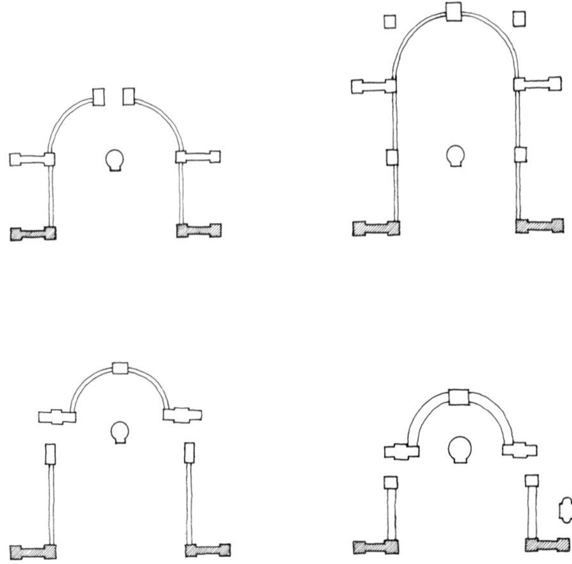

196 Four of Ramée's site plans for Union College, redrawn to the same scale. The shaded buildings in each plan are North and South Colleges. (Author)

shop in 1890 (see Fig. 2).[30] This published plan corresponds closely to engraved and painted views of the design commissioned by Nott (to be examined later), so it probably represents the final site plan that Ramée presented to Nott. The other site plans fall into a sequence that leads logically to this final plan.[31]

All the plans show North and South Colleges in their fixed positions, and all have a circular building as the central focus of the composition. The plans that appear to be the earliest (e.g., Fig. 196, plan at upper left) are somewhat similar in pattern to the original Central Building plan, as if that original plan had been doubled, in a sense, to produce twice as many buildings.[32] This then developed into a plan (represented by three or four of the drawings) showing a large square courtyard with the rotunda at its center, and at its eastern end a large semicircle with a building at its center (e.g., Fig. 193).[33] The next step was to shift two of the large buildings toward the center of the plan, so they would not be hidden behind North and South Colleges and would play a more effective role in the composition, and to move the rotunda toward the back of the courtyard. The changes are found in the most detailed of these drawings: a site plan showing landscaping as well as buildings, carefully drawn in ink and watercolor (and with a last-minute revision on an overlay at the center of the plan). This drawing is clearly intended for presentation to the client (Fig. 194 and color plate 15).[34]

One senses in Ramée's varied site plans – especially in the quickly sketched thumbnail plans drawn in the margins of sheets (Fig. 195) – the architect's delight in exploring the endless possibilities of arranging many buildings and in working on a grand scale. This was the only commission Ramée ever received, as far as we know, that allowed him to conceive a large complex of buildings, planning their overall layout as well as their individual forms, and he clearly wanted to take advantage of the opportunity to find the most successful composition. Indeed, it was perhaps the first group composi-

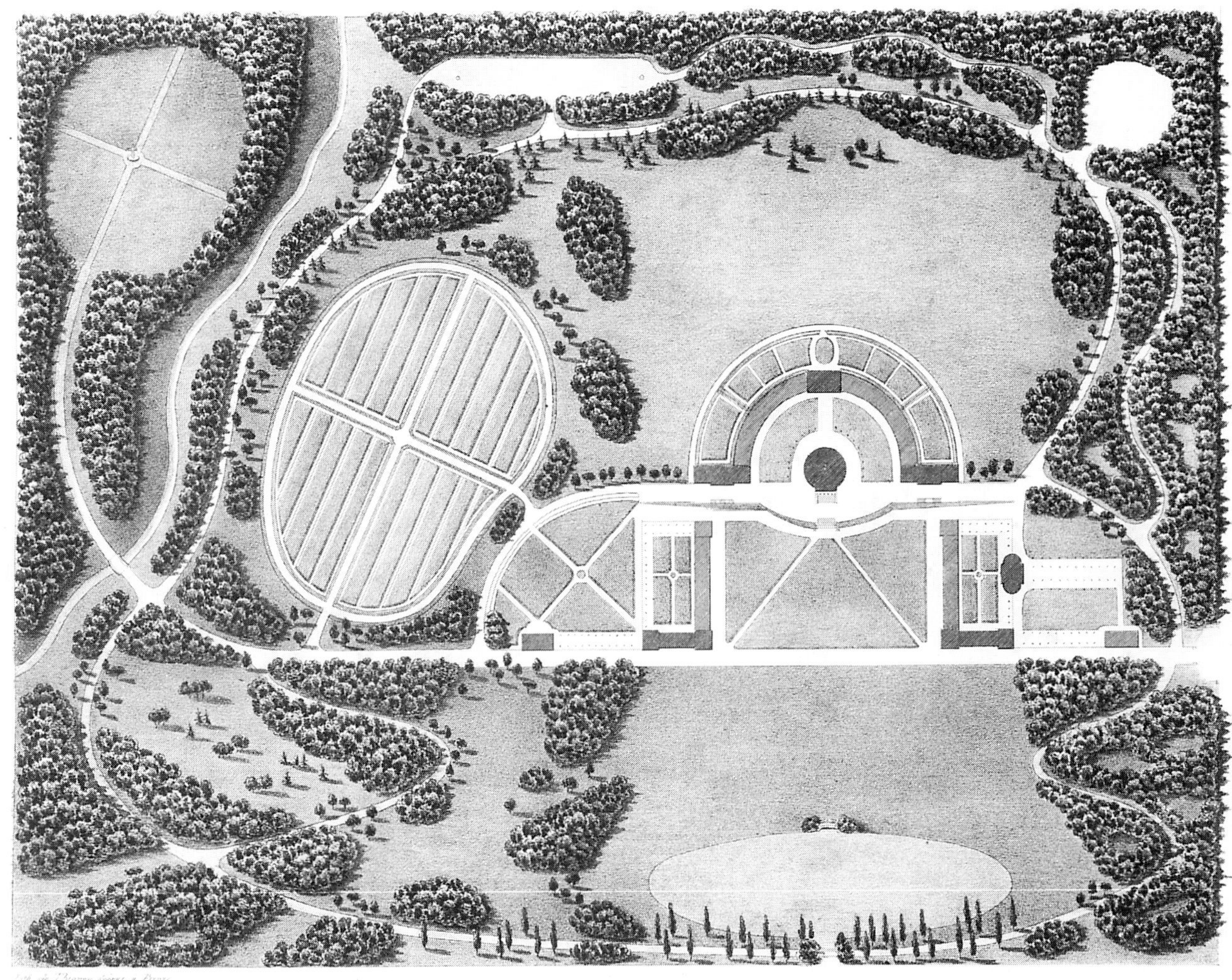

197 Union College. Plan in Ramée's *Parcs et jardins*, pl. 13. (Schaffer Library, Union College)

tion of this type in the United States. Even in Europe, few architects had a chance to build on this scale, in an open environment that allowed a free hand in composing the entire ensemble.

There was a tradition for this kind of plan, however, in the competitions of the French Academy of Architecture. The Academy – reorganized by Napoleon as the architecture section of the École des Beaux Arts – had created a system of design for large groups of monumental buildings in ideal and unrestricted sites. Even if Ramée did not attend the Academy, he was thoroughly familiar with its methods. It is unlikely that while in America he had access to engravings of competition designs; so in designing Union College, he must have drawn on his own knowledge and memories of the academic tradition. His familiarity with this tradition is revealed by a comparison of his Union College site plans – especially two or three of the earlier ones – with the design by an Academy student named Vien for a large hospital, which won one of the Academy competitions in 1787 (Fig. 198).[35] In both cases, a large courtyard, open at the front, is bounded at the sides by ranks of identical and parallel buildings (four, in Ramée's plan, ten in Vien's), closed at the end by a

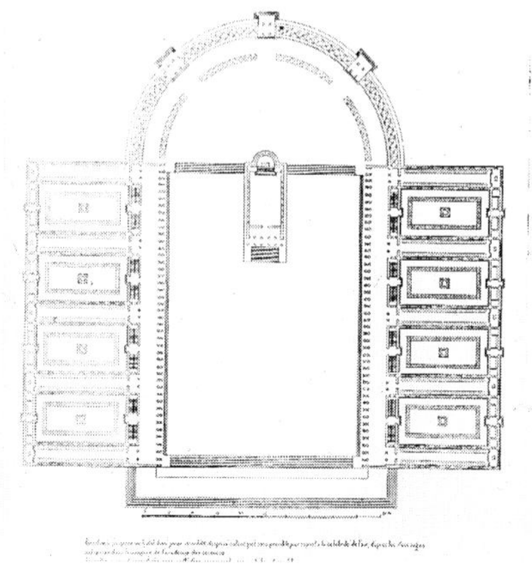

198 Plan of hospital by Vien, for Academy of Architecture competition, 1787, as published in *Collection des prix [de l'] Académie d'architecture* (Paris, c. 1788), pl. 46 (detail). (Collection Centre Canadien d'Architecture/Canadian Centre for Architecture, Montréal)

semicircular arc of buildings or colonnades and having a temple-form chapel in the center of the space.

Vien's plan is just one of many academic designs of the period that are similar, in one way or another, to Ramée's plans for Union College. Ramée probably did not have any particular design in mind as a source; he was simply applying principles of planning he had learned in Paris in the 1780s. Some of these principles represented a new esthetic, which Ramée was perhaps the first architect to employ on a large scale in America. Designs of the period were often composed of identical, repeated parts, creating a regularity very different from the interwoven complexity of Baroque design. Each component of a design tended to have an independent character, though being part of a unified whole. The Union College commission was perfectly suited to this new esthetic. The site was extensive and unencumbered, encouraging the creation of large spaces between buildings. And the collegiate program, whose main elements were identical dormitories and classrooms, was conducive to a pattern of repetition and regularity. Moreover, the wooded site of Union College allowed Ramée to explore another principle: the integration of architecture into natural landscape.

In all these ways, Ramée had a rare opportunity to design on a visionary scale, somewhat in the spirit of the fantastic designs of Ledoux and Boullée or of some of the extravagant Academy designs. That Ramée was caught up in this spirit is revealed by the fact that some of his sketches for Union College show him thinking on a scale too grand even for the broad hilltop site above Schenectady. One quickly penciled sketch, for instance, reveals the architect dreaming of a range of buildings that could never be: buildings connected by arcades that extend about 1200 feet, beyond the limits even of Nott's ambitions (Fig. 199).[36]

In his final plans for the campus, Ramée devised clever means of increasing the impression, if not the reality, of grandeur. For example, the buildings at the rear of the plan were to be on a terrace several feet higher than the rest of the courtyard, following the terrain of the hill, which rose to the east. This change in levels increased the effectiveness of the design as it would be seen from the west: framed by North and South colleges, the great courtyard was on a leveled terrace in the hill, with another terrace at its rear where a second pair of buildings framed the semicircular arcade and the rotunda. The whole composition had a telescopic shape, with spaces that progressively narrowed as they mounted the hill, heightening the sense of perspective depth.

199 Pencil sketch of long arcade, drawn in the margin of one of Ramée's site plans. Detail of sheet no. 25 verso. (Schaffer Library, Union College)

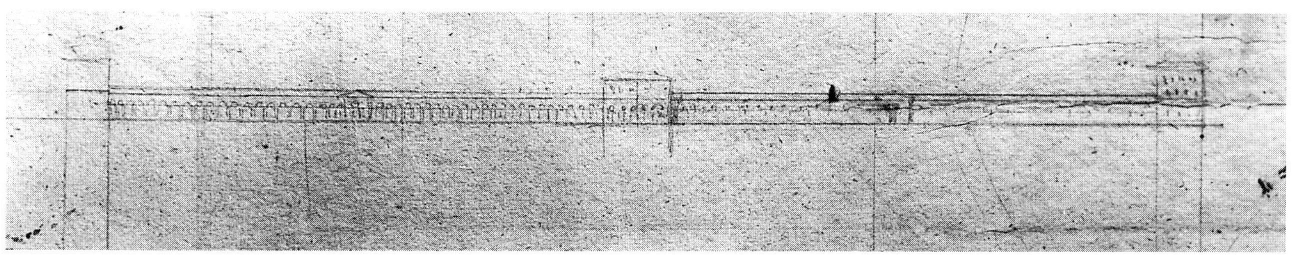

200 Painting of Ramée's design for Union College, by William C. Givens. (Union College)

The Union College Buildings

As Ramée refined his design of the site plan, he was also planning its individual parts, as shown by the rough sketches of buildings that are on the same sheets as some of the site plans. But few of Ramée's completed drawings of these buildings survive. (Of the major buildings, only the President's House is shown in any detail in floor plans and elevation drawings.) To examine the individual components of Ramée's plan for the college, we must turn to additional documents, not actually from the hand of the architect.

When Ramée determined the final form of the Union College design, he must have produced perspective drawings to present to Nott and the college trustees. Perspective drawings are the best way to sell an architectural plan to a client, and Ramée was very good at making them, as seen in the exquisite rendering of his competition design for the Washington Monument in Baltimore (see color plate 18). The list of Ramée's drawings that was made by the college treasurer in the 1850s includes "a large view. . . of all the buildings and foreground."[37] This no doubt was a perspective drawing, but unfortunately it no longer exists. There are two images, however – an engraving and a painting – that are probably copies of lost perspective drawings by Ramée.

The engraving (see Fig. 187) is entitled "View of Union College. . . After the Original Plan" and inscribed with the names of J. Klein (a local Schenectady artist) and an engraver and a printer who were active in Albany around 1818.[38] The painting (Fig. 200) is signed William C. Givens, a Schenectady resident and amateur artist in the early nineteenth century.[39] Both the engraving and the painting represent Ramée's *design* for the college, not the college itself as it ever existed. The two images are similar in the general pattern of buildings they show, but their differences, especially their differing angles of perspective, reveal that they were separately conceived, that is, neither of them began as a copy of the other. It is not likely that Klein and Givens constructed these perspective views themselves. Even if they had access to Ramée's site plans and drawings of all the buildings, it would have been very difficult for them to make the perspective proportions and details correct.

Klein's engraving and Givens's painting must therefore be copies of two separate perspective drawings made by Ramée, which he probably gave to President Nott to show two versions of the design. The major differences are

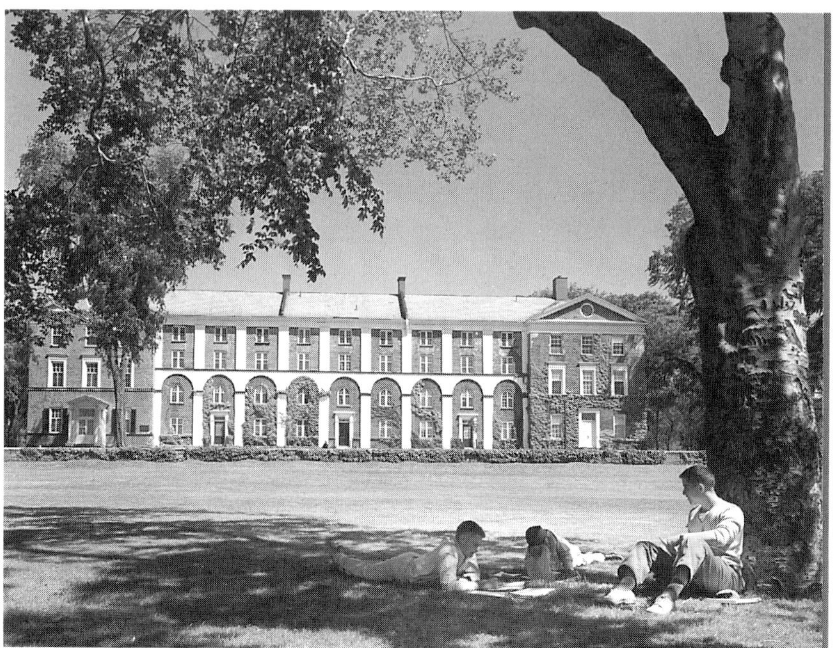

201 South College, viewed from the west. (Union College)

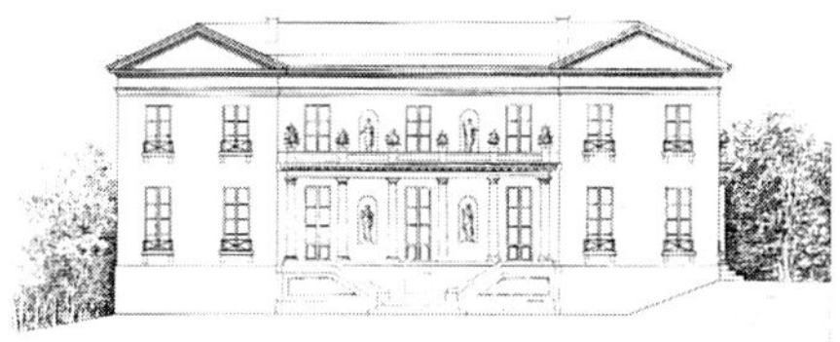

202 Hôtel Leprêtre de Neubourg, near Paris, designed by M. J. Peyre, 1760s. (Krafft and Ransonnette, *Plans . . . des plus belles maisons*, 1802, pl. 38)

203 Hosten House, Paris, designed by C. N. Ledoux, 1792. (Daniel Ramée, ed., *Architecture de C. N. Ledoux*, Paris, 1847, pl. 183. Courtesy of Princeton Architectural Press)

in the landscaping shown in the views. Givens's painting shows an irregular landscape in the foreground, similar to that of Ramée's site plans, while Klein's engraving shows a more geometric pattern of avenues and rows of trees. Another difference is the semicircle of trees around the rotunda in the painting. It is conceivable that these landscape elements were fabricated by Klein and Givens, but there is evidence that they represent different landscape designs by Ramée himself, as will be seen when this part of the design is examined.

These two perspective views show clearly the individual buildings in Ramée's design. At the western edge of the group are North and South Colleges, the first buildings constructed (they were ready for occupancy in September of 1814).[40] Although their foundations had been laid before Ramée appeared on the scene, he redesigned the two buildings, as indicated by the college treasurer's later recollection that the foundations and walls "had to be adapted to the new plan."[41] No drawings by Ramée of North or South College survive, except for a couple of faint sketches in the margins of one of the architect's site plans.[42] But the buildings themselves, as they were executed and still exist today (remarkably well-preserved and unaltered on the exterior), no doubt follow Ramée's design closely, since he was present on the site during their construction in the summer of 1813 (Fig. 201).

Each of these 200-foot-long buildings is composed of three parts: a central section of students' rooms and two end pavilions serving as residences for professors and their families (in accordance with Nott's ideal of a close-knit collegiate community).[43] Although the end pavilions project only slightly from the central part of the building, they are differentiated by their pediments or gables, and by their plain stuccoed walls, in contrast to the central section with its decorative pattern of arches and pilasters, painted white for emphasis.[44] The

204 North College (left) and North Colonnade, terminating in Philosophical Hall. (Schaffer Library, Union College)

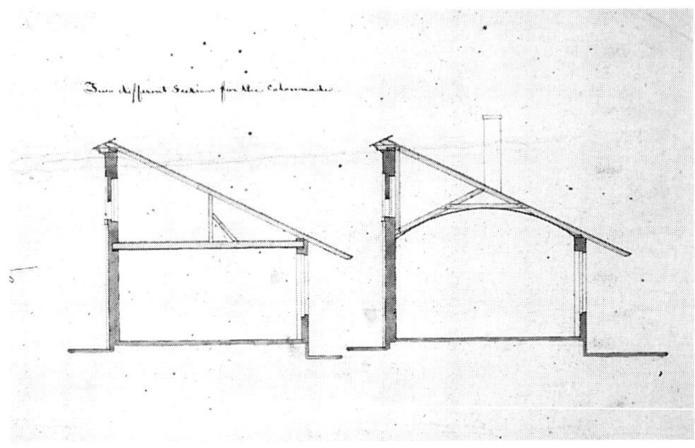

205 "Two different sections for the colonnades." Ink and watercolor drawing, 29 × 46 cm. Sheet no. 41. (Schaffer Library, Union College)

result is a kind of visual ambiguity: the structure can be seen as one building, or as two gabled pavilions connected by a series of columns and arches. In this and other ways, the design was unusual, especially in America. For one thing, it broke with the tradition of emphasizing a building's center, with any projecting or gabled pavilion placed there, not at the ends of the building. Ramée's design exemplifies a new esthetic, developed largely in late eighteenth-century France, which allowed autonomous units and multiple focus, rather than the traditional patterns of hierarchy and single focus. Various precedents for North and South Colleges can be found in French architecture of the period, such as a country house by Marie Joseph Peyre that has the same overall shape, and designs by Ledoux with similar patterns of arcaded walls (Figs. 202, 203).[45] But at Union College, Ramée produced his own interpretation of the new manner and used it to express Nott's ideal of students and faculty living together while retaining their separate identities.

206 Detail of Klein engraving, showing South College (foreground) and building behind it, which was not executed.

A year or two after North and South Colleges, the next components of the plan were built: the two narrow structures connected to the colleges and extending east from them, forming the side boundaries of the central campus (Fig. 204).[46] These structures, 250 feet long and only 25 feet wide, terminate in

207 President's House, elevation drawing. Ink and watercolor drawing, 36 × 59 cm. Sheet no. 43. (Schaffer Library, Union College)

two-storey buildings (erected in the 1850s), 80 by 50 feet in plan, with hipped roofs.[47] In Ramée's drawings, the long structures are referred to as "Colonnades," the name by which they came to be called at the college (though they might more accurately be called arcades). Their façades repeat the pattern of slightly projecting pilasters and arches found on North and South Colleges. But in the Colonnades, this motif creates a more striking effect, since there is more of it and it stands alone: a powerfully simple, nearly two-dimensional rhythm of pilasters and arches, painted white in contrast to the grey stucco of the recessed surfaces of the walls.

Ramée's drawings include several plans, sections, and elevations of the Colonnades, although not shown exactly as they were built. In particular, the drawings show the buildings longer than executed, with an additional structure at the midpoint of the colonnade in some of the drawings; the plans were no doubt reduced in scale for reasons of economy. Ramée's floor plans show rooms of various sizes in the Colonnades, evidently intended to be recitation rooms, scientific "apparatus" rooms, and other types of teaching spaces. This is how the Colonnades were utilized when finally built: the North Colonnade and its terminating building served for scientific instruction, the South Colonnade and building served as classrooms, library, and chapel.[48]

Ramée's section drawings of the Colonnades show him experimenting with structural systems for the wood-trussed roofs of the buildings, one configuration producing a vaulted ceiling inside, another a lower, flat ceiling with a small room above (Fig. 205).[49] Most of the drawings show the roof (as it was executed) with a shedlike shape: a single surface, sloping downward toward the back of the building.[50] This type of roof was so unusual, for any building other than a farm structure or other utilitarian building, that Ramée must have had a specific reason for using it here. Its main effect is to make the roof invisible from the central campus space, thereby creating the impression that the wall of the Colonnade is a thin plane. What was Ramée's motive for doing this? Perhaps he wanted to distinguish these colonnades from the buildings they connected, by making them look lighter and less substantial. Some of Ramée's early site plans suggest that he originally intended to connect the college buildings by true colonnades or arcades – that is, open passageways. In the final design, he may have wanted to preserve the impression of arcaded linkage, rather than solid architecture. Another motive may have been Ramée's general predilection for architectural forms that appear light and planelike rather than heavy and massive. In any case, the result is that the Colonnades produce an ambiguous effect: the observer knows they are solid structures with rooms inside, yet they create an impression of insubstantiality, in contrast to the larger buildings they connect.

208 Detail of Klein engraving, showing the rotunda.

To the east, in Ramée's design, beyond the Colonnades and their terminal structures, are two large buildings that were never executed (Fig. 206). Similar in overall form to North and South Colleges, they probably were meant to have the same function: student housing and professors' residences. In the architect's early site plans, in which these buildings were positioned directly behind North and South Colleges, all four buildings had identical ground plans, with the pavilions at the ends of each structure. But when Ramée shifted the two eastern buildings toward the center of the campus to make them more visible, he altered their design, creating a visual play of forms: in contrast to North and South Colleges, with pedimented pavilions at their ends and an arcaded façade in the middle, the eastern buildings had the pedimented pavilion in the center and arcaded façades at the ends. This type of transformation or rearrangement of forms is reminiscent of the work of Claude Nicolas Ledoux and the new attitude toward design: by disassembling and rearranging the parts of a building, the architect emphasizes the autonomous nature of these parts.

Connecting the two eastern buildings, in Ramée's plan, was to be another "colonnade," forming a great semicircular arc that would close the eastern end of the courtyard. Like the Colonnades attached to North and South Colleges, this one was probably intended for classrooms and other instructional spaces. At the center of this arc was to be the president's house. This building was never constructed (President Nott lived, for most of his tenure, in one of the pavilions of South College), but its design is known because several of Ramée's drawings for it exist: floor plans, elevations, and section drawings.[51] The interior plan of the house was conventional, except that some of its rooms were to be heated not by fireplaces but by stoves (probably Ramée's "Russian" stoves). The most notable drawing of the house is an elevation of its main façade, drawn in ink and watercolor, and showing several bays of the arcaded colonnades on either side (Fig. 207 and color plate 16).[52] Most interesting is the subtle relationship Ramée created between the house and the colonnade: The simple cubic form of the house suggests autonomy and independence, yet it is linked tightly to the colonnade by the continuous arcaded pattern across its façade, as well as the horizontal string-courses, one of which continues the line of the colonnade's upper edge.

This elevation drawing of the President's House is also important because it is the only surviving evidence of Ramée's intentions regarding the

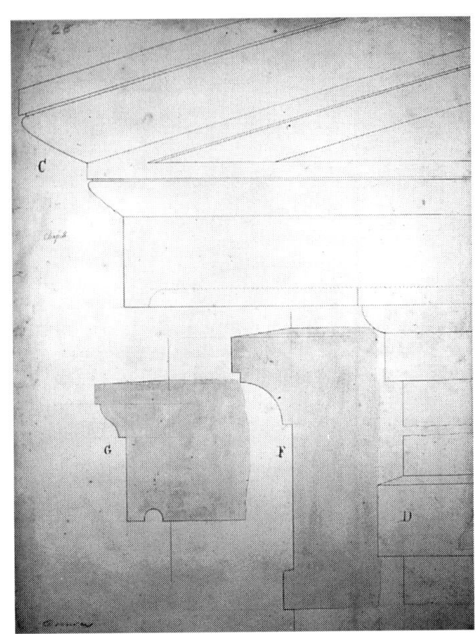

209 The Nott Memorial Building, designed by Edward T. Potter, constructed beginning in 1858. Photograph c. 1903. (Schaffer Library, Union College)

210 Drawing of cornices for the "chapell." Ink and watercolor drawing, 59 × 46 cm. Sheet no. 28. (Schaffer Library, Union College)

211 Thumbnail sketch of the rotunda, drawn in the margin of one of Ramée's sheets. Detail of sheet no. 22 verso. (Schaffer Library, Union College)

212 Detail of Givens painting, showing rotunda. (Union College)

wall surfaces of the Union buildings and their colors. It shows that Ramée planned the buildings – as they were executed – to have a rough-cast surface (a cement or stucco coating over the brick walls), and to emphasize the arcaded pattern by painting the projecting surfaces white or light tan while leaving the recessed surfaces the darker color of the natural rough-cast. This color scheme is more typical of German than French architecture of this period, and thus reflects Ramée's international background.[53]

In the center of Ramée's Union College design is its focal building: the domed rotunda, intended as the chapel (Fig. 208).[54] President Nott, the eloquent preacher for whom religion was the unifying force in education, no doubt encouraged Ramée to make this building imposing and to give it a dominant place in the campus layout. He also hoped to erect it quickly. Treasurer's records of November 1813, when North and South Colleges were still under construction, show that money was spent on "digging at chapel foundation."[55] But work on the rotunda was postponed indefinitely as more essential needs claimed available funds. The college chapel was accommodated first on an upper floor of South College, then in the South Colonnade; it was not until forty years later, near the end of Nott's presidency, that construction of the rotunda actually began. By that time, architectural fashion in America had changed so greatly that Ramée's plans were ignored and the design of the building was entrusted to another architect, Edward Tuckerman Potter.[56] Potter's extraordinary, sixteen-sided structure was one of the first manifestations in America of High Victorian architecture and also was innovative in its use of iron construction (Fig. 209). The design could hardly have been more different from Ramée's, except that both represented the most advanced architectural thinking of their respective times.

The catalogue accompanying Ramée's drawings, discovered at the college in 1932, lists five drawings of the rotunda-chapel that no longer exist.[57]

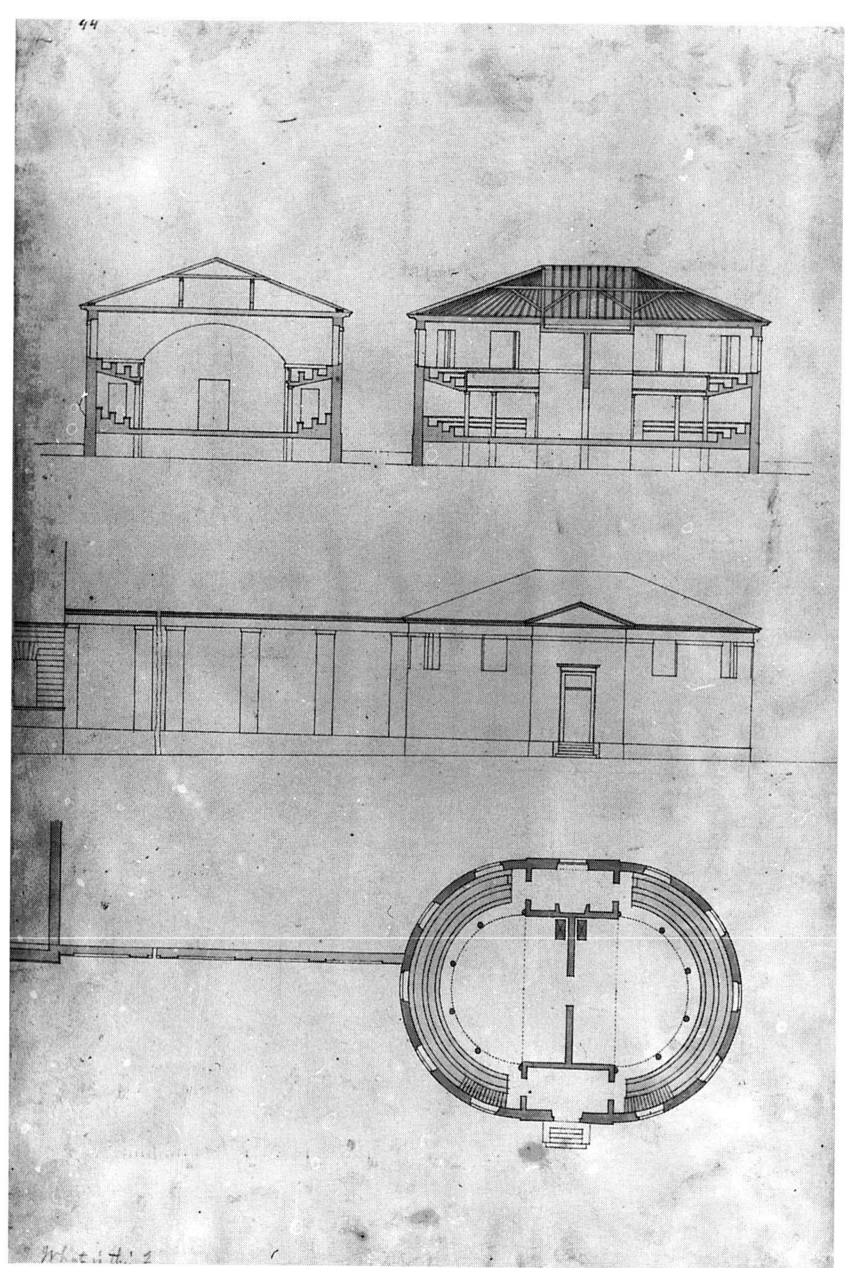

213 Sections, elevation, and plan of elliptical building containing lecture rooms. Ink and watercolor drawing, 49 × 33 cm. Sheet no. 44. (Schaffer Library, Union College)

All that survive are some working drawings of details of the building – the main doorway, column capitals, cornice mouldings (Fig. 210) – and some sketches of the entire building in the margins around other drawings.[58] These correspond closely to the representations of the rotunda in Klein's engraving and Givens' painting, which, as noted earlier, were probably copied from perspective drawings by Ramée. A small, rapidly drawn sketch shows the architect's essential conception of the building: a semicircular dome on a cylinder, with a simple pedimented portico. The building is raised on a small hill (Fig. 211). The ultimate source of this design was the Pantheon of ancient Rome. Following that model, Ramée's thumbnail sketch seems to indicate an oculus at the summit of the dome as the only source of light. Ramée surely intended to glaze this oculus (it could hardly have been left open in a Schenectady winter) and eventually he placed a cupola over it. His working drawings for the building include a profile of the cornice of this cupola, and the perspective views of Klein and Givens show this superstructure, which was to let light into the otherwise windowless chapel (Figs. 208, 212).

The portico of the rotunda was to have six columns (hexastyle, in classical parlance), supporting the pediment and standing at the top of a flight of steps framed by walls: the Roman, not the Greek, temple form. One of Ramée's working drawings shows that the columns were to be of the Doric order. A faint but carefully drawn floor plan of the chapel, in the margin next to one of Ramée's site plans, provides the only information about the interior of the building.[59] It shows a circle of sixteen columns, probably intended to support a balcony or upper floor around the periphery of the interior space. A semicircular platform or dais is indicated opposite the door; behind the platform is a wall or screen, and behind that are flights of stairs that probably led to the upper level.

Domed rotundas had been popular in many periods, but they held a special fascination for the neoclassicists of Ramée's generation, for whom the perfection of the circle was supreme. Circular chapels, temples, or memorials frequently occupied the focal position in group plans by architects of this period, some of whom were almost obsessed with the form. (Étienne Louis Boullée, for example, distilled the rotunda to its ultimate purity in his visionary design for a spherical memorial to Isaac Newton.) Ramée's Union College rotunda is a fine expression of this type of neoclassicism in its emphasis on pure geometry, stripped of nearly all ornament and other distractions.

Givens's painting shows the rotunda partially surrounded by a row of tall poplar or cypress trees (Fig. 212). One might think that this unusual feature was an invention of the painter, but there is evidence that it was a part of Ramée's plan, which he included in some of his drawings and omitted from others. At least two of Ramée's site plans show these trees, as a series of dots forming a semicircle around the back of the rotunda.[60] The notion of a building ringed by trees in this way would have seemed strange to most Americans at this time, but it was familiar to Ramée. The encircling of a monument with trees had its sources in antiquity, especially in funereal architecture; and it had a special attraction for French artists around 1800, as an expression of the romantic combination of nature and classicism.[61] The Lombardy poplar had only recently been introduced to America, and Thomas Jefferson was one of the first to employ it in a monumental setting (in 1803 he lined Washington's Pennsylvania Avenue with poplars).[62]

Two more buildings are represented in Ramée's drawings. One is called the "Steward's House," a college dining hall.[63] The floor plans show pantries and a kitchen in the basement and a large dining room and two parlors on the main floor (with several students' rooms on the upper storey). This is probably the prototype for the two boarding houses that were erected (but no longer exist) at the north and south ends of the terrace wall, which are seen at the edges of the Klein and Givens views.

More remarkable is a sheet with a plan, elevation, and section drawings of an elliptical building, divided into two semicircular rooms (Fig. 213).[64] They are clearly lecture rooms, for they have tiered banks of seats – one on the ground level, one on a balcony above it, supported on columns – with a vaulted ceiling over the space in which the lecturer would stand. This building is connected by a high wall to the corner of another structure (probably South College, since Ramée's published plan of the campus shows an elliptical building behind South College).[65] It is an ingenious design for lecture halls and was perhaps unprecedented in America. But it recalls teaching amphitheaters in France, such as Jacques Gondoin's anatomy theatre at the École de Médecine in Paris, of about 1770. It is another manifestation of Ramée's fascination with primary geometry: cubes, spheres, cylinders, and their inventive combination. This elliptical lecture hall could also be seen as a miniature echo of the geometry of Ramée's overall plan for Union College, with its rectangular central courtyard and appended semicircle.

The Campus as a Park

Almost as important as the buildings in Ramée's Union College design is the landscape around them, which can be reconstructed from several plans and views. These include two of Ramée's drawings found at the college in 1932: the ink and watercolor plan of the entire campus (see color plate 15) and another colored plan which shows the garden area directly behind the President's House (color plate 17).[66] Then there are the ink-drawn plan of the college that was discovered in Paris in 1890 and the nearly identical lithographic plan that Ramée published in his *Parcs et jardins* in the 1830s (see Figs. 2, 197). Finally are the two perspective views by Klein and Givens, which, as we have seen, were probably based on drawings Ramée presented to President Nott (see Figs. 187, 200).

A striking thing about these images is that Klein's view shows a relatively geometric landscape in the foreground, with straight avenues and rows of trees, in contrast to the irregular, naturalistic landscape in all the other plans. Was the more regular design an invention of Klein's? In fact, evidence suggests that Ramée himself devised alternate plans for the landscaping of the campus, some in the irregular "English" style and others in the more geometric "French" tradition.

In the 1850s, Jonathan Pearson (the college treasurer) described in his diary his frustration over the elderly President Nott's stubborn ideas about completing the campus plan. Pearson wrote:

> Remay who planned the buildings also laid out the grounds in true French style with broad straight avenues of eighty feet to one hundred feet in width. No child could have conceived a worse and more inharmonious plan. Here is 250 acres of land mostly covered with trees – uneven and broken – to be cut with city avenues,

contrary to all good taste and common sense, and yet up to this time no mind has been able to break out of this French prison. Fettered by such an absurdity, the "Power that be" [i.e., Nott] ordered the fences to be made – chiefly expensive stone walls – and the trees to be planted along the various avenues, and for thirty years we have labored and spent thousands to attain what in a few years more will be wholly discarded and undone.[67]

This outburst certainly implies that Ramée drew the landscape shown in Klein's engraving, but it is also puzzling. Why would Pearson accuse Ramée of excessive regularity in landscape design, when most of the architect's own drawings show a largely *irregular* layout for the campus? The most likely answer is that Pearson did not understand what had happened, namely that *Nott* had preferred a regular or geometric plan; that he had asked Ramée to draw one, which the architect did (along with his own preferred irregular plans); and that Nott subsequently considered the more geometric plan to be the final one and had it engraved by Klein. In the 1810s, irregular landscape design was still unusual in America, especially in relatively remote areas like northern New York. It was only normal for Nott to object to it and want something more familiar, with rectangular lawns and rows of trees, as at other American colleges of the period.[68] But by the 1850s, public taste in landscape had changed in America and it was normal for Pearson, being of the younger generation, to find the regular plan "inharmonious." (Pearson's antipathy was probably due also to the fact that he resented Nott's insistence on executing Ramée's architectural plan for the campus, which Pearson considered overly grand and impractical; at one point in his diary, he lamented that it was a "pity that Mr. Remay had not remained in Prussia"!)[69]

Ramée thus probably drew the more rigid landscape plan favored by Nott, but his own preference was for a largely irregular design, as seen in most of his drawings of the college. Especially interesting is his ink and watercolor plan, one of the drawings found in 1932 (color plate 15). Toward the west in this plan (that is, at the bottom of the drawing) is a great open field, from which the college was to be approached and viewed. To the north (the left side of the plan) is shown Hans Groot's Kill, the brook that runs through the college grounds. Ramée intended to divert it in order to create a small lake at the western end of the campus. (On the right, Ramée's plan shows another creek feeding the lake, perhaps a diversion of a stream that ran to the south of the campus.)[70] Serpentine roads, passing through groves of trees, are shown next to these creeks, leading up to the terrace and the college buildings. To the east, behind the college (at the top of the plan) is another large open field, bounded by denser woodland.

Interspersed through this part of the campus, however, are several areas laid out geometrically. Most of them are evidently gardens for raising vegetables and other produce, for they are divided in the manner of the traditional French *potager,* as seen in Ramée's own plans for country estates.[71] But one of the geometric parts of the Union plan – the circular area at the left edge of

214 Lithographic view of Ramée's design for Union College, drawn by D. Herron and printed by G. W. Lewis, c. 1858. (Schaffer Library, Union College)

215 View of Jackson's Garden. Photograph c. 1907. (Schaffer Library, Union College)

the drawing, with a small round building at its center – was to be an ornamental garden, whose formal design would contrast with the irregular landscape around it. The geometric parterres shown behind the President's House (at the center of the semicircular colonnade) were probably meant to be both practical and ornamental; they are shown surrounded by rows of trees, perhaps fruit trees. Other such gardens are indicated next to North and South Colleges (the "professors' gardens" mentioned in early college records) and elsewhere on the campus. Ramée thus conceived a landscape that united practical and ornamental elements, providing areas for the cultivation of produce for the college, but integrating these areas into the overall picturesque pattern by using varied geometry and transitional zones that mediate between the formal and the informal.

The plan of the college that Ramée later published shows a larger total campus area, which may account for some of the changes seen in the plan (see Fig. 197). The agricultural gardens are consolidated into one large, roughly oval area. Beyond it, on the north side of Hans Groot's Kill (shown here farther from the college buildings than it should be), is an open space secreted in the woods, with a small pavilion or gazebo at its center. Another clearing in the trees, long and elliptical, is probably a running track.

Nothing quite like Ramée's landscape plan for Union College had been seen before in the United States. The picturesque garden was still a relatively new phenomenon in America, found mainly on the estates of wealthy individuals who had seen or read of prototypes in Europe. Never, it appears, had a public institution in America been planned in an extensive park of this kind.[72] Some parallels might be drawn with Pierre Charles L'Enfant's plan for Washington, of the 1790s, with its vast Mall extending from the Capitol to the Potomac River. But this conception drew mainly from Baroque traditions of planning: the Capitol is at one end of the park, not surrounded by it, and the Mall was originally to be laid out in a geometric, not a picturesque manner. In conceiving an American institution in the midst of a carefully planned, irregular landscape, Ramée was ahead of his time, anticipating the work of Andrew Jackson Downing and Frederick Law Olmsted (a point to be examined further in the next chapter).

Considering the innovative and extensive nature of Ramée's landscape plans for the college, it is hardly surprising that they were not fully implemented. What is remarkable is that some of their essential elements were, in fact, executed. The large area to the west of the college buildings, below the terrace, was kept as an open field, just as Ramée intended. It was called the College Park and served as a pasture for grazing cattle; throughout the nineteenth century, it provided the picturesque, sylvan setting that the architect had envisioned for the college. Artists' views (and then photographs) of the school were invariably taken from the west, across this pasture. Best known among these is an oval lithographic view made in the 1850s, which shows the college buildings as they appeared in Klein's engraving, but replaces Klein's formal avenues with a more accurate portrayal of the college landscape as it actually was (Fig. 214).[73] This area was kept as open space until the mid-twentieth century, when pressure to construct college buildings there became too strong to resist.

Different in character is the large area of naturalistic parkland, called Jackson's Garden, on the north side of the campus. This garden dates from the early years of the college and has been retained largely intact to the present day. The layout of the garden, on both sides of Hans Groot's Kill, was begun shortly after the construction of North and South Colleges by Thomas Macauley, a professor who had worked with Nott and Ramée on the campus plans.[74] Starting in the 1830s, the execution of the garden was carried out by another professor, Isaac Jackson, who had a keen interest in horticulture.[75]

Comprising about twelve acres, Jackson's Garden does not reproduce Ramée's landscape plan exactly, but it follows its principles closely (Fig. 215). There is a great variety of wooded and open spaces, with paths that circulate through the groves and along the edges of more formally planted areas, and rustic bridges over the creek. It was perhaps the first public garden in America that embodied so well the principles of picturesque landscape, and it attracted much attention. The naturalist John J. Audubon praised it after a visit in 1844. An English visitor, in the same decade, wrote that it was "the only real landscape garden I have seen in the United States." And Frederick Law Olmsted is reported also to have visited Jackson's Garden.[76]

Union College and the University of Virginia

Ramée has been known to American architectural historians mainly in regard to a specific question: did his Union College design influence Thomas Jefferson's nearly contemporaneous plan for the University of Virginia? The historian Talbot Hamlin went so far as to suggest that Jefferson may have studied Ramée's rotunda plans, which were missing from the group of Union College drawings discovered in 1932. Hamlin asked, "Had Jefferson seen them? Could they possibly have been borrowed and subsequently lost? The speculation is interesting."[77] Jefferson can be cleared of this suspicion, since the drawings were still in Schenectady in the 1850s when the college treasurer catalogued them. But the question remains whether Jefferson's great campus plan was affected, directly or indirectly, by Ramée's.

The similarities are certainly striking. In both designs there is a large courtyard, bounded by buildings on three sides and open on the fourth, with a domed rotunda as the focal point of the composition (Fig. 216). Both rotundas are based on the Roman Pantheon but, unlike the Pantheon, have a hexastyle or six-columned portico. In both designs, the buildings around the periphery of the courtyard are connected by colonnades or arcades. And parts of the Union plan are similar to Jefferson's in the alternation of pedimented professors' houses with connecting blocks of student lodging. The similarities are remarkable especially as many of these elements, including the Pantheon-like rotunda, were nearly unknown in American architecture up to that time.

Jefferson drew his plan for the University of Virginia in 1817, about four years after Ramée's Union plan. But as early as 1810, Jefferson had conceived certain essentials of his design, especially the pattern of professors' houses linked by colonnaded rows of students' rooms.[78] By 1817, Jefferson's concept had evolved into a plan in which these linked houses and colonnades lined three sides of a large village green. There is no reason to believe that Ramée contributed to this evolution, even if Jefferson knew of the Union plan. But in the spring of 1817 Jefferson solicited the advice of the architects William Thornton and Benjamin Henry Latrobe. The subsequent suggestions of these architects, especially those of Latrobe, led to changes in Jefferson's plan, including the addition of the domed rotunda and a grander conception of all the buildings. It is through Latrobe that Ramée's influence was most likely transmitted.[79]

Latrobe's proposals for the University of Virginia – conveyed in sketches he sent to Jefferson in July of 1817 – included a Pantheon-like structure very similar to Ramée's at Union, and colonnades joining pedimented pavilions (Fig. 217). This pattern is especially similar to one stage of Ramée's plan, which had longer arcades than in the final design and an additional pavilion in the center of each arcade. An elevation sketch by Ramée, showing this

216 University of Virginia, engraved view by B. Tanner, 1827. (Manuscripts Division, Special Collections Department, University of Virginia Library)

217 Drawing by Benjamin Henry Latrobe, in letter to Thomas Jefferson, 24 July 1817. (Library of Congress)

218 Pencil sketch of colonnade and pavilions, drawn in the margin of one of Ramée's site plans. Detail of sheet no. 25 verso. (Schaffer Library, Union College)

arrangement, is remarkably like Latrobe's sketch, in its alternation of pavilions and colonnades (Fig. 218).[80]

Ramée exhibited drawings of his Union College design in Philadelphia in 1814, at the annual exhibit of the Pennsylvania Academy, the main forum for the exchange of artistic ideas in America at that time.[81] Latrobe, who in previous years had also exhibited at the Academy shows, was working in Pittsburgh in 1814, but even if he did not see that year's exhibit, he could have learned of Ramée's design in numerous ways. He was in Philadelphia in late 1813, just as Ramée was working on the Union plan there. And two years later, when the two architects were competing for the design of the Baltimore Exchange, Latrobe mentioned Ramée in correspondence, noting details of Ramée's work that he had learned from Maximilian Godefroy.[82] Godefroy, the French architect working in Baltimore during these years, probably knew Ramée personally, and since Godefroy and Latrobe were close friends and collaborators, Godefroy could have familiarized his friend with the work of his compatriot Ramée. Moreover, Latrobe was an acquaintance of David Parish, who may have introduced him to Ramée or shown him Ramée's designs.[83] In one way or another, Latrobe was surely aware of the Union College design, one of the major architectural projects in America at the time. When consulted by Jefferson, Latrobe naturally may have drawn, consciously or unconsciously, on Ramée's model, especially on the compelling and unprecedented notion of a domed Pantheon as the centerpiece of an American campus.[84]

The courtyard or mall, culminating in a domed structure, became a favored pattern for American campuses, especially in the late nineteenth and early twentieth centuries. The University of Virginia, not Union College, was usually the model for this pattern, since Jefferson's design was better known and had been realized, while Ramée's was only partially executed.

Nevertheless, Ramée's plan was not forgotten. Lithographic and engraved views of the design were produced well into the nineteenth century, both for commercial purposes and as ornaments on Union College diplomas and other documents.[85] Especially as many Union alumni went on to become presidents of other colleges in the nineteenth century, the image of Ramée's plan may have served as a general ideal for campus planning at many institutions. One example of the influence of Ramée's design may be Stanford University in California, whose grand plan was conceived in the 1880s by Frederick Law Olmsted and the university's founder, Leland Stanford.[86] Although different from the Union plan in many respects, the Stanford layout is similar in its formal arrangement of many buildings around a courtyard, linked by arcades. Leland Stanford was born and raised only a few miles from the Union campus; his memory of it may well have been one of the images that contributed to the shape of his own university.

The classical revival that developed in the 1890s in America led to renewed interest among architects in Ramée's design for Union College. It has been suggested, for instance, that McKim, Mead and White were inspired by it in their plan for the University Heights campus of New York University, with its centrally-placed domed building, framed by a semicircular colonnade and connecting buildings.[87] In 1911, the architectural critic Montgomery Schuyler included Union College in a survey of collegiate architecture in *The Architectural Record,* praising Ramée's plan for its logic and foresightedness.[88] A decade later, the landscape architect Richard Schermerhorn, in an article in *The American Architect,* lauded Ramée's design and stated that "the Union College buildings and grounds. . . have been a source of. . . great interest to architects."[89]

Thus the design that helped shape Jefferson's University of Virginia continued, for more than a century, to inspire planners and to serve as a model for American campus planning.

Philadelphia and Baltimore

Chapter 12

Ramée lived in Philadelphia during most of his sojourn in America. He arrived there from Europe in the summer of 1812; after visiting David Parish's North-Country lands at the end of that year, he returned to Philadelphia and spent most of his time there until he sailed back to Europe in 1816. The city directories of Philadelphia show that in 1813 Ramée lived on South Eighth Street, close to Parish's large house on Washington Square.[1] The following year, the architect is found at a nearby address on the northeast corner of Chesnut and Tenth streets. A mid-nineteenth-century view of this block of Chesnut Street shows a three-storey row house with a shop on the ground floor, probably the same building Ramée and his family had inhabited (Fig. 219).[2]

219 Engraved view of buildings on Chesnut Street, Philadelphia, 1851. Ramée and his family lived in the house at the left. (*Rae's Philadelphia Pictorial Directory*, 1851)

220 David Parish's house on Washington Square, Philadelphia. Drawing of 1868. (The Free Library of Philadelphia, Print and Picture Collection)

Although Philadelphia was surpassed in population by New York in the national census of 1810, it was still the premier city of the United States in many respects.[3] Architecturally, it was distinguished by the work of Benjamin Henry Latrobe, who had lived there around 1800 and erected buildings that introduced to America new standards of design and construction.

The careers of Latrobe and Ramée were parallel in certain ways. The two architects were the same age (both born in 1764) and both brought to America a knowledge of architectural design from several countries, as the young Latrobe had lived in Germany and England and had traveled elsewhere in Europe. Some of Latrobe's and Ramée's designs are remarkably similar, especially those relying on simple geometric forms and flat surfaces, broken only by arched recesses. There are differences, however, between their styles. Latrobe never rejected, as Ramée largely did, the traditional use of the classical orders and of porticoes. And some of Ramée's favorite forms were not in Latrobe's repertoire, such as the shallow segmented arch (as seen in the porches of Calverton and David Parish's buildings in Parishville), not to mention the more eccentric forms of Ramée's later designs.

In these respects, Ramée was less conventional than Latrobe. But Ramée surely recognized the great quality and integrity of his main rival's works. He could see important examples of these works in Philadelphia: public buildings such as the Bank of Pennsylvania (with the first large masonry-vaulted space in the United States) and the Center Square Water Works (showing Latrobe's interest in Ledoux), as well as domestic buildings such as the Burd House, just a block from Ramée's residence on Chesnut Street. Even Parish's house on Washington Square was partly the work of Latrobe (Fig. 220).[4] By the time Ramée came to Philadelphia, Latrobe had moved to Washington and then to Pittsburgh, but his influence still dominated the city, both through his own work and through younger architects such as Robert Mills.

Although construction in Philadelphia was depressed by the War of 1812, Parish apparently found clients for Ramée there, as he had done in New

221 Design by Ramée for Washington Monument, Baltimore. Ink and watercolor drawing, 49 × 72 cm. Inscribed "J. Ramée, 1813." (The Peale Museum, Baltimore City Life Museums)

York State. Boulliot's article on Ramée, as noted earlier, states that while living in Philadelphia the architect "embellished that city and its environs with several large and beautiful houses."[5] The identity of these buildings remains a mystery. All that is known of the architect's activity in Philadelphia is that he produced there his designs for Union College and other American works, and that he entered into a business partnership for the manufacture of wallpaper (examined later in this chapter). More is known about Ramée's work in Baltimore than in Philadelphia.

The Washington Monument in Baltimore

In 1813, Ramée entered a design in the competition for the first great American civic memorial, the Washington Monument in Baltimore. Ramée's perspective drawing of his entry survives and is extraordinary not only for the design of the monument but for the drawing itself: a beautifully executed watercolor rendering, one of the finest examples of the architect's drawing skill (Fig. 221 and color plate 18).

Following the Revolution, Baltimore grew and prospered, mainly through exploitation of the Susquehanna Valley, whose produce flowed to the city's mills and wharves. For a while, Baltimore's exports even exceeded those of Philadelphia, and the two seaports were economic and cultural rivals.[6] The

222 Design by Maximilian Godefroy for Washington Monument, Baltimore. (The Peale Museum, Baltimore City Life Museums)

burgeoning civic ambitions of Baltimore help explain why it was this city that built the first important monument to George Washington, thus beginning the rich tradition of memorial architecture in the United States.

In 1810, the Maryland Legislature authorized a board of Baltimore citizens to raise $100,000 by means of lotteries, for the erection of the monument to be located on the site of the old Court House (though it was eventually built on Mount Vernon Place).[7] For the design of the monument, the board turned first to Maximilian Godefroy, the French architect who had come to America in 1805, settled in Baltimore and designed St. Mary's Chapel there, the first important Gothic Revival building in the country.[8] (Despite his considerable architectural talent, Godefroy received few commissions in America and eventually, like Ramée, returned to Europe.) In 1810 Godefroy produced several designs for the Washington Monument, one of which survives (Fig. 222).[9] But the board delayed making a decision, and in March of 1813 it announced a public competition for the design of the monument. The announcement of this event, published in newspapers, included an oddly contradictory statement, inviting Europeans to enter the competition but hinting that Americans would be given preference:

> The board of managers of the Washington Monument Lottery offer a premium of Five Hundred Dollars, for the best design, model, or plan for a Monument to the memory of General Washington. . . accompanied by an estimate of the cost of its execution not exceeding one hundred thousand dollars. . . . The Monument, whether sculptural, architectural, or both, is intended to be placed in the centre of a square 300 feet long and 140 feet wide, crossed in its length by a principal street. The whole space appropriated for it is about 65 feet square.
>
> The sculptors, architects, and other artists of Europe are invited to enter. . . but it is hoped that the American artists will evince by their productions, that there will be no occasion to resort to any other country for a monument to the memory of their illustrious fellow-citizen.[10]

It is not known whether the competition board considered European architects living in America to be Europeans, Americans, or something in between. But the nationalistic prejudice was obvious and must have been disheartening to Godefroy and Ramée, who nonetheless both entered the competition. Godefroy apparently resubmitted his 1810 design that still survives. Besides this drawing and Ramée's, only two entries are known: a design for an obelisk, probably by the gentleman-architect Nicholas Rogers; and Robert Mills's design for a massive, 140-foot-tall column, rising from an elaborate base and bearing a statue of Washington in a victory chariot (Fig. 223).[11]

223 Design by Robert Mills for Washington Monument, Baltimore. (Maryland Historical Society, Baltimore)

Mills's design was clearly too ambitious to be constructed within the board's stated budget of $100,000. But Mills was awarded the prize and his design was eventually executed, in a simplified form. Like many architectural juries, the board was probably overwhelmed by the grandeur of the entry despite its excessive cost. Perhaps they also were swayed by the fact that Mills was 100% American – by birth, education, and citizenship – as Mills had blatantly emphasized in a written statement accompanying his entry.[12]

The designs submitted by Godefroy and Ramée are remarkably similar in overall shape, a fact that the competition board may have interpreted as indicating a particularly French type of design. But a comparison of the two entries reveals differences that help define the nature of Ramée's work and his ideas about monumental urban planning.

Godefroy's and Ramée's designs are both in the form of a triumphal arch with a single arched opening. Both incorporate a statue of Washington – under the arch, in Ramée's design; in front of the arch, in Godefroy's.[13] Both arches, with their plain surfaces and absence of traditional orders, reflect in a general way the radical French neoclassicism of Ledoux and others. And both arches are approached by flights of steps, framed by cubic blocks. We might suspect, in fact, that one of the two designs was inspired by the other. But that seems to be impossible, for Godefroy's design apparently dates from 1810 (judging by its inscription), before Ramée was even in America; and all the significant elements of Ramée's design can be found in his earlier work in Europe. Indeed, one of the remarkable things about Ramée's arch is the way it integrates diverse elements from his earlier designs.

Ramée's drawing, preserved at the Peale Museum in Baltimore, is large (nearly 20 by 28 in.) and exquisitely rendered in ink and watercolor.[14] Inscribed "J. RAMÉE 1813," it was probably executed in late 1813, to meet the competition deadline of 1 January 1814. Ramée's entry must have consisted of several drawings, including at least a ground plan and two elevation drawings. The surviving perspective drawing would have been the "presentation" rendering, meant to show the nonprofessional competition board what the executed arch would look like and how it would relate to its environment.

Perspective drawings were a relatively new phenomenon in architectural practice at this time. Especially in America, most architects still relied on plans and elevations. (Godefroy's and Mills's Washington Monument renderings were both elevations, not perspective drawings.) Latrobe was perhaps the first in America to make broad use of architectural perspectives, but Ramée's Washington Monument drawing introduced a new standard of perspective rendering to American architecture.

Ramée's proposed monument can be compared to his design of 1793 for an arch to commemorate the Austrian recovery of Louvain (color plate 4). Both have plain surfaces which emphasize the geometry of the forms, but the Baltimore arch heightens this effect by eliminating most of the cornices of the Louvain arch, and by altering the proportions so that the main part of the structure (everything but the attic) forms a square. The result is an impression of the purest geometry – squares and circles – which is reinforced by the details of the design: the cubes that frame the steps and the many circular motifs in the sculptural ornament, such as the frieze of wreaths beneath the attic.[15] The legs of the arch, which in the Louvain design were decorated with trophies, are now completely plain. The trophies are moved to the upper part of the surface, replacing the winged victories traditionally placed there. The upper and lower surfaces are separated not by a projecting cornice, as in the Louvain arch, but by a band of tightly packed, low-relief ornament (cannons, drums, flags, and other military objects), of a type that Ledoux had devised and which preserves the flatness of the surface.[16]

But in contrast to the massiveness of Ledoux's works, Ramée's design suggests only volume, as if it were constructed of the thinnest planes. Ramée had been cultivating this effect for some time and it had reached a climax in the perfectly unornamented surfaces of Sophienholm in Denmark. In Ramée's Baltimore arch the effect is heightened, in a strange way, by the addition of ornament – ornament so delicate that it intensifies the impression of lightness and insubstantiality. It is a style distinctively Ramée's, which depends for its effect on the ironic combination of plainness and refined ornament.

The richest ornament is found within the opening of Ramée's arch. As in the Louvain design, Ramée flouted tradition by placing a statue directly beneath the arch: here, a bronze statue of George Washington (Ramée drew it in a delicate green watercolor), set on a high pedestal of bluish-purple marble. Framing Washington on each side of the structure is a screen of Corinthian columns supporting an entablature. Atop the entablature is a fan-shaped array of eighteen star-tipped arrows radiating from a golden eagle, a motif that echoes the arch itself in its semicircular shape.

This combination of statue and columnar screen was unprecedented (as far as I can determine) in the tradition of triumphal arches. That it was Ramée's invention is also suggested by the fact that its component parts are all found in his earlier work. The placement of a statue beneath an arch recalls the Louvain design. The screen of columns within an arch harks back to the façade of Ramée's Börsenhalle in Hamburg, of 1803 (see Fig. 102); its source was no doubt Ledoux's Hôtel Guimard in Paris, in front of which Ramée had built the Perregaux House at the beginning of his career (see Fig. 19).[17]

This pattern of a screen of columns within an arched opening or niche – the "Guimard motif," as it has been called – was one of Ramée's favorite devices. He was to employ it again in America at Calverton, the country house of Dennis Smith. But he never used it the same way twice. His adaptation of the motif for the Baltimore arch was especially original, even daring, since the placement of columns and a statue under an arch violated the traditional notion of a triumphal arch as an opening through which people could march. Ramée probably realized that a memorial arch, such as the Washington Monument, served a different function from a traditional triumphal arch: the emphasis was to be on the image of Washington, which people would approach and contemplate. The purpose of the arch was to focus attention on the memorialized object, not to serve as a passageway.

This purpose is indicated also by Ramée's raising of the arch on a high podium, reached by a broad flight of steps, another violation of the triumphal-arch tradition. Here, too, Ramée drew on one of his earlier designs: the central altar of the *Fête de la Fédération* in Paris, of 1790, with its podium formed of flights of steps and, at the four corners, cubic blocks on which tripods held burning incense, as in the Baltimore arch (see Fig. 35).

As remarkable as the arch itself is the environment that Ramée depicted around it. The competition announcement had noted the intended location of the monument ("a square 300 feet long and 140 feet wide, crossed . . . by a principal street"), but had not indicated that anything more than the monument was to be designed. All the known entries, save Ramée's, presented only the design of the monument. (Mills put some trees in the background, as did Godefroy, who also showed the corners of two typical city houses at the sides; but these were merely indications of what might exist on the site.)

In contrast, Ramée conceived for his design not only a monument but its urban environment. His drawing shows the street forming a circle around the arch, bordered by sidewalks, chain-bearing ballards, lampposts at the ends of iron fences, and semicircles of tall poplar trees (as in the architect's design for the rotunda at Union College [see Fig. 212]). Between the trees we see park lawn, and in the background are continous urban structures with arcaded ground floors. These are similar to the buildings lining the Rue de Rivoli in Paris, designed by Napoleon's architects Percier and Fontaine, which were under construction when Ramée was in Paris just before he went to America (Fig. 224).

224 Rue de Rivoli, Paris. Engraving c. 1830. (A. Pugin and C. Heath, *Paris and its Environs*, vol. 1, London, 1833)

Ramée was thus proposing a complete urban design for this section of Baltimore. It was a type of design still largely unknown in America: a plan for parkland, public monument, traffic circulation, and blocks of buildings, all integrated to reinforce one another and create a unified whole.[18] National pride, following the American Revolution, spurred interest in monumental planning in the cities of the United States and made Americans receptive to new models of design. But truly coordinated planning, involving architecture, landscape, and urbanism, remained rare. The most ambitious urbanistic enterprise was, of course, the planning of the city of Washington by Pierre Charles L'Enfant and others starting in the 1790s, with its immense, Versailles-like spaces stretching from the Capitol to the Potomac River and to the President's House. But the very grandeur of this project, and the problems of its execution, militated against an integrated conception of the parts. The landscaping of the Mall and the design of the public and private buildings bordering it occurred in piecemeal fashion, and they still had not advanced very far by the

1810s.[19] Coordinated urban-planning projects in other cities, such as Charles Bulfinch's Tontine Crescent and Colonnade Row in Boston, were few in number and relatively modest in scale.[20]

Large-scale public urbanism was so unusual in America that the Washington Monument competition board may not have known what to think of Ramée's plan integrating parkland and extensive new buildings. They perhaps wondered why the architect had lavished so much care on depicting things irrelevant to the competition; they may even have perceived a presumptuousness in his redesign of their city. Along with Ramée's unfortunate foreignness, these factors no doubt contributed to the board's rejection of a design that was probably the most sophisticated proposal for a civic monument in America up to that time.

The Washington Monument board made its decision in favor of Mills's plan in May of 1814.[21] The rejection of Ramée must have been especially disappointing to him as he had few other prospects of important work. His planning of Union College was largely completed. Unless he had other commissions of which we are unaware, his only work during this period was for David Parish, who continued to have him produce designs for his North Country properties. But these were relatively minor in scope.[22] In April, Parish had announced to his New York State agents that "Mr. Ramée and his family will probably spend some weeks with me at Parishville this summer," but even this trip did not occur.[23]

In the summer of 1814, several of Ramée's designs were included in the fourth annual exhibit of the Pennsylvania Academy and Columbian Society of Artists in Philadelphia. This was the premier forum in America for artists to bring their work to the attention of each other and to the public. Although architectural drawings constituted only a small part of these Academy shows, the architects Latrobe, Godefroy, Mills, and William Strickland had exhibited in previous years.[24] The exhibition catalogue for 1814 reveals that Ramée submitted at least thirteen entries, representing the broad range of his work as a designer.[25] His submissions included a drawing of his competition design for the Baltimore monument; a "general plan" and a "front elevation" for Union College; a "model of a Russian stove," the ceramic room-heating stove that Ramée had introduced with much success to Ogdensburg, New York; and eight entries listed, collectively, as "Plans, elevations and sections of town and country houses, and designs of Picturesque gardens, with seven explanatory drawings."

Ramée's exhibition of garden designs is especially interesting. None of the other architects who had shown their designs in the Academy exhibits had included such work. In fact, Ramée's entries may have constituted the first public presentation in America of professional designs for naturalistic gardens. It is not known whether Ramée's exhibited plans were of houses and gardens in America (such as his work for Parish and Duane) or in Germany and Denmark. But at least one of Ramée's European gardens was included in the exhibition: a separate catalogue entry under his name was listed as "A view of a picturesque garden on the River Elbe." This sounds very much like the small watercolor drawing of Baurs Park, west of Hamburg, which Ramée made in 1810 and kept for the rest of his life (see Fig. 72 and color plate 13). One wonders what other drawings of his European work Ramée brought to America, to use as models for new work or to show to prospective clients.

Ramée's entries in the Academy exhibition attracted public notice. One reviewer of the show, writing for the magazine *Port Folio,* praised the architect's adherence to "the chaste simplicity of Grecian architecture" and used the occasion to deride the new "semi-barbarous taste. . . for mongrel Gothic architecture."[26] (This writer was obviously unaware that Ramée himself used Gothic forms in some of his designs.) Most intriguing is the reviewer's remark that "we are much pleased to find that Mr. Ramée intends to publish an interesting work on the principles of his art." After returning to Europe, the architect was to produce three publications of his designs, but none of these includes a text. If Ramée did write an essay on his architectural "principles," this reference to it by an anonymous Philadelphia journalist is all we know about it.

Calverton

Of the country estates that Boulliot says Ramée built around Philadelphia, Baltimore, and New York, only Calverton is known. Located about two and a half miles from the center of Baltimore, it was the home of the merchant and banker Dennis A. Smith.[27] Calverton is also the architect's last known commission in the United States and it probably caused him to delay his return to Europe. As usual, Ramée seems to have received the commission through Parish's auspices, for there is correspondence between Parish and Smith about the project, and Parish even handled Smith's payments to the architect: a large fee of $1,500, paid in June of 1816, just before Ramée left America.[28]

Later, in the 1830s, Ramée included his plan of the grounds of Calverton in his publication *Parcs et jardins* and also used a view of it as a vignette illustration on the title page of his *Recueil de cottages et maisons de campagne* (Figs. 225–7). The only other images of Calverton are nineteenth-century engraved and photographic views, for the house burned in 1874 and nothing survives of the estate.

In 1815 Smith engaged Ramée to lay out the grounds of this property and design a new house there.[29] In fact, Smith invited the architect to live with him in Baltimore while making these designs. Benjamin Latrobe mentioned Ramée's presence there in October 1815, and two months later David Parish noted in a letter that Ramée and his family had temporarily "taken up their residence in D. A. Smith's house at Baltimore – they are very much pleased with each other and Ramée is laying out Smith's grounds and building a country house for him in a most splendid style."[30] In January 1816, Parish reported to Smith that "our friend Mr. Ramée and his family arrived here yesterday in good health [and] are highly grateful for all your kindness to them"; several days later Parish wrote that Ramée "has shown me the plan of your country house etc., with which we are all highly pleased here."[31] The building was nearly complete by September of 1816.[32]

Ramée's plan of Smith's entire estate, as he later published it, exemplifies

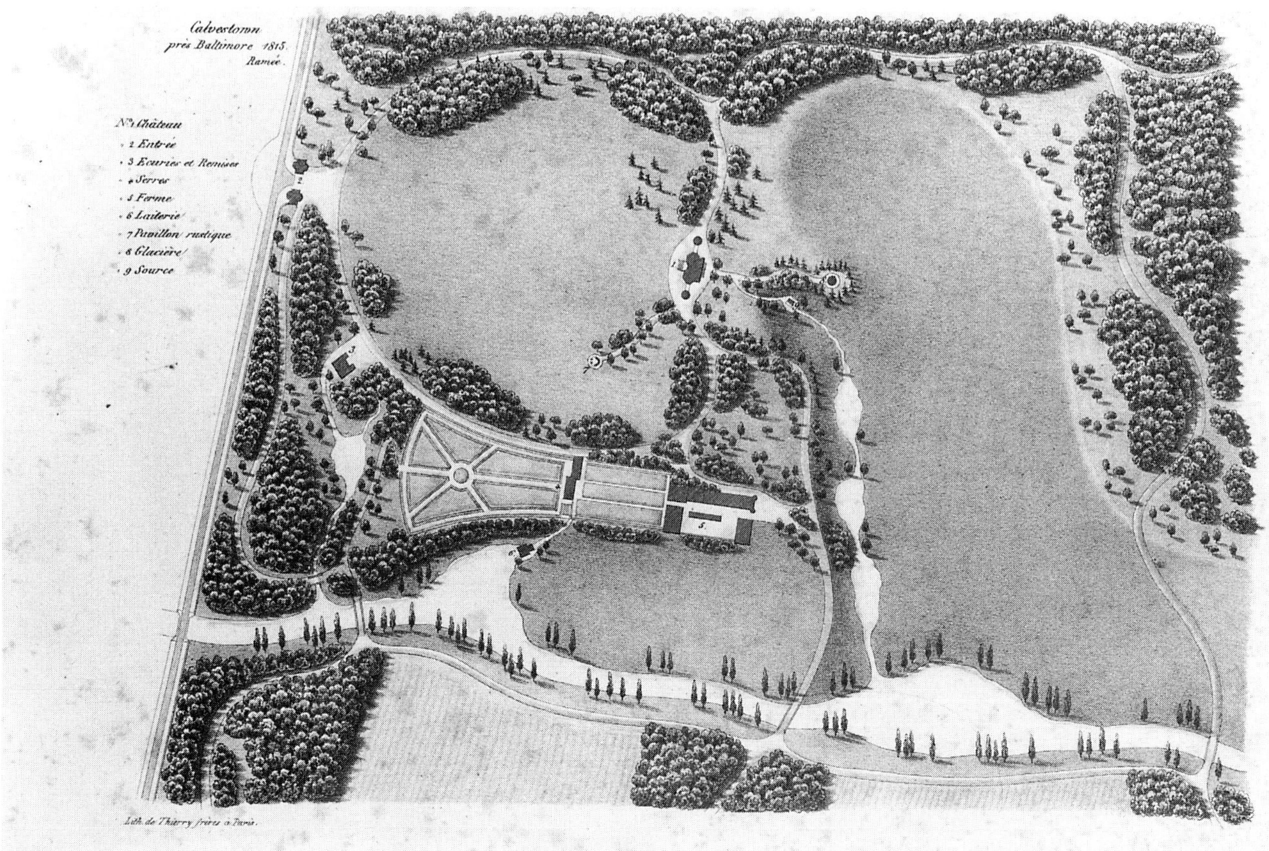

225 Calverton. Plan in Ramée's *Parcs et jardins*, pl. 1. (Schaffer Library, Union College)

his principles of landscape design. Irregular areas of dense woodland encircle most of the property and define large open spaces. The house stands at the juncture of the two main spaces; the house looks across one of them, toward the entry to the estate; in the other direction are more rustic views, with plantings of various species of trees. A spring feeds a small creek, which meanders to a larger stream on one side of the property. The approach to the house from the entry gate circles around, passing the stables, a small geometric garden, greenhouses, a farm, and a *pavillon rustique*. Somewhat farther from the road are the spring house and a circular icehouse.

The design thus created a diversity of types of landscape and architecture, which one would experience while moving through the grounds. But in contrast to the cramped variety of an *anglo-chinois* garden, Ramée strove to keep the overall pattern of the plan simple and to create large open spaces so the eye could enjoy long vistas as well as points of interest at close range. A balance is achieved between simplicity and complexity, as well as between nature and artifice.

The house itself at Calverton had a unusual form: a cubic central block with a large porch, semicircular bays on the sides, a tall cupola on the roof, and two semiattached octagonal or circular pavilions to the sides, each with its own little cupola. The overall effect must have been strangely picturesque, as can be seen in the vignette view of the estate that Ramée later published. In this view, the house is seen through the equally unusual gateway that served as

226 Calverton, plan of the house. Detail of Ramée's site plan in *Parcs et jardins*.

227 Calverton, view of entrance to the estate with house in background. Lithographic ornament on title page of Ramée's *Recueil de cottages et maisons de campagne*, 1837. (© cliché Bibliothèque Nationale, Paris)

the entry to the property. This was a large masonry arch, stepped on the top and supporting a little statue of Eros, the whole construction buttressed at the sides by low, massive, circular structures – with vines growing over it all. If the house and gateway were executed as pictured by Ramée, they represented a type of romanticism nearly unknown in America at this time, integrating picturesque architectural forms and plantings in a manner that was decades ahead of its time.

It is conceivable, however, that Ramée modified the Calverton design when he published it in the 1830s. There is no documentation of the entry gate as it was executed, nor of the octagonal wings flanking the house. But the house itself is seen in a photograph taken shortly before it burned in 1874 (Fig. 228).[33] By this time, the house had long been used for other purposes, first as a civic alms house, then by a Hebrew Orphan Society. The photograph shows the house in poor repair, with the original front steps removed and also without the roof tower (which is seen in an earlier engraved view of the house).[34] Otherwise, however, the building is essentially the same as in Ramée's published drawings.

The most remarkable feature of the house is the large porch, formed by a shallow segmental vault that is supported by two-storey-high square columns. Within this frame, one-storey-high columns support an entablature and a piece of sculpture; at the back of the porch, the wall of the house is recessed to form a vaulted niche, with a large semicircular window above the front door.

228 Calverton. Photograph c. 1874. (The Peale Museum, Baltimore City Life Museums)

229 Design no. 22 of Ramée's *Recueil de cottages*, 1837. (Private collection)

Some of the parts of this composition are awkward in their details and proportions, perhaps because the house was constructed by another architect after Ramée left America.[35] But the basic design is clearly Ramée's. It is another variation of the "Guimard motif" – a screen of columns set in an arched opening – which the architect had used in the Hamburg Börsenhalle and in his design for the Washington Monument. Ramée was to continue to experiment with this motif throughout his career. One variation, found in a house design he published in the 1830s, even uses the segmental vault of the Calverton porch (Fig. 229).[36] As for the sculpture atop the entablature at Calverton, it recalls the similarly placed sculpture on Ledoux's Hôtel Guimard in Paris, where Ramée worked in the 1780s and which was no doubt the source of this motif in his work (see Fig. 19).

Also typical of Ramée was the surface material of Calverton. A local publication of 1822 informs us that the house was constructed "of stone rough cast" – that is, stone walls, covered with cement or stucco. This was Ramée's favorite material for the surfaces of buildings: he used it at Union College and in most of his works in Europe. The 1870s photograph of Calverton shows this roughcast surface still intact, giving the forms a uniformity and flatness that emphasize their geometry and volumes, so typical of Ramée's work.

Virchaux & Company

While living in Philadelphia, Ramée formed a business partnership for the manufacture of wallpaper, the kind of enterprise he had established in Dinant, Belgium. Ramée's partner in Philadelphia was Henry T. Virchaux, one of David Parish's secretaries.[37] As with the firm of Masson et Ramée in Hamburg, Ramée was evidently in charge of the artistic and technical side of the business, while his partner handled financial and commercial matters.

The enterprise was sponsored, in a sense, by Parish. In December of 1812 he mentioned in a letter that

> Ramée is about forming an association with Mr. Virchaux in Philadelphia; they intend to set up or rather to continue a *Tapeten*

> *Fabrik* [wallpaper factory] which the owner, a French gentleman about to return to his native country, has offered them for sale. I think well of this establishment as I have agreed to make them the advances requisite to carry it into effect.[38]

The following year, Parish reported that the business "goes on prosperously," and it was listed in a Philadelphia directory as "Virchaux and Co., paper hanging manufacturers."[39] The fact that Ramée's name did not appear in the firm's title might be due to his having a smaller financial interest in the business than Virchaux, or to Ramée's desire not to become known mainly as a wallpaper maker when he was trying to establish an architectural practice in Philadelphia.

No examples of the firm's products were known until the recent identification, in the Library of Congress, of some early nineteenth-century wallpapers that had been deposited for copyright with the United States government. Among them are ten designs that are designated as the work of Virchaux & Company, deposited for copyright on different dates from 1814 to 1816.[40] Most of the designs consist of two parts, the main wall pattern and a top border. The firm submitted printed captions for the parts of each design, describing them and stating, in most cases, "Messrs. Virchaux & Co. intend to execute the above design of their own invention. . . ." But the captions for the last three designs (dated April 1816) read "Messrs. Virchaux & Co. by right, obtained from Joseph Ramée, intend to execute this design, of his invention."[41] This could be taken to mean that only these last designs were by Ramée. It is likely, however, that he designed all of them. As a partner in Virchaux & Company, Ramée did not need to be named in the copyright applications; only when he left the firm in early 1816 to return to Europe did his authorship have to be specified separately.[42]

In their consistency of quality and boldness of design, the ten wallpapers seem clearly to be the work of one hand. They also reveal a thorough knowledge of contemporary French wallpaper design and printing technology, which they emulate more closely than perhaps any other American-made wallpapers of this period.[43] Most of the patterns are trompe-l'oeil representations of fabric hangings (recalling Ramée's interior decoration of this type, as in the Voght House near Hamburg and the Erichsen Mansion in Copenhagen), surmounted by borders of a more-or-less architectural nature. In some of the designs, the fabric – with various floral and geometric patterns – is shown draped, in others it is stretched; in some cases the gaps between the pieces of fabric reveal columns or other structural or decorative forms. One of the wallpapers ascribed to Ramée in the copyright caption is of this type (Fig. 230). It portrays stretched panels of pale yellow fabric, embroidered with grape leaves and held together by bouquets of flowers, with columns of bamboo between the panels, against a dark green background.[44]

The top borders of the wallpapers have inventive combinations of architectural, floral, and other decorative elements. One recurrent theme is a shallow segmental arch, a shape that Ramée frequently used in his architecture. One of the borders represents a kind of cornice formed by such arches, with

230 Virchaux & Co., wallpaper pattern no. 70, deposited for copyright in 1816. (Library of Congress)

231 Virchaux & Co., wallpaper pattern no. 42, deposited for copyright in 1814. (Library of Congress)

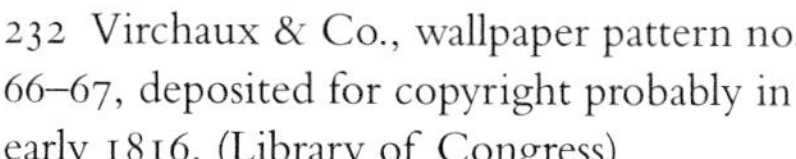

232 Virchaux & Co., wallpaper pattern no. 66–67, deposited for copyright probably in early 1816. (Library of Congress)

gilded eagles and other motifs, and garlands of leaves and flowers hung within the arches (Fig. 231). Like most of the Virchaux papers, this border is printed in rich and varied colors – purple, gold, green, and red, in this case – typical of French wallpaper of the period and dependent on technical know-how not previously evident in America.[45] Some of the ornamental details in these borders have the light, attenuated proportions of the Directoire style, typical of Ramée's earlier interior decorations. But more common in the Virchaux designs are the heavier proportions of the Empire style of this time. The two manners can be seen together in several of the patterns, so it is not a matter of two different artists. Furthermore, the heavier proportions are found even in the designs specifically ascribed to Ramée. They show, therefore, that Ramée was shifting away from the Directoire style and experimenting with the weightier decorative forms then fashionable in France.

Two of the Virchaux wallpapers, both ascribed to Ramée in the copy-

233 Virchaux & Co., wallpaper pattern no. 68, deposited for copyright in 1816. (Library of Congress)

right captions, are more architectural than the others. One depicts a neoclassical iron fence, with piers, posts, and diagonal braces, decorated with rosettes, fan-shaped anthemia, spearheads, and wreaths; the whole structure is gilded and set in stark relief against a blue background (Fig. 232).[46] Railings or fences occasionally figure as subsidiary elements in French wallpapers of the period, but this design, devoted completely to the realistic portrayal of a gilded fence, may be an invention of Ramée.

The other wallpaper ascribed to Ramée also portrays a fence or metal grillwork, but of a more unusual kind (Fig. 233).[47] The main structural members are pairs of closely-spaced columns with decorative bands and grape-cluster decoration, joined by short tie-pieces – all having the appearance of being made of cast iron. Between these pairs of columns are diagonal rails, forming X's, with round disks at their centers. This part of the design is strikingly similar to a pattern found in several of Ramée's plans for *gardens,* such as those for Union College, the Duane estate, and later commissions in France (see Figs. 184, 244, and color plate 17). But the entire structure shown in the wallpaper seems to be unique, with no precedent (that I have been able to find) either in architectural or decorative designs of the period. Moreover, as striking as the structure is the abstract pattern of lines behind it. Printed in a warm brown (in contrast to the steely grays of the structure in front), there are vertical lines behind the columns. These lines merge into concentric circles behind the crossed rails, with fernlike patterns and classical anthemion motifs fitted in between.[48] The whole thing has a dizzying, almost Pop-Art quality, which surely seemed strange and surprising to the wallpaper-buying public in Philadelphia in the 1810s.

When Ramée left America in 1816, Virchaux took a new partner, a man named Borrekens or Borrekins.[49] By 1817, the firm was ordering wallpaper stock from France, and there is no evidence that it continued to design its own patterns.[50] All the evidence indicates that Ramée was the artistic force in Virchaux & Company and that he designed most or all of its original products. Given the high quality of design and craftsmanship of these products, Ramée thus contributed to the development of the decorative arts in America – an aspect of his career completely unknown until the discovery of these wallpapers.

Plans to Return to Europe

Ramée's failure to win the Baltimore Washington Monument competition, at the beginning of 1814, signaled hard times for the architect in America and started him thinking about returning to Europe. Ramée's only known commissions during his last two years in the United States were the design of Calverton and the occasional work that David Parish gave him in connection with his North Country properties. Parish, who felt responsible for the architect in America, naturally tried to find additional jobs for him. In 1815, Parish attempted especially to help Ramée obtain major public commissions, which would have established firmly the architect's reputation in the country.

In March 1815, Parish wrote to General John P. Van Ness, a United States government commissioner, recommending Ramée for the rebuilding of "the public buildings of Washington" – that is, the United States Capitol and the President's House, burned by the British in their occupation of the capital in 1814. Parish spoke of Ramée's "talents and taste," mentioning in particular his layout of Union College, "considered to be unrivalled in the United States."[51] He noted, "In consequence of the late happy events in Europe, Mr. R. is induced to quit this country with his family," but Parish added that "his stay would be prolonged" if he received the work in Washington. Van Ness quickly replied that Benjamin Latrobe and James Hoban (the original architect of the President's House) had just been given the jobs.[52]

"The late happy events in Europe," to which Parish referred, were the fall of Napoleon in 1814, his exile to Elba, and the restoration of the Bourbon monarchy in the person of Louis XVIII. Parish had many reasons to dislike Napoleon, beginning with the Emperor's occupation of Hamburg which had forced Parish's parents to abandon their home and flee Germany. In letters he wrote in 1814, Parish rejoiced in the fall of "the Tyrant."[53] Ramée no doubt shared Parish's sentiments. His career in Germany had been disrupted by Napoleon and he probably believed that the Bourbon restoration would reopen his professional opportunities in France – especially as his former employer, the Comte d'Artois, was now a powerful advisor to his brother the king.

Ramée's plans to return to Europe are revealed in his only surviving American letter, written from Philadelphia in February of 1815 to Joseph Rosseel, Parish's principal agent in the North Country. Ramée and Rosseel had become friends when the architect spent several months in Ogdensburg in late 1812 (Rosseel is the man who wrote to his fiancée about Ramée's fine character). The architect's letter, written in French, has a casual and amiable tone:

My dear Mr. Rosseel,

You will have learned from Mr. P. that I plan to return to Europe and shall probably end up in the neighborhood of your native city. If you wish to charge me with messages for your family, I shall deliver them with pleasure and take advantage of the first opportunity that presents itself.

I looked forward to seeing you again each season in Ogdensburg, but events of various kinds always upset these fine *Brochets* [*ces beaux Brochets*].

[Ramée goes on to inquire about Rosseel's gardening, his wife's progress in learning French, and some items that the two men had sent to one another.][54]

The puzzling word *Brochets* must be a pun, sounding like *projets* ("plans") but literally meaning "pike" – the swift pike being a favorite of sport fishermen in the North Country. Charles Hénard, the French painter who was part of Parish's household in Ogdensburg when Ramée was there, was described by an acquaintance as a man of Fallstaffian good cheer, who especially loved good food and *puns*.[55] So Ramée's remark to Rosseel was a reminder of the good times they had had, in the company of Parish's entourage of French expatriates in the wilds of Upstate New York – an adventure that Ramée was now about to leave behind him.

Joseph Rosseel's native city was Ghent, Belgium. The possible reasons for Ramée's decision to return to Belgium, rather than France, are discussed in the following chapter. Hardly a month after Ramée wrote to Rosseel, however, his plans were disrupted by Napoleon's amazing escape from Elba, his return to France, and his overthrow of the newly restored Bourbon government. War-weary Europe was thrown again into turmoil, as the Emperor raised his army once more to meet the forces of the allied enemies. In July of 1815, Parish wrote to a friend in France: "The Ramée family was planning to return to Europe this year, but they have deferred doing so because of the events that took place there in March."[56]

So Ramée tried again to find work in America. The main architectural project in sight was the Baltimore Exchange – a large building combining mercantile, commercial, and judicial functions – whose architect was being chosen by a board of trustees that included Dennis A. Smith.[57] Several architects submitted drawings, but it appears that the choice was made less on design quality than on political and financial connections. The supporters of Ramée's bid for the job were Smith and David Parish, both of whom were stockholders in the Exchange. Latrobe and Godefroy were also competing for the job, in collaboration with one another. In July of 1815, Latrobe wrote dejectedly to his partner: "Now the fact is, that Ramée will be the architect or Mills, and all we are doing is vain. . . . If our friends can outvote Ramée's, that is Parish's, or Mills', that is Gillmore's, then we shall carry it."[58]

Subsequent correspondence of Latrobe reveals that Ramée made drawings for the Exchange while he was a houseguest of Dennis A. Smith in Baltimore, and that Smith reportedly offered to subscribe $40,000 to the Exchange fund to procure the job for Ramée.[59] But Latrobe and Godefroy ultimately triumphed and received the commission, a decision that was announced in February of 1816.

No drawing by Ramée for the Baltimore Exchange survives. But an exhibition of the competition entries took place, in January 1816 in the Baltimore city council chamber, and sketches of a couple of the entries were made by Robert Mills. One of these sketches may represent Ramée's design (Fig. 234).[60] It shows a façade dominated by a large triumphal-arch entryway, with a screen of columns – the Guimard motif that Ramée liked so much. It is worth noting that Latrobe's final design for the Baltimore Exchange, following the competition, included a screened arch of this type; it was apparently the first time Latrobe used this motif and may therefore represent an influence from Ramée.[61]

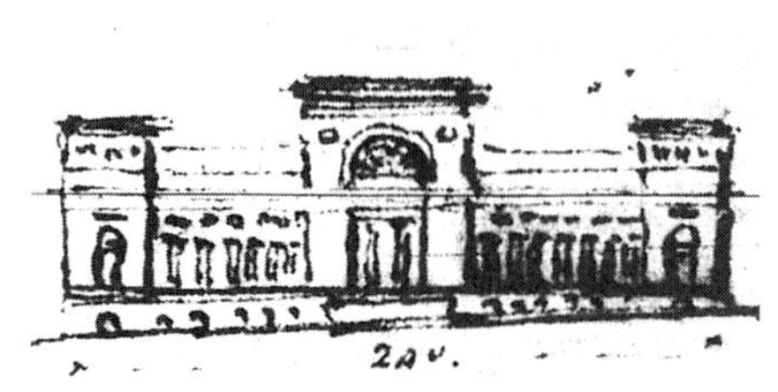

234 Sketch by Robert Mills of one of the designs entered in the Baltimore Exchange competition, 1816. (Library of Congress)

By the time of the Baltimore Exchange competition, Napoleon had been decisively beaten at Waterloo and had gone to his final exile. Louis XVIII had resumed power in France and Ramée could once again plan his return to Europe.

David Parish also had decided to leave America and reestablish himself in Antwerp in Belgium. He turned his North Country lands over to his younger brother George, who came to the United States and made an inspection trip of the properties with David in early 1816. Even in his final months in America, however, David continued to pay close attention to the improvement of his towns in northern New York, and he evidently was still having Ramée draw plans for new buildings there. It was during this period that Parish constructed the church in Antwerp, New York, and talked about plans for several other projects, including a museum to be built in Ogdensburg.[62] He was still a dreamer, fascinated by great schemes.

In the summer of 1816 Parish sold his house in Philadelphia and sailed from New York to Europe.[63] It is not known if he and Ramée sailed together, but the architect and his family did return to Europe at about the same time. Ramée was still in Philadelphia on June 10th, when he received $1,500 from Dennis Smith.[64]

Financially, Ramée's period in America was not a disaster, but it certainly had not brought him wealth, and he still was troubled by the bankruptcy of his Hamburg business with Masson. In January of 1816, Parish transmitted $200 from Ramée to the Marquis de Lafayette, to be paid to the family of Lafayette's friend Archenholtz, who had lost his investment in the firm of Masson et Ramée. In his letter to Lafayette, Parish noted, "Ramée is making a decent livelihood sufficient to maintain his family, but has not yet the means to liquidate the debts of his former establishment at Hamburg."[65]

Ramée's Place in American Architecture

Despite the brevity of his stay in the United States and the small number of important commissions he executed, Ramée made an impact on American design: in architecture, landscape planning, and the decorative arts. The likely influence of Ramée's Union College design on Jefferson's University of Virginia, and on later collegiate planning, has already been suggested. Many American architects must have known of the Union plan, especially after its exhibition in Philadelphia in 1814. They were surely impressed by the grandeur of Ramée's conception, which may have encouraged the trend toward a new scale of unified institutional planning in nineteenth-century America. A similar effect was no doubt made by Ramée's design for the Baltimore Washington Monument, with its vision of integrating architecture and landscape in urban planning.

The influence of more specific aspects of Ramée's architecture is hard to assess. His simple arcaded forms appear to have influenced certain architects, such as Philip Hooker, as mentioned earlier. The "Guimard motif," used by Ramée in the Washington Monument design and at Calverton, became popular with some American architects in subsequent years, but probably not due solely to Ramée.[66] The light and airy quality of Ramée's work, and its use of delicate ornament to contrast with the geometric purity of the overall forms, were distinctive traits and might have influenced American architecture, but they ran counter to the rising tide of the Greek Revival, with its massive proportions. (This observation pertains to Ramée's architecture, not necessarily to his work in the decorative arts, since his wallpaper designs suggest a shift toward heavier proportions.)

Not surprisingly, the foremost chronicler of the Greek Revival in America, Talbot Hamlin, thought that Ramée's designs "looked backward rather than ahead."[67] But this is only part of the picture. Hamlin himself stated, "The remarkable thing [is that Ramée's work] reveals such an adaptable mind – is in fact so American in spirit."[68] Whether or not there was anything particularly "American" about Ramée's work, Hamlin was right about its adaptability. Again and again it adapted to new conditions, clients, and types of work, allowing the architect to survive through the continual upheavals of his professional career.

Besides Ramée's importance for college planning and the possible influence of his wallpaper designs, his most significant contribution in America was probably as a creator of landscape designs integrating nature and architecture. The picturesque garden was known in America before Ramée, but it was generally the work of amateurs: property owners laying out their own estates or those of friends, based on gardens they had seen in Europe or had read about.[69] Ramée was one of the first truly professional landscape architects in America, and he had a new degree of knowledge and specialization in the subject. Latrobe laid out gardens around some of the country houses he designed, and he expressed progressive views on landscape design; but he evidently did not consider it a major part of his professional activity.[70]

Ramée, in contrast, presented himself to the public equally as an architect and as a garden designer. A large proportion of his work in America was landscape design, and "picturesque gardens" were a important part of his contribution to the Pennsylvania Academy exhibit of 1814. It is significant that

Ramée included prominent landscaping even in his architectural designs for which it was not required, such as the Union College plan and the Washington Monument project. For him, the two elements were inseparable: the design of a building was incomplete without its landscaping – a largely new concept in America.

Also significant was Ramée's notion that each landscape design should have its own special character, appropriate to its architecture, site, and intended use, not just a recycled standard garden plan. Each of his American landscape designs was shaped by individual considerations: the agrarian nature of Ogden Island, with working farmland that determined much of the layout; the domestic landscapes at Duanesburg and Calverton, formed by individual topographies and proprietors' needs; the grounds of Union College, appropriate to a large institution in their extent and variety; the urban landscape surrounding the Washington Monument in Baltimore. This emphasis on individuality parallels the views of Humphrey Repton, Richard Payne Knight, and Uvedale Price in England, who criticized earlier landscape designers for the uniformity of their plans. When Ramée later published some of his landscape designs, as *Parcs et jardins,* he emphasized this individuality in the statement he put on the title page: "The author hopes to be useful to lovers of gardens by offering them a series of the most varied motifs, applicable to all sites. . . [and] by the multiplicity of scenes of the most picturesque and differentiated plans. . . which the different localities suggested to the author."[71]

235 View of Livingston Manor (The Hill) on the Hudson River. Engraving in A. J. Downing, *Treatise on Landscape Gardening,* (1841).

236 Barn at Livingston Manor. (Roger G. Kennedy)

A quarter century after Ramée left America, Andrew Jackson Downing transformed garden design in America through his publications, which popularized picturesque landscape and articulated his principles of the art. These principles were similar in many ways to those of Ramée.[72] Downing's models and sources were mostly English, and he never mentioned Ramée in his writings.[73] But Downing must have known Ramée's work. He traveled widely in the eastern United States, seeking out notable scenery and landscape design, and he was thoroughly familiar with the Hudson River Valley, his home region.

Downing was surely aware of Union College, and through his contacts with the Livingston family he may have known Ramée's plans for the Duane estate near Schenectady. The grounds of The Hill, the Livingston estate on the Hudson River (home of Henry W. Livingston, cousin of Ramée's client Catherine Livingston Duane) were among Downing's favorite gardens (Fig. 235). He illustrated the property in his treatise on landscape gardening and called it "perhaps the most remarkable [park] in America."[74] One wonders, in fact, if these grounds at The Hill may have been the work of Ramée – one of his lost designs for estates in New York State.[75] This is particularly plausible as there was a barn at The Hill that had a form similar to the Duane House stable and recalling Ramée's Danish buildings (Fig. 236).[76]

Frederick Law Olmsted, founder of the public park system in America, undoubtedly knew Ramée's work. As mentioned in the preceding chapter, Olmsted reportedly visited Union College to see the gardens there. One of Olmsted's great contributions to American design was a new type of college campus, conceived as a naturalistic park; he advocated this concept starting in

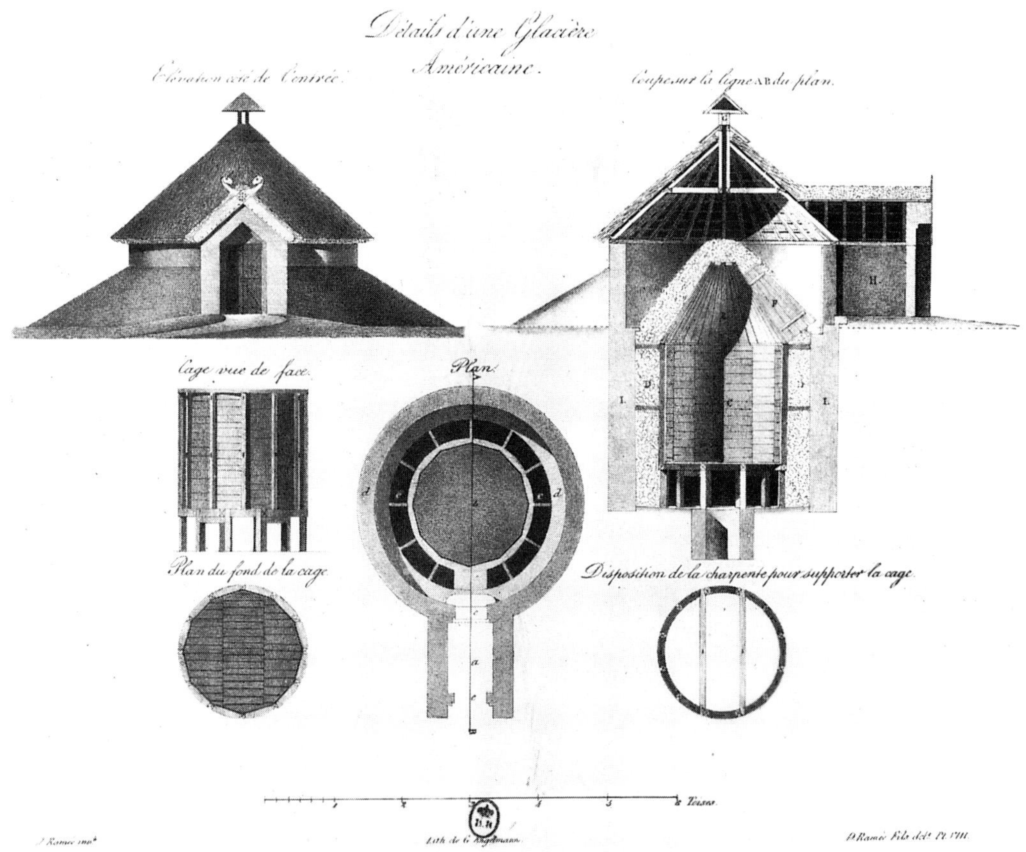

237 Design for "American icehouse." Plate VIII of Ramée's *Jardins irréguliers* (1823). (© cliché Bibliothèque Nationale, Paris)

the 1860s, especially for the new Land Grant institutions.[77] Ramée's plan for Union College, integrating architecture and landscape, was the most significant precedent for this concept of Olmsted's, which subsequently influenced the whole development of the college and university campus in America.

Thus, while Ramée himself was largely forgotten in America after his brief sojourn, the submerged influence of his innovations continued to affect the course of American design.

America's Effect on Ramée

In most of the places where Ramée worked, he not only introduced new forms and styles, but was influenced in turn by things he encountered that were new to him. What did the architect find of interest in America?

Ramée's *Jardins irréguliers,* published in Paris about 1823, contains one design actually identified as American: a "*glacière américaine,*" or American icehouse (Fig. 237).[78] Shown in great detail in plan, elevation, and section, it is a curious structure: circular, with a conical roof and a freestanding wooden cage inside to hold the ice. The "American" designation is puzzling at first. Circular icehouses have never been common in America and some of the details of Ramée's design are positively foreign, such as the thatched roof and the Scandinavian-style gable boards over the doorway, carved with animal heads.[79]

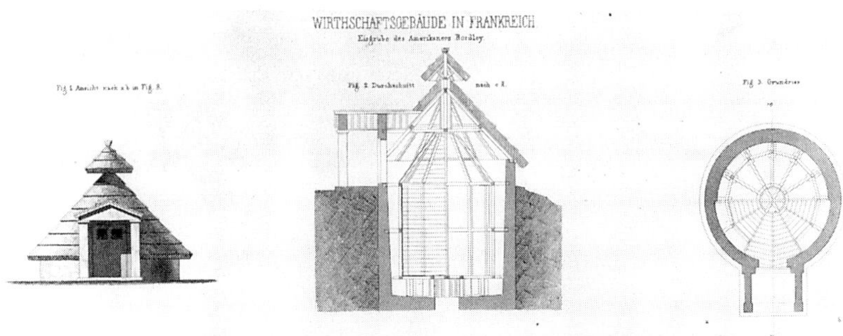

238 Design for icehouse by John B. Bordley, as illustrated in *Allgemeine Bauzeitung* (1854), pl. 652.

It turns out, however, that this design has a specific, American source: a type of icehouse invented by the agricultural expert John Beale Bordley and described in his *Essays and Notes on Husbandry and Rural Affairs,* published in 1799 (Fig. 238).[80] Bordley's main innovation concerned the insulation of the ice, by means of straw packed around a wooden cage or tub, with ventilation at the top of the roof. Bordley states in his text that he constructed an icehouse like this near Philadelphia and that it worked so well that many people came to admire it.[81]

Ramée's interest in Bordley's invention is revealing. Like many Europeans, he was apparently impressed most by American technology and inventiveness. Rather than conventional architectural forms, it was this device for storing ice that Ramée chose to present in his publication as distinctively American. It is also interesting that, starting in America and for the rest of his career, the architect included icehouses – circular in shape and presumably using Bordley's system of insulation – in most of his plans for parks and gardens.[82]

But European visitors to America were perhaps struck most, during this period of burgeoning romanticism, by the country's natural scenery. Ramée evidently shared this attraction. When David Parish described to his father the site of his projected house in northern New York, he remarked, "I have some of the most romantic situations you can possibly imagine, and Ramée. . . declares he never saw anything so fine."[83] Heightening the romantic appeal of the American wilderness, for Ramée, were no doubt the simple, even primitive structures he found there. In northern New York, for instance, one could see numerous log cabins, not very different from the one Ramée later included in his publication *Recueil de cottages* (see Fig. 297).[84] Ramée had known of log houses in Europe (they were, after all, an indigenous Scandinavian building type) and he had included one in his drawing of Baurs Park near Hamburg. But in Europe such structures were considered (by architects, at least) appropriate mainly as picturesque ornaments to gardens. In the American North Country, Ramée saw log cabins and other simple structures inhabited by landowners who would have lived more grandly in Europe. The sharp architectural differentiation between social classes that existed in Europe was blurred in America, especially on the frontier.

There is some evidence that this American tendency toward architectural egalitarianism intrigued Ramée and inspired him to experimentation. It is interesting that the country house Ramée designed for David Parish at Parishville had a degree of humble simplicity that in Europe would have been considered inappropriate for a man of Parish's station (see Fig. 163). It is true that this structure began as the farmhouse for the Parishville estate and was transformed into the main house only when Parish shelved his plans for a "mansion" on the bank of the river. But Ramée was fully in charge of remodeling the farmhouse for use as a country house. When Parish's brother George saw the completed building, he reported that it was "in the cottage stile," as noted earlier. Parish's country house is similar, in fact, to several of the designs Ramée later included in his work *Recueil de cottages* – apparently the first publication in France devoted to this building type. The significance of Ramée's cottage designs will be examined later. But it is relevant here that the architect's interest in cottages as appropriate housing for all social classes seems to have arisen first in America.

More generally, Ramée in America seems to have become increasingly attracted to northern building forms and to have liberated himself increasingly from traditional rules, such as the principle that exotic styles were appropriate only to certain building types. Previously, Ramée had used "Gothic" and other nonclassical styles almost solely for garden pavilions, stables, gardeners' houses, and the like; the main houses at his country estates, as well as other major buildings, were normally classical. Starting with his "cottage stile" house for Parish and his Gothic Revival church at Antwerp, New York, Ramée opened himself up to a much wider range of design possibilities, which was to transform his later work in Europe.

In contrast, American taste during this period was becoming *more* restrictively classical, not less, as the Greek Revival attracted increasing devotion. Ramée no doubt found this unfortunate. Just as Germany and Denmark had sparked his interest in northern-European architectural traditions, America – even farther removed from the classical sources – probably increased his doubts about the universal suitability of classicism. His American experience must have encouraged in Ramée the view he later expressed in *Parcs et jardins,* that "different localities" demand different architectural forms.[85] After his American adventure, his work was to become considerably more varied and eclectic than it had been before.

Return to Europe

Chapter 13

For most historical figures, the ends of their lives are better documented than the beginnings, as their fame increases with age. But in the case of Ramée, the last decades are among the most obscure. The wanderer, having come back to his homeland, was largely unknown there.

The rough outline of the architect's later years is as follows. After returning from America in 1816, Ramée spent about seven years in Belgium, then settled in Paris. In the early 1830s he is found in the Hamburg area. In 1836 he and Caroline Ramée returned to Paris, but three years later moved to Noyon, in northern France; the architect died near there in 1842, at the age of seventy-eight. In these final decades of his life, Ramée executed works in all the places where he lived, in Belgium, France, and Germany. And he published three collections of his landscape and architectural designs.

But within this outline there are large blanks and puzzling questions. Only some of Ramée's executed works can be identified. It is not known why he settled, successively, in Belgium, France, Germany, and then France again. Also in question is the professional relationship between Ramée and his son, Daniel, during these years. It seems that the younger Ramée collaborated with his father, particularly in preparing his publications of designs. To what extent were the late works of Ramée joint creations of father and son? Daniel Ramée went on to become an important figure in mid-nineteenth century French architecture, especially as a restorer of medieval monuments and a writer on architecture. Some of the questions about the late career of Ramée *père* are also relevant to the early career of Ramée *fils*.

Boulliot says about Ramée's activities immediately after he left America:

> Having returned to Belgium in 1816, with the intention of settling there for a while, he built several country houses there and put several parks in order. At this time, he also embellished the Place Verte in Givet. Finally, back in Paris in 1823, he published the first installments of the following work: *Jardins irréguliers*. . . .[1]

Why did Ramée settle in Belgium? Paris would seem to be where his best professional opportunities lay. Napoleon had fallen; the Bourbon king Louis XVIII sat on the French throne; and Ramée's former teacher Belanger, despite his advanced age, was restored to the posts he had held before the Revolution: architect to the king's brother, the Comte d'Artois, and head of the royal office of the *Menus-Plaisirs*. Belanger had followed the career of Ramée and thought highly of him. In 1813 Belanger named him first on a list of his most successful students.[2] He surely could have helped Ramée reestablish a career in Paris.

Some specific opportunity or personal reason must have drawn Ramée to Belgium. In 1815, while still in the United States, the architect had written to his friend Joseph Rosseel that he intended to settle near Ghent.[3] Perhaps David Parish had proposed some kind of business deal for the architect in Antwerp, where Parish established himself after leaving America. But if Ramée did go to Antwerp or Ghent, nothing is known of his activities there.

It appears that the architect spent at least part of this time in Dinant, a Belgian town on the River Meuse, only about twenty kilometers north of the French border and Ramée's native city of Givet. As mentioned in an earlier chapter, there is evidence that before he went to America Ramée established a wallpaper factory in Dinant.[4] In addition, a letter of 1825, written from the Swedish-Norwegian consulate in Paris to the French police inquiring about Ramée, states that the architect "lived for a long time in Dinant in Belgium, where he had established a factory."[5] The only considerable period of time when Ramée could have lived in Dinant is between his return from America and his move to Paris in 1823. It is likely that he was in the Dinant region as early as March 1817, for at that time a copy of his baptismal certificate was made at the city hall of Givet; it was probably acquired by the architect in order to have the necessary documentation for work in Belgium or France.[6]

There is some indication that Caroline and Daniel Ramée went to Hamburg during this period, then rejoined Joseph in Dinant. A mid-nineteenth-century biographical article on Daniel states that after returning from America with his father he "went back to Hamburg, in 1818, [then] made his studies at the *collège* in Dinant."[7] Further evidence of the Ramées' connection with Dinant are two lithographic views of the town, inscribed as having been drawn by Daniel Ramée.[8] They are undated, but it is possible that Daniel drew them while a student in Dinant, for he had precocious artistic talent (as shown by his drawings of his father's designs that were published in 1823). One of the lithographs shows Dinant from the north, the town lying along the River Meuse, dominated by the church with its oddly bulbous tower and by the cliffs and citadel rising behind it (Fig. 239). The other view, drawn from the south, shows the town in the distance and in the foreground the Rocher Bayard, a spirelike rock formation on the east bank of the river. Both views are highly romantic in spirit, focusing on peculiar and irregular forms in nature and architecture. Something of this spirit can be found in Ramée *père*'s landscape designs, but the young Daniel displays it here in a particularly strong way.

Regardless of Joseph Ramée's motive for returning to his native Ardennes region, it is perhaps not surprising that he settled on the Belgium side of the border, for the economy of the region at this time was oriented largely to the north.[9] Southern Belgium, part of the Kingdom of the Netherlands in this period, was enjoying prosperity, due especially to the exploitation of its iron resources. Entrepreneurs who profited from this prosperity were building country estates, and this was no doubt the class of people for whom Ramée, according to Boulliot, "built country houses and put parks in order" in Belgium.

We know the identity of only one of these Belgian estates, however:

239 View of Dinant on the Meuse, drawn by Daniel Ramée. Lithograph of G. Engelmann. (© cliché Bibliothèque Nationale, Paris)

Yves-Gomezée, near Charleroi, about thirty kilometers east of Dinant. Ramée included a plan of the estate, dated 1818, in *Parcs et jardins*. This publication includes plans for two other estates dated about the same time, but these are in France: one at Massembre, just outside Givet, the other at Villers-Agron, near Reims. Two additional plans for estates in northern France – at Flize and Le Mont-Dieu – probably date from this period, when the architect was working in this region.

In these five designs, Ramée's landscape plans are similar to those of his earlier parks. But there is something different about the *houses* on these estates. In the architect's earlier plans, the houses were nearly always new buildings, designed either by Ramée himself (as at Sophienholm) or by other contemporary architects. But in these later designs, most of the houses are old buildings, although some were remodeled by Ramée. One might suppose this to be just a coincidence, or due to economic reasons. But it seems also to represent a shift in taste. In earlier periods, a property owner who was laying out new grounds would normally want a new house too; even in the irregular "English" gardens of the eighteenth century, a new, neoclassical building was the ideal. Now, however, the possession of old buildings was becoming a virtue. This change reflected the new interest in medieval architecture, the desire to reassert historical traditions suppressed by the Revolution, and the increasing appeal of the picturesque esthetic, which favored asymmetry and variety.

The new thinking was expressed in a publication by the aristocrat and artist Alexandre de Laborde, which appeared in installments from 1808 to 1815 and was entitled *Description des nouveaux jardins de la France et de ses anciens châteaux* – "*new* gardens" and "*old* country houses."[10] Ramée evidently knew this work. It seems to have influenced his own publications, and his son Daniel later referred to it in a brief article he wrote on gardens.[11] The plates in Laborde's *Description* illustrate several grand French estates, such as Malmaison, Ermenonville, and Méréville, but the text is applicable to all kinds of country property.

In the first part of his essay, Laborde observes that "rural life acquires a new charm after great revolutions, when men, worn out from events, enjoy relaxing in the calmness of retreat," and he states that the French émigrés, having "wandered far from their country," are now drawn emotionally to "refinding a corner of their forefathers' heritage."[12] Laborde discusses his principles of naturalistic garden design and mentions that he disapproves the term "*jardin anglais,*" preferring "*jardin de la nature*" or "*jardin irrégulier*" (the term Ramée used for the title of his first publication, in 1823). Laborde criticizes the *chinois* version of garden design for its unnecessary complexity. He calls for a more modest approach, in which the existing features of an estate, including its old buildings, are largely retained:

> The true art of gardens seems to me to be the science of producing, in a given spot, the most pleasant appearance appropriate to the site. This rule restrains both the ambition to create and the mania to destroy. It requires following what nature indicates, in the shape of the land, [etc.]. It allows the preservation of most of the old forms and construction. . . and thus reduces greatly the expense, time, and difficulty involved.[13]

Laborde also discusses architectural style. He speaks approvingly of French castles of the Middle Ages and the reign of François I, models which he considers more appropriate to modern French estates than "Greek" buildings (by which he probably means all neoclassical buildings):

> The Gothic style. . . can be adapted to all construction, as it submits to no rigid rule and depends on no fixed proportion. Its disorder is sometimes even charming and pleasing in the midst of the irregularities of the countryside. . . . It is more fitting to our landscapes, because these perpendicular forms, these crenelated or pointed towers, cut into the horizon. . . . Our old châteaux [also preserve] precious traces of our history.[14]

In all these points, Laborde was expressing the new picturesque esthetic, first articulated largely in England, but now finding favor also in France. Ramée, despite belonging to an older generation of architects by this time, quickly assimilated elements of the new thinking – no doubt through the writings of Laborde and others, but also probably through his clients. Ramée, who had adapted his designs to the needs of so many kinds of clients over the course of his career, now found work with some new types, such as industrialists, as well as aristocrats who were rebuilding their lives after the Revolution.

An example of the latter is Louis Marie Joseph, Comte de Lavaulx, for whom Ramée designed a park in 1820. Born in 1781, Lavaulx was of a prominent family of Lorraine, and a nephew of the Duc de Richelieu. During the Revolution, Lavaulx's father fled France, his mother was imprisoned

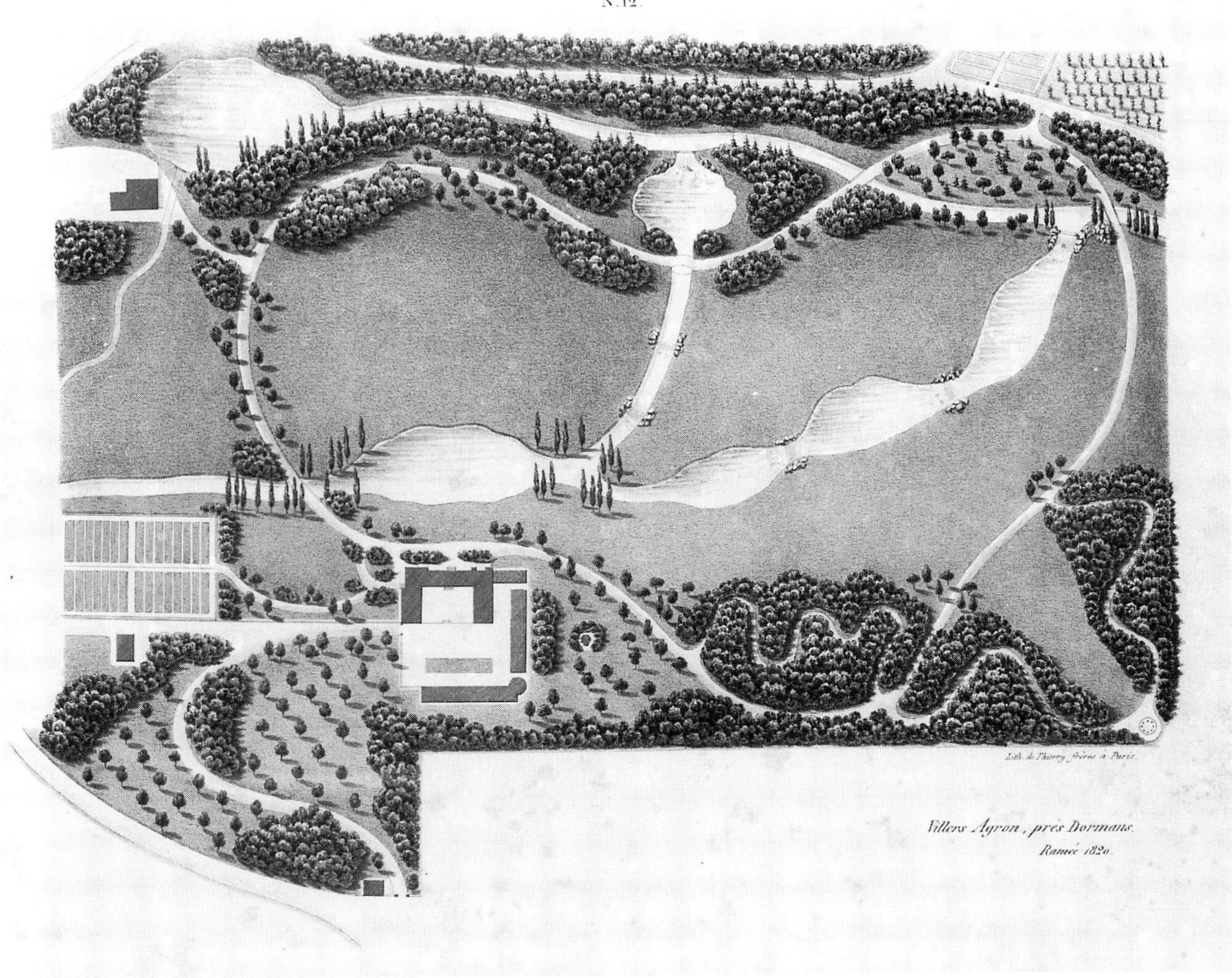

240 Villers-Agron. Plan in Ramée's *Parcs et jardins*, pl. 12. (Schaffer Library, Union College)

for a while, and most of the family properties were confiscated. All that remained was a small estate, Villers-Agron, near Reims, with a dilapidated "château" and some old farm buildings. The young Lavaulx served in the armies of Napoleon and then Louis XVIII, but he quit military service in 1817 to return to Villers-Agron, devote himself to his family, and "*réparer les ruines causées par la Révolution,*" as one of his descendants, the present Comte de Lavaulx, has put it.[15] Lavaulx gradually restored and improved the château, managed his farm successfully, and created a park to the north and east of the house, along the banks of the small River Semoigne.

This is the park designed by Ramée in 1820, according to the plan he later published in *Parcs et jardins*. The plan shows the house and farm buildings at the bottom of the sheet (south) and the river above (Fig. 240).[16] Ramée evidently redrew his plan of Villers-Agron for this publication, altering somewhat the proportions of the property (to fit everything more neatly on the sheet), but all the principal elements of the property are there. The most remarkable thing proposed in Ramée's plan is the creation of additional

241 Château of Villers-Agron and part of its park. (Author)

branches of the river, with basins of water and small waterfalls, by means of locks or sluice gates that could divert the stream. This system was in fact executed by Lavaulx, and some of it even survives to this day. Also executed was the circuit path shown in Ramée's plan, leading from the château through wooded areas, across meadows and back and forth over the various branches of the river. At the lower right in Ramée's plan is a small, circular structure, supported by eight columns; it was built (although it no longer exists) and was called the "kiosque" by the Lavaulx family.

In 1844, Louis de Lavaulx constructed a small tower on the north façade of the château (facing the park), with a tall pointed roof of the sort that Laborde had praised in his essay (Fig. 241). Despite the time that elapsed between Ramée's park plan and the erection of this turret, it is possible that the architect designed it for Lavaulx, to increase the picturesque character of the house as seen from the park. Ramée's *Jardins irréguliers,* published just three years after he planned Lavaulx's park, includes a design for a house that has towers with the same shape as the one at Villers-Agron (see Fig. 258).

Similar towers are found at the château of Flize, directly on the River Meuse near Charleville-Mézières in the Ardennes region of France. Ramée's plan of the estate of Flize, like that of Villers-Agron, appears in his 1839 publication *Parcs et jardins* (Fig. 242).[17] The plan's inscription, "Parc et Château de Flize," is the only one in *Parcs et jardins* that refers to a building, implying that Ramée designed or remodeled the house as well as the garden at Flize. But the plan is undated and the construction history of Flize is obscure. Over the centuries, the château and its subsidiary buildings evidently underwent many changes and were used for diverse functions.[18] In 1816 the property was acquired by two brothers named Chayaux, textile manufacturers who used the buildings partly for their business. In 1828 an iron manufacturer named Gendarme bought the estate; he also employed some of the buildings for industrial purposes, but used the main house as his residence.

Ramée's plan for Flize was therefore commissioned probably by the Chayaux brothers or by Gendarme. But in the absence of documentation on the château during this period, one can only speculate on the nature of

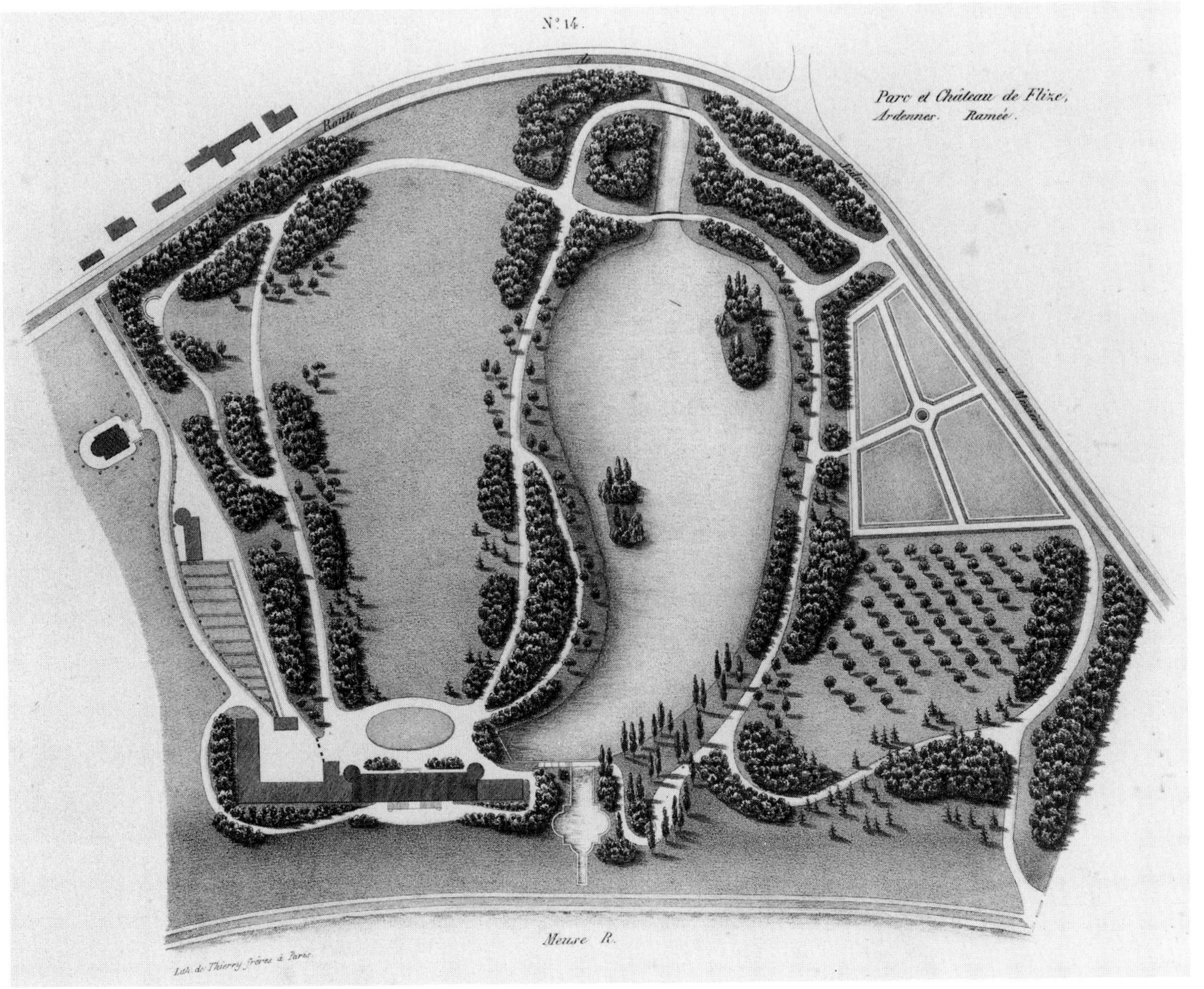

242 Flize. Plan in Ramée's *Parcs et jardins*, pl. 14. (Schaffer Library, Union College)

243 Flize, south side of the château and part of the park. (Author)

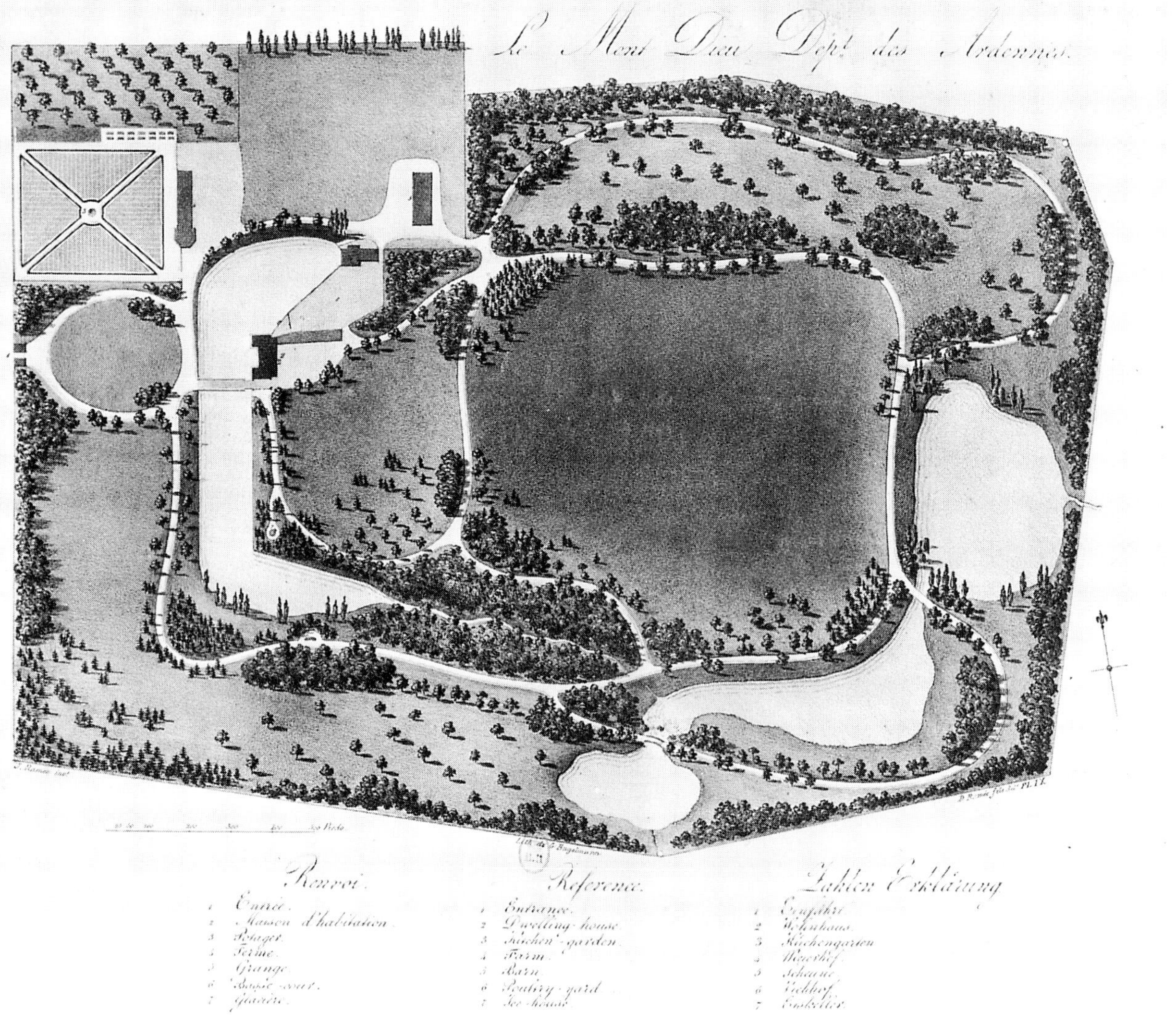

244 Le Mont-Dieu. Plan in Ramée's *Jardins irréguliers*, pl. IX. (© cliché Bibliothèque Nationale, Paris)

Ramée's work. His plan shows the house essentially as it exists today: the main part a symmetrical structure largely classical in form, with a central pediment and large windows, but framed by two round towers with tall pointed roofs (Fig. 243). This odd combination of classical and medieval forms is consistent with a construction date in the early nineteenth century, and with Ramée's work at this time. If Ramée did design or remodel the château of Flize, it is one of his most interesting surviving works.

As for Ramée's plan of the park at Flize, it is typical of his landscape designs. It features an irregular pattern of wooded and open areas, and an artificial lake, to be created by earthmoving and damming the small stream that runs through the property and into the Meuse. Although the lake does not now exist, there are topographical indications that it once did; even the two islands shown in Ramée's plan still rise above the depressed lake bed. So it seems that Ramée's landscape plan for Flize was executed. The unanswered question is what role he played in the design of the château.

245 Le Mont-Dieu, the château. (Author)

Laborde, in his praise of old houses in new gardens, mentioned a specific category of old houses: "These are our former monasteries, which due to the events of the Revolution have become the property of private individuals." Lamenting the fact that so many French monasteries were being destroyed, he spoke of the "picturesque scenes and delightful habitations" that could be created by saving even a portion of a monastery's buildings.[19]

One of Ramée's park plans involved just this phenomenon. The Carthusian monastery of Le Mont-Dieu, near Sedan in the Ardennes, had been founded in the twelfth century and grew into a wealthy establishment, with great landholdings and substantial buildings. Appropriated by the state during the Revolution, Le Mont-Dieu passed through various hands and many of its structures were demolished; but the entry lodge, the archbishop's residence, and several subsidiary buildings survived.[20] One of the owners, a manufacturer from Sedan named Poupart de Neuflize, went bankrupt in 1815 and sold the property in 1820 to the merchant François Camus, whose descendants still inhabit the former monastery.[21] Ramée's publication *Jardins irréguliers,* of 1823, includes his plan for this estate (Fig. 244).[22] Although the plan is undated, it seems likely that it was commissioned by Camus, and therefore was drawn by Ramée sometime between 1820 and 1823.

In the spirit of Laborde's principles of architectural conservation, Ramée proposed no changes to the buildings at Le Mont-Dieu; his plan shows them essentially as they existed at the time, arranged irregularly around a broad moat, which one still crosses on approaching the residence from the entry lodge (Fig. 245). Ramée's landscape plan was meant to heighten the picturesque effect of the architecture and the natural setting by creating promenades around the buildings and the moat, along the edges of the forest, and alongside a series of lakes that were no doubt to be made by damming a stream, as at Villers-Agron and Flize.[23]

Among Ramée's clients in Belgium and France was a new breed of industrialist: a man anxious to create links with the past but also unabashedly proud of his business, proud enough to combine factory and country house on the same property and to portray them together in artists' representations. This was the case at Yves-Gomezée, about halfway between Dinant and Charleroi in Southern Belgium, where Ramée created a park in 1818.[24] The estate, its old house, and its noble title had recently been acquired by Jean Baptiste de Cartier, one of the leading figures in the metallurgic industry that was prospering in this region at the time.[25] The property was evidently appealing both for its historical significance and for its industrial potential, which the new baron Cartier d'Yves exploited fully. He constructed new furnaces, forges, and other facilities around the estate and along the banks of the small stream that runs through it. Ramée's plan for the park at Yves (Fig. 246) identifies several of these industrial structures on the perimeter of the landscaped grounds to be laid out around the "château," and with the entry to the estate right next to the main "*fourneau*" or furnace.

Once more, Ramée proposed to dam a stream to create a small lake, which in this case he shows as a kind of canal, going nearly to the house. It

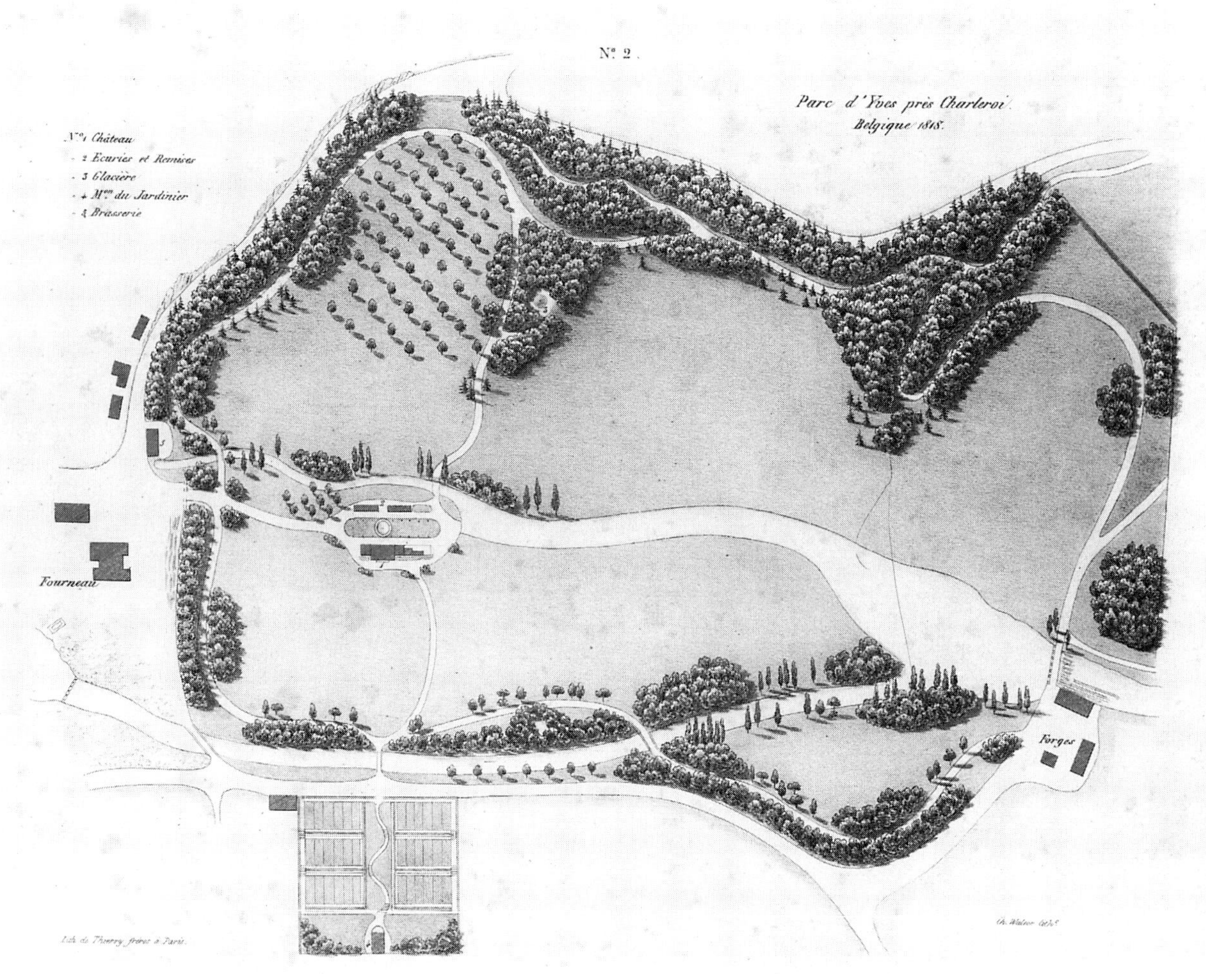

246 Yves-Gomezée. Plan in Ramée's *Parcs et jardins*, pl. 2. (Schaffer Library, Union College)

seems that this waterway was executed, for there is still evidence of an artificial pond on the land today, as well as of the circular fountain that appears on Ramée's plan between the house and the stables.[26] Some of the industrial buildings shown in Ramée's plan also survive, and a couple of them – brick structures with simple arched openings or blind arcades on their façades – look as though they may have been designed by the architect.

The house at Yves no longer survives (it was destroyed in the First World War), but drawings and old photographs show that it was remodeled a couple of times in the nineteenth century. Its early nineteenth-century form, seen in two lithographic views, suggests the hand of Ramée (Figs. 247, 249).[27] A simple, cubic building, evidently with rough-cast walls painted white, it is reminiscent of Ramée's Danish country houses, even down to such details as the narrow window-pediments that float on the façade above the windows, as at Øregaard. The unusual front steps of the house, supported by a segmental arch that springs directly from the ground, are found also in two designs for country houses that Ramée published in 1823.[28] One of the lithographic views of the

247 Yves-Gomezée, lithographic view of house and garden, c. 1840. (Bibliothèque Royale Albert I, Brussels, Cabinet des Estampes)

house also shows a small gate lodge at the entrance to the estate (Fig. 247). Octagonal in plan and with a conical roof, it still stands at Yves (Fig. 248). It also is likely the work of Ramée, for it is similar to designs the architect later published in his *Recueil de cottages* (see Fig. 292).[29]

It is noteworthy that both of the lithographic views show not only the house but the industrial buildings. The view showing the front of the new house includes part of Ramée's garden, with the furnace buildings in the background. The other view (Fig. 249) is drawn from the opposite direction, showing the industrial buildings and their smokestacks in the foreground, with the house and park only partially visible in the background. This view is especially remarkable, as it reveals that the artist – or the proprietor of Yves, who no doubt commissioned the view – considered the industrial component of the estate to be as picturesque and worthy of representation as the house and the park.

248 Yves-Gomezée, gate lodge. (Author)

Two of Ramée's plans in *Parcs et jardins* are dated 1818: the plan of Yves and that of Massembre (Fig. 250).[30] Massembre, just a couple of kilometers north of Ramée's native Givet, is right on the French–Belgian border. In fact, the border follows the stream that runs through the property (and which Ramée, typically, proposed damming to create a small lake). Little is known about the history of Massembre or of its proprietor at the time of Ramée's design.[31] In general, Ramée's plan conforms to the reality of the property at Massembre: the positions of the house, the road leading to it from the entry gate, the stream, and the geometrical *potager* or vegetable garden. But Ramée's plan does not indicate the steep change in grade between the high ground, where the house stands, and the lower land to the west (at the top of the plan), toward the River Meuse.

Moreover, the house in Ramée's plan is composed of three squarish blocks (similar to Sophienholm in Denmark), whereas the actual house at

249 Yves-Gomezée, nineteenth-century lithographic view. In the foreground, the ironworks. Behind, at left, the house.

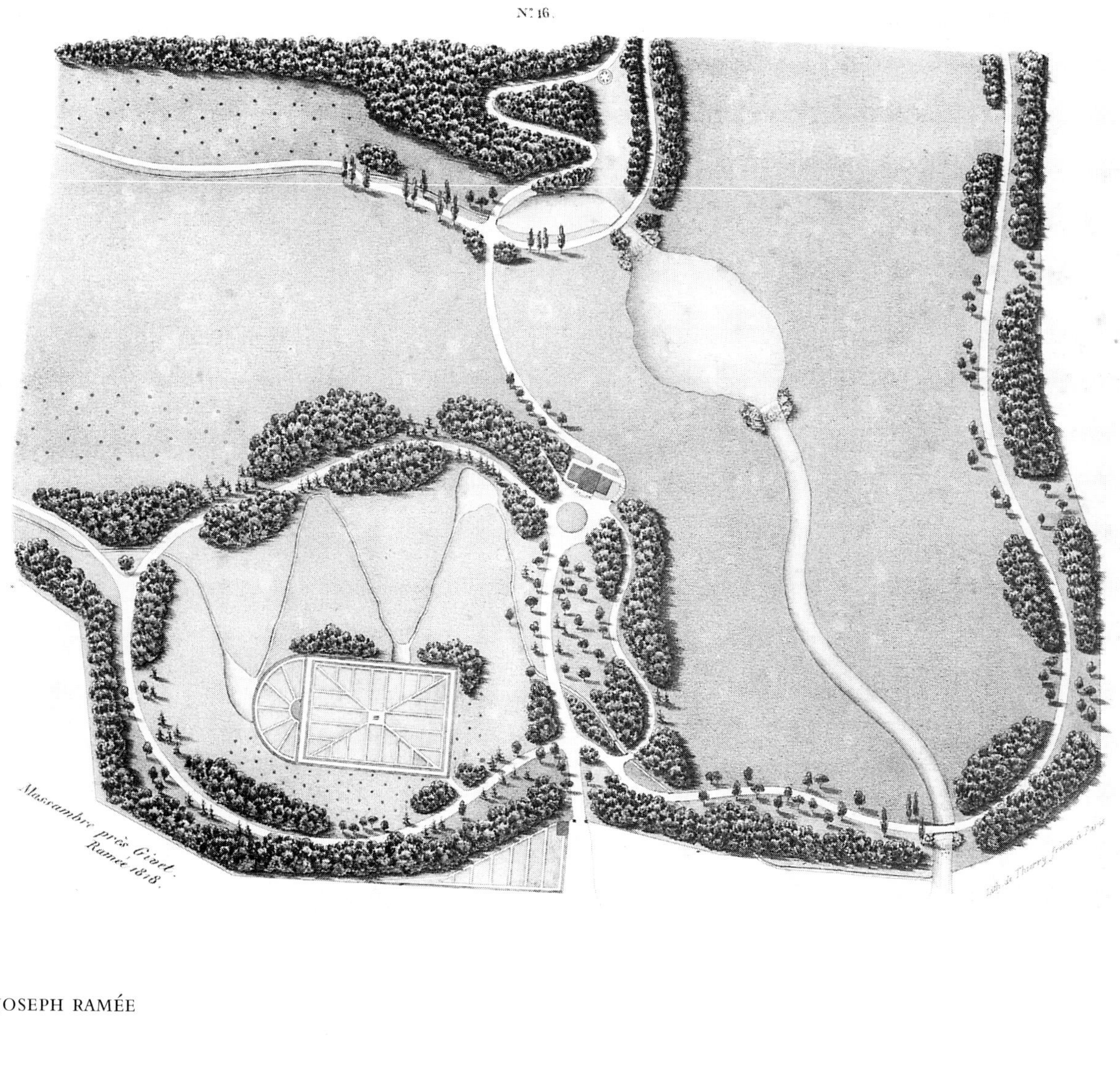

250 Massembre. Plan in Ramée's *Parcs et jardins*, pl. 16. (Schaffer Library, Union College)

251 Massembre, garden side of the house. (Author)

Massembre is one large block, with L-shaped wings that create a small courtyard on the entry side of the house (Fig. 251). The building must date from about the time of Ramée's plan, for stylistically it cannot be much earlier, and it appears on a map of 1823.[32] Did another architect design this house? Or did Ramée produce more than one design for it? Or was his plan modified in construction? Certain details of the building suggest the hand of Ramée, such as the continuous horizontal bands on the façade and the very low pediments over the windows, as in the architect's houses in Denmark (Fig. 252). In the Danish houses, this feature is somewhat different in each one; and here, too, there is a variation on the theme: the window pediments line up with the horizontal bands but distort them, creating a visual ambiguity. If we mentally apply these details to a house shaped as shown in Ramée's plan, with the rough portions of the stone walls stuccoed and painted a light color, the result is very convincingly a work of Ramée.

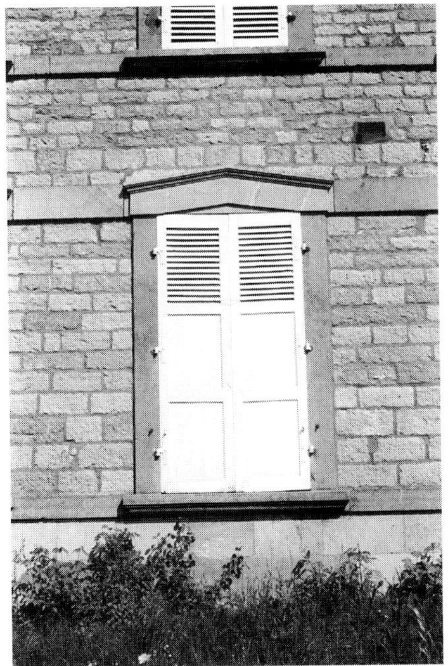

252 Massembre, detail of the house. (Author)

We therefore can identify about four houses that Ramée designed or remodeled when he was living in Belgium after returning from America: those at Massembre and Yves-Gomezée, and possibly Flize and Villers-Agron. Since only one of these is in Belgium, one wonders if Boulliot's article is mistaken in saying the architect "built several country houses" in Belgium. But since Boulliot's information evidently came from Ramée himself, who had no reason to claim that he had worked in Belgium rather than France, it is likely that there are yet-to-be-discovered houses by the architect from this period.[33]

After noting Ramée's work in Belgium, Boulliot states that the architect "embellished the Place Verte of Givet." This square, now called Place de la République, is in Givet-Notre Dame, the part of the city on the right bank of the Meuse. The nature of Ramée's "embellishment" of the square is unknown, but it probably was related to an event of 1817: the legal transfer, from the War Ministry to the city of Givet, of the fountain that was the main feature of the Place Verte. This was a Baroque-style fountain, which had been constructed in 1752 by the Génie Militaire, the military engineering corps (for which Ramée had worked as a boy, in the fortress of Charlemont).[34] The city of Givet may have wanted to replan the Place Verte once it took title to the fountain in 1817, and Ramée may have prepared designs for the landscaping of the square. But no description or visual record of the square in the succeeding years is known, at least until the 1860s when the Place Verte is described (by a resident of Givet who had his own ideas for the square) as "covered with trees, ready to be cut down."[35]

Thus, whatever was the reason that Ramée settled in Belgium after returning from America in 1816, much of his known work during this period was actually in France: in Givet and at country estates such as Massembre, Villers-Agron, Le Mont-Dieu, and Flize. But these jobs could hardly have been enough to support the architect during the seven years before he moved to Paris. He probably was occupied with various kinds of work: additional country houses in Belgium; enterprises such as his wallpaper factory in Dinant; and other activities familiar to this man whose life had forced him to become a jack of all trades.

Paris

Ramée moved to Paris in 1823 and was listed in the city's directories for approximately the next ten years.[36] The reason for his return to the French capital at this time is as uncertain as the reason for his earlier move to Belgium. The architect's mentors, Belanger and Cellerier, were both dead by 1823 (Cellerier had died in 1814, Belanger in 1818). David Parish, Ramée's American patron who had returned to Belgium at the same time as the architect, was in Paris for a while around 1823, conducting business with the French branch of the Rothschild family; perhaps he tried to arrange commissions for Ramée as he had done in America.[37] Another possibility centers on the Comte d'Artois, who in 1823 was assuming almost complete power in France, as his brother Louis XVIII approached death. Artois, who was to assume the throne as Charles X the following year, was a potential patron of Ramée, as the architect had worked for him forty years earlier while an apprentice in Belanger's office. But there is no evidence that Artois rehired Ramée.

One possible motive for Ramée's move has to do with the publications he began producing in 1823, which could be printed and distributed most successfully in Paris. For some time, Ramée had intended to publish something on his work. In Philadelphia in 1814, he was reported to be planning "a work on the principles of his art."[38] But the three publications that Ramée eventually produced, in the 1820s and 1830s, have almost no text; they are simply collections of designs. Like many architects of the period, Ramée probably considered such publications mainly a way to achieve professional recognition and to attract new clients. Paris clearly had more potential in this regard than the provinces.

There is evidence that Ramée's son, Daniel, collaborated with his father in the preparation of these works. Although only seventeen years old in 1823, when the first publication came out, Daniel was already an accomplished artist and drew several of the designs for the lithographer. It is therefore necessary at this point to bring the younger Ramée into the story of his father's career.

Biographical articles on Daniel Ramée, which appeared in the equivalents of today's *Who's Who* starting in the 1850s, provide some sketchy information about his youth.[39] Born in Hamburg in 1806, he accompanied his father on his travels and learned the profession of architecture from him. One of the accounts states that after returning from America and going to Hamburg in 1818, "he studied at the school in Dinant, then in Mézières [center of the Ardennes region of France], where he devoted himself to the arts. In 1823 he went to Paris. Possessing already the basics of architecture, he applied himself especially to the study of the Middle Ages."[40]

In the 1830s, Daniel began his career as a restorer of medieval monuments; much of his work in this field is well documented. But his activities in the 1820s are largely unknown. It seems likely that he worked with his father as a kind of apprentice, both in his designs and in their publication. It also seems that Daniel became interested in the new art of lithography. Invented in Germany in the 1790s, lithography was introduced to France by Godefroy Engelmann, first in Mulhouse, then in Paris starting in 1816.[41] Engelmann exploited the full potential of the technique as a medium for artists, whose drawings could now be transferred directly to the printing stone without the intermediary of an engraver. By 1823, when Ramée's first publication appeared, Engelmann's studio and others in Paris were busy producing lithographs for artists. Four plates in Ramée's 1823 work are lithographs, and they are inscribed as having been printed by Engelmann.[42] Three of these are inscribed as having been "drawn" by Daniel Ramée ("D. Ramée fils del't"), although Ramée *père* is identified as the creator of the designs ("Jos. Ramée inven't"). Engelmann also produced the two lithographic views of Dinant described above, which are inscribed as the work of Daniel. It is possible, therefore, that Daniel introduced his father to the new art of lithography.

The three known publications of designs by Ramée are entitled: *Jardins irréguliers et maisons de campagne, Recueil de cottages et maisons de campagne,* and *Parcs et jardins*. Each is identified on the title page as the work of "Joseph Ramée, architecte." *Jardins irréguliers* bears the date 1823. The other two are undated, but evidence such as the publisher's address and other clues reveals that *Recueil de cottages* was published in 1837 and *Parcs et jardins* probably in 1839. These last two works, which appeared shortly before Ramée's death, will be examined in the next chapter. A puzzling thing about all three publications is their extreme rarity: no more than two or three copies of each one are known today.[43]

The title page of *Jardins irréguliers* is in English and German as well as French (Fig. 253), and the text on some of the plates is also trilingual.[44] Comparison of the three titles is revealing:

> *Jardins irréguliers [et] maisons de campagne de tous genres et de toutes dimensions exécutés dans différentes contrées de l'Europe et de l'Amérique Septentrionale par Joseph Ramée . . .*

> *Drawings and Plans of Gentlemans [sic] Seats, Picturesque pleasure Grounds and Gardens designed, and laid out in different parts of Europe and North America by Joseph Ramée . . .*

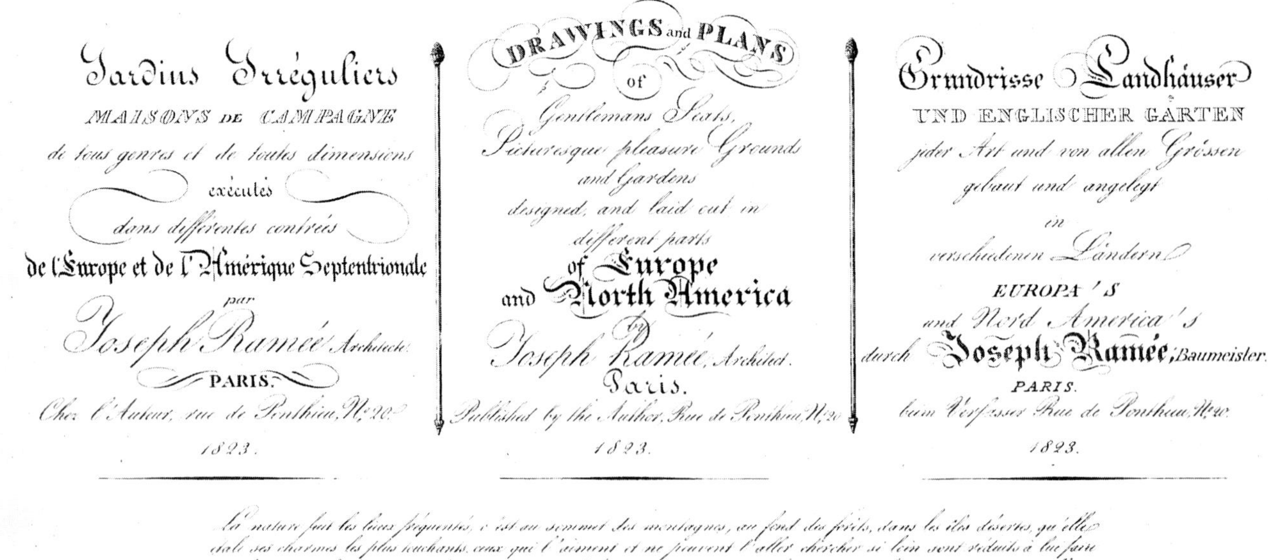

253 Title page of Ramée's *Jardins irréguliers,* 1823. (Kunstakademiets Bibliotek, Copenhagen)

Grundrisse Landhäuser und Englischer Gärten jeder Art und von allen Grössen gebaut und angelegt in verschiedenen Ländern Europa's und Nord America's durch Joseph Ramée . . .

A couple of things are noteworthy here. First, although the English title is somewhat ambiguous and could be read to mean that only the "grounds and gardens" were actually executed by Ramée, the French and German titles state explicitly that the country houses as well as the gardens were constructed by the architect. If correct, this is significant, for none of the three houses shown in the publication has yet been identified as an executed building. These designs may therefore represent some of the missing country houses that Boulliot and others state that Ramée erected in Germany, the United States, and Belgium.

Secondly, it is interesting that Ramée uses three different terms to describe the style of his landscape designs: "*irrégulier,*" "picturesque," and "*Englische Gärten.*" In France, "*jardin anglais*" had long been the most common term for such landscapes. Ramée's choice of the more recent "*jardin irrégulier*" (which Laborde, for instance, used in his essay) implies a desire to distinguish his designs from earlier French models. In any case, Ramée's use of the normal English and German terms for such landscapes indicates that he was familiar with garden design in English-speaking and German-speaking countries, and that he wanted to emphasize to his audience his international experience in the field.

Below Ramée's name, on the title page of *Jardins irréguliers,* is the information "published by the author, Rue de Ponthieu, no. 20" – the architect's address in Paris, according to a city directory of 1824. Ramée thus had the work printed for his own use or distribution. This fact might explain its extreme rarity, only three copies of the work being known in the world today. (However, Ramée's other two publications, equally rare, were handled by a commercial publisher.) At the bottom of the title page is the passage from Jean-Jacques Rousseau's novel *Julie,* about nature and its artificial creation in garden design, which was quoted in Chapter 2.

Like many architectural publications of the period, *Jardins irréguliers* was issued in installments, each consisting of several individual plates. A brief review of the work in a magazine in 1826 noted that two installments had appeared by that time, with a total of thirteen plates. The review adds that "this work will be composed of six parts [*six recueils*], of three installments each [*trois livraisons*], for a total of 108 plates."[45] But it seems that the additional installments were never produced, as the only known surviving plates belong to the first two installments.[46]

These plates have a puzzling diversity. Some are engravings, others are lithographs. Some of the designs are identified, others are not. Included are the following: two plans for parks; plans, elevations, sections, and perspective drawings of three houses (apparently unrelated to the two parks); the design for an "American icehouse" seen earlier; and a view of an entry way to a park (this last plate known only by its mention in the 1826 review, as no copy of it is known to survive). Most remarkable is the diversity of architectural styles represented by the designs, including styles never before seen in the work of Ramée. This variety suggests that Ramée wanted to convey the multiplicity of his talent and experience, acquired from working in many places, as the title of the publication emphasizes.

The two park plans in *Jardins irréguliers* are for the Duane estate in New York and Le Mont-Dieu in Northern France. These are similar in format and drawing style to the landscape plans that Ramée later published in *Parcs et jardins* (the Duane plan, in fact, appears in both publications). The rest of the plates in *Jardins irréguliers* are architectural designs. Because of their diversity, each of them is worth describing.

Four plates illustrate a neoclassical house (with floor plans, elevations, and a section drawing), which is conservative in style, for the 1820s (Figs. 254–7).[47] The tripartite form of the house – two-storey central section with gable roof, and one-storey wings – was a standard eighteenth-century type, found especially in England. Some of the details, however, seem to be drawn from the work of Claude Nicolas Ledoux, such as the arches supported on columns on the garden façade, and the low segmental arch beneath the stairs leading to the porch. The plain surfaces of the house, unframed windows, and starkly simplified classical details are also reminiscent of Ledoux's work, as well as that of John Soane and other English neoclassicists.

In contrast to the conservatism of this design, the other two houses in *Jardins irréguliers* are up-to-date for the 1820s, though unusual in certain respects. One of them is portrayed in a lithographic perspective view, the other in four engravings.[48]

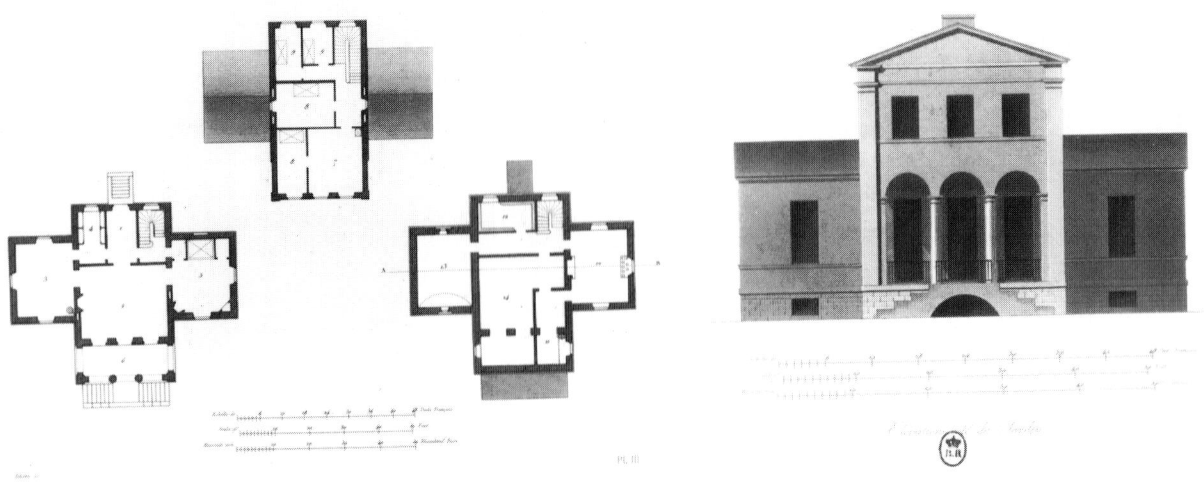

254 Plate III of *Jardins irréguliers*. (© cliché Bibliothèque Nationale, Paris)

255 Plate IV of *Jardins irréguliers*. (© cliché Bibliothèque Nationale, Paris)

The lithographic view (Fig. 258) shows a large park, whose arrangement of lawn, groves of trees, and meandering lake (in the background) is typical of Ramée's landscape plans. But the house is like nothing seen previously in his work; it is a strange mélange of parts and styles. Ramée was clearly trying out the new picturesque manner of design, which had been developing, especially in England, in recent decades. But it seems that Ramée did not pattern his house on the work of other picturesque designers. Rather, he created a potpourri of elements drawn from his own previous designs and from architecture to which he had been exposed in his travels.

The overall plan of the house is symmetrical and relatively classical, as are such details as the windows. The entranceway, a large arched niche, is like the niche in the façade of Ramée's Börsenhalle in Hamburg; even the design of the wall within the niche is similar. And the front staircase, supported by a low arch like that in the previous design, seems derived from designs of Ledoux.

In contrast to these largely classical elements, the medieval turrets – flanking the entrance and at the corners of the house – are similar to those at the châteaux of Flize and Villers-Agron, whose parks Ramée had designed. And the stepped gable of the central part of the house is Flemish or northern German, something Ramée would have known from his years in Belgium and the Hamburg area. Decorative details – the sphinxes flanking the entry, the shield-bearing lions at the apex of the gables, the trophies at the corners of the house – have a whimsical quality and add to the impression that the building is a pastiche of incongruous parts. Indeed, one wonders if Ramée may have conceived this design as a kind of parody of the new picturesque fashion in country houses – as if to say, "Since this is what people seem to want today, I'll show them a real variety of parts, drawn from all the places where I've worked."

The third house in *Jardins irréguliers* has a similarly eclectic character, but is composed of completely different elements and more richly ornamented (Figs. 259–62). There are windows and doorways in about ten different styles,

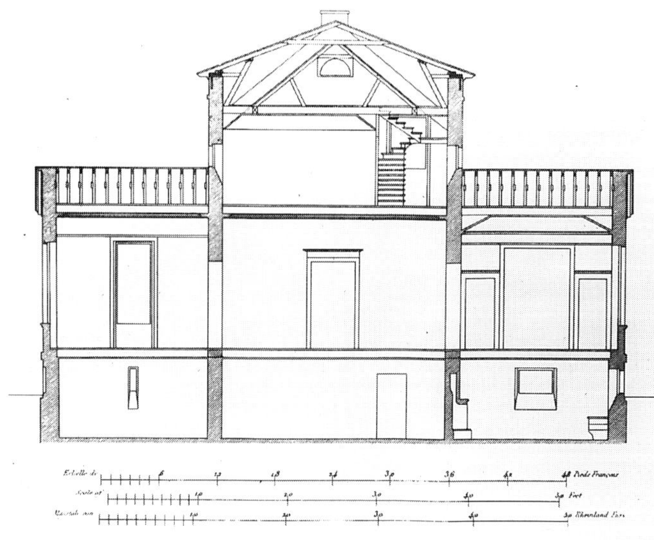

256 Plate V of *Jardins irréguliers*. (© cliché Bibliothèque Nationale, Paris)

257 Plate VI of *Jardins irréguliers*. (© cliché Bibliothèque Nationale, Paris)

258 Plate I of *Jardins irréguliers*. (Kunstakademiets Bibliotek, Copenhagen)

259 Plate X of *Jardins irréguliers*. (© cliché Bibliothèque Nationale, Paris)

260 Plate XI of *Jardins irréguliers*. (© cliché Bibliothèque Nationale, Paris)

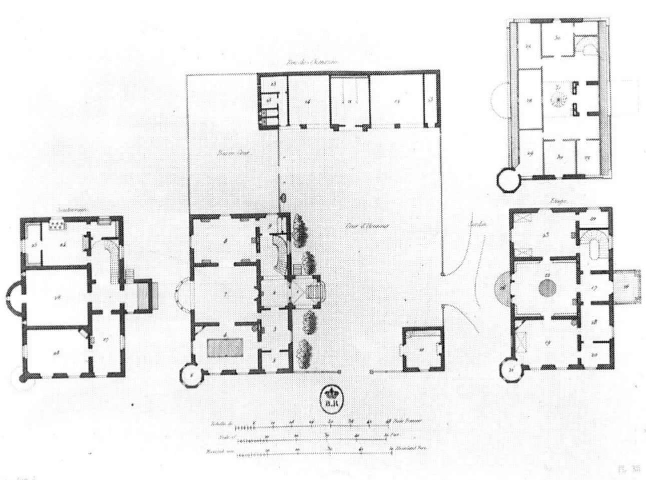

261 Plate XII of *Jardins irréguliers*. (© cliché Bibliothèque Nationale, Paris)

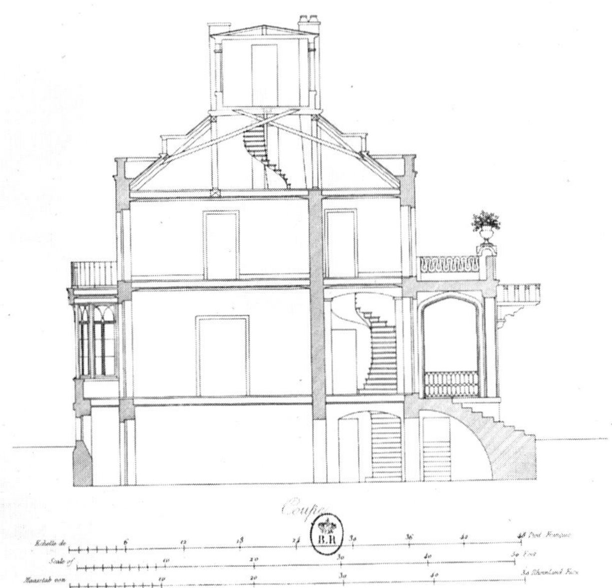

262 Plate XIII of *Jardins irréguliers*. (© cliché Bibliothèque Nationale, Paris)

and numerous decorative treatments and wall patterns. Elements from the late Gothic and French Renaissance predominate, but as in the previous house, the overall impression is of a kind of whimsical pastiche. Among the features are an octagonal corner turret with a heraldic shield on one face and a fancifully decorated dome; a glazed belvedere atop the house; an entry porch with flowerpots and a serpentine balustrade; detached stables with an arcade of low pointed arches and horse motifs decorating a dormer wall; and a gate lodge identified as the "huntsman's house," with an odd-shaped roof and a weathervane in the form of a posthorn. Increasing the picturesque quality of the design, the overall shape of the house and its outbuildings is asymmetrical, although the individual parts are mostly symmetrical. The design is characterized by strange disparities – symmetries and asymmetries, conventional and unconventional forms, unlikely combinations of elements from different periods and place – which one might attribute either to naiveté or to a purposeful desire for incongruity.

Despite their diverse and international eclecticism, none of these house designs in *Jardins irréguliers* has any American component. As if to rectify this deficiency, Ramée included in the publication his design for an "American icehouse (see Fig. 237)." As mentioned in Chapter 12, Ramée based this design on an icehouse devised by John Beale Bordley, with a new system for insulating the ice. The exterior form of Ramée's icehouse follows Bordley's in overall form: circular, with a conical roof and ventilating cap at the top, and a gabled entryway.[49] But Ramée made some changes, especially in the design of the entry, replacing Bordley's rather classical doorway with a pointed opening and a remarkable feature: bargeboards at the edge of the gable, carved with decorative animal heads, a device found in the rural architecture of northern Germany and Scandinavia.[50] Clearly Ramée was not trying to make his icehouse authentically American in every detail. He was more interested in presenting something inventive (both technically and architecturally), and especially in having something in his publication that he could *call* American – to give his work a truly international scope.

Following Ramée's return to Europe, his work thus underwent some radical changes. Although he continued to produce roughly the same kind of landscape designs as before, his architectural work became much more eclectic, picturesque, and idiosyncratic. In this respect Ramée was no doubt influenced by new currents in European design during this period, but it is likely that his American experience had a liberating effect on him, as suggested earlier. It is also possible that Daniel Ramée – still a teen-ager but precocious in artistic talent – played some role in shifting the focus of his father's work.

Also new was Ramée's interest in publishing his work and in using publication as a means of emphasizing the international nature of his career. Previously, the evidence of correspondence and other documents indicates that Ramée had considered the frequent dislocations of his life, quite naturally, as professional misfortunes. After returning from America, however, he apparently came to view his nomadic career in a more positive light, as a distinction worth publicizing and possibly exploiting.

Last Works and Publications

Chapter 14

Nearly twenty years elapsed between the publication of *Jardins irréguliers* and Ramée's death, in 1842, at the age of seventy-eight. Only a few of the architect's activities during these two decades are known. One might suppose that Ramée was simply retiring gradually from work as he grew old. But in fact, most of his known activities are in the second of these two decades: commissions in the Hamburg area in the mid-1830s, two publications of designs in the late 1830s, and landscape work in northern France as late as 1839.

The more mysterious period is the first ten years, before Ramée went to Hamburg about 1833. The architect spent this entire time in Paris, according to the city's directories, which list him at four successive addresses, all in newly laid-out residential streets just north of the Avenue des Champs-Élysées.[1] What was Ramée doing during these ten years? *Jardins irréguliers,* planned in 1823 as a large publication of eighteen installments, halted after two of them (unless there were additional installments that have disappeared). Other than this publication, only three projects by the architect in this period are known: two designs for country estates, and a plan for the Place de la Concorde and Champs-Élysées in Paris, all of which date to the end of the decade, around 1829. For about five years in the mid-1820s, not a single design or other activity of Ramée is known.

Also unknown is the effect that the political events of this period had on Ramée. In 1824, Louis XVIII died and was succeeded by his brother Charles X, the former Comte d'Artois. One would think that Ramée might have profited professionally by the accession to the throne of his old employer, the patron of his teacher Belanger. But there is no evidence of such profit. Then, in 1830, Charles X was overthrown in the "July Revolution" and was replaced by the more liberal Louis Philippe, of the Orleans branch of the Bourbon dynasty. By an odd coincidence, Ramée had personal ties with Louis Philippe as well. In 1792–3, both men had been staff officers of General Dumouriez's army in northern France and Belgium; both were involved in Dumouriez's plot to overthrow the revolutionary French government; and when the plot failed, both escaped into enemy territory. Like Ramée, Louis Philippe then lived for a while in Hamburg and spent many years in exile from France, traveling extensively (even to the United States, though not at the same time that Ramée was there).[2] But there is no evidence that Louis Philippe provided Ramée with architectural commissions when he assumed the French throne.

Ramée's known work in the 1820s is so minimal that one suspects he was involved in some nonarchitectural activity, perhaps a business enterprise such as his earlier wallpaper manufactories in Dinant and Philadelphia. Particularly puzzling is a series of documents of 1825, found recently in the

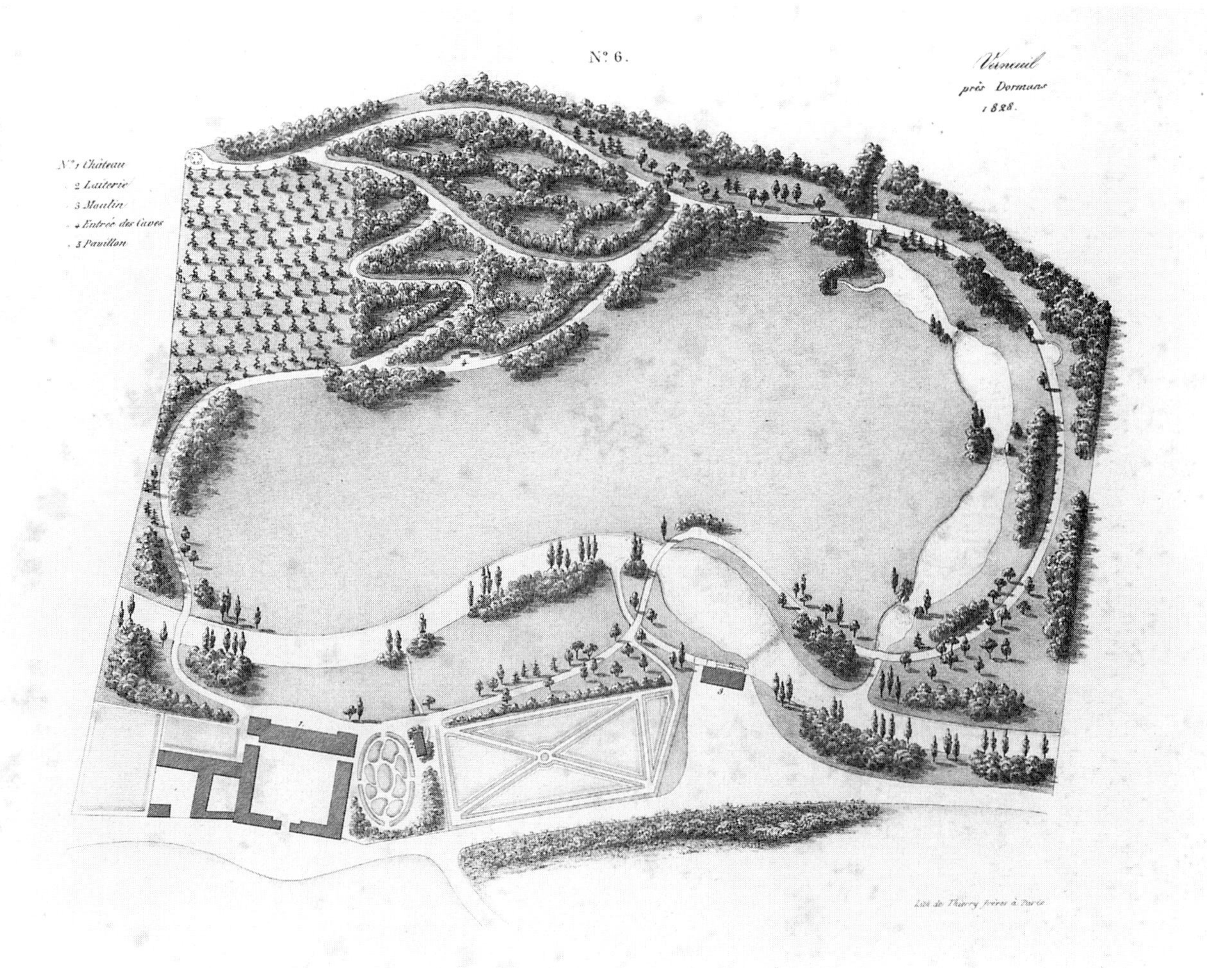

263 Verneuil. Plan in Ramée's *Parcs et jardins*, pl. 6. (Schaffer Library, Union College)

Archives Nationales. These are letters from the Swedish-Norwegian consulate in Paris, to the French police, requesting information on Ramée and his former business partner in Hamburg, André Masson; there is also a response from the police, stating that nothing about the two men could be found.[3] Whether this inquiry was related to the bankruptcy of Masson and Ramée's firm seventeen years earlier, or to more recent activities, is unknown. (In view of the convoluted and somewhat shady political pasts of both Ramée and Masson, one is tempted to imagine such things as secret missions for the Bourbon court, to account for the mysterious years.)

The two plans for country estates that Ramée designed at the end of this period – at Verneuil and Carlepont – are found in his publication *Parcs et jardins* and are dated 1828 and 1829, respectively (Figs. 263, 264).[4] The village of Verneuil (near Dormans, between Paris and Reims) is only a few kilometers from Villers-Agron, so Ramée probably received this commission through his work for the Comte de Lavaulx, described in the preceding chapter. A pre-Revolutionary map of Verneuil shows the property that Ramée later landscaped, identifying it as belonging to the Vicomte de Verneuil; a map of 1832

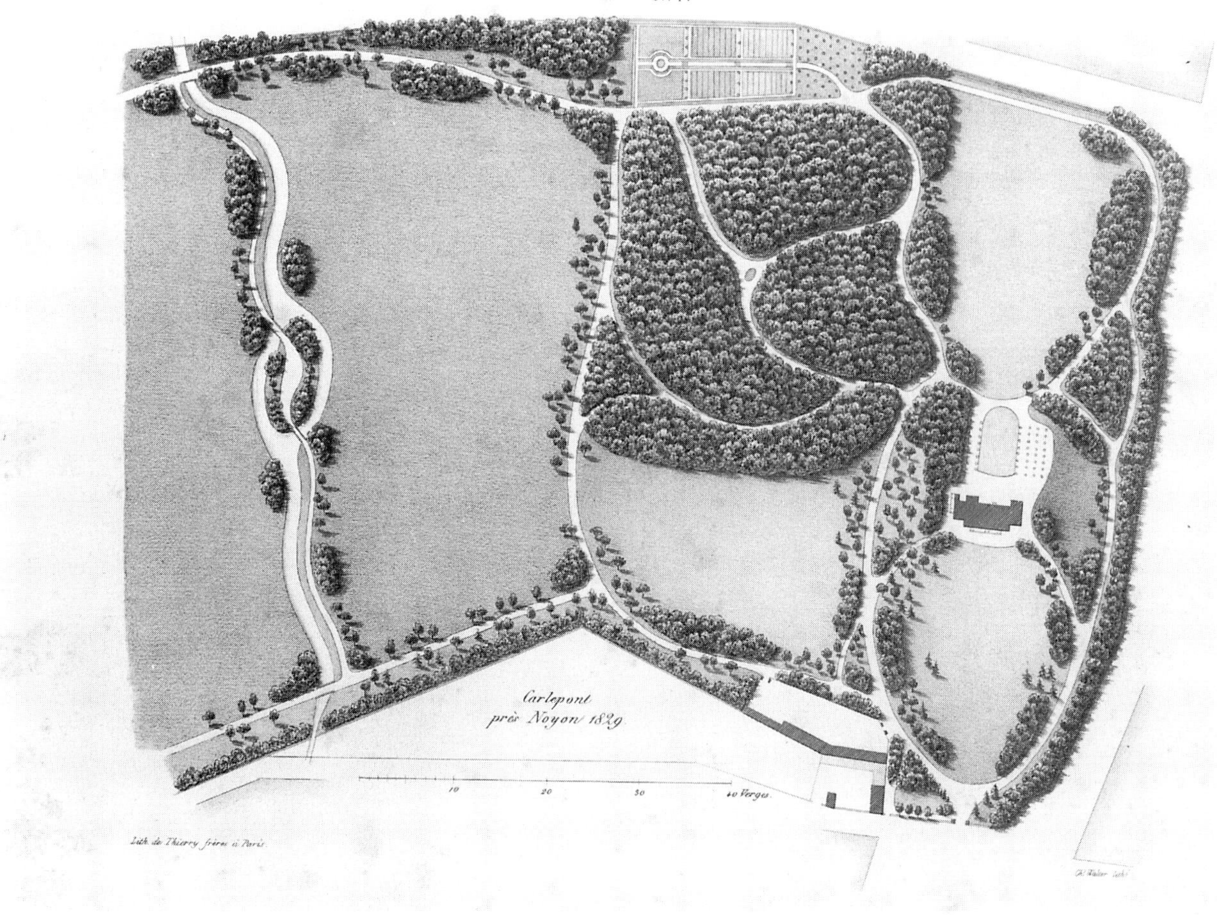

264 Carlepont. Plan in Ramée's *Parcs et jardins*, pl. 7. (Schaffer Library, Union College)

shows the land divided into several properties, most then owned by a certain Pierre Lambert Brion.[5] Ramée's design was perhaps part of a plan by Brion to reassemble the former aristocratic estate and improve it. But the scheme evidently never materialized, and neither the house nor the grounds shown in Ramée's plan survives.

In contrast, the property planned by Ramée at Carlepont – near Noyon, north of Paris – still exists, though it is in poor condition. The estate belonged for centuries to the bishops of Noyon, who built successive country houses there, the last one constructed in 1762.[6] Appropriated by the government during the Revolution, the property passed through several hands and was purchased in 1828 by the Baron de Standish. He evidently engaged Ramée to lay out his grounds the following year. The estate was subsequently owned by other families; the main house was badly damaged in the First World War and is now in ruins, and no records have been found that shed light on Ramée's commission. But enough vestiges of the original layout of the ground – such as patterns of roads and trees – survive to indicate that Ramée's plan was at least partly executed.

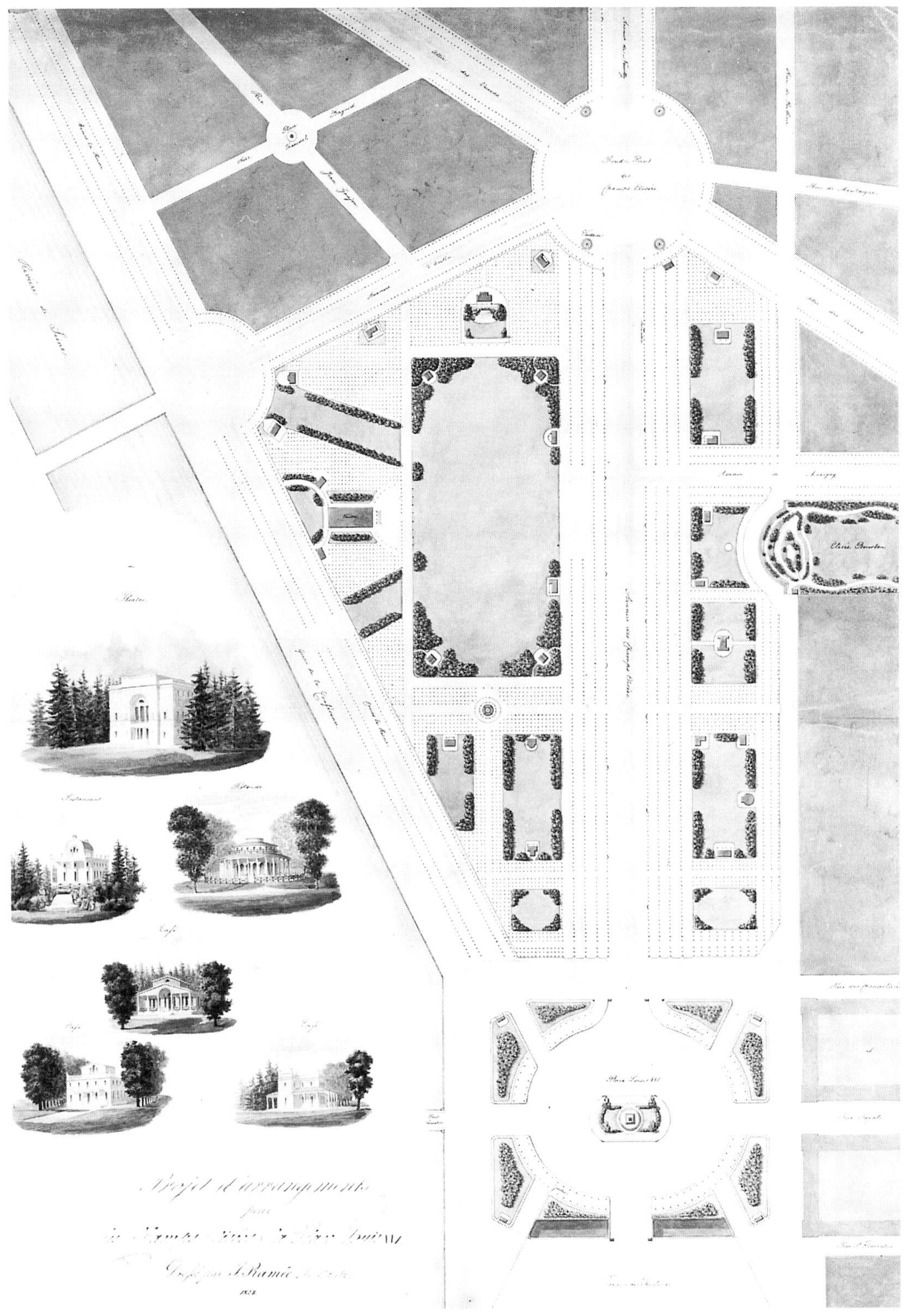

265 Project for the Champs-Élysées and Place Louis XVI, Paris, inscribed "J. Ramée Architecte, 1828." Ink and watercolor drawing, 47 × 68 cm. (Musée Carnavalet, Paris)

The Place de la Concorde and Champs-Élysées

Ramée's most significant work of this period was his redesign of the Place Louis XVI (now the Place de la Concorde) and the Champs-Élysées park, in Paris. Although this project – known by a drawing of 1828 and descriptions of a plan submitted in a competition the following year – was never executed, it seems to have played a role in the process that ultimately shaped these important public spaces.

The drawing, preserved at the Musée Carnavalet in Paris, is inscribed "Projet d'arrangements pour les Champs Élisées & la Place Louis XVI, Dressé par J. Ramée Architecte, 1828." (Fig. 265 and color plate 19)[7] Drawn in ink and watercolor, this plan shows the Place Louis XVI at the bottom of the sheet, the Champs-Élysées above. Also on the sheet are little perspective drawings of garden pavilions and other buildings projected by Ramée for the Champs-Élysées.

In August of 1828, the French government turned these public spaces over to the city of Paris, and in early 1829 a civic competition was held for the redesign of the Place Louis XVI. Ramée was one of the entrants in this competition. Boulliot tells us so, and the architect's plan was described in press accounts of the affair.[8] Although Ramée's competition plan does not survive, the written descriptions of it are detailed enough to show that it was similar to the plan of the square in Ramée's surviving drawing. To understand this design requires some background about the square and the competition.

When laid out in the mid-eighteenth century, as the Place Louis XV, the square's main features were an equestrian statue of the king and decorative moats along the perimeter of the space. During the Revolution, the statue was destroyed and the square (renamed Place de la Révolution and then Place de la Concorde) was the site of the guillotine whose victims included Louis XVI and Marie Antoinette. After Charles X assumed the throne in 1824, he renamed the square Place Louis XVI and conceived a memorial statue of his martyred brother for the center of the space.

At the same time, the square was being used increasingly by the public, as the neighborhoods to the west were developed as residential quarters. To make the place suitable for this traffic, as well as appropriate to the king's memorial intention, the prefect of Paris, the Comte de Chabrol, opened a design competition in 1829.[9] Ten architects were officially invited to enter the competition (receiving a stipend to do so); anyone else could enter on his own. A total of twenty-three designs were submitted and were exhibited at the Hôtel de Ville for three months in 1829. Several Paris newspapers and magazines printed accounts of the competition and the entries.[10]

Included in these accounts are descriptions of Ramée's design for the square, with the information that he was not one of the subsidized competition architects but had entered independently.[11] The accounts reveal that Ramée's entry was similar to, but not exactly the same as, the plan of the square in his drawing of 1828. Despite the date of this drawing, it seems to show an awareness of the competition regulations; perhaps Ramée was apprised of the competition in advance and prepared this preliminary version of his entry.

The competition rules stipulated that four fountains were to be included in the square; that the moats on the west side, next to the Tuileries Garden, were to be retained (the other moats could be filled in); that provision was to be made for vehicular and pedestrian traffic; and that the execution of the plan could cost no more than 1,500,000 francs.[12] The projected memorial statue of Louis XVI was naturally to be the centerpiece of the square.

The newspaper accounts of the competition observed that most of the entries did not adhere well to these stipulations, especially regarding the budget: some of the plans had very elaborate architectural features, such as colonnades. (In fact, Chabrol's jury was not fully satisfied with any of the designs and they asked two of the entrants, Destouches and Lusson, to modify and combine their plans.) Ramée's design was singled out, in some of the accounts, for its adherence to the competition rules and for its simplicity, although there were differing judgments of its success. These accounts are worth quoting, for they are the only evidence of Ramée's entry design, and the divergent opinions they express are revealing. The anonymous writer in *Le Globe* was very favorable:

> We prefer the plan of M. Ramée, who also gives the square an oval shape, but without enclosing it. His plan includes lawns, some groups of trees, and extensive granite sidewalks; it replaces the vegetation presently in the moats with running water and it surrounds the expiatory monument [the statue of Louis XVI] with an elegant and simple parterre. This most natural, most economical and best-conceived plan has another great advantage, in our opinion: it takes the marble giants from the parapets of the Pont Louis XVI . . . and distributes them in the square, surrounding each one with a clump of laurel trees. Thus scattered and shaded, they become less overpowering and grating. In sum, this plan seems to us to fulfill, with pleasing simplicity, all the conditions of the program, and to create an appropriate transition between the architectural beauties of the royal garden [i.e., the Tuileries] and the verdant masses of the Champs-Élysées.[13]

The critic of the *Nouveau Journal de Paris* gave only a brief description of Ramée's plan, but it too was favorable and noted the simplicity of the design:

> This plan joins simplicity and elegance. The four jet fountains are grouped around the monument on a lawn planted with funerary trees [i.e., cypresses]. The twelve surrounding statues and the bodies of water are in perfect harmony with this decoration.[14]

The architectural critic of the *Journal du génie civil,* A. Corréard, provided more details of Ramée's design, though he found less favor with it:

> M. Ramey [sic] is the author of this project. We are grateful to

> him for his efforts to stay within the appropriated sum, 1,500,000 francs. But it is unfortunate that it does not have more nobility. This square with rounded corners makes a poor impression. The author keeps the four moats, reshapes them, and rounds off their jutting angles; he fills them with water, but without explaining how it is retained. He then forms a large oval in the square, bordered with wide sidewalks, and plants grass in the areas between these sidewalks and the moats. On each of these lawns he raises three pedestals with statues. In the center of the square he creates a second, smaller oval, more like a hippodrome, which is also planted with grass, and with cypress trees. In this precinct are four fountains, each with a pedestal, two small basins, and a water jet in the middle. One cannot deny that this latter part of the design is in perfect harmony with the principal monument [i.e., the statue of Louis XVI]; it has the religious spirit that was intended. But it seems that this composition and its elements would be more appropriate for a spot devoted to sepulchers or to a park containing someone's grave, rather than a public square where people will often assemble for ceremonies or festivities. We may observe that M. Ramey did not reflect very well on his subject, or he would have included as many exits as possible, one of the main requirements of a square, and to do this he would have removed the moats, even those on the Tuileries side.[15]

The last two criticisms of Ramée's project were unfair. Corréard personally disliked the religious overtones of the projected memorial to Louis XVI, and he felt that the competition program should have allowed the removal of all the moats; but these were conditions over which Ramée had no control.[16] Corréard's critique does, however, suggest the distinctive traits of Ramée's plan: its informality, its lack of monumentality (or "nobility"), its curvilinearity, and its reliance mainly on plantings – in short, its parklike quality. Ramée's design was quite different from the other competition entries in this respect. Some observers, such as the critic at *Le Globe,* found this refreshing and original. Others, such as Corréard, found it unworthy of a great urban square.

Ramée, having spent so many years abroad working in less monumental environments than Paris, and having specialized in private gardens, may simply have been out of touch with patterns of urban planning on a grand scale. Or he may consciously have chosen to propose a parklike style of urbanism for the Place Louis XVI. The competition jury evidently shared Corréard's disapproval, rejecting Ramée's plan despite its careful adherence to the design regulations.

The plan of the square in Ramée's surviving drawing is similar to his competition plan described above – in its oval shape, wide sidewalks, central planted area, and certain other elements. But in the drawing, only the moats on the Tuileries side are retained, and the peripheral planted areas are therefore different in form from those in the competition plan. Oddly, these points would suggest that the surviving plan was executed *after* the competition, in response to criticism, although the drawing is dated 1828 (before the competition). Whatever the explanation may be, Ramée's overall proposal for the Place Louis XVI – as represented by both of his plans – was unusual and attracted attention at the time of the competition. It also perhaps influenced the design that was eventually executed for the square.

The July Revolution of 1830, which overthrew Charles X, rendered obsolete the competition plans for the Place Louis XVI – now renamed, once again, the Place de la Concorde. But there was still a need to develop this part of Paris, including the Champs-Élysées. In 1833 the project was entrusted to the young architect Jacques Ignace Hittorff. Like Ramée, Hittorff had been an unsuccessful entrant in the 1829 competition.[17] Also like Ramée, Hittorff had been a student of Belanger, though at the end of Belanger's career rather than the beginning. Despite their age difference (twenty-eight years), Ramée and Hittorff surely knew each other. It is therefore significant that the designs Hittorff produced for both the Place de la Concorde and the Champs-Élysées are similar in certain ways to those in Ramée's plan of 1828. Did Ramée's design influence Hittorff's? Did the two architects actually collaborate in some way? One can only speculate on this, but it is worth considering, for Hittorff's plans were largely executed and they helped to shape this part of Paris as we know it today.

After the 1830 Revolution, the statue of Louis XVI in the Place de la Concorde was replaced by the Egyptian obelisk that still dominates the square, and Hittorff drew numerous proposals for the square and its parts.[18] Some of these plans are similar to Ramée's scheme, in their use of plantings to define the boundaries of the square, and in their general simplicity. Starting in 1836, Hittorff's plans were executed, and despite later transformations established largely the modern form of the Place de la Concorde.

Hittorff also played an important role in the development of the Champs-Élysées – in its landscaping and especially in the structures that were executed in this park. Here, too, Hittorff's work bears some similarities to Ramée's 1828 plan for the area, a fact that was noted in a recent historical study of the Champs-Élysées.[19]

The Champs-Élysées, when acquired by the city of Paris in 1828, was an unkempt forest, through which the muddy Avenue des Champs-Élysées ran from the Place Louis XVI to the Rond Point and on to the Étoile, where Napoleon's Arc de Triomphe was still under construction. This wooded area contained few buildings or other public amenities; its main features were several open spaces, the largest of which, the Grand Carré, had been cleared of trees by Madame de Pompadour to create a better view of the Seine from her palace (now the residence of the French president), on the north side of the Champs-Élysées.[20] The land to the north and east of the Champs-Elysées, still open countryside at the time of the Revolution, had just recently been developed as residential neighborhoods (it was here that Ramée lived in the 1820s) and there was now demand to make the Champs-Élysées a safe and comfortable area for public use, with cafés, dancehalls, and centers for amusement and

266 Buildings projected for the Champs-Élysées, in margin of Ramée's plan. Theatre at top. Restaurant and "*Rotonde*" in middle. Three cafés below.

relaxation. In 1820, the landscape designer Gabriel Thouin had published a proposed design for the area, with garden pavilions and restaurants.[21] And in the mid-1820s, Martin Pierre Gauthier, named offical architect of the Champs-Élysées, proposed his own plans, but they were criticized as too lavish and costly.

Ramée's plan of the Champs-Élysées, in his 1828 drawing, is a response to these public needs and financial constraints. It proposes no costly alteration of the land. The Grand Carré and other open spaces in the woods are retained and merely enhanced by dense plantings around their edges, giving them varied rectangular and oval shapes. Distributed through the entire area are structures of differing sizes and shapes. The perspective drawings in the margin of Ramée's plan illustrate six of these buildings: a theatre, a restaurant, a "*Rotonde,*" and three cafés (Fig. 266).

267 C. N. Ledoux, design for river-directors' house, Chaux. (Daniel Ramée, ed., *Architecture de C. N. Ledoux*, Paris, 1847, pl. 110. Courtesy of Princeton Architectural Press)

The designs of these structures are fascinating, for they constitute a kind of summary of Ramée's career and architectural influences. The façade of the theatre is clearly based on the architect's Börsenhalle in Hamburg (see Fig. 102), with a large arched niche over the entrance to the building. One of the cafés (the one at the lower left) is a cubic structure with a gabled attic storey, similar in form to several of Ramée's country houses in Denmark, such as Hellerupgaard and Øregaard (see Fig. 139). Another of the cafés (the one at the lower right) reveals that the architect had been looking at picturesque English country-house designs of the period. The building – asymmetrical and suggestive of a medieval castle or Italian villa, but surrounded by porches – is reminiscent of the villa designs of John Nash and other British architects.[22] Nothing like this is known in Ramée's earlier work. Ten years later, the architect was to publish a collection of cottage designs that reveal somewhat similar English influences. This café for the Champs-Élysées shows that already in the 1820s Ramée was interested in such architectural developments in England – no doubt through publications, but also perhaps from personal visits across the Channel.

268 C. N. Ledoux, design for tollhouse in Paris. (Daniel Ramée, ed., *Architecture de C. N. Ledoux*, pl. 7. Courtesy of Princeton Architectural Press)

The other three structures depicted on Ramées's plan show that the architect was still drawing inspiration from the work of Claude Nicolas Ledoux, who had influenced the young Ramée so strongly in the 1790s. The "*Rotonde*" seems based on two of Ledoux's Paris tollhouses (the Barrière de Monceau and Barrière de Reuilly), though Ramée added a peripheral porch supported by thin columns, appropriate to a park pavilion.[23] Ramée's restaurant is a whimsical variant of Ledoux's extraordinary design for the River Directors' House in the utopian city of Chaux: a house in the shape of a horizontal cylinder, through which the river itself was to flow and create a waterfall (Fig. 267).[24] Ramée separated the two components of Ledoux's design, putting the cylinder on the top of a colonnaded structure, from the base of which gushes the waterfall.

269 J. I. Hittorff, Cirque d'Été on the Champs-Élysées, erected 1840. (E. Texier, *Tableau de Paris*, vol. 1, Paris, 1852, p. 11)

Ramée's third café has a shape that was a favorite of Ledoux: a block with a low-pitched gable roof, an arched opening in the center of the façade, and columns along all or part of the façade (Fig. 268).[25] Ramée altered Ledoux's format mainly by indicating that it was to be built of vertical wood boards, a type of construction Ramée had employed in Denmark (for instance in Frederikka Brun's "Norse House" at Sophienholm) and which was nicely appropriate for a rustic café in a wooded park.

Ledoux's iconoclastic work was held in generally low esteem in the 1820s.[26] Ramée's allusions to it, in these drawings, are especially interesting in light of the fact that Ramée's son, Daniel, was to publish in 1847 the most complete edition of Ledoux's designs. The circumstances of this edition, and even the motivation for it, are unclear and have puzzled historians. Ramée's Champs-Élysées pavilions of 1828 suggest that Daniel Ramée's later edition of Ledoux's work may have been inspired by Ramée *père*'s long-held interest in Ledoux – a question that will be examined in the Epilogue.

In the 1830s and 1840s, Hittorff produced numerous designs for recreational buildings in the Champs-Élysées. Several of these were executed, including the Panorama, Cirque d'Été, Théâtre des Folies-Marigny, and various pavilions and cafés.[27] These structures are reminiscent of the buildings shown in Ramée's 1828 drawing, especially in the cases of the Panorama and Cirque d'Été (Fig. 269), which are similar in form to Ramée's "*Rotonde*."

Ramée's design for the Place de la Concorde and Champs-Élysées is thus significant in several regards. It suggests that the architect's wide-ranging experiences in landscape planning gave him a distinctive, non-monumental approach to the design of urban spaces. Its architectural components serve as a kind of recapitulation of the diversity of Ramée's career. And it played a role in the topographical evolution of this part of Paris.

Return to Hamburg

The Place de la Concorde competition is the last thing mentioned in Boulliot's article on Ramée, published in 1830. From here on, we are deprived of this important source of information on the architect's life and work.

In the mid-1830s, Ramée spent some time in Hamburg again, where he had worked for about fifteen years at the beginning of his career. A nineteenth-century Hamburg publication states that the architect was there starting in 1832, and a family diary reveals that Ramée and his wife returned from Hamburg to Paris in 1836.[28] But the architect probably did not pass this entire period in Germany. The fact that he continued to be listed in Paris directories through 1834 suggests that he may have divided his time between the two places. All of Ramée's known work at this time, however, is in Germany.

Four landscape plans, later published in *Parcs et jardins,* are dated to this period. The first is Baurs Park, at Blankenese on the Elbchaussee, which Ramée had originally planned around 1805 and where he did additional work in 1833 (described in Chapter 6). The other three plans were apparently new commissions. One was for Peter von Lengercke, Jr., a relative of Caroline Ramée.

Peter von Lengercke, Sr., one of Caroline's uncles, had founded in 1781 a successful cotton factory in Wandsbek, a suburb east of Hamburg.[29] His son (who, besides being Caroline's cousin, married one of her sisters) inherited the factory and the family estate, which faced each other across a park, on the shores of the little lake called the Mühlenteich. Ramée's design for this estate is dated

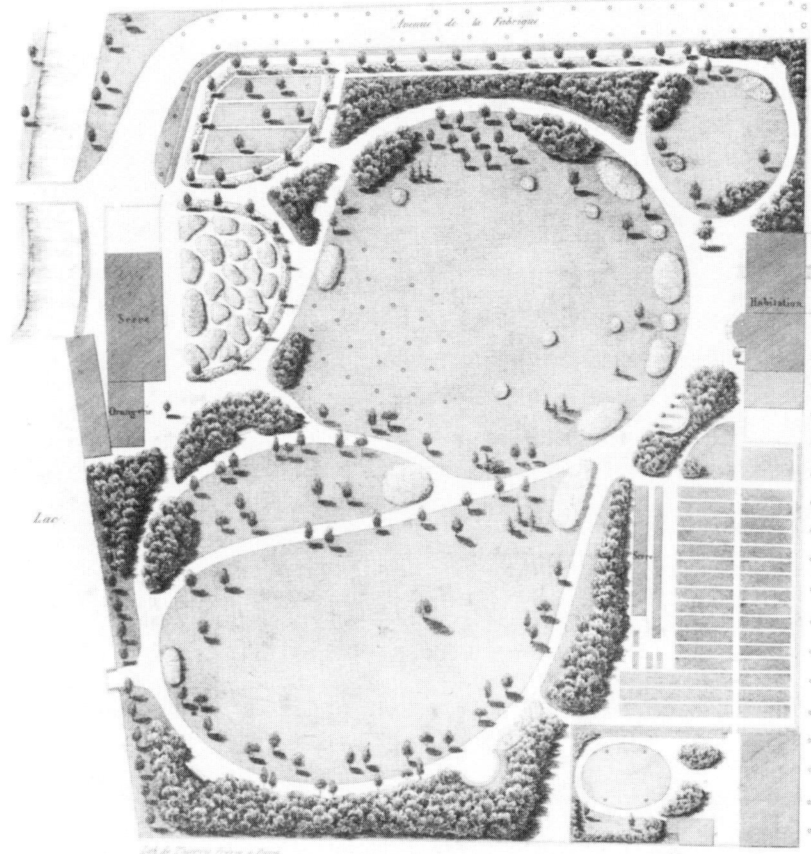

270 Lengercke garden, Wandsbek. Plan in Ramée's *Parcs et jardins*, pl. 11. (Schaffer Library, Union College)

271 Lengercke garden and factories, lithographic view, 1840. (Heimatmuseum, Wandsbek)

1834 in *Parcs et jardins* (Fig. 270).[30] The plan shows two separate gardens. The main one is laid out in a figure-eight pattern of paths and plantings, with the family house at one side and a large "*Serre*" (greenhouse) and an *Orangerie* at the other side, next to the Mühlenteich. (The factory buildings are not included in the plan; they would be to the upper left.) The house faces a street, across which is a second, smaller garden, designed to create a view of lawn backed by dense groves of trees. In a corner of Ramée's plan is a little perspective view of the house, as seen from the main garden. It is a simple neoclassical structure, with a wing on one side that has a semioctagonal bay. The view is too sketchy to allow us to judge whether this house was the creation of Ramée. But it is similar to one of the house designs he later published in *Recueil de cottages*.[31]

A nineteenth-century lithographic view shows the Lengercke estate from the vantage point of the house (Fig. 271).[32] In the foreground is Ramée's park, although the trees and other plantings are shown much reduced in size and number, probably in order not to obscure the buildings in the background. These buildings include the *Orangerie* and greenhouses at the left, and one of the large factory buildings at the right. Whether Ramée had a hand in the design of any of these structures is not known.

Also uncertain is Ramée's possible involvement in construction that Peter von Lengercke carried out in his role of philanthropist. Devoted to social causes, he created workers' housing, a workers' savings bank, and a small hospital, the Wandsbeker Krankenhaus.[33] Lengercke laid the cornerstone of this hospital in 1833 – that is, about the same time that Ramée designed the grounds of his estate. The hospital, known only from old photographs, was a simple, hip-roofed structure, rather typical of utilitarian Hamburg architecture of the period; without additional evidence, there is no way of knowing if Ramée had a hand in its design. Before Lengercke's death in 1848, his philanthropy was awarded with the Dannebrog Order by the King of Denmark, who paid a personal visit to the house and park in Wandsbek.[34]

Another park planned by Ramée during this period was that of the Parish family at Nienstedten, on the Elbchaussee west of Hamburg. These were the grounds that David Parish had referred to affectionately while in America in 1807 (the thought of his parents' leaving their home was like "pulling up by the roots every tree and bush in the garden of Nienstedten"). The estate's elegant stable, as noted earlier, had probably been designed by Ramée before he joined Parish in the New World.[35] In 1826, after returning from America, David Parish committed suicide following a disastrous financial loss in Vienna. His father, John Parish, died shortly thereafter and the Nienstedten estate was inherited by another of his sons, Richard.[36] Richard Parish was as strongly attached to this property as the rest of the family had been, and like his father before him he devoted much attention to developing the grounds and making additions to the house. The fact that Richard engaged Ramée's services in the 1830s, as his father and brother had done earlier, underscores the strong ties the architect had with the Parish family.

Ramée's plan for the Parish estate, published in *Parcs et jardins* (Fig. 272), is dated 1835 and shows many features typical of the architect's landscapes:

272 Parish estate, Nienstedten. Plan in Ramée's *Parcs et jardins*, pl. 10. (Schaffer Library, Union College)

sweeping patterns of paths and plantings, an artificial inlet of water along the river's edge (as at Sophienholm), and even one of the architect's "American" icehouses.[37] But the property, unlike Baurs Park, has not survived intact and it is hard to determine the extent to which Ramée's plan was executed.

Also unknown is whether Ramée played some role in shaping the main house at Nienstedten, which was different from the houses of the other great estates of the Elbchaussee (Fig. 273). Rather than erecting a neat, neoclassical building like those of his neighbors, John Parish had retained an old structure that was on the property when he bought it. In the 1790s he added wings and porches, producing an irregular, multigabled mass that was an early example of the picturesque style of architecture, which Parish perhaps knew from his visits to England. Richard Parish continued making improvements in this vein, for instance adding a cantilevered bay at the end of the eastern wing of the house, surrounded by a porch and set within an elaborate gable; the whole composition had a vaguely Swiss-chalet appearance, somewhat similar to designs that Ramée published in *Recueil de cottages*.[38] These additions to the Parish House were made during the decade following Ramée's plan of 1835, so it is possible that the architect contributed in some way to their conception.

273 Parish House, drawing of 1935, before demolition of the house. (Staatsarchiv Hamburg)

274 Salomon Heine. Lithographic portrait by O. Speckter, 1842.

275 Heine estate, Ottensen. Plan in Ramée's *Parcs et jardins*, pl. 9. (Schaffer Library, Union College)

Another property on the Elbchaussee designed by Ramée in the 1830s was that of Salomon Heine, a Hamburg banker and uncle of the poet Heinrich Heine (Fig. 274).[39] In 1808 Heine had acquired this large estate, at Ottensen, where he spent summers for the rest of his life, surrounding himself with numerous friends and relatives. (His nephew Heinrich, in fact, lived with Heine from 1816 to 1819 and retained fond memories of the Elbchaussee.) Ramée's plan for the estate, as published in *Parcs et jardins,* is dated 1834 and shows the architect's typical landscape patterns of open space and wooded areas, with paths leading down to the river (Fig. 275).[40] The principal buildings shown on the plan already existed, but the architect apparently proposed a couple of small structures: one of his circular icehouses and a garden pavilion labeled "Chaumière" on the plan. This "thatched cottage" has an asymmetrical floor-plan and an open porch around two sides, similar to some of the picturesque designs that Ramée was to publish in his *Recueil de cottages.*

Most intriguing is the question of whether Ramée had a hand in the design of Salomon Heine's *Gartenhaus,* the only original building that survives today on the property (Fig. 276). This modest structure, near the entrance to the estate, was erected in 1832 to serve two distinct functions: gardener's residence and retreat for Heine himself. The second function was accommodated by an elegant room, the *Gartensaal,* occupying the eastern half of the building, where Heine would relax and entertain his intimate friends (Fig. 277).[41] Ellip-

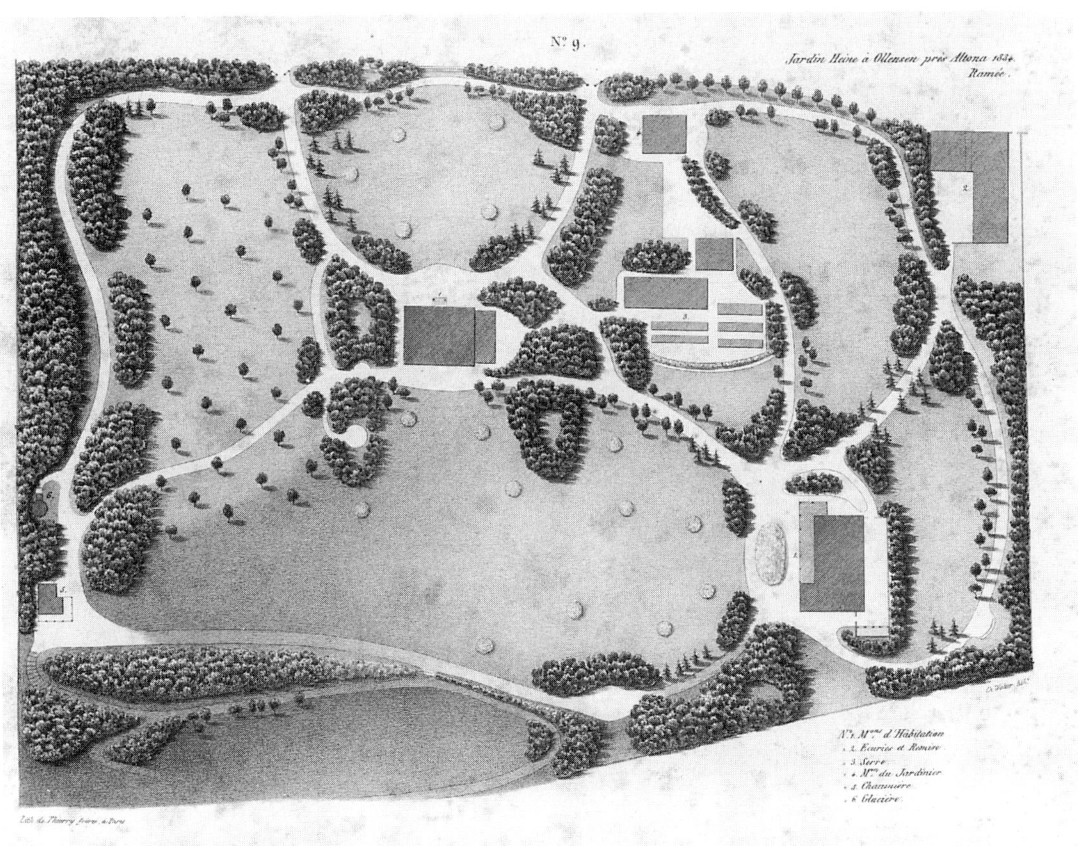

276 Heine's *Gartenhaus*. (Staatliche Landesbildstelle, Hamburg)

277 Heine's *Gartenhaus,* the *Gartensaal.* (Author)

tical in plan, with segmental vaults over the end niches, this room could well be the work of Ramée. The geometry and proportions of this room are compatible with Ramée's interior designs; even the unusual friezes, with small disks or paterae, are found in the architect's other work (in the Perregaux House in Paris, for instance, and at Frederikslund near Copenhagen).

The architect of Heine's *Gartenhaus* is not known.[42] Its exterior form, with a steep hipped roof and plain wall surfaces, is typical of Hamburg architecture of the early nineteenth century. As the building was erected in 1832 – the year that Ramée probably arrived in Hamburg – it is possible that Heine asked the architect to design the interior space after the shell of the structure was in place.

Last Years in France

In 1836, Joseph and Caroline Ramée returned from Hamburg to Paris. This is known from a document that is almost the only source of information on the last six years of the architect's life: a diary written by Stephen Martel, brother-in-law of Caroline Ramée.[43]

Martel was born in 1781 on Saint-Domingue (Haiti). In the 1790s, the bloody revolution there devastated and dispersed his family; apprenticed to a merchant, Martel eventually went into commerce and spent much of his life traveling in Europe and America. For a while in the 1810s he lived in Philadelphia, where he perhaps met Joseph and Caroline Ramée. In 1831, Martel married Caroline's elder sister Wilhelmina, and for the rest of their lives the two couples were very close, even living together much of the time.

Stephen Martel's diary is sketchy and indicates only certain kinds of events, such as voyages the family made. Martel notes that he and his wife and the Ramées left Hamburg in June of 1836, traveled to Le Havre by steamship, and then went on to Paris, settling in the Hôtel du Danube. They apparently lived there for the next couple of years. In the summer of 1838, Martel and the two women spent a month at the baths of Aix-la-Chapelle, then went to Hamburg and Wandsbek (no doubt to visit their relatives, the Lengerckes), then returned to Paris in October. In 1839, there were numerous trips in northern France, by Martel and Joseph and Daniel Ramée, in search of a "*maison de campagne*" to which the double family could retire. In September of 1839 they purchased the "Château de Beaurains," just outside the city of Noyon, where Daniel, then working for the Commission des Monuments Historiques, was documenting the city's great Gothic cathedral and preparing to restore it.[44] The Ramées and Martels lived in Noyon during the remodeling of their new house, into which they finally moved in April of 1841. Ramée *père,* then seventy-seven years old, was to live less than a year thereafter.

In the architect's final years, after he returned to France in 1836, it seems that he continued to do some landscape designing (as shown by a letter he wrote, to be quoted later), but devoted himself mainly to the publication of two collections of his designs: *Recueil de cottages et maisons de campagne* and *Parcs et jardins.* Neither work is dated, but evidence of various kinds reveals that *Recueil de cottages* was published in 1837, *Parcs et jardins* probably in 1839.[45]

Like the earlier *Jardins irréguliers,* these two publications are composed only of plates, with no text except for captions to the illustrations and brief statements on the title pages. But in contrast to the somewhat chaotic *Jardins irréguliers* (with its miscellaneous types of design, some engraved and others lithographed, and of differing sizes), the two later works are focused in content and format. Each has a consistent pattern of plates, all of them lithographs, and each is devoted to one type of design. Rather than being published by the architect himself, as *Jardins irréguliers* had been, the two later works were handled by a commercial publisher, Rittner et Goupil, a prominent firm in Paris at that time.[46]

Despite the more professional manner of publication, copies of these two works are as rare as those of *Jardins irréguliers.* Only two complete copies of *Parcs et jardins* are known, both now in libraries in the United States, plus several loose plates at the Bibliothèque Nationale in Paris.[47] Only three copies (none complete) of *Recueil de cottages* are known: two in the Bibliothèque Nationale and one that remained in the Ramée family and with their heirs.[48] It is not unusual for publications of this kind to be rare, since the editions were often small and, being composed of loose plates, were often broken up and dispersed. But the rarity of Ramée's publications is extreme and may suggest something about the architect's motives in producing them. They were probably not planned as moneymaking enterprises, nor (considering the architect's advanced age) to publicize Ramée's work to prospective clients. The last two publications, in particular, were perhaps intended mainly to document Ramée's work for his family, friends, and professional acquaintances.

This motive is evident especially in *Parcs et jardins,* whose full title is: *Parcs et jardins composés et exécutés dans différentes contrées de l'Europe et des États unis d'Amérique par Joseph Ramée* (Figs. 278, 279). Nineteen of the architect's landscape plans are included: They seem to have been chosen to emphasize the geographical diversity of his work, with plans from France, Belgium, Germany, Denmark, and the United States.[49] A brief statement on the title page notes that the variety of the plans is due to their wide-ranging localities:

Parcs & Jardins

Composés et exécutés dans différentes Contrées de l'Europe
et des Etats unis d'Amérique

par JOSEPH RAMÉE

ARCHITECTE.

L'auteur croit et espère être utile aux amateurs de Jardins en leur offrant une série de motifs des plus variés qui sont applicables à tous les sites et pourront servir de guide à ceux qui s'occupent de ces sortes d'arrangements par la multiplicité de scènes des plus pittoresques et des plus différenciées retracées dans ces jardins et que les différentes localités ont suggéré à l'auteur, cet ouvrage sera plus utile que les longs et volumineux livres écrits sur cette partie de l'art, chacun y trouvera un motif propre à être adapté au local qu'il voudra arranger

On souscrit chez BITTNER *et* GOUPIL, *Editeurs Boulevard Montmartre N.° 15, à PARIS.*

278 Title page of Ramée's *Parcs et jardins*, c. 1839. (Schaffer Library, Union College)

279 Plagerberg, Holstein. Plan in *Parcs et jardins*, pl. 18. (Schaffer Library, Union College)

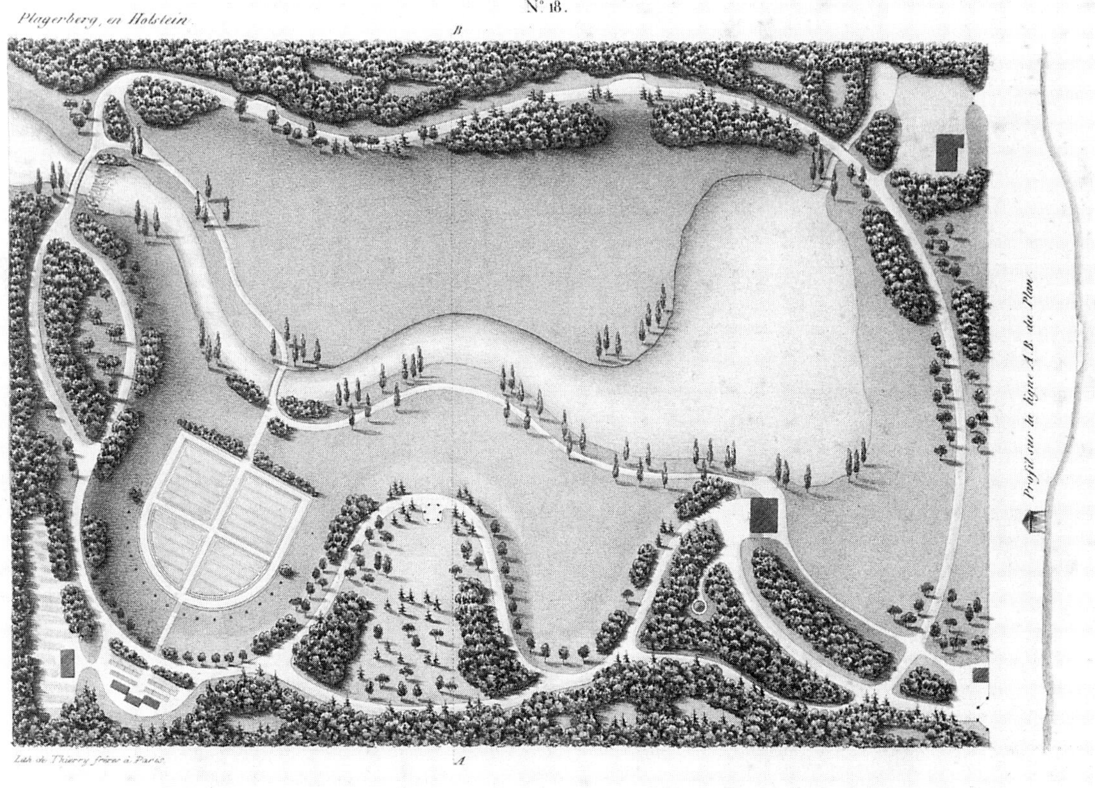

> The author hopes to be useful to lovers of gardens by offering them a series of the most varied designs, applicable to all sites, which can serve as a guide for those concerned with this kind of planning; by the multiplicity of the picturesque and differentiated plans of these gardens, which the different localities suggested to the author, this work will be more useful than the voluminous books written on this art; each will find here a design adaptable to the site he wishes to improve.[50]

The plans in *Parcs et jardins* have been described individually throughout this study, but some general observations can be made here. First is the fact that Ramée must have redrawn his original plans of these landscape designs – spanning a period of over thirty years – to make them consistent in format for the publication.[51] In the process, he no doubt altered some of the designs. But in the roughly half-dozen cases where we can compare the published plans with the originals or with the executed sites themselves, we find that they are largely accurate.[52]

As for the format or presentation of the designs in *Parcs et jardins,* it suggests that Ramée was drawing from several traditions of representing landscape plans. The designs have some traits that were common in the eighteenth century, such as the rendering of trees and other vegetation in perspective (as if viewed obliquely), while the rest of the property is shown in plan, from above. This device was used by Ramée's teacher Belanger, as well as in publications that Ramée would have known from his apprentice years, such as LeRouge's *Jardins anglo-chinois.* Several of the plates in *Parcs et jardins,* however, include an element that Ramée probably adopted later in his career: a section drawing, at the side of the plan, showing the changes in elevation of the property at a given line, indicated on the plan. This seems to have been a particularly English technique; Ramée's use of it can be compared, for instance, to that of G. J. Parkyns in a group of park plans published in John Soane's *Sketches in Architecture* – a copy of which was acquired in 1794 by Ramée's Hamburg client Caspar Voght.[53] Another characteristic of Ramée's plans is a sharp demarcation of the boundaries of the property, produced by a contrast between detailed rendering within and blank surface beyond. This trait is found in a similar manner in a publication of garden designs by Gabriel Thouin, of 1820, designs which are comparable in format to Ramée's in other respects as well, and may have served as one model for *Parcs et jardins.*[54]

Ramée's last publication, *Recueil de cottages,* is devoted to cottages and country houses. As in the case of *Parcs et jardins,* the full title states that the works were "designed and executed in different countries of Europe and the United States": *Recueil de cottages et maisons de campagne de tous genres, de toutes dimensions composés et exécutés dans différentes contrées de l'Europe et des États unis d'Amérique par Joseph Ramée.* This is puzzling, for unlike the plans in *Parcs et jardins,* which are identified by name and are known to be designs of real places, the nature of the works in *Recueil de cottages* is unclear. Only one of the houses is truly identifiable. Several others bear some resemblance to build-

Lith. de Thierry frères Cité Bergère 1.

RECUEIL

de Cottages et Maisons de Campagne

de tous genres, de toutes dimensions composés et exécutés dans différentes contrées de l'Europe et des États unis d'Amérique.

PAR

JOSEPH RAMÉE

Architecte.

On souscrit chez RITTNER & GOUPIL, Éditeurs, Boulevard Montmartre, N°15.

à PARIS.

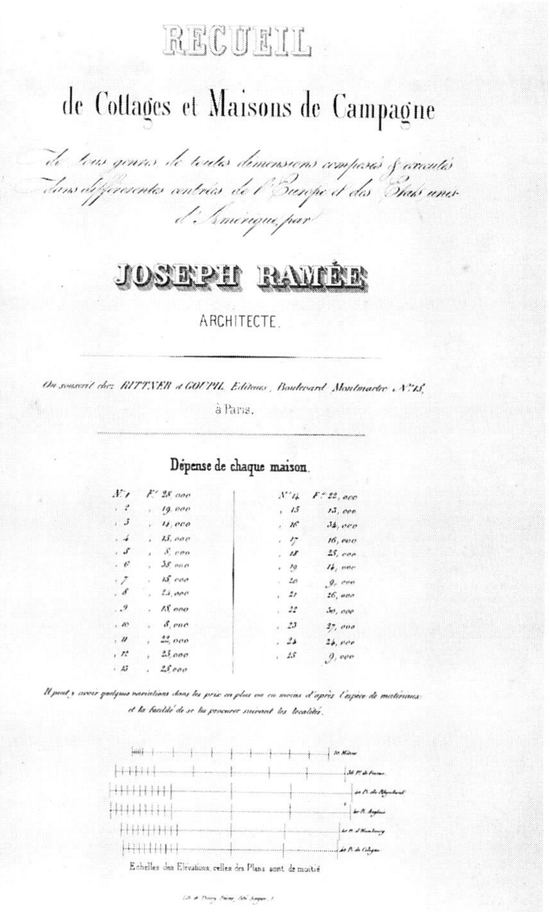

RECUEIL

de Cottages et Maisons de Campagne

de tous genres, de toutes dimensions composés & exécutés dans différentes contrées de l'Europe et des États unis d'Amérique, par

JOSEPH RAMÉE

ARCHITECTE.

On souscrit chez RITTNER et GOUPIL, Éditeurs, Boulevard Montmartre, N°15,

à Paris.

Dépense de chaque maison.

N°	F.s	N°	F.s
1	28,000	14	22,000
2	19,000	15	13,000
3	11,000	16	34,000
4	15,000	17	16,000
5	8,000	18	25,000
6	38,000	19	14,000
7	15,000	20	9,000
8	24,000	21	26,000
9	18,000	22	30,000
10	8,000	23	27,000
11	22,000	24	24,000
12	23,000	25	9,000
13	25,000		

Il peut y avoir quelques variations dans les prix en plus ou en moins d'après l'espèce de matériaux et la facilité de se les procurer suivant les localités.

Echelles des Elévations, celles des Plans sont de moitié.

280 Title page of Ramée's *Recueil de cottages et maisons de campagne*, 1837. (© cliché Bibliothèque Nationale, Paris)

281 Secondary title page of *Recueil de cottages.* (Private collection)

ings by Ramée, but the rest have no known parallel in the architect's work. Is the text of the title mistaken? Or are these truly executed works of Ramée, whose identities are simply not known?

Recueil de cottages consists of two title pages, twenty-five plates (each with the floor plans and an elevation view of a house), and a summary plate that shows all twenty-five designs in miniature perspective views (Figs. 280–282). The main title page is decorated with a view of Calverton, the estate in Baltimore that Ramée had planned in 1815 (see Figs. 225–228). The secondary title page has a chart labeled "Cost of each house," giving a price for the construction of each design (ranging from 8,000 to 38,000 francs), with a note stating that "there may be some variation in the prices, due to the types of materials used and the ease of finding them, depending on the localities."[55] Also on this page are six scales for measuring the dimensions of the designs (in meters, French feet, English feet, and three different regional German feet).[56] The work is thus presented as a series of model designs, to be used by property owners wishing to build, and with the implication – typical of Ramée's international outlook – that they may be constructed in numerous countries.

This kind of publication, with model designs for simple houses, was a particularly English phenomenon.[57] Indeed, the English character of Ramée's

Recueil de cottages is emphasized by its title, for "cottage" is an English, not a French word; when used in French it is an anglicism.[58] (Daniel Ramée, in one of his own publications, referred to "the little country houses called *cottages* by our neighbors across the Channel.")[59] Around 1800, dozens of books on cottages had appeared in England, reflecting new ideas about architecture, landscape and society. Ramée's *Recueil de cottages* was, as far as I can find, the first such work in France.

The cottage – originally, a humble rural dwelling – assumed special significance in the late eighteenth century.[60] The worship of nature, the romanticism of peasant purity, and especially the picturesque esthetic of irregularity and anticlassicism: all these things elevated the cottage to an object of fascination. The mock-peasant "hamlets" created at French estates, such as Marie Antoinette's Hameau at Versailles, were an early manifestation of this interest. But it was in England that the cottage became a widespread phenomenon and a model of new types of domestic architecture. Starting in the 1790s, a stream of publications on cottages, villas, and related types of country houses appeared in England, spurred by public interest in the subject, new printing techniques, and an abundance of architects wishing to publicize their talents.[61] These publications sometimes had a text, but often consisted merely of house plans, elevation drawings, or perspective views. They had a profound influence on nineteenth-century architecture, popularizing the picturesque esthetic and promoting eclecticism through the variety of styles – Gothic, Tudor, Swiss, Italianate, and so forth – represented by the designs.

It was clearly this English publishing phenomenon that inspired Ramée's *Recueil de cottages*. Besides the subject of the work and the use of the word "cottage," the format of the publication follows the English model. Each plate, for instance, bears the elevation drawing of a house at the top and its floor plans below. As in the English books, the designs range in scale from small structures (the true cottages) appropriate for gate lodges, gardeners' houses, and the like, to relatively substantial dwellings (the "*maisons de campagnes*") for middle class residents.

But while the subject and format of the *Recueil de cottages* are fully English, only some of the designs themselves seem to derive from the English cottage books. Most are based on Ramée's earlier works or on other sources. The peculiar and whimsical variety of these designs is, in fact, their most remarkable trait.

Several kinds of classicism are represented. Design number 2 (Fig. 283) is similar to the neoclassical house that Ramée included in *Jardins irréguliers* (see Fig. 255), which resembled earlier designs by Belanger.[62] Number 22 (see Fig. 229) recalls Ramée's Calverton at Baltimore, with its two-storey-high, segmental-arched porch, within which is a screen of columns. There are hints of Ramée's Hamburg Börsenhalle in a couple of the designs, especially number 18 (see Fig. 282), with its large arched niche under a pediment. Numbers 1 and 6 (see Fig. 282) – foursquare houses with hipped roofs and projecting bays on the garden façades – represent a type of simplified English neoclassicism found in several of the English publications on cottages and villas.[63] Number

282 Summary plate of *Recueil de cottages*, showing all the designs in perspective views. Each design is identified by the number in its upper left corner. (Private collection)

4
5
9
10
14
15
19
20
24
25

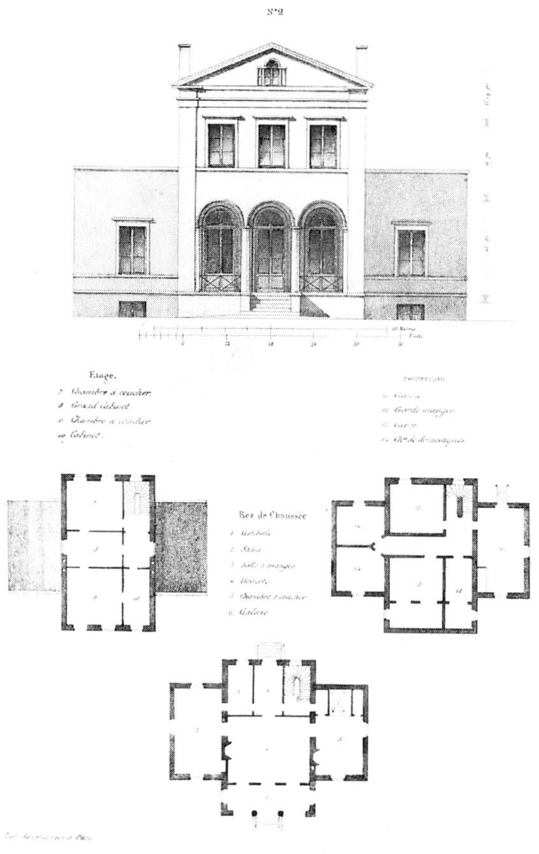

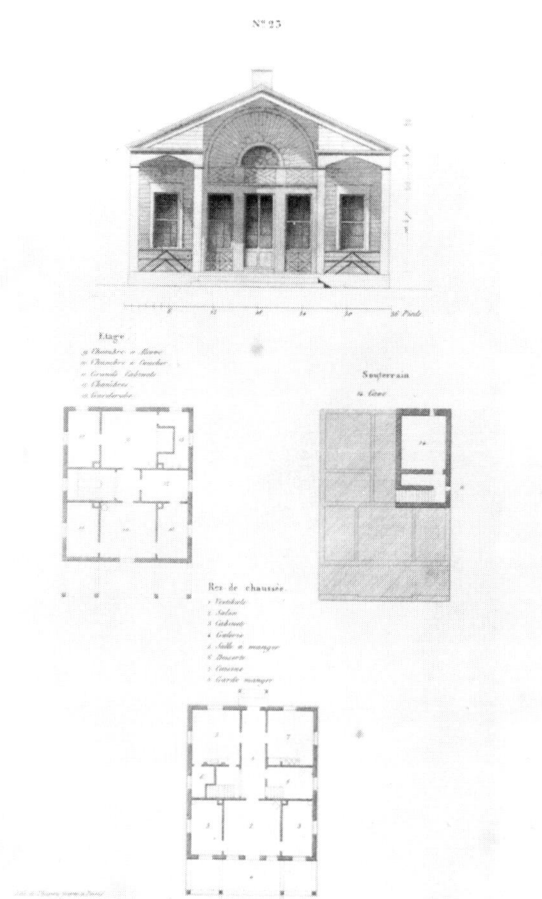

283 *Recueil de cottages*, design no. 2. (Private collection)

284 *Recueil de cottages*, design no. 23. (Private collection)

23 (Fig. 284) is a peculiar classical invention: the pediment of this tiny cottage is broken by an odd triangular opening (with smaller openings of the same shape on the sides), revealing inside the "Guimard motif" of a columnar screen, which Ramée had used in his design for the Washington Monument in Baltimore.

But most of the designs in the *Recueil de cottages* are nonclassical and display a wide range of picturesque alternatives to classicism. Number 8 (Fig. 285) is a small house in a simplified Tudor style, of a sort found in the English cottage books.[64] Number 12 (Fig. 286) is in a mock-castle style, featuring a square tower with a crenelated parapet and little turrets at the corner – somewhat like designs in the English publications and also reminiscent of the medieval tower in Ramée's drawing of Baurs Park near Hamburg (see Fig. 76).[65] Several of Ramée's designs are in a simplified, rustic Gothic style that was especially typical of the English books. Number 20 (Fig. 287), for instance, is similar to a design that appeared in W. F. Pocock's 1807 *Architectural Designs for Rustic Cottages;* and number 3 (Fig. 288) can be compared with a cottage in John Plaw's 1800 *Sketches for Country Houses, Villas and Rural Dwellings.*[66] Plaw's book also seems to have been the source of Ramée's design number 13 (see Fig. 282), with its pattern of Gothic windows and the curving eaves of its thatched roof, though Ramée added wings to Plaw's cottage.[67] And

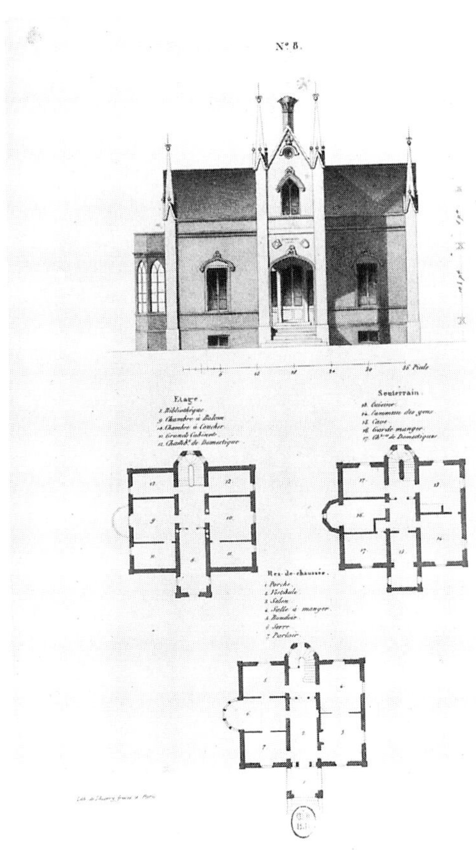

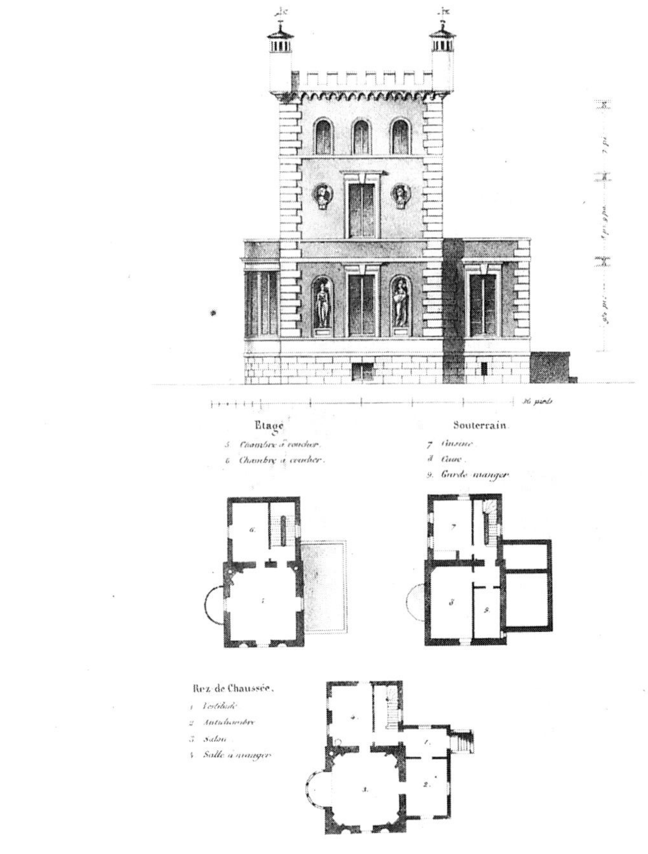

285 *Recueil de cottages*, design no. 8. (© cliché Bibliothèque Nationale, Paris)

286 *Recueil de cottages*, design no. 12. (Private collection)

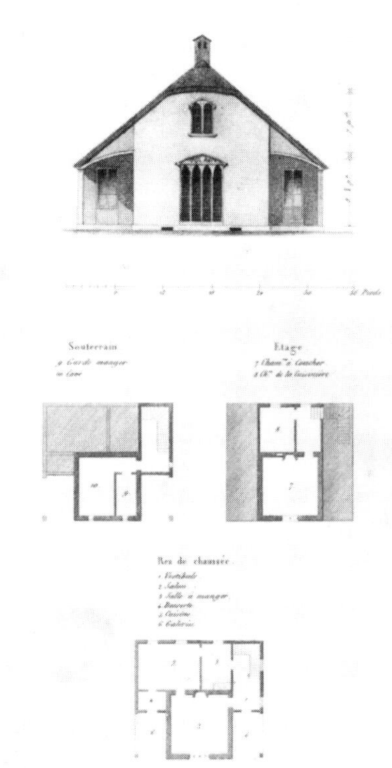

287 *Recueil de cottages*, design no. 20. (Private collection)

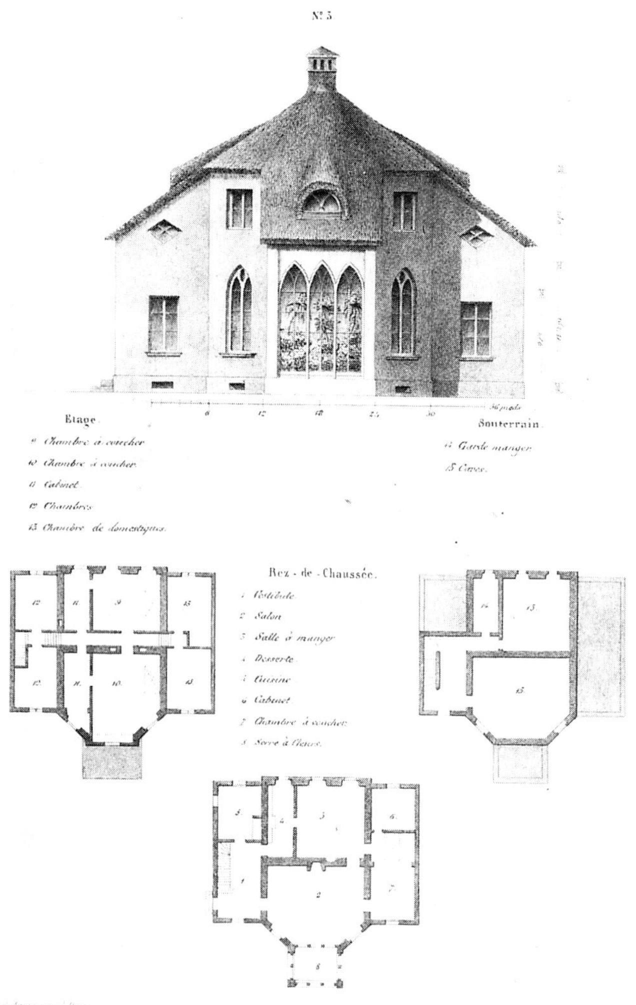

288 *Recueil de cottages*, design no. 3. (Private collection)

Ramée's number 11 (Fig. 289) is similar, but with the addition of a segmental-arched porch that recalls Calverton.

Except for certain incongruous elements such as the segmental arch, these last designs epitomize the picturesque rustic cottage, with their steep thatched roofs, small windows, and occasional medieval details such as simple pointed arches. A variant of this type, number 17 in the *Recueil de cottages* (see Fig. 166), is similar in overall shape to the house that Ramée built for David Parish in northern New York in 1813; this fact suggests that the architect was familiar with the English cottage books before he went to America. (As noted earlier, in fact, Parish's brother George recognized this house as being "in the cottage stile.") Ramée probably first saw the English cottage books in Hamburg. Caspar Voght, as we have seen, acquired one of these publications, Soane's *Sketches in Architecture,* as early as 1794, and hints of the English designs can be seen in the rustic houses Ramée included in his drawing of Baurs Park.[68]

Another design in the *Recueil de cottages* that may have an English source is number 4 (Fig. 290). This house, with its porches and deeply overhanging

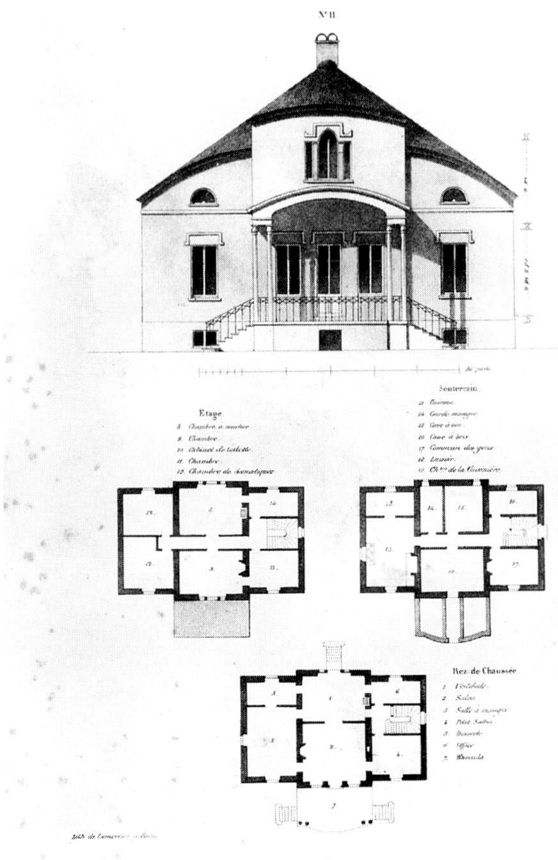

289 *Recueil de cottages*, design no. 11. (Private collection)

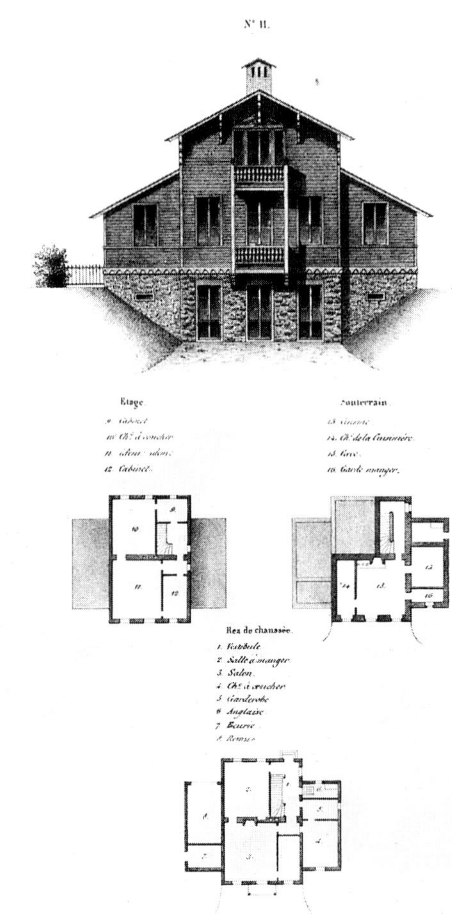

290 *Recueil de cottages*, design no. 4 (misinscribed "No. 11") (Private collection)

roofs, supported by brackets, is evidently intended to be in the "Swiss" manner, which was introduced to England by P. F. Robinson in several cottage publications starting in the 1820s.[69] Ramée, however, gives his house a plainer and more cubic form than the Swiss cottages in the English books.

But at least half the designs in the *Recueil de cottages* are different from anything in the English cottage books. Besides the classical designs based on earlier works by Ramée, many other styles are represented. Number 16 (Fig. 291) is in a kind of French Renaissance style, with details similar to those of one of the houses found in Ramée's *Jardins irréguliers* (see Fig. 259).[70] Numbers 14 and 21 (see Fig. 282) are houses with stepped gables suggesting Flemish vernacular architecture. Number 15 (Fig. 292) is a tiny octagonal cottage with latticework around the entry, somewhat like a garden pavilion published in J. C. Krafft's 1806 *Recueil d'architecture civile*; Ramée has added pointed arches above the windows, giving the design a strangely hybrid character.[71]

At least three of Ramée's cottages, numbers 5, 7, and 10 (Figs. 293–5), were evidently inspired by the designs of Ledoux, though Ramée greatly modified the originals. Number 10 has a barrel-vaulted roof of a sort that was one of Ledoux's most distinctive forms; it is found in several of his visionary

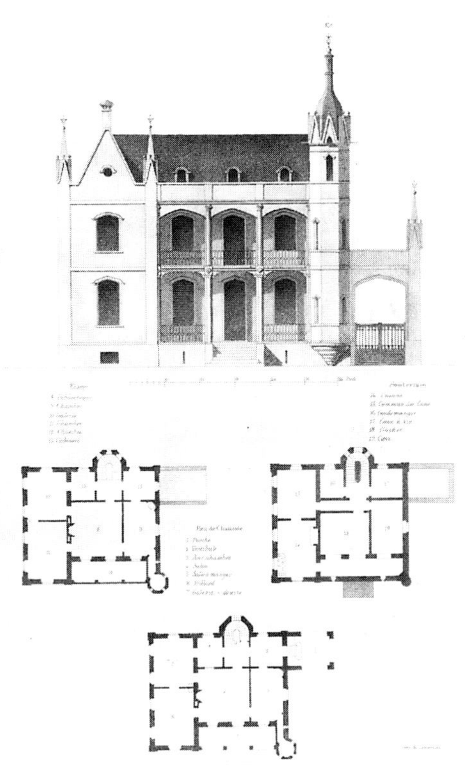

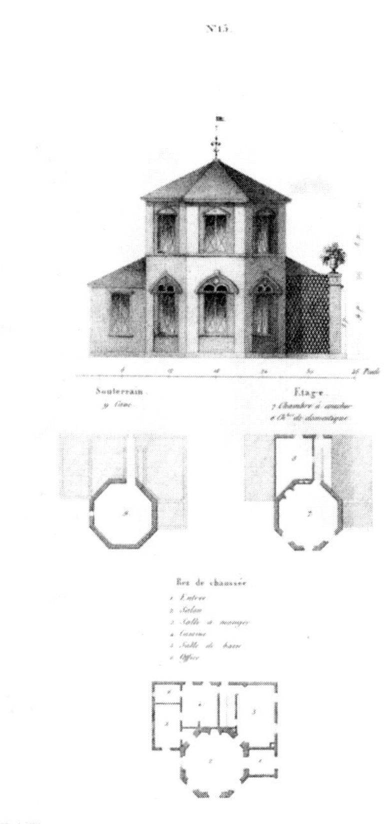

291 *Recueil de cottages*, design no. 16. (Private collection)

292 *Recueil de cottages*, design no. 15. (Private collection)

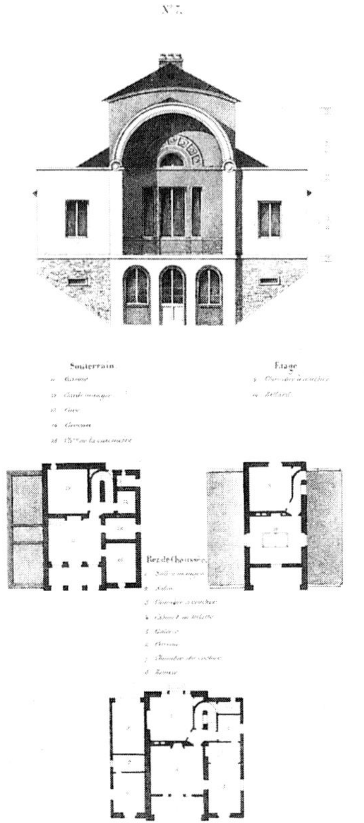

293 *Recueil de cottages*, design no. 7. (Private collection)

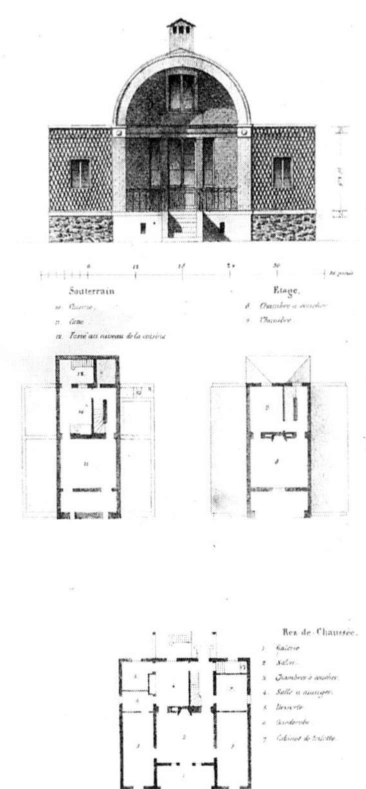

294 *Recueil de cottages*, design no. 10. (Private collection)

295 *Recueil de cottages*, design no. 5 as shown on summary plate.

296 C. N. Ledoux, design for coopers' house, Chaux. (C. N. Ledoux, *L'Architecture . . .*, Paris, 1804, pl. 88)

geometric designs.[72] (Ramée kept the stark character of Ledoux's work in his miniature perspective view of number 10, but transformed it in the elevation drawing, adding trellises and other non-Ledoux details.) Ramée's number 5 (Fig. 295), a tiny house with a large circular hole in the façade serving as entranceway, recalls in a whimsical way Ledoux's astounding design for a barrel-shaped house for the coopers in the utopian city of Chaux (Fig. 296).[73]

Two of Ramée's designs, numbers 19 and 25, are log houses, a building type the architect knew both from Germany and northern New York State.[74] He emphasized the northern character of these log cottages by surrounding them with pine trees, in the plate of miniature views of all the designs. One of these cottages (Fig. 297) is relatively simple, distinguished mainly by a triangular opening over the entryway and a round projection in the thatched roof.

But the other log house, number 19, is the most peculiar of all of Ramée's cottages, an exotic pastiche of elements (Fig. 298). In overall shape, the house is similar to a cottage Ramée had included in his 1810 drawing of Baurs Park – a square log structure with a steep thatched roof and a triangular opening for the entrance (see Fig. 72). But to this basic form Ramée added a foundation of jagged boulders; a surface of vertical boards on the upper part of the front wall, above the log surface; complex patterns of diagonal boards on the wall inside the entryway; little triangular windows in the upper wall of the façade; an "eyebrow" window in the center of the thatched roof, giving

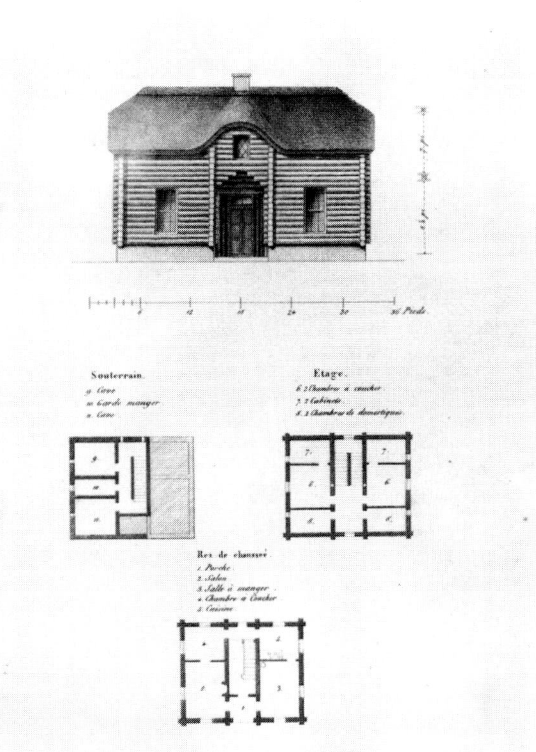

297 *Recueil de cottages*, design no. 25. (Private collection)

the house the appearance of a cyclops's face; a bit of tiled roof atop the thatched roof; and a chimney with a stork's nest on it – complete with stork.

Some possible sources may be noted for this design: log houses that Ramée probably saw in Germany or Scandinavia, a half-timbered barn built by Belanger, and a design for a garden pavilion published by Gabriel Thouin in 1820.[75] But Ramée's bizarre combination of forms gives his log cottage a wholly original, even ridiculous character. It seems to be intended as a kind of parody of romantic cottage architecture.

Indeed, all the designs in the *Recueil de cottages,* when seen together, have a quality of whimsical parody. The styles and sources of the designs are so diverse and are combined in such unlikely ways, that one senses a purposeful arbitrariness and humor in them. In this regard, they are closer to the fanciful garden pavilions of pre-Revolutionary France than to the English cottages. Yet Ramée's designs, like those of the English books, are presented largely as houses for middle-class people to build and live in.

The whimsical character of the *Recueil de cottages* is evident right from the title page, with its vignette view of Calverton, the estate Ramée had designed for Dennis Smith at Baltimore in 1815 (see Fig. 280). The house is seen in the distance, but the real subject of the view is the unusual gate in the foreground. Gates and gate lodges were often featured in the English cottage books of the period.[76] But none had the odd combination of parts found in

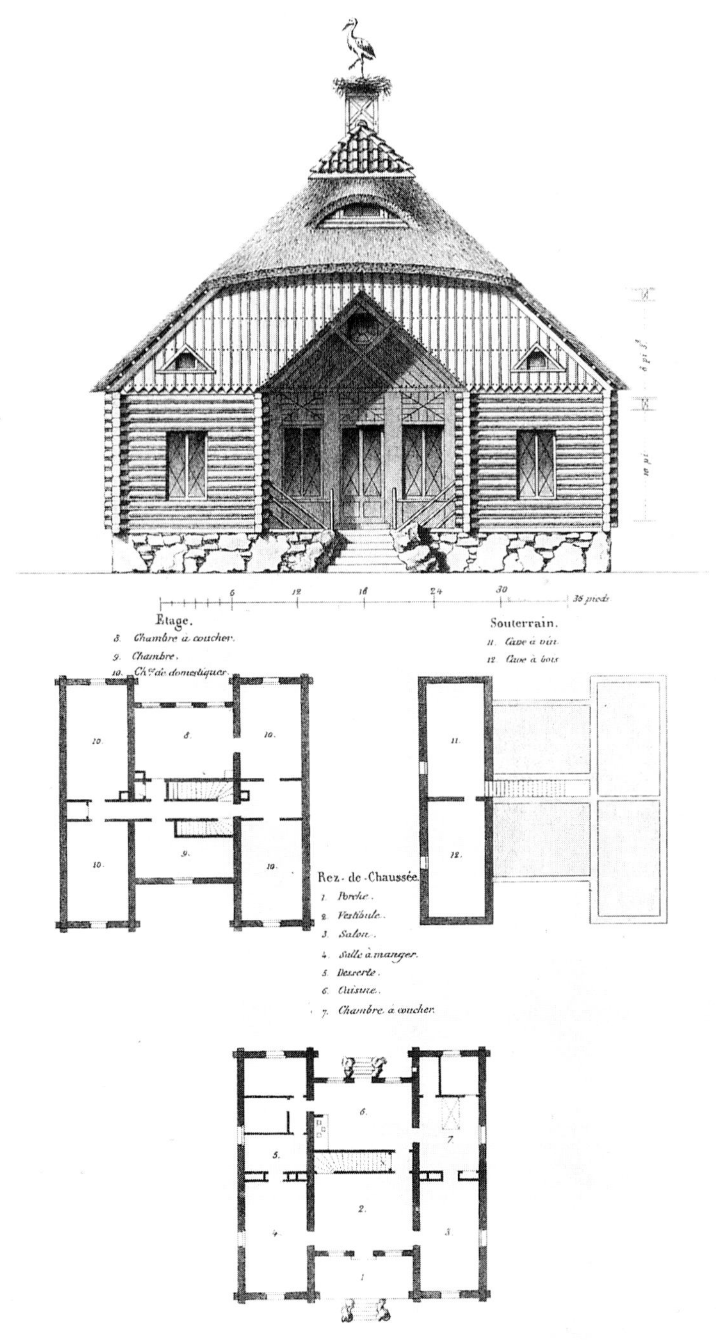

298 *Recueil de cottages*, design no. 19. (Private collection)

Ramée's design: an arch, stepped on the top like a Flemish gable or a crenelated castle wall, flanked by squat circular gate lodges, and at the summit, a statue of Eros (or maybe Diana?) shooting an arrow.[77] Whether Ramée designed this gate in 1815, while in Baltimore, or invented it later for the *Recueil de cottages*, is not known. But combining elements of classicism, medievalism, and romantic fantasy, the design is an appropriate introduction to the strange cottages and villas of this publication.

299 Letter from Joseph Ramée to Daniel Ramée, 19 November 1839. (© Musée National de la Coopération Franco-américaine, Blérancourt, France)

Finally, one must consider the authorship of the *Recueil de cottages*. Did Daniel Ramée play a role in it? Given the fact that Daniel had assisted his father in drawing the plates for *Jardins irréguliers* in 1823, and that he was very close to his father in the late 1830s (as Stephen Martel's diary shows), one might suspect that Daniel helped design these cottages. But this seems unlikely. By the mid-1830s, Daniel had become an important scholar of medieval architecture and had begun his career in the Commission des Monuments Historiques as a restorer of Romanesque and Gothic churches in northern France. He embodied a new kind of serious archeological interest in historical architecture, and it is hard to imagine that he contributed to the pastiche of medieval and classical details in the *Recueil de cottages*.

Daniel Ramée later wrote an encyclopedic work on architecture, *L'Architecture et la construction pratiques,* which contains a section on country houses.[78] One of the designs illustrated here is actually drawn from the *Recueil de cottages*, but it is the sober, neoclassical design number 1.[79] Daniel was influenced by English publications on domestic architecture, several of which he cites; but it was the practical works of John Claudius Loudon that seem to have been his main models, rather than the earlier, more romantic publications that the *Recueil de cottages* typifies.[80]

Moreover, the fact that many of the designs in the *Recueil de cottages* recall earlier works of Ramée *père* (such as Calverton, the Börsenhalle, David Parish's country house, and the structures in Baurs Park) seems to confirm that the publication was the work of the father, not the son. It appears that Ramée, aware of the English cottage books from early in his career, finally used their format as a vehicle for documenting one facet of his international work and experience.

Besides the *Recueil de cottages, Parcs et jardins,* and the diary of Stephen Martel, only one other document is known that sheds light on Ramée's final years. This is a brief letter the architect wrote in 1839 to Daniel, which survives in the Ramée family papers at the Blérancourt Museum (Fig. 299). Written in a trembling hand, the note is hard to read, but it reveals that the architect, now seventy-five years old, was still actively engaged in some kind of landscape work. Written from Charleville in northern France, dated 19 November 1839, and addressed to Daniel in Paris, the letter reads:

> I arrived here yesterday in good health. I waited five hours in Compiègne and seven in Soissons, but then at Notre Dame des Victoires I found first place in the stagecoach, which pleased me greatly. Mr. [Desroux?] has not yet returned from Lorraine, and what is even worse, the trees and shrubs from Margut [a village near the Belgian border] have not yet arrived. According to his promise, they should have left Paris at the beginning of this month. Write him a word and ask him the shipping company that he gave them to. I believe I recall that it is Rue du Jour behind St. Eustache. The wife of [?] has died. I'll write to you by this same mail coach at Noyon. I have checked into the Hôtel du Commerce here. I think I won't stay long in Charleville. Till I see you again, take care of yourself. Ramée[81]

Just a month earlier, the Ramées and the Martels had purchased the "château" at Beaurains, near Noyon. Extensive remodeling was undertaken and the family did not occupy the house until April of 1841, according to Stephen Martel's diary. By the end of that year, Martel was noting the illness of Ramée. No medical details are provided, but several doctors were summoned (one from Paris) and the architect's condition worsened. Daniel, who was apparently living in Paris at this time, made frequent visits to Beaurains in the early months of 1842. Martel's diary records that on May 18, "Daniel arrived from Paris; the same day, at eight o'clock in the evening, Ramée died."[82]

Only twelve days earlier, a great fire had destroyed much of the city of Hamburg, including the Börsenhalle, the building of which Ramée was perhaps most proud. One hopes that the news did not reach the architect on his deathbed.

Ramée was buried in the cemetary of the small church at Beaurains. The gravestone reportedly was inscribed, "Here lies Joseph Ramée, architect, born in Givet 26 April 1764, who yielded his soul to God 18 May 1842. Pray to God for him."[83] Neither this tombstone nor the house at Beaurains survives, for the village was devastated by the Germans in the First World War. But Stephen Martel's diary reveals a touching detail about the architect's burial site. Exactly one year after his father's death, Daniel Ramée erected "a stone from Senlis" at the grave.[84] The Gothic cathedral at Senlis, midway between

Noyon and Paris, was one of the monuments Daniel was restoring at this time. He evidently took a finial or some other carved stone, which he was replacing at the cathedral, and transported it to his father's grave at Beaurains.

Also in 1843, Daniel Ramée published the first of his many books on architecture. Entitled *Manuel de l'histoire générale de l'architecture*, it bears the following dedication: "To Joseph Ramée, my father and master, who accepted the dedication of this book. To his memory."[85]

Epilogue: Daniel Ramée and His Father's Legacy

By the time that Joseph Ramée died in 1842, he was nearly forgotten. Most of his work had been executed so long before and his career had consisted of so many short sojourns in separate places that oblivion had overcome him. The architect's legacy was to be mostly anonymous, residing in the works themselves and especially in the influence Ramée had exerted by transmitting new types of architecture and landscape design from one country to another.

Another part of Ramée's legacy can be found in the work of his son (Fig. 300). Daniel Ramée (1806–87) had a significant architectural career, which was very different from that of his father but was shaped in certain ways by the unusual nature of Ramée *père*'s life and work.

Daniel learned the craft of architecture from his father, whom he accompanied as a child and youth to all the places where the elder Ramée worked.[1] By the age of seventeen, he was skilled enough to assist his father with the publication of *Jardins irréguliers*, and for the rest of his father's life Daniel evidently helped him, when possible, in his architectural practice. But starting in the 1820s Daniel became increasingly interested in history, especially in the

300 Daniel Ramée, self-portrait. Drawing, inscribed "Beaurain, 7 août 1841." (© Musée National de la Coopération Franco-américaine, Blérancourt, France)

architecture of the Middle Ages.[2] When the French government in 1830 created an office of historic monuments, its first director, Ludovic Vitet, chose Ramée *fils* as his staff architect and the two of them made preliminary investigations of medieval churches throughout France. Seven years later, when the Commission des Monuments Historiques was established, Ramée was one of the first architects engaged to restore medieval buildings; he eventually directed the restoration of many important structures, including the cathedrals of Noyon, Senlis, and Beauvais.[3] In the meantime, he had traveled extensively, in Germany, England, Italy, and elsewhere in Europe.[4] And he had begun his career as an author, a career that was to produce over twenty books plus numerous articles, translations from foreign languages, and miscellaneous writings.[5]

As an historian, Daniel Ramée was one of the first to study architecture from a multinational, scholarly perspective, utilizing the experience of his travels and his thorough knowledge of modern languages: French and German learned from his parents, English from his childhood in the United States, and Italian, Dutch, and other languages from his travels. In 1843 an important essay by Ramée was published as the introduction to *Le Moyen-âge monumental et archéologique,* a six-volume collection of views of medieval architecture (many drawn by Ramée himself), edited by Nicolas Chapuy.[6] In his essay, Ramée traced the eighteenth- and early nineteenth-century development of interest in medieval building, surveying in detail the European literature on the subject (noting that the German and English scholarship was more advanced than the French) and outlining the history of Gothic and other medieval architecture. In his conclusion, Ramée pointed out that historians had largely neglected Gothic art because of the traditional focus on Italy and classicism, and he urged that equal attention be given to northern Europe.[7] This essay was perhaps the first historical survey of medieval architecture to make thorough use of scholarly research from throughout Europe.

Also in 1843 appeared Daniel Ramée's *Manuel de l'histoire générale de l'architecture chez tous les peuples*, a work that Ramée was to revise and expand in later years.[8] Although the first edition gave special attention to medieval France, Ramée's preface emphasized (as did the title of the book) that the intention was to document the architecture of all peoples: "In the arts we must study the creations and styles of all countries and times, to find what is beautiful, lofty, and natural in them, to inspire ourselves from these qualities and to use them in the creation of new works."[9] This universalism led Ramée, in his subsequent writings, to examine the architecture of diverse cultures, some largely unknown in the Europe of his day, such as pre-Columbian Mexico, about which Ramée included a commentary in a publication of 1850.[10]

In the preface to his 1843 *Manuel,* Ramée stated that he had first conceived the project of a universal architectural history in 1823. His mention of a specific date implies that he was thinking of a particular event or moment of inspiration. In 1823, at the age of seventeen, Daniel had assisted his father in the publication of *Jardins irréguliers*, whose title page had proclaimed its inclusion of designs from "different countries of Europe and North America." In his 1843 book, Daniel recalled:

> Twenty years ago we were initiated into the principles of architecture. We saw that monuments were studied without any order or chronology. . . . No complete history of architecture existed twenty years ago, nor does it today. We felt the emptiness that the lack of such a book left in the artist's knowledge, and from the beginning of our studies we formed the project of writing a history of this art. . . . Thus was realized the project that we conceived starting in 1823.[11]

One wonders if it was perhaps Ramée *père* who originally conceived the notion of writing a history of architecture from a worldwide perspective. Although there is no direct evidence for this, we recall that in 1814 a journalist reported that Joseph Ramée "intends to publish a work on the principles of his art," which suggests that he had some literary ambitions of his own and perhaps proposed the historical projects that were later carried out by his son.[12] In any case, it seems clear that Daniel Ramée's interest in an international view of architecture had its roots in his family background – not only his childhood travels and multilingual education, but his training in architecture from a father who had a uniquely global experience of his art.

A full assessment of Daniel Ramée's formation as an historian and the significance of his writings would require a lengthy study. His prolific works range from histories of architecture, technology, and the decorative arts to studies of philosophy, religion, and politics, as well as practical books on construction and a dictionary of architectural terms in four languages. Some of Daniel's ideas were complex or obscure, or underwent transformation in the course of his career. Increasingly, during his life, he connected the analysis of architecture to other subjects, such as politics and ethnology; and in his later works an ugly, racist element emerged, in which he used his multicultural approach to architecture to argue the superiority of "aryan" values over those of other races.[13] But in his early writings one finds a much more liberal spirit, genuinely interested in all aspects of the art of building, and motivated, as he said in his 1843 *Manuel*, by the desire to "render impartial justice to the architecture of all peoples."[14] This ecumenical spirit seems to be part of the legacy of Joseph Ramée, whose international career thus contributed, in some small way, to the development of modern architectural scholarship.

Another possible contribution of Ramée *père* to modern architecture, through his son, is more specific but also more puzzling. In the twentieth century, Daniel Ramée has become known mainly for a work that during his lifetime was considered relatively insignificant (and was not even mentioned in most of the contemporary accounts of his career). This is his publication, in 1846–7, of the engraved designs of Claude Nicolas Ledoux, the great neoclassical architect. Ledoux's work fell into disrepute in the nineteenth century but was rediscovered and became influential starting in the 1920s, as his radically geometric designs were seen as precursors of modernism. The circumstances behind Ramée's edition of Ledoux's work are shrouded in mystery. But a review of the story allows some speculation.

For several decades and particularly after the French Revolution ended his official career, Ledoux produced engraved plates for a multivolume publication of his architecture, to include both his built work and his unexecuted and visionary designs. In 1804 he published the first volume of the projected work. Shortly before his death, in 1806, Ledoux sold the engraved copper plates to the architect Pierre Vignon and named three friends (Jacques Cellerier, Emmanuel Damesne, and Léon Dufourny) to assist in the completion of the publication.[15] For some reason, nothing came of these plans. The engraved plates were reportedly still in the possession of Vignon in 1818, but otherwise nothing is known about their whereabouts or ownership until the 1840s, when Daniel Ramée was involved in the publication of a large number of them.[16] In 1846, a volume of Ledoux's work was published in London, containing 230 plates and a preface written by Ramée. The following year, the Paris publisher Lenoir brought out a two-volume edition, with a total of 300 plates and Ramée's preface.[17] It is this "Ramée edition" of 1847 which provides the fullest documentation of Ledoux's architectural designs and thus has preserved them for posterity.

It is not known when or how Daniel Ramée acquired the engraved copper plates for these editions. Nor is it clear *why* he undertook this publishing venture, which is an anomaly in his career as an author. It is his only publication devoted to the work of an individual architect; its neoclassical subject is contrary to his preoccupation with medieval architecture in the 1840s; and it was a publication with little prospect for commercial success, since Ledoux was an unappreciated figure in the mid-nineteenth century.[18] Nor can the publication be explained as motivated by an admiration for Ledoux's work, for it seems that Daniel Ramée had a largely negative view of this work. In his preface to the publication, Ramée acknowledges that Ledoux had great "imagination" and "originality," but he criticizes Ledoux's unwillingness to obey the rules of classicism (in his Paris tollhouses, for example), his eccentricity, and his lack of judgment, which led him to "*bizarreries*" and to the violation of good taste. The only works that Ramée could bring himself to praise were some of Ledoux's early, more conventional buildings. One gets the impression that Ramée was trying to be as generous as possible in his evaluation, by repeatedly acknowledging Ledoux's "imagination" and by suggesting that his errors in taste could be excused as manifestations of the general frivolity of the eighteenth century. Ramée was as kind to Ledoux as he could bring himself to be, but he clearly was not a true admirer of his work.

In view of these facts, what could have motivated Daniel Ramée's publication of Ledoux's designs? It is conceivable that he was simply paid by someone to edit the publication and write the preface. But it seems unlikely that anyone interested enough in Ledoux to subsidize this expensive publication would have hired an editor who was essentially unsympathetic to the work. Another possibility is that there was some Masonic link between Ledoux and Daniel Ramée, since both men had interests in Freemasonry.[19] But in itself this is an implausible motive for an architectural publication, especially as Ramée's preface to the work contains no Masonic references or overtones. The most likely explanation is that Daniel Ramée produced the publication because of some connection his father had with Ledoux or with Ledoux's heirs – and that on Joseph Ramée's death in 1842 Daniel inherited the engraved plates or an obligation of some kind to publish them.

Throughout Joseph Ramée's life, there are numerous indications of his interest in Ledoux's work and of other connections between the two architects. When Ramée was beginning his career in Paris in the 1780s, his two mentors, Belanger and Cellerier, were both friends of Ledoux.[20] Especially close to Ledoux was Cellerier, who, as noted earlier, was one of the acquaintances chosen by Ledoux to assist Vignon in the continued publication of his work. And following Ledoux's death in 1806, Cellerier wrote a eulogy of the architect, praising his work and stressing the importance Ledoux had placed on the publication of the plates he had entrusted to his friends.[21] We have seen that Ramée's own architecture was strongly influenced by Ledoux, starting with the Berthault-Récamier House in Paris, of 1789 (see Figs. 22–5), and later in many ways, such as Ramée's frequent use of Ledoux's "Guimard motif," a screen of columns set within an arch or niche.[22]

Even in the final years of Ramée's career, Ledoux continued to inspire him. Several of the park pavilions shown in Ramée's design of the Place de la Concorde and Champs-Élysées, of 1828 (see Fig. 266), are modeled on designs by Ledoux, as are some of the more fantastic cottage designs in Ramée's 1839 *Recueil de cottages* (see Figs. 293–5). Although it is possible that Daniel Ramée helped his father to prepare this publication, the Ledoux-inspired cottages were surely the work of the father, not the son, for they derive from the stripped-down, visionary projects of Ledoux that Daniel disliked and labeled "bizarre" in his preface to Ledoux's work.

One can imagine various scenarios by which Joseph Ramée played a role in the eventual publication of Ledoux's designs. Cellerier may have enlisted Ramée's help in the project (this would have happened during Ramée's 1810–11 period in Paris, as Cellerier died in 1814), with Ramée later becoming the sole survivor of the group committed to the enterprise. (The other members of the group – Vignon, Damesne, and Dufourny – all died before 1829.) Ramée may have acquired the plates, from Vignon or Cellerier or someone else, and then passed them on to his son. Even if he did not personally possess the plates, Ramée may have felt a moral obligation to see that they were published, as Ledoux had wished, an obligation which he then asked Daniel to assume after his death. In any case, it is much more likely that Joseph was involved in the enterprise than that Daniel undertook it on his own, since Joseph was a fervent admirer of Ledoux's work and Daniel was not. Thus it seems that Ramée *père* played an important role in the preservation of Ledoux's designs and their transmission to the modern period.

The fact that Joseph Ramée retained an appreciation of Ledoux's work into the mid-nineteenth century, long after it had gone out of fashion, underscores the remarkable length of Ramée's career, in a period of great changes in artistic taste. Ramée witnessed the appearance of a multitude of architectural styles and innovations: the neoclassicism of the Louis XVI period and of the

Directoire; the Egyptian and Greek revivals; various versions of the Gothic Revival and the picturesque; and several kinds of irregular landscape planning. Rather than rejecting earlier styles to adopt new ones, as did many artists of the period, Ramée had a curious willingness to embrace them all, adding each new style or concept to his increasingly eclectic repertoire. Ramée's publications, at the end of his life, present an odd multiplicity of forms and styles, some up-to-date and others long out of fashion (such as the sedate neoclassicism of the country house portrayed in *Jardins irréguliers* or the fantastic geometry of Ledoux that is echoed in several of the *Recueil de cottages* designs). To a degree unusual even for the eclectic age in which he lived, Ramée was willing, especially in his later years, to embrace nearly any kind of design he encountered.

Ramée's career was thus ecumenical not only in the geographic sense, but stylistically. In fact, the two traits were linked. Just as Ramée's nomadic life forced him to adapt to many kinds of clientele, so did it give him an unusual artistic tolerance, an openness to nearly all forms of artistic expression. There is something of the historian's mentality in this quality, and it is therefore perhaps not accidental that Ramée's son actually became an historian.

Ramée's career was also universal in its practice of all kinds of design: landscape and urban planning, interior decoration and wallpaper design, as well as architecture itself. As we have seen, this multiplicity was frequently forced on Ramée by the difficult circumstances of his life – as when he had to turn to landscape and interior design after he settled in Hamburg in the 1790s and found himself excluded, as an outsider, from most architectural work. But Ramée came to embrace this diversity and to merge fields of design in ways that gave his work a distinctive character. By the time he went to America, he had developed a conviction that architecture should not be conceived in isolation from its landscaped surroundings. Ramée's view was reflected in his designs for country houses and especially for Union College and the Washington Monument project for Baltimore, producing a type of environmental design that was largely new to America. In Europe, too, Ramée's singular background affected his work in distinctive ways, as in his design for the Place de la Concorde in Paris, whose unusual approach toward urban planning alternately pleased or irritated its reviewers.

The repeated disruptions of Ramée's life were certainly detrimental to his career. If he had not been forced to join the émigré ranks during the Revolution and had pursued the career begun so promisingly with the Perregaux and Berthault-Récamier houses in Paris, he would no doubt have had a more illustrious architectural practice – illustrious in the sense of executing important buildings and making a name for himself. But as an architect without a country, eventually almost forgotten in all the places where he worked, Ramée had a career that is probably more significant, in its transmission of artistic ideas from country to country and in its expression of a uniquely multinational perspective.

Appendix: Boulliot's Article on Ramée, 1830

Abbé Jean-Baptiste-Joseph Boulliot, *Biographie ardennaise, ou Histoire des Ardennais qui se sont fait remarquer par leurs écrits, leurs actions, leurs vertus ou leurs erreurs* (Paris, 1830), vol. 2, pp. 494–6.

RAMÉE (Joseph-Jacques), naquit à Charlemont, le 18 avril 1764. Son goût pour les arts se montra dès sa première jeunesse: souvent il employait ses récréations à former des figures, il cherchait à les tracer avec régularité et avec justesse, avant même d'en connaître le nom, et de savoir qu'il existait une science dont elles fussent l'objet. A l'age de 12 ans, il fut employé par le génie militaire à dessiner des plans de fortification. Un de ses oncles, chanoine de Saint-Pierre de Louvain, l'ayant appelé dans cette ville, ne tarda pas à deviner son talent: il lui mit en main un vignole et des compas; à quinze ans, son neveu donnait des leçons d'architecture.

S'étant rendu à Paris en 1780, ses premiers regards s'ouvrirent sur les chefs-d'oeuvre immortels qui décorent cette capitale. Au bout de neuf mois il entra comme inspecteur dans les bureaux des bâtimens du comte d'Artois, et contribua à l'arrangement du pavillon et du parc de Bagatelle, ainsi qu'à celui de Saint-James, à Neuilly.

A 22 ans, il construisit à Paris une maison où fut employé le premier comble de forme circulaire. En 1790, il fut chargé par M. Beckfort [sic] de faire exécuter une magnifique tente dans le style oriental. Dressée aux menus-plaisirs du roi, cette tente fut transportée de là sur les bords du lac de Genève, où l'artiste givetois se rendit pour diriger les fêtes que ce riche Anglais y donna, et dont la tradition a conservé le souvenir.

S'étant prononcé contre les événemens de la journée du 20 juin 1792 (il était alors capitaine des grenadiers dans son quartier), il fut signalé comme suspect. Menacé de la prison, il ne se déroba aux poignards des assassins des 2 et 3 septembre, qu'en se réfugiant à l'armée de la Belgique, commandée par Dumourier [sic], qui l'employa comme officier d'état major. Mais la défection de ce général, le 4 avril 1793, ramena M. Ramée à Louvain, où il reprit sa première profession.

Lors de la seconde conquête des Pays-Bas par les Français, après la bataille de Fleurus, le 26 juin 1794, il partit pour Erfurt, où le prince primat (M. D'Alberg [sic]) le chargea de diverses constructions; ce qui procura à notre artiste l'arrangement des parcs de Saxe-Mainungen [sic], de Gotha et de Weimar. Passé de cette dernière ville à celle d'Hambourg, il y resta jusqu'en 1802, et y édifia le *Boersin Halli* [sic] (1), lieu où les négocians s'assemblent avant d'aller à la bourse. Il y décora aussi la salle de spectacle des Français, et arrangea encore tous les immenses parcs et jardins qui avoisinent cette cité florissante.

En 1802, il fut appelé à Schwerin par le prince héréditaire de Mecklembourg, pour y arranger son palais. Cinq ans plus tard, il construisit le tombeau de la femme de ce prince, laquelle était soeur de l'empereur Nicolas. A la même époque, il fit de fréquens voyages à Copenhague et dans l'intérieur du Danemarck, afin de présider à l'arrangement de divers châteaux et parcs. Le roi le chargea aussi de la décoration de l'ancien théâtre royal de cette ville, et lui fit dresser des projets pour une nouvelle salle de spectacle dans le parc de Rosenbourg.

M. Ramée revint à Paris en 1810, dans le dessein de s'y fixer. Mais l'horizon politique laissant appréhender de nouvelles catastrophes, il passa dans les États-Unis d'Amérique. De Philadelphie, il se rendit à Ogdensburg, et traversa, dans une étendue de 300 mille [sic], des forêts primitives, aidé seulement de la boussole. L'Angleterre était alors en guerre avec son ancienne colonie. Sur l'invitation du général en chef américain Brocon [sic], notre Ardennais fortifia la petite ville d'Ogdensburg, et la mit, en peu de jours, à l'abri d'un coup de main. Il traça encore plusieurs villes dans l'état de New-York, et y construisit divers établissemens. Dans le même État, il fut appelé à Schenectady, près d'Albany, où il édifia le *collège de l'Union*, monument remarquable par son immense étendue et sa magnifique situation. De retour, à Philadelphie, en 1812, il orna cette ville et ses environs de plusieurs belles et grandes maisons d'habitation, ainsi que Baltimore, New-York, et leurs alentours.

Revenu en Belgique en 1816, dans l'intention de s'y fixer pour quelque temps, il y bâtit quelques châteaux, et y arrangea quelques parcs. A cette époque, il embellit aussi la place Verte de Givet. Enfin, de retour à Paris en 1823, il publia les premières livraisons de l'ouvrage suivant:

Jardins irréguliers, maisons de campagne, de tous genres et de toutes dimensions, exécutés dans différentes contrées de l'Europe et de l'Amérique septentrionale. Paris, 1823, gr. in-4°.

En 1829, il exposa un projet au concours demandé par la ville de Paris, pour les embellissemens de la place de Louis XVI. (*Voy.* le compte rendu de ce projet de M. Ramée, dans le *Journal de Paris* du 1er mai 1829, no 639, et dans le *Globe* du 3 juin 1829, t. VII, no 44.)

(1) M. Weinbrenner, célèbre architecte allemand, a dit dans un de ses ouvrages, que ce monument était le plus beau et le mieux entendu qui existât dans l'Europe.

[Note: Besides the footnote on Weinbrenner's opinion of the Hamburg Börsenhalle, the article has a footnote about the sixteenth-century pretender to the French throne François la Ramée, described as unrelated to the architect Ramée ("étranger à cette famille"). This information probably was added by Boulliot, not provided by Ramée.]

Notes

Introduction

1. Musée National de la Coopération Franco-Américaine, Blérancourt (also called Musée National de Blérancourt), CFA-a-331/3. The oil portrait is signed "Saint Evre, 1832 P[inxit]"; the artist was probably Gillot Saint-Evre, 1791–1858 (*Thieme-Becker Künstler-Lexikon;* C. Grabet, *Dictionnaire des artistes de l'École française au XIXe siècle,* Paris, 1831). The subject of the painting is identified as Joseph Ramée in the records of the museum, an identification evidently made by Madame Edmée La Chesnais (an heir of Ramée's son, Daniel) when she donated the Ramée family documents to the museum in 1937. The Blérancourt Museum was established in 1929 by Anne Morgan, daughter of J. Pierpont Morgan, to promote Franco-American cultural relations; it is not known whether Mme La Chesnais's gift of the Ramée papers to the museum was prompted by the fact that Joseph Ramée spent part of his career in America, or by Joseph and Daniel Ramée's connections with nearby Noyon, or by some other factor.

2. Letter from Joseph to Daniel Ramée, 19 November 1839. Musée National de Blérancourt. See Chapter 14 for the text of the letter.

3. From statements on the title pages of Ramée's *Jardins irréguliers,* (1823), and *Parcs et jardins,* (c. 1839). For these publications, see Chapters 13 and 14.

4. Belanger's statement in Ramée's petition of 1800. See Chapter 2, note 4.

5. *Recueil de cottages et maisons de campagne* [1837]. See Chapter 14.

6. See Anthony Vidler, *The Writing of the Walls: Architectural Theory in the Late Enlightenment* (Princeton, 1987).

7. For French architects working in other countries, see P. Du Colombier, *L'Architecture française en Allemagne au XVIIIe siècle* (Paris, 1954); L. Réau, *Histoire de l'expansion de l'art français* (Paris, 1924–33); L. Réau, *L'Art français aux États-Unis* (Paris, 1926); and P. Lespinasse, *Les Artistes français en Scandinavie* (Paris, 1929). For European architects working in the United States, see Chapter 10.

8. Emil Kaufmann, *Architecture in the Age of Reason* (Cambridge, Mass., 1955).

9. This "environmental" attitude characteristic of the period is discussed in Robin Middleton and David Watkin, *Neoclassicism and Nineteenth Century Architecture* (New York, 1980), pp. 37ff.

10. Neither Joseph Ramée's nor Daniel Ramée's will has been discovered. But the will of Daniel's widow, as well as related documents (in the Archives de la Seine and the Minutier Central des Notaires Parisiens in Paris), reveal the bequest to Edmée Gellion-Danglar (later Madame La Chesnais) and suggest that she was also Daniel Ramée's heir.

11. For the story of the discovery of this drawing, in "an old printshop in Paris" in 1890, see Chapter 11.

12. Abbé [Jean Baptiste Joseph] Boulliot, *Biographie ardennaise, ou histoire des Ardennais qui se sont fait remarquer par leurs écrits, leurs actions, leurs vertus ou leurs erreurs,* vol. 2 (Paris, 1830), pp. 493–6. See Appendix.

13. For this petition, see Chapter 2.

14. Joseph Rosseel to Louisa Miller, 10 November 1812. Owen D. Young Library, St. Lawrence University, Canton, N. Y. See Chapter 10.

15. I myself used the name Joseph Jacques Ramée in my first publications on the architect, before I discovered many of the documents that reveal how he and his family usually gave his name.

Chapter 1

I thank the following people who aided my research on Ramée's origins, family, and youth: Noëlle Baduraux, Patrice Bertrand, Didier Coupaye, Pierre Hubert, André Majewski, M. Nouaille-Degorce, Michel Perpète, Jean Rivière, and Véronique Wiesinger. Michel Perpète has since published some of his findings as "Famille maternelle de Joseph Ramée," in *Ardenne Wallonne* (Sept. 1991), p. 52.

1. This birthdate is given in Ramée's baptismal record (see note 4 below) and in the inscription on his tombstone (which no longer survives; a transcription of it is preserved in the Blérancourt Museum). Boulliot's biography of Ramée, of 1830, gives his birthdate as *18* April 1764, a date that has been perpetuated in subsequent references to the architect. Charlemont is indicated as Ramée's birthplace in his baptismal certificate, his death certificate, Boulliot's article, and elsewhere; his marriage certificate and tombstone give Givet (which had by then absorbed Charlemont) as the birthplace.

2. For Ramée's reported family relationship with Belanger, see Chapter 2.

3. Part of the collection of Ramée documents given to the Blérancourt Museum in 1937 by Madame Edmée La Chesnais (see Introduction). Each copy is entitled "Extrait des registres aux actes de Baptême de la ci devant paroisse de Charlemont. . . ."

4. Text of the French version: "Le vingt six avril mil sept cent soixante quatre est né et le lendemain a été baptisé par moi curé soussigné Jean Jacques fils légitime de Jacques Poisramé et de Anne Dieudonnée Lambert ses père et mère unis en légitime mariage; il a eu pour parain Guillaume Joseph Burette et pour maraine Anne Marie Dembour." Text of the Latin version: "Die vigesima sexta aprilis anno 1764 natus et postridie baptisatus est a me pastore infra scripto, Josephus Jacobus filius legitimus Jacobi Poisramé et Anna Deodata Lambert conjugum: susceptores fuerunt Guillelmus Josephus Burette et Anna Maria Dembour." The original baptismal record was no doubt in Latin.

5. J. Lartigue and A. Le Catte, *Givet: Recherches historiques* (Givet), 1867, p. 267. "Ramée (Joseph-Jacques), célèbre architecte, né à Givet (Charlemont) le 16 avril 1764. On l'appelle aussi Poix-Ramée." Didier Coupaye brought this reference to my attention; he notes that there is a village of Poix-Saint-Hubert twenty miles east of Givet.

6. There was, for instance, a prominent family named de la Ramée in the region south of Givet in the eighteenth century. Boulliot, in a footnote to his article on Ramée, mentions an unfortunate

youth named François la Ramée who was executed in 1596 for claiming a right to the French throne, but Boulliot states that this person was "unrelated to [the architect's] family."

7. Information from Didier Coupaye. Anne Dieudonnée Lambert's baptismal record (obtained by Michel Perpète) reads: "Decima tertia octobris 1720 nata baptizata est anna deodata filia legitima Joannis Lambert et mariae barbarae noel susceptores fuerunt ignatius posson deodata noel carolomontenses" (Registres paroissiaux d'Aubrives, Archives Départementales des Ardennes, No. 5-Mi-11-R-17).

8. Anne Dieudonnée Lambert's godparents are identified in her baptismal record (see note 7 above) as being from Charlemont. Didier Coupaye has discovered that the godfather, Ignace Posson, was the son of one Lambert Posson (1635–90), "gentilhomme de l'artillerie, ou commissaire d'artillerie de Charlemont. . . .entrepreneur des ouvrages, puis contrôleur des fortifications de Charlemont," and that this man's father had held a similar position.

9. Document in the Archives Départementales des Ardennes, no. 3E5220 (found and transcribed by André Majewski). Dated 20 Pluviôse an 11 (9 February 1803), it documents the sale, for 1000 francs, by Joseph Ramée ("architecte et négociant demeurant à Hambourg"), to his sister and brother-in-law (Dieudonnée Ramée and Joseph Torreri, "marchands demeurants [à] Givet") of Ramée's half-interest in a house and garden in Givet (at the corner of the Rue des Vieux Récollets and the Rue du Petit Quartier), which he inherited at the death of his mother, "Dieudonnée Lambert veuve de Jacques Ramée." Ramée was personally present at this transaction in Givet. The document states that Ramée's mother had acquired the house in 1788 from her brother and sister, Jean-Louis Lambert and Marguerite Lambert. Ramée also sold to his sister and brother-in-law, for 2000 francs, his interest in loans or mortgages (*rentes*) that he had inherited from his mother. The date of Ramée's mother's death is not known, but it was probably not long before this transaction in February 1803. She was apparently already a widow in 1797, for a tax record of that year, in Givet, lists a tax for a "veuve Ramée" (document also found by André Majewski). Ramée's mother's house in Givet still stands: a substantial stone structure, it is presently the Hôtel-Restaurant du Nord.

10. In 1726 there were reportedly about 400 civilian inhabitants of Charlemont, living in about a hundred houses, in addition to the army barracks and officers' lodgings (*Charlemont*, "Brochure éditée par le Centre d'Entraînement Commando no. 2", Givet, n.d., pp. 29–30). But a 1771 report ("Atlas des places fortes de France," volume on Givet) states that "depuis que la garnison est réduite à un bataillon, ses habitants ont déserté" (G. Gayot, "Les Cités de la frontière ardennaise au XVIIIe siècle," *Études ardennaises*, vol. 51, October–December 1967, p. 23); and in 1775 the fortress reportedly had only eighty civilian residents (information provided by Didier Coupaye).

11. Abbé d'Expilly, *Dictionnaire géographique, historique et politique des Gaules et de la France* (Amsterdam and Paris, 1764), p. 230.

12. A. Pougin, *Méhul, sa vie, son génie, son caractère* (Paris, 1889), p. 10.

13. Quoted in *Charlemont* (see note 10), p. 33.

14. For the text of Boulliot's article on Ramée, see Appendix.

15. David Chandler, *The Art of Warfare in the Age of Marlborough* (New York, 1976), p. 222; Anne Blanchard, *Les Ingénieurs du Roy de Louis XIV à Louis XVI* (Montpellier, 1979). Didier Coupaye has informed me that the multivolume *Atlas des places fortes*, produced by fortifications director J.-B. de Caux de Blacquetot, was in preparation in the 1770s and that the volume on Charlemont appeared in 1777; it is possible, therefore, that Ramée's employment was in connected with this publication.

16. Daniel Ramée, *Théorie du dessin linéaire, ou Cours de géométrie élémentaire pratique* (Paris, n.d.). Nineteenth-century articles on Daniel Ramée give the date of this publication as 1840.

17. See Appendix.

18. Jean-Louis Lambert, born in Aubrives in 1722, was inscribed in the University of Louvain about 1742 as a "*pauvre*" (a scholarship student) and became a priest. By 1757 he was mentioned in a document as one of the chaplains of St. Pierre (of which there were about forty), residing in one of the houses behind the church, where one or more of his relatives lived with him. His sister Margareta Lambert (born in Aubrives in 1724) died in Louvain in 1788. Jean-Louis himself died there the following year. (Information mostly from Carl Vandenghoer of the archives of the Catholic University in Louvain.)

19. See note 18. The houses behind St. Pierre can be seen in a lithographic view of the center of Louvain by Gustav Kraus (1828), based on a now-lost painting by Domenico Quaglio (C. Pressler, *Gustav Kraus 1804–1852*, Munich, 1977, item 126).

20. Ramée's son, Daniel, for instance, used the word "Vignola" in this generic sense in his introduction to *Le Moyen-âge monumental et archéologique* (vol. 1, Paris, 1843, p. 60), when he noted that there were "no Vignolas or grammars" for Gothic architecture.

21. See Chapter 2.

22. For examples of Ramée's letters, see especially Chapter 9.

Chapter 2

I thank the following people who aided my research on Ramée's training and early work in Paris: Didier Coupaye, Bruno Foucart, Michel Gallet, Denise Gazier, Roy E. Graham, Anne-Marie Joly, Mr. and Mrs. Theodore Kiendl, Monique Mosser, Jean-Marie Pérouse de Montclos, Jacky Plault, Werner Szambien, and Robert Tricoire.

1. See Appendix for the text of Boulliot's article.

2. Alexandre Belanger's letter (in draft form) is preserved in the Bibliothèque Historique de la Ville de Paris (Ms. NA.182, fol. 112–13). Speaking of his father's "*école,*" Alexandre Belanger wrote: "Tous ses parens ont été appelés par des souverains. L'un est premier peintre du Roy de Suède, l'autre premier architecte du Roy d'Espagne et du Prince de la Paix, un autre est à Hambourg où il dirige le goût et les constructions d'une partie des Princes du Nord." In quoting this passage, Belanger's biographer Stern identifies the architect's three "parens" as Louis Belanger, Dugourc and Ramée (J. Stern, *A l'ombre de Sophie Arnould: François Joseph Belanger. . .* ,vol. 2, Paris, 1930, pp. 193–4). Composing the draft of the letter, Alexandre Belanger first wrote the following about Ramée: "un autre est en Russie"; he then crossed out the last two words and corrected them as "à Hambourg." Belanger was from a Parisian family and is not known to have had family connections in the region of Givet.

3. See Appendix.

4. Archives Nationales (no. F^7-5651[1]). The document consists of an inscribed folder, a cover letter, the petition itself (a large sheet folded to create four pages), and a governmental form. Some of the sheets have notes, numbers, or other marks written on them, evidently by officials through whose hands the petition passed. These notations are not included in the following transcription of the document.

[cover letter]

Paris 3. floréal an 8 [23 April 1800]

Le C'en [Citoyen] Perregaux, Banquier rue du mont-blanc
au Citoyen Fouché, Ministre de la Police générale.

J'ai l'honneur de vous adresser une pétition de Joseph Guillaume Ramée, architecte, dont les faits sont certifiés par divers artistes et par le C'en Lagan Consul général de la République française en Basse Saxe, & qui sollicite sa radiation de la liste des Emigrés.

En jettant un coup d'oeil sur mon certificat vous verrez, Citoyen Ministre, que Ramée, injustement porté sur une liste d'Emigrés, n'a cessé de faire du bien à son pays en employant et utilisant les arts & les manufactures de la République, qu'il a constament fait servir aux différents travaux de son Etat dont il était chargé chez nos alliés. Il est d'ailleurs un des artistes les plus distingués que ce pays ci ait produits.

Je vous prie de vouloir bien renvoyer le plutôt possible au ministre de la justice la pétition de C'en Ramée avec les pièces qui y sont joints.

Agréez mes salutations cordiales.

B. J. F. [?] Perregaux [initials hard to read]

[petition]

Au Ministre de la police générale

Citoyen ministre

Joseph Guillaume Ramée, architecte, domicillié Rue du faubourg poissonière municipalité du 3e arrondissement du canton de paris, réclame pour la seconde fois de votre justice sa réintégration dans son titre, et ses droits de citoyen français.

Le C'en Ramée est architecte de profession, élève du C'en Bellanger, comme il est prouvé par les certifficats ci joints tant de son maître que des artistes ses camarades, il l'a été aussi du C'en Celerier.

> [note added in margin at this point, in Belanger's hand:] ce fut lui [Ramée] qui exécuta les plans de ce dernier [Cellerier] au champ de la fédération. B.

Après avoir servi dès les premiers jours de la Révolution avec tout le dévouement d'un vrai patriote dans le bataillon du faubourg montmartre, il crut devoir profiter en messidor an 3 [?] [June–July 1795] du privilège que nos loix accordoient à cette époque aux artistes d'aller se perfectionner, en voyageant dans les pays étrangers amis, ou alliés de la République.

Le C'en Ramée se proposoit de parcourir l'allemagne et l'italie pendant un an ou dix huit mois. Il se trouvoit en vendémiaire an 3 [?] [Sept.–Oct. 1794] dans la basse Saxe où il étoit momentanément employé par le duc de saxe hilburghausen, comme il peut le prouver par pièces authentiques; quand on lui manda de paris que son nom venoit d'être inscrit sur une liste supplémentaire d'émigrés. C'est la dernière qu'on ait publié.

Le C'en Ramée, obligé par la loy du 19 fructidor [5 September 1797] de rester en pays étranger, a réclamé sur le champ. Il a produit un certifficat de son émigration datté 14 [?] messidor an 3 [?] [2 July 1795]. La réclamation signée alors d'un grand nombre d'artistes, et accompagnée des témoignages les plus honorables, est restée déposée au département de la Seine.

Le C'en Ramée demande la Radiation définitive de son nom de la liste des émigrés. Tous les artistes tant ses maîtres que ses camarades, tous ses compagnons d'armes de la garde nationale, les agens de la République dans les pays étrangers, enfin tous ceux de ses concitoyens qui le connoissent, attesteront les droits qu'il peut faire valoir – comme artiste, et comme patriote, à la protection et à la justice du gouvernement, surtout lors qu'il prouvera qu'il fournit de grands débouchés pour le nord, aux fabriques, et manufactures françaises.

Salut & respect. J. G. Ramée

Je Soussigné L'un des architectes des monuments publics, Certifie que Joseph Guillaume Ramé [sic], architecte, a été mon Elève pendant plusieurs années, qu'il s'est distingué dans l'Etude de cet art où il a fait des Progrès Rapides jusqu'au moment où il a mérité d'Employer ses talens pour son avantage particulier,

Qu'il est sorty de mon attelier en 1790, étant nommé par le C'en Celerier premier Inspecteur du Décôre de la fête de la première fédération, à Paris,

Qu'il a construit à Paris une petite Salle de Spectacle, le Corps-de-Logis, sur la Rue, de la maison Peregaux, chaussée D'antin; Rue du Mail la maison du C'en Berthauld ainsi que des jardins à Chantilly &c, &c, &c.

Que les Ouvrages de Cet Artiste ont toujours montré un Talent distingué tant par son Génie naturel que par son Goût pour l'antique, qu'il s'étoit proposé d'aller encore Epurer, par l'Examen des ouvrages des grecs et des Romains, nos véritables maîtres dans cet art; à Paris Ce 2 Germinal an 8 [23 March 1800] de la République française

Belanger

Architecte des monuments publics

Rue du faub'g Poissonnière No. 21.

Je certifie avoir Employé dans mes travaux pendant deux ans et plus le citoyen Ramée, dont les talens distingués m'ont porté à lui confier l'inspection générale des travaux de la fête de la fédération de 1790. J'atteste qu'il en a Rempli ses fonctions avec le plus grand zèle et la plus parfaite intelligence, et que j'ai été portée de Reconnaître dans les travaux dont le C'en Belanger a donné les détails ci dessus l'Empreinte d'un véritable talent. Je déclare d'ailleurs que j'ai toujours connu dans le citoyen Ramée les sentimens d'un homme attaché aux principes de la Révolution.

paris le quatre germinal an huit [25 March 1800].

Cellerier

architecte . . . [illegible]

Je sousigné certifie que le citoyen Ramée, en sa qualité d'Architecte a conduit les travaux du Bâtiment que j'occupe sur la rue du montblanc, ainsi que dans cette occasion et pendant tout le tems que je l'ai connu, il a manifesté et pratiqué tout ce que l'on pouvait attendre d'un bon citoyen sincèrement attaché à son Pays et que d'ailleurs son absence a été remplie par des travaux de son état chez nos alliés pour lesquels il n'a cessé d'utiliser nos manufactures et d'employer les différens artistes de ce Pays.

à Paris le 12 Germinal an 8 [2 April 1800]

B. J. F. [?] Perregaux

Je soussigné domicilié rue Colbert No. 283, ayant résidé à Hambourg en qualité de Consul Général de la République Française en Basse Saxe, certifie qu'il est notoire et de ma connoissance particulière, que le citoyen Joseph Guillaume Ramée architecte y a demeuré, et voyagé dans l'arondissement de mon département depuis environ trois ans; qu'il y a joui de l'estime générale; et qu'il y a porté la cocarde nationale depuis le moment qu'il a été instruit que les citoyens français étoient obligés de porter ce signe en pais étranger. En foy de quoi j'ai signé le présent Paris ce 18 Germinal l'an 8 de la Répub . . . [illegible]

Lagan
consul g'al [général] de la
République française en basse saxe

[At a couple of places in the petition, the following signatures were added between the statements:] Lagrenée / Boizot, sculpteur / Stouf [?], entrepreneur de maçonnerie des hospices civils communaux de paris / Charles Percier / Bouillier [?] / Alexandre Regnier. [See note 7 regarding these names.]

5. See text of petition, note 4.

6. See text of petition, note 4.

7. The signatures on Ramée's petition are: "Charles Percier," "Lagrenée," "Boizot, sculpteur," "Bouillier" [?], "Alexandre Regnier," and "Stouf, entrepreneur de maçonnerie des hospices civils communaux de Paris." Lagrenée was probably Jean-Jacques Lagrenée *le jeune*, as this painter had professional connections with Belanger (Stern, vol. 1, p. 145). Belanger also had dealings with a sculptor named Regnier in the 1780s (Stern, vol. 1, pp. 80, 154), later with a sculptor named Bouillet [sic] (Stern, vol. 2, p. 121), and with the sculptor Boizot (Stern, vol. 1, pp. 71, 80; vol. 2, pp. 121, 359). A sculptor named Jean Baptiste Stouf was active in Paris during this period, but was probably not the "master-mason" Stouf who signed Ramée's petition.

8. For Belanger, see Stern, *Belanger;* Louis Hautecoeur, *Histoire de l'architecture classique en France*, vol. 4 (Paris, 1943–57), pp. 105–9, 302–9; and Allan Braham, *The Architecture of the French Enlightenment* (Berkeley, Calif., 1980). F. Benoît (*L'Art français sous la Révolution et l'Empire*, Paris, 1897, pp. 265–6) wrote: "Avec Ledoux, [Belanger] fut le plus employé des architectes de la fin du 18e siècle et l'on peut le regarder comme un des fondateurs les plus énergiques de l'évolution du goût contemporain en matière de distribution intérieure et de décoration." Alternate spellings of the architect's name that are sometimes found in the literature on him include Bélanger and Bellanger, but he himself normally spelled his name Belanger.

9. For architectural education of this period in France, see J.-M. Pérouse de Montclos, *Les Prix de Rome* (Paris, 1984); C. Cohen, *La Formation architecturale au 18ème siècle en France*, 1980; and R. Chafee, "The Teaching of Architecture at the École des Beaux-Arts," in A. Drexler, ed., *The Architecture of the École des Beaux-Arts* (New York, 1977).

10. For Cellerier, see Braham, pp. 238–9. As for Belanger, I have not found a clear statement of his relationship with the Academy, but Stern's biography (see, for example vol. 2, pp. 163ff.) implies that he was not a member.

11. Information from Hautecoeur, *Histoire,* and other sources.

12. Pérouse de Montclos, *Les Prix de Rome*, information gleaned from the "Index des personnes," pp. 253–60.

13. V. Beach, *Charles X of France: His Life and Times* (Boulder, Colo., 1971), pp. 33, 41.

14. Stern, vol. 1, pp. 56ff. The Comte d'Artois employed 800 workmen to execute the design in the required time.

15. Stern, vol. 1, pp. 193ff, 230ff.

16. Boulliot (see Appendix); Stern, vol 2, p. 280.

17. Information from a "*règlement sommaire*" of 1777. Stern, vol. 1, pp. 53–4.

18. Stern, vol. 1, p. 54.

19. The later document is a letter Belanger wrote in 1813, in which he named Ramée first in a list of his most successful students (Stern, vol. 2, p. 276). Ramée, too, in his petition of 1800, identified himself as an "*élève*" of Belanger. Stern's biography of Belanger states that Ramée was "inspecteur des Bâtiments du comte d'Artois," "sous sa [Belanger's] direction" (p. 280), but does not give a source for this information.

20. For Bagatelle, see Stern, vol. 1, p. 57ff; Hautecoeur, *Histoire,* vol. 4, pp. 105ff; *Le Château de Bagatelle, Étude historique et descriptive* (Paris, n.d).

21. Hautecoeur, *Histoire,* vol. 4, p. 531. Others who contributed to the creation of the Directoire style were Cellerier, the sculptor N. F. Lhuillier, and Belanger's brother-in-law, J. D. Dugourc, all of whom worked closely with Belanger.

22. H. Martin, ed., *Le Style Empire; Le Style Directoire* (Paris, 1933), p. 5; Y. Brayer et al., *L'Empire* (Paris, 1977), p. 35.

23. For Belanger's sketchbook (preserved at the École des Beaux-Arts, Paris), see Kenneth Woodbridge, "Belanger en Angleterre: son carnet de voyage," *Architectural History*, vol. 25 (1982), pp. 8–19. Woodbridge concludes that although Belanger visited many of the important picturesque gardens in England, he was interested mainly in their architectural features and was not much influenced by the latest trends in English landscape design.

24. Stern, vol. 1, pp. 31ff.; Hautecoeur, *Histoire,* vol. 5, pp. 17–18.

25. Stern, vol. 1, pp. 29–30. Belanger's letter is dated "28 ventôse" and therefore was written during the period of the Revolutionary Calendar, 1793–1805.

26. See F. Birrell, introduction to Thomas Blaikie, *Diary of a Scotch Gardener at the French Court at the End of the Eighteenth Century* (London, 1931), pp. 6–7; and the sections on Bagatelle in Stern and Hautecoeur, *Histoire*. Plans and views of the gardens at Bagatelle are found in Georges Louis Le Rouge, *Jardins anglo-chinois*, vol. 12, (Paris, c. 1776–90), pl. 2, 18; and Jean Charles Krafft, *Recueil d'architecture civile* (Paris, 1812), pl. 115–20.

27. Blaikie, pp. 134, 157, 187.

28. These are among the items listed on the plan of Bagatelle in Le Rouge, vol. 12, pl. 2.

29. Blaikie, p. 154.

30. "La nature fuit les lieux fréquentés, c'est au sommet des montagnes, au fond des forêts, dans les îles désertes, qu'elle étale ses charmes les plus touchants, ceux qui l'aiment et ne peuvent l'aller chercher si loin sont réduits à lui faire violence et à la forcer en quelque sorte à venir habiter parmi eux, et tout cela ne peut se faire sans un peu d'illusion." Ramée did not identify the source of this quotation, but it is taken (with minor changes in wording and punctuation) from Rousseau's *Julie, ou la Nouvelle Héloïse* (Part 4, letter 11), first published in 1760.

31. Stern, vol. 1, pp. 135, 147. Plans and views of the house and gardens are found in Le Rouge, vol. 20, pl. 9–13; and Krafft, *Recueil*, pl. 97–114. Baudard was *Trésorier Général de la Marine*. His

title is now usually written Saint-James, although he himself spelled it Sainte-James (it came from a French placename, not from the English name of the apostle). See the *Dictionnaire de biographie française*, vol. 5 (Paris, 1951); and G. Leroux-Cesbron, "Le Baron de Sainte-James et sa folie de Neuilly," *La Revue de Paris* (February 1925), pp. 665–82.

32. Blaikie, p. 181. For descriptions of the Grand Rocher, see Braham, p. 226; Hautecoeur, *Histoire*, vol. 5, pp. 28–9.

33. This use of the Saint-James Grand Rocher design is described in Robert Rosenblum, *Transformations in Late Eighteenth Century Art* (Princeton, 1967), p. 127.

34. See E. de Ganay, *Chantilly au XVIIIe siècle* (Paris, 1925). Amélie Lefêbvre of the Musée Condé at Chantilly informed me that she was unable to find any record pertaining to Ramée (correspondence of 1983). It is possible that Ramée's work at Chantilly was not for the Prince de Condé but for the Berthault family, which had an estate there. (See Chapter 3 for Ramée's design of the Berthault House in Paris.)

35. Ramée's son Daniel, in one of his architectural publications, defined *comble* as: "Ensemble de toutes les pièces de charpente destinées à porter les ardoises, les tuiles, [etc.]" (*Dictionnaire général des termes d'architecture*, Paris, 1868, p. 99). Daniel Ramée included a description of curved roof structures and the "système de Philibert de l'Orme" in his *L'Architecture et la construction pratique*, 4th ed. (Paris, 1881), pp. 314–23.

36. Stern, vol. 1, p. 194.

37. Mark K. Deming, *La Halle au Blé de Paris* (Brussels, 1984).

38. David Gilly, *Ueber Erfindung, Construction und Vortheile der Bohlen-Dächer* (Berlin, 1797). David Gilly's son Friedrich, in Paris in 1797, did drawings of recent buildings there that evidently used this system of roof construction (see, example, *Friedrich Gilly und die Privatgesellschaft junger Architekten*, Berlin, 1987, fig. 24). For Jefferson's interest in the system, see Deming, p. 184.

39. Stern, vol. 1, p. 224.

40. The present shape of the roofs of these buildings on the Rue de Rivoli dates from a remodeling of the 1850s; Percier and Fontaine's original design had a more gently curving profile.

41. For Cellerier's statement in the 1800 petition, see note 4. Ramée's own statement in the petition includes the following: "Le C'en [Citoyen] Ramée est architecte de profession, élève du C'en Bellanger, . . . il l'a été aussi du C'en Celerier."

42. When Cellerier died in 1814, Belanger gave the funeral eulogy for him, in which he alluded to their friendship (Stern, vol. 2, pp. 258–9).

43. Cellerier's Hôtel Laval-Montmorency is illustrated in J. C. Krafft and N. Ransonnette, *Plans, coupes, élévations des plus belles maisons . . . à Paris* (Paris, 1801–3), pl. 41–2. Belanger's somewhat similar Ballue House is illustrated in Krafft, *Recueil*, pl. 2–3.

44. Cellerier's theatrical designs included the civic theatre in Dijon (designed 1787, constructed 1810–25), and the following theatres in Paris: the Wauxhall du Boulevard (c. 1770); the Ambigu-Comique (1770, remodeled by Cellerier 1785); the Salle de Concert of the Hôtel Laval-Montmorency (1786); the Salle de Spectacle of the Hôtel Soubise (designed 1788, but never executed); the Théâtre du Vaudeville (1802); and the Théâtre des Variétés (1807). See Hautecoeur, *Histoire*, vols. 4, 5, and the article on Cellerier by M. Blumer in the *Dictionnaire de biographie française*, vol. 8 (Paris, 1959). For the general subject of theatre design in late eighteenth-century France, see Hautecoeur, *Histoire*, vol. 4, pp. 97–101, 430–54.

45. Stern, vol. 1, pp. 92, 123ff.

46. Cellerier's Salle de Concert is illustrated in Krafft and Ransonnette, pl. 41, 42, 99. Ramée's auditorium-chapel for Union College, which was never constructed, is known from Ramée's drawings, preserved in the Union College Archives. The similarities between the two designs include an apsidal space at the end of the hall, supported by an arcade, and an unusual system of curving stairways.

47. Decoration similar to that of Cellerier's *salle de concert* can be seen, for example, in Ramée's interior decoration of the Erichsen Mansion in Copenhagen.

48. This structure is illustrated in Krafft and Ransonnette, pl. 54. Also see Braham, pp. 238–9, and Hautecoeur, *Histoire*, vol. 4, pp. 119, 370.

49. In the section drawing in Krafft and Ransonnette, a dotted line indicates an additional domed roof (higher than the one shown in detail), which was probably an alternate design.

50. Regarding Boullée's work for Artois, see J.-M. Pérouse de Montclos, *Étienne Louis Boullée* (New York, 1974), pp. 16, 22.

Chapter 3

1. See Chapter 2, note 4, for text of Belanger's statement.

2. Louis Hautecoeur, *L'Art sous la Révolution et l'Empire en France* (Paris, 1953), p. 18. Werner Szambien has recently argued, however, that architectural activity during the revolutionary period was greater than generally thought ("Les Architectes parisiens à l'époque révolutionnaire," *Revue de l'art*, no. 83, 1989, pp. 36–50).

3. "Corps de logis" can mean either "la partie principale d'un bâtiment" or "une construction detachée du bâtiment principal" (*Nouveau Larousse Illustré*). The second sense is evidently meant in Belanger's statement.

4. Articles on Perregaux in *La Grande encyclopédie* (Paris, n.d.); *Nouvelle biographie générale* (Paris, 1862); L. Michaud, *Biographie universelle* (Paris, c. 1854); and G. P. Menais, *Napoléon et l'argent*, (Paris, 1969), pp. 126–31; and P. Jarry, *Cénacles et vieux logis parisiens* (Paris, 1929), pp. 171–86. Some biographical dictionaries give Perregaux's first names incorrectly as Alphonse Claude Charles Bernadin (his son's name). Perregaux's signature on Ramée's petition is difficult to read, but appears to be "B J F [?] Perregaux."

5. See the text of the petition in Chapter 2, note 4. Perregaux evidently was the principal supporter of Ramée's petition, for besides his statement he wrote a cover letter for the petition (dated "3 floréal an 8" [23 April 1800], addressed to "Citoyen Fouché, Ministre de la Police générale"), summarizing Ramée's request for "radiation de la liste des Emigrés," and asking that Fouché forward the petition to the *Ministre de la Justice*.

6. The motif of a niche screened by columns had previously been used by Robert Adam, in the interiors of several of his houses (for example Syon House, of the 1760s) Ledoux, however, was apparently the first architect to employ it on the exterior of a building (as noted in Braham, *The Architecture of the French Enlightenment*, p. 174).

7. This building is Jefferson's Pavilion IX, erected in 1821. See W. Pierson, *American Buildings and Their Architects: the Colonial and Neoclassical Styles* (New York, 1970), pp. 330–3, and H. Rice, *Thomas Jefferson's Paris* (Princeton, 1976), p. 42. For about a year, right after coming to Paris in 1784, Jefferson lived on the Cul-de-sac Taitbout, only one block from the Rue de la Chaussée d'Antin and the Hôtel Guimard. Even after moving to another part of Paris, Jefferson frequently visited friends who lived on the Rue de la Chaussée d'Antin (Rice, pp. 37–43). It is therefore likely that Jefferson saw the changes

that Ramée made to the Guimard property. Also see the remarks on Ledoux and Jefferson by J. Harris, F. Nichols, and J. Pérouse de Montclos in W. Adams, ed., *The Eye of Thomas Jefferson* (Washington, D. C., 1976), pp. 172, 293.

8. Michel Gallet, *Claude Nicolas Ledoux* (Paris, 1980), pp. 84–90. The theatre was apparently removed from the building and installed elsewhere even before Guimard sold the property. (Conversation with Michel Gallet, October 1983.)

9. The history of this property (9, rue de la Chaussée d'Antin) under both Guimard and Perregaux is described in Jarry, *Cénacles*, pp. 171–86, and J. Hillairet, *Dictionnaire historique des rues de Paris*, vol. 1 (Paris, 1963), p. 336.

10. One of these was J.-R. Tardieu's *Pour une épingle* (Paris, 1856), a curious tale about a lady's brooch worn by Perregaux's wife (though the names are changed in the story); the brooch was lost in the courtyard between the residence and the banking house and was found by Jacques Lafitte, who later became Perregaux's partner and Napoleon's principal banker. Concerning this story, see also Jarry, p. 183; Hillairet, p. 336; and André Castelot, *Paris, The Turbulent City, 1783–1871* (New York, 1962), pp. 156–61.

11. Book of Paris block plans, Archives Nationales, Service des Plans, F(31)-74, Ilot No. 15, 9 rue de la Chaussée d'Antin. A comparison of the ground plan of Perregaux's building with a ground plan of Guimard's theatre structure shows that Ramée gave the building a wholly new plan, for example by creating a large stair hall in a part of the building previously occupied by a stable. The two plans are reproduced in Paul V. Turner, "Joseph Jacques Ramée's First Career," *Art Bulletin* (June 1985), fig. 11.

12. This drawing, presently owned by Mr. and Mrs. Theodore Kiendl of Paris, was illustrated in an Hôtel Drouot auction catalogue (27–8 November 1907) as the work of an artist named "Meunier." According to its owners, the drawing is neither signed nor dated. Jarry (pp. 180–1) attributed it to a "Meunier" and identified it as representing the Rue de la Chaussée d'Antin at the end of the eighteenth century. Jarry and Ledoux-Lebard (p. 177) believed it showed Ledoux's building that contained Guimard's theatre. Michel Gallet brought the drawing to my attention and pointed out to me that it must represent the structure as rebuilt by Perregaux.

13. Section drawings of Mademoiselle Guimard's pavilion and theatre structure, showing that the latter had only two floors, are reproduced in Gallet, p. 89.

14. Krafft and Ransonnette, pl. 4, 17, 18, 63. Stern, *Belanger*, vol. 1, pl. opp. pp. 194 and 210.

15. Archives Nationales, Z(1J)1192. Berthault's one-page application is dated 6 March 1789; the eight-page inspector's report is dated 27 March 1789. I thank Anne-Marie Joly of the Service des Plans at the Archives Nationales, who helped me discover this document in August 1983. The present address of the building is 12, rue du Mail.

16. Examples of Ramée's verified handwriting include his statement in the petition of 1800; notes on his drawings for buildings in Germany (1796), Denmark (c. 1800), and the United States (1813); and about twenty letters written by him, most dating from 1804–8. Comparison of Ramée's handwriting with other French hands of the period (such as those of his fellow architects who wrote statements for his petition of 1800) reveals that Ramée's was distinctive, characterized for example by an unusual manner of forming certain capital letters.

17. Hillairet, vol. 2, p. 88. Louis Martin Berthault's birthdate has been given variously in different references to him, but the most recent and thorough article on him gives it as 1770 (entry on Berthault in the 1990 edition of *Encyclopédie universalis*; pre-publication text shown to me by Monique Mosser). The author of this article, J. D. Devauges, has informed me that he considers the attribution of the Rue du Mail house to Berthault an error. Moreover, samples of Berthault's handwriting, provided to me by M. Devauges, are completely different from the handwriting on the drawings for the Rue du Mail house. It is interesting to note that starting in 1798 Berthault worked for Madame Récamier (who lived in the Rue du Mail building from about 1795 to 1798), remodeling her newly-acquired house on the Rue de la Chaussée d'Antin, which was next to the Perregaux House that Ramée had built. (R. and C. Ledoux-Lebard, "La Décoration et l'ameublement de la chambre de Madame Récamier sous le Consulat," *Gazette des Beaux-Arts*, vol. 40 [October 1952], pp. 175–92.) Berthault's family had an estate at Chantilly, where Berthault is said to have exercised his talents as a young man (*Encyclopédie universalis* article); he later published a view of the family's gardens at Chantilly (in *Suite de vingt-quatre vues de jardins anglais exécutés par Berthault, architecte . . .*, Paris, [1820]). One wonders if this was perhaps the garden Ramée worked on at Chantilly, according to Belanger's statement in Ramée's petition. In light of these coincidences, it is conceivable that Ramée and Berthault had some professional relationship in their early years.

18. Stern, vol. 1, p. 82. In his application to build the house, Berthault identified himself as "maître maçon" and "Entrepreneur de Bâtiments à Paris."

19. According to Stern (vol. 1, p. 215), the period from 1785 to the Revolution was the most active in Belanger's career.

20. The three plans have dimensions of about 49 × 52 cm, the section drawing about 52 × 68 cm, and the elevation drawing about 36 × 45 cm.

21. Differences between Ramée's design of the façade and the executed façade are mentioned later in this chapter. The interior of the building is difficult to compare precisely with Ramée's plans, for it has been altered radically (serving in recent times as offices and space for various business enterprises). But enough of the original interior walls survive to reveal that in general the house was executed in accordance with Ramée's floor plans.

22. Gallet, pl. 184. Gallet also illustrates a façade design, very similar to that of the Berthault-Récamier House, which was used for several houses constructed near the Odéon in Paris, in 1789, by followers of Ledoux (Gallet, pp. 205, 206, 248, note 20).

23. The principal examples are Sophienholm, Oregaard, and Frederikslund, all in or near Copenhagen. See Chapter 8.

24. For Ledoux's relationship with Belanger, see Gallet, p. 88; Stern, vol. 1, pp. 41ff, 224–5. Cellerier's eulogy: "Notice rapide sur la vie et les ouvrages de Claude-Nicolas Ledoux," *Annales de l'architecture et des arts* (c. 1807), pp. 3–16. The article is signed "J. C."; this is identified as Cellerier by Gallet (*Ledoux*, p. 287). Following my discussions with Michel Gallet about the Perregaux House, Ramée, and Ledoux, Gallet has written, "ce fut certainement avec l'agrément de Ledoux que J.-J. Ramée . . . transforma sur la chausée d'Antin l'immeuble Guimard, acquis par le financier Perregaux" (*Architecture de Ledoux: Inédits pour un tome III*, Paris, 1991, p. 54).

25. For Daniel Ramée's edition of Ledoux's designs, see the Epilogue. It is interesting that Daniel Ramée used an engraving of the frieze on the front of the Pavillon Guimard for the title page of the second volume of his Ledoux publication.

26. These interior details were intact, at any rate, when I inspected the building in 1986, as it was about to be remodeled. The building at that time was being used as offices.

27. See, for example Krafft, *Recueil*, pl. 2, 104, 117, 118.

28. Martin, ed., *Le Style Empire*, fig. 9; Hautecoeur, *Histoire*, vol. 4, p. 124.

29. The first years of Madame Récamier's marriage are not nearly so well documented as the remainder of her life. Hillairet (II, p. 88) states that she lived in the Rue du Mail house starting in 1795. But her most thorough biographer, E. Herriot (*Madame Récamier*, New York and London, 1925, vol. 1, p. 33), suggests that she lived there from her marriage in 1793 until 1798.

30. See Appendix.

31. See G. Chapman, *Beckford* (London, 1952); B. Fothergill, *Beckford of Fonthill* (London, 1979); and other works cited below. For Beckford's visits to Lake Geneva, see G. R. de Beer, "Anglais au Pays de Vaud: V. William Beckford," *Revue historique vaudoise* (Dec. 1951), pp. 165–80 (brought to my attention by Claire Bonney of the Architekturmuseum in Basel).

32. A. Morrison, ed., *The Collection of Autograph Letters and Historical Documents*, second series, *The Hamilton and Nelson Papers*, vol. 1 (n.p., 1893), p. 165.

33. Stern, vol. 2, p. 40.

34. Letter from Beckford to Hamilton of 31 July 1792, in Morrison, *Hamilton Papers*, vol. 1, p. 169.

35. Ibid.

36. E. Sullivan, ed., *Buck Whaley's Memoirs, Including His Journey to Jerusalem* (London, 1906), pp. 295–6.

37. The Beckford Papers were recently in the possession of Blackwell's Rare Books and unavailable to researchers. However, Peter Fenemore of Blackwell's informed me that Ramée's name does not appear in an index of the papers that was compiled by Boyd Alexander (correspondence of November–December 1983).

38. See Krafft, *Receuil*, pl. 105, 119; Le Rouge, vol. 20, pl. 12; Ganay, p. 98; Dora Wiebenson, *The Picturesque Garden in France* (Princeton, 1978) p. 93 and fig. 94; and Hautecoeur, *Histoire*, vol. 5, pp. 33ff.

39. See Hautecoeur, *Histoire*, vol. 5, pp. 379–80.

40. *Vathek*, written in French and first published in 1787, contains numerous references to *tentes* and *pavillons* (the two words are used interchangeably by Beckford), but they are not described very specifically. See, for example G. Chapman, ed., *Vathek* (Cambridge, 1929), vol. 1, pp. 90, 113–14, and vol. 2, p. 124. As early as 1783, when Beckford was also at Lake Geneva, he had erected "a pavilion composed of glasses, reflecting with a sort of magic confusion the long perspective of the woods, . . ." (Diary entry, quoted in B. Alexander, *England's Wealthiest Son: A Study of William Beckford*, London, 1962, p. 106).

41. For Cellerier's post as public-works deputy in Paris, see L. Gottschalk and M. Maddox, *Lafayette in the French Revolution*, vol. 2 (Chicago, 1973), pp. 158, 159, 171. For Belanger's accommodation to the Revolution, see Pierre Pinon, "Architectes dans la Révolution: Comment le traverser," *Architecture d'aujourd'hui* (June 1989), pp. 58–60. Stern (vol. 2, p. 7) noted that Belanger, despite his links with the aristocracy, essentially "remained a bourgeois."

42. "Après avoir servi dès les premiers jours de la Révolution avec tout le dévouement d'un vrai patriote dans le bataillon du faubourg montmartre, . . ." (See Chapter 2.)

43. See, for example, Monique Mosser and Daniel Rabreau, "Circus, Amphitheatre, Colosseum: Revolutionary Paris as a New Rome," *Lotus International*, vol. 39 (1983), pp. 108–17.

44. A contemporary account of this event is found in *Confédération Nationale, ou récit exact & circonstancié de tout ce qui s'est passé à Paris, le 14 juillet 1790, à la Fédération* (Paris, an 2 [1793–4]). The fête and Lafayette's role in it are described in Gottschalk and Maddox, vol. 2, pp. 503–55. For the physical setting of the event, see R. Etlin, "Architecture and the Festival of Federation, Paris, 1790," *Architectural History*, vol. 18 (1975), pp. 23–42; M. Biver, *Fêtes révolutionnaires à Paris* (Paris, 1979), pp. 11–31; A. Gruber, *Les Grandes fêtes et leurs décors à l'époque de Louis XVI* (Geneva, 1972), pp. 149–53; and P. de la Vaissière, "La Fédération des Français peinte par P.-A. de Machy: Essai d'iconographie de la fête de juillet 1790," *Bulletin du Musée Carnavalet*, no. 2 (1975), pp. 16–35.

45. Quoted in F. Furet and D. Richet, *La Révolution* (Paris, 1965), p. 160.

46. Besides Belanger's identification of Cellerier as the architect of the *Fête de la Fédération* (in Ramée's petition of 1800), Cellerier is identified thus in an engraved plan of the *Fête* in J. Durand, *Recueil et parallèle des édifices de tout genre . . .* (Venice, 1833; following pl. 98), a plan that had also appeared in the 1801 Paris edition of Durand's work, but without Cellerier's name. Further evidence of Cellerier's role as architect of this plan is found in a tract written by the architect G. F. Blondel, *Observations du Sieur Blondel, . . . sur le projet de la Fête de la Confédération, . . .* (Paris, 1790), in which Blondel, evidently disappointed in his attempt to get the commission, compared his own plan for the Fête with that of Cellerier. See Etlin, p. 26 and note 26.

47. See text of Ramée's petition, Chapter 2 note 4.

48. For example, S. Blondel (in *L'Art pendant la Révolution*, Paris, 1887, p. 88) and C. Lucas (in an entry on Ramée in *La Grande encyclopédie*, vol. 28 Paris, c. 1885-1901, p. 119) both credited the design of the *Autel de la Patrie* to Ramée. In 1848, Ramée's son Daniel wrote that his father "a élevé l'autel de la patrie lors de la première Fédération . . ." (Daniel Ramée, "Liberté, Egalité, Fraternité . . .," 1848; copy in Bibliothèque Nationale). A similar attribution was made in G. Vapereau, *Dictionnaire universel des contemporains*, vol. 2, (Paris, 1858), p. 1429. E. Kaufmann (*Architecture in the Age of Reason*, Cambridge, Mass., 1955, p. 183) also made this attribution, without documentation except for reference to Blondel's book. As early as 1858, a biographical dictionary stated that Ramée "erected" the *Autel de la Patrie* (Vapereau, *Dictionnaire*, vol. 2, Paris, 1858, p. 1429), a statement that technically does not mean Ramée designed the structure, but implies it. This statement is found in a biographical entry on Ramée's son Daniel, which may have been provided by Daniel himself.

49. An undated report of the committee (including Cellerier) that planned the *Fête de la Fédération* is contained in *Confédération nationale* (pp. 48–53). It states that the committee first examined proposals of individual artists and then determined the general form of the plan, which thus was "un résultat des idées qu'ils on puisées dans tous les dessins qu'on a mis sous leurs yeux" (p. 51). At this stage, the committee's conception of the *Autel de la Patrie* was "un autel simple, posé sur un stylobate carré, élevé de vingt-cinq pieds, & posé sur de larges gradins" (p. 52).

50. A contemporary engraved plan of the *Fête de la Fédération* ("Plan général du Champ de Mars. . .," by Meusnier and Gauché) identifies the central altar as "Autel de la Patrie élevé de 28 pieds." This engraving also gives the inscriptions on the four corner-cubes

of the altar and those on the triumphal arch.

51. Biver, pp. 47–9; fig. 24. Philippe Duboy (*Lequeu*, Cambridge, Mass., 1987, pp. 16, 345) states that the architect Jean-Jacques Lequeu was involved in the reuse of the setting for a second *Fête de la Fédération* in 1791. Another design of 1791, by the architects Legrand and Molinos, for a "*cirque national*," incorporating an altar similar to Ramée's, is illustrated in Werner Szambien, *Les Projets de l'an II* (Paris, 1986), p. 66. Ramée's altar is also shown in views of "la publication de la loi martiale au Champ de Mars, le 17 juillet 1791" (J. A. Dulaure, *Esquisses historiques . . . de la Révolution françaises*, vol. 2, Paris, 1825, opp. p. 17) and of "the destruction of the emblems of feudalism," 14 July 1792 (Mosser and Rabreau, p. 111).

52. This comparison was pointed out by Kaufmann, p. 183.

Chapter 4

I thank Carl Vandenghoer of the archives of the Katholieke Universiteit in Louvain for his assistance in my research on Ramée's sojourns and work in Belgium.

1. Louis Réau, *Histoire de l'expansion de l'art français*, vol. 2 (Paris, 1928), pp. 234–5.

2. See Chapter 2, note 4, for text of Ramée's petition. In the dates given here as "Year 3," it is hard to tell whether Ramée's cursively written number is a 3 or a 5. In either case, however, the account is inaccurate.

3. See Appendix.

4. *La Vie et les mémoires du Général Dumouriez*, 4 vols. (Paris, 1822–3); article on Dumouriez in *Dictionnaire de la Révolution Française* (Paris, n.d.), pp. 622–6.

5. Document in archives of the French Ministry of War (B1-5), reported by A. Doysie in the 1930s (Larrabee Papers, Union College Archives). According to Doysie's notes, "In the list of the Séconde colonne, lieutenant-général M. Miranda, are the following. Maréchaux de camp: Messrs. Campierre, Stengel, Eustace (American). Adjutants généraux: Messrs. Montjoye, d'Arnaudin. Adjoints: Messrs. Torréry, Chérin, Du Bief, Du Ru, Ramé, Hauchen." A letter written in 1825, from the Swedish consul general in Paris to the French police, inquiring about Ramée, stated that he had held the position of "Major au service de France" (Archives Nationales, F[7]9546; see Chapter 13).

6. Ramée's sister, Dieudonnée Ramée, married a man named Joseph Torreri (see Chapter 1). As this is an extremely rare surname (I can find no other examples of it in France) it seems likely that the "Torréry" who served with Ramée on Dumouriez's staff was of the same family. Moreover, this Torréry was one of the men, including Ramée, who fled with Dumouriez after his failed plot against the French government.

7. Johann Wolfgang von Goethe, *Campagne in Frankreich*; quoted in James J. Sheehan, *German History 1770–1866*, (Oxford, 1989), p. 222.

8. *Vie du Général Dumouriez*, vol. 3, pp. 229, 287–8.

9. Ibid., vol. 3, p. 352.

10. Ibid., vol. 4, pp. 145–7. Among those whom Dumouriez later specifically mentioned in his memoirs as coplotters, were the Duc de Chartres (later King Louis Philippe), generals Valence and Thouvenot, and a Colonel Montjoye, who appeared on the same list of staff officers as Ramée in 1792. The Duc de Chartres's own account of these events is found in *Mémoires de Louis Philippe, duc d'Orléans*, vol. 2, (Paris, 1974), pp. 395 ff.

11. *Vie du Général Dumouriez*, vol. 4, pp. 151, 159.

12. Louis Philippe later noted (*Mémoires de Louis Philippe*, vol. 2, p. 424) that after Dumouriez's escape, his party included Louis-Philippe himself and "Thouvenot, Montjoye, Barrois, Saint-Pardoux, Toreri [sic], Rainville, etc."

13. Service des Plans, Archives Nationales, Paris: drawing no. N II, Dyle 3, 4956. The drawing evidently was taken to Paris during the period of French occupation of Belgium after 1794. The sheet is entitled "Plan général, coupe et élévation d'un entrepôt, projetté pour la ville de Louvain" and signed "Ramée, architecte à Louvain." A drawing that is evidently a copy of this sheet (but without Ramée's signature and certain details of the original) is in the Municipal Museum of Louvain (P.K. 1-10).

14. G. Piot, *Histoire de Louvain depuis son origine jusqu'aujourd'hui*, vol. 1 (Louvain, 1839), p. 343; Edward van Even, *Louvain monumental* (Louvain, 1860), p. 163; and other sources.

15. Petition from the merchants of Louvain to Emperor Joseph II, 2 June 1789.

16. A letter from the Louvain merchants' society to the city authorities, 13 June 1793 (in the Stadsarchief Leuven) proposes the execution of plans for an *Entrepôt* that are apparently those of Ramée.

17. This observation was made by Werner Szambien in conversation with me in 1990.

18. Pérouse de Montclos, *Les Prix de Rome*, p. 225; also pp. 210 (project of Bonnard, 1788), 217 (Normand, 1790), 226 (Bergognon, 1792).

19. For example, the Porte St. Martin and Porte St. Denis in Paris, constructed in the reign of Louis XIV; Ledoux's Hôtel de Thélusson and P. Rousseau's Hôtel de Salm, both in Paris and of the 1780s.

20. Thomas W. Gaehtgens, *Napoleons Arc de Triomphe* (Göttingen, 1974); Uwe Westfehling, *Triumphbogen im 19. und 20. Jahrhundert* (Munich, 1977).

21. Pérouse de Montclos, *Prix de Rome*, p. 211. Le Febvre was a student of L. F. Trouard. Another similar design is an arch that was erected in Paris for a revolutionary *fête* of 10 August 1793 (Hautecoeur, *Histoire*, vol. 5, p. 124), almost exactly contemporaneous with Ramée's design.

22. The question of precedents depends partly on how one defines a triumphal arch. There are examples of sculpture placed within triumphal arch-like forms used as funerary monuments (see, for example, Gaehtgens, pl. 14) or when incorporated into walls, as in the garden wall of Brongniart's house for the Duc d'Orléans in Paris, of 1773 (Krafft and Ransonnette, pl. 30). Robin Middleton has mentioned to me a couple of other possible precedents: an arch designed by Servandoni for the consecration of the Place St. Sulpice in Paris, c. 1754, and a design in Joshua Kirby's *The Perspective of Architecture*, vol. 2 (1761), pl. 55.

23. E. Duller, *Erzherzog Carl von Oesterreich* (Pest, 1859), pp. 118–30.

24. E. van Even, *Louvain dans le passé et dans le présent* (Louvain, 1895), p. 81.

25. For the reference to the *Journal des bâtimens*, see Chapter 9.

26. Stern, vol. 2, p. 114; A. Loiseau, *Notice sur F. J. Belanger* (1818), p. 97. Belanger's address at this time was 21, rue du Faubourg Poissonière.

27. Document of 9 February 1803 (see Chapter 1). Ramée is referred to as "Le Citoyen Joseph Ramée, architecte et négociant demeurant à Hambourg."

28. See Chapter 7.

29. Archives Nationales, Paris (doc. no. T-1687). The report is dated "4e jour complémentaire l'an 4" (20 September 1796), but refers to documents of the dead man that were deposited "22 Thermidor an 4" (10 August 1796) at the Archives du Bureau du Domaine National du département de la Seine; so the man evidently died shortly before this latter date. The man is identified as "Joseph Jacques Ramée, décédé sans héritiers connus, rue et section poissonière no. 23."

30. See Chapter 2.

31. Percier and Fontaine first came to the attention of Napoleon shortly after the coup of 18 Brumaire (9 November 1799), and their advice on artistic matters was being solicited by Napoleon by the beginning of 1800, for example for a ceremony at Les Invalides, 9 February 1800 (J. Duportal, *Charles Percier*, Paris, 1931, pp. 43–5; M. Fouche, *Percier et Fontaine*, Paris, n.d., pp. 38–43). It is not known precisely when Percier signed Ramée's petition, but the dated statements in the petition are of March and April 1800; the signatures of Percier and the other signers were surely added to the document after the statements were written.

Chapter 5

I thank the following people who aided my research on Ramée's work in Saxony. In Erfurt: André Schubart and Herr Nölde of the Angermuseum, Dr. Fischer of the Staatsarchiv, and Herr Thimm of the Institut für Denkmalpflege. In Gotha: Herr Immig and Dr. Ruge of the Staatsarchiv, Dr. Helmut Claus and Frau Gerlach of the Forschungs- und Landesbibliothek, and Dr. Helga Raschke. In Meiningen: Herr Wiegand of the Staatliche Museen. In Weimar: Dr. Wiessner and Frau Fulsche of the Staatsarchiv, Herr Burmeister of the Nationale Forschungs- und Gedenkstätten, and Professors Schädlich and Winkler of the Hochschule für Architektur und Bauwesen.

1. See Appendix.

2. For Ramée's petition, see Chapter 2, note 4.

3. Alfred Overmann, "Das Regierungsgebäude zu Erfurt," in *Mitteilungen des Vereins für die Geschichte und Altertumskunde von Erfurt*, vol. 33 (Erfurt, 1912), p. 99. Other émigrés to Erfurt in 1795 were the Comte Mercy d'Argenteau and the Duc de Narbonne.

4. Karl von Beaulieu-Marconnay, *Karl von Dalberg und seine Zeit* (Weimar, 1879); August Widl, *Die soziale Tätigkeit des Fürstprimas Karl von Dalberg im Fürstentum Regensburg* (Erlangen, 1931).

5. Robert Leroux, *La Théorie du despotisme éclairé chez Karl Theodor Dalberg* (Paris, 1932).

6. Angermuseum, Erfurt. The drawing, in ink and watercolor, measures 44 by 65 cm and is inscribed "Ramée, architecte, 1795." The records of the Angermuseum reveal that the drawing was acquired in 1935 from the museum of the city of Gotha; in Gotha, I could find no evidence of the drawing's previous provenance.

7. Willibald Gutsche, ed., *Geschichte der Stadt Erfurt* (Weimar, 1968), p. 169; A. Overmann, *Erfurt in Zwölf Jahrhunderten* (Erfurt, 1929), p. 304.

8. Dalberg, *De l'influence des sciences et des beaux-arts sur la tranquillité publique* (Parma, 1802), pp. 50–1.

9. Nikolaus Pevsner, "Goethe and Architecture," in Pevsner's *Studies in Art, Architecture, and Design*, vol. 1 (New York, 1968), pp. 164–73; W. D. Robson-Scott, *The Younger Goethe and the Visual Arts* (Cambridge, 1981), pp. 35–44. Ramée's son Daniel was to consider Goethe's essay of prime importance to the development of the appreciation of Gothic architecture, as he stated in his introduction to Chapuy's *Le Moyen-âge monumental et archéologique* (Paris, 1843), vol. 1, pp. 3–4.

10. For the friendship of Dalberg and Karl August, despite their religious difference, see Wilhelm Bode, *Karl August von Weimar: Jugendjahre* (Berlin, 1913), pp. 245–9.

11. For these dukes and their genealogical relationship, see H. Heckmann, ed., *Thüringen: Historische Landeskunde Mitteldeutschlands* (Würzburg, 1986), pp. 38–47.

12. K. Schmidt in "Das erste deutsche Hoftheater," Kurt Schmidt, ed., *Gotha: Das Buch einer deutschen Stadt*, vol. 1 (Gotha, 1931), pp. 364–9; Ann Marie Koller, *The Theatre Duke: Georg II of Saxe-Meiningen and the German Stage* (Stanford, Calif., 1984), pp. 29–30, 56–7 (for Georg I's theatre and that at Hildburghausen).

13. David Watkin and Tilman Mellinghoff, *German Architecture and the Classical Ideal* (Cambridge, Mass., 1987), p. 78; G. Günther and L. Wallraf, ed., *Geschichte der Stadt Weimar* (Weimar, 1976), p. 271. Around 1794, Goethe was also involved in plans for the *Festsaal* in the ducal palace in Weimar; he reportedly rejected designs for this hall by the French architect Clérisseau (Watkin and Mellinghoff, p. 27).

14. Watkin and Mellinghoff, pp. 74–8.

15. Wolfgang Huschke, *Die Geschichte des Parkes von Weimar* (Weimar, 1951); Wolfgang Vulpius and Wolfgang Huschke, *Park um Weimar, Ein Buch von Dichtung und Gartenkunst* (Weimar, 1965); Alfred Hoffmann, *Der Landschaftsgarten* (Hamburg, 1963), pp. 89–99.

16. C. C. L. Hirschfeld, *Theorie der Gartenkunst*, 5 vols. (Leipzig, 1779–85; and published simultaneously in a French edition). For more on Hirschfeld's work, see Chapter 6.

17. Georg Balzer, *Goethe als Gartenfreund* (Munich, 1966).

18. Manfred Kahler, *Goethe's Summer House in Weimar* (Weimar, 1970), pp. 23–4.

19. Alfred Jericke, *Das Römisches Haus* (Weimar, 1967); A. Jericke and Dieter Dolgner, *Der Klassizismus in der Baugeschichte Weimars* (Weimar, 1975), pp. 137–61 and figs. 115–26; Eduard Scheidemantel, "Das Römisches Haus," in *Deutscher Schillerbund: Mitteilungen*, no. 49 (May 1928); information seen in the Weimar Staatsarchiv and the Bauabteilung in the Weimar Schloss.

20. Staatsarchiv Weimar, account book 8570, p. 29: "26 Reichstaler – zum franz. Baumeister J. Ramée für verschiedene Risse u. Zeichnungen zum Röm. Hause."

21. For Schuricht's drawings, see Jericke and Dolgner, pp. 143–5 and figs. 123–4. The drawings for the Vestibule and Blue Room are signed by Schuricht, but not dated. Schuricht worked on the plans for the interior of the Römisches Haus while in Weimar in the summer of 1794, but continued to develop or refine his plans in the following year.

22. Staatsarchiv Weimar, account book 8570, p. 91: "130 Reichstaler – dem franz. baumeister Jos. Ramée für verfertigung eines Plans vom Rothhäuser Berge und Fischhalter Platze, nebst mehreren Zeichnungen, so derselbe auf Serenissimi Befehl zu Behuf des Parcks verfertigt. 20 Carolin." The Carolin was a gold coin used in certain German states; Ramée was apparently paid his fee of 130 Reichstalers in Carolins.

23. According to Huschke (*Geschichte des Parkes von Weimar*, p. 91), "Er [Ramée's plan] ist uns nicht erhalten; wir erfahren auch nichts von Umgestaltungen, die daraufhin dort erfolgt wären."

24. P. Lehfeldt and G. Voss, "Herzogthum Sachsen-Meiningen", in *Bau- und Kunst-Denkmäler Thürigens*, vol. 34 (Jena, 1909), pp. 86–7, 237–43. Koller, pp. 29–30; Wendell Cole, ed., *Max Grube's "The Story*

of the Meininger" (Coral Gables, Fla., 1963), p. 13.

25. Seven of these engraved views are in the Cabinet des Estampes of the Bibliothèque Nationale, Paris (vol. VC-319). Each plate is signed by Thierry and inscribed as representing a feature "im Englischen Garten zu Meiningen": "Eingang" (dated 1794); "Die Eremitage" (1795); "Die Insel" (1795); "Das blaue Haus" (1796); "Die Fischer Hütte" (1797); "Die Meÿereÿ" (1796); and "Tempel der Harmonie" (1797). Impressions of several of these engravings are also in the collection of the Staatliche Museen in Meiningen.

26. Illustrated in Lehfeldt and Voss, pp. 240–1. The Tempel der Harmonie was demolished in the 1880s.

27. Erhard Bansemer, *Der Park Altenstein* (Suhl, 1985), p. 15. Herr Wiegand of the Staatliche Museen in Meiningen brought to my attention the ducal parks of Altenstein and Liebenstein and showed me engravings of them (seven views of Altenstein, one of Liebenstein). Three of these engravings are inscribed "Thierry del./ Gravée à Paris par F. Gaisler [Friedrich Geissler?]; the remaining engravings are clearly of the same series; none is dated, but Bansemer (p. 10) says that two of them were published in 1802 and 1804.

28. Schmidt, ed., *Gotha;* for the ducal garden, vol. 2 (1938), pp. 23–5; for the temple, vol. 1 (1931), pl. 24.

29. Schmidt, Gotha, vol. 1 (1931), pl. 3 (map of Gotha, 1796); P. Lehfeldt, *Bau- und Kunst-Denkmäler Thürigens*, vol. 8, "Herzogthum Sachsen-Coburg und Gotha", (Jena, 1891) p. 109.

30. This suggestion was made to me by Dr. Helga Raschke of Gotha. Klebe's map of the city (1796) indicates the location of these recently-removed walls with dotted lines.

31. Forschungs- und Landesbibliothek Gotha. The bound drawings are identified as "Chart. A 1053." According to Frau Gerlach of the library, its notations indicate that the volume was catalogued by Friedrich Jacobs, the ducal librarian from 1802 to 1841. The sheets, each measuring c. 26 by 41 cm., are attached to the bound pages of the volume. Each sheet is signed and dated "Ramée, 1796."

32. In Ledoux's work, this arcaded motif can be seen, for example in the Hosten House, c. 1782 (illustrated in Daniel Ramée's edition of Ledoux's designs, 1847, pl. 183).

33. Belanger's Rue des Capucines house is illustrated in J. Krafft and N. Ransonnette, *Plans,* pl. 4. The other two houses by Belanger, on the Rue Pigalle and the Rue St. Georges, are shown in Krafft and Ransonnette, pl. 17 and 63. For Ramée's Perregaux House, see Chapter 3.

34. For Bagatelle, see Chapter 2. For the Hôtel Dervieux interiors. see B. Scott, "A Delightful Bonbonnière: Mlle Dervieux's Hôtel, Paris," *Country Life* (20 November 1980), pp. 1902–4. For the interiors of the Rue des Capucines house, see Krafft and Ransonnette, pl. 93.

35. Information from an unpublished manuscript by Dr. Helga Raschke and from conversation with her in Gotha, July 1991.

Chapter 6

I thank the following people who aided my research on Ramée's work in Hamburg: Professors Hermann Hipp and Charlotte Schoell-Glass of the Kunsthistorisches Institut der Universität Hamburg; Dr. Loose and Dr. Richter of the Hamburger Staatsarchiv; Dr. Christian L. Küster of the Altonaer Museum; Frau Ilse Fischer of the Heimatmuseum Wandsbek; and Dr. Renata Klée Gobert.

1. Some references to Ramée in Hamburg state (without supporting evidence) that the architect settled there as early as 1794. But the architect's marriage license (1805) specifies that he had lived in Hamburg for nine years (see text), and the evidence of Ramée's presence in Thuringia in 1795 and 1796 makes it unlikely that he was in Hamburg earlier than 1796.

2. F. J. L. Meyer, *Skizzen zu einem Gemälde von Hamburg,* vol. 1, Heft 3 (1801), pp. 311, 345; vol. 2, Heft 4 (1802), p. 55.

3. Archives Nationales, F[7]6063: "Certificat d'amnéstie" for "Ramée (Jean), ex-officier à l'armée de la Belgique, dem't à Hambourg," dated "15 Fructidor an 11" (2 September 1803).

4. Paul T. Hoffmann, *Die Elbchaussee* (Hamburg, 1977), pp. 50ff. Rainville was one of the men who accompanied Dumouriez (as Ramée apparently did) on his escape from the French army, 4 April 1793 (Louis-Philippe, *Mémoires*, Paris, 1974, vol. 2, p. 424).

5. Vincent Nolte, *Fünfzig Jahre in beiden Hemisphären: Reminiscenzen aus den Leben eines ehemaligen Kaufmannes* (Hamburg, 1854), p. 25. The reference to Ramée reads: ". . . so dass endlich der Französische Baumeister Ramée (derselbe, der die erste Börsenhalle gebaut hatte) den Auftrag erhielt, in dem grossartigen Local des Herrn Godeffroy ein Theater zu errichten." An English version of the work was published at the same time (*Fifty Years in Both Hemispheres . . .*, New York, 1854); in this edition, the reference to Ramée is translated: ". . . so that at length the French architect Ramée, the same who had built our first Börsenhalle, was directed to put up a stage, etc., in the large establishment of Mr. Godeffroy."

6. Meyer, *Skizzen*, vol. 1, Heft 2, (1800), pp. 180ff ("Französische Bühne"); H. Geering, "Emigranten-Theater im alten Hamburg," *Die Volksbühne*, Heft 2–3, (1967), pp. 33–5, 56–8.

7. Ramée's decoration of the French theatre is mentioned in Boulliot (see Appendix); for more information on this work, see Chapter 7. Ramée's third theatre project is noted in Heinrich Sieveking, *Karl Sieveking* (Hamburg, 1928), vol. 3, p. 31 ("Als Platz kam der des alten Domes in Betracht, auf dem schon 1806 ein Herr Ramée ein Theater hatte bauen wollen . . ."); no source is given for this information.

8. See Appendix.

9. For Ramée's listings in the *Hamburgisches Adress-Buch*, see Chapter 7, notes 4 and 19.

10. Letter from David Parish to John Parish, 4 March 1807, in Parish Letter Books, New York Historical Society (book 2, p. 354).

11. Renata Klée Gobert, *Die Bau- und Kunstdenkmale der Freien und Hansestadt Hamburg*, vol. 2 (Altona, Elbvororte), Hamburg, 1959; Hoffmann, *Die Elbchaussee.*

12. Gerhard Wietek, ed., *C. F. Hansen, 1756–1845, und seine Bauten in Schleswig-Holstein* (Neumünster, c. 1982).

13. See, for example, V. Villadsen's article on Hansen in the *Macmillan Encyclopedia of Architects* (New York, 1982).

14. Alfred Aust, *Caspar von Voght*, (Hamburg, 1963). Franklin Kopitzsch, *Grundzüge einer Sozialgeschichte der Aufklärung in Hamburg und Altona* (Hamburg, 1982), pp. 388–98. Voght was named Baron von Voght by the Austrian Emperor in 1802.

15. Michael Goecke, *Stadtparkanlagen im Industriezeitalten. Das Beispiel Hamburg* (Hannover-Berlin, 1981), pp. 161–3 (kindly communicated to me by Renata Klée Gobert). For the phenomenon in England, see William A. Brogden, "The Ferme Ornée and Changing Attitudes to Agricultural Improvement," *Eighteenth Century Life* (January 1983), pp. 39–43. Brogden identifies The Leasowes as a principal representative of the "*ferme ornée*" in England.

16. Wiebenson, *The Picturesque Garden in France*,pp. 98–101; for the phenomenon in England, see David Jacques, *Georgian Gardens* (London, 1983), pp. 18ff. A striking contrast to Voght's moral notion of the ornamented farm is found in a contemporary description of

the "*Hameau*" in the gardens of the Prince de Condé at Chantilly, in which the peasants' houses, fitted out for the Prince's entertainment, were meant to "varier des jouissances [et] transport[er] l'éclat de sa richesse dans le séjour apparent de la pauvreté" (J. Mérigot, *Promenades ou itinéraire des jardins de Chantilly*, Paris, 1791, p. 35).

17. Aust, p. 24.

18. "Der Besitzer und. . .der Schöpfer Flotbecks [i.e., Voght] hat von jeher geglaubt, dass die Kunst der Gartenanlage es hauptsächlich erfordere, eine Reihe von Landschaften zu bilden, deren malerische Beleuchtung für gewisse Tages- wie für die Jahrezeiten berechnet, den dafür empfänglichen Gemüthern nicht allein Natur- und Kunstgenuss zugleich verschaffe; sondern dass es ihr noch höherer Beruf sey, jeder dieser Landschaften den Charakter abzulauschen, den die Natur ihr verlieh;. . .durch den Gesamt-Eindruck das Gemüth zu beruhigen oder zu bewegen im Zaugen des, alles zu neuer Kraft weckenden Frühlings, leise Hoffnungen und frohe Ahnungen im klopfenden Herzen zu erregen oder beym sanftern Eindruck des bey seinem Scheiden sich verschönernden Herbstes den Nachklang lieber Erinnerungen zu erwecken" (Caspar Voght, *Flotbeck in ästhetischer Ansicht,* edited by Charlotte Schoell-Glass, Hamburg, 1990, pp. 11–2. Voght's essay was written in 1824).

19. "Ich habe immer gehofft, dass ich in diesem Lande etwas sehen würde, das mich für eine gewisse Gattung determinierte, aber auch das ist nichts – die wohlhabenden Leute sind zu reich, die Ärmern zu dürftig, und alle haben für bürgerliche Baukunst keinen Geschmack, und für Distribution gar keinen Sinn. Ich schicke Ihnen Soane's Sketches; Sie werden daraus ersehen, wie das ist.

"Ich habe wohl unendlich interessante Hütten gesehen, aber zum Wohnhaus waren sie zu klein, zu ängstlich. – Ich habe recht artige Häuser gesehen, aber sie waren zu schön, zu gross, zu kostbar. Ich habe Gothische Wohnhäuser gesehen – ich möchte ebenso lieb alle Tage die Sagen der Vorzeit lesen, als darinnen wohnen. Das einzige Resultat, das ich mir herausgezogen habe, ist mein Entschluss: ein kleines, ländliches, trockenes, warmes und bequemes Haus zu bauen" (Letter of 14 January 1794, quoted in Aust, p. 27).

20. "Mein Haus müsste zu den übrigen Gebäuden auf dem Hofe passen, kein fremdes Aussehen haben. . .nicht dem Auge eine Masse darstellen, die durch ihre Grösse imponieren soll, sondern viel kleine Teile im gefälligen Verhältnis zueinander" (Quoted in Aust, p. 27; date of letter not specified).

21. "Das Wohnhaus selbst ist, um seine Grösse zu verbergen, zum Theil im Buschwerk versteckt, absichtlich unregelmässig gebaut, um jede architektonische Prätension zu vermeiden und eine Wohnung hinzustellen, die zu den Wirtschaftsgebäuden passte. Es sollte im Innern mehr leisten, als es im Äussern versprach" (Voght, *Flotbeck in ästhetischer Ansicht,* p. 19).

22. Gobert (pp. 210, 211, 284) describes the execution of the house, 1795–6, and dates Ramée's interior decoration to 1796.

23. "Wie prächtig der Saal ist, und wie elegant und comfortable überhaupt das ganze Haus, davon kannst Du Dir nicht leicht einen Begriff machen. Oben, neben der Instrumentenstube ist ein Boudoir, das nichts wie Weichlichkeit atmet; Spiegel bis auf die Erde, ein Sofa in einer Nische unter einem Thronhimmel, rund herum schöne Bücherschränke, und oben darüber ovale, sehr schöne Gemälde, express aus Paris verschrieben. . . . Dieses Kabinett macht wirklich Ramé alle Ehre!" (Letter from Reimarus to his friend Wattenbach, quoted in Heinrich Sieveking, *Georg Heinrich Sieveking*, Berlin, 1913, p. 485).

24. Aust, p. 29.

25. See Chapter 7.

26. The suggestion that these reliefs were manufactured has been made by Hakon Lund, in *Nogle Tegninger af C. F. Hansen* (Copenhagen, 1975), p. 16.

27. For the Hôtel Gouthière, see Martin, ed., *Le Style Empire*, pl. III; Hautecoeur, *Histoire,* vol. 4, p. 124. For the Pompeiian source, see Hans Helge Madsen, *Interiørdekorationer i Erichsens Palae, Fra arkitekten J. J. Ramée's virke i København* (Copenhagen, 1968), p. 36.

28. Madsen, p. 37.

29. Aust, p. 29.

30. Belanger created a military-tent ceiling for the Comte d'Artois at Bagatelle; other tentlike ceilings are found in Cellerier's Laval theatre (Krafft and Ransonnette, *Plans,* pl. 42) and in designs by Dugourc (Hautecoeur, *Histoire*, vol. 4, p. 508).

31. Hans Schroder, *Lexikon der hamburgische Schriftsteller bis zur Gegenwart*, vol. 6 (Hamburg, 1873), p. 157. *Hamburgisches Künstler-Lexikon*, vol. 1 (Hamburg, 1854), p. 196.

32. The gardens for Sieveking, Hosstrup, and G. F. Baur, and that at Hamfelde, are discussed in this chapter. Those for Parish, Heine and Lengercke are in Chapter 14. The evidence for Ramée's garden plan for J. H. Baur (brother of G. F. Baur) is circumstantial; according to Gobert (pp. 214–5), J. H. Baur paid Ramée 1065 Marks Courant in 1808–9, probably for "*Gartengestaltung*" for Baur's estate, Elbschlösschen, at Nienstedten. Ramee's garden at Perdöl, near Neumünster, for which estate C. F. Hansen designed the house, was mentioned by the author August Hennings at the time of Ramée's first stay in Hamburg ("Von Ramä [sic] sehr schön gezeichnete Garten umgebungen"; quoted in P. Hirschfeld, *Herrenhäuser und Schlösser in Schleswig-Holstein*, 1980, p. 221). For Plageberg, see later in this chapter.

33. Meyer, *Skizzen*, vol. 2, Heft 4 (1802), p. 50.

34. Ibid., p. 53.

35. Ibid., p. 55. The other man mentioned was a certain "Schmitt."

36. For The Leasowes: see Christopher Thacker, *The History of Gardens* (Berkeley, 1979), pp. 199–203; Richard Etlin, *The Architecture of Death* (New York, 1984), pp. 176ff. Belanger, too, had seen The Leasowes, but his own garden designs were quite different in character, as noted in Chapter 2.

37. C. C. L. Hirschfeld, *Theorie der Gartenkunst* (Leipzig, 1779–85). See also W. Schepers, *Hirschfelds Theorie der Gartenkunst* (Worms, 1980); and Dorothee Nehring's review of Schepers, in *Journal of Garden History*, vol. 4 (April–June 1984), pp. 197–200.

38. Etlin (p. 210) notes that The Leasowes exemplified Hirschfeld's preferred type of landscape garden.

39. One problem in describing Ramée's early garden designs is that some of them are known only from the plans he published at the end of his life, nearly half a century later – which he might have altered in the meantime. But in the cases where Ramée's designs can be verified by other plans or drawings, they generally prove to be accurate.

40. *Parcs et jardins*, pl. 17. Dr. Wolfgang Prange of the Landesarchiv Schleswig-Holstein, in correspondence to me of 1986, pointed out Daniel Poppe's possession of Hamfelde. Information on the later history of the estate (when it was owned by Albert Ballin, manager of the Holland-American shipping line) was sent to me by Dr. Johannes Habich of the Landesamt für Denkmalpflege Schleswig-Holstein. Daniel Poppe, a Hamburg merchant, acquired Hamfelde some time before 1800; by 1816, it was in the possession of

Daniel Poppe Jr., who retained it until about 1821 (information from Dr. Prange). Ramée's sister-in-law Johanna Louisa Dreyer married the younger Daniel Poppe in 1810 (Dreyer genealogy in the Hamburg Staatsarchiv). I am grateful to Prof. Hermann Hipp, who in 1986 helped me find the Hamfelde estate, and to its present owner, who graciously showed the grounds to Prof. Hipp and me.

41. *Parcs et jardins*, pl. 8.

42. "L'auteur croit et espère être utile aux amateurs de Jardins en leur offrant une série de motifs des plus variés qui sont applicables à tous les sites. . . et que les différentes localités ont suggéré à l'auteur." (Title page of Ramée's *Parcs et jardins*. See Chapter 14.)

43. *Parcs et jardins*, pl. 5. According to Gobert (pp. 170–1, 286), Ramée laid out Sieveking's park in 1793, but this is surely too early. The American statesman Gouverneur Morris, who was in Europe in the 1790s and was an acquaintance of John Parish and other clients of Ramée's in Hamburg, wrote in his journal, 2 May 1797: "I walk[ed] out to see Sieveking's improvements. He is wasting a great deal of money under the auspices of Voght and Ramée, a French architect. With a view to a road down a steep bank of clay soil, they have dug a water course which will take off more earth than Dorkinen can lay in a week" (Journal of Gouverneur Morris, Library of Congress, Microfilm no. 13,518; brought to my attention by Prof. Paul A. Russell).

44. Hoffmann, *Die Elbchaussee*, p. 68.

45. Description by Emilie von Berlepsch (quoted in Hoffmann, p. 69): "Jetzt besah ich mit Poel den Garten und besonders das schöne Bergboskett nach der Elbe hin. Schon aus einer Strohhütte, in der sich die Gesellschaft ohne Verabredung auf verschiedenen Wegen zusammengefunden hatte, ist eine treffliche Aussicht auf die Elbe und ihre Inseln; aber jetzt ist noch ein Berg geebnet worden, der ganz schroff nach der Elbe hinunterging. Oben wird eine Anlage von Tannen gemacht, und hier hat man einen Blick auf die Elbe, der fast einzig in seiner Art ist."

46. Gobert, pp. 229–35; Hoffmann, pp. 262–71.

47. *Parcs et jardins*, pl. 15. The plate is inscribed "Blankmeses," evidently a lithographer's misreading of Blankenese.

48. Gobert, p. 230.

49. Ibid.

50. Watercolor drawing, c. 36 × 50 cm, signed "Ramée 1810" in lower right-hand corner. Musée National de Blérancourt, CFA a 331/1.

51. For Strack and his paintings for Baur, see Altonaer Museum in Hamburg, *"Lieblich zum Auge, gewinnend zum Herzen," Der Ukleisee, Wie um 1800 Ostholsteins Landschaft für die Malerei entdeckt wurde*, exh. cat. (Altona, 1987).

52. This concept of the picturesque landscape was expressed in Knight's *The Landscape* (1794) and *Analytic Enquiry into the Principles of Taste* (1805), and in Price's *Essay on the Picturesque* (1794).

53. Gobert, p. 230. For the motif of a round temple over a grotto, see Monique Mosser, "Le Temple et la montagne . . .," *Revue de l'art*, no. 83 (1989), pp. 27–8.

54. Julie Grüner, *Erinnerungen an das Haus meiner Grosseltern Baur im dänischen Altona* (Hamburg, 1965), pp. 76–8. These memoirs were written in the 1890s.

55. ". . . Unter welchen, Ramé [sic], ein Pariser, und Bunsen [Axel Bundsen, 1768–1832] ein Dane, als die bedeutendsten, viele Arbeit fanden. Im allzuleichten französischen Geschmack und von luftiger Bauart, sind von dem erstern mehrere Landhäuser erbauert" (Meyer, *Skizzen*, vol. 1, Heft 3, 1801, p. 345).

56. Gobert, pp. 235–6 and fig. 253.

57. Gobert, p. 220 (dating of stables to 1806, based on insurance records); R. Ehrenberg, *Das Haus Parish in Hamburg* (Jena, 1905), p. 104 (for Parish family record of 11,600 Marks spent in 1796 for a "neuen Stall" at Nienstedten).

58. Hakon Lund, a specialist in Hansen's architecture, has pointed out to me aspects of this stable which are inconsistent with Hansen's work, such as its use of square piers.

59. Correspondence with Ingrid A. Schubert, 1994. Benjamin Jarvis bought the Plageberg property from the Rantzau family in 1804; documentary evidence suggests that the house was constructed shortly thereafter. Following Jarvis's bankruptcy in 1818 the estate was purchased by a General Danican and was renamed Charlottenberg in 1830. Ramée's lithographic plan of the estate in *Parcs et jardins* (1839) is inscribed "Plagerberg [sic], en Holstein"; it shows the house and several other structures and topographic features in their proper places, although the plan is reversed. It is conceivable that Ramée designed the grounds and house during his second period in Hamburg, in the mid-1830s (i.e., that he replaced or remodeled the original house at this time), but the fact that his plan identifies the estate as Plageberg, rather than Charlottenberg, is evidence that the design was made before 1830 and therefore during the architect's first period in Hamburg. I am grateful to Ingrid Schubert for her assistance in researching the history of the estate, and to Holger Vanselow for providing me with the photograph of the house.

60. J. von Schröder, *Topographie des Herzogthums Holstein*, Oldenburg, 1841, Teil 1, p. 114.

61. See text of Ramée's petition in Chapter 2, note 4.

62. Rudolf Tombo, *Ossian in Germany* (New York, 1901), especially ch. 3, "Ossian's Influence upon Klopstock and the So-called Bards." The possibility of a direct connection between Ramée and Klopstock is suggested by a reference to Klopstock in a letter written by Ramée's partner, André Masson, 28 April 1807 ("Masson & Ramée" to Ludwig Hermann von Mecklenburg; in Mecklenburg correspondence as cited in Chapter 9).

63. Letter of 9 July 1805. See Chapter 9.

64. Hamburg Staatsarchiv, ledger entitled "Hochzeiten Protocoll. de Anno 1805" and "Wedde I / 29 / Bd. 95," p. 550.

65. According to Dr. Schmitt of the Hamburg Staatsarchiv (in correspondence with H. H. Madsen, 1966, provided to me by Mr. Madsen), Ramée acquired "*Bürgerrecht,*" as an architect, on 31 July 1805. Ramée used the names Joseph Guillaume in his petition of 1800.

66. The only known portrait of Caroline Ramée is an oil painting in the collection of Ramée-family items in the Musée National de Blérancourt, signed "Saint Evre 1835 P" (evidently the same artist who painted Joseph's portrait; see Introduction), CFA-a-331/4. The museum records identify the subject as "Mme Joseph Ramée."

67. "Hans Andreas Dreyer. . . und seine grosse Familie," unpublished genealogy compiled by H. Hansen in 1941, in the Hamburg Staatsarchiv.

68. Ramée, *Parcs et jardins*, pl. 11, 17. The Lengercke plan (discussed in Chapter 14) is dated by Ramée 1834.

69. Information from Schmitt–Madsen correspondence (see note 65).

70. Daniel Ramée, *Manuel de l'histoire générale de l'architecture*, vol. 1 (Paris, 1843), p. 314. ("Nous avouons qu'il faut avoir l'âme vigoureusement trempée pour concevoir et entreprendre une abnégation pleine et entière des premiers sentiments de notre enfance,

des souvenirs et des affections de notre jeunesse, des instructions touchantes sur la morale chrétienne que nous donna un père chéri, ou la tendresse d'une mère adorée, pour nous jeter corps et âme dans le passé d'un peuple si différent de nous.") Although Ramée presents this as a general observation, not necessarily autobiographical, it is hard to imagine that he would state it this way (especially in a book dedicated to his father) if it did not apply to his own family.

71. Paris, Archives Nationales, F[7]-3331. There are two nearly identical versions of this police report (perhaps made in connection with Ramée's 1800 petition). The document also states that Ramée's "alleged motive for being in Hamburg" was that he was "à la tête d'un Etablissement"; that he "a fait sa soumission"; and that his name and former army position were: "Ramée, Jean (Ex officier) Ex adjoint ["Ex adjutant" in one of the versions] aux adjutants généraux de l'armée de la Belgique."

72. Document of 3 February 1803; see Chapter 1.

73. References to Philippon (or Phélippon) as a student of Ramée are found in C. Bauchal, *Nouveau dictionnaire d'architecture française* (Paris, 1887), p. 712; Bellier and Auvry, *Dictionnaire général des artistes de l'École française* (Paris, 1880–5), p. 262; E. Delaire, *Les Architectes élèves de l'École des Beaux-Arts* (Paris, 1907), p. 372. Philippon's connection with Ramée was brought to my attention by David Van Zanten.

74. See the text of the petition in Chapter 2, note 4.

Chapter 7

1. Pierre Lespinasse (in *Les Artistes français en Scandinavie*, Paris, n.d. [1929], p. 172) noted that Ramée "introduced to Denmark, or anticipated, one might say, the Empire Style [and the designs of Percier and Fontaine]."

2. H. Sieveking, *Georg Heinrich Sieveking* (Berlin, 1913), p. 485: "Der Madame Sillem hatte Ramé damals [i.e., at the time of his work for Voght] ein Zimmer eingerichtet, das 15.000 M. kostete." This was perhaps the wife of the Hamburg senator M. G. Sillem.

3. E. Meier-Oberist, *Das neuzeitliche hamburgische Kunstgewerbe in seinen Grundlagen* (Hamburg, 1925), p. 73: "Luxus an Möbeln war es denn auch, welcher Fremden zuerst in Hamburg auffiel. Merkel spricht von prächtig möblierten Sälen. . . . Manche Saaleinrichtung koste bis zu 18.000 Mark."

4. *Hamburgisches Adress-Buch* (annual Hamburg directory). Listing for 1800: "Masson et Ramée, Tapeten und Meubelfabr., Herrengr." 1801: same, but address is "Herrengraben no. 168." 1802–3: "Masson et Ramée, Meublen, Tapeten und Niederlage von franz. Porcelain, Herrengraben no. 168." 1804–7: "Masson et Ramée, Kaufl. B. C. unter Herrn F. C. Gräpel, Wbe. et Sohn, Neust. Fuhlentwiete, no. 15."

5. "Il fournit de grands débouchés pour le nord, aux fabriques et manufactures françaises."

6. "Ein ähnliches Lager, ist, weil es erst seit kurzem von den Französen Masson und Ramé angelegt ward, zwar noch nicht von dem Umfang des letztern, wird aber bald seine Stelle ersetzen. Es bietet Mobilien aller Art dar, die nach treflichen französischen und englischen Mustern, in einer nicht weit von Hamburg sich niedergelassnen kleinen französischen Kolonie von Arbeitern, verfertigt werden; ferner, Tapeten, Marmor- und bronzirte Arbeiten, Porzelain, u. dgl. aus deutschen, mehr aber aus Pariser Fabriken. Gute Wahl der Muster und feiner Geschmack zeichnet dieses Lager, vor mehrern deutschen und englischen hiesigen Niederlagen aus; und besonders vor einem Mobilienmagazin aus Fabriken in Berlin, wo Ueberladung mit bunten, fremdartigen Verzierungen und Schnirkeleien, eine eben so herrschende als geschmackverderbende Sitte ist" (Meyer, *Skizzen*, vol. 1, Heft 3 [1801], p. 311).

7. Letters of 6 April, 28 May, 30 May 1825 (Archives Nationales, F[7] 9546). The reason for this inquiry is not specified; perhaps it was instigated by a creditor of Masson and Ramée's failed business. The letter of 6 April states that "[Masson] était Lieutenant Colonel et [Ramée] Major au service de France." For more on these letters, see Chapter 14.

8. *Biographie des hommes vivants*, vol. 4 (Paris, 1818), pp. 376–7. I have not been able to find a copy of "Les Sarrasins en France," which is not listed in the Bibliothèque Nationale catalogue. One also wonders if Ramée's partner may have been the "A. Masson, officier en retraite" who published several political tracts around 1830 (Bibliothèque Nationale catalogue). Masson's first names are given as André Pierre and his life dates as 1759–1820 in Louis R. Gottschalk et al., *Lafayette, A Guide to the Letters* (Ithaca, N.Y., 1975, p. 281), but the editors of this work have not been able to give me the source of this information.

9. Masson de Neuville is mentioned as Lafayette's aide in L. Gottschalk and M. Maddox, *Lafayette in the French Revolution*, vol. 2 (Chicago, 1973), pp. 119, 121, 415; Edmond Cleray, *L'Affaire Favras, 1789–90* (Paris, 1932), pp. 55–8, 68–9.

10. André Maurois, *Adrienne, ou la vie de Mme de La Fayette* (Paris, 1961), pp. 345ff. An English translation of a letter from Masson exists in the Sparks Collection at Houghton Library, Harvard University (undated; recipient unidentified), in which Masson describes the plight of Lafayette and his family in their Austrian captivity, evidently as part of his effort to aid in their release.

11. Information from Dr. Schmitt of the Hamburg Staatsarchiv (in correspondence with H. H. Madsen, 1966; provided to me by Mr. Madsen); *Hamburgisches Adress-Buch*, 1797.

12. B. Whitlock, *Lafayette* (New York, 1929), p. 82.

13. *The Lafayette Letters in the Bostonian Society*, The Bostonian Society Publications, vol. 4, second series (Boston, 1924). The letters are in the Colburn Collection, owned by the Bostonian Society, on deposit at the Massachusetts Historical Society. Regarding Archenholtz, see Friedrich Ruof, *Johann Wilhelm von Archenholtz* (Berlin, 1915). Ramée and Masson are mentioned in this work only as acquaintances of Archenholtz (p. 73). Lafayette's correspondence also reveals that a cousin of Masson, a certain Monsieur Le Febvre de St. Maur, "notaire à Paris et propriétaire d'une terre voisine à Lagrange [Lafayette's home]" made an investment in the business (letter of 23 January 1810, *Lafayette Letters*, pp. 138, 140).

14. "Mes compliments à votre associé: je suis bien heureux du succès de votre établissement, bien sensible aux sentiments qu'il me conserve et que je mérite par les miens pour lui. Vous l'aviez annoncé pour le mois de janvier: il n'est pourtant pas encore arrivé: peut-être le trouverai-je à Paris. . . . je serai fort aise de recevoir votre ami Barbazan, et j'espère que Mr Ramie [sic] me l'ammenera" (*Lafayette Letters*, pp. 118–9). In this publication of Lafayette's letters, Ramée's name is transcribed "Ramie," but my examination of the letters themselves revealed that the name written by Lafayette is in fact "Ramée." I have not been able to discover who "your friend Barbazan" was. A letter from Masson to the Duke of Mecklenburg-Schwerin (2 June 1801) reveals that Ramée had recently returned to Hamburg from Paris (see Chapter 9).

15. Letter of 5 April 1805, from Masson to the Court Marshall of Mecklenburg (see Chapter 9).

16. An anonymous nineteenth-century publication on Dinant states that around 1809 the buildings of the former convent of the Frères-Mineurs contained several enterprises, including "une fabrique de papiers peints appartenant à un français dont le fils, Daniel Ramée, est aujourd'hui un des principaux architectes de France" (*Dinant en poche*, 1887, p. 130; brought to my attention by Didier Coupaye). A letter of 1825, from the Swedish-Norwegian consulate in Paris to the French police, states that Ramée "a longtems habité en Belgique la ville de Dinant où il avait établi une fabrique" (see Chapters 13 and 14).

17. Information from Schmitt–Madsen correspondence. See also Gobert, p. 220.

18. Schmitt–Madsen correspondence.

19. In 1800, Ramée was listed in the *Hamburgisches Adress-Buch* as "Baumeister, Herrengraben, no. 144," from 1801 to 1803 as "Baumeister, Herrengraben, no. 168." From 1804 to 1807: "Baumeister, unter der Firma von Masson et Ramée, Neust. Fuhlentw. no. 15." The 1808 listing is the same except that the street number is 17. In 1809 and 1810, the address given is "Neust. Fuhlentw. hinter no. 17." No subsequent listings for Ramée are given.

20. Schmitt–Madsen correspondence. According to Dr. Schmitt, the two properties were sold at public auction 30 April 1810; they were bought for 62,100 Marks by Peter Godeffroy.

21. Madsen, *Interiørdekoration i Erichsens Palae*, pp. 29–31, 39–40, and elsewhere. According to Madsen, Le Sueur studied in Paris with Jean Pillement, and at the Academy. See also P. Lespinasse, *Les Artistes français en Scandinavie* (Paris, 1929), p. 173.

22. Madsen, pp. 29–31.

23. Madsen, p. 40.

24. Louis Bobé, ed., "August Hennings' Dagbok under hans Ophold i København 1802," *Danske Magazin*, series 7, vols. 1–3 (1934–5).

25. "[S]echs Zimmer sind von Le Sueur an Wänden und Decken recht schön gemahlt, und ein Speisezimmer ist mit Pariser Stukkatur bekleidet. Sollte man nicht glauben, dass eine Façade, die der Rotonde entlehnt ist, und dass so schön dekorierte Zimmer Londoner Feste von einigen hundert Personen fassen müssen? Hier war nur Platz für etwa dreissig Menschen. Für die kleine Zahl schien mir der Aufwand viel zu gross. Für die Decoration hat Ramé 3200 Rdl. erhalten. Unter ihnen sind einige sonderbare. In einem Zimmer sind die Thürstücke zwei Stiere, die sich stossen, und ein Pferd, das einen Panther niederschlägt. An den Wänden sind Sturm, Sonnenaufgang und Mondlicht in den Lambris, und eine mit dem Sturm kämpfende Figur. . . In andern Zimmern sind mythologische Abbildungen, die Arabesken und Malereien sind sanft gehalten, und nicht schreiend, wenn sie gleich bunt sind. Ramé hat auch den Pallast des Étatsraths Brun decorirt. Brun ist aber sehr unzufrieden mit dem, was er hat bezahlen müssen." (Hennings's diary, *Danske Magazin*, p. 13)

26. "Der Salon war wie es schien von Ramé decorirt, wenigstens hatten die in Festons hängenden Gardinen bonnes graces von buntem Musselin mit grünem Taft coupirt" (Hennings's diary, p. 33, 22 July 1802). This evidently was the Bernstorffs' country house, at Bernstorff just north of Copenhagen, built by the architect Jardin in 1759. Hakon Lund, of the Kunstakademi in Copenhagen, believes that Hennings was mistaken about Ramée's involvement here (correspondence with Lund, 1988).

27. "Das ist grösstentheils das Werk Ramées als Künstlers und Brun als Geld-Ausgebers" (Hennings's diary, p. 107). At this point in his diary, Hennings began spelling Ramée's name correctly, rather than "Ramé."

28. "Ramée ist jetzt hier und meublirt verschiedene Häuser, unter andern auch bey Schimmelmann und Erichsen. Er ist unglaublich theuer und daher gesucht, doch ist es eine grosse Thorheit, 25 R. für einen Lehnstuhl zu geben, blos weil er modisch ist. Dieser Werth verliehrt sich bald" (Hennings's diary, p. 196, 5 October 1802).

29. Article on Erichsen in *Dansk biografisk leksikon* (Copenhagen, 1980).

30. H. H. Madsen, *Interiørdekorationer i Erichsens Palae, Fra arkitekten J. J. Ramée's virke i København* (Copenhagen, 1968).

31. Madsen, pp. 36, 37.

32. The relief in the Hôtel Gouthière is illustrated in Martin, ed., *Le Style Empire*, pl. 3. See also, L. Hautecoeur, *Histoire*, vol. 4, p. 124. Other reliefs in the Hôtel Gouthière were used by Ramée in his Berthault-Récamier House in Paris and in the Voght House on the Elbchaussee.

33. Compare, for example, Hautecoeur, *Histoire*, vol. 5, figs. 253, 278.

34. C. Percier and P. Fontaine, *Recueil de décorations intérieures* (Paris, 1801–12), pl. 153.

35. Madsen, *passim*.

36. For Belanger's Dervieux interiors, see Stern, *Belanger*, vol. 1, p. 202ff; Barbara Scott, "A Delightful Bonbonnière: Mlle Dervieux's Hôtel, Paris," *Country Life* (20 November 1980), pp. 1902–4; and J.-F. Barrielle, *Le Style Empire* (Paris, 1982), p. 14. In Mlle Dervieux's bathroom, "the stucco medallions and reliefs were painted in ivory, beige, and terracotta on light blue panels" (Scott, p. 1904), colors found in Ramée's interiors of the Erichsen House.

37. Madsen, pp. 19, 58–9, 68–9.

38. For the thorny question of the relationship of English and French decoration during this period, see D. Stillman, *The Decorative Work of Robert Adam* (London, 1966), pp. 38–40. For Dugourc and "arabesque" ornament, see J. Renouvier, *Histoire de l'art pendant la Révolution* (Paris, 1863), pp. 374ff.

39. Madsen, pp. 64–5.

40. Hennings's diary, p. 13.

41. Drawings labeled Ramée A-2500a, b, and c, in the drawing collection of the Kunstakademi, Copenhagen. Each sheet measures 19 by 24 cm. The drawings are not signed, but the notes written on them, in French, are in Ramée's handwriting, and the drawing style is typical of the architect. According to Hakon Lund of the Kunstakademiets Bibliotek, these drawings were acquired in 1931, having previously belonged to a certain Konrad Møller; nothing more is known of their provenance. Several other rooms in the Brun House are shown in drawings later made for insurance purposes (illustrated in Madsen, figs. 14–5), but their accuracy is questionable.

42. Information from Lisbet Balslev Jørgensen of the Kunstakademiets Bibliotek, Copenhagen.

43. "Er [Brun] beklagte die Kränklichkeit und das Leiden seiner Frau, die jetzt nach Italien ins Bad reisen will, und zeigte mir ein Bad, das er für sie neben ihrem Schlafzimmer bauen lässt, um bey ihrer Zurückkunft ihr zu dienen" (Hennings's diary, p. 25).

44. Stern, *Belanger*, pp. 203ff; Musée Carnavalet, *Alexandre Brongniart* (Paris, 1986), pp. 47-52.

45. Ramée's 1800 petition; see Chapter 2.

46. The relief on the left side of the wall toward the garden, for example, seems to be the same as one in the Hôtel Gouthière, Paris (seen in Martin, ed., *Le Style Empire*, pl. 3) and similar to one in

Belanger's Hôtel Dervieux (Krafft and Ransonnette, pl. 98). The relief on the left side of the opposite wall is similar to ones illustrated in Hautecoeur, *Histoire,* vol. 5, figs 256, 266.

47. For similar interior pedimented doors, see the engraved section drawings of Belanger's Folie St. James and Rue des Capucins houses, in Krafft and Ransonette.

48. Kunstakademiets Bibliotek, drawing labeled "Burmester A-2499e." The drawing is attributed to the "Burmester" whose signature appears on several other drawings of Sophienholm in the Art Academy. But this drawing appears to be closer in style to Ramée than to the less delicate Burmester.

49. *The Øregaard Museum* (Gentofte, 1979), p. 9.

50. Ramée's work for Schimmelmann is mentioned also in *Weilbachs Kunstnerleksikon,* Copenhagen, 1952, p. 15 (article on Ramée, signed "J. R.") and in M. Krohn, *Frankrigs og Danmarks Kunsteriske Forbindelse i det 18. Aarhundrede* (Copenhagen, 1922), p. 194. But these statements may be based only on Hennings's diary.

51. Krohn, p. 194. Valdemars Slot (Castle) was built starting in 1745 (P. Brogaard, H. Lund, H. Nørregaard-Nielsen, *Danmarks arkitektur: Landbrugets huse,* Copenhagen, 1980, p. 156).

52. Letter from Ramée to the Hofmarschall von Mecklenburg, 5 September 1806, in Staatsarchiv, Schwerin (see Chapter 9).

53. Hennings's diary, p. 196.

54. A. Schnapper (*David, témoin de son temps,* Paris, c. 1980, pp. 1745) suggests that the couch in this painting was a studio prop, but notes that it was typical of Madame Récamier's taste.

55. Madsen, pp. 10–11.

56. This room is on the second floor, across the corridor from Ramée's octagonal boudoir; the wardrobe has an oval panel in its central section, as if to frame a painting such as the oval paintings in the boudoir.

57. Letters of 18 October 1804, 6 June 1806. See Chapter 9.

58. Letters of 17 December 1804, 30 April 1805.

59. Letter of 5 April 1805.

60. Gobert, pp. 214–16. Masson et Ramée is mentioned as one of the principal retailers of wallpaper ("Tapeten"), in Hamburg between 1801 and 1806, in E. Meier-Oberist, *Das neuzeitliche hamburgische Kunstgewerbe in seinen Grundlagen* (Hamburg, 1925), p. 322.

61. Françoise Teynac et al., *Wallpaper: A History* (New York, 1982), pp. 101–2. Article on Dugourc in *Dictionnaire de biographie française,* vol. 11 (Paris, 1967), pp. 1497–8.

62. See Chapter 2 for text of Ramée's petition.

63. Nolte, pp. 38–9 (see Chapter 6).

64. H. Sieveking, *Karl Sieveking, Lebensbild eines hamburgischen Diplomaten aus dem Zeitalter der Romantik* (Hamburg, 1928), vol. 3, p. 31.

65. H. Harkensee, "Das französische Theater," in *Beiträge zur Geschichte der Emigranten in Hamburg* (Hamburg, 1896), pp. 12ff.

66. Harkensee, p. 13. Also see W. Melhop, *Alt-hamburgische Bauweise* (Hamburg, 1925), p. 166; Meyer, *Skizzen,* vol. 1, Heft 2, (1800), p. 181.

67. Information from Schmitt–Madsen correspondence.

68. See Appendix.

69. "Royalle Théatre de Copenhague / Mémoire ou Notte / Peinture de deux Décorations complete, et autres partis separé faites pour diférentes pieces. . . d'après les ordres de Monsieur le Général de Walkersdorff, par E. Le Sueur Peintre, pour le compte de MM Masson et Ramé d'Hambourg, depuis le 6 novembre 1800, jusqu'au 27 février 1801" (Madsen, pp. 29–30 and fig. 16).

70. Madsen, p. 30. Madsen states that the "Place Publique" stage-set was still being used by the theatre in the 1820s.

71. See Chapter 9.

72. Gerhard von Hosstrup, *Die Börsen-Halle in Hamburg* (Hamburg, January 1804; copy seen by the author at the Hamburg Staatsarchiv); Victor Dirksen, *Ein Jahrhundert Hamburg 1800–1900* (Leipzig, 1935), p. 214ff; Melhop, pp. 185–6. Much of the text of Hosstrup's booklet was reprinted in an article, "Ueber die Börsen-Halle in Hamburg," in *Zeitung für die elegante Welt* (31 January 1804), pp. 97–102. Accompanying the article was an engraved plate (No. 3) showing the façade elevation and two floor plans of the building. The article states that this representation was "sketched by the able architect Ramée himself," and "communicated [to the journal] through the kindness of Herr von Archenholz." In March 1804 an article on the building appeared in the Paris periodical *Journal des bâtimens* (no. 371, "3 Germinal an 12," pp. 4–6), entitled "Inauguration de la bourse de Hambourg, construite sur les plans de M. Ramée, architecte français."

73. See Chapter 6.

74. Hosstrup, *Die Börsen-Halle,* p. 5.

75. "Mein Wunsch war, etwas in seiner Art Einziges aufzustellen, das nicht von andern Orten entlehnt wäre, sondern selbst Muster werden sollte. Ein Umstand kam mir dabey sehr zu statten und bestimmte um so mehr meinen Entschluss, keine Kosten zu sparen. Dies war der in Hamburg förmlich etablirte französische Architect, Herr *Ramée,* Associé des durch seine trefliche Möbel-Fabrik und durch seinen ausgedehnten Handel mit Luxus-Artikeln bekannten Hauses *Masson und Ramée*; ein durch seinen seltnen Geschmack, so wie durch den Umfang und die Neuheit seiner Ideen berühmter Künstler, der sich schon vor der Revolution als Baumeister in Paris einen Namen gemacht hatte. Er unterzog sich der Unternehmung mit Leidenschaft, und both zu diesem Zweck, unterstützt von seinem thätigen nicht minder geschmackvollen Freunde *Masson,* alle zu seinem Handels-Hause gehörigen Künstler und sehr geschickten Kunstarbeiter auf. Ich kann daher wohl sagen, dass ohne diesen Baumeister und seine Verbindungen, ein Werk dieser Art, so wie man es sieht, nicht hätte ausgeführt werden können" (Hosstrup, pp. 8–9).

76. Engraving, in Hamburg Staatsarchiv, inscribed "Die Börsenhalle in Hamburg" and "Radl del.," "Schnell sc."

77. Melhop, p. 187.

78. A similar design, by E. Damesne, with a triumphal-arch motif topped by a pedimented attic, was published in 1805 in the *Annales du musée* (reproduced in W. Szambien, *J.-N.-L. Durand,* Paris, 1984, fig. 59).

79. Illustrated in G. Wietek, ed., *C. F. Hansen,* pp. 65, 67.

80. This was J. N. Sobre's Théâtre des Jeunes Artistes (see Hautecoeur, *Histoire,* vol. 5, p. 231). Belanger used a somewhat similar motif, at the Folie St. James (see Krafft and Ransonette, pl. 101).

81. "Die Façade ist in einem eleganten Stil. . . . Die Seiten sind glatt und ohne Fenster" (Hosstrup, p. 10).

82. Hosstrup, p. 11.

83. The floor plans are on the engraved plate that accompanied the article on the Börsenhalle in the *Zeitung für die elegante Welt* (31 January 1804). For the engraved interior view, see note 76 above.

84. Hosstrup, p. 13; *Nouvelles des arts,* 1803(?), p. 185.

85. Richard G. Carrott, *The Egyptian Revival: Its Sources, Monuments, and Meaning* (Berkeley, 1978); James Stevens Curl, *The Egyptian Revival* (London, 1982).

86. The source of Ramée's palm capitals was perhaps F. L. Norden's *Travels in Egypt and Nubia* (London, 1757), pl. 144 (reproduced in Curl, p. 97). Another similar palm-column was used by Durand and Thibault for a competition design of 1793, for a monument at the Panthéon in Paris (Szambien, *Les Projets de l'An II*, pp. 62–3). See also D. V. Denon's *Voyage dans la Basse et la Haute Egypte*, Paris (1802).

87. Hosstrup, p. 12. The article on the building in *Journal des bâtimens* (see note 72) similarly describes the hall as being "d'un style simple" (p. 5).

88. Hosstrup, p. 16. ("Unter andern sieht man oben in der Tiefe des Saals, ein Meisterstück der Malerey des berühmten Le Sueur in Paris. . . .") Assuming that it is true that Le Sueur died in 1802 (Madsen, p. 31), the painting mentioned here must have been installed in the Börsenhalle, not executed in place by the artist.

89. Hosstrup, pp. 15–16.

90. See Appendix.

91. F. Weinbrenner, *Architektonisches Lehrbuch* (Tübingen, 1810), pl. 37. The building was erected about three years after this publication. See also A. Valdenaire, *Friedrich Weinbrenner* (Karlsruhe, 1919), pp. 159ff.

92. Melhop, p. 187.

93. E. Brault, ed., *Les Architectes par leurs oeuvres* . . . (Paris, n. d. [1893]), p. 168.

94. Schmitt–Madsen correspondence. The properties were acquired by Peter Godeffroy, one of Ramée's previous clients.

95. John Parish's diary-ledger entitled "Company at Table," p. 134 (in Hamburg Staatsarchiv).

96. "[L]es tems continuent toujours d'être très mauvais pour la ville d'Hambourg, et particulièrement pour nous qui ne faisons [ferons?] presque plus rien" (6 June 1806, in Mecklenburg correspondence; see Chapter 9). In 1804, a blockade of the Elbe and its effect on Hamburg business had been noted in a description of the opening of Ramée's Börsenhalle: "La fermature de l'Elbe avait empêché de donné à cette inauguration le degré de satisfaction de plus, qu'elle aurait eu dans des tems plus heureux" (*Journal des bâtimens* article cited in note 72, p. 6).

97. Schmitt–Madsen correspondence.

98. *Lafayette Letters,* pp. 146–7 (letter of 10 February 1811). Lafayette's letters of this period reveal that after the failure of his business, Masson returned to France, married (in the hope of financial gain, according to Lafayette), obtained employment in the War Department ("l'administration de la guerre") as "adjoint au commissariat," and was in Spain in 1810. (*Lafayette Letters*, pp. 136–46; letters of 23 January and 10 February 1810.)

99. Letter of 24 January 1816, David Parish's letter books (in the New York Historical Society), book 6, pp. 241–2.

Chapter 8

I thank the following people who aided my research on Ramée's work in Denmark: Hakon Lund, Lisbet Balslev Jørgensen, Emma Salling, and Anne Lise Thygesen of the Kunstakademiets Bibliotek, Copenhagen; Hans Helge Madsen; Niels Peter Stilling, of the Søllerød Museum; and Flemming Harboe-Schmidt.

1. Ramée's documented work in Denmark covers the period c. 1800–5. Adding the work attributed to him extends the period to 1797–1808, but 1797 is the date of the doubtful de Coninck house in Copenhagen. The probable period of Ramée's activity in Denmark is c. 1800–8.

2. Ramée's work in Denmark is summarized in H. Lund's article on him in *Dansk biografisk Leksikon*, vol. 11 (Copenhagen, 1982), p. 590. The most thorough study of a part of Ramée's Danish work is H. H. Madsen, *Interiørdekorationer i Erichsens Palae* (Copenhagen, 1968). More general works on Danish architecture or history, containing references to Ramée, include the following: H. H. Engquist, *Danske Landsteder* (Copenhagen, 1949); L. Gotfredsen, *Gentofte, fra Tuborg til Bellevue* (Hellerup, 1952); H. Langberg and H. E. Langkilde, *Dansk Byggesaet omkring 1792 og 1942* (Copenhagen, 1942); A. Linvald, *Historiske Meddelelser om København* (Copenhagen, 1923–4); V. Lorenzen, *Gammel dansk Bygningskultur*, vol. 2 (Copenhagen, 1920); H. Lund, ed., *Danmarks arkitektur*, 6 vols. (Copenhagen, 1979–81); E. Nystrøm, *Fra Nordsjaellands Øresundskyst* (Copenhagen, 1938); Johannes Werner, *Christian Wilhelm Duntzfelt: En dansk Storkøbmand fra den glimrende Handelsperiode* (Copenhagen, 1927); and other works cited in this chapter.

3. Information on French architects in Denmark can be found in the following: M. Krohn, *Frankrigs og Danmarks kunstneriske Forbindelse i det 18. Aarhundrede* (Copenhagen, 1922); Lespinasse, *Les Artistes français en Scandinavie* (Paris, n.d. [1929]); L. Réau, *Histoire de l'expansion de l'art français*, vol. 3 (Paris, 1931).

4. For Hansen, see *Architekt Christian Frederik Hansen,* Altona Museum (1969); G. Wietek, ed., *C. F. Hansen und seine Bauten in Schleswig-Holstein*, Neumünster, 1982.

5. J. L. Mansa published designs for irregular gardens in *Udkast til Hauge-Anlaeg in den engelske Smag* (Copenhagen, 1798). One of the first Danish country houses set in an informal garden, Baekkeskov near Praesto (1796–8, by an unknown architect), is illustrated in P. Brogaard, H. Lund and H. E. Nørregaard-Nielsen, *Danmarks arkitektur: Landbrugets huse* (Copenhagen, 1980), p 174.

6. Correspondence from Ramée and Masson to the Hofmarschall von Mecklenburg, in the Staatsarchiv of Schwerin (see Chapter 9), letter of 27 May 1805.

7. Information from Hakon Lund of the Kunstakademi, Copenhagen.

8. See Appendix.

9. For example, Langberg and Langkilde (*Dansk Byggesaet* p. 114) note that a house of 1802 called Ny-Bakkegaard, in the Frederiksberg section of Copenhagen, was similar in style to Ramée's buildings. (A mid-nineteenth-century drawing of the house, that Hakon Lund showed me, reveals some Ramée-like traits, but no definite attribution can be made.) Examples of interior decoration possibly by Ramée are noted in the preceeding chapter.

10. Brief biographies of Ramée's Danish clients can be found in *Dansk biografisk Leksikon.*

11. When Parish fled French-occupied Hamburg in 1806 and lived for a while in Copenhagen, the dinner guests listed in his "Company at Table" diary (presently in the Hamburg Staatsarchiv) included Erichsen, de Coninck, and C. W. Duntzfelt, another great merchant. Duntzfelt is not known to have hired Ramée himself but was closely associated with nearly all of the architect's Danish clients (J. Werner, *Christian Wilhelm Duntzfelt*).

12. Louis Bobé, *Frederikke Brun og hendes Kreds hjemme og ude* (Copenhagen, 1910), pp. 57, 67, and elsewhere in the text.

13. "Das Gehölze hat Erichsen, es ist von Ramé in Promenaden angelegt" (Louis Bobé, ed., "August Hennings' Dagbok p. 20.)

14. "Am Mittwochen will ich. . . nach Friedrichsthal fahren, und Brun in seinem Landhause besuchen, wovon er mir Ramés Zeichnung gewiesen hat. Ramé hat ihm auch einen Tempel geze-

ichnet, der wie einer in Ordrup bey Erichsen nur eine Spielerei ist. Doch Spielen ist ja die Hauptsache der mehresten Menschen." (Hennings's diary, p. 25)

15. "Auf dem Wege nach Charlottenlund stieg ich bei Hellerup ab, wo der Agent Erichsen sich durch Ramé ein Haus bauen lässt, das mir nicht gefällt. Um dem Hause herum gehet ein ausgemauerter und mit Fliesen gebrückter Graben, der sich im Winter mit Schnee füllen wird und für Kinder, oder bey nächtlicher Zeit, für iedermann halsbrechend ist. Der Garten ist klein, und die Promenaden sind unbedeutend. Die Treiberei ist die Hauptsache und sehr gut unterhalten." (Hennings's diary, p. 27.)

16. "Das ist grösstentheils das Werk Ramées als Künstlers und Bruns als Geld-Ausgebers. . . . Hier gingen wir durch Ramées Naturmalerei nach der Höhe . . ." (Hennings's diary, pp. 107, 108).

17. The house is on Store Kongensgade. Madsen (p. 27) suggests that the attribution to Ramée was first made by F. Weilbach in 1924, "for lack of something better" ["i mangel af bedre"].

18. For examples, see Lund, ed., *Danmarks arkitektur*, volumes on "Enfamilienhuset" and "Landbrugets huse."

19. For the life of Frederikke Brun, see Bobé, *Frederikke Brun*, and the articles on her and her husband in *Dansk biografisk Leksikon*, vol. 2 (1980), pp. 583–7, and *Neue deutsche Biographie*, vol. 2 (1955), pp 676–7.

20. P. Kohler, *Mme de Staël et la Suisse* (Lausanne, 1916), p. 505. References to Brun occur also in G. de Diesbach, *Madame de Staël* (Paris, 1983).

21. Information from Lisbet Balslev Jørgensen of the Kunstakademi, Copenhagen.

22. Article on Constantin Brun, in *Dansk biografisk Leksikon*, vol. 2 (1980), p. 584.

23. The original German text is from Friderike [sic] Brun, *Gedichte*, Fridrich Matthisson, ed. (Zurich, 1798), pp. 2–3. The English translation: *Dublin University Magazine*, vol. 21 (1843), p. 660 (translator not identified).

24. Bobé, *Frederikke Brun*, p. 43: ". . . en nyfrankisk Gartner og Byggerevolutionaer, der uden Hensyn til Klima og Lokalitet elegantiserede alt." Bobé does not specify when Brun said or wrote this, but he gives it as a direct quote.

25. Bobé, *Frederikke Brun*, p 43. The present address of Sophienholm is Nybrovej 401, Kongens Lyngby.

26. I saw Constantin Brun's undated description of Sophienholm, written in German, in a transcription (entitled in Danish "Constantin Bruns egen Beskrivelse af Sophienholm") in the Kunstakademiets Bibliotek, Copenhagen. Added to the transcription (by an unidentified annotator) are notes correcting certain erroneous facts given by Brun such as the date when he purchased the estate. Additonal information on Sophienholm can be found in Bobé, *Frederikke Brun*, pp. 42ff; Lorenzen, *Gammel dansk Bygningskultur*, pp. 35–43; and P. Koch, *Sophienholm* (booklet), Copenhagen, n.d. [c. 1972].

27. *Parcs et jardins*, pl. 3. Ramée's plan is inscribed "Friedrichsthal bei Copenhagen 1804." Sophienholm was originally part of the larger estate Frederiksdal and was apparently called by both names. Hennings also called Sophienholm "Friederichsthal," in his diary of 1802 (p. 107).

28. The drawing collection of the Kunstakademi in Copenhagen contains seven sheets of drawings pertaining to Sophienholm, attributed to Ramée; these, along with the three sheets of drawings of the bathroom in the Bruns' Copenhagen house, reportedly were acquired in 1931 from the drawing collection of Konrad Møller (Madsen, p. 25; correspondence from Lisbet Jørgensen, 1985). The sheets, unsigned but bearing notes in Ramée's hand, are numbered A-2498a, b, c, d; A-2505a, b; and A-2507. (Dimensions, respectively: 26 × 43 cm, 26 × 43 cm, 26 × 43 cm, 35 × 52 cm, 19 × 24 cm, 19 × 24 cm., 24 × 36 cm.) Ramée's notes on the drawings are in French, but the scales are given in Danish "alen." In addition are several sheets signed by or attributed to a certain "Burmester" (A-2499a–e). At least one of these (A-2499e, bearing elevation drawings for the principal room in Sophienholm) is probably from the hand of Ramée.

29. Brun's description (see note 26) includes the following: "Dieser Bau ward durch einen französischer Baumeister nahmens Rammé [sic] besorgt, . . . ferner ward in dieser Zeit von denselben erbaut ein Pferdestall." The references in Hennings's diary: pp. 25 (18 July 1802), 107–8 (24 August 1802).

30. "Im letzten Sommer besuchte ich . . . Dännemark . . . , in Copenhagen sah' ich oft die geistige Brun auf ihrer reizenden Villa Sophienholm." (Letter to Schlegel from Minna van Nuys, quoted in J. Korner, *Krisenjahre der Frühromantik*, vol. 1, p. 244.)

31. Letter from Brun to the poet Friedrich von Matthisson, 3 December 1824, published in *Friedrich von Matthisson's Literarischer Nachlass*, vol. 2 (Berlin, 1832), p. 84. ("Du kennst ja mein Sophienholm und dessen meilenweit romantische Umgebungen! Komm! komm! mit den Schwalben oder spätstens mit der Nachtigall!") Another letter from Frederikke referring to Sophienholm is in the same work, p. 66.

32. The drawing is illustrated in P. Koch, *Sophienholm*, p. 1. Brun's remarks were: "Im Jahre 1805 [sic] erfolgte eine totale Verschönerung, welche darin bestand, das Wohnhaus mitt einer zweiten und dritten Etage zu versehn, samt die bayden Nebenhäuser ebenfalls neu einzurichten, und sämtliche Dächer im Wohnhause mit Blech zu belegen" ("Constantin Bruns egen Beskrivelse af Sophienholm"). The date "1805" is evidently a mistatement for 1800 or 1801.

33. Information from Lisbet Balslev Jørgensen. For Frederikke Brun's visit to Coppet, 1801–2, see Bobé, *Frederikke Brun*, pp. 173–8.

34. Hennings's diary, p. 107.

35. For examples of roofs of eighteenth-century Danish country houses, see Brogaard, et al., *Denmarks arkitektur*, pp. 138–77.

36. Drawing A-2498-d, in the collection of the Kunstakademi.

37. Bonstetten was in Denmark from 1798 to 1801. His presence at Sophienholm during the summers of this period is revealed in a publication of Bonstetten's letters to Frederikke Brun (*Briefe von Karl Viktor von Bonstetten an Friederike Brun*, Frankfurt a. M., 1829); a reference to Sophienholm in a letter of 14 August 1803 is footnoted (by "Fr. Br.") as follows: "Dem Landsitze der Familie Brun, wo, und in dessen Umgebungen, der Verfasser [i.e., Bonstetten] drei Sommer fern von allen Revolutionsstürmen lebte" (vol. 1, p. 152).

38. Karl Viktor von Bonstetten, *Neue Schriften*, vol. 2 (Copenhagen, 1800), pp. 1–87.

39. ". . . Unsere Natur und das ländliche Leben zu verschönern" (ibid., p. 33).

40. Bonstetten specifically complains about suffering from the cold in a house in Copenhagen where he lived for three years – evidently the Brun House (ibid., pp. 10–11).

41. "Unsere nördlichen Gärten mit ihren sonnenmordenden Schatten. . . . Wir haben Ruinen und Einsiedeleien, aber wir frieren nicht selten" (ibid., p. 29).

42. "In Sophienholm ist ein steiler ohngefähr 20 Schuh hoher Rasen gegen Mittag gekehrt, über welchem eine 4 bis 5 Schuh hohe Mauer steht. Dieser sanft eingebogene Rasen bildet die Sektion eines

Zirkels und konzentrirt die Sonnenstrahlen; auf diesem Rasen hörte ich den 20sten November 1799 bei warmer Sonne Heimchen oder Heuschrecken zirpen, wie in warmen Sommertagen" (ibid., p. 15).

43. "Glücklich die Lage des bescheidenen Sophienholm am sanft gebogenen amphitheatralischen Hügel, wo alle Winde hinüberbrausen, ohne die sonnigen zart beschatteten Pfade zu entheiligen. Da blühten in der letzten Hälfte des Novembers eines kalten Jahrs (1799) noch etliche und zwanzig Blumen im Freien; einige Kirsch- und Äpfelbäume hatten noch alle ihre Blätter, dieweil der Sturmwind den nahen Buchenwald ganz entlaubt hatte; die nicht seltenen Nebel des Sees steigen nie bis an das Wohnhaus, das durch die Hügelspitze und den hochgesäulten Buchenwald vor allen Winden geschützt ist" (ibid., pp. 46–7).

44. Ibid., p. 38.

45. "Partout on y a substitué l'utile à l'agréable, et l'agréable y a presque toujours gagné" (ibid., p. 83).

46. Ibid., p. 35, 58–9.

47. "Die wahre Gartenkunst muss jede Szene des menschlichen Lebens nach dem Charakter der wirklichen Natur verschönern, und den Menschen zu seiner wahren Bestimmung, zum Fleiss und thätigen Leben, und zu dauerhafter Glückseligkeit anlocken" (ibid., pp. 68, 86).

48. "See, Inseln, Waldungen, Buchten hinein, Krümmungen umher, Landsitze, Dörfer, Kirchen, Kopenhagen in her Ferne machen eine Mischung, die bey jeden hundert Schritten ein neues Gemälde liefert. Und doch ist Brun bey halb vollendetem Bau schon gesättiget, und suchet andere Nahrung in Antworskow. Dies rührt daher, weil in Friederichsthal [Sophienholm] alles Vergnügen, nichts Nutzen und Geschäfte ist. . . . Brun hat nichts als Divane, Gemälde, Spiegel, Pferdeställe, Schweitzer-, Gärtner-Wohner, Nordisches Haus zur Einsiedelei, gothisches Pförtnerhaus, Chinesischen Pavillon, und nicht eine Kuh, die ihm frische Milch, nicht einen Acker, der ihm Brodkorn giebt" (Hennings's diary, p. 107). Nystrøm (*Fra Nordsjaellands Øresundskyst*, p. 539) states that the "Schweitzer-[Haus]" mentioned by Hennings refers to a peasant hut.

49. "Constantin Bruns egen Beskrivelse af Sophienholm."

50. Hennings's diary, p. 25. This "temple" was probably the circular pavilion shown on Ramée's plan of Sophienholm, on the hill near the entry to the estate. It was perhaps similar to Ramée's domed temple over a grotto at Baurs Park on the Elbchaussee.

51. The pumphouse is illustrated in J. Krafft, *Recueil d'architecture civile* (Paris, 1812), pl. 114. It reportedly supplied water from the Seine for the Grand Rocher in Saint-James's garden (G. Leroux-Cesbron, "Le Baron de Sainte-James et sa folie de Neuilly," *La revue de Paris*, February 1925, p. 671).

52. Drawings A-2507, A-2505a, A-2505b.

53. Constantin Brun described the privy ("Locum") as being made of brick ("Mauersteine") and the gardener's house as cementwork ("Bindungswerk"). A twentieth-century annotation to the transcription of Brun's description states that "the materials of these two buildings are perhaps mistakes due to faulty memory; it is the privy that is cementwork ["Bindingsvaerk"] and the gardener's house that is brick ["Sten"]; but the same annotation states that Brun's description does match Ramee's drawings (Kunstakademiets Bibliotek; see note 26).

54. "Auf dieser Anhöhe ist ein ziemlich geraumiges Haus von Norwegen seewärtz gebracht, von ganzen norwegischen Balken erbaut, und welches ein ziemlich geräumiger Sahl ausmacht, und ein Nebenraum enthält worin eine kleine Küche eingerichtet ist mit besondere Ausgang" (Brun's description of Sophienholm; see note 26).

55. Lorenzen (*Gammel dansk Bygningskultur*, p. 41) states that the original structure still stood, in good condition, in 1920.

56. "Ich wollte, Du wärest hier im nordischen Hause bey mir: wirklich aus Tannenbalken gezimmert, fix und fertig bis aufs Dach, von Norwegen hergesegelt. Es steht auf einer steilen Terrasse am See, und ist von einem so dichten und düstren Kranze von Edeltannen, Weimuthskiefern und Balsambirken umgeben, dass Hühnerweihe und Käuzlein drinn nisten. Von unten herauf wehen blühende Akazienwipfel, und hauchen Düfte, deren Verwandtschaft mit denen der Orangen mich schnell aus dem Norden nach Hesperien versetzt. Unten schimmert der See, von buchenbewaldeten, reitzend aus- und eingebuchteten Gestaden eingefasst. Die Umrisse dieser sanft steigenden Ufer sind leicht in die Luft gezeichnet und weicher im Wasserspiegel abgeschattet. Hier, in meiner geliebten Einsamkeit, arbeite ich nun an einer Revision vom dritten Bändchen meiner Gedichte . . ." (Letter from Brun to Matthisson, 19 June 1819; published in Matthisson, *Literarischer Nachlass*, vol. 2, pp. 62–3).

57. Friderike Brun, *Gedichte*, vol. 2 (Zurich, 1801), p. 57 ("Sophienholm").

58. Information on Conradshøj: Gotfredsen, *Gentofte*, pp. 163–8; Werner, *Duntzfelt*, pp. 228–31; Madsen, *Erichsens Palae*, p. 24.

59. Hennings's diary, pp. 20, 25. ("Das Gohölze hat Erichsen, es ist von Ramé in Promenaden angelegt.")

60. Map illustrated in Werner, *Duntzfelt*, p. 229. There is also a map of 1810 in the Gentofte Historical Association.

61. Mansa, *Udkast til Hauge-Anlaeg*. Another possibility is that the 1809 plan of Conradshøj represents changes made in Ramée's layout after Peter Erichsen's death and the sale of the property to C. W. Duntzfelt in 1805 (Werner, *Duntzfelt*, pp. 228–30).

62. Werner, *Duntzfelt*, pp. 229, 230; map of 1810. The hill was called Ordrupshøj, the lower land Ordrupsdal.

63. Ibid., pp. 229, 230. Painting of Ordruphøj by N. G. Rademacher, in the Øregaard Museum.

64. Photographs illustrated in Gotfredsen, p. 167; Nystrøm, p. 233.

65. Hennings's diary, p. 27. Letter from Countess Sophie Reventlow of 12 June 1810, cited in Madsen, *Erichsens Palae*, p. 28 and note 76. According to Madsen (p. 28 and note 78), Øregaard has been attributed to Ramée at least since 1919.

66. Madsen, p. 27. The construction date of Hellerupgaard is indicated in Hennings's diary, 18 July 1802 (p. 27), in which he states that "Erichsen is having Ramée erect a house" (". . . Erichsen sich durch Ramé ein Haus bauen lässt"), and describes the building from personal inspection.

67. Madsen (p. 28 and note 76) cites fire-insurance records for the information that Frederikslund was still under construction in November 1804. The present address of the building is Frederikslundsvej 21, 2840 Holte.

68. Madsen (p. 28 and note 79) cites fire-insurance records as indicating that Øregaard was largely completed in December 1806 and was finally completed in 1808. The present address of the building is Ørehøjalle 2, 2900 Hellerup. According to Werner (*Duntzfelt*, p. 195), the "Veranda" on the garden side of the house was added in the middle of the nineteenth century.

69. Compare, for example, the houses Svenstrup or Eriksholm, both of the 1780s (illustrated in Brogaard, et al. *Danmarks arkitektur*, pp. 170, 171).

70. Lorenzen (*Gammel dansk Bygningskultur*, p. 35) states that this

semicircular room was added to the house in modern times. A drawing of the garden façade of Hellerupgaard, made by the artist I. F. Bredal in the 1820s (in the Øregaard Museum) shows a small, enclosed porch where the semicircular room was later built; but it is likely that even this porch was not part of Ramée's original design.

71. Belanger had used a similar type of frieze on a couple of his houses in the 1780s (for example, his house in the Rue Pigalle, Paris). See Chapter 3.

72. Hennings's diary, p. 27.

73. Reportedly, recent work on Frederikslund revealed that the original color of the walls was light grey (information received during a visit to the house, 1983).

74. See Hennings's remarks, quoted earlier, about the garden at Hellerupgaard. A painting of Frederikslund and its grounds, c. 1830, is illustrated in Lorenzen, p. 36.

75. Drawing by Søren Laessøe Lange, 1820, in Byhistorisk Arkiv for Søllerød Kommune. Brought to my attention by Hakon Lund.

76. Drawings and photographs in the Kunstakademiets Bibliotek. The drawings, dated 1920, were made for a remodeling of the building. The photographs show the building in both its earlier and later conditions.

77. See for example, an article on Ramée (signed "J. R.") in *Weilbachs Kunstnerleksikon* (Copenhagen, 1952), p. 15. This article also draws a parallel between Ramée's design for Union College and Hansen's later Kommune-hospital in Copenhagen, although it is unlikely that Hansen knew of the Union College design.

78. V. Villadsen, for example, in an article on C. F. Hansen in the *Macmillan Encyclopedia of Architects* (New York, 1982), has noted that Hansen's work reveals a "profound acquaintance with new French theories."

Chapter 9

I thank the following people who aided my research on Ramée's work in Mecklenburg-Schwerin: Dr. Gerd Baier of the Landesamt für Denkmalpflege, Schwerin; Dr. Peter Rakow and Herr Klaus Baudis of the Mecklenburgisches Landeshauptarchiv Schwerin; Frau Hela Baudis of the Staatliches Museum Schwerin; and Herr Hoyer of the Schloss Ludwigslust.

1. See Appendix. The French term "prince héréditaire" (equivalent to the German "Erbprinz") means the heir to a reigning prince.

2. Mecklenburgisches Landeshauptarchiv (Mecklenburg National Archive), Schwerin. Letter from "Masson & Ramée" (probably written by Masson) to "Son Altesse Serenissime le Duc Regnant de Mecklenbourg Suerin," dated "2 juin 1801, Hambourg." The letter reads: "Monseigneur / D'après la permission que vous avez bien voulu nous donner de vous instruire quand M. Ramée architecte, l'un des deux associés de notre maison seroit de retour de Paris, nous avons l'honneur de faire savoir à votre Altesse qu'il prendra vos ordres pour se rendre à Ludwigslust, si son Altesse juge encore convenable de le recevoir." Ramée possibly was brought to the attention of the ducal family through the recommendation of his Danish client Constantin Brun, who had government connections in Mecklenburg-Schwerin (article on Brun in *Dansk biografisk Leksikon*, 1980, vol. 2, p. 583).

3. F. Schlie, ed., *Die Kunst- und Geschichts-Denkmäler des Grossherzogthums Mecklenburg-Schwerin*, vol. 3 (Schwerin, 1900), pp. 265–7. Renate Krüger, *Ludwigslust: eine kulturhistorische Skizze* (Schwerin, 1970), pp. 69–71. According to Krüger, a Gothic-Revival structure (designed by the ducal architect Von Seydewitz) was first begun as the mausoleum, but then it was turned over to the Catholic congregation of Ludwigslust as their parish church and a new mausoleum was planned.

4. The attribution to Lillie is made, for instance, in Schlie's work, cited in note 3 (p. 266); G. Dehio, *Handbuch der deutschen Kunstdenkmäler*, vol. 2 (Berlin, 1926), p. 307; *Thieme-Becker Künstler-Lexikon*, vol. 23 (Leipzig, 1929), article on Lillie; R. Krüger, *Ludwigslust*, caption to photograph of the mausoleum.

5. *Zeitung für die elegante Welt*, vol. 6, no. 33 (18 March 1806), pp. 266–7 and accompanying engraving. In the engraving, the perspective view of the mausoleum is inscribed "Ramée inv.," "die Landschaft von Bartel," and "Hüllman sc. Leipzig."

6. "Das Denkmal, welches der Erbprinz seiner unvergesslichen Gemahlin bestimmte, ist ein Mausoleum. Die Erbauung desselben wurde dem berühmten, in Hamburg lebenden Architekten Ramée übertragen, dessen ausgezeichnete Talente in der Bau- und Gartenkunst bei den jetzigen, diesen Künsten so ungünstigen Zeiten, leider viel zu wenig benutzt werden. Ich rede hier von dem Baumeister der so prächtigen als geschmackvollen Börsenhalle in Hamburg, die ohne diesen Künstler gewiss ungebaut geblieben wäre. Das Mausoleum wurde nach seinen Zeichnungen und unter seiner Leitung aufgeführt. Der von dem Prinzen gewählte Ort bei Ludwigslust war dazu ganz passend: gross, einsiedlerisch und von allem Geräusch entfernt, mit schönen Eichen und Buchen, so wie mit neuen Anpflanzungen von beständig grünenden Bäumen, Weiden, Pappeln und Blumenstöcken. . . / Das Mausoleum ist von Stein, 74 Fuss lang und 44 Fuss breit; eine breite Treppe von 9 Stufen führt zum Eingang, zu einem Peristil, das aus vier Dorischen Säulen besteht, die einen Fronton mit der Inschrift: Helenen Paulownen, tragen, das Thor ist von Mahagonyholz, mit Bronze verziert. Aus dem Peristil tritt man in das Vestibule, wo sich eine Treppe befindet, die zur Griechischen Kapelle führt, die über demselben liegt. Ferner führt das Vestibule ins Innere des Gewölbes, in dessen Mitte zwei Sarkophage stehen. . . . An den vier Ecken der die Sarkophage umgebenden Estrade stehen vier Candelaber von Bronze. Eine kostbare Decke von Carmoisin-Sammet mit Gold gestickt, bedeckt das Ganze. Diess Leichengewölbe hat 38 Fuss im Diameter, und die Höhe ist ebenfalls 38 Fuss. Das Licht fällt von oben herein. Das Innere des Gewölbes ist mit Stukkatur-Arbeit bekleidet, blau mit Sternen von vergoldetem Bronze./ Wir fügen noch hinzu, dass Se. Majestät der Kaiser von Russland bereits Befehle an die Russische Mission in Berlin ertheilt hat, dass Griechische Priester zwei Mal im Jahre sich nach Ludwigslust begeben sollen, um hier eine religiöse Todtenfeier zu halten."

7. A few details of the building, as it presently exists, are not shown in Ramée's engraving and may have been later additions: for example, the acroterial ornament at the peak of the pediment.

8. Mecklenburg National Archive. Letter from Lillie (in Lübeck) to Prince Friedrich Ludwig, dated 25 May 1804: "Durchlauchtigster Fürst, Gnädigster Erb-Printz und Herr / Da ich, seit Einsendung meiner Projecte zum Hochfürstl. Famielien Begräbniss zu Ludwichslust, nicht erfahren habe, ob ich ferner das Glück haben werde für Ew. Hochfürstl. Durchlauchtigheit, in dieser Rücksicht, etwas zu unternehmen, so vermuthe [ich] dass dieser Auftrag einem andern Architecten übertragen ist und erlaube mir zu dem Ende die Freyheit hiermit meine Rechnung zu überreichen. . . ." Accompanying this letter is a bill from Lillie to the prince, also dated 25 May 1804: "Auf Hohen Befehl verfertiget und geliefert / 1804, den 3ten

Febr. / Fünf verschiedene Projecte, bestehend aus gezeichnete Pläne, Facaden und Profiler, zu einem Hochfürstl. Famielien Begräbniss mit zuhörende Beschreibung und Berechnung der Kosten eines Jeden, wofür ich mir zu vergütigen bitte / die Summa 30 Fridr. d'or. . ." A note from Lillie dated 14 September 1804 acknowledges payment of this sum of money. I thank Professor Hermann Hipp for helping me to read and interpret these documents.

9. Lillie's letter of 25 May 1804 (see previous note).

10. For example, Gilly's mausoleum at Dyhernfurth near Breslau, built about 1800 (Berlin Museum, *Friedrich Gilly, 1772–1800*, Berlin, 1984, pp. 161ff).

11. Numerous examples can be found in the sketches of Gilly, as illustrated for example in A. Oncken, *Friedrich Gilly* (Berlin, 1981).

12. Ledoux's project for a house on the Rue Neuve de Berry, published only in Daniel Ramée's 1847 edition of Ledoux's *Architecture* (pl. 213), not in the original edition of 1804. See also Gallet, *Ledoux*, p. 206.

13. See Ledoux's plan for a cemetery at Chaux, pl. 141 of Ramée's edition of Ledoux's *Architecture*; J. N. L. Durand, *Précis des leçons*, (Paris, 1819; orig. ed. 1802–5), vol. 1, pl. 15; and designs of the same period by Vallot, Lahure, et al. (see W. Szambien, *Durand*, Paris, 1984, pp. 305, 308; Szambien, *Les Projets de l'an II*, 1986, p. 68).

14. Staatliches Museum Schwerin. Watercolor drawing, signed and dated "R. Suhrlandt, 1842." The artist Rudolf Suhrlandt was active in Mecklenburg-Schwerin in the early nineteenth century (Hela Baudis, "Rudolf Suhrlandt, 1781–1862," Staatliches Museum Schwerin, n.d.).

15. An inscription under the engraved view of the mausoleum reads "die Landschaft von Bartel." This was probably Friedrich Barthel (1775–1846), an engraver and painter who produced landscape views in Leipzig around 1805 (Thieme-Becker, *Künstler-Lexikon*); but he may merely have drawn the landscaping for the engraver, rather than actually laid out the grounds. Ramée's role in the landscaping of the area around the mausoleum is indicated also by the fact that plants were provided for the Ludwigslust park by James Booth, the Flottbek gardener whom Ramée knew from his work at Caspar Voght's estate. (Itemized bills from Booth, dated 1804 and 1806, are preserved in the Ludwigslust-mausoleum records in the Mecklenburg National Archive.)

16. Photocopies of these documents were kindly provided to me by the Mecklenburg National Archive and the Institut für Denkmalpflege of Schwerin.

17. Letters of 18 October and 17 December 1804, 30 April 1805, 26 June 1807, 1 July 1808, and an undated bill.

18. Letter of 31 September 1804 (written by Ramée in Ludwigslust). "Monsieur le maréchal,/ Le second plan du monument que j'ai communiqué au Prince héréditaire a été rejetté et véritablement il eût été mesquin dans le bel emplacement qui est destiné à cet objet, Je me suis occupé des moyens de diminuer la dépense du premier. il n'y aura plus qu'un seul portique du coté de l'entrée, la chapelle aura toute une autre forme, et aura toujours son entrée particulière, mais qui ne sera pas avancée n'y précedée d'un Péristile. Toutes les colonnes de l'intérieur & la voûte sont suprimées enfin j'espère que par le moyen de ces suppressions, qui ne changeront rien à la grande conception du premier projet, j'espère donc dis-je que la dépense n'excédera pas vingt mille écus, la différence de six à sept mille écus qui existe entre le premier et le second projet ne peut et ne doit pas être une obstacle, à l'exécution du Premier. . ." (The currency referred to in this letter, the écu, was the French term for the German Rixthaler.)

19. Letter of 30 April 1805. "J'espère que le modèle du monument que nous avons eu l'honneur d'adresser à S. A. S. le prince héréditaire sera arrivé sans accident."

20. Letter of 9 July 1805. "Quand [sic] au mur de derrière du monument toute décoration quelconque nuirait à l'effet général, d'ailleurs ce mur ne sera pas si simple puisqu'il est couronné d'une très belle corniche ornée de modillons et surmontée d'un fronton, tout arrangement de croisée ou autres seraient postiches et ôterait cette belle simplicité qui doit caractériser un tel monument." Ramée had just returned to Hamburg from Ludwigslust, as revealed by a letter from Masson to the Hofmarschall, of 5 July 1805. Ramée's reference to "un Stil plus pur" occurs in his letter of 17 December 1804.

21. Letter of 9 July 1805. "J'aurais eu bien du Plaisir à profiter de votre invitation d'aller vous voir à Pluschow, mais j'étais trop pressé de revenir. vous saurez Monsieur le maréchal, que je me marie sous peu et la jeune promise ne permet pas que les absences que je dois faire soyent trop longues. le mariage doit avoir lieu dans les premiers jours du mois prochain, et vers le quinze je compte faire une course à Ludwigslust, et comme vous devez passer une partie de l'été à Pluschow, je me propose de vous y visiter, il serait même possible que je vous y presente Mad. la Baumeister."

22. Letter of 6 June 1806, written from Hamburg. "Monsieur le maréchal,/ Il y a longtems que je n'ai eu l'avantage de recevoir de vos nouvelles, vous étiez en course lorsque je fus la dernière fois à Ludwigslust, je vous y adresse ma lettre dans l'espérance que vous y êtes en ce moment. J'ai à vous communiquer quelques idées sur ce qui reste à faire au tombeau. S. A. S. le prince héréditaire aurait beaucoup desiré que le tout fut terminé à la fin de l'été mais l'ouvrage en Stuck est ce qui nous retiendra. J'avais proposé que la voute fut simplement enduite et peinte en bleu de ciel clair, mais son altesse m'a fait savoir qu'il préférait attendre et qu'elle fut en Stuck; je crois cependant convenable de faire encore une tentative à cet égard; car le Stuck de cette voûte sera très long à faire et nous coutera beaucoup, ensuite le bleu de ciel sur un enduit bien fait, sera à mon avis d'un meilleur effet que le Stuck; nous n'aurions alors que le bas depuis le carreau jusqu'à la corniche à faire, et les Italiens dans le courant de l'été pouraient facilement finir cette partie./ J'ai envoyé des échantillons de Tapis que le prince avait demandé pour la chapelle, mais il n'en a trouvé aucun de son gout, il y en a cependant un qui suivant moi remplirait parfaitement le but, c'est un Tapis très solide très bon marché et d'un très bon effet pour la chapelle, ce tapis est un Jaspé gris avec une bordure à fleurs, il y en a encore un autre qui pourait aussi convenir, celui-cy imite parfaitement la peau de Tigre, mais il faudrait le commander car nous n'en avons pas pour le moment, on ne pourait pas le recevoir avant trois mois./ N'ayant point trouvé une grande différence entre les prix de la fabrique de bronze et ceux de paris j'ai ordonné les toiles à Ludwigslust je leur ai aussi envoyé le dessein en grand pour l'inscription audessus de la porte intérieurement, les Candelabres pour être placés en angles de l'Estrade sur laquelle poseront les deux sarcophages sont entraint et seront j'espère fini à la fin de ce mois, il y aura sur ces candelabres des lampes à double courant d'air qui éclaireront parfaitement la voute lorsque cela sera nécessaire. à mon dernier voyage j'ai determiné le prince à les laisser faire en bois bronzé plutôt qu'en bronze réel, car comme ils doivent être grand ils auraient été extremement chèrs, on travaille à force aux Mascarons pour la Corniche qui probablement seront finis à la fin de la semaine prochaine./ Le fils de mon parent qui m'en-

voye ordinairement de très bon vin de champagne dont vous avez reçu je crois quelques bouteilles, est ici depuis quelques jours, il va à petersbourg avec une forte partie de ce vin qui dans ce moment est à lubec, il desire s'en défaire d'une partie qui lui servirait à acquiter les frais qui sont considérables, Je prend la liberté de vous en envoyer deux bouteilles d'échantillon une de rosé et l'autre blanc le tout mousseux bien entendu, vous m'obligeriez si vous aviez la bonté de le faire proposer au Duc et même à d'autre personne qui pourait en avoir besoin, c'est véritablement une occasion très favorable, il est de première qualité, comme vous pourez vous en convaincre en le goutant, le Prix est trois mark et quatre schelin de notre argent pris à Lubeck et trois m. et six rendu à Ludwigslust, à Suerin, ou à Doberan [town west of Rostock], on le prend par caisse de 50 Bouteilles./ J'aurais une autre prière à vous faire, Monsieur le maréchal, les tems continuent toujours d'être très mauvais pour la ville d'Hambourg, et particulièrement pour nous qui ne fesons presque plus rien, Je vois arriver une époque où ordinairement vos coffres se remplissent, s'il vous était possible, de nous aider de quelque chose vous nous rendriez service, nos avances sont pour le moment d'environ deux milles écus, la moitié de cette somme nous serait d'un grand secours pour le 15 de ce mois./ Depuis notre absence Monsieur le maréchal, j'ai toujours correspondu avec le Jardinier Schmidt par lequel le prince héréditaire m'a transmis ses ordres, ce Jardinier a planté la Partie qui avoisine le Tombeau comme un véritable planteur de choux, sans raisonnement et sans gout, Je me propose bien avec votre secours de rectifier le tout à l'automne prochain, vous m'obligeriez sensiblement Monsieur le maréchal si comme par le passé et si cela ne vous gêne pas trop, de me communiquer vos idées et de vouloir bien me transmettre vous même les ordres du Prince, car Mtre. Schmidt est souvent inintelligible, Je suis persuadé qu'on aurait pu économiser deux cents écus sur les arbres qui ont servi à cette plantation dont probablement une partie sera mort./ Recevez Monsieur le maréchal, l'assurance de mon entier dévouement./ Ramée." (Schmidt was the court gardener at Ludwigslust; he is said to have been the building director ["*Bauleiter*"] of the mausoleum, according to R. Krüger, *Ludwigslust*, p. 71.)

23. This is a draft of a letter addressed to "Monsieur Ramée, associé de Mr Masson, à Hambourg"; it is undated, but references to it in later letters indicate that its date is 14 June 1806. "Monsieur/ La lettre du 6 du courant que vous m'avez fait l'honneur de m'écrire m'a été remise avant hier à Suerin, où j'avais d'abord l'occasion de parler au P. H. [Prince Héréditaire]. S. A. S. renonce au Stucc pour la voute, et consent qu'elle soit simplement enduite et peinte en bleu Je vous prie de donner incessamment les ordres et les instructions nécessaires./ Le choix d'un tapis pour la chapelle n'a pas eu lieu encore. Les échantillons sont à Llust [Ludwigslust]; je ne les ai jamais vu, et je Vous écrirai dès que le P. H. aura pris une résolution sur ce sujet./ Je suis faché que je n'ai pas pu être utile à Votre ami. Les deux échantillons de vin de Champagne, que j'ai fait gouter à plusieures personnes n'ont pas trouvé de l'approbation./ C'est aussi avec un grand regret que je me vois empêché, de Vous envoyer les mille écus que Vous me demandez. Je vous avoue que je ne m'attendais pas à cette demande, et encore moins que Vos avances monteraient de nouveau à la somme de 2/m Thalers. Comment cela est-il possible?/ Je voudrais que je ne m'eusse jamais mêlé de la construction de cette chapelle sépulcrale, qui coute un argent énorme, malgré Vos assurances si positives./ Vous oubliez entièrement Votre premier devis, qui ne montait, y compris une somme considérable pour les frais imprévus, qu'à treize mille Thalers. C'est sur la foi de ce calcul que nous avons commencé cette batisse. Nous avons certainement economisé à Llust autant que possible, et pourtant la dépense déjà faite, surpasse si considérablement cette somme, que déjà nous approchons du double. S'il ne s'agissait que d'un excédent de mille ou de deux mille écus, je ne serais pas surpris ni allarmé, mais ceci est trop fort, et nous ne voyons pas encore la fin./ J'espère, Monsieur, que Vous voudrez bien me communiquer un mémoire justificatif qui explique les raisons d'une différence si étonnante entre le devis et la dépense réelle. Aucun accident n'a eu lieu et aucun changement ne s'est opéré dans le plan du batiment ou dans les prix des matériaux et du travail des ouvriers. Nous devons nous garantir contre les reproches. Comment croyez Vous, que l'Empereur Napoléon accueillerait les comptes, qui monteraient au double de ce que l'architecte lui aurait d'abord demandé?/ Nous n'oserons aussi pas faire aller le tout au hazard, et je Vous supplie de ne pas croire que la somme dont nous aurons besoin soit absolument indifférente./ Vous ne prétendez pas sans doute, que ce soit un problème insoluble en architecture, que de faire un devis exact, et je ne conçois pas, comment un devis fait par Vous avec soin, ait pu s'ecarter si loin de la véritable dépense. De l'autre côté, il est impossible que Vous ayiez fait à dessein un calcul peu juste pour nous entraîner malgré nous dans une dépense considérable. Votre façon de penser, et les sentimens que Vous m'avez constamment marqués, me sont de surs garants, que Vous n'avez pas voulu me compromettre./ Vous vous souviendrez qu'en automne (en Décembre 1805), Vous fites un nouveau calcul des choses que Vous auriez encore à nous fournir de Hambourg. Votre compte Vous mena jusqu'à la somme de 2000 Thalers, qui selon vous ne serait dépassée que de bien peu de chose. Ces 2000 Thalers vous ont été fournis au mois de Janvier, et vous avouerez que j'ai raison d'être un peu surpris de l'avance si forte où vous êtes de nouveau. Si vous nous ménagez encore beaucoup de ces surprises, vous nous ruinerez, et nous serons obligés, d'abandonner l'édifice, malgré qu'il soit près d'être achevé. Agréez, Monsieur, l'assurance de mes civilités./ M. [Mecklenburg]"

24. Letter of 3 August 1806. "Vous croyez peut-être, Monsieur, que le Prince héréditaire est très facile, et que je n'ai qu'à lui présenter les comptes pour être acquite tout de suite. Il est vrai que le Prince est très content du bâtiment. Mais on ne passe pas si vite sur 12 à 15 mille Thalers de frais extraordinaire et inattendus. Aussi n'est ce pas uniquement au Prince que les comptes seront soumis, et je voudrais pouvoir répondre à tout le monde d'une manière satisfaisante. Je vous prie donc, Monsieur, de songer un peu au mémoire que je vous ai demandé./ J'ai trouvé par hazard hier à Ludwigslust les N[os] ci joints du Journal des Bâtimens etc. que je croyais vous avoir rendu depuis longtems. . . ."

25. Letter and statement of 5 September 1806, sent from Hamburg. "Monsieur le maréchal,/ Une absence de quelques semaines, m'a empêché de répondre à votre première lettre du 14 Juin dernier, à mon retour j'ai trouvé votre seconde, et je vais vous donner, Monsieur le maréchal, les éclaircissements que vous désirez avoir sur l'excédent de la dépense relative aux travaux du tombeau. Je crois me rappeller que dans le premier aperçu il n'était pas question du péristil autrement dit portail, qui avec le perron fait une augmentation de dépense assez considérable, ensuite je crois qu'il fut question de faire la corniche du couronnement en Bois, depuis elle a été décidée en pierre, seconde augmentation de dépense, la quantité de cuivre présumée nécessaire pour la couverture a été augmentée de près d'un tiers. J'avais cru premièrement pouvoir faire la goutierre du toit dans la pierre même mais l'ayant trouvé trop porreuse je n'ai pas osé le

risquer, après cela viennent mes voyages, les frais d'inspection, et honnoraire, vous verrez Monsieur le maréchal, par le compte que j'ai l'honneur de vous adresser cy joint qu'il ne contient rien à l'exception de deux ou trois petits articles qui puisse faire partie du 1er aperçu; il y a eu plus de la moitié des pots destinés pour la voute, qui ont du être rejettés étant trop peu cuits et ne ressemblant en rien au model que j'avais eu la précaution d'envoyer, il est possible encore que beaucoup d'autres objets n'ayant pas été mieux soignés que celui là vous verrez Monsieur le maréchal par le compte de mes voyages combien j'y mets d'économie je me dispute souvent avec les postillons qui veulent souvent me forcer à prendre trois chevaux. Je suis de même en dispute avec Taddey [?] le stuckateur qui voulais avoir plus de quatre mille mark pour le stuck du tombeau, Je lui en offre trois et probablement je l'aurai pour ce prix./ Les pappiers publiques vous auront apris Monsieur le maréchal que nous vous proposions de faire dans le courant d'octobre prochain une vente des objets de luxe et autres composant notre magazin, je prendrai la liberté de vous adresser quelques catalogues en vous priant de les distribuer à vos amis et connaissances./ Recevez Monsieur le maréchal, l'assurance de mon entier dévouement/ Ramée."

26. Letter of 1 May 1807. "Messieurs,/ L'état où se trouvent naturellement les affaires du P. h. après les malheurs arrivés à sa patrie, et après que l'on lui a ôté tous les revenus qu'il retiroit du Mecklenbourg doit bien faire excuser auprès de personnes aussi justes et équitables que vous, les delais qui sont mis aux payemens de S. A. S. Croyez cependant, Messieurs, que je n'ai pas oublié votre compte, et que j'espère pouvoir bientôt vous fixer le terme du payement. . . ."

27. Included in the Ramée correspondence in Schwerin is an undated note referring to "les plans et les travaux qui se rapportent au Palais ou au nouveau Château de L'lust [Ludwigslust]." It has been suggested to me, however, that Ramée's palace designs were possibly for Schloss Plüschow, north of Schwerin, a palace that had been acquired in 1802 by Prince Friedrich Ludwig.

28. Letter of 1 July 1808, written from Hamburg. "Monsieur le maréchal,/ Je suis privé depuis longtems de vos nouvelles, j'espère que les quatre candelabres et la glace que j'ai eu l'honneur de vous annoncer seront arrivés en bon état à Ludwigslust, je vous réitère ma prière à l'égard de la réclamation au sujet des travaux fais au nouveau château; j'ai fait quatre voyages dont deux avec mon jeune homme, uniquement pour cet objet je n'ai jamais mis en compte que mes déboursés, de plus le plan général du dit chateau, vue façades sur le jardin, cinq desseins pour la décoration de la grande salle, la salle à manger journalière, le Boudoir ovale, ensuite un projet de salle de spectacle qui devait s'executer dans la grande salle, tous les détails des corniches de chaque pièce, la sculpture qui devait orner ces corniches, a été faite et m'est restée, demême qu'une grande quantité de Baguettes de cuivre que j'ai fait venir de Paris et qui étaient destinées pour les portes que le Prince avait décidé être en acajou, une partie de ces baguettes a été employée depuis, mais il m'en reste encore beaucoup, que je plaçerai difficilement; vous m'obligerez sensiblement, Monsieur le maréchal, si vous avez la bonté de mettre ce petit exposé sous les yeux du Prince et de me mettre à même de recevoir la modique somme que je réclame à ce sujet, je compte sous trois semaines m'absenter d'Hambourg pour quelques mois, et je vous avouerai franchement que j'ai compté sur cette petite rentrée pour faciliter le départ et si vous pouviez y joindre la montant du compte de la maison, ou une partie, vous me rendriez, Monsieur le maréchal un bien grand service; s'il vous est agréable de faire une diminution de cent mark sur la glace qui doit remplacer celle cassée j'y consens avec bien du plaisir./ Agréez Monsieur le maréchal, l'assurance de mon entier dévouement./ Ramée."

29. Letter of 25 March 1808, written from Hamburg: ". . . car je reste encore ici jusqu'à nouvel ordre. Les lettres peu encourageantes que j'ai reçu de paris, et quelques petits travaux qui me sont survenus m'ont fait remettre mon projet à un autre tems."

30. Letter of 6 November 1808. See following note.

31. Letter of 6 November 1808, written from Blankenese. "Monsieur le maréchal,/ J'ai reçu dans le tems[?] les 560 M [?] 7. s. [?] N.2/3 que vous avez bien voulu m'envoyer, je vous dois des excuses de ne pas vous en avoir accusé la réception. J'étais alors très occupé de la salle de fête que le Prince de Ponte Corvo a fait bâtir à l'occasion du jour de naissance de l'Empereur; je le suis encore beaucoup dans ce moment dieu veuille que cela continue et je ne penserai pas à retourner en France de sitot, cy joint les deux reçus que vous désirez avoir./ Agréez Monsieur le maréchal l'assurance de mon entier dévouement./ Ramée."

32. *Der Hamburgische Correspondent*, Nr. 132, 17 August 1808. "Vier bis fünf hundert zu dem Ball des Prinzen eingeladene Personen kamen. . . zu dem Hotel S[eine]r Durchlaucht. . . . Ein Saal, der in einigen Wochen erbauet, aufs glänzendste decorirt worden, und der einem schönen Tempel des Alterthums glich, erregte Bewunderung. Die in dem Sanctuaire befindliche Büste S[eine]r Maj[estät], des Kaysers Napoleon, war der erste Gegenstand, der den Augen auffiel, die durch den Glanz von mehr als 500 Wachslichtern einigermassen geblendet waren." I thank Dr. Richter of the Staatsarchiv Hamburg and Didier Coupaye for bringing this article to my attention.

33. See Appendix.

34. For Ramée's business in Dinant, see Chapters 7 and 13.

35. *The Lafayette Letters in the Bostonian Society,* The Bostonian Society Publications, vol. 4, second series (Boston, 1924), pp. 146–7 (letter of 10 February 1811, written from Lagrange, Lafayette's home, south of Paris).

36. Marie-Louise Biver, *Le Paris de Napoléon* (Paris, 1963), pp. 33–50. W. and A. Durant, *The Age of Napoleon* (New York, 1975), pp. 260–4.

37. Biver, *Le Paris de Napoléon*, p. 33.

38. Ibid., pp. 36, 40.

39. Stern, vol. 2.

40. Deming, *La Halle au Blé de Paris*, pp. 190–7.

41. Biver, *Le Paris de Napoléon*, pp. 124–5. Stern, *Belanger*, vol. 2, pp. 246–7.

42. Biver, *Le Paris de Napoléon*, pp. 255–9.

43. Ibid. pp. 199–207. Jacques Hillairet, *Dictionnaire historique des rues de Paris* (Paris, 1963), vol. 1, p. 155.

44. Biver, *Le Paris de Napoléon*, p. 46.

45. Letter from David Parish to General John P. Van Ness, 25 March 1815, in National Archives, Washington. See Chapter 12.

46. Musée Carnavalet, Paris, drawing no. D-6718, 33 × 48 cm. This drawing was brought to my attention by Professor Damie Stillman.

47. Jean Léonnet, *Les Loteries d'état en France aux XVIIIe et XIXe siècles* (Paris, 1963).

48. Ibid., pp. 58f. The financial records of the lottery administration for the year 1811 are preserved in the "archives du Secrétariat Général de la Loterie Nationale" (Léonnet, p. 100); inquiries to these archives, in 1990, produced no information on Ramée's design.

49. For example, Øregaard and Frederikslund in Denmark, and design no. 22 in Ramée's publication *Recueil de cottages et maisons de campagne.*

Chapter 10

I thank the following people who aided my research on Ramée's work in northern New York State (except for Union College): John Baule, Rev. Peter M. Berg, Claire Bonney, Persis Boyesen, James Bradish, Mary C. Burroughs, Lynn Case Ekfelt, Mr. and Mrs. James Duane Featherstonhaugh, Laura A. Foster, Mr. and Mrs. Joel M. Howard, Eleanor Jones, Roger G. Kennedy, Lowell McAllister, Virginia Ward Duffy McLoughlin, Rev. Liam O'Doherty, Henry V. S. Ogden, Mahlon Peterson, Emma Remington, Norman Rice, Susanne Roberson, Wendy Shadwell, Margaret Shaeffer, Bruce T. Sherwood, Pauline Tedford, Shirley K. Tramontana, and Walter Richard Wheeler.

1. L'Enfant was twenty-three years old when he came to America, Hallet about twenty-six, Latrobe thirty-two, Godefroy forty; Mangin's age is not known. The other principal foreign-born architects of the period were George Hadfield, James Hoban, and William Jay; their respective ages at immigration were thirty-two, twenty-three, and twenty-four.

2. Letter from Joseph Rosseel to David Parish, 10 November 1812; quoted below in the text.

3. Letter from Ramée to Joseph Rosseel, 11 February 1815, SLU (Parish-Rosseel Collection, Owen D. Young Library, St. Lawrence University, Canton, N.Y.), no. 1161. Letters from David Parish to Ramée, 22 March 1813 and 17 March 1814, NYHS (Parish Letter Books, New York Historical Society, New York, N.Y.). Letter from Parish's secretary to Ramée, 3 February 1816, NYHS.

4. Talbot Hamlin, *Benjamin Henry Latrobe* (New York 1955), pp. 396ff.

5. See Appendix.

6. For David Parish and his family, see Richard Ehrenberg, *Grosse Vermögen*, Jena, 1905, vol. 2, *Das Haus Parish in Hamburg*; A. Raffalovich, "John Parish, banquier et négociant à Hambourg," *Journal des économistes*, series 6, vol. 7 (15 August 1905); Philip G. Walters, "David Parish in America 1806–16," bachelor's honors thesis, Harvard University (1942); Philip G. Walters and Raymond Walters, Jr., "The American Career of David Parish," *Journal of Economic History*, vol. 4 (May 1944), pp. 149–66; Roger G. Kennedy, *Orders From France* (New York, 1989).

7. There is disagreement among those who have studied Parish's financial career, about his profit from the Mexican silver scheme. Raffalovich and Walters state that his share was about one million dollars. Kennedy believes it was less than this, but nevertheless calculates that Parish acquired "the modern equivalent of $25 million or more" (*Orders*, pp. 257–9).

8. Walters and Walters, *Parish*, pp 160–1.

9. Letter from David to John Parish, 4 March 1807, NYHS (book 2, p. 354).

10. H. Swiggett, *The Extraordinary Mr. Morris* (New York, 1952); R. L. Hawkins, *Madame de Staël and the United States* (Cambridge Mass., 1930), pp. 10–14; T. W. Clarke, *Emigrés in the Wilderness* (New York, 1941); John H. Hanson, *The Lost Prince: Facts Tending to Prove the Identity of Louis XVII of France and the Rev. Eleazar Williams, Missionary Among the Indians of North America* (New York, 1854).

11. Letter from Gouverneur Morris to Robert Morris, 1790, quoted in Hawkins, *Madame de Staël*, p. 10.

12. Gouverneur Morris, *Notes on the United States of America* (Philadelphia, 1806).

13. Preserved at the New York Historical Society are Parish's "letter books," copies he retained of the letters he wrote (designated "NYHS" in these notes). Preserved at St. Lawrence University, Canton, N.Y. (in the Owen D. Young Library) is the Parish–Rosseel Collection of correspondence and other documents relating to Parish and his agents in the North Country (designated "SLU" in these notes).

14. Letter from Richard to David Parish, 15 June 1812, SLU (no. 623). Letter from David to Richard Parish, 21 June 1812, NYHS (book 3, p. 35).

15. References to "Ramée and family," "Monsieur et Madame Ramée," and so forth, occur in at least nine letters to or from Parish, during the years the architect was in America. Toward the end of his stay in the country, for example, Parish wrote to his friend J. B. Baudry in France, "La famille Ramée comptait retourner en Europe cette année, mais elle a déféré l'exécution de ce plan" (letter of 14 July 1815, NYHS, book 6, pp. 63–4; brought to my attention by Roger G. Kennedy).

16. The "amiable ladies" are mentioned in letters to David Parish from his nephew John Ross (who had accompanied Parish to America), 3 April 1813 and 23 October 1813 (SLU, nos. 758 and 876). Perhaps the Ramées were accompanied to America by Caroline's older sister Wilhelmina, who later lived with the Ramées in France.

17. "Cette dame s'attend à recevoir à l'arrivée de Mons. LeRay en ce pays, le Journal de Modes que vous lui promettez." Letter from Parish to J. B. Baudry (in Nantes), 14 October 1814, NYHS (book 5, p. 386); brought to my attention by Roger G. Kennedy.

18. Rosseel's "return with Mr. Jos. Ramée" from Philadelphia to Ogdensburg, in October 1812, is noted in a summary of Rosseel's diary, at St. Lawrence University. The diary itself was missing when I examined the Parish papers at the university in 1985.

19. This is the route described in the journal of David Parish's brother George, who made the trip in 1816. H. Lasky, ed., "The Journal of George Parish," *New York History* (July 1975), pp. 265–97.

20. The house, like the stone warehouse, was constructed starting about 1809. A letter from Parish to Rosseel, 11 November 1808, SLU (no. 238), refers to "Mr. Newton's plans . . . for the building of the store-house and dwelling house." Jeffrey A. Cohen, of the Latrobe Papers in Philadelphia, has suggested to me that this might be Joseph Newton, a builder in New York City at this time. If Ramée drew the original design for Parish's house, Parish may have had Newton redraw or revise the plans to conform to American measurements and building conventions.

21. Letter from David to John Parish, 1 December 1812, NYHS. Letters from John Ross to Parish, 23 January, 6 and 20 February, and 3 April 1813, SLU.

22. Letter from David to John Parish, cited in preceding note ("[Ramée] has constructed a brick stove on the Russian plan, which is what we want in this cold climate"). Letters from L. Hasbrouck to his wife, 11 December 1812 and 1 January 1813, Ogdensburg Public Library. Letters from John Ross to Parish, 23 January, 20 February, and 23 October 1813, SLU. Letter from Parish to Abraham Ogden, 18 November 1813, NYHS. Lawrence Wright, in *Home Fires Burning: The History of Domestic Heating and Cooking* (London, 1964), p. 138, states that "in the 'German' and 'Russian' stoves, the hot gases were made to circulate through channels, or a series of chambers,

inside the stove, before reaching the flue, so that much less heat escaped unused." In 1814, Ramée exhibited a "model of a Russian stove" at the Academy of Fine Arts in Philadelphia (see Chapter 12).

23. Letter from John Ross to Parish, 3 April 1813, SLU (no. 758).

24. Vincent Nolte, *Funfzig Jahre in beiden Hemisphären* (Hamburg 1854), pp. 195–6 (English edition: *Fifty Years in Both Hemispheres*, New York, 1854, pp. 185–6). Parish's letters reveal that Hénard and other friends frequently accompanied Parish to the North Country.

25. Letter from Rosseel to Louisa Miller, 10 November 1812, SLU (no. 680).

26. *Ogdensburg Palladium* (10 November 1812), quoted in Franklin Hough, *A History of St. Lawrence and Franklin Counties, New York* (Albany, 1853), p. 628.

27. Letter from L. Hasbrouck to his wife, 20 November 1812, Ogdensburg Public Library.

28. For the history of Parishville, see Katy A. Parker, *Sketches from the Early History of Parishville*, [Potsdam, N.Y.?], c. 1910; Charles W. Lahey, "Parishville, A North Country Experiment," *The Quarterly* [St. Lawrence Co. Historical Association journal] (October 1958 and April 1959); Kent Newell, "David Parish's Early Land Developments in St. Lawrence County," *The Quarterly* (April 1979); *Sketches of Parishville, 1809–1976* (Parishville, 1976). The layout of the streets in Parishville is shown in a map, inscribed "A Plan of Parishville by S. Raymond, 1812" (a photograph of which is in the Parish collection at St. Lawrence University). If this layout was conceived by Ramée, it was probably altered in Raymond's plan, for the pattern does not have the clarity one would expect from the architect.

29. Letter from David to John Parish, 1 December 1812, NYHS (book 4, pp. 157–69).

30. Letter from Hoard to Parish, Hoard Letter Book, SLU ("I have been . . . to the spot where the Tavern House was to stand [and] find that the ground is not large enough to set the buildings in the form that Mr. Ramée planned"). Letter from Parish to Church, 23 June 1813, NYHS (book 4, p. 342) (referring to "alterations that might be found necessary in the execution of Mr. Ramée's plans . . . I therefore trust the inconvenience in the plan of the stable and coachhouse for the Tavern has been remedied in the manner you proposed").

31. "Journal of George Parish," p. 290.

32. Hough, *St. Lawrence and Franklin Counties*, p. 424; Parker, p. 80. A series of lithographs of the Parish properties, produced by Salathiel Ellis about 1838, includes a view of a town entitled "Parishville," but it appears to be an imaginary view, as neither the buildings nor the topography seem to correspond to the actual town.

33. Paul V. Turner, "David Parish's Country House Reconstructed," *The Quarterly*, vol. 31 (October 1986), pp. 3–9.

34. Letter from Parish to Church, 19 May 1813, NYHS.

35. Letter from Parish to Hoard, 21 March 1814, NYHS.

36. Letters from Parish to Hoard and Church, 12 April and 9 May 1814, respectively, NYHS.

37. Letter from Smissaert to Parish, 7 October 1814, SLU.

38. "The Journal of George Parish," p. 291.

39. These glass-plate negatives were donated in 1986 to the St. Lawrence Historical Association by Mary C. Burroughs, a descendant of William Abram, who occupied the house in the nineteenth century. The principal description is found in Parker, pp. 83–5.

40. Hough, *St. Lawrence and Franklin Counties*, pp. 448–53. Information provided by Elwood M. Simons of Rossie.

41. Hough, p. 452, suggests that it was built in the 1840s; other sources suggest the 1820s or earlier.

42. It is shown with its chimney in the engraving of Rossie in Hough, opposite p. 452, and in Salathiel Ellis's lithographic view of "Rossie [Ir]onworks"(c. 1838).

43. Hough, *St. Lawrence and Franklin Counties*, pp. 450–1.

44. For Ellis's prints, see Wendy Shadwell, "St. Lawrence County, 1838, as seen through the eyes of Salathiel Ellis," unpublished essay, 1982 (shown to me by Ms. Shadwell, Curator of Prints at the New York Historical Society, which possesses a copy of this series of prints).

45. Shadwell, note 9, citing information from David Houshell, Curator of Technology, The Hagley Museum. See also James M. Ransom, *Vanishing Ironworks of the Ramapos* (New Brunswick, N.J., 1966); John S. Salmon, *The Washington Iron Works of Franklin Co., Virginia* (Richmond, 1986); W. K. V. Gale, *The British Iron and Steel Industry* (Newton Abbot, 1967).

46. *Architecture de C. N. Ledoux* (edition of 1847), pl. 149–50.

47. The construction dates of these houses are given, for example in two articles in a *Watertown Daily Times* series, "Old Houses of the North Country," on file at Jefferson County Historical Association, Watertown, N.Y. In the case of the David Parish House, the Greek-Revival character of certain details of the building indicate a later construction date than the 1810s; if the house was in fact built by Parish, it was no doubt later modified.

48. The photograph was lent to me by Elwood M. Simons of Rossie. Information about the barn is from newspaper clippings and other local sources.

49. Franklin Hough, *History of Jefferson County* (Albany, N.Y., 1854), pp. 85–95.

50. "Journal of George Parish," p. 292.

51. Hough, *Jefferson County*, pp. 86, 94; various newspaper clippings and other documents, provided to me by the rector of St. Michael's Church. I learned of St. Michael's in 1985 from Roger G. Kennedy; its attribution to Ramée had been made in an unpublished paper by Bruce T. Sherwood, of 1975.

52. Letter from Parish to Hoard (Antwerp), 5 April 1816, NYHS (book 6, pp. 282ff); letter from Parish to Hoard, 3 May 1816, NYHS (book 6, p 314); letters from Parish to Rosseel, 3 and 17 May 1816, SLU (nos. 1331, 1336). The last of these letters refers specifically to "the building of the Antwerp church." Letter from Parish to Hoard, 14 June 1816, NYHS (book 6, p. 400).

53. The principal study of the subject is C. Loth and J. T. Sadler, Jr., *The Only Proper Style: Gothic Architecture in America* (Boston, 1975).

54. Letter from Parish to Paul Hochstrasser, 14 April 1813, NYHS (book 4, p. 264).

55. Letters from Van Rensselaer to Parish, 13 June and 9 November 1813, NYHS. Letter from Parish to Van Rensselaer, 1 December 1813, in the Remington Museum, Ogdensburg, according to transcript of the letter in the Larrabee Papers, Union College (the letter could not be found in the Remington Museum when I visited there in 1985). The letters from Van Rensselaer to Parish are in the hand of Stephen Van Rensselaer III (General Van Rennselaer, 1764–1839), according to Norman Rice, of the Albany Institute of History and Art. Van Rensselaer constructed, c. 1817, a house in Albany for his son, Stephen Van Rensselaer IV. This building, which is known only from drawings, has been attributed to the architect Philip Hooker. One may speculate that the plans commissioned from

Ramée were for this house or an early version of it.

56. Ethel C. Olds et al., *Waddington: A Look at our Past* (Ogdensburg, N.Y., 1976); W. O. Wheeler, *The Ogden Family in America* (Philadelphia, 1907); information from Professor Henry V. S. Ogden, 1985.

57. Letters from Louis Hasbrouck to his wife, 20 November and 11 December 1812, 1 January 1813, Ogdensburg Public Library. The letter of 11 December refers to Ramée as "a great architect." Since Hasbrouck and the other Ogdensburg residents would have had little experience for making such a judgment, it was no doubt Parish who introduced Ramée this way.

58. Letter from Parish to Ramée, 17 March 1814, NYHS (book 5, p 146): "Vous trouverez sous ce plis, monsieur, mon check sur la Banque de Pennsylvania pour $550.00 ayant reçu pour votre compte $500. à Schenectady & $50. pour le montant de votre traite sur Mr. D. A. Ogden." There is also a reference to a payment from Ogden to Ramée in a letter from Smissaert to Parish, 16 November 1813, SLU (no. 909): "What am I to do with Ramée's draft on Ogden, in case I should not see Ludlow before I leave town?" Professor H. V. S. Ogden, who has researched the Ogden family during this period, informed me (1985) that "Ludlow" was Thomas Ludlow Ogden, a brother of David A. Ogden, and that "Ogden" was no doubt David A. Ogden.

59. *Parcs et jardins*, pl. 19–20. The plan is identified as "Rapid-long-Island / State of New York." This was probably a variation of the original name of the island, Isle au Rapide Plat.

60. In the mid-nineteenth century, portions of the island were sold by the Ogden family and turned into farms; around 1880 the island was bought by E. S. Crapser, whose descendants continued to use it for farming, until it was acquired by New York State in 1957. Information from Olds et al., *Waddington*, and from Pauline Tedford and Mr. and Mrs. Joel Howard of Waddington, and Cecilia Dewey of Messena, N.Y., all of whom provided me with information about the history of Waddington and Ogden Island.

61. Ethel C. Olds, "The Island House," in *Waddington*, pp. 23–9. The evidence for the later addition of the wings is the fact that their brick walls were reportedly not bonded into the walls of the central part of the house.

62. The best photograph of the coach house (the one reproduced here) is found in the Library of Congress, Prints and Photographs Division. In 1985, I showed it to Mr. Joel Howard of Waddington, who spent most of his life on the island; he said it showed the building as it existed after a fire of 1914, with a new roof and extra dormers, and he thought the photograph was taken by his aunt, Eunice E. Crapser, an accomplished photographer.

63. Joel Howard told me, in 1985, that all the walls of the coach house, including the recessed panels, were solid stone, that the panels were recessed inside as well as outside, and that he believed the stucco coating of the panels was original.

64. A description of the village in 1813 (Hough, *St. Lawrence and Franklin Counties*, p. 344) notes that an "academy" was about to be erected there, which recalls Parish's Academy at Parishville.

65. Olds, *Waddington*, p. 59; "History of St. Paul's Church," *The Quarterly*, vol. 8 (January 1963), pp. 8–15; and various local sources.

66. Olds, *Waddington*, p. 59; "History of St. Paul's," p. 9. This suggestion was perhaps first made by George W. Dalzell, in a letter of 1937 to Harold A. Larrabee, now in the Larrabee Papers at Union College.

67. Church's role is noted in a letter from John S. Chipman to David A. Ogden, preserved at the Waddington Town Hall; it was shown to me in 1985 by Pauline Tedford.

68. My information on Ellerslie comes mainly from correspondence with Professor Henry V. S. Ogden of Ann Arbor, Mich., 1985, and from his articles on the house, in Olds, *Waddington*, pp. 18–22, and *The Quarterly* (April 1976), pp. 4–5, 18, as well as an unpublished manuscript on the Ogden family that he showed me.

69. Letters reveal that Gouverneur Ogden visited Ogdensburg at least twice during the time Ramée was there, at the end of 1812, and that Ogden attended parties at which "Parish and all his family" were also present (letter from Louis Hasbrouck to his wife, 1 January 1813, Ogdensburg Public Library). Parish's "family," in this context, was his houseguests and associates, of which Ramée was one. Moreover, since Ramée was a celebrity in Ogdensburg – because of his fortification designs, his "Russian stoves," and his reputation as a "great architect" (as Hasbrouck stated in one of his letters) – Gouverneur Ogden surely knew of him.

70. The drawing was kindly shown to me in 1982 by Mr. James Duane Featherstonhaugh, present owner of the property.

71. *Jardins irréguliers* (1823), pl. II; *Parcs et jardins* (c. 1839), pl. 4. These two published plans, which are slightly different from one another, are inscribed "Duansburg" [sic]. The present owner of the house possesses a copy of the plate from *Jardins irréguliers*.

72. The original plan and the published versions show somewhat different structures.

73. Information from local newspaper clippings and other sources, in Schenectady County Historical Society.

74. The windows recall, for example, those of Joseph Mangin's New York City Hall, 1802–11. The present porch columns, which have no capitals, are replacements; old photographs show that the original columns had Ionic capitals.

75. These porches are more typical of the work of the Albany architect Philip Hooker, who has been mentioned as the possible architect of the Duane House. (See, for example, the detail of Hooker's Albany Academy, c. 1815, illustrated in Edward W. Root, *Philip Hooker*, New York, 1929, fig. 57.)

76. The oval window in the central part of the stable, however, is not typical of Ramée (who would have preferred a circular window). This stable and its probable Ramée authorship were brought to my attention by Roger G. Kennedy, who mentions it in *Orders From France*, p. 226.

77. Among the buildings in New York State that have been suggested as works of Ramée are the James Le Ray de Chaumont House in Leraysville; the Vincent Le Ray House in Cape Vincent; the Gideon Granger House and Congregational Church in Canandaigua; buildings in Morristown; the Rosseel House in Ogdensburg; Rokeby in Barrytown; and the Livingston House in Hudson. Several of these are discussed in Kennedy, *Orders From France*. For the Le Ray houses, see Claire Bonney, *French Emigré Houses in Jefferson County* (Zurich, 1985), pp. 62–6, 120–8. Bruce T. Sherwood spoke of numerous New York State buildings he believed were by Ramée, in conversation with me in 1985.

78. Wayne Andrews, *Architecture in New York: A Photographic History* (New York, 1969), p. 14; Kennedy, *Orders From France*, pp. 288–91.

79. Kennedy, *Orders From France*, p. 290.

80. Starting about 1815, for instance, Hooker more frequently used an arcaded pattern on the façades of his buildings, as in Ramée's Union College structures. See Douglas G. Bucher and W. Richard Wheeler, *A Neat Plain Modern Style: Philip Hooker and His Contempo-*

raries (Amherst, Mass., 1993), pp. 127, 136, 142, 150, 257.

Chapter 11

I thank the following people who aided my research on Ramée's work for Union College: Ed Polk Douglas, Ruth Ann Evans, Ellen H. Fladger, Daniel Robbins, Ann Seeman, Wayne Somers, and Betty White.

1. For an account of travel by sleigh, see letter from David Parish to John Parish, 8 October 1813, NYHS, book 4, pp. 391–4.

2. Letter from Parish to Joseph Rosseel, 14 January 1813, SLU, no. 701.

3. Letter from Parish to Rosseel, 15 January 1813, described in Larrabee and Hislop's article (see note 9) as being in "Rosseel Coll., St. Lawrence Univ."; I did not find the letter when I examined these documents. According to Larrabee and Hislop's quotation from the letter, Ramée joined Parish in Albany on 15 January 1813, with plans to depart the region the same day.

4. Letters from Parish to Nott, 17 March and 3 November 1813, NYHS, book 4, p. 211; book 5, p. 13.

5. Letter of 17 March 1813, cited in note 4.

6. Payments to Ramée are noted in the college "Treasurer's Vouchers" (Union College Archives), 24 June 1813 ("to Mr. Ramée for drafts and plans 500.00"), 22 March 1814 ("for plan to Ramée 500.00"), and in "Journal of the Treasurer" (according to notes in the Larrabee Papers, Union College Archives), 6 March 1815 ("to cash to Dr. Nott for Ramée $500"). A later college treasurer, Jonathan Pearson, noted Ramée's fee twice in his diary: 25 June 1861 (quoted in text) and 1 June 1858 ("Remay [sic] made a set of drawings at a cost of $1500 for Union College"). The payments to Ramée were apparently made through David Parish; a letter from Parish to the architect, of 17 March 1814, states, "Vous trouverez sous ce pli, monsieur, mon Check sur la Banque de Pennsylvania pour $550.00 ayant reçu pour votre compte $500. à Schenectady. . . " (NYHS, book 5, p. 146).

7. Letter from Parish to General John P. Van Ness, 25 March 1815, National Archives, Record Group no. 24. For more on this letter, and for the exhibition of Ramée's drawings in Philadelphia, see Chapter 12.

8. See note 38 for information on this Klein engraving.

9. The discovery of the drawings is described in Codman Hislop, "The Ramée Plans," *Union Alumni Monthly*, vol. 22 (December 1932), pp. 48–53. The discovery led to research on Ramée by Professor Hislop and especially by Harold A. Larrabee, also a professor at the college. Hislop and Larrabee described their findings in "Joseph Jacques Ramée and the Building of North and South Colleges," *Union Alumni Monthly*, vol. 27 (1938), pp. 1–16. Larrabee alone wrote: "Joseph Jacques Ramée and America's First Unified College Plan," *Franco-American Pamphlet Series*, no. 1 (New York, 1934); "How Ramée Came to Schenectady," *Union Alumni Monthly*, vol. 26 (February 1937), pp. 111–13; "Joseph Jacques Ramée, Architect," *Légion d'Honneur* [New York], vol. 8 (April 1938), pp. 216–21. Larrabee's documentation of his research on Ramée is preserved in the Larrabee Papers, Union College Archives; it has provided the basis of subsequent studies of Ramée's work in America, notably Roy Eugene Graham's "Joseph Jacques Ramée and the French *Emigré* Architects in America," master's thesis, University of Virginia (1968). Also see: Christopher Tunnard, "Minerva's Union," *Architectural Review* (February 1947), pp. 57–62, and "Joseph Jacques Ramée and Union College," *Union Worthies*, no. 19 (1964); and Mendel, Mesick, Cohen, Architects, *The Nott Memorial: A Historic Structure Report* (Schenectady, N. Y. 1973), ch. 1.

10. For the early history of Union College: Franklin B. Hough, *Historical Sketch of Union College* (Washington D. C., 1876); Andrew V. Raymond, *Union University, Its History, Influence, Characteristics and Equipment* (New York, 1907); Codman Hislop, *Eliphalet Nott* (Middletown, Conn., 1971).

11. Hislop, *Eliphalet Nott*, pp. 73, 95.

12. Ibid., pp. 83–4.

13. Hough, *Historical Sketch*, p. 13. Franklin Hough was an alumnus of the Union class of 1841 who became an historian of New York State.

14. Treasurer's records and other documents in the Union College Archives. My research of these documents has been assisted greatly by Ellen Fladger, Union College Archivist.

15. Hooker's Union College building is illustrated in Edward W. Root, *Philip Hooker*.

16. The college adopted this motto in 1796. The influence of eighteenth-century French ideas on Union College in its early years is examined in Samuel B. Fortenbaugh, Jr., *In Order to Form a More Perfect Union* (Schenectady, N. Y., 1978).

17. For Nott's stoves, see Hislop, pp. 255ff.

18. Paul V. Turner, *Campus: An American Planning Tradition* (New York, 1984), pp. 38–46.

19. Treasurer's Vouchers, 20 November 1812 and other dates, Union College Archives.

20. Jonathan Pearson's diary (Union College Archives), entry for 25 June 1861. Pearson added that "some of the alterations may be seen to this day." I can find no evidence of what these "alterations" were.

21. The list is dated and signed "Aug 8/56 J. Pearson." Jonathan Pearson graduated from Union in 1835, joined the faculty as a professor of science in 1839, and was treasurer of the college starting in 1854. His interest in Ramée's drawings was probably due to his involvement, as college treasurer, in new construction on the campus. The numbers written on Ramée's drawings, corresponding to Pearson's numbered list, are in no consistent order (respecting the drawings' chronology, etc.) and evidently were written by Pearson. Each sheet of paper has one number, regardless of how many drawings are on its recto and verso, except for one sheet that bears the numbers 25 and 26 (I refer to it simply as sheet 25 in this text).

22. At first inspection, there seemed to me to be at least three different hands in the drawings, with two distinct ones in the main inscriptions: one a looser, the other a tighter script. But on closer study, they appear to be merely variations of the same hand.

23. Letters from Parish to Nott, 17 March and 3 November 1813, NYHS, book 4, p. 211; book 5, p. 13. "Professor McAuley" was Thomas Macauley, who later concerned himself especially with the layout of the college grounds.

24. The exact duration of Ramée's visit to Schenectady is not known, but it is mentioned in letters from Parish of 14 April and 19 May 1813. Ramée was still in the area (in Albany) in mid-June, as seen in a letter of 13 June from Stephen Van Rensselaer to Parish (for this letter, see Chapter 10).

25. These drawings are on sheets 3–6, 8 verso, 12 verso, 31–4, 38–40. Pearson's list describes some of these drawings as being of the "Rectangular Chapel," evidently to distinquish this structure from the rotunda. The drawings themselves are inscribed simply "Union College." Several of them bear handwriting that is identifiably that of

Ramée (especially sheets 38, 39).

26. These are sheets 8 verso and 12 verso. Ramée reused them to draw plans of the colonnades attached to North and South colleges.

27. The design can be compared, for example, to a "Town Hall" in Isaac Ware's *A Complete Body of Architecture* (London, 1756), pl. 49. The English qualities of Ramée's Central Building help explain Talbot Hamlin's remark (in *Greek Revival Architecture in America*, New York, 1944, p. 42) that Ramée's Union College buildings "are neither French nor English in design; but of the two influences it is the English that predominates." Hamlin illustrated his text with Ramée's drawing of the Central Building façade.

28. For Nott's land purchases, see Trustees' Minutes of 26 July 1815 (Union College Archives).

29. Sheet 27 and the versos of sheets 22, 25, 41. Sheet 22 verso has rough pencil sketches of three different plans. Sheet 25 verso has a small sketch plan in one corner, besides the main plan on the sheet. Sheet 27 has an overlay, glued onto the center of the sheet, with a variation of the plan underneath it.

30. *Parcs et jardins*, pl. 13, inscribed "College de l'union à Schenectady, Etat de Neu-York. Ramée 1813." The discovery of the nearly identical drawing, in 1890 in "an old print-shop in Paris" by a Union College alumnus, is described in *A Record of the . . . 100th Anniversary of . . . Union College* (New York, 1897), p. 52; Raymond, *Union University*, vol. 1, p. 148 (which identifies the alumnus as William E. Benjamin); and the *Union Alumni Monthly* (December 1914), p. 26. The drawing is now in the college archives.

31. My hypothetical reconstruction of the order of execution of the site plans is as follows: 1. Sheet 22 verso, plan in center of sheet. 2. Sheet 41 verso. 3. Sheet 22 verso, plan at left. 4. Sheet 22 verso, plan at right. 5. Sheet 25 verso, plan in center. 6. Sheet 25 verso, tiny sketch in upper-right corner. 7. Sheet 27, original plan (under the overlay). 8. Sheet 27, overlay plan.

32. For example, sheet 41 verso.

33. Sheets 25 verso, 22 verso (the two smaller plans), 27 (the plan under the overlay).

34. Sheet 27.

35. The drawings by Ramée referred to here are on sheets 22 verso, 25 verso, 41 verso. For the design by Vien (whose first name is not known): J.-M. Pérouse de Montclos, *Les Prix de Rome*, p. 202. A design by J. C. Bonnard, similar to Vien's, in the same Academy competition of 1787, had a circular chapel as in Ramée's plan, but was less similar to Ramée's plan in other respects (Pérouse de Montclos, p. 203) The similarity of Bonnard's design to Ramée's was pointed out in Mendel, Mesick, Cohen, p. 13.

36. This elevation sketch is found to the left of the site plan on the verso of sheet 25. The length of the range can be determined because the scale of the elevation sketch is the same as that of the site plan on this sheet, as shown by the placement and dimensions of North College, at the right end of the elevation.

37. The full listing is "a large view (hanging in the Treasurer's Office) of all the buildings and foreground." Pearson, who listed the drawings, was Treasurer at that time. I can find no indication in college records of what happened to this drawing.

38. The engraving, which measures 17 × 30 in., is known in three copies preserved in the Union College Archives. Inscribed: "J. Klein, del't," "Wm Phelps, Printer," "V. Balch, Sculpt, Albany." Balch is listed in Albany city directories in 1818 and 1819, Phelps from 1816 to 1822.

39. This oil painting, measuring c. 23 × 72 in., presently (1987) hangs in the President's House at the college. William C. Givens (1794–1887) was of a hotel-owning family in Schenectady. I have not been able to find other evidence of his activity as an artist.

40. Trustees' Minutes, 25 July 1815. Hough, *Historical Sketch*, p. 14.

41. See earlier reference to Pearson's diary entry of 25 June 1861 in note 20.

42. These sketches, showing only the north end of South College, are on sheet 25 verso.

43. The intended uses of the buildings are described in the Trustees' Minutes of 26 July 1814. Later in the century, Hough (*Historical Sketch*, p. 23) said of North and South Colleges: "The end portions are used as residences for professors and the central part as dormitories for students. This central portion has three separate entrances front and rear, with four rooms on each floor, making, originally, forty-eight rooms in each college."

44. Hough's 1876 account of the college described the buildings as being "of brick, roughcast with ash-colored cement, with pilaster, arches, and trimming in white" (*Historical Sketch*, p. 24). It has occasionally been stated that the Union College buildings were originally built of exposed brick and only later were stuccoed or roughcast. But Ramée's elevation drawing of the President's House shows the walls roughcast and multicolored; and an early description states that North and South Colleges were "of brick, stuccoed in imitation of 'white granite'" (Horatio Gates Spafford, *A Gazeteer of the State of New York*, Albany, 1824, p. 474).

45. For Peyre's Neubourg House, of the 1760s, see Allan Braham, *The Architecture of the French Enlightenment*, p. 85; R. Middleton and D. Watkin, *Neoclassical and Nineteenth-Century Architecture* (New York, 1980), pp. 146–7. For Ledoux's Hosten Houses and other works, see Michel Gallet, *Claude-Nicolas Ledoux*, pp. 209ff. Didier Coupaye has pointed out to me that the Caserne Rougé in Ramée's native city Givet (described in Chapter 1) was similar to North and South College in the functional sense that it had sections at the ends for officers' quarters.

46. These "colonnades" were built in 1815 or 1816. In January 1817 Nott wrote that "two buildings four stories high and 200 feet long are finished, together with a wing to each, two stories high and 170 feet long, besides two houses for boarding with out-houses, etc." (letter from Nott to Samuel Nott, 20 January 1817, Union College Archives).

47. It seems that these terminating buildings were originally called the "small colleges." One of Ramée's drawings shows two cornice designs, labeled "for the two Colonnades" and ". . . of the President's House and small colleges."

48. Hough described these uses in 1876 (*Historical Sketch*, p. 23). The terminating buildings, called Geological Hall and Philosophical Hall, were constructed in the 1850s following plans drawn by William J. Woollett, an Albany architect (Union College Archives), evidently based on Ramée's drawings. Jonathan Pearson wrote (in his diary, 4 June 1855): "The building erected in 1852 for Phil. & Chem. department [i.e., the north building] was originally intended for a professor's or president's house, and to change it . . . was no small difficulty. Ditto, for the one we are now erecting [i.e., the south building, Geological Hall]."

49. Sheet 41, entitled "Two different sections for the Colonnades."

50. One drawing showing part of a colonnade (sheet 43) bears the traces of a horizontal line, subsequently erased; this line suggests

that Ramée was considering whether to make the roof conventional or shedlike.

51. Sheets 13–15, 30, 35, 43.

52. Sheet 43, inscribed "Front elevation of the President's House."

53. Werner Szambien pointed this out to me, in conversation following a talk on Ramée I gave in Paris in 1989, in which I showed the Union College drawings.

54. The identification of the rotunda as a chapel (which has been questioned in previous descriptions of Ramée's design) is supported by various evidence. Pearson, criticizing Ramée's plan in his diary (4 June 1855), wrote, "There was no plan for anything but lodging rooms for the students. . . with a great circular building for a chapel capable of holding at least 2000 persons!" Also, Pearson's list of Ramée's drawings indicates that several of the now-lost drawings of the rotunda were inscribed "The Chapel" (since Pearson put these words in quotation marks; he seems to have used quotation marks in his list only for inscriptions actually on the drawings).

55. Treasurer's Vouchers, 12 November 1813.

56. For this building, now called the Nott Memorial, see Sarah B. Landau, *Edward T. and William A. Potter, American Victorian Architects* (New York, 1979); Mendel, Mesick, Cohen, *The Nott Memorial.*

57. These missing plans of the rotunda were evidently borrowed by the architect Edward T. Potter when he was designing the structure that was actually constructed; the college treasurer, Jonathan Pearson, noted in his diary (3 June 1858) that "Edward Potter called at the Treasurer's office today for the old plans of Remay for the Round Chapel" (Mendel, Mesick, Cohen, p. 140).

58. The working drawings are on sheets 23, 24, 28, 29, and an unnumbered sheet. The marginal sketches are on sheets 22 verso and 25 verso.

59. Sheet 25 verso. The Doric order is shown on sheet 23.

60. This is seen most clearly in the ink-drawn site plan that was discovered in Paris in 1890; it is more faintly visible in the site plan on sheet 25 verso.

61. Circles of trees are found, for instance, in designs for mausolea and other memorial buildings, drawing on Hadrian's tomb and other ancient models. For French examples, see Richard Etlin, *The Architecture of Death.*

62. Therese O'Malley, "Landscape Gardening in the Early National Period," in Edward J. Nygren, ed., *Views and Visions: American Landscape before 1830* (Washington, D. C., 1986), p. 151. See also Monique Mosser, "Le Temple et la montagne. . . ," *Revue de l'art*, no. 83 (1989), pp. 21–35.

63. Sheets 11, 37, 42.

64. Sheet 44.

65. It is puzzling that the connecting wall, in this drawing, is shown with pilasters, not an arcade (as in Ramée's other Union buildings), and that the building to which the wall connects has a rusticated surface (unlike South College).

66. Sheets 27 and 7, respectively.

67. Pearson's diary, 21 April 1855.

68. For contemporary views of Yale and the College of Rhode Island – the colleges Nott knew best – see Turner, *Campus*, figs. 39, 45.

69. Pearson's diary, 22 September 1855. Also see entries of 30 March 1854, 4 June 1855, and 1 June 1858.

70. This was Cow Horn Creek, which no longer exists; its nineteenth-century course, and that of Hans Groot's Kill, are shown on an 1866 atlas of Albany and Schenectady.

71. Such vegetable gardens can be seen in many of the plans in Ramée's *Parcs et jardins*; one of these (pl. 3) identifies the area as "potager." Raymond W. Gastil has shown me a paper he wrote as a student at Princeton, in which he examined this aspect of Ramée's plan for Union.

72. Perhaps the nearest precedent was John Trumbull's master plan for Yale College, of 1792, which included some irregular landscaping, but only behind the buildings (see Turner, *Campus*, fig. 37). Also of interest is an anonymous plan for naturalistic landscaping around the President's House in Washington, which has been attributed to Jefferson or to Latrobe and dated between 1807 and 1818. See Therese O'Malley, "Landscape Gardening," and "Art and Science in American Landscape Architecture: The National Mall, Washington, D. C., 1791–1852," PhD dissertation, University of Pennsylvania, 1989; F. D. Nichols and R. E. Griswold, *Thomas Jefferson, Landscape Architect* (Charlottesville, Va., 1978), pp. 73–4; D. B. Chase, "The Beginnings of the Landscape Tradition in America," *Historic Preservation* (January–March 1973), p. 39.

73. This oval lithograph, probably the most frequently reproduced image of Ramée's plan for Union College, is inscribed "Drawn by D. Herron, junr., of Class '59" and "Lithy. of G. W. Lewis, 122 Fulton St., N. Y." The lithographer George W. Lewis was at this address from 1856 to 1859. There is also a rectangular version of this lithograph, inscribed "Litho. of Lewis & Goodwin, 453 Broadway, Albany, N. Y.," probably executed in the 1860s.

74. Hough, *Historical Sketch*, p. 25. Professor Macauley's participation in the design of the college is noted in a letter from Parish to Nott, 3 November 1813, NYHS, book 5, p. 13 ("Mr. Ramée has promised his attention to Professor McAwley's letter – the plans required of him will be forwarded shortly").

75. For Jackson's Garden, see Richard Schermerhorn, Jr., "Union College and the Jackson Garden," *The American Architect*, vol. 124 (19 December 1923), pp. 541–4; Marian Osgood Fox, "In a College Garden," *House and Garden*, vol. 75 (May 1939), pp. 34, 35, 101.

76. Fox, "In a College Garden." The English visitor is not identified; nor is the date of Olmsted's visit. Susan Hines, of the Frederick Law Olmsted Papers at American University, has informed me that she can find no record of a visit to Union College by Olmsted. After his retirement, however, his firm did some consulting work for the College in 1895.

77. Talbot Hamlin, *Greek Revival Architecture in America* (New York, 1944), p. 42.

78. Turner, *Campus*, pp. 76–87.

79. The possibility that Latrobe transmitted Ramée's influence to Jefferson was suggested by Christopher Tunnard, in "Joseph Jacques Ramée and Union College" (*Union Worthies*, no. 19, 1964, p. 12), and William H. Pierson, Jr., in *American Buildings and Their Architects*, vol. 1 (New York, 1976), p. 475, note 8.20.

80. This sketch and the corresponding site plan are on sheet 25 verso. For Latrobe's letter to Jefferson, of 24 July 1817, see Turner, *Campus*, pp. 83–4.

81. For this exhibition, see Chapter 12.

82. For these letters, see Chapter 12.

83. For Latrobe's acquaintance with Parish, see John C. Van Horne, ed., *The Correspondence and Miscellaneous Papers of Benjamin Henry Latrobe*, vol. 2 (New Haven, 1986), p. 722.

84. Even before Latrobe advised Jefferson on the University of Virginia plan, he may have been influenced by Ramée's Union Col-

lege design. His own plan for a National University in Washington, of 1816, has a three-sided courtyard and a domed church (Turner, *Campus*, pp. 62, 66).

85. Paul V. Turner, "Notes toward a catalogue of early images of Union College architecture," unpublished paper (1982), copy in Union College Archives. Most of the nineteenth-century images of Ramée's design are evidently based on Klein's engraving.

86. Turner, *Campus*, pp. 169–74.

87. Leland Roth, *McKim, Mead and White, Architects* (New York, 1983), pp. 188–90.

88. Montgomery Schuyler, "Architecture of American Colleges, no. IX," *Architectural Record*, vol. 30 (December 1911), pp. 549–53.

89. Schermerhorn, "Union College and the Jackson Garden," p. 541.

Chapter 12

I thank the following people who aided my research on Ramée's work in Philadelphia and Baltimore: Robert L. Alexander, Jeffrey Cohen, Roy Goodman, Dean Krimmel, William Lang, Cheryl Leibold, Mary Markey, Paul F. Norton, C. Ford Peatross, Mark Reinberger, Richard E. Slavin III, and John C. Van Horne.

1. J. A. Paxton, *Philadelphia Directory* (1813): "Ramée J. architect opposite 40 South Eighth." Parish's address was 1 York Buildings, on Walnut Street at Washington Square.

2. *Kite's Philadelphia Directory* (1814): "Ramée Joseph, N.E. cor. Chesnut and Tenth." The view of the buildings on Chesnut Street is found in J. Rae, *Rae's Philadelphia Pictorial Directory* (1851). No Philadelphia directory exists for 1815, and Ramée is not listed in the 1816 directory. See also the entry on Ramée in Sandra L. Tatman and Roger W. Moss, eds., *Biographical Dictionnary of Philadelphia Architects, 1700–1930* (Boston, 1985), p. 642.

3. Edgar P. Richardson, "The Athens of America, 1800–1825," in Russell F. Weigley, ed., *Philadelphia, A 300-Year History* (New York, c. 1982), p. 218.

4. For Latrobe's Burd House, erected ca 1802: Talbot Hamlin, *Benjamin Henry Latrobe* (New York, 1955), p. 150 and pl. 15. David Parish's house, which had the address 1 York Row or 1 York Buildings, was at the southwest corner of the intersection of Walnut and Seventh streets, across from Washington Square. The house had been built after 1807 by John Meany, based partly on plans supplied by Latrobe; see John C. Van Horne, ed., *The Correspondence and Miscellaneous Papers of Benjamin Henry Latrobe*, vol. 2 (New Haven, 1986), p. 456; vol. 3 (1988), p. 523; brought to my attention by Jeffrey Cohen. Parish is recorded in Philadelphia directories as living at this address from 1813 to 1816.

5. See Appendix.

6. Richardson, "Athens of America," pp. 208–9.

7. The story of the monument is documented in J. Jefferson Miller II, "Baltimore's Washington Monument," master's thesis, University of Delaware (1962), and in two publications by the same author, "The Designs for the Washington Monument in Baltimore," *Journal of the Society of Architectural Historians*, vol. 23 (March 1964), pp. 19–26, and *The Washington Monument in Baltimore* (Baltimore, 1966).

8. Robert L. Alexander, *The Architecture of Maximilian Godefroy* (Baltimore, 1974).

9. Alexander, pp. 72–3. Godefroy exhibited six drawings for the monument at the Pennsylvania Academy in 1811; their catalogue descriptions are a bit unclear, but reveal that a couple of the designs were in the form of rotundas, with a statue of Washington beneath or below the dome, and at least two were in the form of arches, as shown in the one drawing that survives. (A. W. Rutledge, *Cumulative Record of Exhibition Catalogues, The Pennsylvania Academy of the Fine Arts, 1807–1870*, Philadelphia, 1955, p. 82.)

10. *The Weekly Register*, Baltimore (20 March 1813), p. 56.

11. Miller (1966), p. 5. The identification of Rogers as the author of the obelisk design was made by Robert L. Alexander, in "Nicholas Rogers, Gentleman-Architect of Baltimore," *Maryland Historical Magazine*, vol. 78 (Summer 1983), pp. 94–5.

12. Miller, "Baltimore's Washington Monument," p. 38.

13. Miller (1964 article, p. 19) states that Godefroy's triumphal arch was "over" the statue of Washington, but the elevation drawing shows that the statue is in front of the arch, and the inscription on the drawing says only that the arch was "designed to *accompany* a pedestrian or equestrian statue" (Alexander, *Godefroy*, p. 75, note 27; emphasis added).

14. Peale Museum, Baltimore, drawing no. CB-5472.

15. These wreaths appear to have dates inscribed in them, but these are merely indicated impressionistically in the drawing, as is the inscription in the attic of the arch. Similar bands of wreaths are found in the work of Percier and Fontaine, for instance in their *Recueil de décoration intérieure* (Paris, 1801), figs. 37, 50.

16. For examples in the work of Ledoux, see *Architecture de C. N. Ledoux* (1849 edition), pl. 29, 287.

17. That Ramée had been inspired by Ledoux's use of this motif is supported by a statement his son Daniel made in the introduction to the 1847 publication of Ledoux's works: "Nous recommandons à l'attention des architectes la jolie façade de la maison de mademoiselle Guimard, qui a été copiée souvent par bon nombre d'architectes." It is possible that Ramée got the idea of incorporating columns within a triumphal arch from a French academic design by F. N. Pagot, which had won the Grand Prix in 1803 and was published in 1806 (Détournelle et Vaudoyer, *Projets d'architecture . . . qui ont mérité les grands prix*, Paris, 1806, unnumbered plate). The elevation drawing of Pagot's design appears to show columns and a sculptural group under a triumphal arch, although in fact the columns and sculpture are in a courtyard behind the façade, as the ground plan shows.

18. Among the few earlier urban designs in the United States that could be compared to Ramée's is Charles Bulfinch's Tontine Crescent in Boston, of the 1790s.

19. John W. Reps, *The Making of Urban America: A History of City Planning in the United States* (Princeton, 1965), ch. 9; Therese O'Malley, "Landscape Gardening in the Early American Period," in E. J. Nygren, ed., *Views and Visions: American Landscape before 1830* (Washington, D. C., 1986); Therese O'Malley, "Art and science in American Landscape Architecture: The National Mall, Washington, D.C., 1791–1852," Ph.D. dissertation, University of Pennsylvania (1989).

20. Harold Kirker, *The Architecture of Charles Bulfinch* (Cambridge, Mass., 1969), pp. 79–85, 258–62. John Reps has remarked on the "unaccountably few American spaces on the London models" in the decades following the Revolution (*Making of Urban America*, p. 145).

21. Miller, "Baltimore's Washington Monument," p. 45.

22. For example, the addition to Parish's house at Parishville (letter from Parish to Daniel Hoard, 21 March 1814, NYHS, book 5, pp. 152–3).

23. Letter from Parish to Daniel Hoard, 12 April 1814, NYHS, book 5, p. 201. Ramée's letter to Joseph Rosseel, of 11 February 1815 (see below), reveals that he had not been to the North Country for several years.

24. A. W. Rutledge, *Cumulative Record of the Exhibition Catalogues, The Pennsylvania Academy of the Fine Arts, 1808–1870* (Philadelphia, 1955). The exhibition took place in the Academy's building on Chesnut Street, close to Ramée's residence at Chesnut and Tenth.

25. *Fourth Annual Exhibition of the Columbian Society of Artists and the Pennsylvania Academy*, Philadelphia (May 1814), pp. 9, 21, 26. Although this catalogue is dated May 1814, the exhibition evidently opened in June. An advertisement in the *True American Commercial Advertiser* (Philadelphia, 8 June 1814) states that the exhibition "will open on Monday, the 16th instant, to continue for six weeks only" (information from Cheryl Leibold of the Pennsylvania Academy of Fine Arts, 1989).

26. "Review of the Fourth Annual Exhibition of the Columbian Society of Artists and the Pennsylvania Academy," *The Port Folio*, 3rd series, vol. 4, no. 1 (July 1814), pp. 94–100 (remarks on Ramée on p. 96). The reviewer is not identified.

27. Paul F. Norton, "The Architect of Calverton," *Maryland Historical Magazine*, vol. 76 (Summer 1981), pp. 113–23.

28. Letter from Parish to D. A. Smith, 10 June 1816, NYHS, book 6, p. 382.

29. It has been suggested that Ramée merely enlarged an existing house at Calverton and created new façades (Alexander, "Nicholas Rogers," pp. 101 and 105, note 28), but Parish's references to Ramée's design, quoted in the text, indicate that it was more than just a remodeling; perhaps the new house replaced an existing one.

30. Letter from Parish to G. Smissaert, 17 December 1815, NYHS, book 6, p. 132. That Ramée was staying only temporarily with Smith is indicated by Parish's reference to some purchases for the architect that "shall be delivered to him when he returns to Philadelphia." Latrobe's reference is in a letter to R. G. Harper, 22 October 1815, quoted in Hamlin, *Latrobe*, pp. 488–9.

31. Letters from Parish to Dennis A. Smith, 12 January and 20 January 1816, NYHS, book 6, pp. 188–9, 207.

32. Letter from Latrobe to Smith, 21 September 1816. Van Horne, *Correspondence of Latrobe*, vol. 3, p. 892, note 10.

33. Peale Museum, Baltimore. The photograph is dated 1874 by the museum.

34. Norton, "Architect of Calverton," fig. 1.

35. Norton, p. 119, proposes that the house was constructed by the architect-builder R. C. Long, Sr.

36. Ramée, *Recueil de cottages*, pl. 22.

37. A letter from G. Simpson to the banker Stephen Girard, 10 July 1812, introducing Virchaux, described the latter as "the confidential clerk of Mr. Parish" (Girard Papers, American Philosophical Library, Philadelphia).

38. David Parish to his father, 1 December 1812, NYHS, book 4, pp. 161–2. P. G. Walters ("David Parish in America," p. 47) states that Parish lent Ramée and his partner $40,000 for this business, but the letters Walters cites do not mention such a loan. In another letter, Parish identified the previous owner of the business as a "Mr. Chardon" (Parish to Vincent LeRay, 12 April 1814, NYHS, book 5, p. 200). Anthony Chardon was a leading wallpaper manufacturer in Philadelphia at this time, but according to Catherine Lynn (*Wallpaper in America*, New York, 1980, pp. 246, 257), he remained in business into the 1820s.

39. David Parish to his father, 8 October 1813, NYHS, book 4, p. 393. The first known references to the firm as "Virchaux & Co." are in the 1814 copyright depositions (see note 40). It is listed in *Robinson's [Philadelphia] Directory* (1816), as "Virchaux and Co., paper hanging manufacturers, 85 Chesnut."

40. These wallpapers were brought to my attention by C. Ford Peatross of the Prints and Photographs Division, Library of Congress. I am grateful also to Richard E. Slavin III, of F. Schumacher & Co. (which is presently reproducing the papers), who provided me with further information about them. On the back of each piece of wallpaper is written the name of the Virchaux firm, the date of copyright deposit, and a number (from 41 to 70, not continuous), corresponding to the number on a separate caption strip. Each caption strip describes the design and its colors and ascribes the design to the firm or to Ramée, as noted in the text.

41. These are designs 66–7 (one design, consisting of several pieces), 68, and 70. The deposit dates of designs 68 and 70 are, respectively, 24 April 1816 and 27 April 1816. The date of design 66–7 cannot presently by ascertained, as the wallpaper is framed for museum exhibition; but it is no doubt just before the other two dates, since the deposit dates of all the other wallpapers follow the order of their design numbers.

42. It is not known exactly when Ramée left the firm, since his name was not in the firm's title, but it is likely that he dissolved his partnership with Virchaux shortly before leaving the country.

43. According to Richard Slavin, "The Virchaux [wallpapers], intended to compete with French imports, [are] of the finest quality. American-made papers up to this time were usually mediocre at best; with this group of wallpapers and borders, Virchaux truly improved the U. S. product" (communication with author, September 1993). For wallpapers of this period, see Odile Nouvel, *Wallpapers of France, 1800–1850* (New York, 1981); Françoise Teynac et al., *Wallpaper: A History* (New York, 1982), ch. 3–4; Lynn, *Wallpaper in America*.

44. This is number 70, described in the copyright caption as: "Ground composed of grape leaves, in bouquets, imitating embroidery; upon one side a spiral garland composed of roses, jessamin and annemone entwined round a bamboo."

45. Number 42. For the use of rich colors, see Lynn, pp. 149–50.

46. This design consists of four separate pieces of wallpaper, two numbered 66, the other two 67. The texts of the caption strips are not presently available, as they have been enclosed behind the wallpaper in a frame, for exhibition. But Ford Peatross tells me that the captions name Ramée as the designer, as in the cases of numbers 68 and 70.

47. This is number 68, described in the copyright caption as: "Design of double columns, ornamented with grape and vine leaves; another part ornamented with losanges, placed horizontally forming the intervals." It consists of two pieces, one having the double columns, the other the "losanges" (the X-shaped rails). The top border for this design is missing; it no doubt bore the number 69.

48. Geometric patterns of a somewhat similar type, in French wallpapers mostly from the 1820s and later, are illustrated in Nouvel (*Wallpapers of France*, pp. 61, 63); therefore, earlier French precedents for Ramée's abstract pattern in this design are possible. But the combination of the geometry and the ironwork fence seems to be Ramée's invention.

49. The company is listed as "Virchaux & Borrek*ins*" in Philadelphia directories of 1817 and 1818; but one of the firm's

receipts (preserved at the Winterthur Museum) is printed thus: "Bought of Virchaux & Borrekens, at their Paper Hanging Warehouse, No. 151, Chesnut St." The only person of either name, listed in Philadelphia directories I have seen, is "Borrekens, H. P., merchant, 85 Chesnut" (*Paxton's Directory*, 1818).

50. For Virchaux & Borrekens's importation of French wallpapers in 1817, see Lynn, *Wallpaper in America,* pp. 216, 217, 249. The firm is listed in the Philadelphia directories (1817–18) as "hanging paper manufacturers," but since Virchaux's known copyright deposits end with Ramée's designs of 1816, it may be that the firm simply continued to manufacture its earlier designs, supplementing them with imports.

51. Letter from Parish to Van Ness, 25 March 1815, National Archives, Record Group no. 42; brought to my attention by John C. Van Horne of The Library Company of Philadelphia.

52. Letter from Van Ness to Parish, 25 April 1815, same source as preceding note.

53. See, for example, letter from Parish to Joseph Rosseel, 7 June 1814, SLU, no. 1031.

54. Letter from Ramée to Rosseel, 11 February 1815, SLU, no. 1161; brought to my attention by Roger G. Kennedy. The full text of the letter is as follows: "Philadelphia le 11. février 1815 / Mon cher Monsieur Rossell [sic], vous aurez apris par Mr. P. que j'avais le projet de retourner en Europe, je me finirai probablement dans le voisinage de votre ville natale, si toutefois vous voulez me charger de commissions pour votre famille, je les ferai avec plaisir, je profiterai probablement de la première bonne occasion qui se présentera. Je comptais vous revoir chaque saison à Ogdensburg mais des événements de differente nature ont toujours dérangé ces beaux *Brochets* [underlined]. / J'espère que vos dames auxquelles je vous prie d'offrir mes compliments auront fais beaucoup de progrès dans le français, et vous dans le Jardinage, j'ai apris que vous rivalisiez du mieux avec l'ami Rosse [probably John Ross, another of Parish's agents in Ogdensburg]. / Cy joint la note des déboursés pour couture gramm. & dictionnaire. Je présume qu'elle balancera le montant de la flanel que vous avez bien voulu me céder. / Agréez je vous prie l'assurance de mon sincère attachem't / Ramée." At the end of the letter is a list of three items and their prices: "Dictionnaire $5.- / grammaire 2.- / couture 1.50 / [total] 8.50."

55. Vincent Nolte, *Funfzig Jahre in beiden Hemisphären* (Hamburg, 1854), p. 196. Nolte described Hénard as "bon enfant, bon mangeur, bon faiseur de calembourgs."

56. "La famille Ramée comptait retourner en Europe cette année, mais elle a déféré l'exécution de ce plan à cause des événemens qui y sont arrivés au mois de mars." Letter from Parish to J. B. Baudry of Nantes, 14 July 1815, NYHS, book 6, pp. 63–4; brought to my attention by Roger G. Kennedy.

57. Mark Reinberger, "The Baltimore Exchange and its Place in the Career of Benjamin Henry Latrobe," PhD dissertation, Cornell University (1988). The architectural competition was announced in the Baltimore newspapers on 30 October 1815, but an informal competition had been going on for several months (ibid., p. 24). The newspaper announcement gave 1 January 1816 as the deadline for submitting plans.

58. Letter from Latrobe to Godefroy, 19 July 1815. Van Horne, *Correspondence of Latrobe*, vol. 3, pp. 674–5.

59. Hamlin, *Latrobe*, pp. 488–9. Van Horne, *Correspondence of Latrobe*, vol. 3, p. 716.

60. The sketch is in one of Mills's journals ("Pocket Memorandum Book for 1816," p. 9; Joseph Toner Papers, Library of Congress). Reinberger, "Baltimore Exchange," p. 271 and fig. 38.

61. Reinberger, "Baltimore Exchange," pp. 269–70.

62. Letter from Parish to his father, 2 April 1816, NYHS, book 6, p. 270.

63. Letter from Parish to Joseph Rosseel, 21 June 1816, SLU, no. 1341. ("On Thursday next I go to New York, with the intention of embarking about the 10th of next month.")

64. Letter from Parish to Smith, 10 June 1816, NYHS, book 6, p. 382. ("Enclosed. . . Mr. Ramée's receipt for $1500 which I have paid him this day.")

65. Letter from Parish to Lafayette, 24 January 1816, NYHS, book 6, pp. 241–2. A subsequent letter from Parish's secretary to Ramée (3 February 1816, NYHS, book 6, p. 257) shows that Parish had paid the $200 to Lafayette from his own funds and then billed the amount to Ramée.

66. Among the architects who used the motif about the time Ramée was in America, or shortly after, were: Latrobe (Baltimore Exchange, as noted in the text); Mills (Washington Hall, Philadelphia; St. John's Episcopal Church, Baltimore); John Haviland (Moody House, Haverill, Mass.); and William Strickland (St. John's Church, Philadelphia).

67. Talbot Hamlin, *Greek Revival Architecture in America*, p. 42.

68. Ibid., p. 42.

69. Examples of the picturesque garden appeared occasionally in America in the eighteenth century. Most notable was Jefferson's layout of the grounds of Monticello, after he had traveled in France and England following the American Revolution. See O'Malley, "Landscape Gardening in the Early American Period"; James D. Kornwolf, "The Picturesque in the American Garden and Landscape before 1800," *Eighteenth Century Life* (January 1983), pp. 93–106. For William Hamilton, probably the most knowledgeable amateur garden designer around 1800 (besides Jefferson), see Richard J. Betts, "The Woodlands," *Winterthur Portfolio*, vol. 14 (Autumn 1979), pp. 213–34. Roger G. Kennedy has pointed out to me the American landscape designs of the Frenchmen C.-J. Sauthier and Pierre Pharoux, in the 1760s and 1790s, respectively (see Kennedy, *Orders From France*, passim).

70. Latrobe's views on landscape are found mainly in his "Essay on Landscape" (devoted principally to landscape drawing and painting), which he wrote for an acquaintance in 1798–9. See Edward C. Carter II, ed., *The Virginia Journals of Benjamin Henry Latrobe*, vol. 2 (New Haven, 1977), ch. 11 and 12.

71. See Chapter 14.

72. The most important of Downing's landscape publications was *A Treatise on the Theory and Practice of Landscape Gardening, Adapted to North America* (New York, 1841). Christopher Tunnard recognized the kinship of Ramée and Downing when he wrote that "[Ramée's] landscapes are full of devices that. . . Downing was to make familiar twenty-five years later – the walk or drive around the periphery, the artificial stream or pond which one came upon as a surprise, the emphasis on tree forms, pointed, as in the case of fir and spruce, or the rounded maple and elm." ("Joseph Jacques Ramée and Union College," in *Union Worthies*, Schenectady, no. 19, 1964, p. 11.)

73. George B. Tatum states that there is no mention of Ramée in Downing's writings; see "Andrew Jackson Downing, Arbiter of American Taste," Ph.D. dissertation, Princeton University (1949), p. 93.

74. Downing, *Treatise*, fig. 2 and p. 30.

75. For The Hill (south of Hudson, New York; house erected c. 1790s, demolished in the 1970s), see H. D. Eberlein and C. V. Hubbard, *Historic Houses of the Hudson Valley* (New York, 1942), pp. 114, 116, pl. 100–2; Kennedy, *Orders From France*, pp. 46–7, 66–9. If Ramée did conduct work at The Hill, his client would have been the widow of Henry Walter Livingston, who died in 1810 (Eberlein and Hubbard, p. 116).

76. The barn at The Hill was brought to my attention by Roger G. Kennedy.

77. For this aspect of Olmsted's work, see my *Campus, An American Planning Tradition* (New York, 1984), pp. 140–50. One of the institutions Olmsted helped plan was Cornell University at Ithaca, N. Y.; it was perhaps at the time of his visits there, around 1867, that Olmsted saw Union College.

78. *Jardins irréguliers*, plate VIII. See the following chapter for information on this publication. Plate VIII is accompanied by a sheet of text, in French, English, and German, describing the numbered parts of the icehouse shown in the section and plan.

79. Among the few circular icehouses in America in Ramée's time was one at Montpelier, James Madison's estate in Virginia, probably designed by Thomas Jefferson (Nichols and Griswold, *Thomas Jefferson, Landscape Architect*, pp. 117, 122); but this structure is very different from Ramée's icehouse. Circular icehouses were actually more common in Europe. One can note, for instance, two designs by an architect named Dubois, published in J. C. Krafft's *Recueil d'architecture civile* (1812), pl. 75, 76. Numerous European examples, of various periods, are illustrated in A. W. Reinink and J. G. Vermeulen, *Ijskelders, koeltechnieken van weleer* (Groningen, 1981). Professor Reinink has kindly corresponded with me on the subject of icehouses.

80. John Beale Bordley, *Essays and Notes on Husbandry and Rural Affairs* (Philadelphia, 1799; second edition, 1801). The chapter on icehouses is found on pp. 364–70 in the first edition, pp. 304–9 in the second. The text refers to an illustration, which however is missing from all the copies of the work I have examined. An Austrian architectural magazine, *Allgemeine Bauzeitung*, in an 1854 issue (vol. 19, pp. 380–5), contains a description of Bordley's icehouse, accompanied by illustrations (pl. 652) that must have been copied from Bordley's missing plate, as they are very similar to Ramée's design.

81. Bordley, *Essays*, second edition, p. 309.

82. Circular icehouses are shown on Ramée's plans for Calverton and Duanesburg in the United States; Yves in Belgium; the Heine and Parish estates near Hamburg; and Villers-Agron and Le Mont-Dieu in France (*Jardins irréguliers*, pl. IX; *Parcs et jardins*, pl. 1, 2, 4, 9, 10, 12). All these plans date from Ramée's American period or later. Two other plans, for Hamfelde and Plagersberg (*Parcs et jardins*, pl. 17, 18), show circular structures that may be icehouses. The dates of these two estates are not known.

83. See Chapter 10.

84. Views of early log cabins in this region were later published, for example, in S. W. Durant and H. B. Pierce, *History of St. Lawrence County, New York* (Philadelphia, 1878), pp. 301, 306.

85. For this statement on the title page of *Parcs et jardins*, see Chapter 14.

Chapter 13

I thank the following people who aided my research on Ramée's late career in Europe and his publications: Noëlle Baduraux, M. and Mme Berlaimont, Patrice Bertrand, the Baron de Cartier d'Yves, Maurice Georget La Chesnais, Didier Coupaye, Ilse Fischer, Philippe Grunchec, Mary Ison, Mme Jacquet-Ladrier, Mme Jestaz, M. Jouët-Pastré, the Comte de Lavaulx, Hakon Lund, Henri Pirot, Dora Wiebenson, and Henri Zerner.

1. See Appendix.

2. Stern, *Belanger*, vol. 2, p. 276.

3. Ramée stated to Rosseel that he would "probably end up" near Ghent (". . . je me finirai probablement dans le voisinage de votre ville natale"). See Chapter 12.

4. Anonymous, *Dinant en poche* [1887], pp. 130–1. Speaking of the childhood in Dinant of the painter Antoine Wiertz, the booklet states that in 1809 the painter's father "entra chez M. Bauwins, directeur d'une filature qui était installée dans les bâtiments de l'ancien couvent des Frères-Mineurs, aujourd'hui l'Athénée Royal. Là se trouvait également une fabrique de papiers peints appartenant à un français dont le fils, Daniel Ramée, est aujourd'hui un des principaux architectes de France."

5. Letter of 30 May 1825, from M. Méfan, consul general of Sweden and Norway in Paris, to M. Franchet Desperrez, French *conseiller d'Etat;* Archives Nationales, $F^7$9546. The relevant sentence reads, "J'ajoute. . . que le Sieur Ramée a longtems habité en Belgique la ville de Dinant où il avait établi une fabrique. . . ." The verb tenses suggest that Ramée established the factory in Dinant *before* living there.

6. The Latin version of Ramée's baptismal certificate, preserved in the Ramée papers at the Musée de Blérancourt, is identified as a copy "délivrée en l'hôtel de Mairie à Givet ce dix sept mars 1817." It is conceivable that someone other than Ramée had this copy made, or that it was ordered by mail, but it seems most likely that Ramée himself acquired it in person in Givet.

7. Biographical article on Daniel Ramée in G. Vapereau, *Dictionnaire universel des contemporains*, vol. 2, p. 1429. The article states that after collegiate study in Dinant, Daniel studied in the French city of Mézières, just south of Givet ("[il] fit ses études au collège de Dinant, puis à Mézières, où il se livra de préférence à des travaux purement artistiques"). This is puzzling, as there was apparently no school in Mézières where Daniel could have studied art at that time. Didier Coupaye has suggested to me that perhaps Ramée *père* was living in Mézières at that time and that Daniel was studying with him.

8. Bibliothèque Nationale, Cabinet des Estampes, Vc-97. The lithographs are inscribed "Vue de la ville de Dinant sur la Meuse" and "Vue de la roche dite de Bayard, près Dinant sur la Meuse." Each is also inscribed "D. Ramée fils del't" and "Lith. de G. Engelmann." For Engelmann, see the text of Chapter 13.

9. Information from M. Henri Pirot of Givet.

10. Alexandre de Laborde, *Description des nouveaux jardins de la France et de ses anciens châteaux*, 16 installments (Paris, 1808–15).

11. The park plans in Laborde's work are similar to those in Ramée's publications in certain respects, such as the manner in which trees and other features are drawn. Also, Laborde's use of French, English, and German on the title page and the plates is similar to that in Ramée's *Jardins irréguliers*. In regard to the possible influence of Laborde's work on Ramée, it is worth noting that among the subscribers to the work was "Le Ray de Chaumont," probably the same man who owned land in New York State and for whom Ramée may have done work while in America. Daniel Ramée refers to Laborde's *Description* in his article on "Jardin" in *Dictionnaire générale des termes d'architecture*, (1868), p. 226.

12. Laborde, pp. 1, 7.

13. Ibid., p. 51.

14. Ibid., p. 52.

15. Information from correspondence, 1990, with the Comte de Lavaulx, who generously provided me with details about Villers-Agron and its state at the time of Ramée's plan.

16. *Parcs et jardins*, pl. 12, inscribed "Villers Agron, près Dormans. Ramée 1820."

17. *Parcs et jardins*, pl. 14, inscribed "Parc et Château de Flize, Ardennes. Ramée." Although the plan is not dated, it is likely that Ramée designed it during the period following his return from America, when he was living and doing other work in the Ardennes region.

18. Article on Flize in Albert Meyrac, *Géographie illustrée des Ardennes* (Charleville 1899), pp. 234–5. Jean Garand, *Un notable ardennais: Jean-Nicolas Gendarme* (Charleville-Mézières, 1988), pp. 130–1 (brought to my attention by Didier Coupaye).

19. Laborde, *Description*, p. 55.

20. Jean Marchal, *Dictionnaire d'histoire monastique ardennaise*, in *Les Cahiers d'études ardennaises*, no. 11 (Charleville-Mézières, 1978), pp. 127–30; and historical plaque on the site.

21. Information from conversation with M. Dominique Jouët-Pastré, current proprietor of Le Mont-Dieu.

22. The plate is inscribed "J. Ramée inv't," "Lith. de G. Engelmann," and "D. Ramée fils del't, Pl. IX." The only copy of it that I know of is in the Bibliothèque Nationale, Cabinet des Estampes, in a collection of prints arranged geographically (Va8, t. 2, Ardennes, H-110921). The plate is not identified as being from *Jardins irréguliers*, but its format, plate number, and other details reveal that it is. *Jardins irréguliers* was published in installments of about six plates each, starting in 1823. This plate may therefore be later than 1823, but is in any case earlier than 1826, when a review of the publication appeared, noting that the first thirteen plates had been published (see note 45).

23. According to the present owner of Le Mont-Dieu, these lakes were not a practical possibility where Ramée showed them. But it is likely that here, as in some of his other published plans, the architect compressed his design to fit a format suitable for publication.

24. *Parcs et jardins*, pl. 2, inscribed "Parc d'Yves près Charleroi, Belgique, 1818."

25. Information on Yves is found in Général Philippe, *Yves-Gomezée, Quelques notes historiques* (Liége, 1938); and J. Schmitz and N. Nieuwland, *L'Invasion allemande dans les provinces de Namur et de Luxembourg*, vol. 6 (Brussels and Paris, 1923), pp. 34–5 (brought to my attention by Mme F. Jacquet-Ladrier of the Archives de l'État à Namur). I thank the Baron de Cartier d'Yves, who provided me with information on the property.

26. Didier Coupaye and I visited Yves in 1990 and spoke with residents of the area who remembered these features and their location on the estate.

27. One of these views, labeled "Château d'Yve [sic], Comm'ne d'Yve-Gomzée [sic], Canton de Walcourt, appartenant à Mr le Baron de Cartier d'Yve, Sénateur," was published in A. Vassé, *La Province de Namur pittoresque* (Brussels, 1840), vol. 1. The other view (inscribed "Ed. Toovey, del. et lith."), of unknown date, was published in Pierre Mardaga, ed., *Le Patrimoine monumental de la Belgique: Wallonie*, vol. 9, tome 2 (Namur: Philippeville) (Liège, 1982), p. 599; brought to my attention by Didier Coupaye. The house shown in these two views was evidently built before 1832, for Van der Maelen's *Dictionnaire géographique de la Province de Namur*, of that date, says of Yves: "On y distingue un beau château construit à la moderne; ce château est la propriété de M. le baron de Cartier."

28. These are the houses shown in pls. I and IV of *Jardins irréguliers*.

29. It may be compared, for example, with pl. 15 of *Recueil de cottages*, and with the octagonal or circular gate lodges shown in the vignette on the title page of this publication, picturing the entry gate at Calverton in Maryland.

30. *Parcs et jardins*, pl. 16, inscribed "Massambre [sic] près Givet. Ramée 1818."

31. The present owners of the property, M. and Mme Berlaimont, showed me the house in 1990 and said they thought that the owner in 1818 was a certain Louis Estivant; I have not been able to find more information than that.

32. The shape of the house as shown on a cadastral map of 1823 was communicated to me by M. Patrice Bertrand of Châlons-sur-Marne. It is not precisely the same shape as the present house, but close enough that it probably represents the same structure.

33. Didier Coupaye has brought to my attention one country house in Belgium that might be a work of Ramée: Mont Garni, near Baudour, a simple neoclassical house with an unusual broad-pedimented façade, constructed in the early nineteenth century. (It is illustrated in J. Bataille and P. Seydoux, *Châteaux et manoirs de Hainaut* (Paris, 1979), p. 27; its architect is apparently unknown.

34. In 1990, M. Nouaille-Degorce, battalion chief of the military base at Charlemont, gave me a copy of a document recording the transfer of the fountain to the city of Givet, August–September 1817. The fountain was demolished in the 1890s.

35. F. Robson, *Embellissement de la Ville de Givet* . . . , (1865), p. 3. Robson describes the Place Verte as "un grand espace encaissé, tout couvert d'arbres bons à abattre."

36. Boulliot states of Ramée, "Enfin, de retour à Paris en 1823, . . ." (see Appendix). For the listings of Ramée's addresses in Paris directories, see Chapter 14, note 1.

37. For Parish's presence in Paris, c. 1823, see G. J. Ouvrard, *Mémoires* . . . (Paris, 1826), part 2, pp. 250–1.

38. For this statement, in a review of the 1814 Academy of Fine Arts exhibit, see Chapter 12. It is possible, of course, that the reviewer was mistaken and that Ramée intended merely a publication of designs, not a written work, as the statement implies.

39. The first such article I can find is in G. Vapereau, *Dictionnaire universel des contemporains* (1858). See also *Nouvelle biographie générale*, vol. 41 (Paris, 1866); P. Larousse, *Grand dictionnaire universel du XIXe siècle* (Paris, 1865–76); Bellier and Auvray, *Dictionnaire général des artistes de l'école française* (Paris, 1885).

40. Vapereau, *Dictionnaire universel*, vol. 2, p. 1429. The article reads, in part: "Il suivit, tout enfant, son père aux États-Unis, revint à Hambourg, en 1818, et fit ses études au collège de Dinant, puis à Mézières, où il se livra de préférence à des travaux purement artistiques. In vint à Paris en 1823. Possédant déjà les principes de l'architecture, il s'appliqua particulièrement à l'étude du moyen âge, et fut bientôt attaché à la commission des monuments historiques." A document in the Ramée papers at Blérancourt states that in 1824 Daniel was admitted to the Église Évangélique in Paris. Some of the accounts of Daniel's life note that through his extensive travels (first as a boy with his father, then on his own), he learned at least four languages besides French (German, English, Dutch, and Ital-

ian), which were to facilitate his later career as a scholar. (See, for example, article on Ramée in *La Grande encyclopédie*, Paris, 1885–1901, vol. 28, p. 119.)

41. Léon Lang, *Godefroy Engelmann, imprimeur lithographe: les incunables, 1814–1817* (Colmar, 1977).

42. Plate VII, of which no copy is known, was also a lithograph, according to the review in *Année française*. (This review does not specify the plate numbers, but its description of the plates allows identification, since all are known except one.) Plates I and VII are described in the review as having been drawn by "Bichebois" – no doubt Louis Bichebois, an artist associated with Engelmann.

43. The known copies of *Jardins irréguliers* are as follows: The Kunstakademiets Bibliotek in Copenhagen has a set that includes the title page and plates I–VI (evidently the first installment of the work). The Bibliothèque Nationale in Paris (Cabinet des Estampes) has two incomplete sets: one consists of the title page, plates II–VI, and a "renvoi" sheet; the other consists of plates VIII, X–XIII, a "renvoi" sheet, and a sheet of text describing plate VIII. The Cabinet des Estampes also has the copy of plate IX (the plan of Le Mont-Dieu) noted in the text and in note 22. A copy of plate II (the plan of the Duane estate in New York) is in the possession of the owner of the Duane estate. The University of Münster, in Germany, once had a copy of *Jardins irréguliers* (described as comprising "zwei Hefte"), but the librarian there has informed me that "Die grossen Tafelbände sind alle im Krieg verbrannt." The author of an article on Ramée published in Hamburg in 1854 (in *Hamburgisches Künstler-Lexikon*, vol. 1, p. 196) also described the work as comprising two installments ("*Jardins irréguliers*. . . , wovon wir zwei Hefte kennen").

44. Two of the known copies of the work (at the Bibliothèque Nationale and the Kunstakademiets Bibliotek in Copenhagen) are in paper folders, evidently the original wrapper in which the first installment was issued; the title on this folder is *Jardins irréguliers et maisons de campagne*. The title on the title page of the work omits the word "et."

45. *Année française ou Mémorial politique, scientifique et littéraire*, vol. 2 (1826), pp. 338–9. Maurice Georget La Chesnais, of Paris, showed me in 1986 a letter, dated 1 July 1826, addressed to Ramée from an editor of the *Année française*, informing Ramée of the review in this magazine and including its text.

46. In addition, Bellier-Auvray's *Dictionnaire général des artistes* (1885) states that Ramée published "les premières livraisons *seulement* [my emphasis] d'un vaste recueil. . . ."

47. These are plates III–VI (all of them engravings): a plate of floor plans, two elevation drawings and a section drawing. Plates III and VI identify the engraver as "Adam"; the other two plates give "Réville" as engraver. A *renvoi* sheet accompanies these plates, listing (in French, English, and German) the rooms of the house, as numbered on the floor plans.

48. The lithographic perspective view is plate I; it is inscribed "Vue perspective de la maison." The other house is represented in plates X-XIII (all engravings, inscribed "Adam, sc."): one plate of plans, two elevation drawings, and one section drawing. A *renvoi* sheet accompanies them, similar to that accompanying plates III-VI.

49. The exterior form of Bordley's design is known mostly from the engraved elevation drawing in the *Allgemeine Bauzeitung* of 1854 (see Chapter 12, note 80). Bordley's written description says only that the icehouse has "a pavilion roof" (probably a conical or tentlike roof) and a vent at the top.

50. Professor Hermann Hipp has pointed out to me that this decoration is particularly distinctive of Lower Saxony or Schleswig.

Chapter 14

1. Ramée's name and addresses appear in Bottin's *Almanach du commerce de Paris* in the years 1824–34. The entries are as follows: 1824–6: "Ramée, architecte, Ponthieu, 20"; 1827–8: "Ramée, architecte, r. de Ponthieu, 6"; 1829: "Ramée, architecte, Oratoire du Roule"; 1830–1: "Ramée, architecte, avenue Chateaubriand"; 1832–4: "Ramée, architecte, avenue Chateaubriand, cité Beaujon." Rue de Ponthieu, Rue de l'Oratoire du Roule (now Rue Washington), Avenue Chateaubriand (now Rue Chateaubriand), and Cité Beaujon (now Square Beaujon) are all now in the Eighth Arrondissement; all were new or relatively new streets in the 1820s. In 1832 and 1833, when Ramée was listed as having two addresses, one was presumably his office.

2. Louis Philippe, *Mémoires de Louis Philippe, duc d'Orléans* (Paris, 1974); Marguerite Castillon du Perron, *Louis-Philippe et la Révolution française* (Paris, 1984).

3. Archives Nationales, no. F[7]-9546. The documents are: two letters from M. Méjan, of the Consulat Général de Suède et Norwège, to M. Franchet Desperrez, Conseiller d'État, 6 April 1825 and 30 May 1825; letter from official in the Préfecture de Police to the Ministre Secrétaire d'État au Département de l'Intérieur, 28 May 1825; draft or copy of letter, on Ministère de l'Intérieur stationery, to the Ministre des Affaires Étrangères, 1 June 1825. The first letter from the Swedish-Norwegian consul reads in part: "Je n'hésite pas à recourir à votre obligeance pour une affaire qui intéresse personnellement un sujet de S. M. le Roi de Suède. . . Il s'agit de découvrir le lieu de naissance et le domicile actuel de MM. Masson de Neuville et Ramée. L'un et l'autre français d'origine. Ces deux MM. dont le premier était Lieutenant Colonel et le second Major au service de France, émigrèrent à la révolution et furent s'établir à Hambourg où ils fondirent ensemble une maison de commerce sous la raison Masson et Ramée; ils habitaient encore cette ville en 1807, ils y éprouvèrent des malheurs et firent faillite. On est aujourd'hui certain que ces deux particuliers sont rentrés en France, on les croit même fixés en ce moment à Paris où ils se seraient rendus pour suivre leurs intérêts en leur ancienne qualité d'émigrés." The second letter from the consul repeats the request for the birthplace and present location of Masson and Ramée, notes that "il est d'une haute importance de posséder promptement [these facts] pour le succès de l'affaire recommandée particulièrement à mes soins par le Gouvernement Suédois," and adds the information that "Ramée a longtems habité en Belgique la ville de Dinant où il avait établi une fabrique." The letters from the Préfecture de Police and Ministère de l'Intérieur state that the questions about Masson and Ramée have been researched but that no information on them could be found. This is curious, since one of the questions – Ramée's present whereabouts – could have been answered simply by consulting the Paris directory.

4. *Parcs et jardins*, pl. 6 and 7. They are inscribed "Verneuil, près Dormans, 1828" and "Carlepont, près Noyon, 1829."

5. I thank Jean Bauchard, of Verneuil, and Didier Coupaye for providing me with this information on the property shown in Ramée's plan of Verneuil.

6. Sources of information on Carlepont were kindly provided to me by Mme Noëlle Baduraux and Didier Coupaye. (See, for example, G. Fleury and R. Capelle, *Essai sur l'histoire de Carlepont*, Compiègne, 1923.)

7. Musée Carnavalet, Paris; catalog no. D-8905. The drawing, executed in ink and watercolor on paper, measures 47 by 68 cm.

8. Boulliot states: "In 1829 [Ramée] entered a project in the competition sponsored by the city of Paris, for the embellishment of the Place Louis XVI" (see Appendix), and he cites two newspaper articles on the competition (see the text of this chapter).

9. Musée Carnavalet, *De la Place Louis XV à la Place de la Concorde* (Paris, 1982), pp. 101–11.

10. The accounts I have seen are: *Nouveau Journal de Paris* (1 May 1829), pp. 2–3; *Le Globe* (3 June 1829), pp. 351–2; and a long essay by A. Corréard, "Examen des projets présentés au concours sur les embellissemens de la Place Louis XVI," in *Journal du génie civil des sciences et des arts* (1829), pp. 322–68.

11. This information is in the *Nouveau Journal de Paris* story. This account gives the architect's name as "Ramey," as does the article by Corréard. But this is clearly Ramée, as the descriptions of the design correspond with that in the story in *Le Globe*, which spells Ramée's name correctly.

12. Corréard's article, pp. 323–4.

13. "Aussi nous préférons le plan de M. Ramée, qui donne également à la place une coupe ovale, mais sans l'entourer d'aucune ceinture: des gazons, quelques groupes d'arbres verts, de vastes trottoirs de granit, des fossés, aujourd'hui cultivés en pépinières, transformés en rivières courantes, et enfin le monument expiatoire entouré d'un parterre élégant et simple, tels sont les dispositions du plan de M. Ramée. Ce plan le plus naturel, le mieux conçu, et le plus économique, a en outre un grand avantage à nos yeux: il fait descendre des parapets du pont Louis XVI ces géants de marbre, épouvantail des petits enfants et des gens de goût qui passent à leurs pieds. M. Ramée les distribue à grands intervalles sur la place, et les entoure d'une touffe de lauriers: ainsi disséminés et ombragés, leurs proportions deviennent moins formidables et leurs formes moins choquantes. En somme, ce plan nous semble remplir avec une heureuse simplicité toutes les conditions du programme, et ménager une transition très convenable entre les beautés architecturales du jardin royal et les masses de verdure des Champs-Élysées. Toutefois, bien que nous donnions la préférence à ce plan pour sa justesse et son élégance peu coûteuse, nous ne pouvons refuser nos éloges d'autres projets. . ." (*Le Globe*, p. 352)

14. "Ce plan joint la simplicité à l'économie; les quatre fontaines à jet d'eau se groupent autour du monument sur une pelouse plantée d'arbres funéraires; les douze statues pédestres environnantes et les pièces d'eau, sont parfaitement en rapport avec cette décoration" (*Nouveau Journal de Paris*, p. 3).

15. "M. Ramey est l'auteur de ce projet: on doit lui savoir gré des efforts qu'il a faits pour ne pas outrepasser la somme affectée aux embellissemens (1,500,000 francs). Il est fâcheux qu'il n'y ait pas plus de noblesse; cette place à angles arrondis fait un mauvais effet. L'auteur conserve les quatre fossés, les redresse et en arrondit les angles rentrans et saillans; il les remplit d'eau, mais sans faire connaître comment il parviendrait à l'y faire tenir; il détermine ensuite un grand ovale dans la place, qu'il borde de larges trottoirs, et sème du gazon dans les parties renfermées entre sa circonférence et les fossés: sur chacun de ces gazons il élève trois piédestaux ornés de statues. Au centre de la place, il détermine un deuxième ovale d'une petite dimension, se rapprochant plutôt d'un hippodrome, également semé de gazon, avec plantation de cyprès: dans cette enceinte sont élevées quatre fontaines à pied-douche et à deux petites coupes, avec un jet d'eau au milieu. On ne peut disconvenir que cette dernière partie de la décoration ne soit en parfaite harmonie avec le monument principal: cela est bien dans le sentiment religieux qu'on a voulu lui donner; mais il semble que cette composition et les accessoires conviendraient mieux à un lieu consacré exclusivement aux sépultures, ou à un parc qui contiendrait les restes d'un particulier, plutôt qu'à une place publique, où le peuple sera souvent appelé à prendre part des fêtes, où des jeux seront peut-être établis pour l'amuser. Nous ferons remarquer que M. Ramey n'a pas bien réfléchi sur son sujet, car autrement il n'aurait pas oublié de conserver à la place Louis XVI le plus d'issues possible, ce qui est une des principales conditions d'une place, et pour atteindre ce but il aurait supprimé les fossés, même ceux du côté des Tuileries" (Corréard, pp. 325–6)

16. Corréard, pp. 356–7.

17. Karl Hammer, *Jakob Ignaz Hittorff, ein Pariser Baumeister, 1792-1867* (Stuttgart, 1968), pp. 128–52; Donald D. Schneider, *The Works and Doctrine of Jacques Ignace Hittorff*, vol. 1 (New York, 1977), pp. 365–430; Musée Carnavalet, *Hittorff, un architecte du XIXème* (Paris, 1986), pp. 75–110, 153–62.

18. Jean Marie Bruson, "La Place de la Concorde," in Musée Carnavalet, *Hittorff*, pp. 75–109.

19. Thomas von Joest, "Hittorff et les embellissements des Champs-Élysées," in Musée Carnavalet, *Hittorff*, pp. 153–61. Referring to Ramée's plan, von Joest states: "Il révèle déjà que le programme de cette promenade impliquera non pas des architectures pittoresques, vernaculaires, exotiques ou gothiques, mais des édifices dont le registre stylistique doit évoquer cette finesse et élégance urbaine, exprimée ici, comme plus tard par Hittorff, dans les termes proches de l'esthétique néo-classique" (p. 154).

20. Hillairet, *Dictionnaire historique*, vol. 1, pp. 298–9; and Maire's 1808 plan of Paris, reproduced at the front of vol. 1.

21. Gabriel Thouin, *Plans raisonnés de toutes les espèces de jardins* (Paris, 1820), pl. 16 and notes on p. 19. The buildings proposed by Thouin for the Champs-Élysées, illustrated at the top of his plan, include a rotunda and various pavilions, one of them employing the "Guimard motif" of columns set in a niche.

22. Ramée's design can be compared, for example, to Nash's Cronkhill, c. 1802, Longner Hall, c. 1805, and West Park Grinstead, c. 1806; John Plaw's *Sketches for Country Houses* (London, 1800), pl. 24; or J. B. Papworth's *Rural Residences* (London, 1818), pl. 17.

23. The Barrière de Monceau and Barrière de Reuilly are illustrated in Daniel Ramée's 1847 edition of Ledoux's *Architecture*, pl. 4, 13.

24. This design appears in the 1804 edition of Ledoux's *Architecture* and also in Ramée's 1847 edition (pl. 110).

25. Variations of this theme are found in Ramée's edition of Ledoux's work, pl. 7, 130, 219, 223.

26. For attitudes toward Ledoux in the early nineteenth century, see Anthony Vidler, *Claude Nicolas Ledoux* (Cambridge, Mass., 1990), pp. ix–x.

27. U. Westfehling, "Le Panorama"; and T. von Joest, "Le Cirque d'Été" and "Des restaurants, des cafés. . . ," in Musée Carnavalet *Hittorff*, pp. 163–205.

28. *Hamburgisches Künstler-Lexikon* (Hamburg, 1854), vol. I, p. 196, states of Ramée: "1832 und 1833 war er wieder in Hamburg."

29. *Neue deutsche Biographie*, article on "Lengerke" [sic]; Georg-Wilhelm Röpke, "Das Geschlecht der Lengercke und Wandsbek," *Der Wandsbeker* (October 1973), pp. 19–26; article on the Lengercke factory in *Wege zur Heimat: Monatsbeilage des Wandsbeker Boten* (April 1939). The information on the relationship between the Lengercke

family and Caroline Ramée, née Dreyer, come from the manuscript Dreyer genealogy in the Hamburg Staatsarchiv (see Chapter 6).

30. *Parcs et jardins*, pl. 11, inscribed "Jardin P. V. Lengerke à Wandsbeck, près Hambourg, 1834, Ramée."

31. *Recueil de cottages*, design no. 1. No copy of plate 1 is known, but the design is pictured in the plate that shows all the designs in miniature.

32. "Kattun-Fabrik des Herrn A. P. P. von Lengercke in Wandsbek / Anno 1840." Ilse Fischer, of the Heimatmuseum in Wandsbek, provided me with a reproduction of this lithograph (no original of which can presently be found).

33. Röpke, "Das Geschlecht der Lengercke," pp. 22–6.

34. Ibid., p. 26.

35. See Chapters 6 and 10.

36. Richard Ehrenberg, *Das Haus Parish in Hamburg* (Jena, 1905), pp. 82ff; Paul T. Hoffmann, *Die Elbchaussee* (Hamburg, 1977), pp. 200–9 ("Die Parishsche Besitzung").

37. *Parcs et jardins*, pl. 10, inscribed "Jardin R. Parish à Menstaden [sic] près Altona. Ramée, 1835." The misspelling of Nienstedten was no doubt a lithographer's error. The inlet of water indicated by Ramée on the plan is puzzling, for the steep topography of the shoreline at this spot (at the present time, at least) would not permit such a feature.

38. This part of the Parish House can be seen in a drawing reproduced in Hoffmann, *Die Elbchaussee*, fig. 19; it was reportedly constructed about 1845 (ibid., p. 207). It may be compared with houses in Ramée's *Recueil de cottages*, for instance no. 4, a Swiss-style house; no. 17, with a bay raised on thin columns; no. 18, with a curved opening in the gable; nos. 1 and 15, with polygonal bays.

39. Renata Klée Gobert, *Die Bau- und Kunstdenkmale der freien und Hansestadt Hamburg*, vol. 2 (Hamburg, 1959), pp. 169–70; Erich Lüth, *Das Heine-Haus an der Elbchaussee* (Hamburg, n.d.); Hoffmann, *Die Elbchaussee*, pp. 56–60.

40. *Parcs et jardins*, pl. 9, inscribed "Jardin Heine à Ollensen [sic] près Altona 1834, Ramée." The misspelling of Ottensen is no doubt a lithographer's error.

41. Lüth, *Das Heine-Haus*. This building was recently restored and is open to the public. Its address is Elbchaussee 31, Ottensen.

42. Information from the curator at the house when I visited it, May 1986. Hakon Lund, of the Art Academy in Copenhagen, tells me that C. F. Hansen cannot have been the architect of this building, as he was not doing work in the Hamburg area at that time.

43. This diary, or series of autobiographical notes by Stephen Martel, is in the Ramée collection in the Musée de Blérancourt (CFA-a 331/29-5, 6, 7). There are two slightly different versions of these notes, both written by Martel; it is not clear whether these are true diaries, composed day by day, or later reconstructions of events.

44. According to Martel's diary, the "Château de Beaurains" was purchased from a Monsieur Desmaretz. I have not been able to discover anything about this house, which evidently no longer exists. A catalogue of the Ramée papers at Blérancourt lists a drawing of the building ("Vue du château de Beaurains, près Noyon, où mourut Joseph Ramée chez Stephen Martel, son beau-frère. Aquarelle par Daniel Ramée"), but on my visits to Blérancourt the staff of the museum were unable to find this drawing.

45. One of the copies of the *Recueil de cottages* in the Bibliothèque Nationale bears a stamp indicating that the library acquired it in 1837. The title page of the work gives the publisher as "Rittner & Goupil, Editeurs, Boulevard Montmartre, No. 15" – an address this firm occupied beginning in 1837 (according to Bottin's Paris directories of the period). As for *Parcs et jardins*, its title page gives the same address for Rittner et Goupil; and Daniel Ramée later referred to the work as having been published in 1839 (Daniel Ramée, *Dictionnaire générale des termes d'architecture*, Paris, 1868, p. 226).

46. The title page of each work states: "On souscrit chez Rittner & Goupil, Editeurs, Boulevard Montmartre No. 15, à Paris." This reveals that the publications were sold by subscription – that is, orders were taken before the prints were actually produced. In the *Recueil de cottages*, ten of the known plates are inscribed "Lith. de Thierry frères"; nine are inscribed "Lith. de Lemercier." In *Parcs et jardins*, all the plates are inscribed "Lith. de Thierry frères à Paris" and several are also inscribed "Ch. Walter lith."

47. The two known complete copies of *Parcs et jardins* are in the Library of Congress and the library of Union College. The Library of Congress copy was purchased in 1977 from a book dealer; its first page bears the signature "Robert W. McLaughlin, Jr." The Union College copy was apparently acquired from the C. W. Leavitt Co., an architectural or engineering firm in New York City; correspondence of Prof. Harold Larrabee of Union College (c. 1936), refers to a copy of the book owned by this firm, which the college wished to acquire. Three plates from the work were published in *Architectural Review* in April 1921 (in an article on American landscape design by R. Schermerhorn), but the source of these plates is not known. At least three individual plates from the work (nos. 1, 2, 4) are in the Cabinet des Estampes of the Bibliothèque Nationale, in albums of prints arranged geographically; this suggests that the Bibliothèque Nationale broke up the work on deposition. One plate (no. 13, the Union College plan) is in the New York Historical Society.

48. Both copies of *Recueil de cottages* at the Bibliothèque Nationale (Cabinet des Estampes) consist of the following sheets: principal and secondary title pages, and plates 8, 15, 17, 20, 22, 23, 24, 25 (all inscribed "Lith. de Thierry frères"). One of these sets has the original cover: a large sheet of brown paper, folded, with the principal title page printed on it. The other known copy of the work was until recently owned by Maurice Georget La Chesnais, of Paris, nephew of Mme Edmée La Chesnais (née Gellion-Danglar), who inherited Daniel Ramée's family papers in the 1890s. This copy (presently in the author's possession) contains the secondary title page, plates 2–4, 7, 10–12, 15–17, 19–20, 22–23, 25, and the summary plate showing all the designs in miniature.

49. The plates in *Parcs et jardins* are labeled as follows: 1. Calvestown [Calverton] près Baltimore 1815; 2. Parc d'Yves près Charleroi, Belgique 1818; 3. Friederichs-thal [Sophienholm] bei Copenhagen 1804; 4. Duansburgh [Duanesburg], Etat de New York; 5. Neumühlen [Sieveking estate] près Altona, Holstein; 6. Verneuil près Dormans 1828; 7. Carlepont près Noyon 1829; 8. Hostrup à Eppendorf, près Hambourg; 9. Jardin Heine à Ollensen [Ottensen] près Altona 1834; 10. Jardin R. Parish à Menstaden [Nienstedten] près Altona 1835; 11. Jardin P. V. Lengerke [Lengercke] à Wandsbeck, près Hambourg 1834; 12. Villers-Agron, près Dormans 1820; 13. College de l'union à Schenectady, Etat de Neu-York, 1813; 14. Parc et Château de Flize, Ardennes; 15. Blankmeses [Blankenese] près Hambourg, 1805 & 1833; 16. Massambre près Givet, 1818; 17. Hamfelde, en Holstein; 18. Plagerberg, en Holstein; 19–20. [a double-size plate, numbered "No. 19 et 20"] Rapid-long-Island, State of Newyork.

50. "L'auteur croit et espère être utile aux amateurs de jardins

en leur offrant une série de motifs des plus variés qui sont applicables à tous les sites et pourront servir de guide à ceux qui s'occupent de ces sortes d'arrangements, par la multiplicité de scènes des plus pittoresques et des plus différenciées retracées dans ces jardins et que les différentes localités ont suggéré à l'auteur, cet ouvrage sera plus utile que les longs et volumineux livres écrits sur cette partie de l'art, chacun y trouvera un motif propre à être adapté au local qu'il voudra arranger."

51. One of the preparatory drawings survives, that of plate 13 (Union College); it is virtually identical to the lithographed plate itself. See Chapter 11 and Figs. 2 and 197.

52. Ramée's original plans for Union College and the Duane estate can be compared with the published plans. The sites at Sophienholm, Baurs Park, and (to a lesser extent) Hamfelde, Villers-Agron, and Union College, were executed faithfully enough and survive well enough to serve as comparison to the published plans.

53. John Soane, *Sketches in Architecture . . . to which are added six designs for improving Grounds . . .* (London, 1803 [first published 1793]). The six landscape plans are at the back of the volume, with explanatory text and an additional title page (dated 1803), attributing them to G. J. Parkyns. Not having seen a copy of the 1793 edition of the work, I do not know if it too contained Parkyns's plates.

54. Thouin, *Plans raisonnés* . It should be noted that the two garden plans in Ramée's 1823 publication *Jardins irréguliers* have the same format and drawing style as the plans in *Parcs et jardins*.

55. "Dépense de chaque maison. . . . Il peut y avoir quelques variations dans les prix en plus ou en moins d'après l'espèce de matériaux et la facilité de se les procurer suivant les localités."

56. The scales are labeled "Echelles des élévations, celles des plans sont de moitié." The three German measurements are "Pieds de Rhynland, Pieds d'Hambourg, Pieds de Cologne."

57. This is pointed out, for example, in Georges Teyssot, "Cottages et pittoresque: les origines du logement ouvrier en Angleterre, 1781–1818," *Architecture, mouvement, continuité* (July 1974), pp. 26–37.

58. Diderot's *Encyclopédie* (1754) describes "cottage" as "un terme purement anglois, qui signifie cabane ou chaumière bâtie à la campagne sans aucune dépendence" (vol. 4, p. 316; quoted in Teyssot, "Cottage et pittoresque," p. 27).

59. Daniel Ramée's *L'Architecture et la construction pratiques*, 4th edition (Paris, 1881; first published 1868), p. 526. Ramée refers to a style "employé en Angleterre d'abord pour les châteaux et ensuite pour les petites maisons de campagne nommées *cottages* [italicized in original] par nos voisins d'outre-Manche."

60. Besides the article by Teyssot, cited in note 57, see Sutherland Lyall, *Dream Cottages, from Cottage Orné to Stockbroker Tudor: Two Hundred Years of the Cult of the Vernacular* (London, 1988).

61. Michael McMordie, "Picturesque pattern books and pre-Victorian designers," *Architectural History*, vol. 18 (1975), pp. 43–59.

62. *Jardins irréguliers*, pl. IV. This and the *Recueil de cottages* design no. 2 can be compared with the garden façade of Belanger's house for the Carmelite convent near Beauvais, as published in Krafft's *Recueil d'architecture civile*, pl. 5.

63. Design no. 1, for instance, is similar in form to the house illustrated in pl. 21 of W. F. Pocock's *Architectural Designs for Rustic Cottages, Picturesque Dwellings, Villas, &c.* (London, 1807).

64. It can be compared with pl. 21 in Pocock's *Architectural Designs* and pl. 5 in J. B. Papworth's *Rural Residences* (London, 1818).

65. This can be compared, for example, to John Plaw, *Sketches for Country Houses, Villas & Rural Dwellings* (London, 1800), pl. 24; T. D. W. Dearn, *Sketches in Architecture . . . Cottages and Rural Dwellings* (London, 1807), pl. 14; P. F. Robinson, *Designs for Ornamental Villas* (London, 1827), pl. 6.

66. Pocock, *Architectural Designs*, pl. 10; Plaw, *Sketches*, pl. 7.

67. Plaw, *Sketches*, pl. 5.

68. For Ramée's Baurs Park drawing, see Chapter 6.

69. P. F. Robinson, *Rural Architecture* (London, 1823), and *Designs for Ornamental Villas* (London, 1827). Somewhat closer to Ramée's design is one in Francis Goodwin's *Domestic Architecture* (London, 1833). A discussion of the Swiss cottage in these English publications is found in Lyall's *Dream Cottages*, pp. 89–95.

70. *Jardins irréguliers*, pl. 10–13. Especially similar are the corner towers in the two houses, and the arcades formed of flattened pointed arches.

71. The design, on pl. 45 of Krafft's publication, is identified as "Pavillon et volière exécutés au jardin de Mr. Fortaÿe, près Marly, par Labbé, Architecte." The latticework here surrounds the parts of the structure serving as the *volière* or aviary.

72. For example, Ledoux's 1847 edition, pl. 19, 29; and especially several houses proposed by Ledoux for Maupertuis, shown in an engraving that did not appear in either the 1804 or 1847 edition of Ledoux's *Architecture*; it is illustrated in Michel Gallet, *Claude Nicolas Ledoux*, p. 38.

73. Ledoux's *Architecture*, 1804 edition, pl. 88.

74. Ramée would have known, for instance, the log "Fisherman's Hut" in the park at Meiningen (see Chapter 5), and he included a log house in his drawing of Baurs Park (see Chapter 6). Log structures were also erected as garden pavilions in pre-Revolutionary France, where they were sometimes called "*maisons russes*." A drawing of one of these, at Raincy, is illustrated in Marie Blanche d'Arneville, *Parcs et jardins sous le premier empire* (Paris, 1981), p. 96.

75. Belanger's "*Ferme Westphalienne*" is illustrated in Krafft's *Recueil d'architecture civile*, pl. 34; see also Gabriel Thouin, *Plans raisonnés de toutes les espèces de jardins* (Paris, 1820), design no. 1, pl. 56.

76. Tim Mowl and Brian Earnshaw, *Trumpet at a Distant Gate: The Lodge as Prelude to the Country House* (London, 1985).

77. The motif of the arched entry gate surmounted by steps can be found in the work of Ledoux, for example in his Barrière du Maine, in Paris, illustrated in Gallet, *Ledoux*, p. 166. The circular gate lodges are somewhat similar to a gate design in Joseph Gandy's *Designs for Cottages, Cottage Farms and other Rural Buildings* (London, 1805), illustrated in Mowl and Earnshaw, p. 70.

78. Daniel Ramée, *L'Architecture et la construction pratiques* (Paris, 1868, and successive editions). In the edition of 1881, the section on country houses is on pp. 523–44, entitled "Du style le plus convenable pour les maisons particulières."

79. *L'Architecture et la construction* (1881 edition), pp. 534–5.

80. Daniel Ramée cites the English works as follows (1881 edition, p. 527): "On trouvera des plans et des façades de cottage dans les ouvrages de F. Goodwin, de Robinson, de Papworth et de J.-C. Loudon." Daniel is probably referring here to Francis Goodwin's publications of the 1830s, P. F. Robinson's publications of the 1820s and 1830s, J. B. Papworth's *Rural Residences* of 1818, and John Claudius Loudon's *Encyclopedia of Cottage, Farm, and Villa Architecture*, first published in 1833. Daniel Ramée's *Dictionnaire général* (1868) does not contain the term "cottage."

81. "Je suis arrivé hier ici en bonne santé, j'ai attendu 5 heures à Compiègne et 7 à Soissons, enfin j'ai trouvé dans [devant?] notre dame des victoires la premiére place dans le coupé, ce qui m'a été

fort agréable. Mr. [Desroux?] n'est pas encore de retour de Lorraine, et ce qu'il y a de plus facheux, les arbres et arbustes de Margut ne sont pas encore arrivés. D'après sa promesse ils ont du partir de paris dans les premiers jours de ce mois. Ecris-lui un mot et demande-lui le roulage où il a du les envoyer. Je crois me rappeler que c'est rue du jour derrière St. Eustache. La femme de [Cassan?] est morte. J'écris par ce même courrier à Noyon, je suis descendu ici à l'hôtel du commerce. Je ne ferai pas je crois un long séjour à Charleville. Au revoir, porte-toi bien. Ramée Charleville le 19 novembre 1839." The letter is addressed, in Ramée's hand, to "Monsieur D. Ramée, architecte, 8, Rue Neuve Luxembourg, Paris."

82. "Daniel est arrivé de Paris - le même jour, 18 may à 8 H. du soir, Ramée est mort" (p. 32 of the notes identified as "CFA a 331/29-6," in the Blérancourt Museum). A copy of Ramée's death certificate, dated 19 May 1842, states in part: "Ramée Jean Jacques Joseph agé de soixante dix neuf ans natif de Charlemont (Ardennes) architecte domicilié à Beaurains fils de défunt Jacques Ramée et de Anne Dieudonnée Lambert époux de Caroline Henriette Cornélie Dreyer Née à Hambourg ville anséatique est décédé hier à huit heures du soir au domicile de Monsieur Martel Stephen sise audit Beaurains. . . " ("Extrait du Registre des Actes de l'Etat civil de la Commune de Beaurains pour 1842," Blérancourt Museum).

83. The inscription on Ramée's tombstone is given in a letter (a partial transcript of which is in the Ramée papers at Blérancourt), written by "A. Ponthieux," 4 November 1937: "Cher Monsieur Girodie,. . . Ramée a été, en effet, inhumé dans le cimetière de Beaurains. La pierre tombale y était conservée avant la guerre (peut-être y est elle encore). Elle portait l'inscription suivante en majuscules allemandes: Ci gît Joseph Ramée, architecte, né à Givet le XXVI Avril 1764, qui rendit son âme à Dieu le XVIII de Mai MDCCCXLII. Priez Dieu pour lui." Ramée's death certificate has not been found. But a death announcement issued by the family (a "faire-part de décès") is in the Archives Nationales in Paris; dated "Beaurains, le 19 Mai 1842" and issued by "Madame Ramée, Monsieur Daniel Ramée, M. et Mme. Stephen Martel," it gives the deceased's name as Joseph Guillaume Ramée.

84. Stephen Martel's diary, for 17 May 1843, notes: "La pierre de Senlis a été posée sur la tombe de Ramée, et aujourd'hui un service d'anniversaire de sa mort a été célébré à l'Eglise de Noyon."

85. "A Joseph Ramée, mon père et mon maître, qui avait accepté la dédicace de ce livre / A sa mémoire / Daniel Ramée" (dedication page of *Manuel de l'histoire générale de l'architecture chez tous les peuples, et particulièrement de l'architecture en France au Moyen-Age*, vol. 1, Paris, 1843). Caroline Ramée lived until 1873; according to information in the Dreyer family genealogy in the Hamburg Staatsarchiv, she died in Argenteuil (near Paris) on 2 November 1873, the same day as her sister Wilhelmina, widow of Stephen Martel, also died.

Epilogue

1. The outline of Daniel Ramée's life is known mainly from articles on him in nineteenth-century biographical dictionaries, and from information in the Ramée family papers at the Blérancourt Museum. The article on Daniel in G. Vapereau, *Dictionnaire universel des contemporains* (Paris, 1858, vol. 2, p. 1429) is the earliest I have found (except for a brief notice in Nagler's *Künstler-Lexikon*, Leipzig, 1835–52) and seems to be the source of most of the information in later articles. Vapereau's article says of Ramée's early years: "Il suivit, tout enfant, son père aux États-Unis, revint à Hambourg, en 1818, et fit ses études au collège de Dinant, puis à Mézières, où il se livra de préférence à des travaux purement artistiques. Il vint à Paris en 1823. . . ." That Daniel was trained in architecture by his father is stated in Bellier and Auvray's *Dictionnaire général des artistes de l'école française* (Paris, 1885, p. 338) and in obituary articles on the architect, such as *La Chronique des arts* (1887), p. 247. Daniel was born in Hamburg, 16 May 1806; was married in Paris, 13 October 1886, to Josephine Clarat Bouillet; and died in Paris, 12 September 1887. I have not found his will, but did locate the will of his widow, who died in Paris, 5 March 1895; she named as her heir Mademoiselle Edmée Gellion-Danglar (apparently an unrelated friend of the Ramées). It was this woman, later Madame Pierre Georget La Chesnais, who in 1937 gave the Blérancourt Museum its collection of Ramée family documents, portraits, drawings, and other items.

2. Vapereau's article on Ramée says: "Il vint à Paris en 1823. Possédant déjà les principes de l'architecture, il s'appliqua particulièrement à l'étude du moyen âge, et fut bientôt attaché à la commission des monuments historiques."

3. Regarding Ramée's work for Vitet and the Commission des Monuments Historiques, see *Centenaire du Service des Monuments Historiques*, tome 1 (Paris, 1935), p. 281; F. Bercé, *Les Premiers travaux de la commission des monuments historiques, 1837–1848* (Paris, 1979), p. 13, and other references. Ramée's work for Vitet around 1830 is mentioned in articles by Vitet in *L'Artiste*, vol. 1 (1831), pp. 161, 202 (brought to my attention by Robin Middleton). The Vitet collection at the Bibliothèque du Patrimoine in Paris contains drawings of medieval buildings made by Ramée on two trips, in 1830 and 1831; among the places he visited are Noyon, Soissons, Bourges, Dijon, Sens, Lyon, Clermont-Ferrand, Auxerre, Valence, Avignon, Tournus, Vienne, Puy, Vézelay, and Arles.

4. According to Vapereau's article, Ramée "visita une première fois l'Italie (1832), vécut deux ans à Florence, parcourut toute la Toscane, et fit de fréquentes excursions en Angleterre et en Allemagne. En 1848, il se trouvait à Rome pour la septième fois." Drawings of medieval architecture by Ramée that were published in Chapuy's *Le Moyen-âge monumental* of 1843 (see below) reveal that he had traveled extensively in France and Germany and had visited Vienna and Prague. Several of the original drawings by Ramée survive, in Houghton Library at Harvard University (PF.MS.Typ.512), and reveal that Ramée executed them on site (a drawing of the city hall of Lübeck, for instance, is signed "Daniel Ramée d'après nature").

5. Daniel Ramée's principal publications (listed in chronological order): *Théorie du dessin linéaire, ou cours de géométrie élémentaire* (Paris, c. 1840); with Nicolas Chapuy, *Le Moyen-âge monumental et archéologique* (Paris, 1840-3); *Manuel de l'histoire générale de l'architecture* (Paris, 1843 and later editions); with M. Vitet, *Monographie de l'église Notre-Dame de Noyon* (Paris, 1845); *Histoire de l'architecture en France depuis les Romains jusqu'au XVIe siècle* (Paris, 1846); *L'Architecture de C. N. Ledoux* (London, 1846 and Paris, 1847); articles in J. Guilhabaud, ed., *Monuments anciens et modernes*, vols. 2-4 (Paris, 1847-50); *Théologie cosmogonique, ou reconstitution de l'ancienne et primitive loi* (Paris, 1853); *La Locomotion, Histoire des chars, carrosses, omnibus et voitures de tous genres* (Paris, 1856); with R. Pfnor, *Monographie du château de Heidelberg* (Paris, 1859); *Le Palais de Fontainebleau* (Paris, 1859); *Histoire générale de l'architecture* (Paris, 1860 and later editions); *La Mort de Jésus* (Paris, 1863 and later editions); *Meubles religieux et civils du Moyen-âge...à Louis XVI* (Paris, 1863); *Sculptures décoratives du XIIe au XVIe siècle* (Paris, 1863); *Action de Jésus sur le monde, ou conséquences du Christianisme* (Paris, 1864); *Le Congrès de Vienne* (Paris,

1866); *Le Palais de l'Exposition universelle au Champ-de-Mars* (Paris, 1867); *Dictionnaire général des termes d'architecture en français, allemand, anglais et italien* (Paris, 1868); *L'Architecture et la construction pratiques* (Paris, 1869 and later editions); *Le Grand perturbateur romain, César* (Paris, 1870); *Le Plébiscite, ce qu'il a été, ce qu'il doit être* (Paris, 1870); *La République, son développement dans l'état et dans la société* (Paris, 1872); *Histoire de l'origine des inventions, des découvertes et des institutions humaines* (Paris, 1875); *Précis de l'histoire des Français* (Paris, 1880); *Recueil de deux cents motifs d'architecture* (Paris, 1886); *Histoire politique et sociale de la Révolution Française de 1789* (Paris, 1887).

6. Nicolas Marie Joseph Chapuy, *Le Moyen-âge monumental et archéologique*, 6 vols (Paris, 1843); Ramée's essay, entitled "Introduction générale," is in vol. 1, pp. 1–62. The illustrations that comprise the rest of the work were apparently published in installments between 1840 and 1843; Ramée's essay probably appeared in 1843, when the work was published in its entirety (information from correspondence with the British Library).

7. *Le Moyen-âge*, vol. 1, p. 60.

8. Daniel Ramée, *Manuel de l'histoire générale de l'architecture chez tous les peuples, et particulièrement de l'architecture en France au moyen-âge*, 2 vols (Paris, 1843). Volume 1 is devoted to Antiquity, volume 2 to the Middle Ages. Revised editions of the two volumes were published in 1860 and 1862 (under the new title *Histoire générale de l'architecture*) and a third volume, on the Renaissance, appeared in 1885.

9. "Dans les arts on doit étudier les créations et les styles de tous les pays et de tous les temps, rechercher ce qu'ils ont de beau, d'élevé, de naturel, s'en inspirer, et le faire entrer dans les oeuvres nouvelles" (*Manuel*, vol. 1, p. ix).

10. Ramée's brief essay on Mexican architecture is one of his contributions to Jules Gailhabaud's *Monuments anciens et modernes*, 4 vols. (Paris, 1839–50); it is in vol. 4 and therefore evidently appeared in 1850. Ramée's other essays in the work (in vols. 2, 3, 4), numbering twenty-one, are mostly on buildings in France and Germany, but also on buildings in Florence, Vienna, and Liége.

11. "Il y a vingt ans que nous fûmes initié aux principes de l'architecture. Nous nous aperçûmes bientôt qu'on étudiait les monuments sans ordre, sans suite chronologique. . . . Il y a vingt ans il n'existait pas plus qu'aujourd'hui une histoire complète de l'architecture. Nous sentîmes ce que l'absence d'un tel livre laissait de vide dans les connaissances de l'artiste, et dès le début de nos études nous formâmes le projet de composer plus tard une histoire de cet art. . . . C'est ainsi que fut réalisé le projet que nous formâmes dès 1823" (*Manuel*, vol. 1, p. vii).

12. See Chapter 12.

13. The development of Daniel Ramée's racist (especially anti-Semitic) views seems to be linked with the rejection of his Christian faith. This faith was still clearly intact when he wrote his introduction to Chapuy's *Le Moyen-âge*, in which he spoke positively of Jewish traditions (see, for example, pp. 1–2). Ramée's later anti-Christian opinions led him to devise an argument that Gothic architecture had little or nothing to do with the Christian religion but was created fully by secular, "freemason" forces; this idea seems to appear first in 1853, in Ramée's *Théologie cosmogonique*, in a chapter entitled "La Cathédrale du XIIIe siècle n'est pas chrétienne."

14. "Nous espérons avoir rendu une justice impartiale à l'architecture de tous les peuples" (*Manuel*, vol. 1, p. vii).

15. Michel Gallet, *Claude-Nicolas Ledoux, 1736–1806* (Paris, 1980), pp. 222–6. I am grateful to M. Gallet and to Anthony Vidler, for their observations, in conversations with me, regarding the possible connections between Ledoux and Ramée *père* and *fils*.

16. Gallet, *Ledoux*, p. 225.

17. The British Museum has a copy of the 1846 London edition (the only copy of which I am aware); Gallet describes it as containing 230 plates and being the "deuxième et dernier volume" (Gallet, *Ledoux*, p. 226); I have not personally seen it. The two-volume Paris edition, of 1847 (published by "Lenoir, Editeur, 5 quai Malaquais") is entitled *Architecture de C. N. Ledoux*; each volume contains 150 plates; Daniel Ramée's preface (called "Avertissement") is two pages long. The New York Public Library possesses a kind of hybrid edition; it was published by Lenoir in Paris in 1847, but otherwise seems to be like the 1846 London edition, having 230 plates in just one volume (called "Second Volume"); it too contains Ramée's "Avertissement." According to Gallet (*Ledoux*, p. 226), Ramée and Lenoir must have used the actual copper plates for their edition (not just sheets previously printed from the plates), judging from the evidence of the paper used. See also Anthony Vidler's introduction to the 1984 Princeton Architectual Press reprint of the publication.

18. References to Ledoux's work in the mid-nineteenth century are generally damning. Typical of their tone are two anonymous articles (reportedly written by Léon Vaudoyer) in the *Magasin pittoresque*: "Les Bizarreries de Ledoux" (vol. 27, 1859, pp. 27–9) and an article on eighteenth-century architecture (vol. 20, 1852, pp. 386–90) which speaks of the "bizarre," "pretentious," and "tasteless" work of Ledoux. For attitudes toward Ledoux in the nineteenth century, see Vidler, *Ledoux*, pp. ix–x.

19. Regarding Ledoux's interest in Freemasonry and various occult subjects, see Michel Gallet, *Claude-Nicolas Ledoux* (Paris, 1980), pp. 24, 269–71. Daniel Ramée's attraction to Masonic ideas and historical interpretations can be seen in his writings starting in the 1850s, such as *Théologie cosmogonique* (1853).

20. For Ledoux's relationship with Belanger and Cellerier, see Chapters 2 and 3. Handwritten notes on Ledoux and his work are found in Belanger's papers in the Bibliothèque Historique de la Ville de Paris (MS.NA.182, following sheet no. 115).

21. "Notice rapide sur la vie et les ouvrages de Claude-Nicolas Ledoux," *Annales de l'architecture et des arts* (1807 ?), pp. 3–16; signed "J. C." Gallet (*Ledoux*, p. 287) identifies the author as Cellerier. The reference to the continued publication of Ledoux's work is on p. 15.

22. In his preface to the publication of Ledoux's work, Daniel Ramée refers to the façade of the Guimard House, "qui a été copiée souvent par bon nombre d'architectes, qui se sont bien gardés de faire connaître l'original." This is puzzling, as one assumes that Daniel was aware of his father's use of the Guimard prototype and thus was including him in this implied criticism.

Documents and Bibliography

I. Documents

Listed here first are the locations of the most important known primary documents of Ramée's life and work. Other documentation is cited in the notes to this monograph. In addition, the London art dealer B. Weinreb reportedly possessed (in the 1960s or 1970s) drawings signed by Ramée, but my attempts to discover what happened to them have been unsuccessful.

Denmark

Copenhagen, Kunstakademiets Bibliotek. Drawings for the house and outbuildings at Sophienholm (A-2498a, b, c, d; A-2505a, b; A-2507, A-2499e); drawings for bathroom of Brun House (A-2500a, b, c); plates of *Jardins irréguliers*.

France

Blérancourt, Musée National de la Coopération Franco-Américaine (Musée National de Blérancourt). Collection (CFA-a-331) of Ramée family items given to the museum in 1937 (see Introduction), including portraits of Joseph, Caroline and Daniel Ramée; drawing by Joseph of Baurs Park, 1810; letter of Joseph, 1839; Joseph's death certificate and copies of birth certificate; drawings, letters, and manuscripts of Daniel; diaries of Stephen Martel; other family documents and papers.

Paris, Archives Nationales. Documents and drawings for Berthault-Récamier House (Z^{1J}-1192); plan for Louvain entrepôt (N-II-Dyle-3-4956); Ramée's 1800 petition (F^7-5651^1); diverse documents (T-1687; F^7-3331; F^7-6063; F^7-9546, etc.).

Paris, Bibliothèque Nationale. Plates of *Jardins irréguliers* and *Recueil de cottages* (Cabinet des Estampes, S.N.R.-Ramée).

Paris, Musée Carnavalet. Drawing for Loterie Impériale, 1811 (D-6718); plan for Champs-Élysées and Place Louis XVI, 1828 (D-8905).

Germany

Erfurt, Angermuseum. Drawing of the Erfurt Domplatz, 1795.

Gotha, Forschungs- und Landesbibliothek. Drawings for country house, 1796 (Chart. A-1053).

Hamburg, Staatsarchiv. Ramée's marriage certificate, 1805, and other documents of his Hamburg years; genealogical data on Caroline Ramée's family.

Schwerin, Mecklenburgisches Landeshauptarchiv. Letters of Ramée and other documents of his work for the Mecklenburg court, 1804–8.

Weimar, Staatsarchiv. Records regarding Ramée's work in the ducal park and Römisches Haus, 1795–6.

United States

Baltimore, Peale Museum. Drawing for Washington Monument, 1813 (CB-5472).

Canton, N. Y., St. Lawrence University. David Parish papers; letter of Ramée, 1815 (Owen D. Young Library, Parish-Rosseel Collection). (Cited as "SLU" in the Notes.)

Duanesburg, N. Y., James Duane Featherstonhaugh. Plan of Duane estate, 1813; plate II of *Jardins irréguliers*.

New York, New York Historical Society. David Parish letter books.(Cited as "NYHS" in the Notes.)

Schenectady, N. Y., Union College. Thirty-four sheets of plans and drawings for Union College; additional plan for the college (acquired in Paris, 1890); treasurer's records of payments to Ramée and other documentation of the design and its execution; copy of *Parcs et jardins*; Harold A. Larrabee Papers (Schaffer Library Archives).

Stanford, Calif., Paul V. Turner. Plates of *Recueil de cottages*.

Washington, Library of Congress. Copy of *Parcs et jardins*; examples of wallpapers designed by Ramée (Prints and Photographs Division).

II. Works on Ramée

Following are publications on Ramée and Ramée's own publications of designs. Not included are articles on the architect in biographical dictionaries or encyclopedias (except for Boulliot's important 1830 article), nor publications that deal with Ramée only as part of a larger subject. Fuller bibliographies for specific aspects of the architect's career are provided in the notes of this monograph. An unpublished study that should be mentioned here is Roy Eugene Graham's "Joseph Jacques Ramée and the French Émigré Architects in America" (master's thesis, University of Virginia, 1968).

Boulliot, Abbé [Jean Baptiste Joseph]. Article on Ramée in *Biographie ardennaise* (Paris, 1830), vol. 2, pp. 493–6.

Hislop, Codman. "The Ramée Plans," *Union Alumni Monthly* (December 1932), pp. 48–53.

——— and Harold A. Larrabee. "Joseph Jacques Ramée and the Building of North and South Colleges," *Union Alumni Monthly* (February 1938), pp. 1–16.

Larrabee, Harold A. "Joseph Jacques Ramée and America's First Unified College Plan," *Franco-American Pamphlet Series*, no. 1 (New York, 1934).

———, "How Ramée Came to Schenectady," *Union Alumni Monthly* (February 1937), pp. 111–13.

———, "Joseph Jacques Ramée, Architect," *Légion d'Honneur* (April 1938), pp. 216–21.

Madsen, Hans Helge. *Interiørdekorationer i Erichsens Palae: Fra arkitekten J. J. Ramée's virke i København* (Copenhagen, 1968).

Norton, Paul F. "The Architect of Calverton," *Maryland Historical Magazine* (Summer 1981), pp. 113–23.

Ramée, Joseph. *Jardins irréguliers, maisons de campagne, de tous genres et de toutes dimensions, exécutés dans différentes contrées de l'Europe et de l'Amérique Septentrionale, par Joseph Ramée, architecte* (Paris, 1823).

———. *Recueil de cottages et maisons de campagne, de tous genres, de toutes dimensions, composés et exécutés dans différentes contrées de l'Europe et des États unis d'Amérique par Joseph Ramée, architecte*

(Paris, Rittner et Goupil, [1837]).

———. *Parcs & jardins, composés et exécutés dans différentes contrées de l'Europe et des États unis d'Amérique par Joseph Ramée, architecte* (Paris, Rittner et Goupil, [probably 1839]).

Tunnard, Christopher. "Joseph Jacques Ramée and Union College," *Union Worthies*, no. 19 (1964), pp. 5–15.

Turner, Paul Venable. "Joseph Jacques Ramée's First Career," *The Art Bulletin* (June 1985), pp. 259–77.

———. "David Parish's Country House Reconstructed," *The Quarterly* [St. Lawrence County, N. Y., Historical Association] (October 1986), pp. 3–9.

———. "Joseph Ramée's Design for Baltimore, 1813: A New Type of Urban Monument in America." W. Böhm, ed., *The Building and the Town, Essays for Eduard F. Sekler* (Vienna, 1994), pp. 294–304.

III. Frequently cited works

Following are publications cited frequently in the Notes. See also the works on Ramée listed above.

Bobé, Louis, ed. "August Hennings' Dagbok under hans Ophold i København 1802," *Danske Magazin*, series 7, vols. 1-3 (1934-5). (Cited as "Hennings's diary" in the Notes.)

Braham, Allan. *The Architecture of the French Enlightenment* (Berkeley, Calif., 1980).

Gallet, Michel. *Claude-Nicolas Ledoux, 1736–1806* (Paris, 1980).

Gobert, Renata Klée. *Die Bau- und Kunstdenkmale der Freien und Hansestadt Hamburg* (Hamburg, 1959).

Hautecoeur, Louis. *Histoire de l'architecture classique en France* (Paris, 1943-57).

Hillairet, Jacques. *Dictionnaire historique des rues de Paris* (Paris, 1963).

Hirschfeld, C. C. L. *Theorie der Gartenkunst* (Leipzig, 1779–85).

Hoffmann, Paul T. *Die Elbchaussee* (Hamburg, 1977).

Krafft, Jean Charles. *Recueil d'architecture civile* (Paris, 1812).

——— and N. Ransonnette. *Plans, coupes, élévations des plus belles maisons et des hôtels construits à Paris* (Paris, c. 1802).

Le Rouge, Georges Louis. *Jardins anglo-chinois* (Paris, c. 1776-90).

Meyer, F. J. L. *Skizzen zu einem Gemälde von Hamburg*, vols. 1-2 (Hamburg, 1801-2).

Nolte, Vincent. *Fünfzig Jahre in beiden Hemisphären: Reminiscenzen aus den Leben eines ehemaligen Kaufmannes* (Hamburg, 1854).

Pérouse de Montclos. J.-M., *Les Prix de Rome* (Paris, 1984).

Ramée, Daniel. *L'Architecture de C. N. Ledoux* (Paris, 1847).

Stern, Jean. *A l'ombre de Sophie Arnould: François Joseph Belanger, Architecte des Menus Plaisirs* (Paris, 1930).

Index

Pl. 1 Berthault-Récamier House, Rue du Mail, Paris, 1789. Elevation drawing of façade, ink and watercolor on paper, 36 × 45 cm. (Archives Nationales, Paris, Service Photographique)

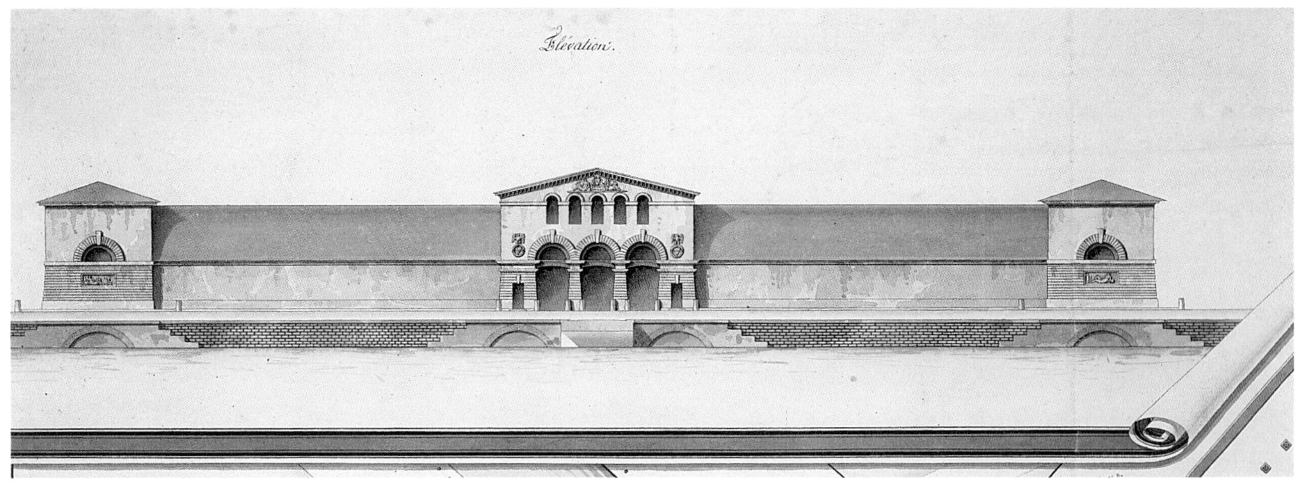

Pl. 2 Design of *Entrepôt* for Louvain, 1793. Detail with elevation drawing of building, ink and watercolor on paper. (Archives Nationales, Paris, Service Photographique)

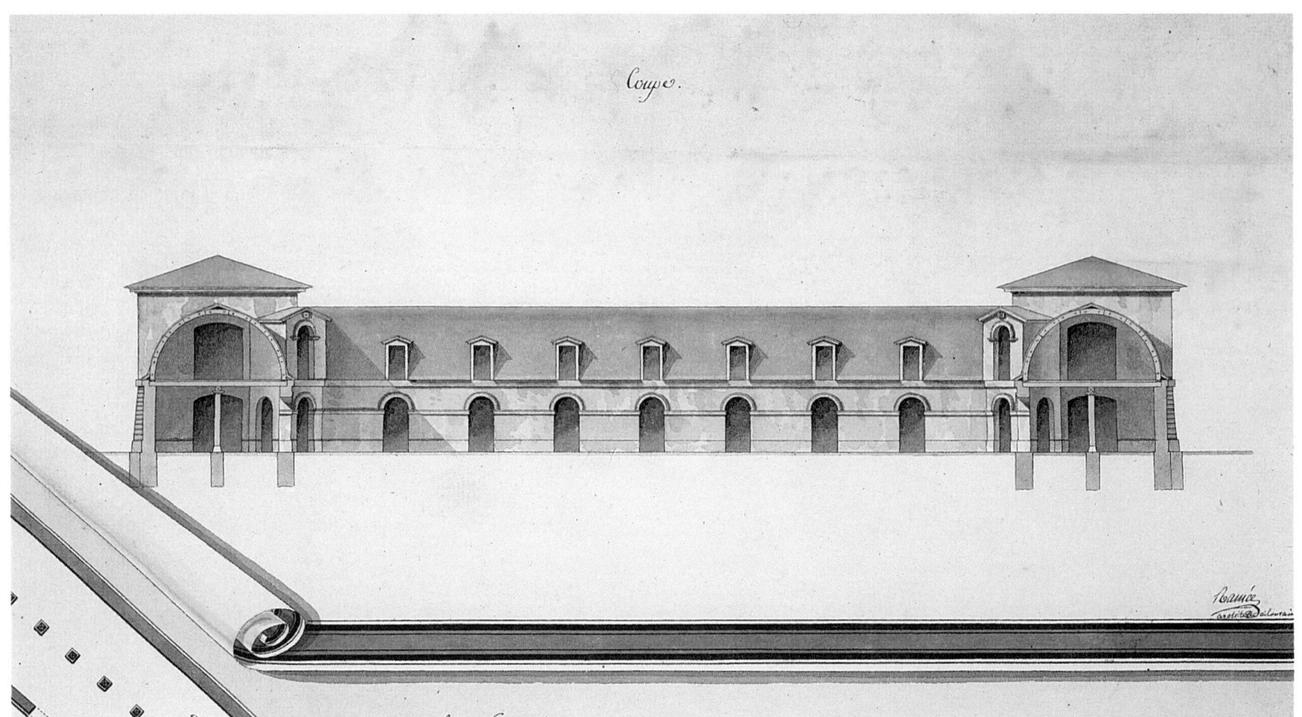

Pl. 3 Design of *Entrepôt* for Louvain, detail with section drawing of building. (Archives Nationales, Paris, Service Photographique)

Pl. 4 Design of *Entrepôt* for Louvain, detail with commemorative arch, ink and watercolor drawing, signed "Ramée, architecte à Louvain." (Archives Nationales, Paris, Service Photographique)

Pl. 5 View of Domplatz (Cathedral Square), Erfurt. Ink and watercolor drawing on paper, 44 × 65 cm, signed "Ramée, architecte, 1795." (Angermuseum, Erfurt)

Pl. 6 Perspective view and site plan of country house. Ink and watercolor drawing on paper, 26 × 41 cm, signed "Ramée, 1796." (Forschungs- und Landesbibliothek, Gotha)

Vüe perspective et Plan général d'une Maison de Campagne
Partie du Jardin
Maison
Cour des Ecuries.
Remises et Ecuries. avec logemt. de Domestiques au dessus.
Logement du concierge et des valets de la Basse cour.
Basse-cour.
Sortie.
grille.
Entrée.

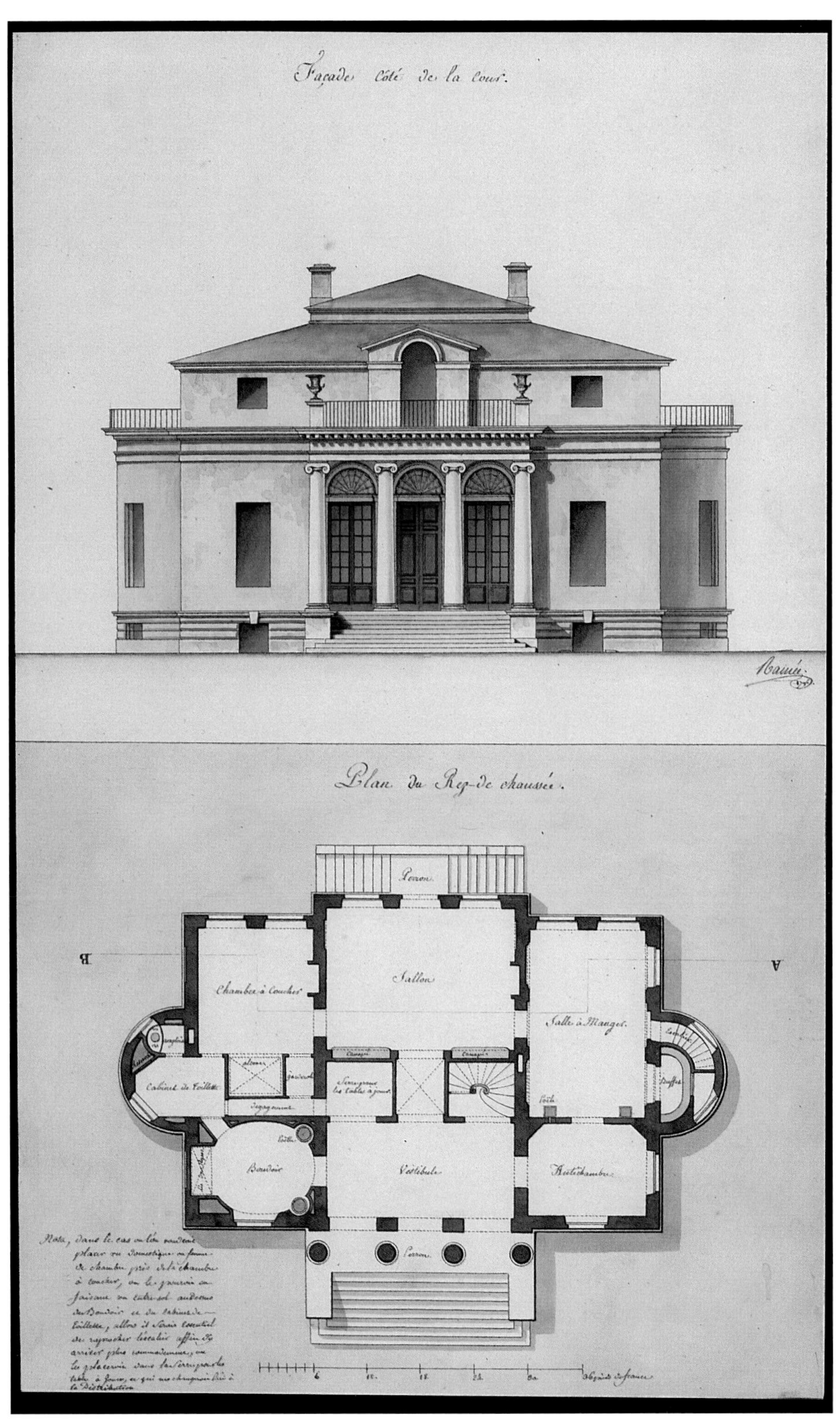

Pl. 7 Elevation drawing of entry façade and main floor plan of country house. Ink and watercolor on paper, 26 × 41 cm, signed "Ramée, 1796." (Forschungs- und Landesbibliothek, Gotha)

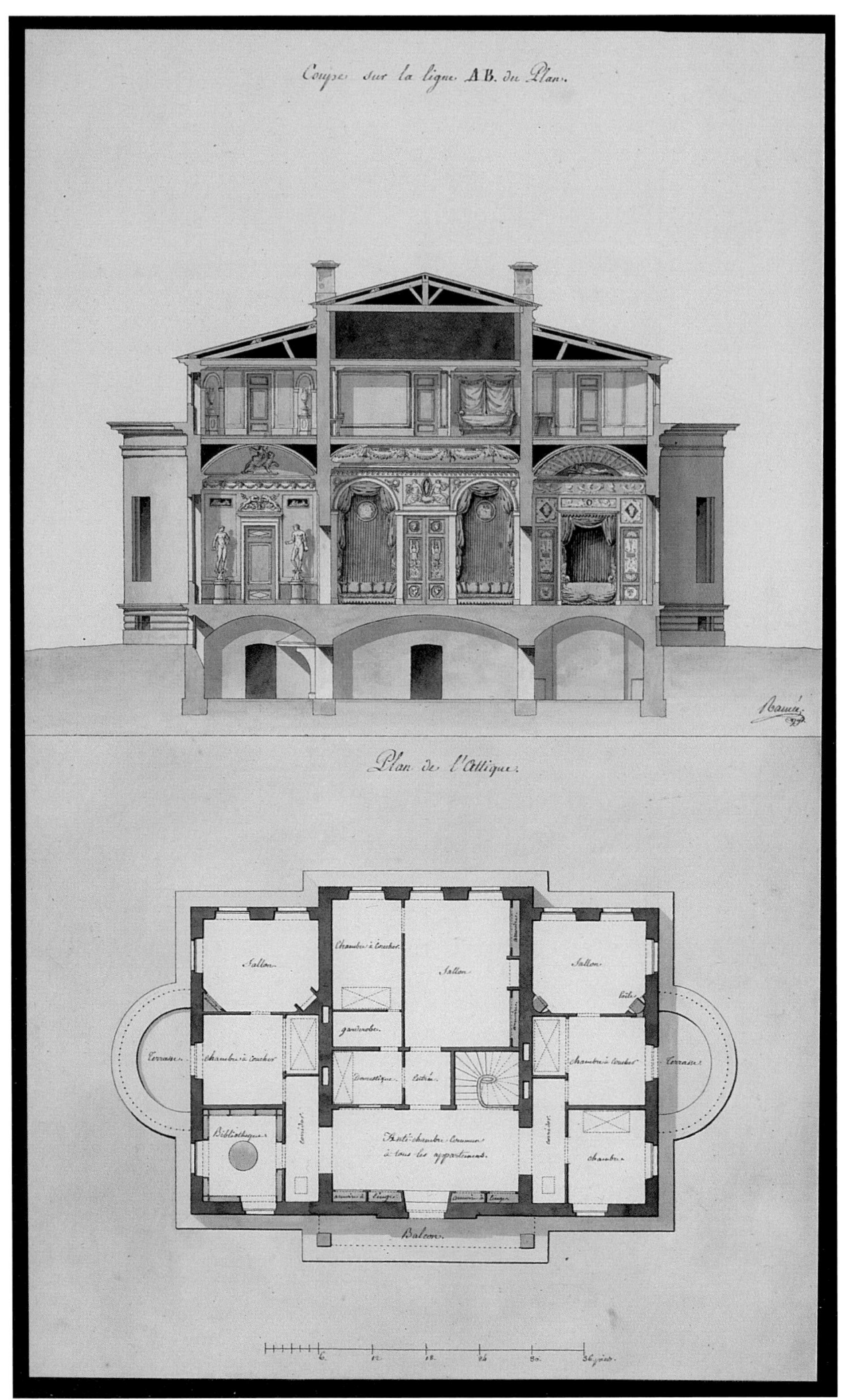

Pl. 8 Section drawing and attic floor plan of country house. Ink and watercolor on paper, 26 × 41 cm, signed "Ramée, 1796." (Forschungs- und Landesbibliothek, Gotha)

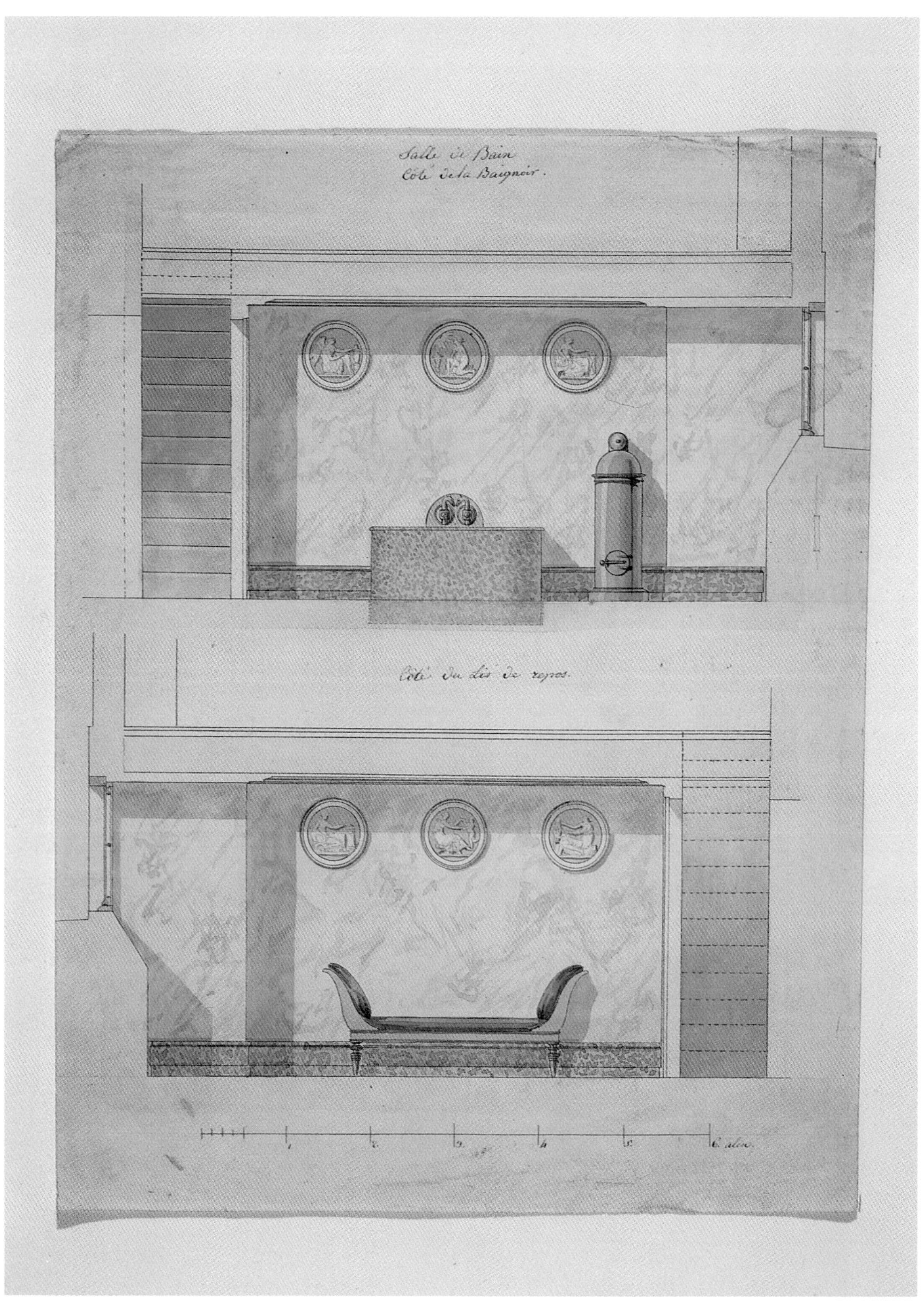

Pl. 9 Design for bathroom in Brun House, Copenhagen, c. 1802. Elevation drawings of two walls, ink and watercolor on paper, 19 × 24 cm. (Kunstakademiets Bibliotek, Copenhagen)

Pl. 10 Brun House bathroom. Elevation drawings of two walls, ink and watercolor on paper, 19 × 24 cm. (Kunstakademiets Bibliotek, Copenhagen)

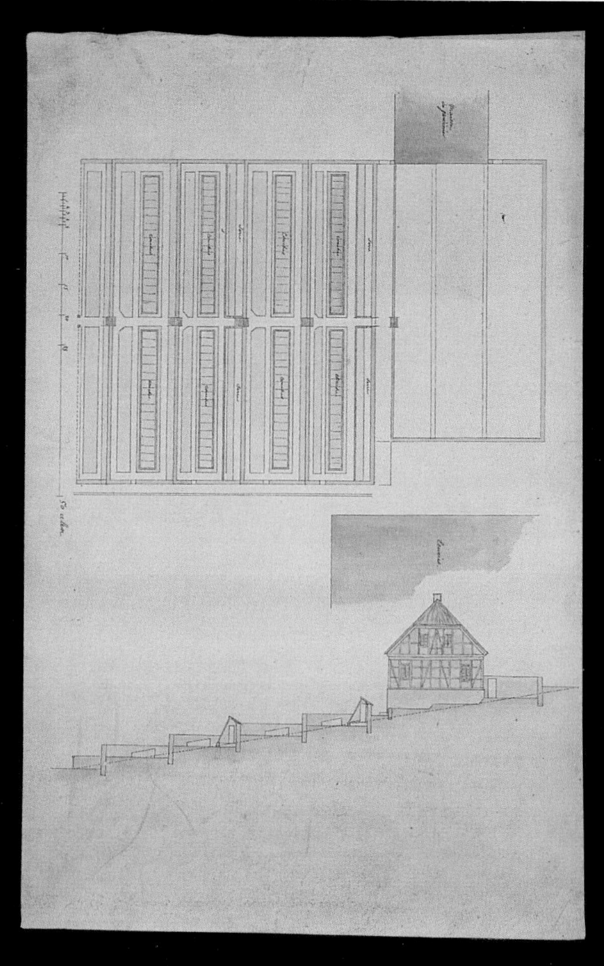

Pl. 11 Sophienholm, two elevation drawings of privy, c. 1802. Ink and watercolor on paper, 19 × 24 cm. (Kunstakademiets Bibliotek, Copenhagen)

Pl. 12 Sophienholm, plan and elevation drawings of gardener's house and planting beds, c. 1802. Ink and watercolor on paper, 24 × 37 cm. (Kunstakademiets Bibliotek, Copenhagen)

Pl. 13 View of Baurs Park from the Elbe River. Watercolor drawing on paper, 36 × 50 cm, signed "Ramée, 1810." (© Musée National de la Coopération Franco-américaine, Blérancourt, France)

Pl. 14 Elevation drawing of "Loterie Impériale de France." Ink and watercolor on paper, 33 × 48 cm, signed "Ramée, 1811." (Musée Carnavalet, Paris; cliché, Musées de la Ville de Paris © by SPADEM)

Pl. 16 Elevation drawing of President's House, Union College, probably 1813. Ink and watercolor on paper, 36 × 59 cm. (Schaffer Library, Union College)

Pl. 17 Plan of gardens behind President's House (at bottom), Union College, probably 1813. Ink and watercolor on paper, 33 × 46 cm. (Schaffer Library, Union College)

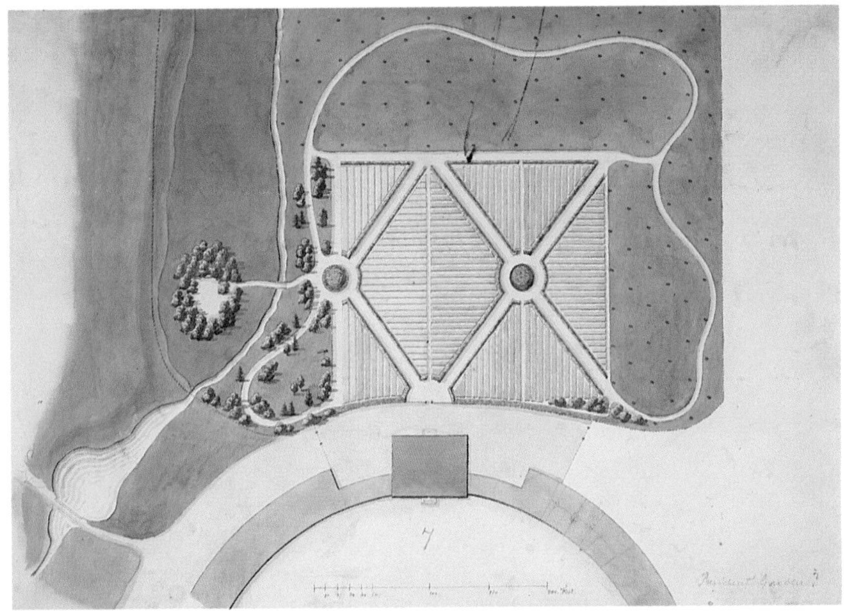

Pl. 15 Site plan for Union College, Schenectady, New York, probably 1813. Ink and watercolor on paper, 46 × 28 cm. (Schaffer Library, Union College)

Pl. 18 Design for Washington Monument, Baltimore. Perspective drawing, ink and watercolor, 49 × 72 cm, inscribed "J. Ramée, 1813." (The Peale Museum, Baltimore City Life Museums)

of general George Washington, to be erected at Baltimore.–
J. RAMÉ
1815.

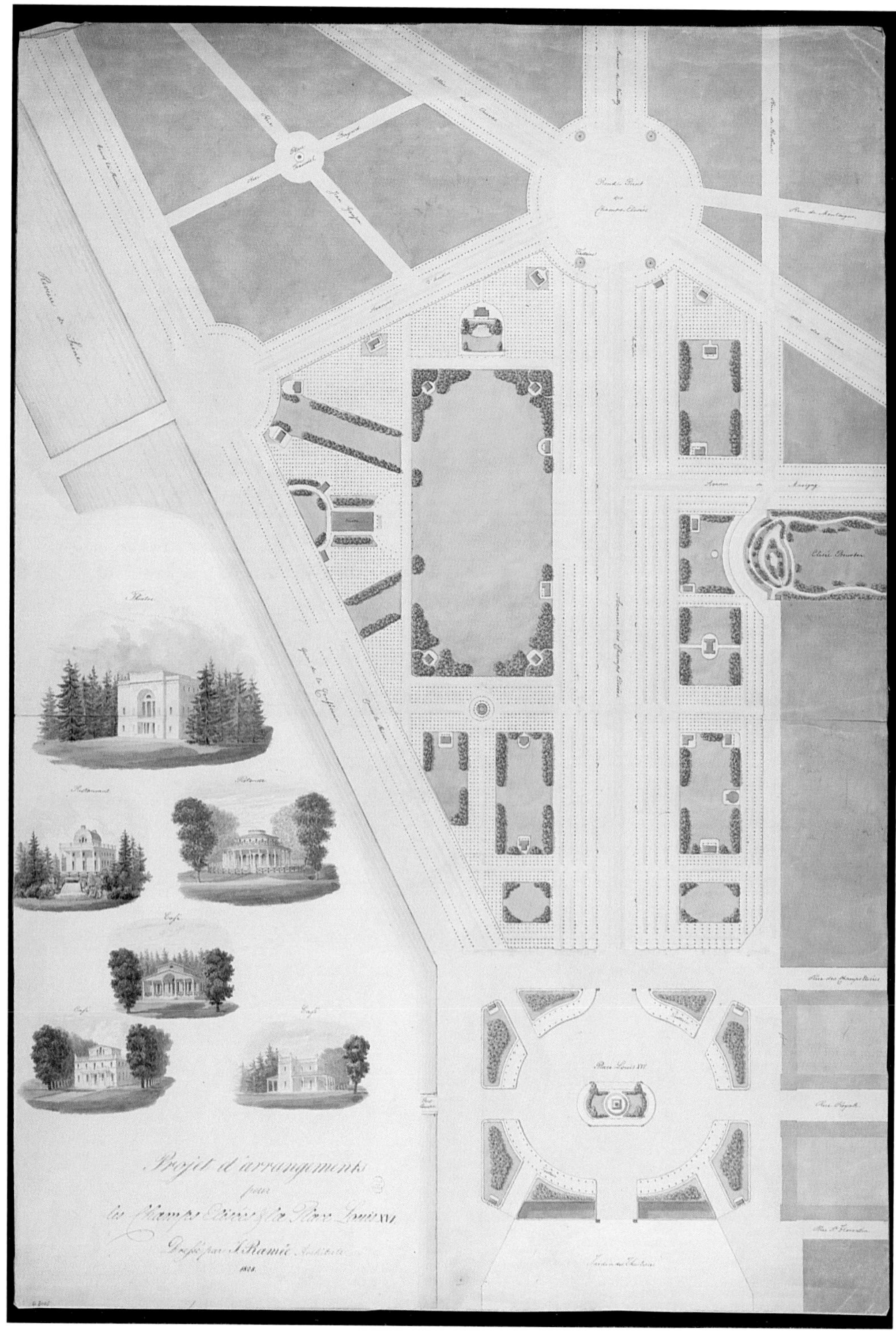

Pl. 19 Design for Champs-Élysées and Place Louis XVI (now Place de la Concorde), Paris. Ink and watercolor on paper, 47 × 68 cm, inscribed "J. Ramée, Architecte, 1828." (Musée Carnavalet, Paris; cliché, Musées de la Ville de Paris © by SPADEM)